Lecture Notes in Computer Science 7522

Commenced Publication in 1973
Founding and Former Series Editors:
Gerhard Goos, Juris Hartmanis, and Jan van Leeuwen

Marc Herrlich   Rainer Malaka
Maic Masuch (Eds.)

Entertainment Computing - ICEC 2012

11th International Conference, ICEC 2012
Bremen, Germany, September 26-29, 2012
Proceedings

 Springer

Volume Editors

Marc Herrlich
Rainer Malaka
Universität Bremen
Technologie-Zentrum Informatik und Informationstechnik (TZI)
Postfach 33 04 40, 28334 Bremen, Germany
E-mail: {mh, malaka}@tzi.de

Maic Masuch
Universität Duisburg-Essen
Abteilung für Informatik und angewandte Kognitionswissenschaften
Forsthausweg 2, 47057 Duisburg, Germany
E-mail: maic.masuch@uni-due.de

ISSN 0302-9743 e-ISSN 1611-3349
ISBN 978-3-642-33541-9 e-ISBN 978-3-642-33542-6
DOI 10.1007/978-3-642-33542-6
Springer Heidelberg Dordrecht London New York

Library of Congress Control Number: 2012947147

CR Subject Classification (1998): K.8.0, K.3.1, K.4.3, H.5.1-2, I.3.7-8, J.5, C.5.3, D.2.1-3, D.2.13

LNCS Sublibrary: SL 3 – Information Systems and Application, incl. Internet/Web and HCI

Typesetting: Camera-ready by author, data conversion by Scientific Publishing Services, Chennai, India

Printed on acid-free paper

Springer is part of Springer Science+Business Media (www.springer.com)

Preface

We are proud to present the proceedings of the eleventh International Conference on Entertainment Computing (ICEC 2012). After Seoul (2010) and Vancouver (2011) ICEC was back again in Europe and we were honored to host this event in the city state and Free Hanseatic City of Bremen, Germany.

Bremen – the tea and coffee capital of Germany – with its strong mercantile tradition has always been a place of exchange between people and cultures from all over the world. Thousands of people started their endeavor for a better life and future into the New World from the port of Bremerhaven.

Considering the world-famous fairy tale of the iconic Bremen Town Musicians it is fair to say that Bremen also has a long history in entertainment. The University of Bremen founded in 1971 is already known as a major center of research in northern Germany and has recently become one of eleven German Universities of Excellence.

Although it has been said that the people in northern Germany are sometimes not of the most emotional type, we were very excited and delighted to welcome so many guests from all over the world. Together, we made this ICEC an exciting, enjoyable, and scientifically valuable event.

Entertainment computing is a diverse field bringing together computer science, social and cultural sciences, psychology, art, design, and many other disciplines. Therefore, entertainment computing is the prototype of interdisciplinary and open research and one focal point of exchange between these different disciplines, as was again demonstrated by the variety and scientific quality of this year's program.

Overall, we received 53 full and 17 short paper submissions and 45 submissions to the other categories, giving a total of 115 submissions from 30 countries. After a rigorous peer-review and meta-review process, 21 full papers, 13 short papers, 16 posters, 8 demos, 4 workshops, 1 tutorial, and 3 doctoral consortium submissions were accepted. We would like to thank all members of the program committee and all additional external reviewers for their work and commitment. We are very proud of the final selection of papers, which would not have been possible without their efforts and support.

The doctoral consortium was a premier at this year's ICEC and allowed young researchers to take the opportunity to get feedback on their PhD work from renowned experts in the field. Also, for the second time, the ICEC was organized as a single-track conference to foster the dissemination and discussion of the presented scientific results within the community.

This year's ICEC was co-located with the third International Conference on Serious Games Development and Applications (SGDA). Participants were free to visit sessions of both events, providing additional opportunities to increase exchange and exposure within a greater scientific community. The workshop and tutorial program complemented the main conference by focusing on special topics of interest. We decided to include 14 peer-reviewed workshop submissions in the proceedings of the main track because we think they consitute valuable scientific contributions that are of interest to all ICEC participants.

The conference presented three inspiring keynotes from speakers coming from different backgrounds who shared their specific view on important topics of entertainment computing. Steve Ince – artist, game designer, and writer – brought his long-time industry experience and shared his ideas on game creation, design, and storytelling. Espen Aarseth – principal researcher and professor at the Center for Computer Games Research, Copenhagen – looked at games and narration from a researcher's point of view. Olga Sorkine – professor at the Institute of Visual Computing at ETH Zurich – presented her insight into the technological aspects of entertainment computing in her talk about real-time modeling and animation.

We thank our sponsors and supporting organizations: InnoGames, Clickworker, the German Research Foundation (DFG), the German Informatics Society (GI), the Center for Computing and Communication Technologies (TZI) at the University of Bremen, and the University of Bremen. We also thank our media partners: Making Games and Interaction-Design.org. Additionally, we are grateful for the support of the IFIP TC 14 committee, especially Matthias Rauterberg and Ryohei Nakatsu. The help and information provided by last year's organizers also proved invaluable and we want to specifically mention Sidney Fels and Junia Anacleto for supporting us in this regard. Furthermore, this event would not have been possible without the assistance of all the great people from our respective groups at the universities of Bremen and Duisburg-Essen, including of course our technical staff and student assistants and volunteers. We would like to specifically thank Irmgard Laumann and Florian Lütkebohmert for the technical support before and during the conference, Franziska Lorz for maintaining the ICEC website and for designing most of the fliers and other information material, and Dmitry Alexandrovsky for his aid in the editing process of the proceedings and throughout the conference.

July 2012

Marc Herrlich
Rainer Malaka
Maic Masuch

Conference Organization

Conference Chair

Rainer Malaka   University of Bremen

Conference Advisory Committee

Ryohei Nakatsu   National University of Singapore
Matthias Rauterberg   Technical University of Eindhoven

Program Chair

Maic Masuch   University of Duisburg-Essen

Workshop Chairs

Lynne Baillie   Glasgow Caledonian University
Rod McCall   University of Luxembourg

Industry Chairs

Don Marinelli   Entertainment Technology Center, Pittsburgh
Jörg Niesenhaus   University of Duisburg-Essen/GTCC.NRW

Doctoral Consortium Chairs

Matthias Rauterberg   Technical University of Eindhoven
Ryohei Nakatsu   National University of Singapore
Esteban Clua   University of Sao Paulo

Social Media Chair

Lennart Nacke   University of Ontario Institute of Technology

Local Organization Chair

Marc Herrlich   University of Bremen

Local Organization Committee

Gerald Volkmann	University of Bremen
Markus Krause	University of Bremen
Jan Smeddinck	University of Bremen
David Wewetzer	University of Bremen

Program Committee

Valter Alves	University of Coimbra
Junia Anacleto	Federal University of São Carlos
Manuela Aparicio	DCTI/ISCTE
Lynne Baillie	Glasgow Caledonian University
Regina Bernhaupt	University of Toulouse, IRIT
Rafael Bidarra	TU Delft
Anthony Brooks	Aalborg University
Marc Cavazza	University of Teesside
Paolo Ciancarini	University of Bologna
Esteban Clua	University of São Paulo
Philippe Codgnet	CNRS / Keio University
Fionnuala Conway	University of Dublin
Nuno Correia	New University of Lisbon
Carlos Costa	DCTI/ISCTE
Henry Duh	National University of Singapore
Sidney Fels	University of British Columbia
Owen Fernando	National University of Singapore
Mathias Funk	Eindhoven University of Technology
Oscar Garcia-Panella	Universitat Ramon Llull
Chris Geiger	University of Applied Sciences Düsseldorf
Timo Goettel	HTW Berlin, Germany
Pedro González Calero	Complutense University of Madrid
Nicholas Graham	Queen's University, Kingston
Marco A. Gómez-Martín	Universidad Complutense de Madrid
Stefan Göbel	TU Darmstadt
Brenda Harger	Carnegie Mellon University
Letizia Jaccheri	NTNU Norway
Javier Jaen	Polytechnic University of Valencia
Bill Kapralos	University of Ontario Institute of Technology
Haruhiro Katayose	Kwansei Gakuin University
Rilla Khaled	IT University of Copenhagen
Christoph Klimmt	Hanover University of Music, Drama, and Media
Joseph Laviola	Brown University
Seungyon Lee	SangMyung University
Christoph Lürig	FH Trier
Rainer Malaka	University of Bremen
Regan Mandryk	University of Saskatchewan

Additional Reviewers

Alejandro Catala
Lutz Dickmann
Anders Drachen
Katharina Emmerich
Kathrin Gerling
Thomas de Groot
Marc Herrlich
Jarrod Knibbe
Markus Krause
Jose A. Mocholi
Frederic Pollmann

Robert Porzel
Sue A. Seah
Jonas Schild
Ralf Schmidt
Jan Smeddinck
Aneta Takhtamisheva
Tim Tutenel
Robert Walter
Benjamin Walther-Franks
Dirk Wenig
Job Zwiers

Supporting Organizations and Sponsors

International Federation for Information Processing (IFIP)
German Informatics Society (GI)
German Research Foundation (DFG)
Center for Computing and Communication Technologies (TZI)
University of Bremen
InnoGames
Clickworker

Media Partners

Making Games
Interaction-Design.org

Table of Contents

Storytelling

Serious Games (Learning and Training)

Self and Identity

Interactive Performance

Mixed Reality and 3D Worlds

Serious Games (Health and Social)

Player Experience

Tools and Methods I

Tools and Methods II

User Interface

Posters

Demonstrations

Industry Demonstration

Doctoral Consortium

Co-located Event

Workshops

Harnessing Collective Intelligence with Games

Game Development and Model-Driven Software Development

Mobile Gaming, Mobile Life - Interweaving the Virtual and the Real

Exploring the Challenges of Ethics, Privacy and Trust in Serious Gaming

Tutorial

Open Source Software for Entertainment

Social Interaction for Interactive Storytelling

Edirlei Soares de Lima[1], Bruno Feijó[1], Cesar Tadeu Pozzer[2], Angelo E.M. Ciarlini[3],
Simone Diniz Junqueira Barbosa[1], Antonio L. Furtado[1],
and Fabio A. Guilherme da Silva[1]

[1] PUC-Rio – Department of Informatics, Rio de Janeiro, RJ – Brazil
{elima,bfeijo,simone,furtado,faraujo}@inf.puc-rio.br
[2] UFSM – Department of Electronics and Computing, Santa Maria, RS – Brazil
pozzer@inf.ufsm.br
[3] UNIRIO – Department of Applied Informatics, Rio de Janeiro, RJ – Brazil
angelo.ciarlini@uniriotec.br

Abstract. In recent years interactive narratives emerged as a new form of digital entertainment, allowing users to interact and change stories according to their own desires. In this paper, we explore the use of social networks as a way of interaction in interactive narratives. We present the interaction interface of an interactive storytelling system that allows users to interact and change stories through social networks. To validate our approach we conducted a user study with 24 participants. The preliminary results show that our method improved the user satisfaction and experience. The proposed methods can be adapted to other applications that require social interaction.

Keywords: Interactive Storytelling, Social Networks, Social Interaction.

1 Introduction

Interactive narratives have been presented as a new form of digital entertainment, in which users can interact and change stories according to their own desires. Although the idea of interactive narratives can be traced back to the 1970s [1] and important experiments on agent-based storytelling can be found in the 1990s [2], the 2000s can be considered the decade of the most intensive and influential research works on interactive storytelling systems. In more recent years, we have been exposed to new demands for richer interactive experiences in storytelling, such as transmedia storytelling [3] and social interaction between groups [4]. We believe that those new demands require the development of new interaction mechanisms and, in particular, the use of social networks as an interaction interface. Williams *et al.* [4] argue that after playing a game, gamers love to discuss the events that just took place and comment on the memorable events, contributing to the culture of the game. The same can be said of interactive storytelling on digital TV.

An interactive narrative designed for TV and shared by thousands of viewers requires new interaction mechanisms and interfaces that support the social interaction between viewers. Moreover, attractive interaction mechanisms are necessary to incentive viewers to interact with the narratives. The popularization of social network services (such as Facebook, Twitter and Google+) puts social computing in the everyday

M. Herrlich, R. Malaka, and M. Masuch (Eds.): ICEC 2012, LNCS 7522, pp. 1–15, 2012.

life. Social networks are like windows to virtual worlds, where people can interact with friends, family, or even strangers.

In this paper, we explore the use of social networks as a way of interaction in interactive stories. We implemented a prototype of the proposed interaction interface in Logtell [5], an interactive storytelling system based on temporal logic and non-deterministic planning. The interactive story implemented in our system corresponds to a short story in the genre of swords and dragons (Figure 1).

Fig. 1. Dramatization of the swords-and-dragons story performed by Logtell

The paper is organized as follows. Section 2 presents the previous works. Section 3 proposes the architecture of the social interaction interface. Section 4 presents the proposed methods of social interactions. Section 5 describes a preliminary evaluation of the proposed system. Section 6 contains concluding remarks.

2   Previous Works

There are several works on forms of interactions for interactive storytelling in the literature. They cover the subject from traditional GUI interfaces [6][7] to more complex interaction mechanisms, such as speech recognition [8][9][10], body gestures combined with speech [11][12][13], hand-drawn sketches [14][15] and physiological inputs [16]. However, few of these works consider multiuser interactions. Moreover, none of them proposes the use of social networks as a form of interaction interface. The need for social interactions between groups watching interactive TV is analyzed by Williams *et al.* [4]. However, the authors do not propose any specific form of interaction.

Likavec *et al.* [17] propose a framework that allows a social/collective narrative from several story fragments created by several authors interacting on social networks. However, the authors are not dealing with interaction interface methods. Moreover they are not considering interactive digital storytelling narratology. Pittarello [18] presents an architecture for mobile interactive storytelling that includes Facebook. However, his work does not propose forms of social interaction.

3   Social Interaction

The method of interaction presented in this paper is based on the idea of using social networks (such as Facebook, Twitter and Google+) as an interaction interface. This method, here called "**social interaction**", expands the boundaries of human-computer interaction towards new forms of multiuser applications. It can be used in any story-telling system that generates plots organized by chapters. This idea is demonstrated in this paper through an interface prototype that we created to our interactive storytelling system called Logtell [4].

Interactive storytelling applications usually require multiuser settings, especially the ones designed for interactive television (iTV), where narratives are shared by thousands of viewers. The Logtell system fits in this category and requires an interaction mechanism that is at the same time attractive to users and allows such a large-scale multiuser interaction.

3.1 Basic Architecture

Figure 2 illustrates the basic architecture of the social interaction interface and how it communicates with the interactive storytelling system. The Storytelling Server gene-rates and controls the execution of the stories, administrates multiple clients who share the same narrative, and informs the Social Interaction Server about valid sug-gestions for the next chapters. The Social Interaction Server is the interface between interactive storytelling system and social network. It is responsible for accessing the social networks looking for user interactions, translating the users desires into valid story suggestions, and informing the Storytelling Server about the user's choices. The Client Drama Viewer is responsible for simply displaying the generated plots to the viewers. Users can access the social networks using their own social network applica-tions. The interaction system also has a special page in the social networks. Users who want to participate and interact with the story must "follow" (Twitter and Google+) or "like" (Facebook) this page, so they are able to receive the update messages from the interaction system.

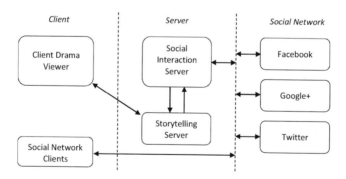

Fig. 2. Basic architecture of the proposed interactive storytelling system with social interaction

3.2 Flow of Activities

Our method is designed for storytelling systems that are organized by chapters. In these systems, users' desires can be fulfilled in the next chapter or during current dramatization. The storytelling system is constantly sending messages to induce facts to the user or provoke him/her, which we denominate "induction messages". We can use Activity Diagrams [19] to specify the dynamic behavior of the system, where messages are exchanged and dramatizations are performed. Figure 3 presents the activity diagram for the proposed system, in which the moments of social interactions are indicated by a cloud illustration and a shaded box. When the system starts, the induction message is an introduction to the story. Users receive this message as an update in the social network and are able to comment on the message (Facebook and Google+) or use hashtags (Twitter) to indicate suggestions. The introduction message describes the story characters, places, gives some tips about what could happen in the story and incentive the users to comment what they would like to see happening in the story. In our prototype, we present a fairy tale as shown in Figure 4.

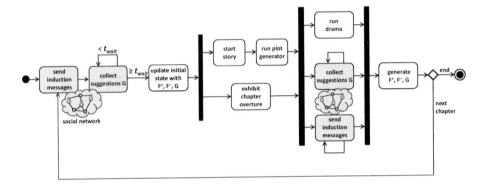

Fig. 3. Activity diagram of the proposed system

"*Once upon a time there was a charming princess, called Marian, lady of the White Palace, and two brave young men, sir Brian and sir Hoel, knights of the Gray Castle. Not far away in the sinister Red Castle, lurched Draco, the evil dragon, ready to seize the princess, despite her guardians, and keep her with super-human strength. But there was also the silent wizard of the Green Forest, Turjan the mage. Whoever approached him with due courtesy could hope for a gift of great fighting power. Uncountable stories can be told in this world of fantasy. Will the princess be abducted by the dragon? Or killed by the monster? Will one of the knights save her or revenge her death, with or without the mage's help?*

A new interactive story is about to begin. Comment here what you would like to see happen with the characters of this story."

Fig. 4. Example of an introduction message

The system keeps collecting suggestions for t_{wait} minutes (as indicated by the looping arrow), after which the initial state of the chapter is update. Three sets of facts are considered: F^+ (facts generated by the system that are added to the state), F^- (facts generated by the system that are removed from the state), and G (suggestions created by the user that may be considered by the plot generator if they are not inconsistent with the ongoing story). The system considers the G facts that are more frequently mentioned by the users.

The thick black bars indicate parallel activities. We should notice that a chapter overture is exhibited (*e.g.* audio, text, and/or video) while the system runs the plot generator module (the most demanding processing time). Also we can see that interactions occur during the dramatization process (*i.e.* in parallel with the box "run drama" of Figure 3). The induction messages in this dramatization stage are suggestions for the next chapter (*e.g.* "*Would you like to see Turjan giving strength to Brian in the next chapter?*") or an invitation for a poll (*e.g.* "*The villain should defeat the guards? Yes or No?*"). The users do not have to wait or pay attention to induction messages – they can keep sending any kind of messages (*e.g.* "*The princess should die!*") anytime.

The last activity in the process is to generate the sets of facts F⁺, F⁻, and G for the next chapter. This set G will probably be expanded or edited in the beginning of the new cycle, during the initial t_{wait} minutes.

During the interaction process, the behavior of the users is analyzed by the interaction system. If it detects that only a small number of users is contributing with story suggestions through comments, the system creates a poll in the social network where they are able to select and vote by clicking on the poll option. The votes are combined with the votes from the other interaction methods to decide the events for the next chapters.

4   Methods of Social Interactions

We propose three basic ways of interacting with the stories: (1) **interaction by comments** – where users explicitly express their desires through comments in natural language; (2) **interaction by preferences** – where users express satisfaction or state preferences; and (3) **interaction by poll** – where a poll is created and users vote in what they want. Adaptations are necessary for each type of social network. For example, Twitter does not allow direct comments on the posts as Facebook and Google+, but allow users to use hashtags to indicate suggestions to the stories.

The above-mentioned methods of interaction define the architecture of the Social Interaction Server (Figure 5). In this architecture, the Suggestion Manager controls the interaction mechanisms and centralizes the users' suggestions and poll results. The next sections describe those three methods of interaction in more details.

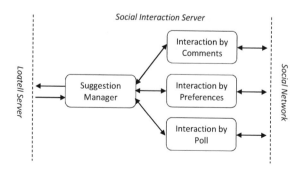

Fig. 5. The architecture of the Social Interaction Server

4.1   Interaction by Comments

The interaction by comments allows users to explicitly express their desires through comments on the social network. The interaction system accesses the users' comments and extracts valid suggestions using natural language processing techniques. The most often mentioned suggestions are incorporated into the story.

The process of extracting valid suggestions from the users' comments involves natural language processing [20]. A traditional natural language processing task consists of two main phases: (1) **syntax parsing**, where the syntax tree and the grammatical relations between the parts of the sentence are extracted; and (2) **semantic analysis**, which is the extraction of the meaning of words or phrases.

In the proposed interaction system, we adopted the Stanford Parser to perform the syntax parsing of the sentences [21]. The Stanford Parser [22] is a probabilistic parser that represents all sentence relationships as typed dependency relations instead of using phrase structure representations. However, it also produces phrase structure trees.

The Stanford Parser produces 55 different typed dependencies [23]. These dependencies reflect the grammatical relationships between the words. Such grammatical relations provide an abstraction layer to the pure syntax tree and provide information about the syntactic role of all elements. Figure 6 (a) shows a phrase structure tree generated by the Stanford Parser for the sentence "*Draco should kill Marian!*". The corresponding typed dependencies are listed in Figure 6 (b). Typed dependencies facilitate the analysis of semantic relationships between words based on both their grammatical relationships and overall sentence syntactical structure.

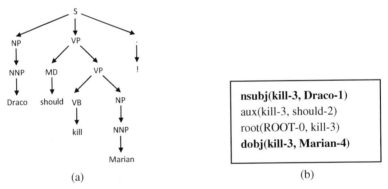

(a)   (b)

Fig. 6. Phrase structure tree (a) and the typed dependencies (b) of "*Draco should kill Marian!*"

The typed dependencies are all binary relations, where a grammatical relation holds between a "governor" and a "dependent". In the above example, the relation *nsubj* (nominal subject) relates the noun "*Draco*" with the corresponding verb "*kill*", whereas the relation *dobj* (direct object) relates this verb with the object "*Marian*". In this way, the sentence elements are extracted and the sentence structure can be translated into simple first-order logic sentences. In the above example, the following sentence is extracted:

kill(Draco, Marian)

which means that "*Draco*" must perform the action "*kill*" and the victim is "*Marian*".

In the present work we generate simples logic sentences composed by a disjunction of predicates, *e.g.* from *"Brian and Hoel fights against Draco"* is generated the sentence *fight(Brian, Draco)* and *fight(Hoel, Draco)*.

With this dependency chain, the system is able to extract "subject – direct object" relationships from sentences. However, for this pattern to be valid, four conditions must be met: (1) a nominal subject (*nsubj*) dependency must exist; (2) the dependent of the *nsubj* dependency must be a family member (in the phrase structure tree); (3) the governor of this dependency must be a verb, which means that a family member is the head noun of the subject of a clause which is predicated by the verb; and (4) a direct object (*dobj*) dependency must exist and the governor of this dependency must match the index of the governor of the *nsubj* dependency – then we assume that the dependency of the *dobj* relation is paired with the family member found initially.

In the example above, the extracted logical sentence already contains the semantic meaning necessary to our interaction system infer a valid suggestion to the story. However, there are some cases where the subjects are not directly referenced. For example, in the sentence *"Brian save Marian and marry her."*, the pronoun *"her"* refers to *"Marian"*. However, when we compute the typed dependencies for this sentence (Figure 7), we see in the relation *"dobj(marry-5, her-6)"* that the pronoun *"her"* was not resolved and, in some cases, it's not possible to solve it using only the phrase structure tree. The process of resolving what pronoun or a noun phrase refers to is called **anaphora resolution**. To solve this problem, we used another tool from the Stanford Natural Language Processing Group, the Stanford Deterministic Coreference Resolution System [24], which is able to indicate precisely the correct reference of any unknown pronoun.

nsubj(save-2, Brian-1)
nsubj(marry-5, Brian-1)
root(ROOT-0, save-2)
dobj(save-2, Marian-3)
conj_and(save-2, marry-5)
dobj(marry-5, her-6)

Fig. 7. Example of anaphora problem in the sentence *"Brian save Marian and marry her."*

The parser also verifies the occurrence of negations. For example, in the sentence *"Draco should not kill Marian!"*, the adverb *"not"* completely changes the meaning of the sentence. To identify negations, the parser analyses the occurrence of negation modifiers (*"neg"*) in the typed dependency list. Figure 8 illustrates the typed dependency for the example above and occurrence of the negation modifier.

nsubj(kill-4, Draco-1)
aux(kill-4, should-2)
neg(kill-4, not-3)
root(ROOT-0, kill-4)
dobj(kill-4, Marian-5)

Fig. 8. Example of negation in the sentence *"Draco should not kill Marian!"*

After translating the "subject – direct object" relations into first-order logic sentences, the parser also needs to validate the sentences. For example, the predicate "*fight(CH₁, CH₂)*" requires a nominal subject CH_1 that is a valid character and a direct object CH_2 that also is a valid character in the story context. Moreover, the verb "*fight*" also must be a valid action. To perform this validation, the parser has access to a list of valid actions, characters and places. In this way, the parser is able to identify the elements that the words represent. However, almost all words have synonyms and to deal with this, the parser also incorporates a dictionary of synonyms associated with each action, character and place. So, it is able to parse sentences such as "*The hero should annihilate the villain!*", where the verb "*annihilate*" is an synonym of the action "*kill*", and the objects "*hero*" and "*villain*" are, respectively, the roles of the characters "*Brian*" and "*Draco*".

Ideally, the parser expects sentences that contain at least one verb, one nominal subject and a direct object. However, it not always happens, in some cases the subject, the direct object, or both are omitted. For example, the sentence "*Kill the princess!*" do not express directly who should perform the action "*kill*", but indicates the direct object "*princess*" (Figure 9). In this case, the parser is still able to generate a partial logic sentence to represent it:

kill(*, Marian)

which means that someone "***" must perform the action "*kill*" and the victim is "*Marian*" (identified by its role in the story ("*princess*")). The operator "***" can be replaced by any valid character to complete the logical sentence.

> root(ROOT-0, Kill-1)
> det(princess-3, the-2)
> **dobj(Kill-1, princess-3)**

Fig. 9. Example of omitted subject in the sentence "*Kill the princess!*"

The entire process of extracting valid first-order logic sentences from text phrases is illustrated in Figure 10. In the Syntax Parsing step, the Stanford Parser receives a text phrase S_x as input and generates a Dependency Tree and the Typed Dependencies for the sentence. Using this information, in the Semantic Analysis phase, the parser performs the Anaphora Resolution process to resolve the pronouns of the sentence and find valid synonyms using the Synonym Dictionary. Finally, the parser checks the integrity of the sentences using some Logic Rules and returns a list of valid first-order logic sentences (P_x^n).

After extracting all users' suggestions from the comments in the social network, the interaction system relates comments that express the same suggestions and count how many votes the suggestions received. In the case of Facebook and Google+, besides writing a comment, users are also able to "like" or "+1" a comment of another user, which indicates that they liked what the comment says. In this way, the interaction system considers the number of users that directly wrote that something should happen and the number of users that liked the respective comments. After counting the number of votes of each suggestion, the module that manages the Interaction by Comments sends this information to the Suggestion Manager (as illustrated in Figure 5).

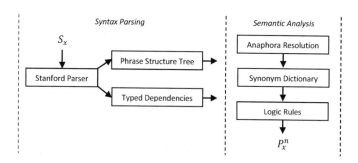

Fig. 10. The process of extracting valid first-order logic sentences. S_x is the input text phrase and P_x^n is the output list of predicates

4.2   Interaction by Preferences

The interaction by preferences allows users to express their satisfaction with the story suggestions through social networks. Instead of directly writing a comment express-ing a desire, users are able to "like" (Facebook) or "+1" (Google+) a suggestion gen-erated by the interaction system. Users can also write comments on the generated suggestions expressing their satisfaction with the proposed events. The interaction system checks the users' responses and the most well received suggestions are incor-porated into the story.

The process of extracting user's satisfaction also involves natural language processing, more specifically the area of Sentiment Analysis [25]. However, in this work, instead of using complex sentiment analysis techniques, we adopted a more simplistic approach to solve this problem. As the generated suggestions are more like questions (e.g. "*Would you like to see Draco attacking the White Palace in the next chapter?*"), the users usually respond it positively or negatively, i.e. agreeing or disa-greeing. In this way, the parser only needs to identify positive and negative answers in the users' comments.

The approach adopted by our parser to identify positive and negative answers uses a list of words, where each word W_i is associated with a numerical score $W_i^s \in [-1.0, +1.0]$. High negative scores represent very negative words and high positive scores represent very positive words. Considering C_x a user commentary, the senti-ment $St(C_x)$ is given by:

$$St(C_x) = \frac{1}{n}\sum_{i=1}^{n} W_i^s \quad if \quad (W_i \in C_x)$$

where $St(C_x) \in [-1.0, +1.0]$ indicates if C_x is a positive commentary $(C_x > \beta)$ or a negative commentary $(C_x < \alpha)$, in which α and β defines a precision threshold where uncertain commentaries are ignored (classified as neutral).

To illustrate this process, let's consider $\alpha = -0.3$ $\beta = +0.3$, and the following user commentaries for the suggestion $S_1 = $ "*Would you like to see the princess Marian dying in the next chapter?*":

1. "*Yes!! :)*"
2. "*I would love to see it happening!!! ;)*"
3. "*No!! I love the princess... :(*"
4. "*This story is boring... :(*"

For case (1), the word "*Yes*" and the emoticon "*:)*" have both the score +1.0; giving the sentiment $St(C_1) = +1.0$ and classifying it as a positive commentary. In case (2), the word "*love*", "*see*" and the emoticon "*;)*" have the scores +0.8, +0.5 and +0.9 respectively; giving the sentiment $St(C_2) = +0.73$ and classifying the sentence as a positive commentary. In case (3), the word "*No*", "*love*" and the emoticon "*:(*" have the scores -1.0, +0.8 and -1.0 respectively; giving the sentiment $St(C_3) = -0.4$ and classifying the sentence as a negative commentary. Finally, in case (4) the word "*boring*" and the emoticon "*:(*" have the scores -0.7 and -1.0 respectively; giving the sentiment $St(C_4) = -0.85$ and classifying the sentence as a negative commentary.

There are some cases where the users also complement their opinion with other story suggestions (*e.g.* "*No!!! The hero must save the princess!*"). For this reason, the interaction system also performs the process of extracting story suggestions from user comments (described on section 4.1) in the comments created on posts designed for the interaction by preferences. In the above example, the system would be able to classify the commentary as a negative commentary (counting a negative vote for the system suggestion) and extract a new vote for the suggestion "*save(Brian, Marian)*".

When the system completes the process of classifying the comments as positive or negative, the number of votes is computed. Positive comments count as positive votes to the suggestion described in the post and the negative comments count as negative votes. The number of users that "like" (Facebook) or "+1" (Google+) the suggestion also count as positive votes. Then, the module that manages the interaction by preferences sends this information to the Suggestion Manager (as illustrated in Figure 5).

4.3   Interaction by Poll

The interaction by poll allows users to choose what they want through polls in the social network. Instead of directly writing a comment or waiting for the desired suggestion appear (posted by the interaction by preferences), they are able to see all available options and vote in the suggestion of their choice. The interaction system checks the poll results, and the most voted suggestions are incorporated into the story.

The process of extracting users' choices from a poll does not require any complex algorithm. However, the importance of this method should not be underestimated, because it provides an easy way of interaction where users that don't like to write or don't know exactly what they want are able to interact just by clicking on a poll option.

After computing the number of votes of each poll option, the module that manages the Interaction by Poll sends this information to the Suggestion Manager (as illustrated on Figure 5).

5   Evaluation

To evaluate the social interaction interface, we performed two tests: (1) a user evaluation test to check the interface usability from a Human-Computer Interaction (HCI) perspective, and (2) a technical test to check the performance and accuracy of the proposed methods of interaction. The following sections describe these tests.

5.1   User Evaluation

We have conducted a preliminary user evaluation with 24 high school students, 14 male and 10 female, aged 16 to 18 (mean of 17). Sixteen of them play video games at least weekly. None of them had previous experiences with interactive storytelling systems. Twenty of the participants use social networks at least once a day; the other four use few times a week. We divided the participants in two groups and conducted separated evaluation sessions for each group. The participants of each session were on the same room, but we asked them to don't interact between them physically.

We asked participants to interact with two versions of our interactive storytelling system, one based on a traditional GUI interface (described in [26]) and the other using the social interaction interface here presented. In order to reduce learning effects, one group used the traditional GUI interface first, and the other used the social interaction interface first. Facebook was the most popular social network between the participants, so all participants used it to interact with the social interaction interface. Six participants decided to use their cell phones to access the social network, while the others used desktop computers. The GUI interface was used by all participants through desktop computers.

After using each version, the participants filled out a questionnaire derived from the IRIS Evaluation Toolkit [27][28]. We evaluate the system usability, the correspondence of system capabilities with user expectations (user satisfaction), the interaction effectiveness and the user experience (curiosity, flow and enjoyment). Each statement was given on a five-point Likert scale ranging from "strongly disagree" (1) through "neutral" (3) to "strongly agree" (5). After having interacted with both versions of the system, the participants were interviewed about their experience.

Figure 11 summarizes the results of the questionnaires. The GUI interface produces slightly better usability and effectiveness when compared with the social interaction interface, probably because it requires less effort for the interaction. On the other hand, the social interaction interface clearly increases the user satisfaction and improved the user experience. As far as the interviews are concerned, all participants stated that they preferred to interact using the social network, because it was more interesting, attractive, exciting, and innovative. Some participants pointed that they had some difficult to understand what kind of suggestions they could write. We believe that this difficult can be overcome by adding some discrete tips in the story (*e.g.* by making the characters to think out loud what they could do). We noticed during the analysis of the results that users that used cell phones to access the social network had better experiences, especially regarding the usability of the system.

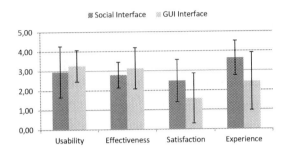

Fig. 11. Average and standard deviation of questionnaire topics in both versions of our system

5.2   Technical Evaluation

The technical evaluation concerns the accuracy and the real-time performance of the interaction system. The evaluation was based on two experiments: (1) the recognition rate test, to check the accuracy of the predicted suggestions; and (2) the performance test, to check the time needed to process the input comments and recognize the suggestions as first-order logic sentences. For both tests we used the comments derived from the user evaluation experiment described on section 5.1. In this way, we were able to evaluate the methods with real comments and check how well the system performed in the experiment.

During the user evaluation test we collected a set of 107 text comments, including 81 comments that were manually classified as valid suggestions. For the recognition rate test, we used our method to extract valid story suggestions from the comments and then compared the results with the results obtained through the manual classification. As result we get a recognition rate of 90.6%, with only 10 valid comments being incorrectly classified as invalid suggestions. The main reason for the incorrect classifications was the occurrence of spelling mistakes in the comments.

To evaluate the performance of our method, we again utilized the collection of 107 comments collected during user evaluation, and calculated the average time necessary to perform the recognition of the suggestions as first-order logic sentences. The computer used to run the experiments was an Intel Xeon E5620, 2.40 GHZ CPU, 24 GB of RAM using a single core to process the algorithms. As result we get the average time of 2.7 milliseconds to process an input comment and recognize the suggestion as first-order logic sentences (standard deviation of 1.3 milliseconds).

Similarly, we evaluated our method to recognize user satisfaction. During the user evaluation test we collected a set of 43 text comments expressing user satisfaction. We used our simplistic method of sentiment analysis to classify the comments as positive and negative comments then compared the results with the results obtained through a manual classification. As result we get a recognition rate of 97.6%, with only 1 positive comment incorrectly classified as negative. The time consumed by the algorithm is almost insignificant (less than 0.001 milliseconds).

In our experiments, the social interaction interface presented good results. However, natural language processing is not a trivial task; it is possible that our parser don't recognize correctly every possible valid sentence, but we believe that it is able to recognize the sentences in the most part of the cases without the audience be aware of mistakes. The time necessary to process the user comments is small, but it grows according to the number of comments to be processed. With a large number of users interacting at same time, the parallelization of this process may be necessary to guarantee the real-time execution of the narrative.

6   Conclusions

In this paper, we explore the use of social networks as a way of interaction in interactive stories. We present the interaction interface of an interactive storytelling system that allows users to interact and change stories through social networks. This method, here called "social interaction", expands the boundaries of human-computer interaction towards new forms of multi-user applications. As far as we are aware, this is the first time this form of interaction is explored in an interactive narrative.

The prototype was built over the Logtell system; however its architecture is generic enough to be adopted by any interactive storytelling system organized by chapters. Moreover, the interaction methods can be adapted to other systems that require a social user interaction. This form of interaction fits very well in the context of interactive narratives designed for digital TV. It doesn't require any direct interaction through the TV. Spectators interact through the social network clients, using smartphones, tablets, or personal computers without having to install any additional software. The activity that results from the user interactions in the social network may attract more viewers to the broadcasting channel (increasing the audience). In addition, viewers can make new friends through the interaction in the social network.

Acknowledgements. This work was partially supported by CAPES (Coordination for the Improvement of Higher Education Personnel, linked to the Ministry of Education) under grant RH-TVD 01/2007 No. 133/2008 and by Research Productivity Grants of CNPq (National Council for Scientific and Technological Development, linked to the Ministry of Science and Technology) under grant PQ 304090/2009-3.

References

1. Meehan, J.R.: TALE-SPIN, An Interactive Program that Writes Stories. In: Proceedings of the 5th International Joint Conference on Artificial Intelligence, pp. 91–98 (1977)
2. Loyall, A.B., Bates, J.: Hap: A Reactive, Adaptive Architecture for Agents. Technical Report CMU-CS-91-147, School of Computer Science, Carnegie Mellon University, Pittsburgh, PA (1991)
3. Cheshire, T., Burton, C.: Transmedia: Entertainment reimagined, Wired UK, http://www.wired.co.uk/magazine/archive/2010/08/features/what-is-transmedia (accessed April 20, 2012)
4. Williams, D., Ursu, M.F., Meenowa, J., Cesar, P., Kegel, I., Bergström, K.: Video mediated social interaction between groups: System requirements and technology challenges. Telematics and Informatics 28, 251–270 (2011)
5. The Logtell Project Website, http://www.icad.puc-rio.br/~logtell (accessed April 19, 2012)

6. Ciarlini, A.E.M., Pozzer, C.T., Furtado, A.L., Feijo, B.: A logic-based tool for interactive generation and dramatization of stories. In: Proceedings of the International Conference on Advances in Computer Entertainment Technology, Valencia, pp. 133–140 (2005)

7. Grasbon, D., Braun, N.: A morphological approach to interactive storytelling. In: Proceedings of Cast 2001, Living in Mixed Realities, Sankt Augustin, Germany, pp. 337–340 (2001)

8. Mateas, M.: An Oz-Centric Review of Interactive Drama and Believable Agents. In: Veloso, M.M., Wooldridge, M.J. (eds.) Artificial Intelligence Today. LNCS (LNAI), vol. 1600, pp. 297–328. Springer, Heidelberg (1999)

9. Cavazza, M., Charles, F., Mead, S.: Character-based interactive storytelling. IEEE Intelligent Systems, Special issue on AI in Interactive Entertainment 17(4), 17–24 (2002)

10. Cavazza, M., Pizzi, D., Charles, F., Vogt, T., André, E.: Emotional Input for Character-based Interactive Storytelling. In: Proceedings of the 8th International Conference on Autonomous Agents and Multiagent Systems, Budapest, Hungary, pp. 313–320 (2009)

11. Cavazza, M., Charles, F., Mead, S.J., Martin, O., Marichal, X., Nandi, A.: Multimodal acting in mixed reality interactive storytelling. IEEE Multimedia 11(3), 30–39 (2004)

12. Cavazza, M., Lugrin, J.-L., Pizzi, D., Charles, F.: Madame bovary on the holodeck: immersive interactive storytelling. In: Proceedings of the 15th International Conference on Multimedia (MULTIMEDIA 2007), pp. 651–660 (2007)

13. Lima, E.S., Feijó, B., Barbosa, S., Silva, F.G., Furtado, A.L., Pozzer, C.T., Ciarlini, A.E.M.: Multimodal, Multi-User and Adaptive Interaction for Interactive Storytelling Applications. In: Proceedings of the 10th Brazilian Symposium on Computer Games and Digital Entertainment (SBGames), pp. 1–10 (2011)

14. Lima, E.S., Feijó, B., Barbosa, S.D.J., Furtado, A.L., Ciarlini, A.E.M., Pozzer, C.T.: Draw Your Own Story: Paper and Pencil Interactive Storytelling. In: Proceedings of the 10th International Conference on Entertainment Computing (ICEC), Vancouver (2011)

15. Kuka, D., Elias, O., Martins, R., Lindinger, C., Pramböck, A., Jalsovec, A., Maresch, P., Hörtner, H., Brandl, P.: DEEP SPACE: High Resolution VR Platform for Multi-user Interactive Narratives. In: Proceedings of the 2nd Joint International Conference on Interactive Digital Storytelling, pp. 185–196 (2009)

16. Gilroy, S., Porteous, J., Charles, F., Cavazza, M.: Exploring Passive User Interaction for Adaptive Narratives. In: Proceedings of the International Conference on Intelligent User Interfaces (IUI). ACM (2012)

17. Likavec, S., Lombardi, I., Nantiat, A., Picardi, C., Dupré, D.T.: Threading Facts into a Collective Narrative World. In: Aylett, R., Lim, M.Y., Louchart, S., Petta, P., Riedl, M. (eds.) ICIDS 2010. LNCS, vol. 6432, pp. 86–97. Springer, Heidelberg (2010)

18. Pittarello, F.: Designing a Context-Aware Architecture for Emotionally Engaging Mobile Storytelling. In: Campos, P., Graham, N., Jorge, J., Nunes, N., Palanque, P., Winckler, M. (eds.) INTERACT 2011, Part I. LNCS, vol. 6946, pp. 144–151. Springer, Heidelberg (2011)

19. OMG. UML Superstructure Specification, v2.4 (2011), http://www.omg.org/spec/UML/2.4/Superstructure/Beta2/PDF (accessed April 19, 2012)

20. Jurafsky, D., Martin, J.H.: Speech and language processing: An Introduction to Natural Language Processing. In: Computational Linguistics, and Speech Recognition. Prentice-Hall (2000)

21. Klein, D., Manning, D.C.: Accurate Unlexicalized Parsing. In: Proceedings of the 41st Meeting of the Association for Computational Linguistics, pp. 423–430 (2003)

22. Stanford, Stanford Parser, http://nlp.stanford.edu/software/lex-parser.shtml (accessed April 20, 2012)

23. Marneffe, M., Manning, C.D.: The Stanford typed dependencies representation. In: Proceedings of the Workshop on Cross-Framework and Cross-Domain Parser Evaluation, Manchester, pp. 1–8 (August 2008)
24. Raghunathan, K., Lee, H., Rangarajan, S., Chambers, N., Surdeanu, M., Jurafsky, D., Manning, C.: A Multi-Pass Sieve for Coreference Resolution. In: Proceedings of the 2010 Conference on Empirical Methods in Natural Language Processing, Boston, USA (2010)
25. Liu, B.: Sentiment Analysis and Subjectivity. In: Indurkhya, N., Damerau, F.J. (eds.) Handbook of Natural Language Processing, 2nd edn. (2010)
26. Camanho, M.M., Ciarlini, A.E.M., Furtado, A.L., Pozzer, C.T., Feijo, B.: A model for interactive TV Storytelling. In: Proceedings of the 7th Brazilian Symposium on Games and Digital Entertainment, Rio de Janeiro, Brazil, pp. 197–206 (2009)
27. Klimmt, C., Roth, C., Vermeulen, I., Vorderer, P.: The Empirical Assessment of The User Experience In Interactive Storytelling: Construct Validation of Candidate Evaluation Measures. Technical Report, Integrating Research in Interactive Storytelling - IRIS (2010)
28. Roth, C., Vorderer, P., Klimmt, C.: The Motivational Appeal of Interactive Storytelling: Towards a Dimensional Model of the User Experience. In: Iurgel, I.A., Zagalo, N., Petta, P. (eds.) ICIDS 2009. LNCS, vol. 5915, pp. 38–43. Springer, Heidelberg (2009)

Gaming after Dark

Visual Patterns and Their Significance for Atmosphere and Emotional Experience in Video Games

Ivana Müller, Petra Sundström, Martin Murer, and Manfred Tscheligi

Christian Doppler Laboratory for Contextual Interfaces,
ICT&S Center, University of Salzburg,
Salzburg, Austria
firstname.lastname@sbg.ac.at

Abstract. Design Patterns help a range of designers, architects, and others. However, there is surprisingly little such guidance for game artists. In this paper, we present our look at late 19th century art works and the emergent set of visual features commonly used to create an atmosphere of horror in visual art. Further, we show how we transformed these features into a set of seven patterns to be used in interactive artistry, based on an analysis of six well known survival horror games. Finally, we provide the full description of one of these patterns, the *Visual Contrast*.

Keywords: Design Patterns, Visual Art, Atmosphere, Survival Horror Games.

1   Introduction

Game designers and artists constantly encounter new challenges that emerge from the increasing variety of advanced technical upgrades, as well as the demanding expectations of the audience. This has had the effect that the art department often find it hard to keep up. The art often suffers from an uninspired application of these technological, engine-based presets [1]. In this context, a set of visual patterns could also potentially provide the art department with some guidance as to what game engine/technology may be the most suitable for translating a certain style.

One might argue that art is not something that can or should be limited to a set of pre-defined parameters, or that using patterns could diminish creativity and an individual approach to the work performed, but that would be a lack of understanding of what patterns are and in what way they can aid creative process. Patterns are by no means repetitive. They should be considered as hypotheses and/or a collection of ideas, there to act as inspiration and guidance. As every artist would probably agree, it is much easier to be creative if one knows the tools and masters the various methods of expertise.

As a first attempt in this direction, this paper decribes our viewing of an exhibition on uncanny art in Vienna and how the essential aesthetic traits used to evoke a feeling of unease were extracted, adjusted and examined according to how well they mapped

M. Herrlich, R. Malaka, and M. Masuch (Eds.): ICEC 2012, LNCS 7522, pp. 16–29, 2012.

to six well-known survival horror games. We end this paper by providing an example of how a pattern for visual contrast during enemy encounter in video games can be staged and used.

2   Background

Design patterns were first introduced in architectural design by Christopher Alexander [2], but were soon adopted and became a very popular tool in other design-related fields, such as software engineering [e.g. 3], and user experience and experience centered HCI [e.g. 4]. Lately, design patterns have also become an important tool for video game designers, providing many effective problem-solving approaches. The question is, why is there no such help for game artists?

There are, however, tendencies that show that this will happen. For example, Galda from Electronic Arts talked at the FMX'11 conference about their new artistic approach for creating emotionally appealing and cinematic experiences in the game *Fight Night Champion*. Also, Jonathan Jacques Belletete, the art director of the long awaited game *Deus Ex Human Revolution* stated, when being interviewed for Gamasutra [5], about their visual concept: *"They're motifs. They are patterns. That's the direction we chose"*. And even if these efforts do nto qualify as visual patterns as of yet, the trend of a structured artistic approach is clear, making this investigation relevant. Introducing the theory of patterns in art could be the basis for another successful brainstorming tool and further, a tool for offering ideas, solutions and methods for a practical translation of artistic concepts into the engine-based 3D space of the game, while preserving significant aspects of art and style.

In terms of already existing pattern-approaches for art, El-Nasr [6] has introduced several patterns for color and lighting techniques for creating the desired visual effect inspired by the staging of style in movies. His patterns were formulated on the basis of a qualitative study of over thirty movies. Such framework can serve as an important additional approach when extending the idea of visual patterns for game designers. Further, Ravaja and colleagues [7] have investigated emotional patterns in video games in terms of sensation seeking. They have also examined emotional responses of joy, relaxation or anger and pointed out that games with different characteristics (different genres) elicit different emotional response patterns.

There are also other works in this direction outside the field of gaming. For example Ståhl and colleagues [8] have explored how shapes, colors and animations can enhance an emotional experience when sending text messages. Also the principles of Gestaltanalysis [9] could be mentioned here as they describe how perception is related to abstractions, symbolism and form.

With the work presented here, our aim is to add to those works and in the longer perspective together form the basis for a set of tools and structures as guidance to game artists.

3   An Analysis of Visual Art

The starting point for this work was an analysis of traditional works of art, which we conducted to derive the key visual features that contribute to an uncanny atmospheric experience in visual art. The horror as used in video games is mainly based on two components; *body horror* that describes the fear of extreme abnormality and disfigurement of formerly known shapes, and *unconscious panic* that arises when confronted with the destruction of familiar forms and social aspects. Different from individual personal phobia, these two sources of fear expand beyond the boundaries of society. [10] The analyzed paintings were therefore chosen to cover both of the two themes and even though these paintings were non-interactive, we argue that interactive gaming and interactive art can learn a lot from the more established art traditions.

We looked at several exhibitions. One was *Edvard Munch und das Unheimliche*, exhibited in 2009/2010 in the Leopold Museum, Vienna. It contained a variety of paintings from Munch, Klinger, Ensor, Kubin and many other painters from the late 19th century, but also offered several essays and concepts from famous personalities, like the psychoanalyst Sigmund Freud and the writer Edgar Allan Poe, both of whom discussed the issue of the uncanny. Different from the usual Christian medieval illustration of horror that was based on portraying death, war or the terrors of hell, artists, writers and psychologist of the 19th century focused on the diffuse fear of obscure emotions and an uncanny atmosphere of the unconscious that, according to them, could be found in everyday life and within our dreams.

3.1   Visual Features

To define what visual features to look for, we made use of methods from image analysis [11] as it is applied in traditional art. As our final aim was game play, these features were slightly adjusted, perhaps most apparently in the visual features named *Characters* and *Contrast during Encounter*. The visual features we ended up looking for were:

Style. First of all, we analyzed style in general, as it determines basic parameters for all relevant visual factors and decides on the degree of abstraction of the look. Also the visual composition that results from style includes light placement, colors, camera angles, field of view, movement, textures and many more aesthetic features. In games, such art decisions have strong impact on how the game environment is perceived by the players [12]. If the style is well defined and seamlessly pursued throughout the whole work, it helps a lot in experiencing a believable and authentic environment.

Colors, Contrasts and Temperature. The next element we looked at was color and the subsequent scene temperature. Even in 'real' life, we decode at least forty percent of all received information through colors. Colors help us to orientate, to estimate distances and spaces. With nuances of colors, one is able to express the temperature of an image, [13] as well as evoke feelings of ease or unease, pleasure or disgust.

Light. The aspect of lighting was considered next. Light and shadow are inevitable components for creating the atmosphere. They provide clues concerning the spatial relationships of objects and reveal, to some extent, the information hidden from the current point of view. [14] Low-key scenarios or strong, dramatic light-effects build tension and expression into the environment. In video games, they also support motion and work as visual guidelines, as the eye reacts rapidly to light-and-dark changes.

Shapes and Geometry. This feature deals with the staging of the environment, based on the principles of geometry. Depending on the overall style, different forms are suitable for providing information about the environment. Cozy and safe rooms are portrayed in completely different shapes than hostile spaces, which employ sharper and edgier shapes.

Characters. Even though paintings show characters or introduce a *hero*, they are rather impersonal when compared to how they are used in video games, where the character is the main aspect of the story. Defining the looks of the protagonist, as well as various antagonists, is, to a large extent, the task of the art department. It is an essential one, as the player is usually accompanied by the main character throughout the whole game, and the protagonist is the main source of empathy experienced by the player [15]. In survival horror games, the character is usually weak, helpless and left alone in an hostile environment. On the contrary, monsters are creatures that threaten the player's goals and evoke feelings of disgust and fear. Their design usually fits with the style and through their appearance and movement, they directly mirror the attributes of the game atmosphere.

Contrasts during Encounter. This feature is also better represented in games than in paintings, as paintings only can show one single event at a time, while games offer the player a whole palette of visual experiences. This is essential for the changes of atmosphere related to events encountered during gameplay. The visual contrasts during enemy envounter are therefore one of the most subtle yet important aesthetic features in survival horror. This pattern refers to environmental changes that appear throughout the game and is, in other words, the displaying of release and tension through visual manners.

Visual Semantics. Finally, visual semantics deal with special objects, colors, or elements that are easily recognized by the audience as visual leitmotivs and symbolize certain events. Whether they are portrayed in an alienation effect or are an obvious recurring mark, they evoke certain emotional responses. In games, this is a rather easy tool to use, nevertheless a powerful and effective technique for guiding the player's attention and to support the storyline.

To provide an example of a painting we analyzed using the above listed visual features, we present our analysis of *Hatred* by Pietro Pajetta, painted in 1896. This specific painting was one of the many pieces at the exhibition *Edvard Munch und das Unheimliche*. The painting presumably deals with the topic of necrophilia and portrays a scene of interfering with the dead. It was chosen because it provides a good example for further game aesthetic analyses, as it not only resembles the semirealistic style of survival horror games, but also introduces characters and distinguished shapes, as often used in game design.

3.2   An Analysis of the Painting *Hatred*

A representative of the European art scene of the late 19th century, the painting deals with the topic of death in its own subtle yet macabre way. At first sight, the painting shows a man tenderly bending over a woman. Only at second glance can it be noticed that the woman is lying in a coffin and must therefore be dead. The tenderness of the man then seems vaguely strange and leaves the outcome to the viewer's imagination, causing a feeling of unease and anxiety.

Style. The style combines realistic methods with abstracted approaches to underline the topic and to lead the audience's eye to focus on the center of the painting. Even though at first, the painting looks realistically painted, it isn't: The painter carefully focused on the character of the dead woman and added lots of detail to her clothes, especially her white skirt, to make it the most outstanding part of the painting. The second character is almost a mere silhouette, with lack of details. It hovers like an ambiguous shadow over the first character and is nearly as stylized as the nature in the background, which is just implied by its shapes (the trees and the horizon). The level of detail increases with the immediate proximity, while the shapes in the distance appear blurry.

Fig. 1. Hatred by Pietro Pajetta, oil on canvas

Colors, Contrasts and Temperature. The colors used in the painting all share a similar tone of sepia, except for the dark shades of the forest and the figure in the front. The colors used for the background (sky and horizon) are faint and desaturated, while those in the front appear in various shades of rich brown. The only parts that stand out can be found in the shining white skirt of the woman and her slightly dusky pink blouse, which still match the yellowed undertone of the painting. The colors used are not pleasant, as they suggest something rotten, supporting the theme of death.

Fig. 2. Color codes as used in *Hatred*

The contrasts are visible and distinctive, starting with the most obvious display of the dark, almost black man, bending over the white woman. The two opposite colors touch in an almost exact diagonal that separates the whole painting. The contrasts are visible in the entire image, but especially in the center of the picture, where they are presented by the two characters.

The image also uses contrasts to describe negative spaces: The upper part of the painting, consisting of the lighter background (horizon and sky) serves as contrast to the dark silhouette of the man, while the lower part is almost the exact counterpart of this display, showing it as a negative (in reverted colors). See Figure 3.

The colors also play an important role for displaying the distance within the painting (apart from the contrasts of dark proximity and light background). The closer the scene is to the audience, the warmer the colors become and the more the shades of sepia take over.

Fig. 3. Contrasts and Geometry as used in *Hatred*

Light. The light in the painting is flat and non-realistic. While the sky suggests dusk or late dawn, the lighting is different than it should be at twilight. The warm light coming from the right could be explained by an additional light source not visible in the image, but the way the dead woman is illuminated is reminiscent rather of the surrealist approach to lighting. While every other element within the painting is dark, the figure of the woman is overexposed.

Shapes and Geometry. The painting works strongly with essential geometric shapes, see Figure 3. Each character or object represents one shape and the nature divides the image into two sections. Additionally, all basic shapes are in the very center of the piece. The shapes of the two characters are interesting; the man is represented by a circle (or rather an oval/egg-shaped form), while the woman with her dress is positioned as a triangle. While round shapes usually suggest safety and cosines, the man is dark and appears unpleasant, even dangerous. On the other hand, the unusual shape of the dead woman suggest her vulnerability, as she is lying there, unbent and stiff, directly exposed to the dark mass of the man, hovering over her body.

Characters. The painting introduces two characters, contradicting in many aspects: first, there is the body of a dead woman, shown in faint, pastel colors and strongly illuminated. Compared to her counterpart, she suggests something fragile and pure, while the second character appears dark and dangerous, threatening her peace. She is remarkably detailed, whereas the second character, the mysterious man, is painted in dark, undistinguished colors, reminiscent of a huge shadow. Even though he may look gentle at first sight, the colors and the context presents him as doubtlessly malevolent.

Visual Semantics. Not only the colors, light and contrast, but also the choice of the characters themselves suggests a duality portrayed in the painting. Starting with obvious differences, such as the bold use of black and white, the symbolism is carried on with the contrariety of man and woman and taken a step further, the dichotomy of the dead and the living.

About ten paintings were analyzed this way. This gave us a collection of visual features used for illustrating the themes of horror and fear. We then set ourselves the task of analyzing how well these features already were used in interactive gaming, and also to look for other tools and features that we had not seen used in the paintings.

4   An Analysis of Six Survival Horror Games

Six famous survival horror games were chosen for our analysis of how well these visual features were already used (and if they were used at all) in successful game titles; three western and three Japanese (or eastern, but incidentally, all three were Japanese). These games were chosen after interviews with 14 people who consider themselves fans of the survival horror genre. We asked them about their preferred games, as well as games they experienced as extraordinarily frightening. Apart from these interviews, we also looked at several online communities[1] devoted to the subject and looked at their top lists for the most popular games in the genre. The final selection was made according to how uncanny these games were considered to be, and to their use of body horror and unconscious panic. The final set of games was:

Dead Space 1. Developed by the U.S. studio Visceral Games and EA Redwood Shores and published by EA in 2008, this 3rd person shooter game follows the storyline of Isaac Clarke, an engineer who has to survive on board of the USG Ishimura, an interstellar mining ship infested with mutant human-like creatures called Necromorphs.

Silent Hill 2. Konami's survival horror classic from 2001 that relies mainly on dynamics of aberrant psychology as its most essential element, was the second game analyzed. The game evolves around the protagonist James who receives a letter from his late wife Mary, inviting him to meet her at their special place in a small town called Silent Hill. As soon as James arrives there to solve the mystery, his nightmarish journey through distorted realities and obscure locations begins, constantly walking the thin line between sanity and madness.

Alan Wake. A story-driven survival horror game, developed by the Finnish studio Remedy Entertainment and published by Microsoft Game Studios in 2010, was the

---

[1] Gamasutra.com (with various contributions), Dreamdawn.com, Compactiongames.about.com, Joystickdivision.com, Vsrecommendedgames.wikia.com, Thegamershub.net, Gameranx.com

third game we looked at. This game skillfully adapts the strengths of psychological thrillers with a cinematic look and feel. The plot follows Alan Wake, a novel writer on his journey to uncover the mysteries of the small town Bright Falls in Alaska and investigate the disappearance of his beloved wife. The main idea of the game is to fight darkness with the use of light.

Amnesia - The Dark Descent. The third western game looked at, developed and published by Swedish Frictional Games in 2010, features the unarmed protagonist named Daniel, suffering from amnesia. The player guides the character through a dark and foreboding castle, avoiding terrible creatures and dangerous obstructions, while trying to regain his memory.

Project Zero (Fatal Frame). The Japanese survival horror game named Project Zero, but known as Fatal Frame in the USA, was released in 2001 by Temco. It has a unique plot that deals with ghosts, exorcism and dark, evil Shinto rituals. The game follows the young girl Miku Hinasaki on the search for her missing brother. Equipped only with an old camera, the player must survive among lost, hostile souls and make his/her way through a haunted mansion.

Haunting Ground (Demento). This highly disturbing survival horror game developed and published by Capcom in 2005 was the last of the Japanese games we looked at. The plot revolves around Fiona Belli, who awakens in a sinister castle after surviving a car accident. Even though her memories seem too vague to figure out what happened, she soon realizes that she must quickly escape from the castle. Accompanied by a German Shepherd, Fiona tries to evade and hide from the odd personnel of the castle that is stalking and hunting her down, trying to kill her.

Each of the six games was analyzed using the list of visual features defined above. For that purpose, we sat next to persons playing these games and took notes while talking to the players about their experiences in various game-play situations. Our focus was on the aesthetic display of the game. Due to space limitations, this paper only presents the analysis of one of the games, *Alan Wake*.

4.1   The Analysis of the Game *Alan Wake*

Style. This game pursues an almost photorealistic look that supports the cinematic approach. It fits well with the concept of displaying the journey of Alan as TV- like episodes. Due to its overwhelming visual style, the game is very touching and immersive and draws the player gradually into the world of *Alan Wake* with an intensity that goes under the skin.

Colors, Contrasts and Temperature. The use of colors is intuitive; see Figure 4 for the color code. As the change of day and night plays a crucial role in the game, the scenes change, not only in terms of color, but also in contrast, hue and saturation. The night is basically deep blue, with highly saturated tones of indigo. It has passages of pure black and the contrast is set high. Overall, the night conveys an intense color experience. However, once inside a building, there are almost no traces left of the strong saturation. The colors, even though basically staying the same bluish teints of violet or green, seem to be washed out, grey rather than colorful. There are also shades of sepia mixed with the colors. Still, the shadows remain deep black, providing a hard contrast between fair and dark areas. The daylight, on the other hand, appears colorless in comparison to the night. The exterior is very bright with low contrast, mainly filled with shades of sepia and grey, both in very low saturation. The interior is similar, just a little bit darker and denser, reminiscent of the color codes of other survival horror games. The illustrative change starts with the dusk, when darkness approaches. First of all, the contrast settings improve even though the hues do not change. Dark areas filled with grey shadows become deep dark and seem to expand. After that, the hues take on shades of violet and brown with a higher saturation that evokes an eerie feeling, and finally the intense blue hue merges with the other colors.

Fig. 4. Color codes as used in *Alan Wake*

Light. The lighting also depends on how day and night changes in this game. The light during the night almost always outshines its source and causes strong rimlights to accentuate silhouettes. On the contrary, shadows appear deeply dark, in both static and moving conditions. Glowing spots and haze in the background signify darkness. Again, daylight is extremely radiant and almost purely white. Even though it should improve the feeling of security during a sunny day, the fact that the light is colorless and white makes it appear sterile and cold, almost without any shadows at all. The third aspect of light in this game is related to the torchlight that is an indispensable tool for Alan. It provides the protagonist with an enhanced view in darkness and is essential during the fights against dark creatures. The emblematic cone of light that shines down on Alan from time to time is displayed by dense, strong light, piercing through darkness, shielding and protecting him.

Shapes and Geometry (Environment). As the setting is the small town of Bright Falls, the game world is open and provides the player with interiors as well as open landscape with forests, lakes and meadows. The nature is shown in a beautiful, almost poetic way, while turning vile and wild when roamed by the Dark Presence. The buildings are rustic and country-style, reminding one that the town used to be an Indian colony.

Characters (and Monsters). The protagonist Alan Wake is a very natural looking character with a likable face. It is easy to empathize with him and even become attracted to his looks. The main antagonist in the game is known as the Dark Presence and is a dark and evil force responsible for the nightmares haunting Bright Falls. Visually, the Dark Presence is manifested as heavy fog, bleach smoke, dense shadow, swarms of birds or even swarms of people. The player encounters the Dark Presence mostly as dangerous dark, humanoid, faceless creatures, immortal unless pierced by the torchlight.

Contrast during Encounter. The contrast during an encounter with enemies is a visually impressive experience. The whole screen changes color and fades to apparently unrelated shades. The colors become expressive in hue and saturation, shifting between blue-green, blue-violet and red or pink. Any light sources are strongly outshined, adding glowing and sparkling accents to the scene. The shadows appear more vivid, dancing around in wild motion. At the same time, the player is exposed to slow motion, motion blurs and bloom post effects, while shiny sparks emit more confusing lights. The camera is shaking and when hit, the whole screen turns red. The signs of enemy approaching include exploding light sources that can be noted immediately before the actual encounter.

Visual Semantics. The main theme of *Alan Wake* is light and darkness, and not only in terms of daytime vs. nighttime, but also in terms of mental sanity. This is visualized through visual responses within the game: the day is desaturated, almost colorless and faint, and the night nearly bursts in intense colors. It is during the night that Alan must pursue his quest and during daytime that he has to face his challenges with advancing logics that evoke doubts about his mental state and sanity, dealing with his nightly encounters with the Dark Presence.

In addition to the analysis of the six games, we watched several walkthrough-videos of each of these games, put online by various players. As many of the walkthrough videos were commented, we could easily identify the moods and anxieties various players were experiencing during the game, even though we never were in direct contact with any of the players. This resulted in descriptions of each of the games, same as the one presented above for *Alan Wake*.

5   Visual Patterns

In the final step, we extracted the information about each of the visual features from the six descriptions we had obtained by game analysis. These extractions were then summarized in the basis of their similarities and adjusted into a pattern description along the lines of the pattern template as used in game design [16]:

Name. A single word or a short phrase, defining the main concept of the pattern.

Core Definition. A brief sentence describing the core content of the pattern. The idea behind core definitions is to provide an initial overview for browsing through an extensive pattern collection.

General Description. A short, general description of properties that provide the fundamentals of the pattern, as well as the motivation for its name. General properties are stated by using game examples and concepts that occur in the component framework. The general description is concluded by some explicit examples of various aspects and games that contain the pattern.

Use of the Pattern. A variety of choices which can be helpful when applying the pattern are listed.

Consequences. This part provides information about issues that may appear when a pattern is found in a game. For our purposes, this section is directed toward analyzing visual aspects to help solve artistic problems in an already existing visual design, or to suggest other patterns to instantiate in the art of the game.

Relations. This section lists the relations that exist between the analyzed pattern and other patterns. Basically all patterns occuring in any game design concept are in relation to each other, due to the interactivity of a game. Any related pattern is sorted into five categories with different kinds of relations: *Instantiates* (meaning the presence of the pattern requires the presence of a second pattern), *Modulates* (the pattern changes certain aspects and features of a second pattern), *Instantiated by* (the pattern can be instantiated by the presence of a related pattern), *Modulated by* (if additional patterns are applied, this will happen to this specific pattern) and *Potentially conflicted with* (using this pattern makes the use of another pattern impossible).

Examples. Here, the direct inspirations for creating the pattern are listed, as well as some descriptions of the main aspects of the pattern.

Due to space limitations, we can only present one pattern we created in this paper. Also, this paper is mainly concerned with the proces of creating patterns and the arguments for using them, and not so much with the patterns themselves (that would be a different kind of publication). The pattern *Visual Contrast during Encounter* was chosen to represent the created patterns, as it not only combines various aesthetic aspects, such as light and color, but also refers to important components of interactivity essential for the game experience. The other six patterns emergent from our work were: *Style, Color, Light, Geometry, Characters* and *Visual Semantics*.

5.1   The Pattern for Visual Contrast during Encounter

Core Definition. This pattern describes how to apply visual changes to the overall style during certain events within the game, to guide the player's attention and increase immersion.

General Description. Visual Contrast during Encounter with enemies is strongly connected to tension during gameplay, as (especially in the survival horror genre) the player is left with doubts about the outcome of the battle and the game at large. Emotional cues during such moments are expressively visualized in various ways in order to emphasize the fact that the player is not fully in control of the events and more importantly, of his/her character.

Example from *Haunting Ground*. When encountering an enemy stalker during gameplay, Fiona, the heroine of *Haunting Ground*, may panic. Her vision becomes limited to a few essential things, her focus shifts and colors change in contrast and saturation. Her movements are restricted by adding a freeze-frame effect, combined with strong motion blur and camera shakes.

Using the Pattern. The presence of enemies, deadly traps as well as player character killing and player character elimination are the basis for the existence of factors attempting to inflict damage on the player and thus create a feeling of tension. In the survival horror genre, the player expects these factors all the time, which puts him/her in a constant state of tension. This feeling can be even improved by the actual encounter with such a factor – usually in the form of an enemy. Encounters are a strong visually impressive experience for the player and have two main purposes: on the one hand, it is important to visually emphasize the immediate danger coming from the encounter and urge the player to change the situation, whether it is through fighting or running; on the other hand, they strengthen the connection between the protagonist and player, as the protagonist's fears are directly communicated, showing his/her limited vision and abilities caused by the panic s/he experiences.

Making use of various elements to support this situation, the image is filled with disturbing visuals, such as swaying and shaking of the camera, change of saturation and hue, stronger contrast and often also movement of lighting, combined with additional light sources that increase spaces of lit areas, and darkest shadows. The survival horror genre introduces some key features, such as the third-person perspective (in most cases) that allows for the showing of the scenery framed in high-or low angle long shots or distorted lenses in order to increase the feeling of vulnerability and isolation and especially to enhance the shock experienced during an encounter. These features add dramatic tension to the scene, allowing the player to see things that would usually remain lost, such as the approach of monsters and the protagonist running for his/her life at the same time. The tension of an encounter reaches its visual peak when the monster is able to grab the protagonist – this is the moment when the character usually panics the most. Often, this moment is displayed in a short negative shot – an image with reversed tones – followed by the most advanced dissociation of the usual look and feel. The camera might move around way too fast or in very slow motion, while the character and the monster's movements can appear excessively jerky, with the overall representation of the horrific game world possibly becoming very confusing.

Consequences. The visual representation of an encounter serves mainly the purpose of shifting the focus of the player, directly influencing the perception of the horrific atmosphere when experiencing loss of control. Considerations of a probable threat lead to a state of constant emotional anxiety which is a good base for experiencing shock, as this exact scenario is more or less expected by players of survival horror games. According to Power and Dalgleish [17], the fear reactions are mainly triggered by expecting the threat, rather than observing it. The immediate encounter is the climax of such expectations, resulting in the peak of a visually disturbing alienation. The entire graphic representation focuses on communicating the experience of shock and loss of control to the player; it integrates elements of cinematography, light and color as well as multiple post effects within the scene in order to change the image to its utmost expressive and vertiginous extent. The pattern for *Visual Contrast during Encounter* points out which visual elements are essential for triggering both emotions: the anxiety that slowly grows when the player starts to suspect hostile changes within the environment, as well as the initial shock that is experienced when the confrontation with the long-expected fearsome enemy actually happens. Apart from this conceptual inspiration, the pattern also offers suggestions about the use of different tools and techniques to achieve the desired emotional response within the game, such as post effects, camera shakes, animation of lights, desaturation or shifting of colors or freeze-frame animation. In terms of lighting for improving tension, several game titles already embraced the utility of cinematic lighting effects for projecting peaks of excitement and fear in gameplay.

"Examples include flickering lights interjected at specific moments in the game, darkly lit environments or the use of saturated red." [6]

Fig. 5. Visual Contrast during Enemy-Encounter in *Haunting Ground*

Relations[2]

- *Instantiates*: Emotional Immersion, Tension, Disruption of Focused Attention, Fear, Emotional Response, Visual Acceptance, Field of Vision
- *Modulates:* Focus of Attention, Perception of Environment, Imperfect Information, Player Behavior, Character Behavior
- *Instantiated by*: Monsters, Penalties, Combat, Damage
- *Modulated by*: Time Limits, Character Killing, Player Behavior
- *Potentially conflicting with*: Visual Style, Gameplay

6   Conclusion

This paper outlines our attempt to take the first steps towards the creation of a set of visual patterns for game artists. We took visual features obtained by image analysis, and used them as a basis for an analysis of the manner in which visual art conveys an atmosphere of horror. Then, we explored how it is used within game design. We used these findings to generate a set of seven patterns specifically for the survival horror game genre, with the pattern for *Visual Contrast during Encounter* included in this paper. More research and experiments are needed in order to formulate a working collection of visual patterns to enhance the game art workflow in terms of concept and production. Visual patterns for genres other than survival horror are, of course, also necessary to be created and worked on. It is important to note that different genres will stimulate different visual clues, and thus different emotional responses within the game [e.g 18, 19] and result in a variety of different visual patterns; however, the overall aim remains the same – visual patterns should provide game artists with:

1. Inspiration and overview of artistic approaches to use within the specified genre.
2. A wide range of possibilities and tools to translate a visual direction into technologies and game-engines that are likely to be used without losing the genuine artistic approach to the engine's technology.

---

[2] The Relations-section was added to the pattern for the sake of completeness. It will become more relevant when used with the set of future visual patterns that influence and relate to eachother, just as described above.

Acknowledgements. We greatly acknowledge the financial support by the Federal Ministry of Economy, Family and Youth and the National Foundation for Research, Technology and Development (Christian Doppler Laboratory for "Contextual Interfaces") and the project "AIR – Advanced Interface Research" funded by the Austrian Research Promotion Agency (FFG), the ZIT Center for Innovation and Technology and the province of Salzburg under contract number 825345.

References

1. Bunt, B.: Obliquereflections: softwareart & the 3d gamesengine. In: CyberGames 2006, Perth, Western Australia (2006)
2. Alexander, C., Ishikawa, S., Silverstein, M.: A Pattern Language: Towns, Buildings, Constructions (Center for Environmental Structure Series). University Press, Oxford (1977)
3. Gamma, E., Helm, R., et al.: Design Patterns: Elements of Reusable Object-Oriented Software. Pearson Education Corporate Sales Devision, Indianapolis (1995)
4. Obrist, M., Wurhofer, D., et al.: CUX patterns approach: Towards contextual user experience patterns. In: PATTERNS 2010, Lisbon, Portugal (2010)
5. Remo, C., http://www.gamasutra.com/view/feature/4325/past_and_future_tension_the_.php
6. El-Nasr, M.: Projectingtension in virtualenvironmentsthroughlighting. In: CHI 2006, Montréal, Québec, Canada (2006)
7. Ravaja, N., Salminen, M., et al.: Emotional responsepatternsand sense ofpresenceduringvideogames: Potential criterion variables forgame design. In: NordiCHI 2004, Tampere, Finland (2004)
8. Ståhl, A., Höök, K., Sundström, P.: A Foundation for Emotional Expressivity. In: DUX 2005, San Francisco, USA (2005)
9. Von Ehrenfels, C.: Übergestaltqualitäten. Vierteljahrsschriftfürwissenschaftliche Philosophie. n/a (1890)
10. McCrea, C.: Horror Video Games: Essays on the Fusion of Fear and Play. McFarland & Company, Inc., Publishers, North Carolina (2009)
11. Welton, J.: Eyewitness Art – Looking at Paintings. Dorling Kindersley, London (1994)
12. El-Nasr, M., Zupko, J., Miron, K.: Intelligent lightingfor a bettergamingexperience. In: CHI 2005, Portland, Oregon, USA (2005)
13. Marschall, S.: Farbeim Kino. SchürenVerlag GmbH, Marburg (2009)
14. Eisemann, E., Assarsson, U., et al.: Casting shadows in real time. In: SIGGRAPH ASIA 2009, Yokohama, Japan (2009)
15. Schaap, R., Bidarra, R.: Towards emotional characters in computergames. In: ICEC 2009, Taipei, Taiwan (2009)
16. Björk, S., Holopainen, J.: Patterns in Game Design. Charles River Media, Inc., Hingham (2005)
17. Power, M., Dalgleish, T.: Cognition and Emotion: From Order to Disorder. Psychology Press Ltd., Hove (1997)
18. El-Nasr, M., Yan, S.: Visual attention in 3d videogames. In: ACE 2006, San Antonio, Texas, USA (2006)
19. Jie, L., Clark, J.: Game Design Guided by Visual Attention. In: Ma, L., Rauterberg, M., Nakatsu, R. (eds.) ICEC 2007. LNCS, vol. 4740, pp. 345–355. Springer, Heidelberg (2007)

Information-Gathering Events in Story Plots

Fabio A. Guilherme da Silva[1], Antonio L. Furtado[1], Angelo E.M. Ciarlini[2], Cesar Tadeu Pozzer[3], Bruno Feijó[1], and Edirlei Soares de Lima[1]

[1] PUC-Rio, Depto. de Informática, Brasil
{faraujo,furtado,bfeijo,elima}@inf.puc-rio.br
[2] UNIRIO, Depto. de Informática Aplicada, Brasil
angelo.ciarlini@uniriotec.br
[3] UFSM – Departamento de Eletrônica e Computação, Santa Maria
pozzer3@gmail.com

Abstract. Story plots must contain, besides physical action events, a minimal set of information-gathering events, whereby the various characters can form their beliefs on the facts of the mini-world in which the narrative takes place. In this paper, we present an approach to model such events within a plan-based storytelling context. Three kinds of such events are considered here, involving, respectively, inter-character communication, perception and reasoning. Multiple discordant beliefs about the same fact are allowed, making necessary the introduction of higher-level facilities to rank them and to exclude those that violate certain constraints. Other higher-level facilities are also available for pattern-matching against typical-plan libraries or previously composed plots. A prototype logic programming implementation is fully operational. A simple example is used throughout the presentation.

Keywords: Plot Composition, Communicative Acts, Perception, Deduction, Abduction, Plan Recognition, Plan Generation, Logic Programming.

1 Introduction

Story plots typically include action events, but another class of events is also needed for the sake of realism: the *information-gathering* events, which enable the various characters to mentally apprehend the state of the world. Without such events, one would have to assume that the characters are omniscient, being aware of all facts that currently hold and of how they change as a consequence of the action events. In order to create and analyze more plausible story plots, we propose an approach to model *information-gathering* events.

Here we shall recognize a sharp distinction between the facts themselves and the sets of *beliefs* of each character about the facts that hold at the current state of the world, which constitute, so to speak, their respective *internal states*. Beliefs can be right or wrong, depending on their corresponding or not to the actual facts. Moreover, we have taken the option that acquiring a belief does not cancel a previous belief. As a consequence, we allow a character to simultaneously entertain more than one belief with respect to the same fact, possibly with a different degree of confidence which

M. Herrlich, R. Malaka, and M. Masuch (Eds.): ICEC 2012, LNCS 7522, pp. 30–44, 2012.

depends on the provenance of the beliefs. We consider three types of information-gathering events, each type associated with a set of operations: *communication events*, supported by the operations `tell`, `ask` and `agree`; *perception events*, supported by the operations `sense` and `watch`; and *reasoning events*, supported by the operations `infer` and `suppose`.

All operations refer to beliefs on facts, except `watch`, whose object is some action event witnessed by a character. The operations are defined in terms of their pre-conditions and post-conditions, in the same way operations corresponding to action events are defined, i.e. using the STRIPS formalism [1]. The pre-conditions are logical expressions commonly involving affirmed or negated facts and beliefs, whereas post-conditions denote the effect of the operation in terms of beliefs that are added or deleted to/from the current internal states of the characters involved. The specification of the operations is deliberately kept at a minimum to be independent from the context. It is however, complemented, both with respect to pre-conditions and post-conditions, by separate *conditioners* that express the peculiarities of the different characters participating in the stories.

The approach described here is going to be integrated with the **Logtell** interactive storytelling system [2, 3]. **Logtell** uses a *plan-generation* algorithm that deals with nondeterministic and partially-ordered events to compose plots. Since the present work focuses on the construction of an information-gathering package, to be later integrated to the design of full-fledged narrative genres, we decided to initially use a simpler planner that deals only with deterministic events. In addition, a single action event will be mentioned in our example. This event, associated with the `go` operation, consists of the displacement of a character from a place to another, which is needed because presential verbal interaction is the only form of communication that we currently cover.

All features discussed were implemented in a logic-programming prototype, and a simple running example is used as illustration. Section 2 explains how the example was formulated so as to run in a plan-based context. Section 3 describes the information-gathering events. Section 4 adds some higher-level facilities, which help to analyze the resulting beliefs and to make comparisons by means of *plan-recognition*. Section 5 reviews related work, and section 6 contains concluding remarks.

2   Example in a Plan-Based Context

2.1   Conceptual Specification

Our conceptual design method involves three schemas: static, dynamic and behavioural. The *static schema* specifies, in terms of the *Entity-Relationship* model [4], the entity classes, attributes and binary-relationships. The information-gathering package requires the Prolog clauses below to describe entities, attributes and relationships:

```
entity(person,name).
attribute(person,gender).
relationship(current_place,[person,Place]) :-  taken_as_place(Place).
attribute(person,believes).
relationship(trusts,[person,person]).
```

Similarly to what happens to `believes`, we have defined `sensed`, `watched`, `inferred`, `supposed` and `asked` as attributes of the entity `person`. Also, notice that the specification of the `current_place` relationship associates the entity `person` with a still undetermined entity, represented by the variable `Place`. Putting the package together with a story context, other clauses can be added. In our example, we use the following:

```
entity(country,country_name).
entity(city,city_name).
attribute(person,hair_colour).
attribute(person,daltonic).
relationship(born, [person,country]).
relationship(home, [person,country]).
relationship(citizen, [person,country]).
taken_as_place(city).
```

The *dynamic schema* defines a fixed repertoire of operations for consistently performing the state changes corresponding to the events that can happen in the mini-world of the application. The *STRIPS* [1] model is used. Each operation is defined in terms of pre-conditions, which consist of conjunctions of positive and/or negative literals, and any number of post-conditions, consisting of facts to be asserted or retracted as the effect of executing the operation. The operations that constitute the core of the information-gathering package will be described in section 3.

Currently our *behavioural schema* specifications mainly consist of goal-inference (a.k.a. situation-objective) rules. Since our present running example does not employ such rules, we shall not discuss them here (cf. [2]).

2.2   States of the Stories

States of the story are sets of ground clauses denoting valid instances of the specified static schema. These clauses are facts (positive literals) specifying the entity instances, their attributes and relationships. Whenever a fact is not part of a state, it is assumed to be false. Beliefs and facts that describe what is told, asked, sensed, watched, inferred and supposed by characters are attributes of the characters and can also be part of a state and mentioned in pre- and post-conditions of the events. These facts about facts can speak about both positive and negative literals (e.g. a character can believe that a certain fact is not true).

To generate a plot, it is necessary to populate the initial database state. Informally speaking, the mini-world of our example comprises four characters, John, Peter, Mary and Laura, three countries, UK, USA and Canada, and two cities, both in the UK, London and Manchester. The recorded information does not provide a uniform coverage. It registers where Mary, Peter and Laura were born but does not indicate John's birth-place. About Mary it adds that her domicile (home) is also in the UK and that she has red hair, whereas Laura — who, in spite of having been born in the USA, is a Canadian citizen — is blond. Peter is said to be daltonic. John, Peter and Mary are currently in London, and Laura in Manchester. Contrary to the other characters, whose beliefs are initially confined to their explicitly recorded properties, John is aware of all registered facts.

2.3   Main Features of the Plan-Generator

The plan generator follows a backward chaining strategy. For a fact F (or not F) that is part of a given goal, it checks whether it is already true (or false) at the current state. If this is not the case, it looks for an operation Op declared to add (or delete) the fact as part of its effects. Having found such operation, it then checks whether the precondition Pr of Op currently holds – if not, it tries, recursively, to satisfy Pr. Moreover, the plan generator must consider the so-called frame problem [5].

In view of the needs of the information-gathering package, we specified pre_state(Op,S) as one more effect of every operation Op, which allows to capture in S the *prefix* of operation Op, i.e. the entire plan sequence, starting at the initial state, to which Op will be appended. Indeed, sequence S supplies a convenient operational denotation of the state immediately before the event denoted by Op, to which we may, in particular, apply the holds predicate to find out who was present at some place associated with the occurrence of the event. This is important, in particular, because (at least for the time being) we assume that, to watch an event, a character should be at the place where the event occurs.

Like goals, pre-conditions are denoted by conjunctions of literals. We distinguish, and treat differently, three cases for the positive or negative facts involved:

1. facts which, in case of failure, should be treated as goals to be tried recursively by the plan generator;
2. facts to be tested immediately before the execution of the operation, but which will not be treated as goals: if they fail the operation simply cannot be applied;
3. facts that are not declared as added or deleted by any of the predefined operations.

Note that the general format of a pre-condition clause for operation Op is precond(Op, Pr) :- B. In cases (1) and (2), a fact F (or not F) must figure in Pr, with the distinction that the barred notation /F (or /(not F)) will be used in case (2). Case (3) is handled in a particularly efficient way. Since it refers to facts that are invariant with respect to the operations, such facts can be included in the body B of the clause, being simply tested against the current state when the clause is selected.

An example is the precondition clause of operation tell(A,B,F), where character A tells something to character B. We require that the two characters should be together at the same place, and, accordingly, the Pr argument shows two terms containing the same variable L to express this location requirement, but the term for B is barred: /current_place(B,L), which does not happen in A's case. The difference has an intuitive justification: character A, who is the agent of the operation, has to either already be present or to go to the place L where B is, but the latter would just happen to be there for some other reason.

The proper treatment of (1) and (2) is somewhat tricky, because of the backward chaining strategy of the planning algorithm. Suppose the pre-condition Pr of operation Op is tested at a state S_1. If it fails, the terms belonging to case (1) will cause a recursive call whereby one or more additional operations will be inserted so as to move from S_1 to a state S_2 where Op itself can be included. But it is only at S_2, not at S_1, that the barred terms in case (2) ought to be tested, and so the test must be *delayed* until the return from the recursive call, when the plan sequence reaching S_2 will be fully instantiated. Delayed evaluation is also needed, as one would expect, for instantiating the `pre_state` predicate mentioned before.

Once generated, a plan can be processed via the `execute` command, thus effecting the desired state transition, i.e. adding and/or deleting facts to/from the current database state. As a side effect, the `log(S)` clause (initially set as `log(start)`) is updated by appending to `S` the plan executed. At any time, the entire story thus far composed can be narrated, in pseudo-natural language, by entering "`:- log.`".

To finish this partial review of the plan features, we remark that the planning algorithm `plans(G,P)` can be called in more than one way. More often `G` is given, as the goal, and `P` is a variable to which a generated plan will be assigned as output. However an inverse usage has been provided, wherein `P` is given and `G` is a variable. In this case, the algorithm will check whether `P` is executable in view of the initial state and of the interplay of pre- and post-conditions, and, if so, assign its net effects (a conjunction of `F` and `not F` terms) to `G`.

2.4   Templates for Pseudo-natural Language Generation

Both for facts and events, we resort to *templates* for description and narration in pseudo-natural language. The template device allows, to begin with, to list all properties registered in the initial database state (or in the current state reached by executing a plan), via the `facts` predicate. The templates for operations and facts are combined in a way that favours a fairly readable style. Consider, as an example, operation `tell(A,B,F)`, in which `A` tells fact `F` to `B`. Suppose fact `F` corresponds to a property of character `C`. Concerning the identity of the three characters, we can distinguish three situations:

- They are all distinct: `tell('John','Peter',hair_colour('Mary',red))`
- C is the same as A: `tell('Mary','Peter',hair_colour('Mary',red))`
- C is the same as B: `tell('John','Mary',hair_colour('Mary',red))`

The `def_template` algorithm that drives the application of the templates produces for the above events:

```
John tells Peter: "- Mary has red hair".
Mary tells Peter: "- My hair is red".
John tells Mary: "- Your hair is red".
```

The algorithm duly uses gender information, rendering for example `infer('Mary',citizen('Mary','UK'))` as:

```
Mary infers that she is a citizen of UK.
```

Negative facts in the several operations, and the occurrence of variables in the `ask` operation, are treated as expected by the algorithm. So, again for the `hair_colour` property, one will have, respectively:

```
tell('John','Laura',not hair_colour('Laura',red))
    John tells Laura: "- Your hair is not red".
ask('John','Laura',hair_colour('Laura',X))
    John asks Laura: "- What is the colour of your hair?".
ask('John','Laura',hair_colour(X,red)))
    John asks Laura: "- Who has red hair?".
```

Analogous templates are provided for rendering in pseudo-natural language the information-package facts, such as `told`, `asked`, `sensed`, `watched`, `inferred`, `supposed`, `believes` and `trusts`. These templates are generic and can be used in different story contexts.

3   The Information Gathering Events

Our information gathering events change the current state by adding clauses that represent when facts are believed, told, asked, sensed, watched, inferred and supposed by characters. They were modeled by a generic schema of the corresponding operations, which extends the set of pre-conditions in accordance with context-dependent rules. In this section such schema is described.

3.1   Communication Events

In the Computer Science community, communication between characters immediately brings to mind the communication processes executed by software agents in multi-agent environments [6]. In particular, the Agent Communication Language consists of formally specified operations similarly defined by their pre-conditions and post-conditions [7]. However software agents differ from fictional characters (and, ironically, from human beings in general) in that they are supposed to only transmit information on which they believe, to agents that still lack such information and need it in order to play their role in the execution of some practical service.

In contrast, certain characters are prone to lie, either for their benefit or even out of habit. In general they may ignore the conversational maxims prescribed by philosophers of language, such as [8]. The bare specification of our `tell(A,B,F)` operation does not even require that A has any notion of the fact F to be transmitted to B. It is enough that both characters are at the same local L; if they are not, a `current_place(A,L)` sub-goal is recursively activated, which may cause the displacement of the teller (character A) to L, where B currently is (note the "/" sign before `current_place(B,L)`, as showed in section 2.3, to indicate that B would not be expected to move). And the only necessary effect of the operation is merely that F is told by A to B. Whether or not B will believe in F will depend on the execution of the `agree` operation, which in turn depends on whether or not B trusts A.

The `ask` operation is similarly defined, and its effect is just that A has `asked` F from B, who may respond or not. The fundamental character-dependent conditioners are established, respectively, by separate `will_tell` and `will_ask` clauses. These clauses specify the conditions for telling or asking about a fact within a certain story context. Such conditions are automatically considered as part of the pre-conditions of an event `tell` or `ask` by the planning algorithm.

Example 1: Mary is willing to ask John about his current whereabouts. She asks, he replies and, since she trusts him, adopts the belief that he is in London.

```
Goal: believes(Mary, current_place(John, A))
Mary asks John: "- Where are you?". John tells Mary: "- I am now in
London". Mary agrees with John.
```

3.2   Perception Events

Perception is the faculty whereby people keep contact with the world through their five senses (sight, hearing, touch, smell and taste). At the present stage of our work we do not make such distinctions, and merely consider a generic `sense` operation to apprehend any sort of fact, with a variant version that makes provision for defective sensing. For correct sensing of a positive or negative fact F, F must be successfully tested. Distorted sensing is accompanied by a side-remark on the true fact. In any case, besides the effect that F was `sensed` by the character, a `belief` clause is immediately added, since direct perception does not depend on a third party who might not be trusted.

The `watch(W,O)` operation was harder to implement, requiring the inclusion of the already mentioned `pre_state(O,S)` clause as an extra feature, where O is the operation witnessed by W, and S denotes the state previous to the application of O (i.e. the sub-sequence of the generated plan that precedes O). It becomes possible then to check the location of character W at the time when O happens.

As before, the definitions are left to be completed by conditioners, respectively `sense_rule` and `watch_rule` clauses. For `sense`, it is required that, to ascertain a positive or negative fact F involving an entity instance E currently at place L, a character W must be at L, either originally or as the result of pursuing `current_place(W,L)` as a sub-goal. For `watch`, normally applicable to action events only, the `current_place` requirements depend on what is being watched, which justifies their being left to the special `watch_rule` clauses, to which the `current_place(W,L)` information, checked as described before, is passed. For instance, `go(A,L1,L2)` can be watched partly by persons at L1 (origin) and partly by those present at L2 (destination). Naturally the agent (character A) is able to watch the action in its entirety.

Example 2: Peter obtains three different indications concerning the colour of Mary's hair. Only the first, supplied by trustworthy John, was correct. Laura was lying, and Peter himself, being daltonic, failed to perceive the true colour.

```
Goal: believes(Peter, hair_colour(Mary, A))
John tells Peter: "- Mary has red hair". Peter agrees with John.
Laura goes from Manchester to London. Laura tells Peter: "- Mary has
blond hair". Peter agrees with Laura.
Peter wrongly senses that Mary has green hair -- in fact Mary has red
hair.
```

3.3   Reasoning Events

Deduction, induction and abduction are complementary reasoning strategies. For deduction, if there is a rule $A \rightarrow B$ and the antecedent A is known to hold, it is legitimate to *infer* that the consequent B holds. In the case of induction (fundamental to the natural sciences), the systematic occurrence of B whenever A occurs may justify the adoption of rule $A \rightarrow B$. Abduction is a non-guaranteed but nevertheless most useful resource in many uncertain situations: given the rule $A \rightarrow B$, and knowing that B holds, one may *suppose* that A also holds. This is a type of reasoning habitually performed by medical doctors, who try to diagnose an illness in view of observed symptoms. The trouble is, of course, that it is often the case that more than one illness may provoke the same symptom — in other words: there may exist other applicable rules $A^1 \rightarrow B$, $A^2 \rightarrow B$, ..., $A^n \rightarrow B$, suggesting different justifications for the occurrence of B. In abduction, one is led to formulate hypotheses rather than the firm conclusions issuing from deduction over deterministic rules.

Our infer and suppose operations utilize, respectively, deduction and abduction. The conditioners for both can be the same rules of inference (inf_rules) to be traversed forward in the former case or backward in the latter. In the case of infer over a rule P=>F adopted by character A, the antecedent P furnishes the beliefs to be tested as pre-condition, whereas A's belief in F will be acquired as an added effect (another addition being an inferred clause) upon a successful evaluation of P. Conversely, in the case of suppose, the belief on the consequent will motivate the addition of a belief in some fact present in the logical expression of the antecedent.

We must stress that the inference rules adopted by the characters in a given story do not have to be scientifically established rules. Informally, in our example, the rules are:

1. if person A was born in a country B, and A's domicile is also in B, then A is a citizen of B.
2. if person A is daltonic, and says that the colour of B's hair is C1, but a daltonic when looking at an object coloured C2 would mistakenly perceive that colour as C1, then the colour of B's hair is C2.
3. if person A was observed departing from location L to some other location, then A is no longer at L.
4. if person A was observed arriving at location L, coming from some other location, then A is currently at L.

Rules **3** and **4** are trivial, representing a more general case: watching an event from an appropriate place allows the observer to conclude that the direct and indirect effects of the event should hold. We point that rule **1** does not really cover the legal citizenship requirements prevailing in most countries, and rule **2** represents a naive understanding (taking red for green and vice-versa) of one variety of colour blindness (cf. [9]).

Example 3: As a goal that, so we thought, should fail, we enquired how red-haired Mary could come to believe that her hair was not red. The planner found a solution using inference in a most devious way: John gives Peter the correct information, which he transmits to Mary. However, having first noticed that Peter is daltonic, Mary is led to apply our (naive) inference rule dealing with red-green colour blindness.

Goal: believes(Mary, hair_colour(Mary, A)), not A=red
Mary senses that Peter is daltonic. John tells Peter: "- Mary has red hair". Peter agrees with John. Mary asks Peter: "- What is the colour of my hair?". Peter tells Mary: "- Your hair is red". Mary infers that she has green hair.

4   Higher-Level Facilities

In order to analyze composed plots and the resulting beliefs, we have implemented a set of higher-level facilities. In the current prototype, the predicates implementing the higher-level facilities are, so to speak, external to the narrative, to be applied as an instrument of analysis after plot composition. Future work may promote their inclusion in the repertoire of events, especially in the context of detective stories, where the critical examination of past facts and events plays a fundamental role. In this way the analysis of the plot so far might become part of the narrative (more on that in section 6). To run the higher-level facilities with a specific application, a number of clauses must be specified. The facilities and the corresponding additional information necessary to use them are described in the sequel.

4.1   Surveying and Ranking Multiple Beliefs

Since multiple beliefs about the same fact are allowed, one needs a device to rank them on the basis of their provenance. The survey predicate collects all beliefs of a character about an indicated fact, together with their provenance (operation whereby they were acquired) and puts them in decreasing order with respect to the appropriate weights. These must have been declared by a conditioner; for the example below, we shall   assume   the   following   one: `weights('Peter',   hair_colour(X,Y),` `[1:sensed('Peter',_), 2:told('John',['Peter',_])])`.

Example 4: Peter collects all possible inputs on the colour of Mary's hair. He then ranks the results, according to his pre-defined list of weights based on provenance. As far as hair-colour is concerned, what he hears from John is ranked (weight 2) above the evidence of his own defective eyesight (weight 1). He trusts Laura, but never thought of assigning a weight to her opinion (weight 0 is the default). By using our facility to survey and rank Peter's beliefs towards Mary's hair color, the following output can be obtained.

```
Surveying: hair_colour(Mary, A)
sensed(Peter, hair_colour(Mary, green))
told(John, [Peter, hair_colour(Mary, red)])
told(Laura, [Peter, hair_colour(Mary, blond)])
Ranking the results:
2:hair_colour(Mary, red)
1:hair_colour(Mary, green)
0:hair_colour(Mary, blond)
```

Another stricter surveying facility, when collecting the various inputs rejects those that cause the activation of any `violate_rule`. Such rules play a central role in the higher-level facility described in the next section.

4.2   Validating a Belief

Certain beliefs may not make sense in that they violate some natural law, or legal norm or even some convention of the chosen story genre. An elementary kind of violation refers to the schema definition itself: e.g. instances of a relationship are not acceptable if not declared between existing instances of the entity classes over which the relationship was defined. Also, similarly to naive inferences, a `violate_rule` established for a story genre may reflect its conventions, rather than the real world.

The `violations` predicate, illustrated below, checks a given expression in view of the established `violate_rules`. If a rule is violated more than once, the rule identifier will be repeated an equal number of times in the resulting list.

In our example, both `violate_rules` are about the `citizen` relationship. According to rule r1, any instance thereof is considered not valid if the first parameter is not a `person` or the second is not a `country`, whereas rule r2 excludes the possibility of plural citizenship (although such cases are often encountered in practice).

Example 5: When checking a belief corresponding to the conjunction of the facts `citizen('Mary','UK')`, `citizen('Mary','London')`, `citizen('Mickey','USA')`, rule r1 is activated twice: London is not a `country` and Mickey is not a `person`. A violation related to rule r2 is also detected, since there should be no more than one clause declaring Mary's citizenship.

4.3   Recognizing a Library Plan from Events Observed

Typical plans can be extracted from previously existing plots, and, after their parameters are consistently replaced by variables, be stored under this plan-pattern form in a library, for future reference. Our tiny example library comprises two short plans:

```
lib([start=>go(A,L1,L2)=>go(B,L1,L2)=>sense(A,current_place(B,L2)),
    start=>go(A,L1,L2)=>go(A,L2,L1)]).
```

In the former, two characters A and B follow the same itinerary and, next, A senses that they are now together at place L2. The latter just shows A leaving from and returning to the same place.

One of the uses of a library is to match one or more observed events against each plan-pattern. If all the observations supplied, ideally in a small number, unify with plan events that must lie in the same sequence but do not have to be contiguous, one gains the following complementary benefits: (1) anticipating what the characters are trying to achieve in the long run and (2) extending the few events to a larger plot, consisting of the matching plan pattern, with some (or all) variables instantiated as a consequence of unification.

To obtain further intuitive understanding of what (1) means, take the commonplace example of a person being observed to hail a taxi and go to an airport. These observations would match a plan-pattern with events such as buying an air ticket, hailing a taxi, loading a number of bags on the taxi, going to the airport, etc., etc., checking-in, boarding the plane, etc. But they might also match a similar plan in which the person would be going to the airport not to embark but to meet another person in an arriving flight. The fact that the same observations can match alternative plans shows that recognition can, in general, be hypothetical.

On the other hand, a prospective author would have, in view of (2), one or more possible plots obtained by extending an initial fragmentary sketch. So, curiously, both plan-generation (as shown in the previous sections) and plan-recognition provide useful story composition strategies. Indeed plan-recognition brings to mind the notion of reuse, and in the literary domain is in consonance with the remark in [10] that "any text is a new tissue of past citations".

Example 6: Two observed `go(X,Y,Z)` events are matched against the given library of typical plans. The first event is fully instantiated, whereas the second seems to result from a vague observation: the only clue is that the agent was either John himself or a woman. With the first option, the library plan wherein the same character travels forward and then backward is recognized; with the second, the recognized plan is that two different characters embark on the same trip, and the former notices the presence of the latter when they have both reached their destination. Calling the plan-generator to validate the plans has the effect of restricting the choice of the female character to Mary, who happens to be initially in London as required. By using our facility to recognize plans the following output can be obtained.

```
Observed: [go(John, London, Manchester), go(A, B, C)]assuming that A was
either John himself or some person of the female genderLibrary plans
recognized - and executable:
John goes from London to Manchester. John goes from Manchester to Lon-
don.
John goes from London to Manchester. Mary goes from London to Manches-
ter. John senses that Mary is now in Manchester.
```

4.4   Recognizing a Pattern in a Generated Plan

Pattern-matching can also take an opposite direction, working on an existing plot and checking whether it contains some not necessarily contiguous subsequence to which a pattern may be matched. Both verifying that the match succeeds and, if so, extracting the matching subsequence are relevant to the analysis of plots.

Example 7: A pattern expressing a going and returning trip performed by some character is matched using our facility against an existing plot, which, among its events, contains an instance of the pattern — which is duly found. The following output can then be displayed.

```
Applying the pattern: [go(A, B, C), go(A, C, B)]
to the given sequence: start=>go(John, London, Manchester)=>
go(Laura, Manchester, London)=>go(John, Manchester, London)
one finds: [go(John, London, Manchester), go(John, Manchester, London)]
```

5   Related Work

Within the Interactive Storytelling area, the problem of controlling the diversity and coherence of the stories has been tackled by means of the specification of reactive behaviour, such as in Façade [11], or by means of deliberative planning, such as in [12-14], where techniques such as hierarchical task networks-HTN [15] and partial-order planning are applied. In our **Logtell** tool [3], partial-order planning and HTN are combined to conciliate flexibility and efficiency and to treat nondeterministic events. In this paper, we propose a generic approach to deal with information gathering events that could be adapted to different story contexts. In order to simplify the reasoning process about beliefs, we have resorted to a simpler backward chaining linear planner, and used logic programming to infer pre-conditions and post-conditions of the events. As we intend to incorporate this approach to **Logtell**, it will be adapted to deal with partially-ordered nondeterministic events.

Reasoning about beliefs in order to perform actions is a major characteristic of the Belief–Desire–Intention (BDI) software model [16]. The model's architecture purports to implement the principal aspects of the theory of human practical reasoning originally proposed by Bratman [17]. Efforts to formulate logical models to define and reason about BDI agents have led to formal logical descriptions such as BDICTL [18] and, more recently, LORA (the Logic Of Rational Agents) [19]. In [20], beliefs, and their respective strengths, are recognized from the surface form of utterances, from discourse acts, and from the explicit and implicit acceptance of previous utterances. Communicative operations can be performed with the aid of the Knowledge Query and Manipulation Language (KQML) [21]. ACL is a proposed standard language for agent communications in multi-agent systems, whose semantics are based on the BDI model of agency [7]. KQML and ACL define a set of *performatives* (operations performed by the agents) and, more fundamentally, rely on speech act theory [22-23]. In our approach, we explicitly reason about beliefs in order to achieve goals of the characters, and such goals can be generated by means of goal-inference rules, which can represent each character's desires. In spite of the similarities with BDI models, there is a fundamental difference: instead of being concerned about the actual communication between software agents, we are focused on creating coherent plots in which characters' actions can be justified by their beliefs.

Regarding the use of templates, one important issue in applied Natural Language Generation (NLG) is deciding between the usage of complete NLG systems, or the option – which we favoured in our current work – for template-based approaches [24]. Although some scholars have stressed the disadvantages of template-based systems in comparison to full-fledged NLG systems [25-26], some more recent studies do not concur with this point of view [27]. In fact, they are considered Turing-equivalent computational systems [25]. Reiter [28] compares the two techniques, showing the advantages in each case. Indeed, template-based approaches are easier to implement, and generate texts more quickly than traditional approaches. Yet, on the other hand, rigid templates are inflexible and difficult to reuse. An Augmented Template-Based approach is proposed in [29] as a means of yielding templates that should prove more flexible and reusable.

There surely exists a good deal of interesting research about the automatic generation of texts for different purposes, in some cases with the use of templates (cf., for example, [30-31]). More specifically, NLG methods have been applied to interactive storytelling systems (e.g. [32-34]). However we still find that the automatic rendering of a given plot in a high quality text is more often than not a complex task [35].

6   Concluding Remarks

Besides the simple-minded example used as illustration, we have already applied some of the information-gathering events to enhance the Swords-and-Dragons genre that runs in **Logtell**, by dropping the unrealistic omniscience assumption. Now a damsel watches the villainous Draco kidnapping Princess Marian, runs to `tell` Sir Brian about the mischief, and he `infers` that, as a kidnapped victim, she should have been carried to the villain's dwelling, whereto he promptly rides to rescue his beloved.

But the availability of information-gathering events will, probably after further elaboration, open the way to more sophisticated genres. In particular, we have been examining the requirements of detective stories. It has been convincingly argued [36] that such narratives actually contain two stories: one covers the crime and the other the investigation. The first story ends before the second begins. And the characters of the story of the investigation do not predominantly act — they *learn* —, which is well within the scope of the package discussed here.

Future work should extend the repertoire of events to contemplate other speech acts, for example to allow a character C1 to solicit or to order another character C2 to execute an action of C1's interest, which C2, but not C1, is empowered and in a position to perform. Moreover, in stories of even moderate complexity, behaviour should be characterized as a decision-making process affecting the participation of each character in every kind of event, either involving physical action or the information-gathering activities of the present study — and this process hinges on both cognitive and emotional considerations [37- 42], further influenced by the goals and plans of the other characters [43]. We have done some initial work on drives, attitudes, emotions, and mutual interferences among agents [44], but a full integration within the **Logtell** system still remains to be achieved.

References

1. Fikes, R.E., Nilsson, N.J.: STRIPS: A new approach to the application of theorem proving to problem solving. Artificial Intelligence 2(3-4) (1971)
2. Camanho, M.M., Ciarlini, A.E.M., Furtado, A.L., Pozzer, C.T., Feijó, B.: Conciliating coherence and high responsiveness in interactive storytelling. In: Proc. of the 3rd International Conference on Digital Interactive Media in Entertainment and Arts, pp. 427–434 (2008)
3. Silva, F.A.G., Ciarlini, A.E.M., Siqueira, S.W.M.: Nondeterministic Planning for Generating Interactive Plots. In: Proc. Ibero-American Conference on Artificial Intelligence, Bahía Blanca, Argentina, November 1-5, vol. 162 (2010)
4. Batini, C., Ceri, S., Navathe, S.: Conceptual Design – an Entity-Relationship Approach. Benjamin Cummings (1992)
5. Lloyd, W.: Foundations of Logic Programming. Springer (1987)
6. Sadek, M.D.: Logical task modelling for man-machine dialogue. In: Proceedings of the Eighth AAAI Conference, Boston, MA (1990)
7. FIPA Review of FIPA Specifications (2006), http://www.fipa.org/subgroups/ROFS-SG-docs/ROFS-Doc.pdf
8. Grice, H.P.: Logic and conversation. In: Cole, P., Morgan, J.L. (eds.) Syntax and Semantics, Speech Acts, vol. 3. Academic Press, New York (1975)
9. Dalton, J.: Extraordinary facts relating to the vision of colours: with observations. Memoirs of the Literary and Philosophical Society of Manchester 5, 28–45 (1798)
10. Barthes, R.: The Theory of the Text. In: Young, R. (ed.) Untying the Text: A Post-Structural Reader, pp. 31–47. Routledge, Boston (1981)
11. Mateas, M., Stern, A.: Structuring content in the Facade interactive drama architecture. In: Proc. Artificial Intelligence and Interactive Digital Entertainment Conference, AIIDE (2005)
12. Cavazza, M., Charles, F., Mead, S.: Character-based interactive storytelling. IEEE Intelligent Systems, Special Issue on AI in Interactive Entertainment 17(4), 17–24 (2002)
13. Young, R.: An overview of the mimesis architecture: Integrating narrative control into a gaming environment. In: Working Notes of the AAAI Spring Symposium on Artificial Intelligence and Interactive Entertainment, pp. 78–81. AAAI Press, Stanford (2001)
14. Riedl, M., Young, R.M.: From Linear Story Generation to Branching Story Graphs. IEEE Computer Graphics and Applications 26(3), 23–31 (2006)
15. Erol, K., Hendler, J., Nau, D.S.: UMCP: A sound and complete procedure for hierarchical task-network planning. In: Proceedings of the International Conference on AI Planning Systems (AIPS), pp. 249–254 (1994)

16. Rao, A.S., Georgeff, M.P.: BDI-agents: From Theory to Practice. In: Proceedings of the First International Conference on Multiagent Systems (ICMAS 1995), San Francisco (1995)
17. Bratman, M.E.: Intention, Plans, and Practical Reason. CSLI Publications (1999)
18. Dastani, M., van der Torre, L.: An Extension of BDICTL with Functional Dependencies and Components. In: Baaz, M., Voronkov, A. (eds.) LPAR 2002. LNCS (LNAI), vol. 2514. Springer, Heidelberg (2002)
19. Wooldridge, M.: Reasoning About Rational Agents. The MIT Press (2000) ISBN 0-262-23213-8
20. Carberry, S., Lambert, L.: A Process Model for Recognizing Communicative Acts and Modeling Negotiation Subdialogues. Computational Linguistics 25(1), 1–53 (1999)
21. Finin, T., Weber, J., Wiederhold, G., Gensereth, M., Fritzzon, R., McKay, D., McGuire, J., Pelavin, R., Shapiro, S., Beck, C. (eds.): DRAFT Specification of the KQML Agent-Communication Language. PostScript (June 15, 1993), http://www.cs.umbc.edu/KQML/kqmlspec.ps
22. Searle, J.R.: Speech Acts An Essay in the Philosophy of Language. Cambridge University Press, Cambridge (1969)
23. Winograd, T., Flores, F.: Understanding Computers and Cognition: A New Foundation for Design. Ablex Publishing Corp., Norwood (1986)
24. Reiter, E., Dale, R.: Building Natural Language Generation Systems. Cambridge University Press, Cambridge (2000)
25. Reiter, E., Dale, R.: Building applied natural language generation systems. Nat. Lang. Eng. 3, 57–87 (1997)
26. Busemann, S., Horacek, H.: A flexible shallow approach to text generation. In: Proceedings of the Ninth International Workshop on Natural Language Generation, Niagara-on-the-Lake, Ontario, Canada, pp. 238–247 (1998)
27. van Deemter, K., Krahmer, E., Theune, M.: Real versus Template-Based Natural Language Generation: A False Opposition? Comput. Linguist. 31, 15–24 (2005)
28. Reiter, E.: NLG vs. Templates. CoRR. cmp-lg/9504013 (1995)
29. McRoy, S.W., Channarukul, S., Ali, S.S.: An augmented template-based approach to text realization. Nat. Lang. Eng. 9, 381–420 (2003)
30. Stenzhorn, H.: XtraGen: A Natural Language Generation System Using XML- And Java-Technologies. In: Proceedings of the 2nd Workshop on NLP and XML, vol. 17, pp. 1–8 (2002)
31. Piwek, P.: A flexible pragmatics-driven language generator for animated agents. In: Proceedings of the Tenth Conference on European Chapter of the Association for Computational Linguistics, vol. 2, pp. 151–154 (2003)
32. Gervás, P., Díaz-Agudo, B., Peinado, F., Hervás, R.: Story plot generation based on CBR. Knowledge-Based Systems 18(4-5), 235–242 (2005)
33. Szilas, N.: A Computational Model of an Intelligent Narrator for Interactive Narratives. Applied Artificial Intelligence 21(8), 753–801 (2007)
34. Montfort, N.: Generating narrative variation in interactive fiction. PhD dissertation, Computer and Information Science - University of Pennsylvania (2007)
35. Callaway, C.B., Lester, J.C.: Narrative prose generation. Artificial Intelligence 139(2), 213–252 (2002)
36. Todorov, T.: The Poetics of Prose. Cornell University Press (1977)
37. Brave, S., Nass, C.: Emotion in Human-Computer Interaction. In: Sears, A., Jacko, J. (eds.) The Human-Computer Interaction Handbook, pp. 77–92 (2008)

38. Loewenstein, G., Lerner, J.S.: The role of affect in decision making. In: Davidson, R.J., Scherer, K.R., Goldsmith, H.H. (eds.) Handbook of Affective Sciences, pp. 619–642. Oxford University Press (2003)
39. McCrae, R.R., Costa, P.T.: Validation of a five-factor model of personality across instruments and observers. J. Pers. Soc. Psychol. 52, 81–90 (1987)
40. Goldberg, L.R.: The Development of Markers for the Big-Five Factor Structure. Psychological Assessment 4(1), 26–42 (1992)
41. O'Rorke, P., Ortony, A.: Explaining Emotions. Cognitive Science 18(2), 283–323 (1994)
42. Ortony, A.: On making believable emotional agents believable. In: Trappl, R., Petta, P., Payr, S. (eds.) Emotions in Humans and Artifacts, pp. 189–211. The MIT Press (2003)
43. Willensky, R.: Planning and Understanding - a Computational Approach to Human Reasoning. Addison-Wesley (1983)
44. Barbosa, S.D.J., Furtado, A.L., Casanova, M.A.C.: A Decision-making Process for Digital Storytelling. In: Proc. IX Symposium on Computer Games and Digital Entertainment - Track: Computing (2010)

Design and Evaluation of Parametrizable Multi-genre Game Mechanics

Daniel Apken[1], Hendrik Landwehr[1], Marc Herrlich[1],
Markus Krause[1], Dennis Paul[2], and Rainer Malaka[1]

[1] Research Group Digital Media, TZI, University of Bremen
[2] Interaction and Space, University of the Arts Bremen

Abstract. Designing digital games is primarily interaction design. This interaction manifests as a meaningful change in the game world. An aspect of a game can only change dynamically with a parametric model of this aspect available. One aspect of digital games is yet missing such a systematic description: the genre of a game is currently only determined by its designer. This paper introduces a new approach that allows for dynamic blending between genres. We describe a set of game mechanics that express the characteristics of different game genres. We extract a parametric model from these mechanics to allow dynamic blending. The paper illustrates the possibilities of this approach with an implementation of a multi-genre-game. It also provides empiric evidence that the described model successfully generates different game genres.

Keywords: multi-genre games, genre blending, parametrizable game mechanics, game mashups.

1   Introduction

The design of many computer games is based on common and very stereotypical genre patterns. The mechanics of different first-person shooters, role-playing games (RPG), or platform games are very similar in comparison. Exceptions are so-called "genre mash-ups", e.g., games combining puzzling with action or strategy with RPG. Not only does combining well-known game patterns in new ways give existing genres an interesting twist but this could also broaden the target audience of a game by providing a more personalized game experience. Imagine the player being able to tailor the specific mix of game mechanics to her taste and mood or the game automatically adapting to the player's preferred playing style over time.

However, currently it is exclusively the designer that decides on the specific mix, which is fixed after shipping the game. At the same time, it is important to not take all creative control away from the designer because this would clearly diminish the game experience as good game design is anything but random and arbitrary. The goal is to strike a balance between creative control and influence of the designer and customizability and flexibility regarding mechanics and user preferences. What is needed are fundamental building blocks that allow

M. Herrlich, R. Malaka, and M. Masuch (Eds.): ICEC 2012, LNCS 7522, pp. 45–52, 2012.

designers to incorporate dynamic genre mixing and switching in their games in a systematic, controlled, and understandable way. Such building blocks should be easily customizable, ideally using only a floating point variable to switch or blend between different game characteristics. They should facilitate clearly distinguishable play styles at an equal level of quality for each style. From an engineering perspective they should generalize to a wide variety of games.

In this paper we introduce our approach to customizable multi-genre game mechanics. We present the design and evaluation of three specific multi-genre game mechanics: movement metaphor, puzzle factor and AI factor. We show how our multi-genre game mechanics fulfill the requirements discussed above. We report on a conducted user study, providing empirical evidence that our mechanics successfully support different play styles while maintaining a near constant and high level of quality of the overall game experience. We discuss how our approach is generalizable to other games and mechanics.

2   Related Work

Numerous computer games already use procedural game elements. Automated map and asset creation are popular techniques. A very successful example of procedural world creation is Minecraft [3]. It uses an algorithm that imitates nature by heavily relying on perlin-noise [6] to create structures such as fields, hills, or lakes. Other games, e.g., the Diablo series[1], create procedural worlds from pre-created interchangeable pieces to convey unpredictability. "Rogue-like" games in general often use similar techniques to create seemingly unique items by randomly selecting from a predetermined attribute range, e.g., a sword with a special attack type, damage value, or player class requirements [12]. Other systems rely on behavioral models such as "rhythm groups" [9,10]. Search-based content generation [11] or difficulty calculating algorithms [2] are examples of yet another class of related methods. The appearance of assets can also be altered using the mentioned methods, applying slight differences to otherwise similar objects [13]. Façade is an interactive drama [5] employing different techniques, e.g., natural language understanding, to alternate the progress of the story depending on the player's choices. Lopes et al. [4] describe adaptive games, in which parts of the game are altered according to the user's behavior. In some games, e.g., Mario Kart[2] or Max Payne[3], the difficulty is altered based on the player's performance, e.g., providing increased aiming assistance if the player dies too often.

The mentioned works cover procedural content for game worlds, levels, assets, their graphics, and story. However, to our knowledge, there are no examples of games that allow to vary fundamental game mechanics such as the movement metaphor based on a continuous parametrization.

---

[1] http://www.blizzard.com/games/

[2] http://www.mariokart.com/wii/launch/

[3] http://www.rockstargames.com/maxpayne/

3   Multi-genre Game Mechanics

A prototype has been developed that provides customizable fundamental game mechanics based on easily changeable numerical parameters. The main goal is to provide game mechanics that can be altered at any time, resulting in clearly distinct game types or genres while at the same time maintaining a high quality and comparable overall game experience. In effect that means that it should be possible to generate games of different genres or blends of such games at the same quality level, which would still work as self-contained games, including all the usual elements of games [7,8].

3.1   Prototype Genres

While our mechanics can in principle be varied "continuously" as they are represented by floating point parameters, for the prototype and the following user tests we developed three distinct parameter sets, each corresponding to a specific setup as listed below. We selected three popular and distinct genres we wanted to emulate by customizing our mechanics. The goal was to potentially appeal to a variety of player types [8].

Platformer setup. The primary aim of this game variant is to jump and collect items. The player is automatically moved to the bottom. With increasing height the items being collected are also increasing in value.

Shoot 'em up setup. The primary aim of this game variant is to shoot enemies while dodging obstacles. The player is automatically moved to the right. Enemies are getting stronger as the player progresses.

Puzzle setup. The primary aim of this game variant is to solve puzzles by changing the color of at least three hexagons. The player is not automatically moved. Puzzle difficulty increases with each one solved.

3.2   Static Mechanics

In addition to the customizable "dynamic" mechanics described below, all games (or game variants) include basic "static" mechanics that work similarly independent of any parametrization. This includes a collecting mechanic and a score system. Collecting items, killing enemies, and solving puzzles yields the player points, which provide a measurable outcome and goal to the player.

Additionally, we devised a simple interaction mechanic independent of the game variant. The player can click on game objects to make the game avatar launch box-shaped projectiles at these objects. This "shooting" mechanic is static across variants, however, the result is based on the respective target object type, which may vary. In effect this allows the player to remove obstacles, attack enemies, or solve puzzles using the same basic interaction method.

3.3 Dynamic Mechanics

The principle of dynamic mechanics, being controlled by parameters, has been applied to several core mechanics of the prototype. One of the most fundamental mechanics is movement. In principle, movement can be customized through the following parameters: direction, acceleration, speed, automatic or manual movement, linear or non-linear movement. Furthermore, movement possibilities are heavily dependent on the surrounding game world and objects, e.g., types of barriers, walls, or platforms. The specific type of movement and obstacles have a great impact on the perceived game genre and are not independent. In order to parametrize movement for different genres we investigated common movement patterns [1]. We developed a special kind of barrier which is only passable from one side and which is automatically rotated according to the movement parametrization. Although other movement parameters (listed above) are also slightly adjusted according to the specific setup, the movement metaphor is mainly parametrized by a single floating point parameter – "gravity" – that determines the direction of forced or non-forced (by setting gravity to zero) player movement. The barriers as well as other movement parameters and player controls are adapted according to this parameter.

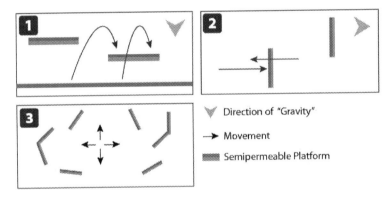

Fig. 1. Three different movement and obstacle combinations controlled by "gravity" are used to model three different game genres

In the platformer setup (figure 1, box 1), the gravity is directed downwards. As the desired direction in this setup is upwards, the player can use a jumping motion to get there. The platforms align according to the gravity, allowing the avatar to stand on top of them and jump through them from below. Additionally, movement to the left and right is not impeded. The gravity in the shoot 'em up setup (figure 1, box 2) draws the player rightwards. The goal is to shoot and avoid enemies, which is the easiest when moving with the gravity. The avatar can move up and down freely. The platforms serve as obstacles that impede the players progress, instead of supporting it. In the puzzle setup (figure 1, box 3), there is no gravity at all, which means the avatar can move freely in all directions.

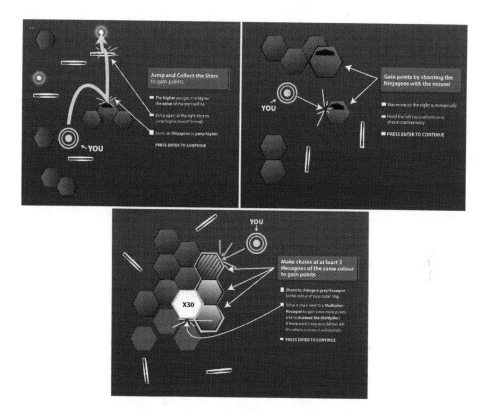

Fig. 2. Instruction screenshots for the three different game variants modeled in the prototype: Platformer (top left), Shoot 'em up (top right) and Puzzle (bottom)

In this case, it cannot be predicted where the player will navigate next, so the platforms "align" in random directions.

Another fundamental mechanic is the type of non-player objects/agents the player can interact with. To customize objects to a wide variety of uses they should be of a simple shape, while still providing enough possibilities to give them an interesting appearance and functionality. Furthermore, they should work as individual objects but they should also be combinable into larger clusters. We found that simple hexagons fulfill these requirements. They can represent obstacles, enemies, or puzzle pieces (hexagons of different colors), depending on the intention of the player and/or goal of the game (figure 2). This is realized by providing a certain behavior when creating new hexagons in a level. Most hexagons being spawned are neutral and act as obstacles or platforms to stand or jump on. Two parameters called "puzzle" and "aggressiveness" factor, respectively, are used to alter this spawn rate, providing more objects of either kind. Additionally, the aggressiveness is used to determine the initial behavior of enemies, making them more passive or active and the puzzle factor determines the puzzle complexity as it influences the number of colors used.

Enemies that are being hit become more aggressive, approaching the player faster and stealing points when reaching her. All other hexagons that are hit (except for special puzzle hexagons) adopt the color of the projectile. When three or more hexagons of the same color are connected to each other, they explode and the player gains points but only a few. When a special puzzle hexagon (a hexagon showing a number) is connected to them, the points gained are multiplied by its number and the number itself increases, making it possible to gain even more points when destroying other hexagons connected to it. Enemies that are not aggressive at all will not approach the player and cost her no points when she touches them. However, they still push her off, making them ideal to be used as trampolines, supporting the jumping mechanic. Larger formations of neutral hexagons can often impede the player's way. The puzzle and shooting mechanics can be used to connect three of them, make them explode and clear the way.

4   User Study

An online user study was conducted to empirically confirm the suitability of the described approach. The main goals of the study were to confirm that the multi-genre game elements actually work for each genre and that at the same time each genre is still clearly distinguishable by the user.

The game was implemented in Java and could be downloaded from our website. We invited users to participate by circulating the access link both over internal and external mailing lists and social network sites of our university. In the disclaimer, users were instructed that we wanted to test new game designs but no specifics on multi-genre or generative game design were provided. We used a within-subjects design with each user playing all three game variants (platform, shoot 'em up and puzzle setups as described in section 3.1). The order of game variants was randomized using a latin square across participants. Participants were asked to select the three most important concepts specific to each game variant from a list of 14 items (see below). They were asked to rank all variants in comparison and additionally to rate each individually on a 5-point Likert scale. We collected similar ratings on graphical quality, story, and game play for each version.

Overall 64 people participated in the study. After removing invalid data, we still retained 44 valid data sets for further analysis. Of these final 44 participants, 37 were male and 7 female with an average age of 25.66 (SD 4.2) years. Friedman tests revealed no significant differences between the three game variants regarding ranking, ratings (overall, graphical quality, story, gameplay), perceived fun, learnability of the controls, and clarity of the game goal. Mean values for perceived fun (5-point Likert scale; $1 = $ better; $5 = $ worse) were 2.52 (SD 1.0), 2.45 (SD 1.13), and 2.32 (SD 0.983). Overall rating mean values were 2.61 (SD 0.754), 2.55 (SD 0.761), and 2.45 (SD 0.820). Mean values for learnability of controls (5-point Likert scale; $1 = $ worse; $5 = $ better) were 4.75 (SD 0.534), 4.73 (SD 0.694), and 4.70 (SD 0.701). Mean values for clarity of gaming goal (5-point Likert; $1 = $ clear; $5 = $ unclear) were 1.52 (SD 0.628), 1.45 (SD 0.875), and 1.77

(SD 0.886). Application of Cochran's Q revealed significant or highly significant differences between the three game variants for the following concepts: logical thinking ($\chi^2(2) = 33.583$, $p < 0.01$), reaction speed ($\chi^2(2) = 11.760$, $p < 0.01$), collecting ($\chi^2(2) = 29.727$, $p < 0.01$), shooting ($\chi^2(2) = 26.963$, $p < 0.01$), jumping ($\chi^2(2) = 70.205$, $p < 0.01$), problem solving ($\chi^2(2) = 17.077$, $p < 0.01$), aiming ($\chi^2(2) = 14.519$, $p < 0.01$), dodging ($\chi^2(2) = 8.667$, $p < 0.05$), and attacking ($\chi^2(2) = 24.4$, $p < 0.01$). For maneuvering, tactical thinking, hand-eye coordination, concentration, and exploration the differences were found to be not significant, although the p-value for tactical thinking ($p = 0.07$) missed the 5% threshold very narrowly.

5   Discussion

As reported above, no significant differences have been found between the three game variants in relation to perceived quality and fun. All variants were comparable in terms of ranking, ratings and sub-ratings (such as graphical quality etc.). The absolute ratings reinforce the results of the relative rankings and they additionally show that all variants were not just rated equally, but equally good. This also pertains to the learnability of the controls. On the other hand nine of 14 concepts exhibited statistically significant differences. This shows that the participants were indeed very aware of differences in game play and that they very clearly attributed different concepts and core mechanics to each game instance.

In summary this shows that our approach successfully led to the creation of three very distinct and different games while maintaining a good quality and working game mechanics for each game individually. Switching between these games – or genres – is now just a matter of adjusting the three main parameters (gravity, puzzle, and aggressiveness), which are floating point variables and thereby also enable simple blending between different variants.

Our participant base was biased towards young, male, hard-core gamers. The results of the study are therefore limited to this audience at the moment. However, one could also interpret this audience as being an audience of computer game experts.

6   Conclusion and Future Work

With regard to our initial research question, the results of the reported user study show that we were able to successfully create three distinct gaming experiences the participants clearly related to three different game genres while maintaining a comparable level of high quality across all game variants.

Our approach currently rests on three main pillars: a variable motion mechanic, the puzzle factor, and the AI (or aggressiveness) factor. All games that feature the exploration of space could potentially benefit from dynamic motion mechanics. What is needed to implement genre-blending is a "natural" mapping of a floating point game attribute to a motion metaphor, such as gravity in our case. Examples could be other physical properties related to motion like friction, buoyancy, or permeability. Our puzzle factor can be generalized to dependencies between other game elements. Thus increased puzzle factor means more dependencies. Again a mapping function is needed that maps a floating point variable to more complex dependencies. The AI factor influences if the player perceives other objects as static object, neutral agents, or enemies. This maps rather directly to some sort of "aggressiveness" factor in most simple game AI systems.

So far we only tested three distinct game variants. In the future we plan to add additional variants to investigate further the scalability of our approach. The parametric approach in principle allows to blend game variants at runtime. When and how to blend has to be determined and evaluated to ensure a convincing gaming experience.

References

1. Bjork, S.: Patterns in Game Design, 1st edn. Charles River Media, Hingham Mass (2005)
2. Compton, K., Mateas, M.: Procedural level design for platform games. In: Proc. AIIDE 2006, pp. 109–111 (2006)
3. Handy, A.: Markus 'Notch' Persson talks making Minecraft (2010), http://www.gamasutra.com/view/news/27719/Interview_Markus_Notch_Persson_Talks_Making_Minecraft.php (last accessed: April 20, 2012)
4. Lopes, R., Bidarra, R.: Adaptivity challenges in games and simulations: A survey. IEEE Transactions on Computational Intelligence and AI in Games 3(2), 85–99 (2011)
5. Mateas, M., Stern, A.: Facade: An experiment in building a fully-realized interactive drama. In: Proc. GDC 2003, San Jose, CA (2003)
6. Perlin, K.: Improving noise. In: Proc. SIGGRAPH 2002, pp. 681–682. ACM, New York (2002)
7. Salen, K., Zimmerman, E.: Rules of Play: Game Design Fundamentals. MIT Press, Cambridge Mass (2003)
8. Schell, J.: The Art of Game Design: A Book of Lenses. Elsevier/Morgan Kaufmann, Amsterdam (2008)
9. Smith, G., Cha, M., Whitehead, J.: A framework for analysis of 2d platformer levels. In: Proc. SIGGRAPH 2008 Symposium on Video Games, pp. 75–80. ACM, New York (2008)
10. Sorenson, N., Pasquier, P., DiPaola, S.: A generic approach to challenge modeling for the procedural creation of video game levels. IEEE Transactions on Computational Intelligence and AI in Games 3(3), 229–244 (2011)
11. Togelius, J., Yannakakis, G., Stanley, K., Browne, C.: Search-based procedural content generation: A taxonomy and survey. IEEE Transactions on Computational Intelligence and AI in Games 3(3), 172–186 (2011)
12. Toy, M., Wichman, G., Arnold, K., Lane, J.: Rogue by artificial intelligence design (1983)
13. Watson, B., Muller, P., Wonka, P., Sexton, C., Veryovka, O., Fuller, A.: Procedural urban modeling in practice. IEEE Computer Graphics and Applications 28(3), 18–26 (2008)

A Virtual Training Tool for Giving Talks

Oswald D. Kothgassner[1], Anna Felnhofer[1], Leon Beutl[2],
Helmut Hlavacs[2], Mario Lehenbauer[1], and Birgit Stetina[3]

[1] University of Vienna, Faculty of Psychology,
Working Group Clinical Psychology,
Liebiggasse 5/3, 1010 Vienna, Austria
http://psychologie.univie.ac.at/
[2] University of Vienna, Faculty of Computer Science,
Research Group Entertainment Computing,
Lenaugasse 2/8, 1010 Vienna, Austria
http://cs.univie.ac.at/
[3] Webster University Vienna Campus, Faculty of Psychology,
Berchtoldgasse 1, 1220 Vienna, Austria
http://www.webster.ac.at/psychology

Abstract. In this paper we present two studies concerning the application of a virtual environment for public speaking anxiety. We have created a program simulating a virtual lecture room, which can be filled with a large number of listeners behaving in different ways. The purpose of the scene is to train people who are anxious to give talks in front of a large audience. We present the results of two studies, showing the impact of this kind of virtual exposure. Results indicate that people do experience such a situation as realistic, as well as report social insecurity and show heightened psychophysiological arousal (HR). Furthermore, we show that especially curious people, and people with high social insecurity rate the system as useful.

1 Introduction

Social phobia (or social anxiety disorder, SAD) is a well-defined disorder in the DSM-IV. Individuals with social phobia suffer from a marked and persistent fear of one or more social or performance situations in which the patient is exposed to unfamiliar people or possible scrutiny by others. These patients suffer from maladaptive cognitions concerning the self-image and/or their own behavior in social situations (including a ruminative cognitive style) and furthermore they experience a physiological hyperarousal.

For treating phobia in general, people with social anxiety are often exposed to situations they are afraid of, and try to gradually adapt to them, thus decreasing the subjectively felt fear. Examples include, e.g., fear of certain animal types like spiders or dogs, fear of heights, places, situations, etc. Social phobia is special since it always involves other people, and treatment as described above involves the presence of a possibly large number of real humans, a scheme that is often impractical for psychological training and therapy.

M. Herrlich, R. Malaka, and M. Masuch (Eds.): ICEC 2012, LNCS 7522, pp. 53–66, 2012.

In contrast, exposing people with social anxiety to virtual situations by using videos or computers offers the potential of creating arbitrary situations with limitless other (virtual) human beings. In virtual reality (VR) one can interface with the environment, usually through peripheral devices, such as head-mounted displays and keyboards. By watching the scene through a head-mounted display, the patient should be immersed into the virtual scene, and ideally perceive the same or comparable stimuli as in real situations.

However, virtual exposures to flight, heights and social settings are well studied for psychological practice and can be more cost- and time-effective for both therapists and patients, thereby improving the accessibility of therapy to individuals who may previously have been unable to afford treatment. Newman et al. [15] estimated a savings of 540-630 per client when compared with standard individual therapy. Also, the use of inherently motivating virtual reality scenarios containing gaming aspects such as stimulating content and diverse levels of achievements has recently become very attractive. Especially so called serious games are increasingly applied in psychological therapy and training as they constitute a valuable endorsement of common cognitive behavioral approaches (for a detailed description see below). However, it is still an open question whether virtual exposure always achieves the same impact on patients compared to real situations, and which factors determine the efficacy of virtual exposures.

In this paper we demonstrate the efficacy of the virtual training tool for giving public lectures in front of an audience. The scene is 100% virtual, rendered in a computer using modern graphics cards and an open source render engine. We describe the software and results from experiments with a large sample size.

2   Related Work

Psychophysiological theories suggest that patients who suffer from social phobia experience heightened physiological arousal when they enter social situations. They interpret this arousal as an indication of danger or anxiety [9] and this leads to increased symptoms of anxiety (e.g., a racing heart, blushing). Individuals therefore learn to avoid social situations to evade this psychophysiological arousal [1,14]. Cognitive models of SAD highlight the centrality of fear of negative evaluation in the onset and maintenance of this disorder [5,12].

The goal of our approach is guided by the psychophysiological assumptions as mentioned above and the cognitive model by Clark and Wells [5]. According to this model, anxious people who enter feared situations believe, that (1) they are in danger of behaving in an unacceptable manner and (2) that such behavior will have disastrous consequences. The avoidance behavior is a complex constellation of cognitive, behavioral and psychophysiological changes, the danger is more imagined than real with anxiety responses (both physical and cognitive) being mostly inappropriate [5]. Cognitive-behavioral treatment methods (CBT) focus on changing maladaptive cognitions, psychophysiological reactions and include body relaxation training (such as biofeedback). Patients who undergo this kind of treatment report gaining a sense of empowerment and knowledge about how to best control their physiological symptoms [18].

The efficacy of technology-aided exposition methods has been shown to be comparable to traditional face-to-face settings [7,15,16,18]. VR can be combined with the compelling and motivating character of (serious) games which offer huge varieties of social interactions with other users or computer generated agents [4,11]. There are several serious games for health with promising results available, such as *Re-Mission* (provides knowledge about cancer), *Snow-World* (to distract burn recovery patients from pain), or *Sparx*, an online role-playing game for the treatment of depression[1]. Yet, for serious game developers it is a great challenge to find the right balance between a sufficient level of stimulation and motivation and at the same time satisfy the requirements of the cognitive behavioral treatment approach. Thus, studies concerning the users' perceptions of such scenarios as well as investigations regarding efficacy, usability and usefulness are required to provide entertainment computing specialist with sufficient knowledge.

In this paper we present the results from two studies concerning virtual exposures to a lecturing situation. It is well known that many people fear giving talks in front of large audiences. Examples for virutal training of giving public speeches are the products of *Virtually Better*,[2] often a mixture between pure virtual surroundings and real people filmed by video, or *Virtual Reality Medical Center*[3], a video that is presented through a visor. Another example using real people as a virtual audience is the Internet based tool *Talk To Me* [2], whose efficacy is researched in [3].

In contrast, we created a purely computer based scenario, using only virtual surroundings and artificial characters, in order to be able to synthesize different settings (e.g. varying sizes of the audience, different emotional expressions of the listeners). We present results from detailed analyses of the experiments, both indicating the efficacy of the virtual exposure and identifying factors which determine the usefulness of such a tool.

3   Virtual Training for Lecturing

This application allows users to virtually act out a situation in which they are supposed to give a lecture to an adjustable amount of people. The virtual environment consists of a room with space for about a hundred people. Since this room is supposed to resemble a lecturing hall, it has high walls with large windows, and small lights placed on the ceiling. Within the room there are two seating areas, a main one consisting of eighty seats in the middle of the room and a tribune in the back, resting on two columns. This main seating area is separated into a left and a right part, with a corridor between them. In this area

---

[1] http://sparx.org.nzfor

[2] http://www.virtuallybetter.com/

[3] http://www.vrphobia.com/therapy.htm

3 dimensional virtual avatars are placed in rows of red seats, with a table in front of each row. The last rows and the tribune are, when adjusted, filled up with 2 dimensional sprites, which is not noticeable at this distance and increases the performance of the application. As an example, Figure 1 shows the room with 70 people and fill sprites in the back.

Fig. 1. 70 avatars with fill sprites

To increase the realism of the scenario additional items which may be brought to a lecture are added for each avatar, like bags, magazines or laptops. The 3 dimensional avatars, both males and females, who simulate the audience have a number of animated seating poses, between which they change independently after a certain amount of time to create some liveliness. Additionally there are three different facial expressions, neutral, happy and hostile which can be changed in the options menu. The avatars also blink in irregular time steps and close their eyes when they mimic a sleeping position. The view of the test person is from a small, slightly elevated stage in front of the main seating area. Small stairs to the right and left of the stage lead up to it. On the stage there is a large screen behind and to the left of the test person, and a podium in front of him. The podium provides an additional small screen and a virtual microphone. On both screens slides for the lecture are displayed. The position of the test person is fixed, only his view is controllable. A virtual avatar is placed on the same position, so when the test person looks down, he sees parts of his body. After adjusting the settings explained in Section 3.1, the simulation starts and the test person has to give a lecture as he would do in front of a live audience. While doing so, the 3 dimensional avatars will display different poses and expressions during the speech, happy, hostile or tired ones. If adjusted, a request to speak louder or laughter will be heard after a certain amount of time, similar to a real lecture. Also, the real slides of the lecture can be imported into the application and are then displayed upon the big screen behind the test person and the small one on the podium. These slides can be switched upon pressing a button and can aid the lecturer during the speech.

3.1   Options

Before starting the application there are some settings that can be adjusted to alter the appearance and the perception of the simulation. The following list describes the available options:

1. **Number of people:** Here the number of 3 dimensional audience avatars is adjustable, and ranges from zero to seventy, which is about the maximum the main seating area can hold. This option has the most influence on the performance of the application, since visualizing the avatars is the most intensive in terms of computation.
2. **Percentage of happy people:** With his option the expression of a certain number of people can be changed. It defines the percentage of avatars with a smiling expression. What avatars this expression is assigned to is decided by change.
3. **Percentage of sleeping people:** This option allows to define a number of sleeping avatars, which do not change expression but rest their head on their arms on the table before them, mimicking a sleeping pose.
4. **Percentage of hostile people:** With this option the expression of a certain percentage of avatars can be changed to hostile, which will result in a frowning face with lowered mouth corners.
5. **Background sound:** Currently there are only two possible sounds, a rather silent one with only quiet talking and some coughing, and a noisy one. These can be used to fit the number of people or to set a certain mood for the lecture.
6. **PowerPoint Slides:** This option defines the number of slides to be used in the application. All available slides are stored in a predefined folder and have to have a consecutive numeration. However, with this option it is possible to use only a certain number of slides in the current test.
7. **Time offset for request:** This defines the number of seconds after which a request to speak louder will be heard from the audience (see Figure 2). The values reach from zero to 1800, where zero means no request at all.
8. **Time offset for laughter:** This defines the number of seconds after which a loud laughter from the audience will be heard. The values reach again from zero to 1800, where zero means no laughter at all.
9. **Add sprites:** If the maximum of seventy avatars is not enough for a test, and an even bigger audience should be simulated, then this option provides the possibility to fill the back of the main seating area and the tribune with 2 dimensional sprites.

Fig. 2. A person asking the participant to speak louder. Some listeners are sleeping.

3.2   Technical Implementation

The application was developed by a group of students during a practical course at the University of Vienna, using Visual Studio C++ Express and the Ogre3d graphics engine in combination with QuickGUI. All the 3 dimensional models were created in Blender3D and the textures were processed using Gimp.

For the creation of the models, especially the human faces, a simple technique was helpful by which a photograph of the front and the side of the object are loaded into Blender3D. Using these images as a guide the object can then be modelled to fit the pictures. The only thing to keep in mind is, since the modelling happens in a 3D environment, that each vertex of the model has to fit both of the pictures. Additionally this technique helps greatly in the texturing process. Blender3D allows to project a picture upon a model and then bake this projection into the uv-map. Also a combination of projections is possible. Unfortunately the border at which the two images are merged together is clearly visible on the final uv-map, and has to be processed in a image processing software as a final step. All the smaller objects, like bags or magazines, were modelled using only a single picture as a reference and as texture input. A single rig was created for all the human models, and the animations were created in a way that they are all based on a base pose. This base pose is important for the switching between poses, since it is the only one that has a seamless transition into the different poses. So to change from pose A to pose B, the avatar hast to change from pose A to the base pose, and from there then into pose B. The facial animations were created using shape keys, which allow to alter all the vertices of a model and save these deformations in relation to a base position. In case of the faces the base position is the neutral facial expression with open eyes, and in relation to this the different expressions, hostile, happy and blinking were created. These shape keys can then be exported as Ogre3d pose animations.

Ogre3d, which was used as a graphics engine, uses a node tree to visualize the scene. Each created element is therefore part of the RootNode, and can itself have children on its own. The different parts of the room, walls, doors etc. were therefore modeled in Blender3d and then put together in the source code. For the positioning in Ogre3d it is important to know where the center of each model is, because it is used as the base point for position, rotation and scale. Since there are lots of repetitions in the room design, like the chairs in the main seating area, most work could be handled by simple loops. The animations of the audience avatars, as well as the facial animations, textures and additional items, like backpacks etc. were implemented in a random fashion, allowing the scenario to be slightly different each time the application starts. QuickGUI is a simple independent GUI system which works well together with Ogre3d, and it was used to implement the user interface. It provides all the necessary methods and images needed to create simple menu items. All the additional images were created with Gimp. All the PowerPoint slides that are to be used in the simulation have to be put as consecutive numbered .jpg files into the /slide folder in the main directory. Joypad support was added via SDL. A simple wrapper for it was used to get the necessary inputs from the device. Since Ogre3d does not support sound on its own, OpenAL was used for the playback of the sound files, which are provided in .wav format.

4 Psychological Experiments

Two psychological studies were conducted on public speaking anxiety using the above described virtual lecture hall. The objective of the first study was the comparison of two groups holding a presentation either in front of a virtual audience (experimental group) or an imagined audience (control group). The groups were evaluated with regards to their social insecurity as a speaker, reported anxiety and physiological arousal as well as the perceived reality experience of the virtual and the imagined environment. The second study investigated predictors of the perceived usefulness of the virtual public speaking scenario in a larger sample. Both of the studies were conducted at the Department of Psychology at the University of Vienna in accordance with the current version of the Declaration of Helsinki. Prior to participation all participants signed an informed consent form indicating the experiments procedure and the possibility to terminate participation at any time. All statistical analyses were conducted using SPSS Version 15 (SPSS, Inc. Chicago, USA) considering an alpha error of 5%.

4.1 Study 1

Participants. The overall sample ($N = 50$) consisted of students who were recruited from several courses at the University of Vienna and received a course credit for their participation. The mean age of the virtual group ($N = 25$) was 23.44 years ($SD = 3.355$) ranging from 20 to 35 years. Eight percent were male ($N = 2$). The mean age of the control sample was 24.84 years ($SD = 3.023$). In this group the percentage of males was a little higher with an overall of N=8 males (32.0%).

Procedure. Upon arrival to the lab, participants were randomly assigned to either the control group or the experimental group and instructed to hold a 5 minute presentation after a 10 minute preparation period. All participants were given a printed version of the 20 slide presentation to get acquainted with it. In order to ensure the novelty of the subject across participants, a fairly unfamiliar theme was chosen: the description of the kingdom of Bhutan. After preparation, the experimental group was presented with the virtual lecture hall using a head mounted display (eMagin Z800 3D, Bellevue, Washington). A standardized protocol was used for the lecture hall resulting in an overall audience of 20 viewers (both male and female) among which 2 characters were bored and seemed to be asleep on the desks and 2 were laughing out loud once during the presentation. Furthermore, half of the remaining audience was showing neutral emotions. The slides were presented in the virtual environment and controlled by the presenting participant, who - like the participant's virtual self - was standing up during the presentation period. In contrast to the experimental group presenting in the virtual environment the controls were asked to merely imagine an audience. The participants were instructed to stand up in front of a small computer screen containing the presentation slides and speak out loud while imagining a lecture hall around them. To facilitate the imagination of the audience, a short imagination exercise was conducted prior to the start of the procedure.

Measures. Table 1 provides an overview over all psychological questionnaires used in study 1 and 2. The two-factor solution of the questionnaire Personal Report of Confidence as a Speaker (PRCS) [10], was used to assess the participants social insecurity (6 items) and anxiety (12 items) during the public speaking task on a 4 point Likert scale. The participant was asked to rate statements on a 4 point Likert scale (*does apply - does not apply*). Trait social anxiety was measured by the 20-item version of the Social Interaction Anxiety Scale (SIAS) [13] on a 5 point Likert scale (*not at all - extremly*). Additionally, a single 4-point-Likert-scaled item (*strongly agree – strongly disagree*), from the iGroup Presence Questionnaire, IPQ [17], was used to measure the perceived reality of the virtual and the imagined environment. To measure stress related sympathetic activity the participants heart rate during the speech was recorded using M-EXG (Schuhfried BFB 2000 x-pert, Moedling, Austria). EKG was assessed using three one-way electrodes (3M Medica RedDot electrodes, Perchtoldsdorf, Austria). Heart rate was monitored at 5s intervals throughout the speech; 60s intervals were computed using the Schuhfried BFB 2000 x-pert software for analysis.

Table 1. Psychological assessments

	Factor	Description	Example for item wording
Personality facets	Neuroticism	anxiety, depression, self-consciousness and vulnerability to stress	I am easily concerned.
	Extraversion	assertiveness, activity and excitement seeking	I am a very active person.
	Openness for experience	fantasy and ideas	I often try new and foreign dishes.
	Conscientiousness	competence, order and self-discipline	I work hard to reach my goals.
	Agreeableness	altruism, compliance and modesty	I always try to act considerate and sensible.
Technology facets	Curiosity	inquisitive thinking about technology and the desire to explore new technological tools and devices	I was curious to use computer based applications like the VR.
	Usability	comfort and effortlessness of the technology usage	It was easy to transfer what I intended to do into the VR.
	Perceived Usefulness	enhancement of performance or well-being caused by the usage of the technology	Computer based applications like the VR constitute a good preparation for a speech.
State facets	Social Insecurity	competence in social situations (inverse items)	I look forward to an opportunity to speak in public.
	Anxiety	apprehension when the subject is faced with the audience	My hands tremble when I try to handle objects on the platform.
	Realness	experience of realism in the virtual world	Do you experience the audience as real?
Trait facets	Social Anxiety	insecurity and anxiety in social situations	I am nervous mixing with people I don't know well.

Results. Neither heart rate, measured in a 60s interval previous to the task, $(t(48) = 1.589, p = 0.119)$ nor trait social anxiety measured by SIAS $(t(48) = 1.442, p = 0.156)$ did differ at baseline level.

Psychological questionnaires: In order to estimate whether the two groups showed any differences on the measures of social insecurity and anxiety during the public speaking task and perceived reality group comparisons using t-tests were conducted. Figure 3 shows the different distributions between groups on the PRCS scales and the perceived reality (means±SEM). The group presenting in front of the virtual audience differed significantly $(t(48) = 2.759, p = .008)$ from the group imagining the scenario, in sum reporting a higher perceived realness of the situation (experimental: $M = 4.64$, $SD = 1.380$; control: $M = 3.56$, $SD = 1.386$). Additionally, the virtual group ($M = 27.56, SD = 6.980$) showed higher levels of reported anxiety than the control group ($M = 21.72, SD = 6.509$) $(t(48) = 3.590, p = 0.004)$ and at the same time, the experimental group ($M = 18.76, SD = 4.064$) reported significantly higher levels of social insecurity than the control group ($M = 15.32, SD = 4.028$) $(t(48) = 3.006, p = 0.004)$.

Physiological Measures: A repeated measures ANOVA comparing the two groups was employed. Additionally, a Greenhouse-Geisser adjustment was used to correct the violation of the sphericity assumption ($\epsilon = 0.48$). Heart rate

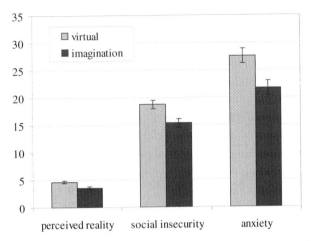

Fig. 3. Differences between the virtual and the control group in perceived reality, social insecurity and anxiety (means± SEM)

interval analysis indicates a significant main effect of time ($F(2.392, 114.819) = 77.007$, $p < 0.001$), a significant difference between the groups ($F(1, 48) = 7.110$, $p < 0.010$) and an interaction effect time x group ($F(1.617, 114.819) = 6.547$, $p < 0.001$). While both groups showed a higher heart rate (more physiological arousal) at the beginning of the speech it symmetrically declined for both groups during the speech. Yet, the virtual group showed an a priori higher heart rate than the control group, in sum indicating higher physiological stress and anxiety during the virtual exposition ($p < 0.001$). Figure 4 depicts the heart rate means (±SEM) according to the 60s intervals over the 5 minute speaking period.

4.2   Study 2

Participants. The sample consisted of $N = 137$ Psychology students recruited from several courses at the University of Vienna. The mean age was 24.18 years (SD= 3.565) ranging from 20 to 40 years. Approximately fifteen percent of the sample were males ($N = 20$) whereas the majority consisted of female students ($N = 117$, 85.4%). Most of the participants ($N = 109$) stated to have a lot of experience with public speaking (>5 presentations). Nineteen participants reported fair experience (4-5 presentations) and only nine persons had little experience (1-3 presentations). The majority ($N = 123$) of the sample was right handed (only $N = 14$ were left-handed). 133 participants were analyzed, 4 datasets were excluded because of missing values.

Procedure. The procedure was the same as for the experimental group in study 1 including the same instructions, the same subject and length of presentation and the same settings of the virtual lecture hall. Again, the virtual environment was presented using a head mounted display (eMagin Z800 3D, Bellevue, Washington) and the participant was standing up while presenting.

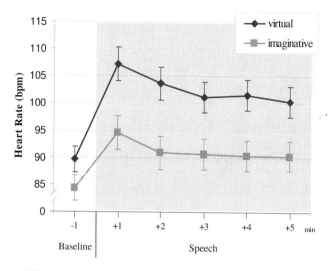

Fig. 4. Group differences between heart rates during a 5 minute speaking period (means±SEM)

Measures. In addition to the PRCS (described in study 1 above) a German version of the NEO-Five-Factor-Inventory (NEO-FFI) [6], was used in the second study (see table 1 for item wording). The 60-item NEO-FFI assesses 5 personality factors known as the Big Five on a 5 point Likert scale (*strongly agree – strongly disagree*). Furthermore, a self-constructed 12-item scale regarding the attitude towards technology (see Technology Acceptance Model, TAM) [8] was applied. It consists of 3 scales assessing curiosity towards technology use, usability of the technology and perceived usefulness of the technology on a 7 point Likert scale (*essential – unessential*).

Results. The perceived usefulness of the virtual lecture hall was rated by the participants after the exposition with the protocol. According to the average ratings over the 4 items 56% of the participants rated the system as *useful* or higher (28% rated the system as *very useful* or *essential*. In contrast, 21% rated the system as *unessential, very useless,* or *useless,* while 23% rated the system as *neither useful nor useless*. A multiple linear regression analysis was conducted to identify the best predictors of the technology's perceived usefulness. Both, the five personality factors (personality facets) and the two subscales of the technology facets curiosity and usability were entered as predictors in the regression model, additionally the variable social insecurity as speaker was included into the analysis.

The current results indicate that the participants' social insecurity as speaker during the speech and both technology facets (usability and curiosity) were encouraging predictors of the dependent variable. Assuming a higher alpha level at 0.10, two personality facets (extraversion and conscientiousness) would have shown a predictive value as well. Table 2 reports the standardized coefficient,

Table 2. Linear Regression analysis to predict perceived usefulness

		Beta	t	p
Personality facets	Neuroticism	0.032	0.367	0.715
	Extraversion	0.144	1.805	0.073*
	Openness for experience	-0.041	-0.517	0.606
	Agreeableness	0.106	1.366	0.175
	Conscientiousness	-0.145	-1.860	0.065*
Technology facets	Curiosity	0.297	3.872	0.000**
	Usability	0.408	5.095	0.000**
State facets	Social insecurity	0.245	2.817	0.006**

Notes: Dependent variable: Perceived Usefulness; * p< 0.10, **p<0.05

t-coefficient and significance level for each independent variable. Nevertheless, the usability of the system seems to predict the usefulness of the virtual lecture hall best, followed by the person curiosity towards technology use and high values of social insecurity. In sum, predictor variables included in the final regression model accounted for almost 31% of the variance ($R^2 = 0.35$; adj. $R^2 = 0.31$; $F(9, 124) = 8.460$, $p < 0.000$; Durbin-Watson= 1.756).

5   Conclusions

Results from Study 1 offer encouraging evidence that in comparison with the control group, which was asked to imagine the audience, the virtual lecturing scenario tends to decrease the participants' self-confidence as speaker and evoke insecurity as well as self-reported anxiety during the speech task. Also, the virtual group showed a significantly higher increase in heart rate (a psychophysiological indicator of stress and arousal) than the control group. These observations indicate the efficacy of the virtual lecture hall as a means for virtual exposition therapy. Additionally, participants of the virtual group had higher ratings than their controls when asked about the perceived level of realness of the lecture hall. In accordance to our findings, previous studies indicate that stronger feelings of actually being present in the virtual environment both positively alter the perception of its realness and vividness and evoke behavioral and psychophysiological reactions that are similar to those in a comparable real life situation. Thus, the more a person who is immersed in a virtual environment behaves like in a comparable real environment, the better the transfer of knowledge and learned skills will be. It therefore seems crucial to develop virtual scenarios with the best possible stimulating and rich content in order to enhance presence and therein increase the efficacy of the training tool. As demonstrated in the current study, a virtual lecturing scenario may indeed evoke satisfying emotional and psychophysiological reactions in order to be effectively used to train public speaking competencies.

In Study 2 curious and socially insecure persons were identified to rate the virtual lecture hall as more useful. We assume that these findings are a result of the participants' individually different motivations to use the technology. Thus, future research should take individual differences in terms of motive and motivation into account. Moreover, participants perceiving the system as usable and easy to use reported higher perceived usefulness of the virtual lecture hall; this result is consistent with Davis' technology acceptance model (1989), which indicates a strong causal relationship between the usability and the perceived usefulness of a technology or a technological system. Thus, if such virtual reality tools shall be designed for use in therapy and treatment a great focus should be put on their ease of use, including both, the programming of the virtual simulation and the application of immersive technologies such as head mounted displays. The user's satisfaction with an easy to use navigation through the virtual environment and a highly effective head tracking system may lead to a higher acceptance of the system and thus, enhance motivation to use it again. Also, if the user identifies a system as useful, he may be more prone to engage in it and develop a sufficient level of presence for the VR to be effective (see above).

Regarding personality facets, extraverted persons seem to rate the virtual technology as more useful than introverted persons, possibly reflecting the generally more positive attitude of extraverted persons towards new (social) experiences such as the experimental situation in general. In contrast, conscientious persons showed a negative trend in rating the technology as useful. The high achievement standards of the highly conscientious participants might have been counteracting with the satisfaction of their virtual presentation and hence, with the positive ratings of the technology altogether. These results are highly valuable, since they indicate that not all users may equally engage in and thus, benefit from these virtual scenarios. Yet, more research is needed if these findings shall effectively be used to identify a person to be unsuitable for a VR treatment or let alone to establish ideal user types for VR scenarios. In future, interdisciplinary approaches covering both, the development of the technologies and the area of their application are called upon extending their collaborations in order to study such phenomena more broadly.

Acknowledgments. We would like to thank Jasmine Gomm, Nathalie Hauk, Anna Hoffmann, Elisabeth Kastenhofer, MSc., Nora Poesl and Janka Scharfenberger for helping us with the acquisition of the data.

References

1. Anderson, E.R., Hope, D.A.: The relationship among social phobia, objective and perceived physiological reactivity, and anxiety sensitivity in an adolescent population. Journal of Anxiety Disorders 23, 18–26 (2009)
2. Botella, C., Hofmann, S.G., Moscovitz, D.A.: A self-applied Internet-based intervention for fear of public speaking. Journal of Clinical Psychology 60, 1–10 (2004)
3. Botella, C., Gallego, M.J., Garcia-Palacios, A., Guillen, V., Banos, R.M., Quero, S., Alcaniz, M.: An Internet-Based Self-Help Treatment for Fear of Public Speaking: A Controlled Trial. Cyberpsychology, Behavior and Social Networking 13(4), 407–421 (2010)

4. Caplan, S., Williams, D., Yee, N.: Problematic Internet use and psychosocial well-being among MMO players. Computers in Human Behavior 25, 1312–1319 (2009)
5. Clark, D.M., Wells, A.: A cognitive model of social phobia. In: Heimberg, R.G., Liebowitz, M.R., Hope, D.A., Schneier, F.R. (eds.) Social Phobia: Diagnosis, Assessment and Treatment, pp. 69–93. Guilford Press, New York (1995)
6. Costa, P.T., McCrae, R.R.: Revised NEO Personality Inventory (NEO-PI-R) and NEO Five-Factor Inventory (NEOFFI) professional manual. Odessa: Psychological Assessment Resources (1992)
7. Cote, S., Bouchard, S.: Virtual reality exposure for phobias: A critical review. Journal of CyberTherapy & Rehabilitation 1(1), 75–91 (2008)
8. Davis, F.D.: Perceived usefulness, perceived ease of use, and user acceptance of information technology. MIS Quarterly 13, 319–340 (1989)
9. Gerlach, A.L., Mourlane, D., Rist, F.: Public and private heart rate feedback in social phobia: a manipulation of anxiety visibility. Cognitive Behaviour Therapy 33, 36–45 (2004)
10. Hook, J.N., Smith, C.A., Valentiner, D.P.: A short-form of the Personal Report of Confidence as a Speaker. Personality and Individual Differences 44, 1306–1313 (2008)
11. Kothgassner, O.D., Stetina, B.U., Lehenbauer, M., Seif, M., Kryspin-Exner, I.: Behavior beyond the world of online gaming. In: Welker, M., Geiler, H., Kaczmirek, L., Wenzel, O. (eds.) General Online Research, pp. S53–S54. DGOF, Pforzheim (2010)
12. Laposa, J.M., Cassin, S.E., Rector, N.A.: Interpretation of positive social events in social phobia: an examination of cognitive correlates and diagnostic distinction. Journal of Anxiety Disorders 24, 203–210 (2010)
13. Mattick, R.P., Clarke, J.C.: Development and validation of measures of social phobia scrutiny fear and social interaction anxiety. Behaviour Research and Therapy 36, 455–470 (1998)
14. Mauss, I.B., Wilhelm, F.H., Gross, J.J.: Autonomic recovery and habituation in social anxiety. Psychophysiology 40, 648–653 (2003)
15. Newman, M.G., Szkodny, L.E., Llera, S.J., Przeworski, A.: A review of technology-assisted self-help and minimal contact therapies for anxiety and depression: Is human contact necessary for therapeutic efficacy? Clinical Psychology Review 31(1), 89–103 (2011)
16. Parsons, T.D., Rizzo, A.A.: Affective outcomes of virtual reality exposure therapy for anxiety and specific phobias: A meta-analysis. Journal of Behavior Therapy and Experimental Psychiatry 39, 250–261 (2008)
17. Schubert, T., Friedmann, F., Regenbrecht, H.: The experience of presence: Factor analytic insights. Presence: Teleoperators and Virtual Environments 10(3), 266–281 (2001)
18. Wiederhold, B.K., Wiederhold, M.D.: Virtual Reality Therapy for Anxiety Disorders. American Psychological Association, Washington (2005)

Stories from the History of Czechoslovakia, A Serious Game for Teaching History of the Czech Lands in the 20th Century – Notes on Design Concepts and Design Process

Vít Šisler[1,2], Cyril Brom[1,2], Jaroslav Cuhra[3], Kamil Činátl[1], and Jakub Gemrot[1,2]

[1] Charles University in Prague, Faculty of Arts,
Nám. Jana Palacha 2, Prague, Czech Republic
[2] Charles University in Prague, Faculty of Mathematics and Physics,
Malostranské nám. 2/25, Prague, Czech Republic
[3] Academy of Sciences of the Czech Republic, Institute of Contemporary History,
Vlašská 9, Prague, Czech Republic

Abstract. In the context of curricular history education both commercial entertainment games as well as serious games specifically tailored for educational purposes were employed. Especially the latter types of games were reported as being promising concerning instructional effectiveness. Still, there are not many complex serious games for history education, particularly in the secondary schools context. In this work-in-progress paper, we report on the progress of project *Stories from the History of Czechoslovakia*, a serious game for teaching history of the Czech lands in the 20th century. We introduce main game concepts, describe two main design challenges we have been facing during the development and how we have addressed them and overview our feasibility study on 71 high-school students. This paper can be informative for researchers and designers working on similar projects.

1 Introduction

Digital game-based learning refers to employing a videogame as an educational aid. In the context of curricular history education, both commercial "off-the-shelf" entertainment games as well as serious games specifically tailored for educational purposes were employed and their learning effects empirically examined. While usage of commercial games turned out to be problematic in this context (e.g. [4, 14]), the studies of serious games, such as various 3D virtual reality cultural heritage games [10] or *Frequency 1550*, a mobile city game [6], reported more promising results (see also [12, 15]).

In the Czech Republic, descriptive methods, the focus of which is the reproduction of extensive knowledge, still prevail in the teaching of history. However, the recently introduced curricular reform puts an emphasis on the development of key skills and competencies [7]. At the same time, history textbooks which shall be in accordance with the reform are largely not available. Serious games are oftentimes based on the

M. Herrlich, R. Malaka, and M. Masuch (Eds.): ICEC 2012, LNCS 7522, pp. 67–74, 2012.
© IFIP International Federation for Information Processing 2012

knowledge of factual account of events. More importantly, they aim to develop skills and abilities of students to comprehend, compare and analyze sources of facts and create their critical judgments. Serious games thus arguably provide an alternative teaching aid to traditional history textbooks in accordance with the above-mentioned curricular reform.

In this paper, we introduce a complex educational serious game which is currently being developed at the Faculty of Arts and the Faculty of Mathematics and Physics of the Charles University in Prague and the Institute of Contemporary History of the Academy of Sciences of the Czech Republic. The main target audience is 13 to 19 years old high-school students. The general educational objective of the game, developed under the working title *Stories from the History of Czechoslovakia* (SHCS), is to present to the students the key events of the history of Czechoslovakia in the second half of 20th century (to 1989) and to enable them to "experience" these events from the perspective of different actors. By doing so, the game aims to develop deeper understanding of the complex and multifaceted political, social, and cultural aspects of this time period. Emphasis is given on the diversified historical experiences of various segments of the population.

The game is a single-player dialog-based adventure game with a strong narrative, featuring interactive comics and authentic audio visual materials. Importantly, the content of SHCS is based on personal testimonies of eyewitnesses of the respective periods. The player assumes a different role in individual modules and interacts with the eyewitnesses in the present and "travels" back in time on memories of the eyewitnesses yielded during conversations. The educational methodology also supports in-class discussions concerning the given periods and events.

The purpose of this paper is to introduce game concepts, main design decisions (Section 2), describe two main design challenges we have been facing during the development and how we have addressed them (Section 3) and overview concept evaluation (Section 4). This paper can be informative for researchers and designers working on similar projects.

2   Game Concepts and Background Historical Research

The main educational goal of SHCS is to develop deeper understanding of the complex and multifaceted political, social, and cultural aspects of the key events of the history of Czechoslovakia between 1938 – 1989 by presenting these events from a perspective of multiple actors. At present we plan to develop 4-5 different historical modules, each covering a different chronological period (1938 – 1945: The dissolution of Czechoslovakia and establishment of the Nazi Protectorate of Bohemia and Moravia; 1945 – 1948: The immediate postwar era, including the reconstruction of Czechoslovakia, the expulsion of its German-speaking citizens and the rise to power of the Communist Party; 1948 – 1960: The radicalization and then stabilization of the communist regime; 1960 – 1968: The gradual liberalization of the regime, or "Prague Spring," and Soviet occupation in 1968; and 1969 – 1989: The restoration of a hardline Communist regime and the so-called "Normalization," which led to the "Velvet revolution" in 1989). At the time of writing this paper, the first module and the game engine are half finished. The whole game should be finished before 2013.

On the level of content, the game stems from applied historical research of the possible manifestations of experiencing the history of the 2nd half of 20th century in Czechoslovakia. This research has been conducted at the Institute of Contemporary History of Academy of Sciences of Czech Republic. The research a) focuses on mapping the personal histories of the citizens of Czechoslovakia between 1938 and 1989, b) explores the key events of the above mentioned period, and c) analyzes their broader social, cultural, and political impact. At the same time, the content of SHCS is based on personal testimonies of eyewitnesses of the above-mentioned periods, collected by the nongovernmental organization Post Bellum [9]. Nevertheless, SHCS does not adapt these real stories in a literal fashion; rather it uses them as source for constructing realistic and appealing narratives (note the target audience appreciates this concept - see Sec. 4). By doing so, SHCS enables us to produce appealing stories with a number of authentic details without "gamifiying" the real-persons' – oftentimes emotionally and ethically loaded – testimonies. Yet, the game is enhanced by a multimedia encyclopedia which presents to the students both with additional factual information as well as authentic testimonies of real people from the above mentioned period.

On the level of structure, the game is organized hierarchically. It is divided into individual modules, which could be accessed independently. Each module covers one historical period, accessed through a key event or series of interlinked events, from a perspective of multiple actors. Correspondingly, each module is divided into blocks which are dedicated to memories of particular persons. Furthermore, each block is divided into scenes which present the player with separated, yet interlinked "micro-stories". Scene is thus a molecular unit of the game. From a designer's perspective, there are four types of scenes in the game: animation, interactive comics (Fig. 1), interactive game, and video interview. Each type utilizes different graphical style and design concept. Simultaneously, it provides different educational possibilities for the teachers and different affordances for the players. Essentially, animations and interactive comics serve as vehicles for "pushing" the story forwards and providing the player with real-world background, including multimedia and textual materials. Every module features several interactive games, each of which can be based on a different game genre, including point-and-click adventure, logical game, simple strategy game, or action game. Yet, each interactive game is intertwined with learning outcomes of the scene and these two do not constitute separate elements, which turned out to be problematic in previous studies [8, see also 5]. Finally, video interviews represent the core element of the game, i.e. an interactive interview with the "real" protagonist, whose memories the player just followed in the interactive comics and interactive game. Each block contains all of the above mentioned types of scenes, effectively combining them and utilizing their full potential.

SHCS deals with topics of Czech and Central European modern history which are often subject to discussion and debates in the public space. Given the design of the game, every student can progress through it via different people's stories and ask these people different pre-scripted questions, including ethically and emotionally contested issues. Every student can choose different path in the interviews and thus has to a certain extent unique gaming experience. Importantly, the students' in-game experience is then subject to debriefing, an important part of the educational methodology [10]. Not only serves the game as a data source in itself, it also naturally stimulates debates in a framework of multi-perspectivity. Following the ideas of pedagogical constructivism, students are taught that "history is neither a closed past nor a collection of events and definite conclusions, but rather a platform for questions to be asked" [11].

Fig. 1. Screenshot from *Stories from the History of Czechoslovakia* (Charles University in Prague, 2012). Graphic design by Petr Novák and Richard Alexander.

3   Design Challenges

The development team comprises about 20 people, including game designers, historians, educationalists, programmers, and artists. The team's roles are more diverse than in a typical entertainment game development team. Therefore, we have faced a challenge how to organize the teamwork so that the game content can be produced with minimal communication overhead. This includes bridging terminology used by team members with different background and reconciling their sometimes contradictory requirements and expectations, e.g. on entertaining elements and game flow (a game designer's perspective), the amount and character of learning content (an educationalist's perspective), and historical accuracy and possible schematizations (a historian's perspective). In addition, we faced a challenge to obtain authentic materials, such as photographs or radio recordings, to build the game's narratives around real personal stories, and finally, to mediate this realness to players.

We addressed the first challenge very early in the preproduction phase by several means. The most important turned out to be development of a rigid formal structure for specification of modules' scenarios. Essentially, the structure organizes modules' elements described in Sec. 2. into a two-level hierarchical finite state machine (hFSM), in which some of the lower level states comprise dialog trees for capturing dialog possibilities with individual characters. This structure is formal yet simple enough to enforce a common design language among all team members, which has allowed us to do two things. First, we have employed a top-down design process, during which designers refine incrementally the game scenarios together with historians, educationalists and artists. Second, we have completely separated game content data from the engine, exploiting benefits of the data-driven software architecture. Consequently, it has become possible to develop an authoring tool, StoryBuilder, in the preproduction phase. Because StoryBuilder structures game content data in the same way as designers and historians do when they specify the scenarios, these team members can encode the resulting scenarios using StoryBuilder themselves. Although we still do need the role of a level designer, who maintains the flow of the game play, the direct involvement of historians in the process eases keeping the historical accuracy and avoiding schematizations.

The second challenge is addressed by creating semi-real stories, based on authentic personal testimonies as has been described above. Due to our collaboration with historians, we can also capitalize on results of their applied research and the use of archival materials.

From the technical perspective, we have chosen to use Adobe Flash platform utilizing Adobe AfterEffects for creating visually appealing animations, including videos, and Adobe Flash Pro for sequencing them. Animations are then imported into StoryBuilder forming some of the game scenes. Other scenes comprise dialogs with game characters or interactive games. Together, these scenes serve as states of the game hFSM. StoryBuilder is then utilized to provide conditional transitions between these scenes thus providing means for plot formalization. Each module can be separately exported and interpreted by StoryEngine.

4   Concept Evaluation

In past, our team developed several different educational games for secondary education and conducted empirical research on their acceptance in the context of curricular schooling and their learning effects, e.g. [2, 3]. From our previous experience, we know that acceptance of a new educational game is far from guaranteed and many students are skeptical towards games in the formal education (cf. [4, 13]). At the same time, our experience suggests that at least above-average students understand that the quality of graphics of serious games will be lower than that of AAA entertainment games, and our empirical data support the idea that real-world grounding of a game's content is of crucial importance, e.g. [3]. With these facts in mind, we have conducted a small scale feasibility study with two questions:

1. Would the concept of an adventure game combining comics-based graphics and videos be appreciated by students in the context of history education?
2. To which extent should the game's content be based on real stories?

The study had two parts. First, questionnaires accompanied by demonstrations of example graphics were administered in two above average high-school classes (n=44; m=20; f=24). Second, slightly modified questionnaires accompanied by demonstrations of example graphics were administered in another above-average high-school class (n=27; m = 14; f = 13), students of which then participated in group interviews. In the questionnaires, mostly Likert items with 4-point scale were used (1 = strong yes; 4 = strong no). The questions of present interest were: 1) "Would you accept the following game genre should you play a serious game in history classes"?

2) "Would you like to play such a game when the module concerns the following historical period?" (cf. Sec. 2); 3) "Would you accept the following graphical style for such a game?"[1] In addition, we asked them 4) whether "Stories of the in-game characters should..." a) "exactly correspond to real stories", b) "be based on real stories", c) "be specifically fabricated for the educational purposes", d) "does not matter". The results are depicted in Tab. 1.

Table 1. The questionnaires' outcomes (means and standard deviations for Questions (1), (2), and (3); numbers of answers for Question (4))

Question	n						
1	44	Adventure	Logical	action game	detective	RPG	multi-player
		2.02 (0.87)	2.05(0.9)	2.35(0.95)	2.21(0.83)	1.84(0.92)	1.89(0.87)
2	71	1939 – 45	1945 – 48	1948 – 62	1962 - 72	1972 - 89	
		1.71 (0.91)	2.11 (0.96)	2.28 (0.9)	2.2 (0.89)	2.1 (0.87)	
3	44	Comics	Video	3D VR			
		2.4 (0.87)	2.23 (0.95)	2.03 (0.84)			
4	44	a) real	(b) semi-real	(c) fabricated	(d) doesn't matter	no answer	
		10	26	5	2	1	

We see that the concept of adventure game scored relatively well, though a multi-player RPG might be a better genre. We see that students tended to prefer 3D graphics, but a comics and video-based styles were also accepted. These two outcomes are actually in line with our observation stated above. Finally, students' attitude towards any of the time periods was positive. Not surprisingly, the most positive attitude was towards the 2nd World War period. Note however that this period is already well covered by existing educational materials in the Czech Republic. Finally, students strongly preferred stories that are based on real stories, but are not necessarily exact copies of real stories. This agrees with our previous results [3].

Thus, concerning our first question, quantitative data suggest that students do not have insurmountable issues with our game concept. They would perhaps appreciate more a 3D multi-player RPG, but the development of such a game is an order of magnitude more expensive. Concerning our second question, our concept of semi-real stories seems to suit perfectly for our purpose.

Detailed analysis of students' preferences of different comics styles revealed large between style differences, which is not very surprising. This suggests that graphics evaluation with the target group of users is vital during the production of the game.

The qualitative data from interviews supported our caution concerning students' acceptance of serious games in general and history education in particular. Majority of students is mildly skeptical towards usage of games in formal schooling system and detailed analysis of their statements supports the idea that games should be used as a supplement only and that the teachers role and consecutive contextualization of the game play and discussions are vital, cf. [1, 10, 13]. Representative sample of citations of high-schools students 18 or 19 years old:

---

[1] The following demonstrations were used for the comics, video and 3D virtual reality, respetivelly: Aqua (Games Distillery, 2010), The Curfew (Channel 4, 2010), Fahrenheit (Quantic Dream, 2005).

"Simulations [in education] are fine, but it depends on teachers how they will use them." (girl)

"We want a discussion, not a game." (girl)

"Simulations [in education] are not just games. We do have computers so why not to use them?" (girl)

"I more or less agree with [usage of educational] games, but everything in moderation." (boy)

"A good teacher will be always better than a simulation." (girl)

"[Serious games] can make education more engaging." (girl)

"[Serious games] can help a below average teacher to increase quality of education." (boy)

This is in line with previous data, e.g. [4]. The notable limitation of the present study is relatively low number of students and the fact that all of them were from above average high-schools. It would be useful to supplement these results with date from average and below average schools, which is one of our on-going efforts.

5 Conclusion

In this paper, we have reported on progress of the project *Stories from the History of Czechoslovakia*, a complex single-player serious game for teaching history of the Czech lands in the 20th century. The main target audience is high-school students and the primary objective is to develop deeper understanding of the complex and multi-faceted political, social, and cultural aspects of respective time periods. The main elements of the game are video-dialogs with eyewitnesses of the given time periods, through which a player can "travel" back in time, and animations, interactive comics and interactive mini-games, through which the player can perceive the respective historical periods from the perspective of the eyewitnesses. The game offers every player to a certain extent unique gaming experience, which helps a teacher to set-up consecutive in-class discussion. The game is to be enhanced by a multimedia encyclopedia, enabling students to study the topics at several levels of details.

Development of such game would have been impossible without having not only game designers, programmers, and artists, but also historians and educationalists on board. Our main challenge to organize teamwork and to enable people with various backgrounds to understand each other was addressed by imposing a rigid formal structure for specifying the game scenarios, which become a ground for a shared "language" among all team members. Our main design decision that the game content will be based on personal testimonies of eyewitnesses of the respective periods but not appropriating these real stories in literal fashion, has been supported by outcomes of our concept evaluation with the target audience. At the same time, the evaluation has suggested that we may not need a cutting-edge 3D graphics to engage students in playing the game; nevertheless, the above average high-school students might be, no matter the graphics quality, mildly skeptical towards the idea of using games in the context of formal schooling system. This suggests that the game should be designed from the beginning with the idea that it will be later integrated within the formal schooling system. Designing supplementary activities and supporting teachers is vital.

Acknowledgments. This paper was supported by the grant project DF11P01OVV030 "Příběhy z dějin československého státu: výzkum a experimentální vývoj softwarových simulací pro výuku historie českých zemí ve 20. století" financed by the Czech Ministry of Culture in 2011-2014. The authors would like to thank to Tereza Selmbacherová for her assistance with data collection and analysis.

References

1. Anderson, E.F., McLoughlin, L., Liarokapis, F., Peters, C., Petridis, P., de Freitas, S.: Developing serious games for cultural heritage: a state-of-the-art review. Virtual Reality 14, 255–275 (2010)
2. Brom, C., Preuss, M., Klement, D.: Are Educational Computer Micro-Games Engaging And Effective For Knowledge Acquisition At High-Schools? A Quasi-Experimental Study. Computers & Education 57, 1971–1988 (2011)
3. Brom, C., Šisler, V., Slavík, R.: Implementing Digital Game-Based Learning in Schools: Augmented Learning Environment of Europe 2045. Multimedia Systems 16(1), 23–41 (2010)
4. Egenfeldt-Nielsen, S.: Beyond Edutainment: Exploring the Educational Potential of Computer Games. PhD thesis. University of Copenhagen (2005)
5. Habgood, M.P., Ainsworth, S.E.: Motivating children to learn effectively: Exploring the value of intrinsic integration in educational games. Jn. Learning Sciences 20(2), 169–206 (2011)
6. Huizenga, J., Admiraal, W., Akkerman, S., ten Dam, G.: Mobile game-based learning in secondary education: engagement, motivation and learning in a mobile-city game. Journal of Computer Assisted Learning 25(4), 332–344 (2009)
7. Janík, T., et al.: Kurikulární reforma na gymnáziích. Případové studie tvorby Kurikula (Curricural reform at gymnasiums: Case studies from creating the curriculum). In: VÚP Praha (2011) (in Czech)
8. Jantke, K.P.: Games that do not exist: Communication design beyond the current limits. In: Proc. ACM Conference on Design of Communication (2006)
9. Bellum, P.: Paměť národa, Memory of Nation (April 16, 2012), http://www.pametnaroda.cz/ (in Czech)
10. Peters, V.A.M., Vissers, G.A.N.: A simple classification model for debriefing simulation games. Simulation & Gaming 35(1), 70–84 (2004)
11. Rámcový vzdělávací program pro základní vzdělávání (Framework Education Programme for Basic Education). VÚP Praha (2007), http://www.vuppraha.cz/wp-content/uploads/2009/12/RVPZV_2007-07.pdf (April 16, 2012) (in Czech)
12. SELEAG project consortium: TimeMesh game (2011), http://www.timemesh.eu/site (April 16, 2012)
13. Šisler, V., Brom, C.: Designing an Educational Game: Case Study of 'Europe 2045'. In: Pan, Z., Cheok, D.A.D., Müller, W., El Rhalibi, A. (eds.) Transactions on Edutainment I. LNCS, vol. 5080, pp. 1–16. Springer, Heidelberg (2008)
14. Squire, K.: Replaying history: Learning World History through playing Civilization III, PhD thesis, Indiana University (2004)
15. The Education Arcade: Revolution game (2004), http://educationarcade.org/node/357 (April 16, 2012)

Cognitive Processes Involved in Video Game Identification[*]

Christopher Blake[1], Dorothée Hefner[1], Christian Roth[2],
Christoph Klimmt[1], and Peter Vorderer[3]

[1] Department of Journalism and Communication Research,
Hanover University of Music, Drama and Media,
Expo-Plaza 12, 30539 Hannover, Germany
[2] Department of Communication Science,
VU University Amsterdam,
De Boelelaan 1081, 1081 HV Amsterdam, The Netherlands
[3] Department of Media and Communication Studies,
University of Mannheim,
Haus Oberrhein (602), Rheinvorlandstr. 5, 68159 Mannheim, Germany
christopher.blake@ijk.hmtm-hannover.de

Abstract. Identifying with video game characters is one potentially important process in game enjoyment. Based on a theoretical model of video game identification as transformed self-perception, cognitive processes in video game identification were explored. An experiment with N = 60 male players revealed that increased cognitive accessibility of character-related concepts should be considered as element of the identification process. Moreover, shifts in players' self-perceptions were observed so that players of a shooter video game (*Call of Duty 2™*) described themselves as less gentle and more soldier-like than a control group. Overall, the study suggests that shifts in self-related cognition occur as part of the gaming experience. Implications for future research on game enjoyment and long-term game effects are discussed.

Keywords: Video games, entertainment, identification, priming, experiment, lexical decision task.

1   Introduction

Many contemporary video games contain rich narratives and offer a specific character (e.g., a war hero) or a certain role (e.g., military commander) to players. In the scientific discussion of the remarkable fascination and enjoyment of video games, such narrative elements have been suggested to facilitate emotional player responses because of processes of identification [1-3]. While the term identification has been used quite differently across studies, media types (e.g., novels versus TV), most scholars

[*] This research was funded by the European Commission, project "FUGA: The fun of gaming" (NEST-PATH-IMP 28765). We thankfully acknowledge the Commission's support.

M. Herrlich, R. Malaka, and M. Masuch (Eds.): ICEC 2012, LNCS 7522, pp. 75–84, 2012.
© IFIP International Federation for Information Processing 2012

would agree that identification refers to cognitive and emotional bonds media users (such as gamers) develop with a target media character such as their avatar in a video game. Oatley has proposed a simulation metaphor of identification which suggests that media users imagine the story events 'through the character's eyes', which leads to cognitive and affective responses in media users that are similar to what the character her-/himself is experiencing [4]. In a similar fashion, Cohen has defined identification as strong empathetic response to a media character combined with a loss of self-awareness in media users [5]. Metaphorically speaking, video game players who are identifying with their game character or role 'become one' with the character.

A recent theoretical account of video game identification by Klimmt, Hefner & Vorderer has translated the notion of users 'melting' with their game character into a social-psychological process of transformed self-perception [1]. Based on basic research by Goldstein and Cialdini, they argue that identifying with a game character becomes manifest in a modified self-perception so that the player sees (some of) the attributes of the character also as element of her/his current self [6]. Identification, in this sense, would thus mean transformed self-perception. Because many game characters display extreme attributes, such as great physical strength or moral superiority, it is likely that adopting character attributes into one's self-perception (e.g., perceiving oneself as more courageous than in everyday situations) reduces self-discrepancies [7]. Players who experience reduced self-discrepancies, that is, who perceive themselves to get closer to their preferred "ideal" self, typically respond with positive emotions that feed into overall game enjoyment [1]. Bessiere, Seay, and Kiesler found, for instance, that many MMO players design their avatars in a way that represents (parts of) their ideal selves; an empirical observation that directly supports the present theoretical account of video game identification [8].

2   Video Game Identification and Cognition

The purpose of this study was to explore the cognitive processes involved in video game identification as transformed self-perception. One mode of cognition that should occur as a consequence of the theorized identification phenomenon is an increased accessibility of character-related concepts as implicit cognitive prerequisite of identification. Close identification with, for instance, a soldier role in a first-person shooter should come along with 'thinking in a soldier's categories', such as friend or foe, attack and withdraw, weapons, tactics, camouflage, tanks, explosions, et cetera. To the extent that a player identifies with a character or role, concepts that are related to the character or role should thus be activated frequently in the player's mind during game play. As a consequence, these concepts should be more salient and more accessible for automatic processing during and immediately after game play. Implicit measures addressing accessibility of concepts should thus reveal cognitive traces of identification. Accordingly, we hypothesize that players of a military first-person shooter video game display greater cognitive accessibility of soldier-related concepts than players of a non-military video game (H1).

From the perspective of Klimmt et al.'s model, such cognitive accessibility of character-related concepts should be considered as necessary, but not sufficient condition of identification [1], because strong involvement [9] without identification could also result in higher accessibility of concepts related to the character or game world. Still, concept accessibility is theoretically linked to identification, and its empirical occurrence would be interpretable as a milestone on the way towards full video game identification.

In addition to concept accessibility, residuals of changed self-experiences through video game identification should be observable in players' self-descriptions after game play. Goldstein and Cialdini (study 1) found that people who read an interview with a target person and were instructed to empathize with that person described themselves as more similar to that target person afterwards than a control group [6]. Klimmt et al. interpret this finding as a result of merged identities between observer and target person [1]. In the video game context, then, we assume that players who identify with a video game character during game play should describe themselves as more similar to the game character than a control group, due to the merger of their own and the character's identity, which is a change of players' 'normal' self-image. For instance, players of military first-person shooters who identify with a soldier character should describe themselves as braver, more courageous, loyal etc. than a control group. Accordingly, we assume that players of a military first-person shooter video game describe themselves as more similar to a soldier immediately after playing than players of a non-military video game (H2).

The identification process that leads to such changes in self-description may be automatic and not accessible or noticeable for players; the altered self-description may thus serve as an implicit measure of a cognitive residual of video game identification. This means that while players explicitly describe themselves, they are not necessarily aware of the reason why they assign certain attributes to themselves (i.e., prior identification with a game character).

3   Method

An experiment with 60 voluntary university students aged between 20 and 34 years ($M = 24.97$, $SD = 3.32$) was conducted to test the hypotheses. All respondents played video games at least sometimes ("2" on a scale from "1" = never to "5" = very often), 72% of them even played video games often or very often. For two reasons only male students were recruited: First, male students are more likely to be familiar with first person shooter games and second, the limitation leads to a more homogenous sample. This is beneficial with regard to the internal validity of our experimental approach. Participants were randomly assigned to either play a military first person shooter (*Call of Duty 2*™, a popular World War II shooting game), which was intended to facilitate identification with an infantry soldier, or the popular puzzling game *Tetris* that did not include any military content at all and certainly no soldier character to identify with. Randomization procedure was only partly successful. While participants in the two conditions did not differ concerning their use of video games, World War II shooting games or *Call of Duty 2*™, there was a significant difference concerning participants' age ($M_{CoD} = 24.0$, $SD = 2.4$; $M_{Tetris} = 26.0$, $SD = 3.8$). In order to account for the unequally distributed age, this variable was used as a covariate in each of the following statistical tests.

To examine the accessibility of soldier-related concepts (H1), players were confronted with a Lexical Decision Task after ten minutes of game play [10, 11]. This implicit procedure presents letter sequences on a screen and requires participants to decide whether the letters make a real word or not as fast as possible. Letter sequences that do not make real words (non-words) could be a word at first sight. They are made up of a real word with one letter exchanged (e.g., "Morch" instead of "March"). Concept accessibility is measured by the time participants need to identify words semantically related to the concepts under study in comparison to words unrelated to that concept. For instance, strong accessibility of the concept 'soldier' should result in very fast decision times for words such as rifle, mine or tank but not speed up decision times for unrelated words such as elephant, coffee or cake. Following the procedure described by Macrae et al., a lexical decision task was implemented to measure cognitive accessibility of soldier-related concepts [10]. It presents words that reflect soldier-related contexts or are unrelated to that context (for the purpose of comparison). Specifically, a set of 14 words with connection to the soldier role and 14 words unrelated to that role were presented to participants in random order.[1] The same number of 28 non-words was added to the list of target words appearing on screen. Each word/non-word was visible on screen for 75 milliseconds. Participants were requested to press either 'd' on a computer keyboard if the presented word was a real word or to press 'k' if the word was a non-word. Response times between target word onset and press of the key was measured in milliseconds (with the Inquisit 2 software by Millisecond, Inc.). H1 was thus translated into the prediction that players of the shooter game will display greater cognitive accessibility and thus faster decision times if words related to the soldier role appear on screen (compared to words unrelated to the solider role and in comparison to players in the *Tetris* control group).

Following standard procedures for LDT measures [12], we eliminated five participants from the data set due to their performance (they had assorted more than 25% of the words incorrectly, too fast (<300 ms) or too slowly (>1400 ms $\approx$ 2 standard deviations above the mean).

To test H2, the self-description procedure applied by Goldstein and Cialdini (study 1) was adapted to the present context [6]. Participants were given an attribute list and asked to rate each attribute concerning the extent to which it was true for themselves. Ratings were made on an 11-point scale with 1 meaning "the attribute describes me much less than the average person" and 11 meaning "the attribute describes me much

---

[1] Words reflecting a soldier-related context (translated from German): to attack, bunker, defilade, explosion, firing, cannon, rifle, grenade, helmet, mine, to reload, tank, soldier, to blow up (Reaction time: $M = 624.2$ ms, $SD = 91.1$). Words reflecting a soldier-unrelated context: to bake, to shop, elephant, bottle, spring, to water, cellphone, to marry, coffee, chamber, cake, bar, street, to perform magic (Reaction time: $M = 634.6$ ms, $SD = 83.7$).

more than the average person". The scale mid-point 6 was labeled "the attribute describes me about the same as the average person." Half of the attributes were soldier-related (e.g., brave, patriotic, assertive), the other half was semantically distal to the soldier concept (e.g., warm-hearted). Following H2, it was predicted that identification with the infantry soldier should lead to higher ratings of soldier-related attributes and lower ratings of distal attributes in players of *Call of Duty 2*™ than in *Tetris* players.

Upon entering the laboratory, participants first played the game that was randomly assigned to them (*Call of Duty 2*™ or *Tetris*) on a laptop computer with a 17 inch display, headphones, and external mouse device. After ten minutes of game play, the experimenter kindly interrupted game play by pausing the game and invited the participant to perform the LDT on a second laptop computer. After completion of the LDT, participants were asked to resume game play for another ten minutes (to re-establish identification). Afterwards, the experimenter finished the game and handed a questionnaire to participants that included the self-description task as described above, an item to measure prior use of world war games similar to *Call of Duty 2*™, various other brief questions and some demography items. Finally, participants were thanked, offered information on study results, and received 10 EUR as financial compensation.

4   Results

To test H1, experimental groups were compared in LDT performance. Specifically, the average response times for those target words were analyzed that had a semantic connection to the soldier role. Following H1, the prediction was tested that players of *Call of Duty 2*™ would display greater cognitive accessibility and thus faster decision times (compared to *Tetris* players) for this kind of target words. In reverse, words unrelated to the soldier role (neutral words) should not produce significant differences in the mean reaction time between the two experimental groups.

A repeated measure ANCOVA with the word category (soldier-related vs. neutral) as within-subjects factor and the experimental condition (Game played: *Call of Duty 2*™ or *Tetris*) as between-subjects factor was conducted (see Figure 1). Age was included as a covariate due to its unequal distribution between the two experimental groups. The hypothesized interaction effect for word category and game occurred ($F(1,52) = 12.97$; $p<.01$; $\eta^2 = .20$). There was no main effect for the within- subjects factor word category ($F(1,52) = 0.20$; *ns*).

The interaction of game and word category occurred because reaction times to soldier-related words were significantly faster in players of the shooter game than in *Tetris* players while there was only a marginal difference concerning the neutral words between the two groups. H1 thus received empirical support: Players of the military shooter game displayed substantially greater accessibility of soldier-related concepts compared to the control group of *Tetris* players.

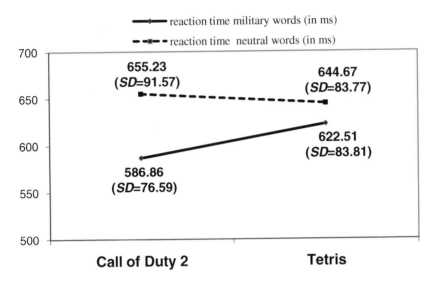

Fig. 1. Effect of the stimulus game (Shooter: *Call of Duty 2*™ versus *Tetris*) on reaction times for military words and neutral words (N = 55)

In order to test H2, the items of the self-description scale were submitted to a factor analysis first (principal component analysis with VARIMAX rotation). For various reasons, 11 of the 26 items were removed step-by-step (because of factor loadings <0.5, bad interpretability along with other items in a factor, and/or lack of semantic clarity). The final factor solution was based on 15 items and comprised four dimensions explaining 58.68% of the variance (see Table 1). All factors had an eigenvalue of at least 1.7 after rotation and 1.4 before rotation. Three factors reflected typical soldier attribute dimensions (factor 1: tenacity and discipline, factor 3: aggressiveness, and factor 4: courage) and one attribute dimension contrasted typical soldier attributes (factor 2: gentleness).

A MANCOVA with "Game played" as between-subjects factor, age as covariate and the factor values of the four dimensions as dependent variables was then conducted to test H2 (Table 2). Results lend partial support to H2: While those participants who played *Tetris* display higher values for the factor "gentleness", respondents who played the shooter game held higher values on the dimensions "tenacity-and-discipline" and "aggression", which implies a greater tendency to ascribe soldier-related attributes to themselves. A marginally significant multivariate group difference across all four dimensions was observed. Factor-wise analysis revealed that the experimental group difference was only significant for the second factor "gentleness" (Table 2). Thus, H2 received modest empirical support.

Table 1. Extracted personality trait dimensions

	Factor 1	Factor 2	Factor 3	Factor 4
disciplined	.772			
tough	.735			
persevering	.604			
proactive	.587			
persistent	.523			
kind		.850		
helpful		.797		
warm-hearted		.614		
aggressive			.712	
courageous			.632	
adventurous			.628	
assertive			.560	
anxious				-.738
composed				.641
brave				.553

Principal component analysis with VARIMAX rotation. Factor loadings < .51 are not displayed. Rotation converged in 5 iterations. Excluded items: cultivated, easygoing, tolerant, loyal, trusting, patient, chaotic, imaginative, sportive, lame, shy.

Table 2. Effects of the stimulus game on the self-assessment of certain attributes

Stimulus game	Factor 1: Tenacity and discipline Mean (SD)	Factor 2: Gentleness Mean (SD)	Factor 3: Aggressiveness Mean (SD)	Factor 4: Courage Mean (SD)
Call of Duty	0.11 (0.94)	-0.34* (1.03)	0.11 (1.22)	0.02 (0.88)
Tetris	-0.11 (1.06)	0.34* (0.86)	-0.11 (0.73)	-0.02 (1.12)

Multivariate effect: $F(1,52) = 2.11$; $p < .10$; $\eta^2 = .14$.
*Univariate effect for "gentleness": $F(1,55) = 6.91$; $p < .05$; $\eta^2 = .11$.

An explanation for the observed moderate effect might be that not only the experimental stimulus but also prior experience with similar world war games affects participants' self-perception. This could result in within group variance that suppresses the experimental effect on the three soldier-attribute dimensions. In order to check this, another MANCOVA including prior use of world war games (yes/no) as a second factor besides the experimental manipulation was conducted. Age was controlled by including it as a covariate. Results neither yielded a main effect of prior use of war games on the four personality dimensions, nor an interaction effect between "game played" and prior experience with war games.

5   Discussion

The experiment was designed to search for traces of video game identification manifest in players' cognitive accessibility of role-related concepts and in post-game self-descriptions. Findings from the Lexical Decision Task suggest that playing a soldier role indeed increases cognitive accessibility of soldier-related concepts. In the context of the model of video game identification (see above), the cognitive salience of words connected to the protagonist or role that a player is identifying with is an empirical confirmation of automatic processing of character-related information as part of the identification process during game play. The LDT cannot reveal automatic shifts in self-perceptions (as expected by the model), but already demonstrates that video games affect players' cognitive processing in a way that prepares actual identification by increasing salience of character-relevant concepts. Players 'think in the categories of' or 'from the perspective of' the game character or role they are adopting during game play, and we suggest interpreting concept salience as measured by the LDT as a cognitive prerequisite of this pre-stage of video game identification.

The self-description task used to test H2 revealed only limited experimental support for our assumptions. Identifying with a video game character seems to affect players' self-rating in a post-game questionnaire only marginally. However, we suggest an optimistic interpretation of this result, because in the situation of inquiry, participants were likely to take some time to reflect about themselves, which renders (implicit) effects of the prior game experience less relevant. Therefore, no strong effect of the prior video game identification should be expected. In the foundational study by Goldstein and Cialdini (study 1, see above) [6], a very similar measure also produced rather small group differences (with $\eta^2 = .03$). From this perspective, we consider the occurrence of even small experimental differences as indication that the contention of identification as change of self-perception holds empirical relevance.

While there is a need to continue empirical testing of the theoretical account of video game identification as transformed self-perception, the present results suggest that basic cognitive processes, priming and transformation of self-perceptions, are involved in players' responses to character-based video games. Of course, the generalizability of our results is limited due to the specific group of respondents (male university students) and the chosen stimulus genre (a first-person shooter). Nevertheless, related work applying the Implicit Association Test recently found automatic associations between character attributes and players' self-concept for a racing game as well [13]. The mentioned study compared players of *Need for Speed: Carbon* with *Call of Duty 2*™ players concerning the associations between racing- vs. military-related concepts and players' self: While associations between self-concept and military words were stronger compared to those between self-concept and racing-related words in players of the military game, the opposite pattern emerged for players of the car-racing game. Thus, there is empirical evidence suggesting the applicability of the theoretical approach to a greater variety of genres than the one that was chosen in this study.

In line with similar lines of research [8, 14], the self-relevance of digital characters emerges as an important aspect of the video game experience. Further research is needed to explore the implications for game enjoyment [1] as well as the long-term implications of game players' transformed self-perceptions. It is, e.g., highly plausible that identification with self-selected favorable roles in digital games facilitates game enjoyment via mitigating self-discrepancy at least during gaming. A relevant follow-up question would of course be if resp. how long this reduced self-discrepancy persists. Does it – in the long run – foster self-esteem of, e.g., adolescent males striving for the feeling of strength and masculinity? Or does it – contrary to that – even lead to a reduced self-esteem after playing, because players then 'return' to their own life and self?

Another effect could be the long-term incorporation of role-attributes into one's self-construal, e.g. of more aggressive concepts [15] or the adoption of high moral standards of a favorite policeman game character. For the moment, video games emerge as machines of effective temporary self-alteration, with potentially interesting implications for short-term fun and long-term (self-)development.

References

1. Klimmt, C., Hefner, D., Vorderer, P.: The video game experience as 'true' identification: A theory of enjoyable alterations of players' self-perception. Communication Theory 19, 351–373 (2009)
2. Lewis, M.L., Weber, R., Bowman, N.D.: "They be pixels, but they're MY Pixels": Developing a metric of character attachment in role-playing video games. Cyber Psychology and Behavior 11, 515–518 (2008)
3. Peng, W.: The mediational role of identification in the relationship between experience mode and self-efficacy: Enactive role-playing versus passive observation. Cyberpsychology and Behavior 11, 649–652 (2008)
4. Oatley, K.: A taxonomy of the emotions of literary response and a theory of identification in fictional narrative. Poetics 23, 53–74 (1994)
5. Cohen, J.: Defining identification: A theoretical look at the identification of audiences with media characters. Mass Communication and Society 4, 245–264 (2001)
6. Goldstein, N.J., Cialdini, R.B.: The spyglass self: A model of vicarious self-perception. Journal of Personality and Social Psychology 92, 402–417 (2007)
7. Higgins, E.T.: Self-discrepancy: A theory relating self and affect. Psychological Review 94, 319–340 (1987)
8. Bessiere, K., Seay, A.F., Kiesler, S.: The ideal self: Identity exploration in World of Warcraft. Cyberpsychology and Behavior 10, 530–535 (2007)
9. Wirth, W.: Involvement. In: Bryant, J., Vorderer, P. (eds.) Psychology of Entertainment, pp. 199–213. Lawrence Erlbaum Associates, Mahwah (2006)
10. Macrae, C.N., Bodenhausen, G.V., Milne, A.: The dissection of selection in social perception: Inhibitory processes in social stereotyping. Journal of Personality and Social Psychology 69, 397–407 (1995)

11. Meyer, D.E., Schvaneveldt, R.W.: Facilitation in recognizing pairs of words: Evidence of a dependence between retrieval operations. Journal of Experimental Psychology 90, 227–234 (1971)
12. Perea, M., Carreiras, M.: Sequential effects in the lexical decision task: The role of the item-frequency of the previous trial. Quarterly Journal of Experimental Psychology 56, 385–401 (2003)
13. Klimmt, C., Hefner, D., Vorderer, P., Roth, C., Blake, C.: Identification with video game characters as automatic shift of self-perceptions. Media Psychology 13, 323–338 (2010)
14. Yee, N., Bailenson, J.: The Proteus effect: The effect of transformed self-representation on behavior. Human Communication Research 33, 271–290 (2007)
15. Uhlmann, E., Swanson, J.: Exposure to violent video games increases automatic aggressiveness. Journal of Adolescence 27, 41–52 (2004)

An Annotation Scheme for Social Interaction in Digital Playgrounds*

Alejandro Moreno, Robby van Delden, Dennis Reidsma,
Ronald Poppe, and Dirk Heylen

Human Media Interaction, University of Twente,
P.O. Box 217, 7500 AE Enschede, The Netherlands
{a.m.moreno,r.delden,d.reidsma,r.w.poppe,d.k.j.heylen}@utwente.nl

Abstract. This paper introduces a new annotation scheme, designed specifically to study children's social interactions during play in digital playgrounds. The scheme is motivated by analyzing relevant literature, combined with observations from recordings of play sessions. The scheme allows us to analyze how key social interactions are related to different stages of play and the physical activity levels associated to them. We can use this information for two goals. First, we can identify relations between social interactions and the impact that changing game dynamics have on their occurrence. Second, it facilitates the analysis of automatic recognition of these social behaviors. Results obtained are useful for both goals. They show that it is possible to identify social interactions and their relation to game dynamics. Finally they also allow for further analysis into the possibility of their automatic recognition.

Keywords: Observation scheme, children's play, social interaction, digital playground.

1 Introduction

"... civilization is, in its earliest phases, played. It does not come from play... it arises in and as play, and never leaves it." Huizinga [9] stated that play has a major role in shaping human behavior. Even though people of every age play, children's play in particular has attracted a lot of interest in research fields such as health and well-being, psychology, medicine, among others. Some studies have identified a relation between obesity and children's current play habits [21]. Another study showed that children who fail to engage in social interaction during play, or show irregularities while doing so, can be linked to several specific mental or social impairments such as autism or mental retardation [7].

Children's play often takes place at playgrounds. Playgrounds can take many forms ranging from the traditional school or park playground to novel interactive digital playgrounds. Digital playgrounds differ from traditional ones in that they are augmented with different kinds of technologies that can enhance engagement,

---

* This publication was supported by the Dutch national program COMMIT.

M. Herrlich, R. Malaka, and M. Masuch (Eds.): ICEC 2012, LNCS 7522, pp. 85–99, 2012.

entertainment, social interaction, physical exertion and immersion [3,15]. For instance, Wyeth et al. [23] designed an interactive floor to promote social and physical interaction among mentally challenged people. Soler and Parés designed an interactive slide to counter the lack of physical activity and socialization of children [18]. Seitinger et al. developed the Interactive Pathway to research how children's play patterns could be affected by modifying the playground itself [16].

We aim to develop a new type of interactive playground that is able to automatically sense social behavior during children's play and respond to it. To accomplish this we need data to train algorithms for the recognition of social behavior. This means that reliable ground truth needs to be obtained through annotation schemes. These schemes serve three main purposes. First, they would allow digital playgrounds to be capable of online, automated sensing of interesting behavior, trained from prior offline annotation. Second, they facilitate the evaluation of reaching higher end goals such as learning social skills, facilitating play for specific target groups [23] or increasing physical interaction [12]. Third, they would help in understanding the impact of the responses of the playground on social behavior. However, due to the lack of annotation schemes, progress in the field is hampered [1]. Moreover, existing observation schemes are either very general (applicable to different settings but lacking depth) or are tailored and designed with specific settings in mind (only applicable in the intended setting).

We propose an observation scheme designed specifically to evaluate children's social interactions during play in digital playgrounds. It was designed by analyzing theories and schemes from literature and recorded play sessions. For the latter, we used the Interactive Playground, a digital playground developed to encourage physical activity, competition and cooperation [20]. Our scheme provides an in-depth observation methodology focusing on the social domain that allows the annotation of key social interactions along with useful information such as physical activity. From a bottom-up processing standpoint, it would allow for online, automatic social signal processing by identifying low level features related to specific social behaviors (modeled from offline annotations). From a top-down processing standpoint, it would facilitate evaluating the impact of modifying game dynamics such as success in promoting/reducing specific behavior, enhancing/reducing levels of engagement, immersion and fun. It must be noted that we present a scheme to describe social behavior, not a user experience evaluation scheme, which will help design socially aware digital playgrounds.

2   Existing Observation Schemes

Below we present a list of some of the widely used or recently created observation schemes focused on children's play in playgrounds. For more schemes to measure (anti-)social behavior from a clinical standpoint, please refer to [4,10].

2.1   Play Observation Scale

The Play Observation Scale (POS) was proposed by Rubin in 1989 and revised in 2001 [14]. Rubin tried to combine the two mainstream theories used in studying

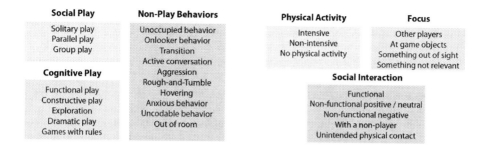

Fig. 1. Play Observation Scale composition

Fig. 2. Outdoor Play Observation Scheme composition

children's play: the social one proposed by Parten and the cognitive one promoted by Piaget. The purpose of this scale is to assess children's free play preferences. The scale is separated into three main play categories, each of which contains different aspects of play (Figure 1). The social play category deals with grouping and children's interactions, the cognitive play category is related to the type and role of play, and finally the non-play behaviors category addresses a broad range of items including social interactions as well as items outside of the actual play. The cognitive play category is nested into the social play category e.g. the child can show solitary-functional play, group-constructive play, etc.

The annotation is done by observing a child for 10 seconds, and then selecting the predominant behavior within this time lapse from a list of predefined actions. No child should be observed for more than five successive minutes to avoid subjective annotations. In total at least 15 minutes should be analyzed, thus several sessions are needed to be able to evaluate a single child.

According to Rubin, the scale is useful in identifying age and sex differences in play, effect of ecological setting in play and identifying children 'at risk' of developing psychological problems. This scheme was conceived to be very general, which has the advantage of making it applicable under different contexts to study children's play. However, when in need of more detailed behavior analysis, the categories are too coarse. For instance the distinction between competitive and collaborative play is not clearly present in the scheme. Also, there is no measurement for physical activity. Non-play behaviors do include some relevant social behaviors, such as aggression, rough-and-tumble and onlooker/unoccupied behavior.

2.2   Outdoor Play Observation Scheme

The Outdoor Play Observation Scheme (OPOS) was proposed by Bakker et al. in 2008 [1] and can be seen in Figure 2. They stated it was imperative for the HCI community to develop a structured methodology for observation of play. They were specifically interested in an observation scheme applicable in the evaluation of Head-Up games (HUGs) which are instrumented games for children that can be played without the need to look down [19].

In OPOS, two different types of approach are considered: event coding (frequency-based approach) and state coding (duration-based approach). Event coding is related to event-sampling; i.e., registering specific point-events such as yelling. On the other hand, state coding refers to actions that are continuous in nature, or at least have a measurable duration such as running. They also decided it was beneficial to analyze every child individually to avoid missing important information not measurable when taking the whole group as the basic unit.

OPOS is composed of four different behavioral categories. One of the categories was added just for practical purposes such as annotating children being out of sight. This category, named "general", is therefore not present in Figure 2. The physical activity category refers to the level of physical exertion exhibited by the players, the focus category indicates the player's gaze object of interest, and lastly the social interaction category deals with communication (verbal and non-verbal) in the broadest sense of the word.

OPOS was tested by evaluating a game called Lighthouse. The authors obtained a multi-rater κ measure of .7 for physical activity, .45 for focus and .24 for social interaction when comparing individual classified items among three coders. When comparing the total amount of occurrences of any of the items, all κ's increased (.9, .74, .73 respectively). Even though the scheme proves useful in finding differences in play, we find that the social interaction category is too coarse (functional vs non-functional only) for our purpose. For instance, there is no way to indicate social interactions such as competition/collaboration, rough-and-tumble or leadership. The physical activity category, however, is useful.

2.3   Manchester Inventory Playground Observation

Manchester Inventory Playground Observation (MIPO) was proposed by Gibson et al. in 2011 with the goal of evaluating children's play for clinical analysis [6]. They tried to determine social skills problems in children during play since previous studies showed that developmental disorders were associated to social functioning difficulties [7]. Playgrounds, which are fairly challenging social environments that require complex social interactions, lend themselves for useful studies of real time social information processing.

MIPO was designed to be a real-time social interaction observation scheme usable both for clinical analysis and research in general. It was structured so that it could identify several different patterns of social impairments across several disorders. It is composed of four main categories of peer socialization; each one containing different observations resulting in 28 different items as seen in Figure 3. The pro-social skills category mainly deals with grouping behavior and inclusion. The conflict management deals with types of aggression. Confiding and care concerns helping behavior. Atypicality deals with indicators of unusual, unwanted social behavior such as shouting out for no reason.

Each of the items was rated on a 4-category, rank-ordered rating scale that went from socially competent in this domain to marked difficulties. The annotators first observed the behavior of a randomly chosen child from a control group with no psychopathologies.

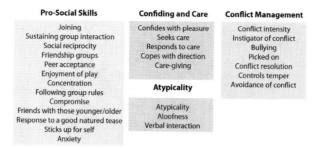

Fig. 3. Manchester Inventory Playground Observation composition

We found that MIPO was one of the most complete observation schemes in terms of social interactions. However, it neglects other areas relevant to children's play such as the phases of play and the level of physical activity. Evidently, since the scheme was designed specifically for clinical identification of social skill impairment, there was no need to observe other type of actions or behaviors.

2.4   Overall Conclusions

We found that current schemes provide several useful categories and items such as physical activity and some non-play behaviors (rough-and-tumble, aggression, etc). However, we found that the social categories did not suffice for our purpose. We are interested in studying a wide array of social behaviors (similar to MIPO), but also how they are related to play itself. We noticed that current schemes are built around play implicitly; they observe play through related categories but never address it as is. Morrison et al. proposed a set of terms to categorize phases that may emerge during play in the context of interactive art installations [13]. They proposed terms such as speculative play, interactive play or comprehension stages that we found applicable to describe play in interactive playgrounds as well. We decided that studying real play sessions in a digital playground was necessary to define other important items that could be added to the scheme.

3   The Interactive Playground

The Interactive Playground was implemented by Tetteroo in 2010. It was designed to stimulate physical activity, collaborative and competitive behavior during children's play. It is composed of a top-down projector and a near-infrared camera located on the ceiling, several hats with infra-red reflectors on it, balls and wristbands worn by the children, both with wireless motion sensors (Sun SPOTS). The projection on the floor of the room has several shapes like triangles, circles and squares that can be interacted with. Music is played and several sound effects are also emitted when certain events happen. The most important system interactions are listed below:

- If a player with a ball enters the playground he is surrounded with a colored shape; if entering without a ball, a short trail of shapes will follow him.
- If a player chases a free shape long enough the shape is added to his trail.
- If a player shakes the ball it will produce 'venom', killing nearby player's shapes. For every shape killed, his colored shape will grow.
- If a player with a ball is being chased by another player with a ball, he will lose the last shape of his trail to the chasing player.

3.1 Experimental Setup

Children were instructed to play in groups of two to four befriended children. A play session was composed of two sub-sessions of about ten minutes and a short break between the two sub-sessions. During the break, the functioning of some of the system interactions was explained to the children. In total, 39 children (aged between six and twelve) and around four hours of play were recorded. The system has been evaluated in a darkened controlled environment. At the end of every play session, a group discussion was carried out to get a better insight in the children's level of understanding of the provided interactions and their experiences. A complete description can be found in [20].

3.2 General Behavioral Observations

Tetteroo noticed that although some interactions were targeting collaboration, most interactions witnessed were based on individual play with the system or were competitive by nature. Nonetheless, even when the children were engaged in individual play, some social interaction between players still occurred. For instance, explaining out loud how certain interactions worked, which sometimes led to responses from the other players.

Tetteroo concluded that most interactions with the system could be triggered easily and were attainable in several seconds mainly because of the limited size of the playground. This might have led to the relatively low occurrence rates of cooperation and intensive physical activity. Although children were observed sitting or standing still, the predominant behavior was non-intensive physical activity. Because of the diverse interactions, children took some time to realize / understand how the playground responded to their actions and explored with different possibilities. This, in turn, gradually led to further discussion amongst them and the discovery of new interaction forms.

An interesting observation is the remarkable number of times that rough-and-tumble play occurred. Children were seen pushing one another, chasing / kicking each other and frantically throwing balls at each other. Very often the children were trying to step on the shapes on the floor and, sometimes, on other children's feet. They were also observed dragging each other around when someone fell down or was tripped by a sliding tackle. Sometimes, but not often, violent behavior was exhibited; i.e., having the intention to physically harm another. Aside from the physical contact, some children executed performances

Phase of Play	Social Behavior
Not playing [not]	Leadership [lea]
Exploration [exp]	Rough-and-Tumble [rat]
Playing (with the system) [pws]	Violence [vio]
Playing (not with the system) [pns]	Helping [hel]
	Performance [per]
Physical Activity	Mimicking [mim]
None [non]	Cooperation [coo]
Normal [-]	Competition [com]
Intense [int]	Other social behavior [osb]

Fig. 4. Final annotation scheme composition with abbreviations between brackets.

like swimming on the floor, spins, tricks, and dances. They were sometimes followed by others that showed the same kind of behavior on their own initiative or after being told or hinted to do so by another player.

4 Proposed Observation Scheme

The information gathered from observing play in the targeted context helped define and corroborate items that should be available in the scheme. We designed an observation scheme for interactive playgrounds with a focus on social interactions between children. Our goal is to analyze children's play from a social interaction standpoint; identifying the different interactions present and studying how playground characteristics influence their occurrence. The scheme borrows concepts from the previously discussed schemes, social and psychological theoretical background, but also proposes new categories and observable behaviors especially in the social domain. The scheme was refined iteratively in two rounds (a pilot and final evaluation). The proposed scheme can be seen in Figure 4.

The scheme is composed of three main categories covering the social interactions we want to focus on, the higher end goal of increasing physical activity and the relation to the phase of play a child is in. The social interactions included in the scheme were chosen because they occur often, their relation to play is important, can possibly be influenced by changing game dynamics and hopefully can be automatically detected.

Our observations were carried out on a per child basis to prevent generalizing and avoid the risk of missing important individual behavior such as normally inactive participants suddenly engaging in play, increasing physical activity or social interaction [1,23]. Also, one of the main annotators did not use the sound of the footage, neither in the pilot nor the final annotation, to analyze the suitability of using computer vision algorithms for automatic recognition in the future.

4.1 Units of Annotation

When annotating, the first decision to make is whether predefined time slots or manually annotating the exact duration of an action is more beneficial. Using time slots makes the annotation easier and faster, increasing the efficiency of the annotation. It also allows the annotation of several children concurrently. However, when only one label can be assigned to a time slot and two or more actions take place simultaneously, the dominant one should be chosen, which can lead to discrepancies. One could solve this by allowing multiple labels in one time slot when the nature of the category allows this. On the other hand, annotating the exact duration of an action gives more accurate labeling (useful for machine learning) but is much more time consuming since each child needs to be annotated individually and the entire video needs to be watched for each of the children. If time slots are chosen, another issue would be to define the duration of the time slots.

We noticed that for phase of play, a longer duration is useful since phases will not change that rapidly (we chose eight second sequences). In the case of social behavior, smaller sequences are more appropriate since most are usually completed rather quickly (we chose two second sequences). Lastly, physical activity will mostly show normal intensity, with bursts of intense/no activity, and thus the duration of the bursts was manually annotated. This led to the problem of thresholding which will be explained in the next section.

4.2   Detailed Description

Phase of play refers to the different stages that a child can go through when playing and are based on [13]. This dimension gives an indication of how simple the game is and whether children will play it. The observable behaviors are annotated exclusively, which means only one of them can be labeled in each time slot. One might find relationships between the phase of play and certain social behaviors. These findings could help in preventing or triggering certain social behaviors and in improving social signal processing.

Social behavior is the category that identifies different social interactions that occur when children play. Arguably, this might be one of the most important aspects of play. According to Bandura's *Social Learning Theory*: "Learning would be exceedingly laborious, not to mention hazardous, if people had to rely solely on the effects of their own actions... most human behavior is learned observationally through modeling: from observing others..." [2, p22] . In the same line, Vygotsky's *Social Development Theory* encompasses that social interaction plays a fundamental role in the process of cognitive development [22]. Lastly, Erikson's *Psychosocial Development Theory* defines a specific stage (*macrosphere play*) where children master social interactions and realize they can be successful in the larger social world [5].

The social behavior dimension contains two items based on POS: *Violence* (based on their item of aggression) and *Rough-and-Tumble*. Making the distinction is important because, according to Hughes [8], aggressive play should not be discouraged as it allows children to release their anxiety. It should, however, be controlled. He also mentions that play should be nonliteral, which is related to the *performance* item (such as dancing or doing flips) which was observed quite often in the recordings and is also mentioned in [12]. *Helping* can be linked to the more detailed caring category of MIPO. *Mimicry*, besides being a specific interest of our research, is mentioned in [13]. Erikson mentioned that during the third stage of psychosocial development (Initiative vs. Guilt) children need to lead or direct play and social interactions in their attempt to assert their power over the world [5]. *Leadership, cooperation* and *competition* were witnessed in the recordings and therefore found relevant to code in relation to play. The last item, *Other social behavior* (OSB) refers to any interaction not covered by the other items in the social behavior dimension, that would imply that 2 or more children are interacting and belong to a group for the duration of this interaction.

The social behavior dimension may inform whether the playground, or parts of the playground, increase these social interactions or if unwanted social behavior like violence could be diminished. At the same time, it paves the way for a more socially aware digital interactive playground. These behaviors are non-exclusive and thus multiple labels can be assigned simultaneously.

Physical activity categorizes the amount of physical effort that the children are doing at a given time. In [8], Hughes mentions that play should keep children actively engaged, involved psychologically and physically. This conveys why this category is one of the common goals in interactive playgrounds. One might benefit from automatic measurement of this dimension by using, for instance, the number of steps [11], motion energy images or skeleton tracking. This is an exclusive category.

The complete table with an explanation of the specific observable behaviors can be found in the supplemental material provided[1]. Potential uses of this scheme include possible identification of ambiguous social signals, physical cues related to certain social interactions, identifying how playground characteristics affect social interactions and its effect on the phases of play, among others.

5   Analysis and Evaluation

5.1   Training and Annotation Setup

We annotated a subset of the videos using our proposed scheme. The annotation was performed using ELAN [17] from the Max Planck Institute for Psycholinguistics in Nijmegen, the Netherlands. Four annotators were involved in the coding. Two of the annotators, closely involved in the creation of the scheme, participated in both sessions. Two external annotators, one participating in the pilot and the other one in the final evaluation, had no participation in the creation of the scheme. The two main annotators had a training session of coding three minutes of footage. The two external annotators were given an explanation of the scheme and its use followed by a training session and a discussion of the labeled fragments. For the pilot scheme training, the explanation lasted 30 minutes and the training video lasted 30 seconds. For the final scheme training, the times were twice as much to provide a better explanation. The training sessions

---

[1] hmi.ewi.utwente.nl/playground-annotation-scheme-manual.pdf

covered most items; examples of the unseen items from the scheme were shown by fast forwarding through the training video.

For the pilot annotation, all annotators went through 10 minutes of video, separated into three videos of three minutes and 20 seconds each. The subsets of the three videos covered the beginning, middle and end of different sessions, respectively. For the final evaluation, only three minutes and 20 seconds were annotated. As explained before, one of the main annotators did not use the sound of any of the footage.

5.2   Shortcomings of the Pilot Scheme

Comparing annotators in the pilot study resulted in rather low Cohen's κ-values for all the dimensions. For a dimension such as social behavior, which can be quite ambiguous or subjective, this could be expected. However, the physical activity [11] and grouping dimension are considered objective dimensions and should have obtained a high agreement. Phase of play, on the other hand, should have obtained at least a modest agreement.

We identified some problems both in the scheme design and evaluation procedure. In regards to the design, we noticed that some items were not defined explicitly which led to ambiguities when annotating. For example, it was not stated if *rough-and-tumble* was to be used for every physical contact, intentional or not, or if it should be labeled for both children or only the one doing the contact. This problem was solved with a more comprehensive description of each item in the scheme manual and a more thorough training session. Besides this, we had also included a grouping dimension which created a lot of confusion due to distance restrictions between children and amount of interaction required to be labeled a group. Since physical grouping can be obtained accurately using computer vision, manual annotation seemed redundant. We decided to move towards a higher level meaning of grouping where intention, and not location, was the focus. We added the *other social behavior* item to the social behavior dimension and removed the grouping dimension.

In regards to the evaluation procedure, the physical activity dimension was first coded using defined time slots of eight seconds. However, agreeing on which was the dominant behavior for some time slots was problematic. To try to overcome this problem, we manually labeled bursts of *intensive* or *none* physical activity in the final version.

5.3   Results and Analysis of Final Scheme

Phase of Play Dimension had a fair agreement between the two main annotators (κ of .41). However, it had a low reliability when comparing the external annotator (κ of .08 and .09). When grouping together *playing with the system* and *exploration*, the resulting κ with the external annotator went up to .53 and .51 respectively (see Table 1). Tetteroo's Digital Playground is designed to allow

Table 1. Confusion matrix for the category of phase of play of the two main annotators, κ is .41

	not	exp	pws	pns	-
not	**0**	0	0	0	0
exp	0	**35**	15	1	0
pws	0	8	**28**	0	0
pns	0	0	0	**0**	0
-	0	7	3	0	**3**

Table 2. Confusion matrix for the physical activity category of the two main annotators, κ is .32

	non	int	-
non	**23**	0	2
int	0	**30**	4
-	26	21	

Table 3. Confusion matrix for the physical activity category of the external annotator and main annotator A, κ is .0.5

	non	int	-
non	**24**	0	2
int	0	**30**	7
-	11	6	

Table 4. Confusion matrix for the physical activity category of the external annotator and main annotator B, κ is 0.29

	non	int	-
non	**31**	0	5
int	0	**29**	6
-	24	23	

children to explore and interact freely with the system, find new interactions, explore and interact with the system again. Our results show that differentiating *playing with the system* from *exploration* will be challenging in playgrounds that promote free play and emerging interactions due to the numerous phase transitions in the sessions. In these settings, combining both items would yield a higher inter-observer reliability while still providing useful information about the phase of play. For games with more strict or structured phase transitions it will be easier to annotate this dimension.

It is noteworthy that audio played some role in the ability to correctly annotate this dimension. For instance, sometimes children were asking "how can you get the Pacman?", clearly indicating it was an exploratory endeavor that could not be coded correctly without the use of audio. Nonetheless, the degree to which audio affected the results was not high.

Physical Activity Dimension had a low agreement between the main annotators (κ of .32), especially considering physical activity ought to be an objective measurement, shown to have high agreement when observers are intensively trained using strict protocols [11]. When comparing the external annotator to the main ones, we obtain κ values of .5 and .32. Two important observations were seen i)*intensive* and *none* items were never confused (see Tables 2 and 4) and ii) whenever either annotator A or the external annotator labeled a burst of activity, annotator B almost always agreed (92% for none and 88% for intensive with annotator A, 86% and 83% for the external annotator). Thus, we can conclude that the problem is the threshold at which the annotators separate intensive activity from normal, and normal from none. For very intensive or obvious lack of physical activity, the agreement is extremely high, but in cases where the activity is somewhere in between, agreement is lacking.

Agreeing on a threshold for physical activities proves quite challenging: first, because expressing this with words is not trivial, second, because listing every action the children could execute is near to impossible. Using for instance up to two steps as threshold for no physical activity would not suffice as children might be intensively shaking using their entire upper body while standing still. The reliability of this dimension will depend on the type of playground, or on being able to define strictly the threshold between the level of activities before the annotation. For playgrounds with a lot of freedom of movement it will be hard to annotate this dimension.

Social Behavior Dimension had a high agreement between the main annotators with a κ of .67 (see Table 5). On the other hand, agreement between the external annotator and main annotators A and B was κ 0.28 and 0.37 (see Table 6) respectively. Agreeing on when a behavior happened was problematic, thus we also analyzed, when both annotators agreed some behavior was underway, if they agreed on which one it was. The results showed that the agreement was quite high considering this is a subjective dimension (External annotator - main annotator A 0.66, External annotator - main annotator B 0.67, two main annotators 0.92).

Rough-and-tumble was the most frequently annotated behavior and it was often accompanied by signs of *competition* (although the external annotator failed to see several occurrences of quick physical contact) which shows that identifying relations between social interactions is possible. *Performance* was also seen often during various parts of the game where the kids wanted to show off or just have more fun. There were some discrepancies in *leading* but when the videos were analyzed, all but one could be accounted to not using audio by one of the annotators. It is interesting that actually all but one coded instance of leadership were accompanied with speech. The influence of speech was also seen in *help*, where helping verbally could not be annotated without audio.

It can be seen in Tables 5 and 6 that interestingly, *competition* and *cooperation* were not confused even without the use of sound. In many cases speech contained information about the correct social signal, however it was often accompanied with clear physical cues. We noticed that various types of social interactions can be identified accurately without using audio but could benefit from it nonetheless. This seems promising for the automatic recognition of social signals in digital playgrounds using computer vision. For instance, sudden invasion of personal space by other children could signal aggressive behavior or competition, whereas synchrony in movement and actions could signal cooperation.

Table 5. Confusion matrix for the social category of the two main annotators, κ is .67 (when taking out the empty slots, κ is 0.92)

	-	lea	rat	vio	hel	per	mim	coo	com	osb
-	204	0	3	0	0	9	0	1	12	6
lea	8	2	1	0	0	0	0	1	0	0
rat	3	0	67	0	0	0	0	0	0	0
vio	0	0	1	1	0	0	0	0	0	0
hel	5	0	0	0	2	1	0	0	0	2
per	5	0	0	0	0	18	0	0	2	0
mim	1	0	0	0	0	0	5	0	0	0
coo	5	0	0	0	0	0	0	3	0	0
com	2	1	0	0	0	0	2	0	35	0
osb	27	0	0	0	0	0	0	1	1	22

Table 6. Confusion matrix for the social category of main annotator B and the external annotator, κ is 0.37 (when taking out the empty slots, κ is 0.67)

	-	lea	rat	vio	hel	per	mim	coo	com	osb
-	186	6	1	0	3	3	3	1	12	14
lea	5	5	0	0	1	0	0	1	0	0
rat	34	1	27	0	1	2	0	3	0	2
vio	0	0	2	0	0	0	0	0	0	0
hel	4	0	0	0	6	0	0	0	0	0
per	9	1	1	0	1	9	0	0	2	2
mim	6	0	0	0	0	0	0	0	0	0
coo	1	0	0	0	0	0	0	7	0	0
com	19	1	0	0	0	0	0	0	19	1
osb	27	2	0	0	3	0	2	3	6	8

6   Conclusions

We have proposed a new annotation scheme for observational studies in digital playgrounds. The scheme is composed of three dimensions and focuses on children's social interactions during play, and their relation to play itself. It was designed using relevant elements from current schemes, psychology and sociology theories and observations from recorded play sessions. On average, the agreement was fair which means the scheme still needs to be refined. Nonetheless, results show that the scheme is useful in identifying relations between different social interactions. This provides information directly related to the impact that changing certain game dynamics to promote a specific kind of interaction can have on the game. They also show that, for certain social interactions, automatic recognition could be possible with a reasonable accuracy even without the use of audio. The scheme was designed having our own goals in mind, however it remains generic enough to be used in other settings. We regard the current state of the scheme as a good starting point, either as a base scheme for more specific ones, or for further development in creating a general socially focused annotation scheme for the evaluation of digital playgrounds.

References

1. Bakker, S., Markopoulos, P., de Kort, Y.: OPOS: an observation scheme for evaluating head-up play. In: Proceedings of the Nordic Conference on Human-Computer Interaction, NordiCHI 2008, New York, NY, USA, pp. 33–42 (2008)
2. Bandura, A.: Social Learning Theory. Prentice Hall (1977)
3. Bichard, J.P., Waern, A.: Pervasive play, immersion and story: designing interference. In: Proceedings of the International Conference on Digital Interactive Media in Entertainment and Arts, DIMEA 2008, New York, NY, USA, pp. 10–17 (2008)
4. Cook, F., Oliver, C.: A review of defining and measuring sociability in children with intellectual disabilities. Research in Developmental Disabilities 32(1), 11–24 (2011)
5. Erikson, E.H.: Childhood and Society. W. W. Norton & Company (1993)
6. Gibson, J., Hussain, J., Holsgrove, S., Adams, C., Green, J.: Quantifying peer interactions for research and clinical use: the Manchester Inventory for Playground Observation. Research in Developmental Disabilities 32(6), 2458–2466 (2011)
7. Guralnick, M.J., Hammond, M.A., Connor, R.T., Neville, B.: Stability, Change, and Correlates of the Peer Relationships of Young Children With Mild Developmental Delays. Child Development 77(2), 312–324 (2006)
8. Hughes, F.: Children, Play, and Development. SAGE (2009)
9. Huizinga, J.: Homo Ludens: A Study of the Play Element in Culture. Roy Publishers (1950)
10. Leff, S.S., Costigan, T., Power, T.J.: Using participatory research to develop a playground-based prevention program. Journal of School Psychology 42(1), 3–21 (2004)
11. Loprinzi, P.D., Cardinal, B.J.: Measuring Children's Physical Activity and Sedentary Behaviors. Journal of Exercise Science & Fitness 9(1), 15–23 (2011)
12. Lund, H.H., Jessen, C., Klitbo, T.: Playware technology for physically activating play. Artificial Life and Robotics 9(4), 165–174 (2005)
13. Morrison, A., Viller, S., Mitchell, P.: Building sensitising terms to understand free-play in open-ended interactive art environments. In: Proceedings of the Conference on Human Factors in Computing Systems, CHI 2011, New York, NY, USA, pp. 2335–2344 (2011)
14. Rubin, K.H.: The Play Observation Scale (POS). Published by the Center for Children, Relationships, and Culture of the University of Maryland (2001), http://www.rubin-lab.umd.edu/CodingSchemes/
15. Seitinger, S.: An ecological approach to children's playground props. In: Proceedings of the Conference on Interaction Design and Children, IDC 2006, New York, NY, USA, pp. 117–120 (2006)
16. Seitinger, S., Sylvan, E., Zuckerman, O., Popovic, M., Zuckerman, O.: A new playground experience: going digital? In: CHI 2006 on Human Factors in Computing Systems, Montréal, Québec, Canada, pp. 303–308 (2006)
17. Sloetjes, H., Wittenburg, P.: Annotation by Category: ELAN and ISO DCR. In: LREC (2008), http://www.lat-mpi.eu/tools/elan/

18. Soler-Adillon, J., Parés, N.: Interactive slide: an interactive playground to promote physical activity and socialization of children. In: Proceedings of the International Conference on Human Factors in Computing Systems, CHI EA 2009, New York, NY, USA, pp. 2407–2416 (2009)
19. Soute, I., Markopoulos, P., Magielse, R.: Head Up Games: combining the best of both worlds by merging traditional and digital play. Personal Ubiquitous Comput. 14(5), 435–444 (2010)
20. Tetteroo, D., Reidsma, D., van Dijk Nijholt, A.: Design of an interactive playground based on traditional children's play. In: Proceedings International Conference on Intelligent Technologies for Interactive Entertainment (INTETAIN 2011), Genoa, Italy (2011)
21. Vandewater, E.A., Shim, M., Caplovitz, A.G.: Linking obesity and activity level with children's television and video game use. Journal of Adolescence 27(1), 71–85 (2004)
22. Vygotsky, L.S.: Mind in Society: The Development of Higher Psychological Processes. Harvard University Press (1978)
23. Wyeth, P., Summerville, J., Adkins, B.: Stomp: an interactive platform for people with intellectual disabilities. In: Proceedings of the International Conference on Advances in Computer Entertainment Technology, ACE 2011, New York, NY, USA (2011)

Philosophy Meets Entertainment: Designing an Interactive Virtual Philosopher

Xuan Wang[1,2], Eng Tat Khoo[3], Sanath Siriwardana[1],
Horathalge Iroshan[1], and Ryohei Nakatsu[1,2]

[1] Keio-NUS CUTE Center, Interactive and Digital Media Institute,
National University of Singapore
{wangxuan,hssiriwardana,idmhorat,elenr}@nus.edu.sg
[2] NUS Graduate School for Integrative Sciences and Engineering, Singapore
[3] Eon Reality, Singapore
engtat@eonreality.com.sg

Abstract. To many people, philosophy seems to be a difficult and daunting subject. Our research seeks to make the esoteric philosophical ideas and concepts more accessible to people in the modern world, and make philosophy learning an entertaining activity by allowing people to directly interact with virtual philosophers from the past. With Artificial Intelligence technology, we have created a virtual philosopher that can automatically respond to user's input in natural language text. It is hoped that the added interactivity can help to increase the appeal of philosophical subject to the users, and the users can have a better idea of the philosophy after an entertaining experience talking with the virtual philosopher. In this paper, we share our considerations for designing the system, the system architecture, and our preliminary user study on the interaction with the virtual philosopher.

Keywords: Virtual philosophers, interactive philosophy, artificial intelligence, conversational agent.

1 Introduction

To many people, philosophy seems to be a difficult and daunting subject. Though philosophical concepts are hard to grasp, learning about them do benefits us [4]. Traditionally, the main channel for the public to learn about philosophy is through reading books. Recently, the advent of digital technology is reshaping the way people learn about things [12]. Passive media such as books are gradually losing its appeal to the new interactive digital media - people now possess a higher level of digital literacy, and are more inclined to acquire knowledge through the modern networked and digital media.

Observing this trend, we started to look into this question: is there a way to make philosophy less intimidating and more interesting, so that even today's born-digitals would like to know more about it? Drawing inspirations from the field of Edutainment, which makes learning more fun by adding new media

M. Herrlich, R. Malaka, and M. Masuch (Eds.): ICEC 2012, LNCS 7522, pp. 100–113, 2012.

elements such as video games, our research tries to leverage people's digital literacy, and bring traditionally esoteric philosophical ideas and concepts into an entertaining context, in order to make them more appealing and more accessible to the general public.

New entertainment technology needs to offer an active experience in order for users to reach enjoyment [8]. Based on this theory, we have designed a system that makes philosophy learning interactive. Rather than trying to get a grip of the ideas through thousands of lines in the books or sit back and watch a video, people can directly speak 'face to face' to the philosophers through the activity of online chat. We hope to promote philosophy learning, or at least dispel the common stereotype about philosophy, by creating an interactive system with fun interface but also deep meaning behind. We are interested to see how people respond to such system, and whether such a system can actually be used in the real world as a new way for learning and interacting with philosophy.

In this paper, we present our system, iSage, a virtual conversational agent that models philosophical knowledge and impersonates sages in the past. We discuss the design considerations of creating a virtual philosopher, and present the architecture of our prototype system. We share the lessons learnt from making the system and the user testing, and discuss the future directions of this research.

2   Design Considerations

As reasoned above, one of the issues with philosophical books is its huge volume and esoteric appearance. In fact, there has been endeavours in making traditional texts more friendly to the modern readers by means of adding modern language interpretations and even caricatures. Efforts have also been made to bring the thoughts and even the life experiences of the sages into digital media in the production of films and cartoons series. Electronic resources are also available on the internet in the form of online databases and ebooks. However, in these situations, the interaction between the user and the medium is still one-way, and the user still largely remains as a passive receiver rather than an active explorer.

Speaking of sages, most people naturally feel a distance towards them, thinking they are lofty ideals that are beyond normal people's understanding. Modern philosophers see this problem and try to relate philosophy in people's everyday life and explain it in ways that are easy to understand. Askphilosophers.org is a web site that gathers talents and knowledge of trained philosophers to answer questions from the general public [1]. The site has attracted people at all stages of life and successfully proves that philosophy can be explained in intelligible ways and be used to help people. However, this site needs to be managed by people, and it takes time to get the answers as the answers are all given manually by the real philosophers.

---

[1] http://www.askphilosophers.org/

Different from the approach of askphilosophers.org, we want to develop an automatic system that is interactive and appealing to users. We have identified the following three characteristics that are necessary:

- *Interactivity.* Users should not be just passive receivers, but instead active enquirers. Active experience is one of the important conditions that lead to enjoyment [8]. More freedom should be given to user to freely explore things in which they are interested. It does not necessarily have to follow a linear or logical path (as in the case of book reading or film watching), but a path of interest.
- *Short and fast interaction.* The system should be easy to get access to and readily available. Users do not need to take the time and read a huge book, but can interact and get an idea in a very short time.
- *Easy-to-use interface.* No prior knowledge is required to interact with the system. In other words, we should take advantage of the digital literacy that people already own, and present it in a medium that is familiar to most of the people today.

The above considerations lead to the decision of making a virtual recreation of sages in history with a mobile interface. We want to let the sages speak for themselves, share their life stories, reveal their admirable charisma, and become advisors or even friends to people. People can easily use the system to talk freely to the sages, whether for a casual chat or to seek insights of the profound philosophy. In this way, it tailors to the specific needs of each individual and offers a personalized dialogue experience with a virtual sage of choice.

3   Related Work

Chat bots, also known as conversational agents, have appeared long ago. One of the first chat bots, Eliza, was invented as early as in the 1960s [15]. It is a simulation of a Rogerian psychotherapist that can talk to patients. Since then, numerous chat bots have been created [2]. However, the focus of such chat bots is to use various techniques to disguise as a human being [7]. Generic answers are given when the question is out of bounds of the knowledge base, which often does not offer real help to the user. On the other hand, virtual conversational agents have also been used for online help, as we can see on many companies' websites, and they have been used in museums as museum guides [6]. They are used for learning as well, for example, to learn a foreign language [2]. Researchers have also built a chat bot for people to access the Quran, the central religious text of Islam [11]. Most of these systems usually have no understanding of the input, but solely rely on pre-programmed questions and answers. As a result, the output is confined within the scope of trained patterns, which means limited ability to handle user request.

Compared to these chat bots, our virtual philosopher differs in two important ways:

---

[2] e.g. Cleverbot, http://www.cleverbot.com/ and Jabberwacky, http://www.jabberwacky.com/

1. *Understanding*: The normal chat bots usually rely on pattern matching to provide an answer. In cases when a template cannot be matched, tricks such as asking the question back are used to make it appear like understanding. However, for users who would like to seek advice from the virtual agent, this does not offer any help, and can sometimes be frustrating. Therefore, in our system, we attempt to handle unseen inputs by syntactic and semantic analysis, and relate the input to the knowledge base entries via semantic closeness.

2. *Authenticity*: Unlike many of the chat bots which are arbitrarily created characters that handle small talks and are just for fun, our system represents a real existed person. Moreover, it represents the renowned historical giants, to whom people naturally have much respect and expectations. This also presents great technical challenges to model the philosopher's thinking accurately.

4   Creating a Virtual Confucius

Among the many influential schools of thought, we decided to choose Confucianism as our first attempt in interactive philosophy. This is mainly because we are a lab based in Asia where Confucianism is very influential. Though this Asian philosophical system is more than 2500 years old, it is still being studied nowadays, and classic Confucian ideas such as filial piety, respect for elders and man's relation to his society are still very relevant to the modern society.

4.1   Building the Knowledge Base

The first step of creating a virtual Confucius is to gather large amounts of data and build a knowledge base. Because this is a highly specialized domain of knowledge, we have to work together with the domain experts. We collaborated with researchers specializing in Confucius philosophy in our university. They helped us to gather data from classical texts: the *Analects*, the *Mencius*, the *Book of Rites* and the *Classic on Filial Piety*. These four texts constituted a major part of educational curriculum for children in China [13].

The whole set of Confucius knowledge base is divided into three broad categories, according to the nature of the statements. We believe that due to the distinctive nature of the information in each of these categories, they should be treated separately both in terms of the knowledge representation as well as retrieval methods. The first category is domain specific factual knowledge, including information about Confucius as an individual, for example, his age, his date of birth, his hometown, etc., as well as introductory statements about the figures appearing in Confucius's responses (mostly Confucius's disciples). We gather this information from the earliest reliable historical text of Shiji by Sima Qian (ca. 110B.C.). As information in this category is straightforward factual knowledge, we choose to store them in Artificial Intelligence Markup Language (AIML) scripts [14], which is good for handling such query. For instance, if the user asks "who is Yan Hui", Confucius's reply will directly be taken from the scripts saying, "Yan Hui is my favourite disciple".

The second category is the major part of the knowledge base, which contains all Confucius's sayings and ideas, collected from the above mentioned classical texts. Moreover, paragraphs in these texts are separated into short but self-sustained statements. For instance, the opening passage of the *Analects* becomes three entries in our database: 1. Is it not pleasant to learn with a constant perseverance and application? 2. Is it not delightful to have friends coming from distant quarters? 3. Is he not a man of complete virtue, who feels no discomposure though men may take no note of him? In this way, a total of 2069 entries were collected and stored in an SQL database.

For each sentence, the domain experts tagged it with 1-3 topic(s). The reason for this manual work is due to the special nature of the domain knowledge, which often contains implicit meanings that are impossible to deduce from the literal understanding of the sentence using natural language processing technology. A total of 309 topics were identified. These topics are used later in our algorithm to compare the relatedness of the entry with the user inputs. These topics were further tagged with specific senses in the context of Confucius's teaching. This is necessary because many of the topics in this domain have particular meanings, and literal word level tagging cannot convey the precise meaning and would lead to confusion. For example, the topic 'way' in Confucian context means 'a course of conduct', rather than direction or path. Therefore, for the topic 'way', it is tagged as 'way#n#5', which is the fifth meaning of the word 'way' in the WordNet lexical database [1]. We chose to use WordNet because of its comprehensiveness and its ontology that makes possible the comparisons of semantic similarities between words. By tagging the sentences with the topics, it effectively transforms them into points in a high dimensional space, where each dimension represents one topic.

WordNet is a general ontology. Though it is good in handling everyday concepts, it is not sufficient to cover all the concepts in the Confucian knowledge base. Therefore, it is necessary to create a separate knowledge base with domain-specific terminologies. For instance, names of classical texts from which Confucius often quotes, and Confucian terminologies such as Junzi (the morally ideal man in Confucian philosophy) and Ren (benevolence, or the 'way of being' that of an exemplary person), etc, need to be captured and denoted specifically. As these words do not have semantic meanings, entries related to these terminologies are tagged with the literal words and stored in the SQL database. Some sentences from the second category are also tagged with keywords if they contain certain terminology. A total of 319 sentences were tagged with such keywords.

4.2   System Architecture

The core of the system is a virtual sage thinking engine, which analyses user inputs, calculates and extracts the most appropriate answer. A front-end mobile application is used to interact with the virtual philosopher. Figure 1 shows the architecture of the system.

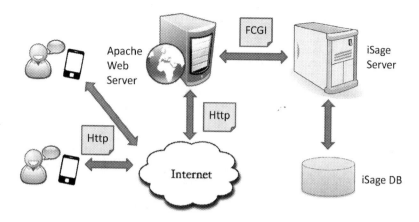

Fig. 1. Architecture of iSage system

The virtual sage thinking engine consists of three different modules: a pattern matching module, a keyword matching module, and a semantic closeness matching module. Figure 2 shows an overall composition of the virtual sage thinking engine. Each of the modules is designed to handle different part of the knowledge base, as described before.

The Pattern Matching Module. The pattern matching module contains pre-scripted templates and their matching rules. This is a technique commonly used in many chat bots, which has been proven to be very effective in providing good responses as long as the question falls within the pre-scripted set. It also helps to make the bot converse more like a person. We have used a modified A.L.I.C.E. AIML [14] knowledge base in our system. Unrelated templates are deleted, and many of the templates are modified to be more Confucius-like with the help of the domain experts, according to the information collected in the knowledge base building phase. The quality of an answer from this module is assessed by how much the pattern matches the input. If there isn't a readily available answer for the input, the answer selection process will go onto the next stage.

The Semantic Closeness Matching Module. We certainly cannot predict all the questions that will be possibly asked and prepare an answer for each. Especially for the case of building a virtual Confucius, doing so would require very good knowledge on the subject and would be extremely time-consuming. Therefore, sophisticated natural language processing and reasoning are necessary to automatically extract the answer for unseen input. In the semantic closeness matching module, a series of NLP techniques are employed to find important words in the sentences as well as their meanings, and then match them with a relevant answer based on their semantic closeness. There are three stages: important words identification, topics identification, and database entry selection. As

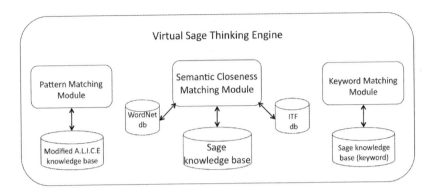

Fig. 2. Composition of the virtual sage thinking engine

mentioned before, a lexical database called WordNet [1] is used to find semantic
relations of English words.

In the important words identification stage, the user input is first fed into a
parser [5] that analyses the grammatical structure of the sentence. The last noun
of each noun phrase is selected as the important word [3]. Furthermore, we employ Inverse Term Frequency (ITF) to find additional important words, based on
the idea that the more frequent word such as 'the', 'and' do not contribute much
to the real meaning of the sentence, whereas the less frequent words, 'loyal',
'conflict', for example, are more important. An ITF database is built by calculating the frequency of appearance of each word in a large corpus. Combining the
results from the above two methods, a list of important words can be extracted
from the user input. Furthermore, the user input is passed through a Word Sense
Disambiguation (WSD) module [10] to get the meaning of these words in the
context. This information, together with the important words selected, is used
to compare the semantic closeness against a list of pre-defined topics in the sage
knowledge base. This is done using a WordNet-based similarity module Word-
Net::Similarity [9], which computes a semantic similarity score for any given pair
of words. Each important word selected is compared with the list of topics. The
final value for each topic is based on the summation of the similarity scores with
each important word. Scores that are below a certain value are discarded to reduce noise. After this step, the input sentence is digitized as a point in the high
dimensional space of topics. It can be represented as a vector $\boldsymbol{v}$:

$$\boldsymbol{v} = \sum_{i=1}^{m} \varphi(sim(w_i, p_1))\boldsymbol{t_1} + \cdots + \sum_{i=1}^{m} \varphi(sim(w_i, p_n))\boldsymbol{t_n} \tag{1}$$

where m is the number of important words extracted from the input sentence,
n is the total number of topics, $\boldsymbol{t_n}$ is the basis vector representing the nth topic,
$sim(w, p)$ is the similarity score between word w and topic p, and

$$\varphi(x) = \begin{cases} x & \text{if x is greater than threshold} \\ 0 & \text{otherwise} \end{cases}$$

Finally, the process enters the database entry selection stage. Here, the user input sentence is represented as a vector in a high dimensional space constructed by the list of topics. Similarly, each database entry is also determined as a vector in this high dimensional space, according to the taggings by the domain experts. The fitness of a sentence as an output to a certain input is assessed by the Euclidean distance between the two points. The database entry with the closest distance is selected as the output, if the distance is below a certain threshold value.

The Keyword Matching Module. In the Keyword Matching Module, a simple string comparison between the keywords in the database with the user input is carried out. Each matched word would increase the matching score for the sentence by 1. If the highest sentence score is more than a threshold, the corresponding entry is deemed as suitable for output. If, at this stage, still no suitable answer can be extracted, the system will ask the user to rephrase the question, or to change the topic.

User inputs go through a layered process and are analysed by the above three modules sequentially. The suitability of output is evaluated by computing a quality score. These three methods handle different types of inputs and thus complement each other. Figure 3 shows a simplified flow diagram of the system.

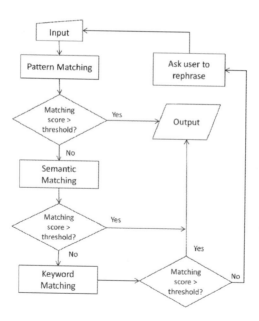

Fig. 3. A simplified flow diagram of the virtual sage thinking engine

4.3   Example Usage

Following are some example outputs given by this algorithm.

- *Question: What is love?*
- *Answer: Love commences with respect as its basis. To neglect respect is to leave affection unprovided for.*
- *Question: How should I treat my parents?*
- *Answer: A son of all comprehensive virtue serves his parents as he serves Heaven.*
- *Question: I am worried.*
- *Answer: If a man takes no thought about what is distant, he will find worries near at hand.*
- *Question: Tell me something about the Book of Poetry.*
- *Answer: It is said in the Book of Poetry: be always studious in order to be in harmony with the ordinances of Heaven, you will certainly get for yourself much happiness.*

4.4   The Application

We have created a Android application, iSage Confucius, which allows people to talk to the virtual Confucius on their smart phones by typing their questions. After receiving the query, the mobile application sends the request to the iSage server, where the virtual Confucius thinking engine is located. The server processes the incoming request, and returns the answer given by our algorithm. The answer is then displayed on the user's phone as Confucius's reply, as if the user is having a real conversation with the sage. Figure 4 shows two screenshots of the application.

To make it more fun for users, we also added a function for sharing the answer to social networks such as Twitter and Facebook. Users can also rate the answer if they think it is a very profound answer, a funny answer, or a bad answer. They can also go to another page to see the questions asked by other people and the answers given by Confucius, ranked according to the query time or the ratings, as is shown on the right in Figure 4. This is to add more diversity to the application other than a robot that simply answers. The rating function serves research purpose as well, because we can get a better idea of the quality of the system through human feedback.

5   User Evaluations

To see people's reactions to this system as a new way to interact with philosophy, and to gather feedbacks to improve the system, a pilot user testing was conducted.

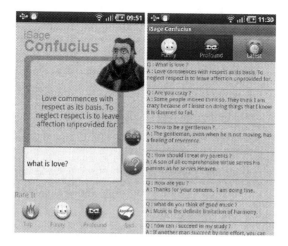

Fig. 4. Screenshots of the iSage Confucius application

5.1   Participant Demography

Twenty participants were recruited for the study (15 male and 5 female). All of them are under the age of 35, and nineteen of them have experiences or are very familiar with mobile applications. The participants come from a variety of ethnic groups, but are all Asian except one. 7 of them indicated that they knew nothing about Confucius's philosophy, 11 said they knew "a little", and 2 had a moderate amount of knowledge. About their interests in Confucianism, 2 indicated that "I have great passion for it", 12 "would like to learn about it if possible", 4 are "not interested, but do not mind to know more", and 1 participant indicated "not interested at all". When asked about the reasons that prevent them from knowing more about the Confucian culture, 11 of them said it is because of a lack of time. Besides reasons like "too difficult to understand", or "just don't like it", other reasons reported by the participants include "not enough interest to look for information on my own, and not enough reported in the media". This implies that an application that can offer fast and entertaining interaction might be useful and attractive to them.

5.2   Procedure

The participants were first informed that he/she was going to interact with a virtual Confucius, which is a computer program that tries to mimic the real Confucius. They could use this mobile application to converse with Confucius, and they could ask any questions they like. The participants were asked to interact with the system for about 10 minutes and fill in a questionnaire afterwards to report their experience with the application.

We did not impose any constraints on questions to be asked and restricted them to the topics that are more suitable to be answered by Confucius, partly because we are curious what users have to say to a virtual Confucius, but also because we would like to see the system's ability to handle arbitrary questions and user's reactions to the answer (be it good or bad) given.

5.3 Results

In the questionnaire, the participants were asked to rate their experiences and opinions based on a 5-point Likert scale. The responses to the questions are presented as bar charts in Figure 5. Many of the participants were excited to use the system, and all participants except one indicated that they enjoyed interacting with the application. 60% of the participants said they became more interested in Confucian culture and would like to know more. Some comments from the participants are "it is very user friendly and interesting", "the idea and the vision is interesting", "answered some of my questions pretty logically, and seem to comprehend the nature of my question".

17 out of 20 participants agreed that interacting with the application is more fun than reading a book. However, when asked whether they think it can achieve the same effect as reading a book, most of them hold a conservative view: only 7 agreed or strongly agreed. This is not surprising, as book reading has always been considered the traditional and proper way to acquire knowledge, especially for this kind of philosophical knowledge which requires one to take time to delve

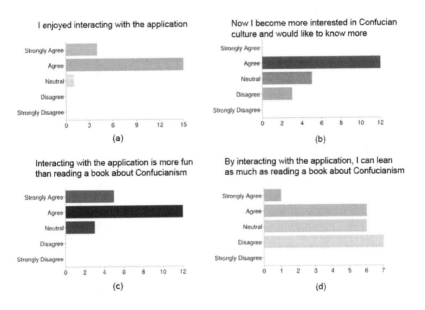

Fig. 5. Results of the questionnaire from the user study

into, to reflect and distil. However, for some people, they may never pick up a book and read the *Analects*, but if they are presented with an entertaining interactive system, they are much more likely to try it out and play with it. This is also one of the important motivations and goals of building this system - to make philosophy learning more enjoyable and to introduce Confucianism to more people.

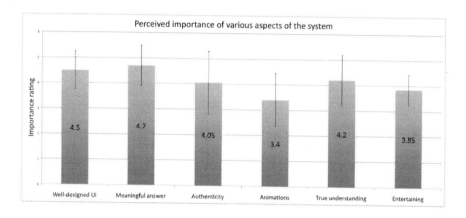

Fig. 6. Participants' perceived importance of various factors of the system

In addition, the participants were asked to give a rating of the importance of various factors of the system based on a 5-point Likert scale, with 1 being the least important and 5 being the most important. The candidate options are: well-designed UI, meaningfulness of the answer, authenticity (i.e. whether it truly represents the opinion of Confucius), animations of Confucius showing emotions, true understanding (note that this is different from meaningfulness, as the system can have no understanding of the user but still output a sensible answer, as in the case of many chatterbot systems), and entertainment value. Participants were explained in more detail if they were not sure what the option means. The results of the average ratings are shown in Figure 6. Quality of the answer, or the meaningfulness of the answer is deemed as the most important aspect of the system, and plays an important role in providing a satisfying experience. Participants care relatively less about whether the system truly understands them or not, but they expect the answers to be *meaningful*. In terms of 'authenticity', participants hold a more varied view, with some thinking it is very important, but some considering it not so important. UI design is also considered an important factor, as people expect to have an easy-to-use system. Entertainment value is somewhat important, but much less so as compared to the answer's meaningfulness. Other interaction modalities, for example, the use of animations, are deemed as the least important among all the factors.

6   Conclusion and Future Work

In this paper, we have presented our efforts in making philosophy interactive by creating a virtual philosopher. A mobile application, iSage Confucius, is developed. We hope it can allow more people to be able to interact with the valuable pool of knowledge and draw upon the ancient wisdom in an easy and entertaining way. From our pilot user testing, we can see that this mode of interaction is liked by users, but there are many more that needs to be improved. Rather than constraining our research in a lab environment, we want to push our research results into the wild and benefit the general public. At the same time, we hope that real world usage of our application can provide us valuable insights and information to improve our system.

From the results of the pilot user study, we can see that people have high expectations of the answers given by a virtual sage. Our current algorithm sometimes gives unrelated answers, and lacks the ability to comprehend words without semantic meanings such as people's names. In future works we should focus on designing better AI algorithms. One of the possible improvements is to look up information on the internet for words that it does not understand, and use the relevant information for further inference. For example, if the user asks about Obama, the system should search on the internet and find Obama is a political leader, then look in the knowledge base for politics-related views such as how to govern a country. In addition, we want to test the effectiveness of the current structure of the system by conducting controlled studies where people use varied versions of the system containing only part of the modules in the virtual sage thinking engine.

Apart from improving the system, we also want to know the effects of this application. This work is done under the original intention of promoting philosophy and let it be known and liked by more people, we should test whether this goal can be achieved. However, unlike mathematics or physics where there can always be a definite answer, philosophy is very abstract and often subjective. Thus, it is very difficult to assess how much knowledge about philosophy people gain after using the system. Evaluation of such kind of systems is an interesting and important question to be addressed in future works.

To make a virtual recreation of great sages in the past is clearly not an easy task, and we are just beginning the first step. We believe that philosophy learning can be made into an entertaining activity using interactive new media technology.

Acknowledgements. This research is supported by the Singapore National Research Foundation under its International Research Centre @ Singapore Funding Initiative and administered by the IDM Programme Office.

References

1. Fellbaum, C.: WordNet: An Electronic Lexical Database. MIT Press, Cambridge (1998)

2. Fryer, L., Carpenter, R.: Bots as Language Learning Tools. Language Learning & Technology 10(3), 8–14 (2006)
3. Huang, Z., Thint, M., Qin, Z.: Question classification using head words and their hypernyms. In: Proceedings of the Conference on Empirical Methods in Natural Language Processing, Morristown, NJ, USA, pp. 927–936. Association for Computational Linguistics (October 2008)
4. Kindersley, D.: The Philosophy Book. Dorling Kindersley Ltd. (2011)
5. Klein, D., Manning, C.D.: Accurate unlexicalized parsing. In: Proceedings of the 41st Annual Meeting on Association for Computational Linguistics - ACL 2003, pp. 423–430 (2003)
6. Kopp, S., Gesellensetter, L.: A Conversational Agent as Museum Guide – Design and Evaluation of a Real-World Application. In: Panayiotopoulos, T., Gratch, J., Aylett, R.S., Ballin, D., Olivier, P., Rist, T. (eds.) IVA 2005. LNCS (LNAI), vol. 3661, pp. 329–343. Springer, Heidelberg (2005)
7. Mauldin, M.L.: Chatterbots, Tinymuds, and the Turing Test Entering the Loebner Prize Competition. In: Machine Translation, pp. 16–21 (1994)
8. Nakatsu, R., Rauterberg, M.: A New Framework for Entertainment Computing: From Passive to Active Experience. In: Kishino, F., Kitamura, Y., Kato, H., Nagata, N. (eds.) ICEC 2005. LNCS, vol. 3711, pp. 1–12. Springer, Heidelberg (2005)
9. Pedersen, T.: WordNet::Similarity - Measuring the Relatedness of Concepts. In: Proceedings of the Nineteenth National Conference on Artificial Intelligence (AAAI 2004), San Jose, CA. Number Patwardhan 2003, pp. 1024–1025 (2004)
10. Pedersen, T., Kolhatkar, V.: WordNet::SenseRelate::AllWords: a broad coverage word sense tagger that maximizes semantic relatedness. In: Proceedings of the North American Chapter of the Association for Computational Linguistics - Human Language Technologies 2009 Conference, Boulder, CO., pp. 17–20. Association for Computational Linguistics (2009)
11. Shawar, B.A., Atwell, E.: Accessing an Information System by Chatting. In: Meziane, F., Métais, E. (eds.) NLDB 2004. LNCS, vol. 3136, pp. 407–412. Springer, Heidelberg (2004)
12. Tapscott, D.: Growing up digital: The rise of the Net Generation. McGraw-Hill (June 1998)
13. Theodore de Bary, W.: Confucian Education in Premodern East Asia. In: Tu, W.-M. (ed.) Confucian Traditions in East Asian Modernity, pp. 21–38. Harvard University Press, Massachusetts (1996)
14. Wallace, R.: The elements of AIML style. Alice AI Foundation (2003)
15. Weizenbaum, J.: ELIZA-a computer program for the study of natural language communication between man and machine. Communications of the ACM 9(1), 36–45 (1966)

Spotting the Difference: Identifying Player Opponent Preferences in FPS Games

David Conroy, Peta Wyeth, and Daniel Johnson

Queensland University of Technology,
Science and Engineering Faculty,
Brisbane, Australia
{david.conroy,peta.wyeth,dm.johnson}@qut.edu.au

Abstract. This paper describes a study designed to understand player responses to artificially intelligent opponents in multi-player First Person Shooter games. It examines the player's ability to tell the difference between artificially intelligent opponents and other human players, and investigates the players' perceptions of these opponents. The study examines player preferences in this regard and identifies the significance of the cues and signs players use to categorise an opponent as artificial or human.

Keywords: Video Games, Artificial Intelligence, Indentification Processes, User Study, Multi-player.

1   Introduction

Artificially intelligent (AI) opponents or bots[1] are an important feature of First Person Shooter (FPS) video games. There have been many advances in the field of bot AI technology, particularly in relation to attempting to better mimic player-like behaviour. Despite these advances, there are still unanswered questions about what players expect from FPS AI and how bots impact on the player experience. The FPS genre of videogames can be defined as a virtual world in which the player moves in a first-person perspective to achieve the goals of the game. These game goals can vary depending on the different kinds of play or combat mode [1][2]. In the game mode dubbed 'deathmatch', the objective is to gain points by killing or 'fragging' other opponents in a free-for-all style. During a match, a player will interact with other opponents who can be controlled by other human players or by the game itself through AI controlled bots. The types of games that are the focus of this research are these deathmatch style games.

The study detailed in this paper forms part of a program of research designed to investigate claims that current AI designs are unrealistic, predictable and exploitable and influence game play negatively [3]. The current paper examines player preferences for in-game opponents. It explores the contrast between the behaviour of real

---

[1] Bots – computer controlled agents that mimic player behaviours performing game play tasks.

M. Herrlich, R. Malaka, and M. Masuch (Eds.): ICEC 2012, LNCS 7522, pp. 114–121, 2012.

players and AI controlled bots in the game. The focus of the study is to better understand players' views through:

- Investigating the extent to which players are able to identify human players and bots in multiplayer environments; and
- Discerning which opponent behaviours are the most useful in assisting players identify bots from human opponents.

This paper is not an analysis of the algorithms underlying the control of bot AI systems in FPS games or an examination of the psychological characteristics of participants that make them perceive AI agents the way they do. The research is designed to understand how readily a player can identify bots from humans and the types of opponent behavior traits they use in this identification.

2   Background

There is evidence that players have different experiences playing against computer controlled opponents as opposed to competing against human players, especially with respect to presence, flow and enjoyment [4]. Results show that most people generated higher physiological arousal and more fun while playing against another human. It may be that the exploitive and repetitive nature of NPCs in games reduces player enjoyment and   causes them to look for more challenging game play experiences [5]. Interviews have identified that, while players appreciate challenging bots that give players a chance to practice and improve their skills, they also flag negative aspects such as unrealistic behavior, unexpected behaviour (e.g. not taking cover or retreating), problems with coordination and unfair game advantages [6]. "Subhuman" behaviour, behaving in predictable ways that made it easy for human players to ascertain the weaknesses of bots and invent unconventional ways to defeat them, was identified as a particular weakness of opponent AI.

Human control of a game avatar and bot controlled AI are inherently different. Players do not naturally have a fully intuitive sense of orientation and action in virtual environments and must invest time and energy to master the control interface and learn the mechanics of games [7]. They require time to master game actions, e.g. shooting at targets [8]. Conversely, bot AI often includes a notion of shooting inaccurately through the random 'missing' of targets. This process doesn't consider improvement or progression in expertise. When expert judges were asked to identify the human player from the game play of a human and a bot in a one-on-one deathmatch environment, little correlation between skill levels and ratings of humanness was found [1]. Such results might call into question the necessity to create bot AI with multiple skill levels (e.g. [9]). Dynamic game systems that change the priority of a tactic depending on success ratings might be more akin to the play style of human players, especially in fast paced environments such as FPS games [5]. Research has demonstrated that it might be useful to consider bot play-styles based on survival as this play style has been shown to improve performance of bots [2] and strongly rewards human players as well [9].

Previous studies that have examined players' categorisation of human and bot opponents have demonstrated that it is not necessarily easy to judge accurately. Hingston [1] determined that people found it difficult when asked to observe a human and a bot in a one-on-one deathmatch environment and rate the likeness to the play style to a human player. Judges were often far from accurate. High aggression, adaptability and tactical game play were the characteristics that judges most easily recognised as human. Missing behaviours, stupid behaviours and low aggression also indicated bot-like game play. A study involving functional magnetic resonance imaging (fMRI) found higher levels of brain activity when participants believed they were competing against other human participants as opposed to a bot, even if in actual fact they were not [10]. Participant's also commented they were convinced of the alleged opponent's humanity and found those games to be more compelling.

From the literature it is clear that there are still unanswered questions related to players' abilities to identify bots from humans, and their perceptions of both. It is equally clear that we need this understanding to guide the future development of bot AI, to ensure that a positive player experience results.

3   Method

A user study was conducted to examine players' responses to bot and human opponents. The study consisted of two components; a multi-player gameplay session and a participant questionnaire. Five groups of four participants were involved, resulting in total of 20 participants taking part in the user study. The game used for the study was Quake III: Arena by iD games. The Quake III game client was used mainly for its ease of modification and setting up of dedicated multiplayer games.

3.1   Multiplayer Game Play Sessions

Each multiplayer game play session required four participants to play four multiplayer death matches consecutively with a brief questionnaire acting as intermission between games. Participants were positioned in a room with dividers blocking their view of the other participants. Participants were briefed on set-up procedures and were provided with simple step by step instructions. Each participant was required to wear headphones to eliminate vocal noises emitted by other participants. For each participant, two of the four multiplayer games were against a single opponent (1v1). Each of these games lasted approximately seven minutes. The other two games consisted of three opponents, making them four player matches (1v1v1v1). Each of these games lasted approximately 10 minutes. Two of the four games, one 1v1 and one 1v1v1v1, had bot opponents for the players to compete against. The order of presentation of the first two 1v1 games was randomized for opponent types. The 1v1v1v1 game that contained bot opponents had two bots and two human player. By the end of the study session each participant would have competed against three bots and every other participant in the room at least once.

3.2   Participant Questionnaire

The participant questionnaires consisted of a series of questions that players answered prior to playing any games, immediately after playing specific game session types and finally, after all games were completed. Questions asked before playing related to player demographic information. After each multiplayer session, participants rated the humanness level of all opponents on a Likert scale between 1 and 7, with 1 definitely being a bot, 4 being neutral/undecided and 7 definitely being a human. Any participant who rated a bot between 1 and 3 (being a bot) could be described as correctly rating the opponent as a bot. If they rated the bot from 5 to 7, they have incorrectly rated the bot as a human. Anyone who felt they could not decide rated the opponent a 4 and were therefore neutral about their decision. This same process is applied to when the opponent was a human, but in reverse.

After the first two 1v1 matches, players were queried on which opponent they preferred (Opponent 1 or Opponent 2). After all games were completed, participants completed a final section of the questionnaire regarding how useful they felt certain behaviours were in identifying whether an opponent was a human or bot. This consisted of a list of 11 behaviours (e.g. dodging, aiming) and another Likert scale to rate the extent to which each behaviour assisted in identifying a bot from a human. A 5 point scale was incorporated for this assessment, with 1 indicating that a behaviour failed to assist in classification and 5 indicating that it provided strong evidence to guide a player's decision. The 11 behaviours chosen for this identification process were actions found through previous research [3][11] to be most prevalent in participants playing FPS games. These behaviors were extracted and analysed from previous research data using an adapted time and event sampling technique [12]. Participants were not permitted to communicate with the other participants in any way either during game play or when completing the questionnaire.

4   Results

4.1   Two Player Participant Data

The 1v1 data allowed for a direct comparison of each participant's ratings after playing a single bot and a single human player. Each of the 20 participants only competed against one bot and one human in 1v1 games, making 20 ratings for each opponent type (bot and human). The results can be found in Fig. 1.

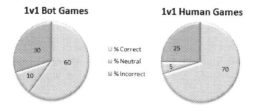

Fig. 1. 1v1 Participant Assessment Totals: green – correct, orange – neutral and red – incorrect

The results from the 1v1 participant data in Fig. 1 show that players are able to correctly categorise a bot and a human in a majority of instances, with only a small number of participants maintaining a neutral stance. Participants more accurately identified humans correctly. Participants were generally more definite in their assessment when categorising an opponent as human – 55% as "definite" or "most likely" as opposed to 40% for bots. The number of incorrect identifications made in the 1v1 games appears to be similar between both the bot and human games. However, while 3 participants recorded the bot as "definitely a human", no participants rated their human opponent as "definitely a bot".

4.2   Four Player Participant Data

The four player deathmatch games provided data that allowed for comparison between participant ratings of human and bot opponents in games with multiple opponents. Each participant played one match against 1 human and 2 bot opponents and one match against 3 human opponents. This resulted in a total of 40 possible bot identifications and 80 total human identifications across all the participants. Results are displayed in Fig. 2.

4 Player Bot Games   **4 Player Human Games**

Fig. 2. Four Player Participant Assessment Totals

The data from Fig. 2 reveals that people can correctly identify bots from humans more often than not. However, the percentages for both opponent types decreased in comparison to the 1v1 data, with a larger number of participants choosing incorrectly. Compared to the 1v1 participant data in Fig. 1, there is a significant increase in the number of participants who were indecisive or neutral in their decision. Many participants did not rate all 3 opponents as human in the final 4 player human game sessions. While most participants did manage to rate human opponents on the correct side of the scale (i.e. a rating between 5 and 7), some participants believed there to be at least one other bot in the game, if not two, or could not decide (see Table 1). There were more examples of participants gravitating towards an indecisive vote (i.e. a rating of 3 or 4) for the four player, all-human games. Thirteen of the 18 incorrect assessments of humans as bots, occurred in the 4 player all-human game sessions. The three examples where participants assessed human opponents as "definitely a bot" also occurred in these sessions.

Table 1. Final Four Player Game Participant Ratings

Bot->Human Rating Scale	1	2	3	4	5	6	7
Human Opponents (60)	3 (5%)	6 (10%)	4 (6.6%)	11 (18.3%)	12 (20%)	12 (20%)	12 (20%)

4.3   Opponent Preferences

Information about opponent preferences was gathered from 1v1 gameplay scenarios. A question asked participants which opponent they preferred. Participants were not aware of whether an opponent was a human or a bot. Seventeen participants chose the opponent who was human while only three chose the opponent that was a bot. Interestingly, most participants preferred the opponent who was human, even if they categorised that opponent as a bot. Two participants indicated that they preferred the human opponent, yet perceived it as a bot. The three participants who preferred the bot opponent, perceived the opponent as a human.

4.4   Opponent Behaviour Identification Data

The final section of the questionnaire was used to examine which opponent behaviours are most useful in assisting players in identifying bots from human opponents. The mean and standard deviation of this data is displayed in Fig. 3. The data was analysed to identify which behaviours were deemed most important in identifying human opponents from bot opponents. Behaviours identified as most important in the assessment process, with high mean and mode scores, were detecting, aiming, camping, response to player, fleeing and pursuing.

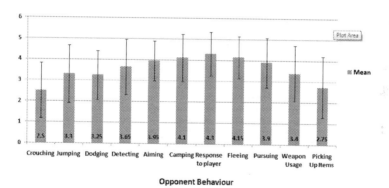

Fig. 3. Opponent Behaviour Identification Data

5   Discussion

The data concerning player's preference in opponent type yielded interesting results. In the 1v1 games, participants preferred the human opponent to the bot at a ratio of 17:3. There were two participants who perceived both their 1v1 games as having bot opponents, yet indicated their preference for the game where the opponent was a human. From these results it appears that players have a greater preference for human opponents; even those participants who chose bots, perceived them as human. The level of accuracy in classifying bot opponents (60% for 1v1 games and 45% for 4 player games) was lower than expected. For the four player games, this reduction in accuracy may be attributable to more participants being unsure, with neutral assessments increasing in count. While accuracy in determining human players also decreased in four player scenarios (70% in 1v1 versus 60% in 1v1v1v1), the decrease was not as marked. This may indicate that players became more adept at identifying characteristics of human opponents while bot-like activity remains ambiguous for longer.

Players were consistently better at determining human opponents from bot opponents. They also did so with more confidence in the 1v1 scenarios. The data indicates that game opponents are consistently harder to classify if they are bots. Accuracy differences of 10% in 1v1 games and 15% in four player games needs to be examined. When uncertain within the bot scenario, participants appear to be more likely to guess human. When uncertain in the human scenario, they may be more likely to select human. A possible interpretation is that players expect bots to behave in certain "bot-like" ways and when bots don't meet these expectations, players classify them as human. Consequently, further exploration of "bot-like" behavior is necessary in order to design bots that meet player expectations and have the appeal of human opponents.

Results related to the behaviours deemed most useful for opponent type were informative. The data presented in Fig. 3 shows that behaviours related to the reactions an opponent has to player actions are more useful in determining bots from humans. From the data, detecting, camping, aiming/inaccuracy, pursuing, fleeing and general response to player actions were found to be the major contributors to opponent identification. These behaviours have a higher percentage of participants determining them useful for identifying opponents with little variation in distribution across the behaviour identification rating scheme.

6   Conclusions and Future Work

The research described in this paper was conducted to support a larger research program. The current study examines the players' ability to tell the difference between bot and human opponents based on exhibited behaviours. This user study was designed to understand the situation from the player's point of view. While the study revealed some unexpected results, data analysis supports much of our existing research, especially with respect to player preferences for human opponents. Players were capable of identifying bots from humans more often than not, yet with slightly less capability than expected. This shows identification is not straightforward, and the reasoning around decisions, while generally indicating that reaction and response are the key indicators, needs further exploration.

The data generated from the existing study has revealed information which can be applied to future research. In particular, the data describing which behaviours both bots and humans perform that reveal their true identity has provided a stronger argument for the much larger research study. To illustrate with example, the bot's response to the player was deemed a better predictor than correct weapon usage, or jumping. This is not to say that the way bots jump in FPS games is human-like, it simply implies that the act of jumping does not act as a clear predictor. Response to the player's presence on the other hand appears to be a good predictor. Investigation of which behaviours have been used by those participants who accurately identified humans from bots is a logical next step. From this data it is possible to develop a picture of how one might better design AI behaviours that players find more engaging. It supports the notion of modifying bot AI to better respond to player actions, particularly concerning attacking, retreating, fleeing and hiding. This information will be integrated into the expanding program of research currently being undertaken. Future work will expand on this study, to develop a model of bot AI that players find more interesting and engaging to compete against.

References

1. Hingston, P.: A Turing Test for Computer Game Bots. IEEE Transactions on Computational Intelligence and AI in Games 1, 169–186 (2009)
2. Esparcia-alc, A.I., Member, S., Mora, A., Merelo, J.J., Garc, P.: Controlling bots in a First Person Shooter Game using Genetic Algorithms. Environment (2010)
3. Conroy, D., Wyeth, P., Johnson, D.: Modeling player-like behavior for game AI design. In: Proceedings of the 8th International Conference on Advances in Computer Entertainment Technology - ACE 2011, p. 1. ACM Press, New York (2011)
4. Weibel, D., Wissmath, B., Habegger, S., Steiner, Y., Groner, R.: Playing online games against computer- vs. human-controlled opponents: Effects on presence, flow, and enjoyment. Computers in Human Behavior. 24, 2274–2291 (2008)
5. Hartley, T.P., Mehdi, Q.H.: In-game tactic adaptation for interactive computer games. In: 16th International Conference on Computer Games (CGAMES 2011), pp. 41–49 (2011)
6. Clarke, D., Duimering, P.R.: How computer gamers experience the game situa-tion: a behavioral study. Computers in Entertainment 4, 6 (2006)
7. Przybylski, A.K., Rigby, C.S., Ryan, R.M.: A motivational model of video game engagement. Review of General Psychology 14, 154–166 (2010)
8. Rayner, C.: Player Modelling for Cursor-Driven Games. Challenges (2007)
9. Laird, J.E.: Using a computer game to develop advanced AI. Computer 34, 70–75 (2001)
10. Krach, S., Blümel, I., Marjoram, D., Lataster, T., Krabbendam, L., Weber, J., van Os, J., Kircher, T.: Are women better mindreaders? Sex differences in neural correlates of mentalizing detected with functional MRI. BMC Neuroscience 10, 9 (2009)
11. Conroy, D., Wyeth, P.: Building Better Bad Guys: A New Framework for Game AI Design. In: Proceedings of the 7th Australasian Conference on Interactive Entertainment, IE 2010, pp. 0–2. ACM Press (2010)
12. Bushnell, D., Irwin, M.: Observational Strategies for Child Study. Rinehart and Winston, Holt (1980)

AR Paint: A Fusion System of a Paint Tool and AR

Suwon Lee, Jinki Jung, Jihye Hong, J.B. Ryu, and Hyun S. Yang

Dept. of Computer Science,
KAIST, Republic of Korea
{swlee,jk,jihyerish,jbmagic,hsyang}@paradise.kaist.ac.kr

Abstract. In this paper, we present AR Paint, a fusion system of a paint tool and Augmented Reality (AR) that can augment in-place hand-drawn paintings onto an object. The system allows users to draw anything using the paint tool and then augment it onto an object whenever they want while providing a new experience and enjoyment during the process. It also has potential value if used in industry or for medical purposes. The hand drawing and visualization for AR is done through the screen of a mobile device, and all processes of the system are performed in real time.

Keywords: Augmented Reality, AR, AR Paint.

1   Introduction

Have you ever desired to draw something directly onto a famous painting? When you visit an art gallery, you may wonder how a painting would look if something you drew could be added to the painting. For example, you can imagine drawing Mona Lisa's eyebrows onto the painting Mona Lisa by Leonardo da Vinci. This impossibility has motivated us, and we made it possible using Augmented Reality.

Augmented Reality (AR) is a type of human-computer interaction that enhances our perception and helps us to see, hear, and feel our environments in new and enriching ways while providing local virtuality [1, 2]. With AR technology, we can gain a better understanding of education, find guidance through processes, be instructed in the assembly of objects, and have new experiences that we otherwise could not.

In this paper, we present a fusion system of a paint tool and AR termed AR Paint. The system allows users to draw anything using the paint tool and augment it onto an object in real time while providing a new experience and enjoyment during the process. The drawing and visualization for AR is done through the screen of a mobile device, and all processes of the system are performed in real time. The system also has the potential to be used in industry or for medical purposes. For example, surgeons may need to mark specific blood vessel for tracking while performing surgery. In such a situation, AR Paint can be the best choice when it supports full 3D object tracking with drawing in 3D space. In the AR Paint system, however, we currently consider only 2D surface tracking while drawing on a surface.

M. Herrlich, R. Malaka, and M. Masuch (Eds.): ICEC 2012, LNCS 7522, pp. 122–129, 2012.

The rest of this paper is organized as follows. In Section 2, we first present the AR Paint system with its scenario and framework. We then show a demonstration with a performance evaluation in Section 3. Finally, we conclude with a brief summary and discussion in Section 4.

2   AR Paint

In this section we present the AR Paint system from a scenario based on end users' viewpoints to detailed accounts of its processes. The system can take many different forms depending on its application, but in this paper, we describe our system via an AR Paint application for an art gallery for a clear understanding of its capabilities.

2.1   Scenario

In the Louvre Museum in Paris, a man is standing in front of Mona Lisa, Leonardo da Vinci's most famous painting. While looking at the painting, he wonders how different the painting would look if Mona Lisa was given eyebrows. He runs the AR Paint application on his smart phone and then he points its built-in camera at the painting. The boundary of the painting is marked and tracked in every frame. Once he touches a screen of the smart phone, the current frame is fixed and the GUI for the paint tool pops up. He starts drawing the eyebrows on the touch screen using his fingertip. Once he finishes this task, the eyebrows he drew are visualized and tracked in every frame.

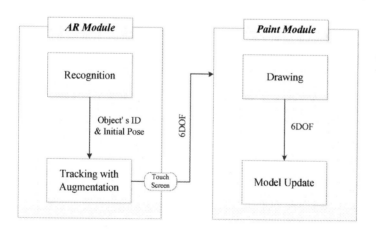

Fig. 1. The framework of AR Paint

2.2   Framework

For the AR Paint system, only a mobile device equipped with a camera and a supporting touch-screen input are necessary, both of which are available on the latest smart phones. AR Paint system is composed of two main modules: the AR module and the Paint module, as shown in Fig. 1.

In the AR module, recognition and tracking are performed using training data that is learned from recognizable objects. The recognizable objects and the distribution of the training data depend on the application. In our application, the recognizable objects are limited to 2D paintings and the distribution of the training data is done in advance when the application is installed on the mobile device.

The AR module switches to the Paint module when the user touches the screen while tracking an object. When switching, the three-dimensional position of the object is remembered for use later. Users can add something to the painting in the current fixed frame using the paint tool. The three-dimensional position is used to remove any distortion from the user's drawing and update the model which will be augmented in the AR module.

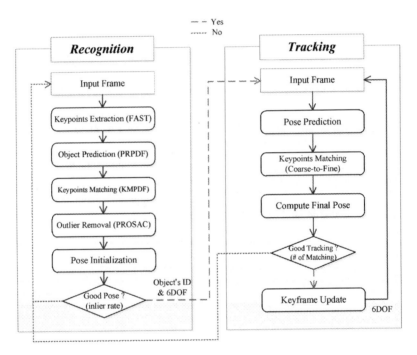

Fig. 2. Recognition and Tracking process in the AR module

2.3   AR Module (Recognition and Tracking)

Fig. 2 shows the entire process of the AR module, which is described in this section. The recognition process is initially performed for every frame captured by the camera. For real-time object recognition with pose estimation, we use a Generic Random Forest (GRF) [3]. The GRF is designed to be capable of simultaneous object recognition and keypoint matching through one pass over the original Random Forest [3, 4]. As shown in Fig. 3, a GRF consists of N_T random trees, and each tree conducts D binary tests comparing the intensities of two pixel locations of the input image patch surrounding a keypoint. Every leaf node of each tree stores $n + 1$ probability distributions (1 distribution is for object recognition, and each of the n distributions is for the corresponding object's keypoint matching). Therefore, for an image patch surrounding a keypoint, the GRF returns two results ('where' is the keypoint from among n objects, and 'what' is the keypoint from among the k keypoints of the corresponding object). For every frame, several keypoints are extracted via a FAST corner detector [5].   Every keypoint is passed through the GRF and the candidate object is predicted with matching pairs. Outliers are eliminated by the computation of a homography using PROSAC [6], and only matching pairs with reprojection error amounts of less than 10 pixels become inliers. If the number of inliers is smaller than a threshold, the candidate object is rejected for recognition; otherwise, the initial six-degree-of-freedom (6 DOF) pose of the candidate object is calculated [7].

Once an object is recognized, its ID and 3D pose are estimated and the tracking process is started. During the tracking process, a new pose of the object in a new frame is predicted using the previous 3D pose and the current camera motions. For the predicted new pose, coarse-to-fine matching is conducted to calculate the final pose and the opportunity to update the keyframe is given only in the case of good tracking. All of the aforementioned tracking processes are performed in the same manner as [8]. While an object is tracked, the boundary of the object is marked with a red line whose inner area becomes the canvas in the Paint module. Moreover, if there are some drawings of the object, they have to be augmented onto the object. In order to complete these tasks simply, we put one virtual layer per object and refer to the virtual layer as a model. The model is initialized by a transparent canvas with a red boundary considering corresponding to the object's shape and size. As a result, we can easily facilitate both augmentation and model update (Fig. 5).

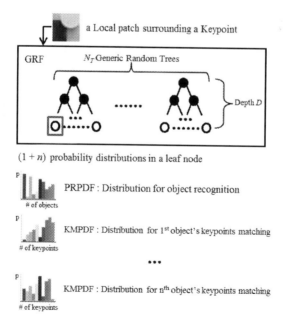

Fig. 3. Generic Random Forest

Fig. 4. Ready for drawing (fixed frame with the GUI of the paint tool)

2.4   Paint Module (Drawing and Model Update)

When the system is tracking, the current frame has an augmented model on the object as its image. By touching the screen during the tracking process, the current frame is fixed and the GUI for paint tool is displayed on the screen, as shown in Fig. 4. This state is ready for drawing and the inner-area of the model's boundary becomes a canvas for drawing. Users can draw something on the touch screen using their fingertip or a touch pen. In our application, currently, drawing is limited to 2D space, as our recognizable objects are 2D paintings and because the drawing is added onto their surfaces.

Once the drawing task is finished, the system starts the tracking process again and the users can see their drawing become augmented. This means the model for the object is updated immediately. When users draw something onto an object, the 3D position of the object differs depending on the viewpoint of the users. Therefore, we need to remove distortion in the drawing before applying it to a model. As shown in Fig. 5, the drawing is inversely warped to remove its distortion using 6 DOF pose of the object and the model is then updated according to the result.

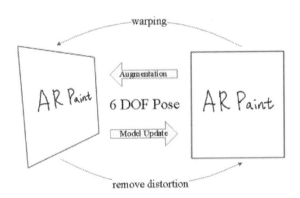

Fig. 5. Augmentation and Model Update

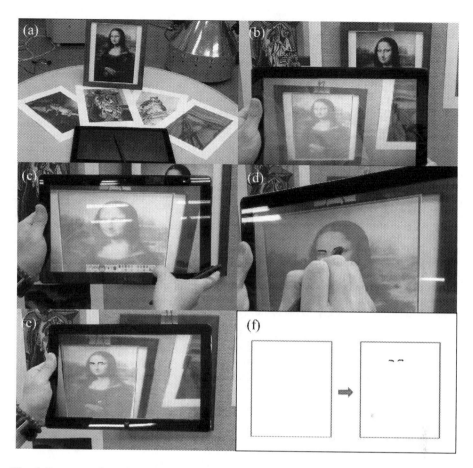

Fig. 6. Demonstration of AR Paint System (a) Environments: Tablet PC and target objects (b) Tracking with model augmentation (c) GUI for drawing   (d) Drawing on a touch screen (e) Updated model in next tracking   (f) Model update

3   Demonstration

To test our system, we implemented the AR Paint application on a tablet PC with a 1.4GHz dual-core processor and 1GB of RAM. For target objects, we printed out 100 paintings and trained them using a GRF which consisted of 40 trees of 12 depths, as mentioned in Section 2.3. At runtime, the application works as described in Section 2.1. Fig. 6 shows the demonstration of the application. All processes of the application were performed in real time.

For an evaluation of the performance, we first measured the recognition rate and recognition time as the number of training objects increased from 20 to 100. We randomly synthesized 100 new images per object, and they were used to measure the recognition performances. The average recognition rate and recognition time are shown in Table 1. We then measured the tracking time using a test movie with 500 frames. The test movie includes various events with tilts, scale variations, rotation, and fast movement. The averaged tracking time over all of the frames was 5.2*ms*. With the recognition time, it achieves more than 30 fps considering the total time requirements. This demonstrates that our system is fast enough in terms of its frame-rate performance.

Table 1. Recognition Rate and Recognition Time

# of training objects	20	40	60	80	100
Recognition Rate (%)	99.0	98.8	98.6	98.3	98.1
Recognition Time (*ms*)	18.9	19.2	19.6	20.2	21.0

4   Conclusion

In this paper, we presented AR Paint, a system which is able to augment in-place hand-drawn paintings onto an object. With the AR Paint system, users can immediately add their own drawing to a well-known painting, and the system provides a new experience and enjoyment for users as they use it. In the proposed AR Paint system, currently only 2D drawings on 2D surfaces are allowed. However, by allowing 3D drawings on 3D objects, it will become feasible to use this system for various purposes. As a future work, we first intend to find needs the AR Paint system can fulfill by conducting user studies. We also have plans to expand the system to support 3D drawings on 3D objects.

Acknowledgement. This work was supported by the IT R&D program of MKE/MCST/IITA, [Development of learner-participational and interactive 3D Virtual learning contents technology].

This research was supported by Basic Science Research Program through the National Research Foundation of Korea(NRF) funded by the Ministry of Education, Science and Technology (2011-0018291 / 2012-0005793).

References

1. Azuma, R., Baillot, Y., Behringer, R., Feiner, S., Julier, S., MacIntyre, B.: RecentAdvances in Augmented Reality. IEEE Computer Graphics and Applications 21(6), 34–47 (2001)
2. Krevelen, D.W.F., van Poelman, R.: A survey of augmented reality technologies,applications and limitations. Int. J. of Virtual Reality 9(2), 1–20 (2010)
3. Cho, K., Yoo, J., Yang, H.: Markerless Visual Tracking for Augmented Books. In: Joint Virtual Reality Conference of EGVE-ICAT-EuroVR, pp. 13–20 (2009)
4. Lepetit, V., Fua, P.: Keypoint recognition using randomized trees. IEEE Transactions on Pattern Analysis and Machine Intelligence 28(9), 1465–1479 (2006)

5. Rosten, E., Drummond, T.W.: Machine Learning for High-Speed Corner Detection. In: Leonardis, A., Bischof, H., Pinz, A. (eds.) ECCV 2006. LNCS, vol. 3951, pp. 430–443. Springer, Heidelberg (2006)
6. Chum, O., Matas, J.: Matching with PROSAC-progressive sample consensus. In: Proc. IEEE Conference on Computer Vision and Pattern Recognition, pp. 220–226 (2005)
7. Schweighofer, G., Pinz, A.: Robust Pose Estimation from a Planar Target. IEEE Transactions on Pattern Analysis and Machine Intelligence 28(12), 2024–2030 (2006)
8. Cho, K., Jung, J., Lee, S., Lim, S., Yang, H.: Real-time recognition and tracking for augmented reality books. Computer Animation and Virtual Worlds 22(6), 529–541 (2011)

Pictures at an Exhibition: Design of a Hybrid Puppetry Performance Piece

Ali Mazalek[1], Michael Nitsche[1], Claudia Rébola[2], Paul Clifton[1],
Andy Wu[1], Nick Poirier[1], and Firaz Peer[1]

[1] Digital Media, Georgia Institute of Technology,
Atlanta, GA 30332, USA
{mazalek,michael.nitsche,party,andywu,nick.poirier,firazpeer}@gatech.edu
[2] Industrial Design, Georgia Institute of Technology,
Atlanta, GA 30332, USA
crw@gatech.edu

Abstract. *Pictures at an Exhibition* is a physical/digital puppetry piece that uses tangible interface puppets to modify a virtual scene projected at the back of the stage in real-time. The piece merges traditional puppeteering practices with tangible interaction technologies and virtual environments to create a novel performance for the live stage. This paper describes the design and development of piece, as well as our lessons learned from this process and from on-stage performances of *Pictures at an Exhibition* in a puppetry theatre.

Keywords: physical/digital puppetry, performance, experimental theatre, tangible interaction, virtual space.

1 Introduction

Digital technologies are increasingly shaping novel performance practices [3] [4]. Hybrid performance formats are found in traditional theatrical settings, as well as in film and video games. In theatre, digital media are used to augment performances, e.g. in the form multimedia projections, in a manner similar to traditional visual effects. Artists and researchers have also explored digital media in combination with real-time computation in order to create interactive experiences for audiences or performers. In film and television, the use of digital puppetry and motion capture technologies is a widespread production process. More recently, the emerging machinima art form uses real-time game engines as platforms for digital puppetry in the creation of short animated films.

Building on these ideas, our work explores the merger of traditional puppetry with tangible interfaces and virtual environments. In *Pictures at an Exhibition*, five physical puppets equipped with sensors communicate data about their movements to a virtual scene projected at the back of the stage, which changes in response (see Fig. 1). The piece was inspired by Zbig Rybczynski's *Tango*, which uses 36 overlaying loops to build a video performance. In order to create *Tango*,

M. Herrlich, R. Malaka, and M. Masuch (Eds.): ICEC 2012, LNCS 7522, pp. 130–143, 2012.

Rybczynski had to draw and paint roughly 16,000 cell-mattes and make several hundred thousand exposures on an optical printer, a lengthy process that took seven months [14]. Instead of looping the recorded image, our piece captures animation data from puppets during the live performance. This data directly affects the virtual scene but is also looped and layered much like the actions in *Tango*. However, recording and looping happens in real-time. The virtual space becomes a lasting reflection of the story unfolding in the physical space. The abstract mapping between puppets and virtual scene addresses key questions of digital performance that deal with the relationship of the body to the digital realm in hybrid performance pieces.

Fig. 1. Performance of *Pictures at an Exhibition* during the XPT show at the Center for Puppetry Arts

Pictures at an Exhibition was created through a process of physical/digital co-design and was realized as a joint project across classes on experimental media, industrial design, and expressive virtual space. In this context, the conceptual, physical, and digital aspects of the piece co-evolved. The design and development of each aspect–story and performance, physical puppet interfaces, virtual environment–thus informed and altered the design of the other two. The process concluded with the performance of the piece on stage as part of the Xperimental Puppetry Theater show at the Center for Puppetry Arts in Atlanta, GA. The project enabled us to better understand the nature of hybrid performances that bridge the physical and digital worlds, and how to foster them in an interdisciplinary collaboration between artists and researchers.

First, this paper looks at related work from traditional and experimental puppetry. Next, we provide an overview of *Pictures at an Exhibition* and describe the design process across the physical, digital, and performance aspects of the piece. We discuss experiences and observations from the performances and conclude with lessons learned about the design of hybrid performance pieces for the live stage.

2   Related Work

Our work is inspired and informed by traditional puppetry and by digital technologies in performance arts, especially virtual environments and games. We offer an overview of related work in these areas.

2.1   Traditional Puppetry

As we have discussed elsewhere, there is a roughly inversely proportional relationship between ease of use and expressive potential with respect to traditional puppetry techniques [8]. Marionettes, which use strings to control individual parts of the puppet, can lead to a very fine degree of control over the puppet. However, each body part requires an additional string, and each string adds a degree of complexity to the puppet's control. At times, the control is shared. In the Bunraku tradition, three puppeteers control a single puppet. The main puppeteer controls the right arm and the head, while the other two control the left arm of the puppet and its legs. Each puppeteer has a fine degree of control over one or two body parts, which leads to an extremely expressive but also complex performance. Mastering these formats often takes years of practice.

Hand and rod puppets are more limited in their manipulation. However, as Jim Henson's Muppets have shown, in the hands of a skilled puppeteer they can be very expressive. Hand and rod puppets are controlled using one hand inside the puppet and the other hand to move a rod attached to one of the puppet's hands. While hand and rod puppets do not provide a fine degree of control of each individual part of the puppet's body, they do provide a balance between ease of use and expressive range. They can gesture using their arms and can direct their gaze at the important parts of a scene. Certain features, like the eyes, are simplified and exaggerated. *Pictures at and Exhibition* uses hand and rod puppets designed as described below.

2.2   Digital Technologies in Theatre Performance

Pinhanez describes theatre practices that actively use computers during live performance while maintaining the dynamics of live theatrical performance [10]. This includes human-controlled digital lighting and scenery, as well as artificially intelligent actors sharing the stage with a human actor. For example, in Mark Reaney's production *The Adding Machine*, off-stage computers control 3D projected props and scenery that users at computer terminals move to simulate movement of the live actors on stage. This literally shifts the perspective of the audience. Off-stage actors are also projected in 3D. The size and angle of the projection changes as they interact with the actors performing on the stage [13]. Computation in *The Adding Machine* is used to frame the viewers' experience in a way that would not be possible otherwise. In comparison, *It/I* creates a digital character that reacts to the performance of the actor and to audience participation. The digital character communicates with words, pictures, videos, sounds, and stage lighting [11].

In puppetry, digital technology has been used primarily for stage effects. Meridiano Theatre's *Genesis* uses projections to move the scene from underwater to outer space, and projection mapping to highlight certain props with changing surface textures [12]. In Terrapin Puppet Theatre's *The Falling Room and the Flying Room*, a projected television screen acts as a character in the performance. Animated versions of the puppets and actors move back and forth from the animated world to the real world. While the animated events are pre-rendered, careful staging and skilled puppeteering make the interactions look seamless [16]. Digital technologies also allow new forms of audience participation. Naked Puppets' *Dark Earth* uses technology to enable the audience to affect the scenery, soundscape, and imagery of the performance [9]. In both theatre and puppetry performances, computer vision and projection mapping have been the tools of choice for facilitating interaction between performers, puppets, and digital content. Embedded sensor technology, though, remains undeveloped in live theatre, with few examples of puppets that sense their own movement, like we implemented in *Pictures at an Exhibition*.

2.3   Digital Puppetry and Virtual Environments

Ever since users gained control over interactive digital characters, this interaction has been characterized as a form of dramatic performance [7] and digital puppetry [5]. A player character's actions usually depend completely on a user's input – much like that of a physical puppet. Calvillo-Gamez and Cairns draw a parallel between users learning game controls and puppeteers learning the functionalities of a puppet [2]. But due to the standardized nature of video game systems, the puppet analogy also has deficiencies.

One problem is mapping the limited control schemes of existing interfaces onto the near limitless range of expression. The hardware limits the input to certain set parameters. Keyboard, mouse, joystick, gamepad, motion-control device, etc. each have their own restrictions. In traditional puppetry, each puppet features a control scheme customized for its particular construction. Since games depend on standard input devices, such fine-tuning is difficult. Mappings can be adjusted, as players can set their own control preferences, but remain limited by the hardware. Another challenge is the principle difference in design between games and performances. Video games are defined as goal-driven systems that encourage players to fulfill a certain objective [6]. They emphasize the notion of interaction as making a "choice" [15] that has certain consequences in the game world. Due to the limitations of interaction possible in these worlds, these choices are often simplified (shoot the enemy or not, help the thief or the victim). In contrast, a theatrical performance consists not only of the action a character does, but also how any activity is performed. Due to the dominance of either pre-produced motion captured animations or procedural animation systems such fine-tuned control remains largely inaccessible to users.

Cases of successful digital puppetry grow in emergent play formats, when players either modify or repurpose game elements to achieve a level of expression that was not envisioned by the game designer. For example, fighting moves might be re-interpreted as dance for a machinima music video (see Bainst's *Dance Voldo Dance*). More open systems, like *Second Life*, allow creation of new animation cycles that can be used by virtual performers like the Ballet Pixelle [1] to stage choreographies with multiple dancers steered in real time by their users. However, their character control is achieved through elaborately timed animation activation. The players have no direct control over individual body parts of their dancing avatars.

Few titles allow for such a direct control over limbs, head, and expression through the interface. Media Molecule's *Little Big Planet* (2008) features typical jump'n run gameplay but allows players direct control over some facial animations and body parts of the virtual puppet. These expressions have no effect on achieving the main game objective but illustrate the focus on player involvement that is a key component of *Little Big Planet*. The game includes elaborate creation tools for players to generate game levels and customize their characters. It highlights a shift away from the pre-fabricated goal driven game and exemplifies the expressive range of digital puppetry. As it stands, this shift in commercial video games most often still depends on the inventive use of the underlying platform by the player and is rarely actively supported by the original producer.

3 Pictures at an Exhibition

Pictures at an Exhibition is a six-minute physical/digital puppetry piece that tells the story of a heist in an art gallery in seven scenes. The cast features five characters: security guard, cat, old lady, small boy, and gangster, each represented by a tangible interface puppet controlled by a single puppeteer. The piece is set in one room of the art gallery, where the old lady, small boy, and gangster conspire to steal a painting (represented on stage by a physical prop), while the security guard and cat try to foil their efforts. Another artwork is projected at the back of the gallery room and acts as a virtual mirror of the characters' actions, reflecting them in abstract animations on its surface, which are looped and layered over time. The piece is a comic reflection on the way the stories of visitors to an exhibition become part of the exhibited paintings themselves. Inspired by the structure of Rybczynski's *Tango*, the performance unfolds as follows:

– *Scene 1*: a performer (security guard puppeteer) enters stage and tells a story with their puppet. This puppetry leaves traces on the artwork in the background. Once this section of the story is completed, the performer and puppet leave the stage, but the animations repeat in an endless loop on the artwork at the back of the stage.
– *Scene 2*: another performer (cat puppeteer) enters and their actions with the puppet animate another part of the virtual canvas. They are soon followed by the first performer (security guard puppeteer), whose new actions are reflected onto the painting and layer with those of cat. As the scene ends, the performers leave the stage but their past actions continue to loop on the virtual canvas.

- *Scenes 3-5*: These scenes repeat the pattern, each bringing a different group of characters onto the stage as the story builds up to its climax. At the end of scene 5, the painting prop is stolen and all characters leave the scene while the artwork reflects the frenzy of actions.
- *Scenes 6-7*: As the story resolves itself with a comic twist involving the whole cast of characters, the layered animations on the painting build up to reveal the fully assembled image as the curtains close.

The story is conveyed through the puppet performance, which is set to a specially composed sound track that uses a different instrument for each character and helps to pace the performance. All puppets are custom-designed variations on hand and rod puppets with sensors at key points of articulation to capture expressive actions. The sensors in each puppet are connected to an Arduino and XBee, which transmit data to a computer that controls the virtual space.

4   Design Process and Performance

The piece was designed as part of a joint project across three research and studio classes on experimental media, industrial design, and expressive virtual space at Georgia Tech in spring 2011. One of our goals in producing the piece was to explore, engage in, and ultimately better understand how an interdisciplinary physical/digital co-design process can be applied to the creation of hybrid performance pieces that use real-time computational media on the live stage. Crucial to this is the seamless integration of the physical performance and the digital media on stage. Tangible interaction and puppetry are especially suited for this, since the puppets themselves can serve as an interface between the physical and digital worlds. The performers tell the story through the movements they make with their puppets, while the puppets capture real-time data of these actions and communicate them to the virtual space. The puppets can also serve as reflections of the captured data, for example through LED lights embedded in their bodies.

The project began with an initial concept of the structure and story for the piece. The realization of this concept unfolded across the three classes in a tightly coordinated manner. The progress in each class informed the work in the other two, and also evolved and altered the structure and story to its final state. Students in the three classes worked in teams to develop the different aspects of the piece. In the industrial design course, students did studies of form, materials, and movements, in order to inform the conceptual and physical design of the puppets. In the experimental media course, students explored physical interactions and sensor technologies, in order to realize the design, prototyping, and development of the puppet interfaces. In the expressive virtual space course, students explored the structure and animation potential of visual artworks, in order to create real-time animated versions that could reflect the story of the puppets into the virtual space.

The co-design process required sharing work-in-progress material across all three classes, including design sketches, renderings, technical specifications, and prototypes. E.g. an OSC-based communication protocol between the physical interfaces and virtual artwork was developed and refined as the piece evolved. Over the course of the semester, students from each class presented deliverables in the other two classes at key stages in the design process. Subsequent deliverables in those classes built on the ideas and artifacts presented: industrial design students built on the conceptual puppet designs from the experimental media students and presented additional design explorations back. Experimental media students used their output to revise their concepts and develop prototypes of the puppet interfaces. These prototypes were presented to the expressive virtual space students, who in turn used them to inform the design of the virtual artwork.

The Xperimental Puppetry Theatre (XPT) show at the Center for Puppetry Arts in Atlanta accepted our piece. So, in addition to our class collaboration, we also worked with professional puppeteers involved in XPT. These puppeteers provided feedback on the puppet designs, story, and staging of the piece throughout the design process, and helped to coach the performers. One of the puppeteers was a composer and created the music for the piece.

4.1   Puppets and Story

The experimental media class was divided into five teams of 3-4 students. Each team was assigned one of the five story characters and tasked with building its corresponding puppet interface. The creation of the puppets and the script evolved in iterations, from concept designs, through two rounds of prototypes, to final products. The two industrial design students worked as a team, producing design concepts and prototypes, which were informed by and inspired the work of the experimental media students.

Phase 1: Concept Designs. Experimental media students first generated conceptual designs for their puppets. The group visited the workshops, stage, and museum at the Center for Puppetry Arts to draw inspiration from traditional puppetry. As they developed their designs, each team was encouraged to consider:

- How their characters personality could be reflected in the puppets physical design and expressive movements;
- How their puppets actions could be captured with sensing technologies and in turn reflected within its body;
- How their characters relationship with other characters could be conveyed through interactions with them; and
- What kinds of story scenarios might unfold between the characters in the art gallery setting.

This conceptual design exercise yielded puppets with a lot of complexity in their mechanical design and operation, and a lot of detail in their physical appearance. The designs supported many different interactions between characters, and thus

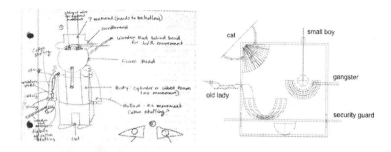

Fig. 2. First design concept for the gangster puppet with complicated control mechanisms (left) compared with the heavily abstracted puppet designs (right)

many possible relationships and story scenarios. The next task was to constrain and significantly simplify these designs.

The industrial design students worked from the initial design concepts, distilling each character's personality to one primary emotion. They explored how these emotions could be conveyed through abstractions of form and movement, and built a cardboard prototype that embodied the five characters as geometric shapes that were integrated into the space of the stage and interacted with one another through simple but evocative movements (see Fig. 2). This prototype was presented to the experimental media students, and encouraged them to radically re-think the nature of character and story in stage performance. Inspired by the work of the industrial designers, the experimental media students then revisited their initial concepts in order to represent each character as a simple geometric shape that communicated its essential qualities: the short stocky gangster was represented by a square, the broad-shouldered security guard was represented by an upside down triangle, the active chubby small boy was represented by a circle, the little old lady in a long dress was represented by a triangle, and the sleek cat was represented by a sideways oval.

Phase 2: Prototyping. Following the initial concept design phase, the experimental media and industrial design students went through two rounds of prototyping. The first prototype focused on the physical design of the puppets, including form, appearance, movement, control, and sensing. Each puppet was designed with sensors (accelerometers, bend sensors, and rotary potentiometers) at key points of articulation, which were connected to an Arduino microcontroller board. Puppets were also equipped with LEDs that highlighted key physical features. E.g., the cat could arch its back and its LED eyes would go from blue to red. The arching movement was detected by two accelerometers placed in the forward and rear segments of the cat's body. The second prototype refined the physical designs, and served as a step in wirelessly communicating puppet data to a computer via XBee, where it was visualized using 2D avatars created in Processing. A standardized XML format was developed to describe the moving parts and data value ranges for each puppet in order to enable calibration and mapping of the sensor data to the virtual artwork running in Unity.

Fig. 3. Final gangster puppet (left) and electronics housed inside the gangster's coat (right). The gangster used a bend sensor to detect movement in his rod-controlled elbow, a force sensing resistor (FSR) to detect contact of his cigar with his mouth, and two 3-axis accelerometers (one in the head, on in the body) to detect head and body movements.

Phase 3: Final Puppets. Building on the two rounds of prototyping, the industrial design students did studies and design exercises with different materials in order to improve the production quality, consistency, robustness, and performance controls of the final puppets (see Fig. 3). For example, they refined the production of the cat's eyes (using halved ping pong balls) in order make the LEDs more visible on stage, and they added volume to the old lady's dress so that she would better retain her shape while performing.

Story Script. As the puppets and their personalities took shape, so too did the story and dramaturgy. After the first prototypes were built, a story workshop was held with the experimental media students and professional puppeteers. Different story scenarios were storyboarded and eventually turned into a precisely timed script, which was shared with the expressive virtual space students, who used it to refine their designs for the virtual artwork. The script continued to evolve throughout the remainder of the design process, until the puppets, the virtual artwork, and the music were all finalized and the piece was in the final stages of rehearsal.

4.2   Virtual Artwork

The expressive virtual space class was divided into 4 teams of 3-4 students. Their task was to design and animate a virtual environment based on an existing artwork. They remained updated on the development of storyline and characters in the parallel course throughout the process.

Phase 1: Selection and Design. Students had to select an existing artwork to adapt for the virtual canvas. They explored materials and art historical references to envision interaction and animation designs that would reflect its specific qualities. The goal was interactive re-interpretation rather than reproduction. Four reference pieces were selected: French's *Summer* (1978), Kandisky's *On White II* (1923), Warhol's *Silver Clouds* (1966), and van Gogh's *Starry Night over the River Rhone* (1888); all created in different periods, using different techniques, and engaging audiences in different ways.

For each artwork, the mappings from expressive movements of the puppets to animations on the artwork were done in different ways. Each piece featured some specific quality that was highlighted in the interaction design. E.g., the design for *Summer*, a virtual stained glass window, referenced glass material in the animations (light reflections, melting, shattering, and bending glass based on external input). *On White II*, ultimately chosen for the performance, referenced the artist's abstract geometrical art. It does not claim to truly incorporate Kandinsky's complex approach, but uses its distinct components, breaks them into individual 3D objects (see Fig. 4), and maps them onto different characters. The designers looked for features in the painting that would reflect the story characters and their puppets, and the animations follow the lines of movement in the artwork in a way that relates to the key actions made by the puppets. For example, the black cat puppet who leaps and bounds across stage in the performance is reflected in the leaps of the black diagonal segments that cross in the center of the painting, while the gangster smoking his cigar creates bubbles that emerge from the smoke-like curves in the upper left.

Phase 2: Implementation. All four teams created 3D models of their pieces in Maya and imported them into Unity as real time rendered environments. Then they coded the interaction design. Changes in the digital artworks were planned in correlation to the storyline as it evolved from the parallel class.

The most challenging part was connecting the puppet data to the virtual artwork. Seamless communication and clear mappings between the two had to be established. Each puppet had different sensors, which changed throughout the design process. The mapping to animations in the virtual Kandinsky had to cater for these changes. Even during the rehearsal stage, this mapping was adjusted in collaboration with the puppeteers and puppet designers. Unity also had to record the animations in real-time and provide instant playback. This was achieved via a database that recorded all input from the puppets and fed it back into the

Fig. 4. The virtual artwork – a 3D digital recreation of Kandinsky's *On White II*. Complete front view (left) and animated portion (right).

render engine when activated by an operator. This system allowed the operator to orchestrate a smaller version of layered animation as seen in Rybczynski's *Tango* in real-time. We also included pre-set animations that reflected the intended effects. This allowed us to test the artwork while the puppets were still being built. It also served as back-up in case the connection to the puppets was lost.

4.3   Live Performance

The XPT show (see Fig. 5) consisted of five performances preceded by five nights of dress rehearsals. Overall, the system worked solidly during all rehearsals and dress rehearsals. However, some initially small inconsistencies observed in the the connection between puppets and virtual artwork became more prominent after the first two show performances. This forced us to sidestep the live-recorded animation playback during two of the performances and employ our back-up plan of playing pre-recorded animations on the virtual Kandinsky painting.

Despite the technical difficulties we experienced, the piece received laughter from the audience at the right moments (e.g. when the old lady hit the boy with her cane) and much applause. The feedback received from audience members after each performance was positive, and many people approached us to say how much they enjoyed the piece. Nobody we spoke with had experience of real-time computation used in performances, and many were intrigued by the idea and interested to see more similar works. While everyone perceived the connection between the puppets and the virtual artwork in our piece, relatively few understood how the different characters' stories played out on the virtual canvas. This indicated that the mappings between the puppets' actions on stage and the virtual artwork were too abstract, and would have benefited from simplification.

Fig. 5. Performers manipulate the puppets on stage during the XPT performance of *Pictures at an Exhibition*. The puppets' actions are mapped to the virtual painting in real time.

5   Discussion and Conclusions

We provide here a brief summary and discussion of lessons learned from the design and performance of the piece.

Communication. One of the most important aspects of design of a hybrid performance piece is effective and timely communication between members of the interdisciplinary team that is realizing the physical and virtual aspects of the piece. The communication between the industrial design and experimental media students worked well at the first, but became more challenging as the prototypes progressed. Since much of the ideation took place separately, as the designs progressed, students from the two classes were not always in line with their refinements and design iterations. In the same way, communication between experimental media and expressive virtual space students met with challenges throughout the process. Most significantly, the expressive virtual space class would have benefited from having a complete set of captured data earlier in the design process, however this was impossible for the experimental media class to deliver as the piece and technologies were continually evolving. Overall, a more tightly integrated design process in which all three classes participated in all design sessions together would have been beneficial, but this was not feasible due to institutional constraints, such as class scheduling and coordination across different units.

Mapping. Hybrid performance pieces need to consider how the physical world on stage and the projected virtual world interact. We aimed for a balance between the two. However, the mappings were not obvious enough to the audience, and so the action on stage took precedence over the changes happening to the virtual canvas. In retrospect, this could to some extent have been avoided if we had been able to incorporate the virtual artwork into the rehearsals earlier on. But due to timing constraints and technical challenges, the real-time communication between the puppet interfaces and the artwork was not in place early enough for the rehearsals to happen with the virtual canvas running. A lot of rehearsing/coaching with the professional puppeteers thus focused on the physical performance, and the changes in the artwork did not seem to be designed into the story action from the outset. In the future, it would be worthwhile to explore how to mock up the virtual scene and rehearse with it early in the design process even as the puppet designs, technologies, and storyline continue to evolve.

Balance. Hybrid performances need to consider how to balance between action on the physical stage and action in the virtual space. There is no one correct way to realize this balance since it depends on the story and director's vision. However, it is difficult for the audience to focus in many places at once, so a hybrid piece should give the audience time to take in and switch between action on the physical stage vs. on a projection screen. In our case, replaying animations on the virtual canvas after each scene gave the audience time to process and relate the virtual performance to the physical one. This was especially important given the fast pace of the actions unfolding on stage.

Control. The physical actions made by puppeteers when their focus is on controlling a virtual entity are different than when their focus is generating a physical performance. Our puppeteers performed actions regardless of how they were unfolding on the virtual canvas. Even when communication lagged between the puppets and virtual artwork, the puppeteers maintained their focus on the physical performance. Shifting their focus to control of the virtual, e.g. to make an adjustment or accommodate latency, would have been at the expense of expressivity and narrative communication of the physical puppets. In this sense, a physical performance with a physical controller can be at odds with a virtual performance with a physical controller. This poses a challenge for the creation of hybrid pieces that blend both physical and virtual performances.

Error-Handling. Hybrid performance practices need to develop methods for real-time error handling that do not disrupt the performance in progress. Technological devices and networks rarely work flawlessly. However, common error-handling methods usually involve pausing the normal workflow in order to address the error (e.g. respond to an error dialog, restart the application, restart the machine, etc.). This is not an option in a live performance, where any disruption will break the fourth wall for the audience. Having a backup plan is important, however the decision to use it needs to be made in a timely manner, before the performers are on stage. Solutions enabling the seamless transition to a backup plan in mid performance could be worth exploring in future hybrid performance works.

Acknowledgments. We thank students in our spring 2011 classes at Georgia Tech, puppeteer collaborators Lee Bryan, Dolph Amick, Mauree Culberson and Lynn Talley, XPT director Michael Haverty, the Center for Puppetry Arts, and BlinkM.

References

1. Ballet Pixelle (2011), `http://psg.com/~pixelle/`
2. Calvillo-Gamez, E.H., Cairns, P.: Pulling the strings: A theory of puppetry for the gaming experience. In: Guentzel, S., Liebe, M., Mersch, D. (eds.) Proc. of The Philosophy of Computer Games Conference, pp. 308–323. Potsdam University Press (2008)
3. Dixon, S.: Digital Performance. MIT Press, Cambridge (2007)
4. Giannachi, G.: Virtual Theatres: An Introduction. Routledge, London (2004)
5. Hayes-Roth, B., van Gent, R.: Improvisational Puppets, Actors, and Avatars. In: Pahlka, J. (ed.) CGDC Proceedings, pp. 199–209. Miller Freeman, San Francisco (1996)
6. Juul, J.: Half-Real: Video Games between Real Rules and Fictional Worlds. MIT Press, Cambridge (2005)
7. Laurel, B.: Computers as Theatre, 2nd edn. Addison-Wesley Publishing Company, Reading (1993)
8. Mazalek, A., Nitsche, M., Chandrasekharan, S., Welsh, T., Clifton, P., Quitmeyer, A., Peer, F., Kirschner, F.: Recognizing Self in Puppet Controlled Virtual Avatars. In: Proc. Fun and Games 2010, pp. 66–73. ACM (2010)
9. Naked Puppets: Dark Earth. Naked Puppets Theatre Company, Olympia, WA, USA (2006), `http://www.nakedpuppets.org`
10. Pinhanez, C.S.: Computer Theater. Tech Report 378, Perceptual Computing Group, MIT Media Lab (1996)
11. Pinhanez, C., Bobick, A.: It / I: A Theater Play Featuring an Autonomous Computer Character. Presence: Teleoperators and Virtual Environments 11(5), 536–548 (2002)
12. Ravicchio, G.: Genesis. Meridiano Theatre, Denmark (2006), `http://www.meridiano.dk/`
13. Reaney, M.: Virtual Scenography: The Actor/Audience/Computer Interface. Theatre Design and Technology 32(1), 36–43 (1996)
14. Rybczynski, Z.: Looking to the Future: Imagining the Truth. In: Penz, F., Thomas, M. (eds.) Cinema & Architecture: Melies, Mallet-Stevens, Multimedia, pp. 182–198. BFI, London (1997)
15. Salen, K., Zimmerman, E.: Game Design and Meaningful Play. In: Raessens, J., Goldstein, J. (eds.) Handbook of Computer Game Studies, pp. 59–81. MIT Press, Cambridge (2005)
16. Terrapin Puppet Theatre: Hobart, Tasmania, Australia (2011), `http://www.terrapin.org.au`

Follow the Grass:
A Smart Material Interactive Pervasive Display

Andrea Minuto, Gijs Huisman, and Anton Nijholt

Human Media Interaction Group, University of Twente
PO Box 217, NL-7500 AE Enschede, The Netherlands
{a.minuto,gijs.huisman,a.nijholt}@utwente.nl

Abstract. Smart materials offer new possibilities for creating engaging and interesting forms of interaction and ways of displaying information in a material way. In this paper we describe Follow the Grass, a concept of an interactive pervasive display for public spaces. The display will be built up out of a number of blades of grass that are actuated in eight directions using nitinol muscle wires (i.e. a shape-memory alloy). A Microsoft Kinect-based tracking system is employed to detect users' presence. Follow the Grass can be used for entertainment purposes by displaying animations through movement of the grass, as well as for indoor way-finding and ambient persuasive guidance. We present a number of scenarios with varying scales of interaction, and different applications, followed by a description of the initial hardware design of a single blade of grass and its actuated root. We will give a description of the tracking system, and how it tracks users and is capable of identifying individuals. Finally we will provide suggestions for the further development.

Keywords: Smart material interface, quiet computing, ambient, organic, display.

1 Introduction

For two decades researchers and designers have actively explored new methods of physical interaction with computer systems [7]. The seminal work of Ishii and Ullmer [11] helped spur the development of tangible interfaces; interfaces that allow users to manipulate physical objects that modify digital information. With technological advances, tangible interfaces have started to incorporate smart materials [10]. These materials are characterized by having physical properties that can be altered in a controlled way. Interfaces that incorporate such materials can be referred to as Smart Material Interfaces (SMIs [18]). In essence, where "traditional" tangible interfaces couple physical objects to digital information often displayed on a screen, smart materials allow the digital information to be represented by the physical state of the material. An advantage of this is that the information can be directly embedded into the materials of the physical environment. Furthermore, the use of smart materials allows for new forms of silent, energy efficient and more natural ways of actuating physical output (e.g. Sprout I/O [4]; Lumen [20]).

M. Herrlich, R. Malaka, and M. Masuch (Eds.): ICEC 2012, LNCS 7522, pp. 144–157, 2012.

In this paper we will present a concept of an interactive pervasive display that uses nitinol shape memory alloy (SMA) wires to actuate an artificial blade of grass in eight directions. These blades of grass can be thought of as physical pixels, and, when multiplied, can form a physical ambient display. Such a display can be employed for entertainment, indoor way-finding, or ambient persuasive guidance.

We will first review related work on ambient displays, ambient persuasive guidance and smart materials. Then we will present a detailed outline of the "Follow the Grass" concept, present a number of scenarios, and offer a description of the hardware prototype of the blade of grass and actuated root, and software design of the tracking system. We will conclude by providing suggestions for the further development of the hardware and software.

2   Related Work

2.1   Ambient Technology

The interest in Tangible Interaction [11] is part of a development in HCI research that is moving away from the typical "window, icon, menu pointing device" (WIMP) interaction [13]. Reality-based interaction (RBI) encompasses interfaces and interaction styles that support humans' existing knowledge about the physical world [13]. In this sense, the vision of *ubiquitous computing* is particularly relevant. Weiser's view [26] of ubiquitous computing holds that computing can be unobtrusively integrated into everyday objects and environments. This proposes a direct coupling of computation and the "real" physical world, in an integrated natural manner. Furthermore, distributed networks and sensor technology can make such systems intelligent, resulting in objects and environments that can naturally adapt to their users [27]. Examples of such systems being used for presenting information or providing entertainment are plentiful. The ambientROOM [12] uses lights, sounds and movement to unobtrusively communicate a host of background information, such as the physical presence of others or the activity of an actual hamster. Similarly, Hello.Wall [21] consists of a grid of lights integrated into a wall, information can be presented by changing light patterns, that react to the proximity of the user to the installation. Another example is The Information Percolator [9], which displays information through air bubbles rising up in a number of transparent tubes filled with water. One application of The Information Percolator tracks people's movement along a corridor and represents this information in the ambient display. A more physical approach to ambient displays is implemented in Super Cilia Skin [22], which is a magnetically actuated display that makes cilia (i.e. individual actuators) move lightly to emulate the physical touch of a finger or a gesture trace. A similar approach has been used in the artistic installation Project Dune (Studio Roosengaard[1]), which is composed of large amounts of fibers that brighten according to the sounds, touch and motion of passing users, accompanying them along the walk.

---

[1] http://www.studioroosegaarde.net/project/dune/info/

For an overview of similar ambient displays we refer the reader to Vande Moere [24]. What all of these ambient displays have in common is that they display information in an unobtrusive, yet aesthetically pleasing and fun way.

2.2   Persuasive Ambient Technology

Recent evidence suggests that ambient technology can also be employed for persuasive purposes (for example Breakaway [14] and Twinkly Lights [23]). The fact that such ambient systems are integrated into the environment, means they do not explicitly tell people to change their behavior. Instead they can suggest alternatives for a certain behavior [23], or provide implicit visualizations of 'bad' behaviors [14]. The strength of this approach lies in the notion that people are not consciously aware of the ambient intervention, yet still adjust their behavior [23].

There has been a substantial amount of research investigating the effects of static persuasive cues on the way people navigate public spaces. Such studies typically use textual [2] or visual cues [23] to guide people in a certain direction, for instance towards the stairs instead of the escalator. Examples of visual cues include lines that, when viewed from a certain angle, form guiding arrows [1]. Others used lenticular lenses to produce the illusion of lines moving to one side with the goal of guiding pedestrians [8].

Compared to the use of static visuals, the advantage of using ambient technology for persuasive purposes is that the system can be dynamically adapted to the users' behavior and to individual differences, as Kaptein says in [16]. This makes it more suitable for individual users, as well as allowing the system to adapt based on situational circumstances. For example a suddenly appearing obstacle that requires changing the direction in which pedestrians are guided. Here the use of smart materials is promising, because they offer both the ability to change dynamically as well as the ability to blend into the environment.

2.3   Application of Smart Materials

Considerable efforts have been made to explore the possibilities of applying smart materials in interfaces. For example, Surflex [3] consists of a foam with coiled nitinol muscle wires embedded. The muscle wires can be used to reshape the foam. This principle has been applied as a way to use SpeakCup [6], a device used to record and replay messages by physically manipulating its shape (Shape-changing interfaces [6]). Another suggested application of Surflex is as a form of physical computer-aided design. Indeed, Parkes and Ishii [19] presented just such a design tool, for motion prototyping and form finding, named Bosu. Bosu consists of a number of flexible modules that can be physically manipulated (e.g. bent, twisted). The physical manipulations can then be played back thanks to nitinol muscle wires embedded in the modules.

Apart from design tools such as Bosu, smart materials have been used in the creation of novel ambient displays. Shutters [5] is a curtain with a grid of shutters that are actuated by nitinol wires. Shutters can be used to regulate the amount of light and air flow that enters a room, as well as serving as an ambient display by creating patterns using the grid of shutters. An ambient display that aims for a more tangible experience is Lumen [20]. A grid of cylindrical physical pixels are actuated to move up and down, using nitinol wires. The physical pixels contain LED's that allow Lumen to display animations both visually, and physically.

While nitinol is by far the most widely applied smart material, others have used ferro fluids and thermo-chromic materials to create physical ambient interfaces. WeMe [17] for example, is an ambient display that visualizes the presence of members of remote families represented by bubbles of ferro fluid. Wakita et al. [25] note how, in the design of such interfaces, the materials and colors are felt as part of the emotional communication of the interface. Using the property (in this case colors) of the material directly, their aim is to communicate mood by changing the color of the Jello Display-Keyboard using IR-chromic material.

The application of smart materials in interfaces enables designers to build interfaces that can take advantage of human tactile senses and perceptions of movement to improve interaction [15]. This allows for the complete abandonment of the digital display in favor of shapes and movements, creating a more direct way to communicate with the user and establishing a novel design language that could reduce the cognitive load (unlike WIMP interfaces which add new symbols interpretation).

In the next section we will present our idea of applying smart materials in an ambient pervasive display that can be used for entertainment, indoor way-finding and ambient persuasive guidance. The keys to communication here are the shape and movements of the artificial blades of grass. As was mentioned in [18] we want to try to keep the perception of the interface as analog as possible, experimenting with materials and shapes.

3   Follow the Grass

Follow the Grass is an interactive pervasive display made of artificial blades of grass. By moving individual blades of grass sequentially, it is possible to create animations (e.g. a Mexican wave-style animation[2]). Such animations can be used to communicate information to users. While the grass-pixels were designed for general use as an ambient display, their appearance and movement capabilities, make them particularly well suited for giving directions in indoor way-finding, or for ambient persuasive guidance and entertainment.

Follow the Grass mimics the way grass waves in the wind, not by representing only a single pixel but a mass of objects. In a large field installation it would be possible to emulate a virtual wind by moving the grass in waving patterns. Such a 'virtual wind' blowing through the grass field can be initiated by the presence of the user (see chapters Scenarios and following). Using a dedicated tracking system that follows and records the identity of users, it is possible to distinguish between different users, and to address them individually.

---

[2] Mexican wave-style: it is a large scale example of a metachronal wave. These movements produce the appearance of a travelling wave.

The grass-pixels were born out of the idea that, by using smart materials, we can create interaction in a less traditional manner (no WIMP) and convey information through the materials' properties (shape, position, colors, etc.). By using a muscle wire[3] we can accomplish a variety of movements allowing the blade to bend toward a specific direction (for now four cardinal point plus the four diagonals), with different speed to accentuate certain movement just by increasing the reaction time. Furthermore nitinol wires are highly reliable and resistant to many kinds of stress. Compared to servo-motors, the nitinol wires operate silently, not drawing the users' attention to the hardware operating behind the scenes. This allows a more seamless experience of the grass, making it ideal for pervasive applications.

Some previous works involved display methods similar to the one used in the Follow the Grass concept. The Project Dune has fibers with LED's embedded in the tips, that respond to sound. However, these blades of grass are not actuated and therefore lack the capability to address a certain direction. In Super Cilia Skin [22] the set of cilia creates a visual approximation of a contiguous deformable surface. Differently, the Follow the Grass concept attempts to make use of individually actuated blades of grass to address direction, or create a path by orienting individual blades of grass in unison. Compared to Coelho's work Sprout I/O [4] that uses nitinol wires to bend a fabric grass in a linear movement (left-right only), we make active use of two degrees of freedom (see next sections for more details of implementation and movements). Sprout I/O was born as a remote control device and interactive actuated interface. The Follow the Grass concept, on the other hand, was conceived instead as an actuated pervasive display, envisioned to be mass produced and to be put in different public spaces. In addition Follow the Grass should provide interaction designers with a flexible infrastructure to develop animations to be depicted in the grass.

Unlike real grass, on which you can walk, it is not possible to step on the artificial grass at this stage, however, in the future we will be able to build a more robust base which would allow users to walk on the grass. But a limited number of blades can be put on a pedestal, or, in the case of a grass field, under a transparent floor, allowing the user to walk over the grass still perceiving its presence and animations.

We envision the interaction to take place in public spaces where the users are free to walk such as a hall of a complex building, a crossing of corridors or just the entrance of a building. The tracking system handles the tracking of all individuals that pass the installation, and adds a special profile to each one of them. For example if you are in a hospital, and you need to know where the office of Dr. Red is, you can register your request at the reception desk. At this point the system can track your movements, and attach your request to you as an individual. By animating the grass in the direction of the office of Dr. Red, the only thing left to do is follow the grass distributed along the way.

---

[3] Flexinol or muscle wire is special kind of nitinol wire that change shape by contraction its length.

4   Scenarios

For the application of our system we illustrate several kinds of scenarios. In each of the scenarios the hardware and software will be the same, but in some cases adjustments are needed to adapt to the specific interaction. In every scenario the individual roots and blades of grass are the same. In some scenarios we assume that we know the objective of the user (such as: path or game objective), for example an existing "Helpdesk" or a pre-filled user profile.

4.1   Field

In this scenario (Fig.1 and 2) we imagine a large-scale public installation, where a field of artificial grass is placed underneath a transparent floor. The users walk over the field without touching it, while the system tracks the identities of the users and produces personalized animation patterns under each user, by moving the nearby blades of grass. This can be used purely for entertainment purposes by simply displaying animations. For example a rippling effect, similar to a drop of water being dropped onto a water surface, causing concentric waves to form around the user. Another example is simulated wind that causes blades of grass all over the field to move in a natural manner. The field can also be used to guide individual users in a certain direction, by bending the blades of grass to form a path. A similar approach can be used to draw attention to specific objects in the space, by bending the blades of grass towards the object. Such an approach could be relevant for museum exhibitions or serious gaming purposes.

Fig. 1. Scenario Field. The users are walking on a transparent floor over the grass,.

4.2   Lawn

In the "Lawn" scenario (Fig.3) the total number of blades of grass is reduced by placing strips of grass (lawns) along the walls of a public space. This

Fig. 2. Scenario Field. The grass bends creating a path from under the user to his/her goal.

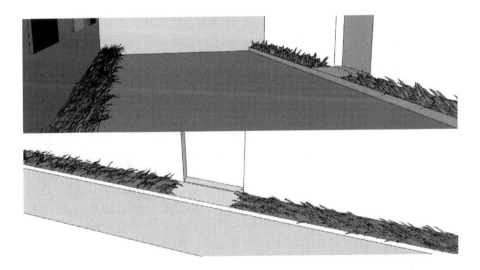

Fig. 3. Scenario Lawn. On the top the grass bends toward the door on the right side and toward the corridor on the left. On the bottom the detail of the grass bending toward the door.

approach preserves part of the entertainment possibilities of the "Field" scenario and maintains the possibility to provide personalized guidance to users. Users could simply follow the direction of the waving grass along the wall. Attention can be drawn to specific areas along the wall, for example the office of the person the user is looking for.

4.3   Map

Here, a specific location is addressed using a scale model of an area (Fig.4 and 5), for example a university campus. The scale model will represent the surrounding area, with the space between the models covered in the artificial grass. Users can interact with the scale models through gestures (using the Kinect included in the system) in order to ask for directions. The grass will respond by forming a path from the users current location to the requested destination. This setup can also be used to highlight events in a specific part of the area, by playing animations that focus on the area in which the event takes place.

Fig. 4. Scenario Map. Installation from the side.

4.4   Patch

The last scenario (Fig.6) is a small scale field (3x3 blades of grass) coupled with the tracking system. The patch of artificial grass can be placed on a pedestal at the place where a corridor splits. In the presence of the user, the grass will attract the users attention in *entertainment mode* (waving in different pattern or bending toward the user) and if profiled, address a direction in *guiding mode*.

Fig. 5. Scenario Map. The grass is bending toward the tower.

5   System: Tracking and Actuation

The system is composed of two distinct components: one for the physical output
(the grass) and one for the input, which is the presence of the users detected by
the tracking software.

With the system, it is possible to track a specific person in a small group of
people. This makes it possible to address this specific person individually, and
provide him/her with personalized information, such as specific directions at the
right time.

The interaction starts when people enter the area covered by the tracking
system.

5.1   Software

A Kinect[4]-based tracking system is being developed to be able to address and
track all the users in its sight. The idea is to have a system that is able to
track identities from a simple blob tracker[5]. We intend to identify the user by
knowing the tracking faults of the blob tracker itself and solving the problem
in two phases. First, each time a blob merges with another we will trace and

---

[4] http://www.microsoft.com/uk/wave/hardware-kinect.aspx
[5] With BLOB we refer to regions with no fixed shape in the image that differ in
properties compared to the surrounding. E.g.: brightness or color.

Fig. 6. Scenario Patch. The grass bends indicating a direction to the incoming user.

save the previous and new relation (and related information), creating a sort of logical history of relation of blobs (with "AND" and "OR" logic conditions). Second, we will try to confirm the identity (between the observed ones) using logical operation and matching with hints that the software acquires from the behavior and features analysis of each blob (in development).

The user can be identified in one of the specific checkpoints (if needed for giving personalized information) or just by entering the sight zone, a numeric ID is attached to the blob and tracked during the movements.

When the system is unable to track the user, there are three possibilities:

- The user is out of sight.
- The blob has merged with someone else's blob. In this situation we aggregate the information in "AND" until the system is able to address the blobs again.
- The blob has split into two or more parts. The information of the old blob is inherited in a doubt condition, i.e. an "OR" mode, on the generated blobs.

This way we generate blobs with some of the information precisely (aggregation of reliable information in "AND") and others in doubt (separation of blobs, in "OR" condition). To solve the "OR" condition we use a feedback loop that checks the features of the new blobs from time to time (shape, contrast, color, height, etc.) with the one from before. Basically giving hints on which one is the most reliable solution. We then backward propagate on the other blobs to solve other pending doubt conditions.

The system has some limitations and can only be used in a controlled environment (at the moment only inside the field of view of the Kinect). However, it is modular so that it will be further developed with other tracking features and the possibility to extend the field of view by connecting more units together.

5.2 Physical

Each grass-pixel is made of three parts: the controlling electronics, the "root", or actuator base (Fig.7), and the externally visible blade of grass. The electronic component consists of an Arduino[6] board that controls the power on a specific duty cycle to the muscle wire, using a PWM (Pulse-Width Modulation). This way it is possible to control the amount of power used to heat the wire. It is possible to vary the duty cycle to make the heating process faster or slower, resulting in faster or slower movement of the grass, allowing for controlled organic movements and animations.

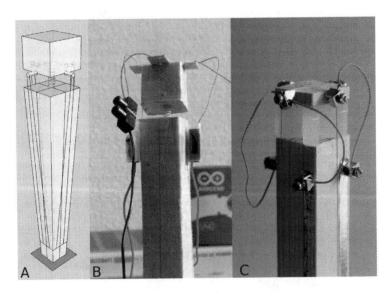

Fig. 7. Physical actuator element, It is possible to see the movable head of the "root", where the blade of grass will be attached. A) the original 3D model for the project, B) the cardboard prototype with spring, C) latest prototype update with silicon "spring".

The root is the physical actuator that forms the base on which the blade of grass is placed. The root is hidden from view, leaving only the blade of grass visible. Originally made of a long cardboard prism with squared base, it is now

---

[6] Arduino is an open hardware platform http://arduino.cc, one board controls one blade of grass, but with some optimization, the number of blades can be incremented.

substituted with a more practical wood splint. The base measures 20 centimeters in height, to allow enough contraction space for the muscle wire. The wires contract longitudinally about 4% of their total length. Attached to the main structure is a spring that holds a square that serves as the platform on which the blades of grass are attached. At the end of each edge of the top, a nitinol muscle wire is attached. The other end of the wire is connected to the lowest part of the main structure. The wires were originally kept in tension by a spring, but this created a balancing problem. The latest version has a soft silicon mold for enhanced stability.

The blade of grass will be affixed to the top part of the root, and will be made out of a flexible material so that when the base moves, the blade of grass gently sways.

The reaction time of the actuator is relatively fast, taking about half a second to contract. Here we refer to the complete contraction time, from resting position to the end of the animation. In order to avoid a "switch-click" effect (sudden movement from initial position to the final), we slowed down the reaction to a more "organic" contraction speed of around one second. Combined with a relaxation time of around one-and-a-half seconds[7], the animation of a waving piece of grass is nearly symmetrical.

6   Conclusion and Future Works

Our aim in this paper was to describe the ongoing work in building an interactive physical pervasive display, that can be used for indoor way-finding, ambient persuasive guidance, as well as for entertainment. Following the visions of ubiquitous computing and tangible interfaces, the Follow the Grass concept offers an engaging way for users to interact with their environment. As it has been demonstrated in [23] and [8] it is possible to change the behavior of people by giving peripheral visual cues. Follow the Grass has the potential to have the same effect. Furthermore, the tracking system enables the interface to react dynamically to the users' presence, making it possible to give the correct information at the right time to the correct individual. This creates a more personalized experience for the user. The capability of the artificial grass to display animations adds to the expressiveness of the interface, and creates opportunities to engage and entertain the user.

The design of the actuated root is still ongoing. We are working to improve on a number of issues, including the precision of the addressed direction, as well as more secure and unobtrusive attachment of the nitinol muscle wires to the base. Once we have a sufficiently robust version of the actuated root we aim to realize the 'patch' scenario consisting of a grid of 3x3 blades of grass. Future developments for the actuated root could include installing a tilt sensor on top which would reduce the number of nitinol wires required, from four to three. The sensor would enable measurement of the angle of the platform to which the blade of grass is attached, allowing fine adjustments to be made using only

---

[7] This amount of time is required for relaxing without forcing the wire.

three muscle wires. The next step would be to make a serializable version of the root for creating a larger field of artificial grass. Miniaturizing the electronic components and constructing a dedicated controller module, would make the system more suitable for modular deployment. The tracking software will have to be improved and optimized for larger scale interactions (e.g. big rooms and halls). We are in contact for a possible future version of "Lawn" in a museum.

Acknowledgements. This publication was supported by the Dutch national program COMMIT and a CTIT-ITC collaboration project.

References

1. Boehm, G.: Ambient persuasive guidance. In: Proc. of the 5th International Conference on Tangible, Embedded, and Embodied Interaction, TEI 2011, pp. 431–432. ACM, New York (2011)
2. Brownell, K., Stunkard, A., Albaum, J.: Evaluation and modification of exercise patterns in the natural environment. American Journal of Psychiatry (1980)
3. Coelho, M., Ishii, H., Maes, P.: Surflex: a programmable surface for the design of tangible interfaces. In: CHI 2008 Ext. Abstracts on Human Factors in Computing Systems, CHI EA 2008, pp. 3429–3434. ACM, New York (2008)
4. Coelho, M., Maes, P.: Sprout I/O: a texturally rich interface. In: Proc. of the 2nd International Conference on Tangible and Embedded Interaction, TEI 2008, pp. 221–222. ACM, New York (2008)
5. Coelho, M., Maes, P.: Shutters: a permeable surface for environmental control and communication. In: Proc. of the 3rd International Conference on Tangible and Embedded Interaction, TEI 2009, pp. 13–18. ACM, New York (2009)
6. Coelho, M., Zigelbaum, J.: Shape-changing interfaces. Personal Ubiquitous Computing 15, 161–173 (2011)
7. Fitzmaurice, G.W., Ishii, H., Buxton, W.A.S.: Bricks: laying the foundations for graspable user interfaces. In: Proc. of the SIGCHI Conference on Human Factors in Computing Systems, CHI 1995, pp. 442–449. ACM Press/Addison-Wesley Publishing Co., New York (1995)
8. Furukawa, M., Yoshikawa, H., Hachisu, T., Fukushima, S., Kajimoto, H.: "Vection field" for pedestrian traffic control. In: Proc. of the 2nd Augmented Human International Conference, AH 2011, pp. 19:1–19:8. ACM, NY (2011)
9. Heiner, J.M., Hudson, S.E., Tanaka, K.: The information percolator: ambient information display in a decorative object. In: Proc. of the 12th Annual ACM Symposium on User Interface Software and Technology, UIST 1999, pp. 141–148. ACM, New York (1999)
10. Ishii, H., Lakatos, D., Bonanni, L., Labrune, J.B.: Radical atoms: beyond tangible bits, toward transformable materials. Interactions 19(1), 38–51 (2012)
11. Ishii, H., Ullmer, B.: Tangible bits: towards seamless interfaces between people, bits and atoms. In: Proc. of the SIGCHI Conference on Human Factors in Computing Systems, CHI 1997, pp. 234–241. ACM, New York (1997)
12. Ishii, H., Wisneski, C., Brave, S., Dahley, A., Gorbet, M., Ullmer, B., Yarin, P.: ambientroom: integrating ambient media with architectural space. In: CHI 1998 Conference Summary on Human Factors in Computing Systems, CHI 1998, pp. 173–174. ACM, New York (1998)

13. Jacob, R.J., Girouard, A., Hirshfield, L.M., Horn, M.S., Shaer, O., Solovey, E.T., Zigelbaum, J.: Reality-based interaction: a framework for post-wimp interfaces. In: Proc. of the 26th Annual SIGCHI Conference on Human Factors in Computing Systems, CHI 2008, pp. 201–210. ACM, New York (2008)
14. Jafarinaimi, N., Forlizzi, J., Hurst, A., Zimmerman, J.: Breakaway: an ambient display designed to change human behavior. In: CHI 2005 Ext. Abs. on Human Factors in Computing Systems, CHI EA 2005, pp. 1945–1948. ACM, New York (2005)
15. Jung, H., Altieri, Y.L., Bardzell, J.: Skin: designing aesthetic interactive surfaces. In: Proc. of the Fourth Conf. on Tangible, Embedded, and Embodied Interaction, TEI 2010, pp. 85–92. ACM, New York (2010)
16. Kaptein, M., Markopoulos, P., de Ruyter, B., Aarts, E.: Persuasion in ambient intelligence. Journal of Ambient Intelligence and Humanized Computing 1, 43–56 (2010), doi:10.1007/s12652-009-0005-3
17. Masson, N., Mackay, W.E.: WeMe: Seamless Active and Passive Liquid Communication. In: Jacko, J.A. (ed.) HCI International 2009, Part II. LNCS, vol. 5611, pp. 694–700. Springer, Heidelberg (2009)
18. Minuto, A., Vyas, D., Poelman, W., Nijholt, A.: Smart material interfaces: A vision. In: Proc. 4th International ICST Conference on Intelligent Technologies for Interactive Entertainment (INTETAIN 2011). LNICST, vol. 78, pp. 57–62. Springer (2011)
19. Parkes, A., Ishii, H.: Bosu: a physical programmable design tool for transformability with soft mechanics. In: Proc. of the 8th ACM Conference on Designing Interactive Systems, DIS 2010, pp. 189–198. ACM, New York (2010)
20. Poupyrev, I., Nashida, T., Maruyama, S., Rekimoto, J., Yamaji, Y.: Lumen: interactive visual and shape display for calm computing. In: ACM SIGGRAPH 2004 Emerging technologies. SIGGRAPH 2004, p. 17. ACM, New York (2004)
21. Prante, T., Stenzel, R., Röcker, C., Streitz, N., Magerkurth, C.: Ambient agoras: Inforiver, siam, hello.wall. In: CHI 2004 Ext. Abstracts on Human Factors in Computing Systems, CHI EA 2004, pp. 763–764. ACM, New York (2004)
22. Raffle, H., Joachim, M.W., Tichenor, J.: Super cilia skin: An interactive membrane. Human Factors, 808–809 (2003)
23. Rogers, Y., Hazlewood, W.R., Marshall, P., Dalton, N., Hertrich, S.: Ambient influence: can twinkly lights lure and abstract representations trigger behavioral change? In: Proc. of the 12th ACM International Conference on Ubiquitous Computing, Ubicomp 2010, pp. 261–270. ACM, New York (2010)
24. Vande Moere, A.: Beyond the tyranny of the pixel: Exploring the physicality of information visualization. In: 12th International Conference on Information Visualisation, IV 2008, pp. 469–474 (July 2008)
25. Wakita, A., Shibutani, M., Tsuji, K.: Emotional Smart Materials. In: Jacko, J.A. (ed.) HCI International 2009, Part III. LNCS, vol. 5612, pp. 802–805. Springer, Heidelberg (2009)
26. Weiser, M.: The computer for the 21st century. Scientific American, 94–104 (1991)
27. Wisneski, C., Ishii, H., Dahley, A., Gorbet, M., Brave, S., Ullmer, B., Yarin, P.: Ambient Displays: Turning Architectural Space into an Interface between People and Digital Information. In: Yuan, F., Konomi, S., Burkhardt, H.-J. (eds.) CoBuild 1998. LNCS, vol. 1370, pp. 22–32. Springer, Heidelberg (1998)

The ICOCOON Virtual Meeting Room: A Virtual Environment as a Support Tool for Multipoint Teleconference Systems

Aljosha Demeulemeester[1], Katriina Kilpi[2], Shirley A. Elprama[2],
Sammy Lievens[3], Charles-Frederik Hollemeersch[1], An Jacobs[2],
Peter Lambert[1], and Rik Van de Walle[1]

[1] Ghent University - IBBT,
Department of Electronics and Information Systems, Multimedia Lab,
Gaston Crommenlaan 8 bus 201, B-9050 Ledeberg-Ghent, Belgium
[2] IBBT-SMIT, Vrije Universiteit Brussel, Pleinlaan 9, B-1050 Brussels, Belgium
[3] Alcatel-Lucent Bell Labs, Copernicuslaan 50, B-2018 Antwerpen, Belgium

Abstract. Globalization and increasing collaboration between remote teams drive the need for teleconference systems. However, currently no videoconferencing system matches the face-to-face experience for a business meeting with many participants in a flexible and affordable manner. In search for a better solution, we created a Virtual Meeting Room (VMR) application that visualizes key events detected using computer vision (e.g., participant entering the meeting room, talking, presenting) in a 3D virtual environment. The goal was to provide a good sense of overview to users when many meeting participants - represented by 3D avatars - from remote locations join a teleconference. In this paper, a technical overview of the working prototype - built using 3D game technology - is presented. Also, feedback from multiple user tests performed during the development of the prototype is discussed and presented as a set of recommendations. From the technical perspective, we found that existing 3D game technology is mature, affordable and contains the features needed to build the VMR application. From the users' and experts' feedback, we conclude that the VMR has merits as a teleconferencing support tool accompanying a video stream that conveys more detailed non-verbal communication of the active speaker.

1 Introduction

Teleconferencing systems are omnipresent in modern business environments. They range from basic phone conferencing systems, which allow many persons to join a phone conversation, to more elaborate setups using high-definition video streams displayed on large screens. Teleconferencing allows remote teams to collaborate without loss of time in traveling, which leads to cost and energy savings [1]. However, current-generation systems are lacking as users still report the need for face-to-face meetings, particularly when many participants are involved. Some of the central complaints about the current teleconferencing tools, on top

M. Herrlich, R. Malaka, and M. Masuch (Eds.): ICEC 2012, LNCS 7522, pp. 158–171, 2012.
© IFIP International Federation for Information Processing 2012

of the complicated setups, are the lack of a clear overview of the entire meeting situation and the lack of the co-presence experience due to the way in which the audiovisual data is presented. The multidisciplinary ICOCOON project[1] aimed to tackle these issues by extracting knowledge by means of computer vision from audiovisual streams captured by a visual sensor network from multiple locations involved in a teleconference. This knowledge is then used to automatically select the most relevant video stream (e.g., someone presenting or asking a question) among all video streams from all locations to present to the user. Additionally, the project investigated the possibility of visualizing the captured knowledge in a virtual environment (VE)[2] resulting in our *Virtual Meeting Room (VMR)* application, which is the focus of this paper. Our approach aimed to visualize the high-level interpretation of captured knowledge in the context of a business meeting (see Section 3). The main goal of the VMR is to provide the same sense of overview (and more) one has during a conventional face-to-face meeting where all parties are present in the same location. The basic premise was that this could be valuable, especially in business meetings with many participants where only one participant is shown in a video feed to remote participants. Using a virtual environment, 3D humanoid avatars can convey actions of meeting participants in a way that can be interpreted intuitively by a user. Also, this approach offers a lot of flexibility on the way knowledge is visualized. This allows for an abstract representation of what is happening in the real world which facilitates the feeling of overview.

In this paper, we present a technical overview of our working teleconferencing prototype. Additionally, we present recommendations on the use of the VMR and the way knowledge should be visualized. The recommendations are derived from user evaluations and expert reviews, performed at different stages in the development of the prototype. The paper is structured as follows. After the overview of related work in Section 2, Section 3 discusses the semantics of captured knowledge and its representation in the VE. In Section 4, a high-level technical overview of the complete system is given. Section 5 describes the visualization module that renders and animates the virtual environment and the 3D avatars that represent the meeting participants. Section 6 describes the user research methods used and the set up of the proxy meeting technology. In Section 7, we formulate recommendations based on the feedback of the users and experts which we discuss further in Section 8.

2   Related Work

The next generation of teleconferencing goes beyond merely displaying a captured video stream of one or multiple meeting participants. The immersive 3D videoconferencing system of Kauff and Schreer [3] uses a shared virtual table environment. Participant video streams are modified using image-based rendering

---

[1] Immersive COmmunication by means of COmputer visiON [2].

[2] Bringing in physical elements into a predominantly virtual space is sometimes referred to as Augmented Virtuality.

to enable natural representation of gestures, eye contact and gaze. As a downside, the amount of participants is limited and they require a specialized setup for the purpose of teleconferencing.

Teleconferencing using a large amount of participants has been explored by IBM [1] using Second Life (SL), the massively multi-user online game-like 3D virtual world for social interaction. Users in SL are represented by a customizable 3D avatar in the virtual world and can interact with each other through spatial voice chat, text chat and avatar animation. The avatar is explicitly controlled by the user. The authors report positive feedback from the participants of a conference held using SL with over 200 participants. Kantonen et al. [4] enabled two types of participant: the first (virtual) participant uses a SL viewer and explicitly controls his avatar in the VE, the second uses augmented reality to visualize virtual participants in the physical meeting room. Hand tracking is performed to allow interaction with the augmented virtual world and to allow gesturing with their avatar. Regenbrecht et al. [5] present an augmented virtuality system for teleconferencing with video streams of participants being visualized inside the VE. Recent work by Lou et al. [6] focuses on informal communication in work settings. Their system called PresenceScape provides an immersive and interactive virtual office environment for the informal communication in the office space.

Using 3D avatars for communication has been extensively studied, both from the technical point of view as from the user perspective. A self-animated avatar in an augmented virtuality setup directly reflects the movement of a human in the real world. This allows using gestures and body language to convey a message [7]. The appearance (i.e., surface texture and geometry) of the avatar is usually predefined and the animation is done by manipulating the virtual bones of the character. A real-time motion capture system can track the position of all human limbs. However, to decrease the required network bandwidth, and to increase the amount of expressiveness in the avatar visualization, Arita et al. [8] symbolizes the raw motion capture data using knowledge on the communication context (e.g., teleconferencing, tele-teaching). The captured symbols, which represent intentions of communication, are sent over the network and transformed into high resolution motion data suitable to animate different avatars. This is comparable to our approach of detecting meeting participant actions that are relevant, sending this knowledge to all visualization clients and visualizing this in the most appropriate way in the VE. However, our system currently does not use detailed human motion capturing. This technology is not mature enough to capture human limb movement of many participants in one room full of obstructions (e.g., chairs, tables) without imposing many restrictions. Detailed non-verbal communication of participants is conveyed through the video stream that accompanies the VMR. As an alternative to motion capturing, the surface geometry of humans can be continuously captured using real-time 3D reconstruction from video streams [9]. These geometry sequences are implicitly animated and can be directly visualized in a VE. However, due to the lack of a control structure such as an animation skeleton, the geometry cannot easily be modified automatically to adapt the participant's virtual representation to the VE and other avatars (e.g., pointing or looking in the right direction). Also, 3D reconstruction requires more network bandwidth than streaming (symbolized) motion data.

While little research has focused on avatars in formal settings, Inkpen and Sedlin [10] investigated the use of 2D avatars for workplace videoconferencing. Their findings suggest that users are concerned how they are represented as avatars, but not about the representation of the ones they interact with. Focusing more on showing behavior than the design of avatars, Reidsma et al. [11] developed a virtual meeting room that can translate observations (such as gestures and gaze) from audio and video to animations in an avatar based virtual meeting room.

3   Meeting Observations in the VMR

A typical teleconference has participants from two or more locations. To enhance the feeling of co-presence, the avatars are represented in a single virtual (meeting) room which is the background for the visualization of captured knowledge. Similar to Reidsma et al. [11], we recognize that the observed knowledge from the physical world can be interpreted on progressively more complicated levels. For example, the exact position of the hand of a user can be detected. Depending on the position, this can be interpreted as hands being held up, which in itself can be interpreted as voting behavior or asking to speak. What we define as a *meeting observation* in our system are the high-level interpretations of the observed knowledge. These need to be visualized in the most recognizable way. Thus, the avatars in the VMR (see Figure 1) do not necessarily reflect participant actions directly. For example, the exact position of a meeting participant is not relevant so the result of the people tracking (see Section 4) does not need to be visualized exactly. Incidentally, it is not straightforward to map coordinates of multiple locations into one virtual location. However, proximity to certain objects (e.g., presenting board, other participant, etc.) is meaningful and is thus categorized as meeting observation. Using 3D humanoid avatars is an intuitive presentation form of meeting observations as opposed to text. This has the additional advantage that, when no high level interpretation of the collected knowledge can be made, the knowledge can be visualized directly to be interpreted by the user. For our earlier hand tracking example, this means that the avatar's hand position directly reflects the participant's hand position while leaving the user to decide on the meaning of the hand gesture.

In a teleconference scenario, knowing who is present is essential. This has to be interpreted as being part of the meeting in some way. Derived from presence are a number of meeting observations that we identified: participant enters the meeting, participant leaves the meeting temporarily (e.g., to restroom), participant exits the meeting permanently, participant re-enters after temporary leaving and participant joins unexpectedly. Additionally, it is visualized which participant is speaking, who is presenting and where each participant is looking

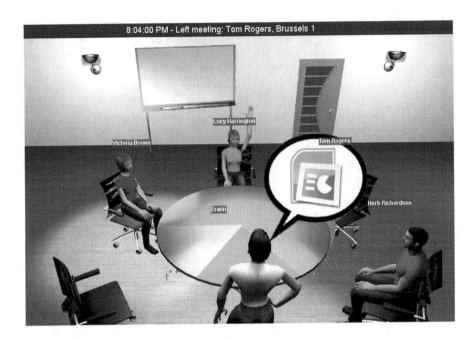

Fig. 1. The VMR application showing participant Erwin as presenting using a speech bubble with powerpoint logo; participant Victoria as speaking using a spotlight; participant Lucy with raised hand

(e.g., is s/he paying attention). As a form of metadata about the physical world, detailed information of each participant (e.g., name, company, meeting role, etc.) is also shown in the VE.

4   Overview of the Teleconference System

The entire system can be subdivided in three main parts. First, information about each location is captured using a visual sensor network comprising of multiple spatially distributed cameras per location (smart rooms). This information is processed by a multitude of computer vision algorithms to attain knowledge about each location. The high-level vision algorithms each monitor a single property of one or multiple objects at a location (e.g., position of participants, are hands up/down, etc.) with high accuracy. The gathered knowledge is sent over the network to the central aggregator using JSON formatted messages. Second, the aggregator enriches and corrects the received knowledge and sends the consistent knowledge to the last subsystem, namely the visualization component (i.e., the VMR application). The latter consists of the visualization server and a visualization client per participant. The server is responsible for adapting the virtual world state to reflect what is happening in the physical world based on the received knowledge. Also, it distributes the virtual world

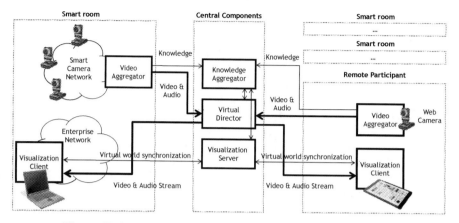

Fig. 2. High-level overview of the VMR teleconferencing system

state to the visualization clients that each render their own unique view on the virtual world.

The architecture of the overall detection system consists of multiple smart rooms and the network infrastructure (see Figure 2). Each installed smart room comprises a calibrated smart camera network and one video aggregator. The smart cameras capture, resize, compress and send the video streams towards the video aggregator. The video aggregator extracts knowledge out of the captured video streams and sends this to the knowledge aggregator located in the network. In our smart room prototype, four overview cameras are mounted high and have a full view of the meeting room while three front-view cameras are mounted at eye height for capturing an optimal frontal view. Current extracted knowledge per location consists of a person's position and identification, gaze direction and activity status (e.g., sitting, walking, presenting, hands up/down). Four computer vision algorithms are used: face recognition by use of parabolic edge maps [12], people tracking [13], gaze detection [14] and hand detection and tracking. In our prototype, knowledge on people's position is used for extracting the behavior (e.g., entering, sitting, presenting) of the persons involved, based on the location of the person in the physical world (e.g., at the presenter board), the walking direction and speed and the size of each person. The people tracking module is also tightly coupled with the face recognition module that processes all people entering the meeting room and sitting at the table so that each moment in time the correct activity can be linked to the correct person. The person's gaze is extracted using a combination of face recognition and the upper-body detector module. In addition to the smart rooms, participants can also join from other locations. In this case, only the web cam of their personal computing device is used with a video aggregator running locally on that device (see Figure 2). The only difference for this kind of participant is that the types of meeting observation that can be made are reduced.

5   The VMR Visualization Client

In business meetings, it is common for participants to bring their own computing device (e.g., laptop, tablet, etc.). The VMR client is intended to run on these devices. This approach eliminates the need for dedicated hardware. Also, this allows participants to observe the meeting using the VMR even if they are not in one of the smart rooms. Therefore, the VMR client should run on the widest possible array of devices and require the minimum amount of memory and computing power possible. Because each client renders its own view on the virtual world, real-time 3D rendering, accelerated by common graphics hardware, is the preferred option to visualize the VE. As many avatars can be present in the VE, the avatar animation system should be highly optimized for speed. From these requirements, it was clear that modern 3D game middleware technology (i.e., game engine) is a good fit as it enables state-of-the art simulation and rendering while staying within the limits of commodity hardware. The Second Life system also offers many features relevant for our application but was not chosen because it is less flexible.

To manage and visualize the VE, the Unity 3D game engine[3] was selected as the foundation of the VMR application because of its range of features, its ease of use and its limited cost. The features critical to our application are a rendering engine for 3D graphics, scripting of object behavior and appearance, data driven animation and networking support. Equally important, Unity 3D deploys on most platforms, including iOS or Android mobile devices. The in-game Unity Editor enables the placement and configuration of objects in the virtual world. C# scripts are used to animate rigid objects. Unity 3D can load most popular mesh and animations formats and provides a system to play, blend, and cross-fade prerecorded (avatar) animation clips. No free open source engines were found that provide this combination of features. However, advanced path planning and Inverse Kinematics (IK) support is currently not present. The latter is used for automatically calculating joint rotations when directly animating hand and foot positions of a human avatar. Our VMR application requires only basic path planning and IK so this was not seen as a problem. Custom IK can be performed by overwriting the output of the Unity animation system for parts of the bone hierarchy.

To animate the VE and specifically the avatars, a set of controllers were designed that each modifies a (limited) set of virtual object properties. The navigation controller uses a graph based search algorithm to guide an avatar to an object or place (e.g., presenting board, chair) in the VE without collisions with other virtual objects. The animation controller manages a set of artist created animation clips. The clips are scheduled and cross-faded depending on the current desired end state (e.g., sitting, walking). The animation system needs at least one animation clip for each of the (currently six) states. All the avatars used have the same bone structure, avoiding the need for animation retargeting. Currently, avatar customization is limited to dynamically setting surface

---

[3] Unity 3D: http://unity3d.com

properties (e.g., shirt color) or replacing the avatar's head. Render assets (i.e., geometry and textures, e.g., head scans) are loaded from a web server when needed. The procedural animation controllers use IK to directly control the head gaze and the avatar's hands. New controllers are easily added to the system. To ensure a consistent virtual world state, the visualization server calls the controllers running on the visualization clients. This uses less bandwidth than frequently sending the result of the controllers to the clients. Also, this allows for more customization of the visualizations at the client by the participant.

6   User Evaluation of the VMR

To improve and to evaluate our design of the next generation teleconferencing tool we used a multimethod approach. For this we introduced the Virtual Meeting Room to both users and experts with experience in teleconferencing. We conducted six group interviews with users after showing a video demonstration of the proposed system. Secondly, we conducted two expert reviews using heuristic evaluation with a working prototype of the system. Due to time limitations of the project, an evaluation of the prototype with users was not possible. This section describes our findings.

6.1   Video Demonstration and Group Interviews

The goal of the demonstration was to provide the users with the possibility to experience a close-to-realistic next generation teleconferencing system and create the feeling of immersion (see Figure 3). The demonstration was followed by group interviews. The setup of the meeting consisted of a table in a meeting room around which the users and two researchers (one leading the discussion, the other one observing) were sitting. The demonstration consisted of three screens: the first screen showing the video stream presenting the remote participants in the meeting (a video clip shot and edited beforehand), with next to it the VMR application demo film. In addition, one meeting participant (played by someone on the video stream) presented slides shown on a third screen. To create a connection between the participants in the VMR and the ones on the mocked up video stream, one of the researchers had a speaking role (i.e., asking a question). The videoconferencing system was reviewed by using variations of VMR visualizations as a starting point for discussion. The six group interviews had 3 - 5 participants each (mean group size = 3.8), which resulted in a total of 23 participants. The users' ages ranged between 22 and 50 years old (average = 33 years). The users came from different organizations and had different professional backgrounds such as a researcher, a manager and a historian. All users except for two had experience with both teleconferences and videoconferences. About 44% (n = 10) of the users had experience with virtual world applications.

Fig. 3. Left: Setup during group interviews with three screens: video stream, VMR and presentation slides. Right: Setup during expert reviews: the VMR, the video stream from remote locations and a feedback image of themselves.

6.2 Expert Reviews with Working Prototype

The prototype was reviewed by having a videoconferencing meeting between two locations (see Figure 3). The experts, each with a laptop, sat around a table. Each laptop displayed the VMR, a live video stream of the remote location and a feedback image of their own location. Both expert reviews were conducted with 3 - 4 people who all had a background in user experience, two of them especially in virtual world applications.

7   Results and Recommendations

After the group interviews on the mocked up technology, recommendations were formulated and applied to the prototype. The experts thus evaluated a system that had fundamentally been shaped by the user feedback from the group interviews. Similarly, after the expert reviews, the prototype was adjusted based on the findings of the experts. Although the mockup provided users with too much information, the expert reviews with the working prototype showed that this was no longer the case. This was most likely due to the reduction from three to two screens. Rather, the experts found the VMR to be a useful awareness tool during big meetings (i.e., more than 5 persons) where maintaining a good overview of the situation is harder. For instance, the VMR can provide support by showing what is going on in the real meeting room (e.g. who is speaking at the moment). Also, it gives a useful overview of who is present in the meeting, a feature, which was suspected to become more useful in bigger meetings with more remote participants. However, the findings suggest that the VMR might be of little use in a small videoconferencing meeting where a video stream covers all participants at once. Other changes after the user reviews include the implementation of a feedback image and the possibility to use a working interactive system (as opposed to the static mockup). In addition, the animations in the VMR that the users preferred were used during the expert reviews. In the next paragraphs, we list the recommendations pertaining to the VMR and highlight each recommendation with examples from our research.

VMR Should Provide an Overview. Users and experts viewed the VMR application as an awareness tool that supports the users' knowledge on who is present in the room. Especially in a meeting with many locations and participants, users reported difficulties in keeping track of people's activities as they move in and out of the room. In addition, getting back on track after a moment of distraction was also viewed as being hard. Visualizations on presence status and meeting observations could support the user in having a more efficient meeting experience.

Design for Immersion, Though It Is not Always Needed. The experts reported feeling immersed when using the prototype because of the interactivity between participants across rooms that the video stream facilitated. This had mostly to do with the video stream. However, depending on various aspects of the meeting such as relevance, commitment and interest, the users argued that immersion is not always needed. According to our users, it is common practice that when a user is not expected to actively contribute to a meeting, this passive follower might choose to multitask during the meeting. Although multitasking can be detrimental to some aspects of meetings, it is not always negative and can even positively impact meeting effectiveness and efficiency (cf. Lyons, Kim and Nevo [15]). The VMR can help the multitasking participant to get back on track.

Provide Background Information about Users. In teleconferencing meetings, especially with unknown participants, people sometimes miss someone's name, job title or other relevant information. Stemming from this need, the users suggested displaying basic useful information (i.e., name, job title and company) about other meeting participants. We chose to display a person's name close to each avatar, and allow the retrieval of additional information in a pop up when hovering over a specific avatar with the mouse cursor (see Figure 4).

Visualization Should Be Instantly Clear and Leave No Room for Misinterpretation. To allow the participant to focus on the meeting itself, all functionalities of the VMR should be instantly clear. Although some users found the size of the pie chart (see Figure 4) intimidating, most users appreciated the pie chart because it provided an overview of the location each participant belongs to. However, the functionality of the prototype, in which one could request additional information about avatars was not clear enough for the experts. Therefore, we suggest using visual cues (for instance a button) to make the functionality more explicit.

Visualizations Should Not Distract. The users found the moving and the blinking of the animations distracting. Some users however pointed out that in certain situations a blinking animation could help to draw the attention of the participant who is otherwise preoccupied. To achieve a balance, we decided to show animations at certain events, such as the event of entering by showing a walking avatar. Some users considered this animation interesting to watch when participants were waiting for the meeting to start. However, when a participant joined a meeting at a later point in time, this animation had to be subtle and non-distracting, which was visualized by the avatar instantly appearing into an empty chair.

Allow Users a Degree of Control. The users indicated that they should be given more control over the information presented in the VMR. For instance, some users argued that some information should be made optional, since it is not always needed. By giving users the possibility to customize which types of information they want to view, their feeling of control is increased. Users should also be allowed to control the appearance of the avatar representing them. While some users reported being satisfied with the minimum adjustments of the default avatar (i.e., avatar's shirt color matches shirt of meeting participant), others wanted more control over the avatar's looks to feel comfortable with their representations. Therefore, allowing customization of avatars based on user needs is recommended.

Connect with Reality. To help users understand the VMR and to enhance immersion, observations visualized in the VMR should correspond to reality. This means that any gesturing or actions tied to a direction should translate realistically to the VMR. For example, when a person A is facing person B, the two avatars should also face each other in a similar way. In addition, the seating arrangements of the avatars should correspond to the same sitting order of the participants in same physical locations. During the group interviews, the importance of this connection was not a central topic to be investigated. At the expert reviews, however, this lack of connection turned out to be of importance, when dealing with own feedback image, on the VMR and on the video stream.

8   Discussion

The VMR was primarily viewed by both users and experts as a possible support tool for bigger meetings with multiple locations and more than six participants. For instance, the VMR can be used to convey information about any meeting participant, but also to provide an overview of the other locations. In addition, the VMR can offer a viable solution in situations where video stream is not possible to certain parties of the meeting (e.g. due to low bandwidth).

We have contributed by exploring the kinds of support people would benefit from in meetings held in VMRs, as proposed by Hasler, Buecheler and Pfeifer [16]. Although experts reported feeling immersed, they, like the users, found that

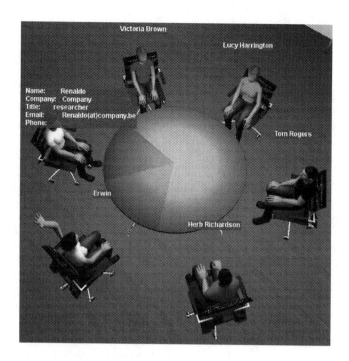

Fig. 4. Top down view in the VMR showing the pie chart table overlay that indicates the location of each participant. Also, the user information of Renaldo is shown.

full immersion is not always needed (cf. Bowman and McMahan [17]), depending on the type of meeting. The design of a VMR should be clear and not contain elements that are distracting to the meeting participants. Also, the information presented in the VMR should be coherent with reality. Finally, we recommend to allow users more control, both regarding the amount of information presented and the customization of avatars.

Moreover, we recommend using a proxy technology tool to allow users the possibility to simulate the future technology. Although only a simulation, the proxy works as a starting point for discussion. It also allows the user researchers to contribute to the development of the technology with user insights, while the developers can continue working on the VMR. Through the iterative process, the prototype could be adapted incrementally, leaving enough time for the changes to be made and allowing the implemented recommendations to be investigated.

Because the prototype of the VMR used for the expert reviews only allowed testing with small meetings (e.g. up to five people), our findings are limited to smaller meetings. Future research could include testing the prototype with a larger group of people in more than one remote locations. This would allow us to investigate whether the usefulness of the VMR increases with more people as we hypothesize. Also, since meeting dynamics might differ in large meetings, the amount or type of information needed could change. For instance, we could investigate the added value of providing additional information, such as the agenda points still to be covered.

Another important aspect of the ICOCOON system is immersion. Even though some research participants reported that it is not always necessary to be immersed during meetings, it would be interesting to study how different camera views and perspectives, specifically first person view, would affect the level of immersion. Further research should be conducted to investigate these research questions.

9   Conclusion

Game technology provides a good foundation for an experimental VMR application. Our choice of game engine was a good fit for prototyping, incremental design and implementation. Unity 3D strikes a good balance between ease of use and the amount and the complexity of the provided features, which results in a limited amount of software development knowledge needed. From our discussions with users and experts, we conclude that our VMR approach has merits as a teleconferencing support tool without the need for an immersive experience. We strongly feel that the benefit of the VMR rises with increasing amount of participants and locations. However, we could not confirm this due to the limited amount of test users in one session. Essential to our application are avatars that are immediately recognizable as their corresponding participant. Our future research focuses on pre-meeting scanned, photo-realistic avatars. In our current prototype, most non-verbal communication is conveyed through the video stream because our users stressed the fact the redundant information is confusing. Additional research could identify how much of the physical world needs to be brought into the virtual world to make the video redundant. This would change the VMR from a support tool to a communication tool.

Acknowledgements. We would like to thank the following people for their contribution: Erwin Six, Kris Naessens, Donny Tytgat, Vinay Namboodiri, Maarten Aerts, Lizzy Bleumers, Koen Willaert, Bram Lievens, Ralf De Wolf and Chris Poppe. Also, we thank the interviewed participants. The research activities in this paper have been performed in the context of the ICOCOON project[2] and were funded by Ghent University, the Interdisciplinary Institute for Broadband Technology (IBBT), the Institute for the Promotion of Innovation by Science and Technology in Flanders (IWT), the Fund for Scientic Research-Flanders (FWOFlanders), the Belgian Federal Science Policy Office (BFSPO), and the European Union.

References

1. Linden Lab: How Meeting In Second Life Transformed IBM's Technolgy Elite Into Virtual World Believers. Technical report (2009)

2. ICOCOON (2010), http://www.ibbt.be/en/projects/overview-projects/p/detail/icocoon-2, IBBT

3. Kauff, P., Schreer, O.: An immersive 3D video-conferencing system using shared virtual team user environments. In: Proceedings of the 4th International Conference on Collaborative Virtual Environments, CVE 2002, pp. 105–112. ACM, New York (2002)

4. Kantonen, T., Woodward, C., Katz, N.: Mixed reality in virtual world teleconferencing. In: 2010 IEEE Virtual Reality Conference (VR), pp. 179–182 (March 2010)

5. Regenbrecht, H., Ott, C., Wagner, M., Lum, T., Kohler, P., Wilke, W., Mueller, E.: An augmented virtuality approach to 3D videoconferencing. In: Proceedings of the Second IEEE and ACM International Symposium on Mixed and Augmented Reality, pp. 290–291 (October 2003)

6. Lou, Z., Bouwen, J., Willaert, K., Van Broeck, S., Van den Broeck, M., Zubic, S., Van Raemdonck, W., Van Herreweghe, H., Dams, D.: PresenceScape: Virtual World Mediated Rich Communication. Bell Labs Technical Journal 16(4), 219–242 (2012)

7. Dodds, T.J., Mohler, B.J., Bülthoff, H.H.: Talk to the Virtual Hands: Self-Animated Avatars Improve Communication in Head-Mounted Display Virtual Environments. PLoS ONE 6(10), e25759 (2011)

8. Arita, D., Taniguchi, R.: Real-time Human Proxy: An Avatar-based Communication System. J. UCS 13(2), 161–176 (2007)

9. Lien, J.-M., Bajcsy, R.: Skeleton-Based Compression of 3-D Tele-Immersion Data. In: First ACM/IEEE International Conference on Distributed Smart Cameras, ICDSC 2007, pp. 347–354 (September 2007)

10. Inkpen, K.M., Sedlins, M.: Me and my avatar: exploring users' comfort with avatars for workplace communication. In: Proceedings of the ACM 2011 Conference on Computer Supported Cooperative Work, CSCW 2011, pp. 383–386. ACM, New York (2011)

11. Reidsma, D., op den Akker, R., Rienks, R., Poppe, R., Nijholt, A., Heylen, D., Zwiers, J.: Virtual meeting rooms: from observation to simulation. AI Soc 22(2), 133–144 (2007)

12. Deboeverie, F., Veelaert, P., Philips, W.: Face Analysis Using Curve Edge Maps. In: Maino, G., Foresti, G.L. (eds.) ICIAP 2011, Part II. LNCS, vol. 6979, pp. 109–118. Springer, Heidelberg (2011)

13. Grünwedel, S., Jelaca, V., Niño Castañeda, J., Hese, P.V., Cauwelaert, D.V., Veelaert, P., Philips, W.: Decentralized tracking of humans using a camera network. In: Roning, J., Casasent, D.P. (eds.) The International Society for Optical Engineering. Proceedings of SPIE, vol. 8301, p. 9. SPIE (2012)

14. Marin-Jimenez, M., Zisserman, A., Ferrari, V.: Here's looking at you, kid. detecting people looking at each other in videos. In: British Machine Vision Conference (2011)

15. Lyons, K., Kim, H., Nevo, S.: Paying Attention in Meetings: Multitasking in Virtual Worlds. In: First Symposium on the Personal Web, Co-located with CASCON, vol. (2005), p. 7 (2010)

16. Hasler, B.S., Buecheler, T., Pfeifer, R.: Collaborative Work in 3D Virtual Environments: A Research Agenda and Operational Framework. In: HCI, vol. 12, pp. 23–32 (2009)

17. Bowman, D.A., McMahan, R.P.: Virtual Reality: How Much Immersion Is Enough? Computer 40(7), 36–43 (2007)

Playing with the Weather

Sofia Reis and Nuno Correia

CITI, DI, Faculdade de Ciências e Tecnologia, Universidade Nova de Lisboa
2829-516 Caparica, Portugal
se.reis@campus.fct.unl.pt, nmc@di.fct.unl.pt

Abstract. In this paper the contribution of real time weather data to player enjoyment was tested and evaluated. To gauge the contribution of weather to player engagement an adaptronic, multiplayer, location based game, where real time weather data is key to the gameplay, was created. In this game the player assumes the role of a wizard and confronts other players in duels where the current weather plays a decisive role. A survey was conducted and results indicated that the weather contributed positively to the enjoyment of players and to their feeling of a connection between the real world and the game.

Keywords: game, casual game, pervasive game, weather, adaptronic games, multiplayer games, location based.

1 Introduction

According to Bo Walther, adaptronic games "are games consisting of applications and information systems that simulate life processes observed in nature. These games are embedded, flexible, and usually made up of 'tangible bits' that oscillate between virtual and real space". To be adaptronic a game should react to changes in the environment in real time [1]. Sharkrunners is an example of an adaptronic game. In Sharkrunners the game uses the position and movement of real sharks out in the ocean to influence the gameplay [2]. Another example is Boktai, a game where sunlight charges the player's weapon [3].

Other way for a game to be adaptronic is to resort to the real weather. According to Stenros [4] this may be too conceptual and not enough to give players the feeling that the game is merging with real life. Peter Molyneux, who included real weather patterns in a game so that it matched the real weather outside the player's window, goes further on this argument and looking back on the experience considers that is was "a dumb, stupid idea" [5]. So, is this argument final and true? Is using the real weather really a lost bet? We decided give it one more try and address this question in more detail. Perhaps the way the weather is included in the game may make a difference. Just mimicking the weather outside the player's house may not be much fun or contribute to the gameplay. But, if the weather is closely bound to the gameplay, instead of being a mere background feature, then perhaps that may cause a difference. The key contribution of our work is to shed further light on how real time weather data can contribute to the gameplay as an example of integrating real world elements in games.

M. Herrlich, R. Malaka, and M. Masuch (Eds.): ICEC 2012, LNCS 7522, pp. 172–184, 2012.
© IFIP International Federation for Information Processing 2012

Some other researchers have already made interesting work in using weather information in games. This work is addressed in Section 2. In Section 3 we propose a game that revolves entirely around the weather and present the results of the user study. In Section 4 the conclusion and future work are presented.

2   Related Work

Several games have already resorted to the weather to influence the gameplay. In the game Free All Monsters, monsters can be freed according to the weather conditions. With this game the authors considered how location based games should be redesigned to accommodate the increase of scale and addressed the participation inequality of players [6]. However, specific results about the influence of the weather in the players' interaction are not presented.

In Weatherlings each player has a deck of cards with weather dependent creatures. The players battle each other in arenas that correspond to real locations. The choice of arenas is limited to U.S. cities. Even though the game makes use of real weather conditions the weather data is not real time, so this game cannot show how the use of real time weather data influences a game [7].

Mythical the Mobile Awakening [8] is another adaptronic game where players perform magic rituals to enhance their magical skills. The authors show an interesting comparison of several types of contexts (environment, spatio-temporal, proximity, and social) in the gameplay. However the weather is not analyzed in detail.

Heroes of Koskenniska is about raising environmental awareness among visitors of a Biosphere Reserve in Finland. The game resorts to temperature, humidity and illumination sensor data, however this is not the focal point of the game but an accessory to the game's storyline [9]. Furthermore, contrary to the game we are proposing (Section 3.1) this game cannot be played everywhere. In Epidemic Menace virus motion is influenced by the wind direction and strength [10]. Similarly to what happens in Heroes of Koskenniska this game can only be played in a specific place.

In Samurai Romanesque, if it rains in Tokyo players cannot use their muskets and their mobility in the game becomes limited. Weather conditions were supplied by the Japanese Weather Bureau [11]. Flightgear [12], Realistic 3-D Golf and the Driving Game [13] are all games that resort to real weather conditions to achieve more realism. In Black & White the weather in the game matches the weather outside the player's house [5]. AgriVillage also resorts to the weather to influence crops, but the weather is simulated by the game [14]. Levee Patroller is another game where the weather is simulated. When it rains the player's sight becomes limited and playing the game is therefore more difficult [15].

So, even though several games have already somehow resorted to the weather, none of the mentioned previous work provides an analysis specifically focused on the influence of the weather in the gameplay and in player enjoyment. To find out how the weather contributes to the gameplay we propose a game that is presented in the next Section.

3   Our Proposal

In Weather Wizards the weather is the core of all the gameplay. The initial idea for Weather Wizards was previously presented [16, 17]. Here we present detailed info about the game (Section 3.1), the user tests concerning the influence of the real time weather data in player enjoyment (Section 3.2) and the results and discussion of the user tests (Section 3.3).

3.1   Weather Wizards Game

In our game, the player assumes the role of a wizard and duels other players. During the duels, the player's chances of winning are directly related to the weather at the duel location.

Weather Wizards was implemented as an application for mobile phones (Figure 1 (a)). The game can be downloaded from Google Play [18]. Our game is, as far as we know, the first Android native application that resorts to real time weather data.

Weather Wizards is a multiplayer game. All the players' data is stored on a server. For that reason, a connection to the Internet is required to play the game. The mobile phones send the player's data to the server where the fate of the duels is decided. Real time weather data is retrieved via Weather Underground's API [19] and the name of the place corresponding to the latitude and longitude of the player's current location was obtained with Google's Geocoding API [20]. Weather Underground's API and Google's Geocoding API are contacted by the server.

In Figure 1 (b) the player's profile is presented. Here, the player can check her level, experience, life, coins, location and the weather at her location. In front of the experience points there is a green bar that provides a graphical representation of how many points are left to reach the next level.

(a) Game running in several mobile phones

(b) Player's profile

Fig. 1. (a) Weather Wizards running in several mobile phones and the (b) player's profile

If the user presses the Fight button (Figure 1 (b)) a list of possible rivals is presented (Figure 2 (a)). There are two Fight buttons because some mobile phones' screens are very small. So, if the user scrolls down to see the rest of the options and the first Fight button is no longer visible in the screen it will not be necessary to scroll up again in order to start a duel. All the game revolves around duels that are affected by the weather so we wanted the buttons that allow a duel to start to be as available as possible.

For each wizard in the list (Figure 2 (a)), the name, level, location and weather at the player's location are presented. It is possible to find out more information about a wizard by pressing the Info button. After pressing the Info button the profile of the possible rival appears (Figure 2 (b)). The first wizard in the list is chosen randomly from among all the wizards whose level is inferior or equal to the player's level. The second wizard is chosen randomly from among all the wizards whose level is superior to the player's level. The third wizard in the list is chosen randomly from among the ones who are nearby the player. So, even though the wizards in the list are randomly chosen, diversity was forced. There will always be a wizard who is equal to the player or weaker than the player, a wizard stronger than the player and finally another wizard who is close by. If the player is not happy with the presented possible rivals it is possible to ask the game to search again and other wizards will be presented.

(a) Duel list   (b) Rival's profile

Fig. 2. (a) Duel list and (b) rival's profile

To start a duel the player presses the Fight button, in the duel list, corresponding to the wizard she wants to fight with (Figure 2 (a)). Optionally it is also possible to press the Duel this Wizard button in the rival's profile (Figure 2 (b)). After pressing the Fight button the player's wizard teleports to the rival's real location. The duel's background shows the weather at the rival's location. In Figure 3 several different weather conditions, during a duel, are presented. The sun may be shinning (Figure 3 (a)), it may be a cloudy day (Figure 3 (b)), it may be raining (Figure 3 (c)), it may be a foggy day (Figure 3 (d)), it may be snowing (Figure 3 (e)) or there may be a thunderstorm (Figure 3 (f)) or a thunderstorm with rain (Figure 3 (g)) at the rival's location. The player is the black colored figure on the left and the rival is the red colored figure on the right. During the duel each wizard will take turns to attack the opponent casting spells. The health bar of each wizard, represented at the top of the screen, will gradually decrease for each successful attack. Eventually, the health of one of the opponents will decrease to zero and the duel ends. The victorious wizard is the player whose health is above zero. The wizard whose health is equal to zero loses.

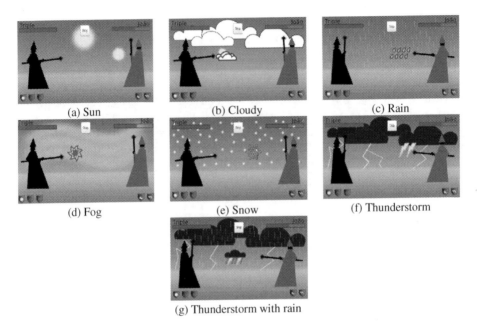

(a) Sun   (b) Cloudy   (c) Rain

(d) Fog   (e) Snow   (f) Thunderstorm

(g) Thunderstorm with rain

Fig. 3. Wizards dueling in different types of weather

Each wizard can cast different types of spells. There is one basic attack spell that is available to all wizards but which is not very powerful. The really powerful spells are the weather spells. The available weather spells are: clear sky, cloud, rain, fog, snow, thunderstorms and thunderstorms and rain. Each of those spells becomes stronger if the weather element it corresponds to is present during the duel. So, if it is raining at the rival's location and the player casts a rain spell, that spell will become stronger.

The spell to cast, in each turn, is chosen randomly from among all active spells in the wizard's grimoire. Spells are stored in the wizard's grimoire (Figure 4 (a)). In the Grimoire a wizard can buy, upgrade and activate or deactivate spells. If a spell is deactivated that spell will not be cast during a duel. So, if the wizard has a strong rain spell and the rival to duel is at a rainy location it will be convenient to deactivate all the spells, except for the rain one, in order to maximize the chances of success.

To better protect herself, a player can also buy defense spells. Similarly to what happens in the attack spells there are also clear sky, cloud, rain, fog, snow, thunderstorms and thunderstorms and rain defense spells. A defense spell will decrease the health damage received by the wizard when attacked with the corresponding attack spell. Defense spells are represented bellow each wizard during the duel (Figure 3).

When the player presses a spell in the grimoire more information about that spell can be visualized (Figure 4 (b)). Initially, some of the spells are locked (Figure 4 (c)). However, as the player gains more experience those locked spells will progressively become available.

(a) Options to buy lives and buy, upgrade and activate or deactivate spells

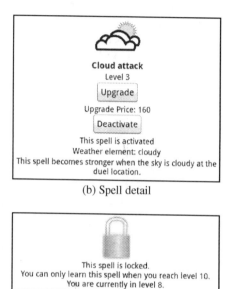

(b) Spell detail

(c) A locked spell

Fig. 4. Grimoire

After a player acquired enough experience that player can become master of the wizards defeated during the duels, who turn into lackeys. Having a master is not entirely devoid of advantages as the master concedes a daily scholarship to the lackeys (Figure 5). The higher the level of the master the higher is the value of the scholarship. With the scholarship's coins the wizard can buy more spells for the grimoire or upgrade spells that are already in the grimoire. Another way of wining coins is trough duels. When a duel ends the player always receives coins, whether she wins or loses. However, more coins are awarded when defeating higher level wizards.

Fig. 5. Master functionality

A wizard can find out who is her master by pressing the Master button and check on her lackeys by pressing the Lackeys button in the Profile (Figure 1 (b)). Some wizards may not have a master. For example, the player whose profile is presented in Figure 2 (b) was, at the time of writing, the most experienced wizard in the game and had no master. That is why there is no Master button is his profile. Similarly, in a wizard without lackeys, the Lackeys button will not appear.

To motivate and provide visibility to the most successful players, Weather Wizards has two types of ranks: the Power Rank (Figure 6 (a)) and the Lackeys Ranks (Figure 6 (b)). In the Power Rank wizards are ordered by experience and in the Lackeys Ranks they are ordered by the number of lackeys. The ranks are accessible through the menu button of the Android phone.

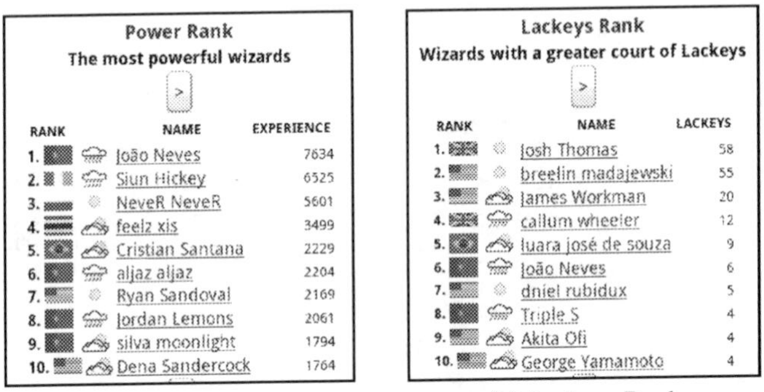

Power Rank The most powerful wizards		
RANK	NAME	EXPERIENCE
1.	João Neves	7634
2.	Siun Hickey	6525
3.	NeveR NeveR	5601
4.	feelz xis	3499
5.	Cristian Santana	2229
6.	aljaz aljaz	2204
7.	Ryan Sandoval	2169
8.	Jordan Lemons	2061
9.	silva moonlight	1794
10.	Dena Sandercock	1764

Lackeys Rank Wizards with a greater court of Lackeys		
RANK	NAME	LACKEYS
1.	Josh Thomas	58
2.	breelin madajewski	55
3.	James Workman	20
4.	callum wheeler	12
5.	luara josé de souza	9
6.	João Neves	6
7.	dniel rubidux	5
8.	Triple S	4
9.	Akita Ofi	4
10.	George Yamamoto	4

(a) Power Rank   (b) Lackeys Rank

Fig. 6. (a) Power Rank and (b) Lackeys Rank

To test how the use of the weather affects player enjoyment, a user study was conducted. The user study is addressed in the next section.

3.2   User Study

To test Weather Wizards we deployed the application on Google Play. We could have sent the application's APK file to a few selected users and ask them to install it in their phones. However, we thought that deploying the game on Google Play would provide us with the more realistic scenario possible, rather than merely having the players sitting at the lab to experiment the game [21]. In order to create a realistic scenario, and so that our game would be subjected to all the same constraints that other games are subjected to when they are deployed in the wild, no rewards were offered to players for installing and playing the game. The game was advertised on the research group's web page, on social networks and on mailing lists.

The application was deployed on Google Play in 27 December 2011. Until the moment of writing there were 306 user installs. The evolution of the active device installs is presented in Figure 7.

When the game is installed players are asked what their gender is. 70% of our users are male, 20% are female and 10% preferred not to answer that question.

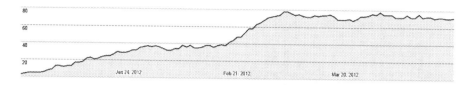

Fig. 7. Evolution of active device installs

To evaluate the game and influence of the weather in player enjoyment we resorted to both the logs of the player data stored in the server and to a survey that the players filled via the web. We sent an email to players asking them to fill the survey. 21 players responded to our survey. 81% of those players are male and 19% are female. Their average age is 28.6 years old. 86% of the players use their phone to play games. The remaining 14% do not use their phones to play games (so probably, ours was the first they installed). 9 of the players were students, 6 worked in areas related to informatics and finance, 5 were researchers and 1 did part time jobs.

3.3   Results and Discussion

57.2% of the players agree or strongly agree that the weather made them feel that the game was dependent from the real world (Figure 8 (a)). Perhaps this percentage could be higher. During the duels, the weather that was displayed in the mobile phone was the weather at the rival's location. Eventually, that rival could be far away from the user so the sense that the weather was real could not be so evident.

71.5% of the players agree or strongly agree that using real weather data was fun (Figure 8 (b)). None of the players thought that using real weather data was not fun. 28.6% of the players neither agree nor disagree. So, there were players who even though didn't feel that the game was dependent from the real world, nevertheless found the user of weather data fun.

We asked players if they would prefer randomly generated weather data instead of real weather data. 86% of the users prefer real weather data. 14% would rather have randomly generated weather data (Figure 9).

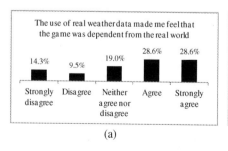

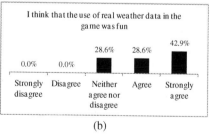

(a)   (b)

Fig. 8. Players' opinion about (a) how much the use of real weather data made them feel that the game was dependent from the real world and (b) how much the use of real weather data in the game was fun

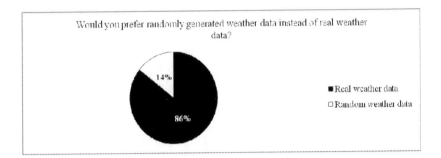

Fig. 9. Players' opinion about using real weather data or randomly generated weather data

As Weather Wizards depends of the user's location, we asked users if they thought it was fun to know the real location of the other players (Figure 10 (a)). It is possible to know the real location of another player through that player's profile (Figure 2 (b)). In the ranks (Figure 6) there is also a flag that indicates the country where the player is. 85.7% of the players agree or strongly agree that it is fun to know the real location of the other players. This percentage was higher than the one that refers to the use of the weather (Figure 8 (b)).

Since the game was made available on Google Play, until the time of writing, players have fought 10335 duels. These duels were initiated by 125 distinct users. In 66.9% of those duels the spell that corresponded to the weather at the rival's location was activated.

We also asked players if the game responds quickly to their actions. To obtain the real time weather data the phone needs to contact the server and the server needs, in turn, to contact Weather Underground's API. Those two steps could cause some delay. Surprisingly, 71.4% of the players agree or strongly agree that the game responds quickly to their actions (Figure 10 (b)).

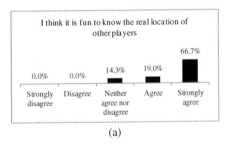
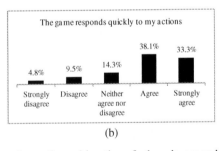

(a)   (b)

Fig. 10. Players' opinion about (a) how fun it is to know the real location of other players and (b) about how quickly the game responds to their actions

In the survey, players were asked a series of questions based on the Game Flow. People experience flow when they do an activity for the sole sake of the activity, for enjoying themselves and not to receive material rewards [22, 23]. In one of the questions we asked players to what extent did they have a sense that the game kept them concentrated while they were playing. This question was related to the concentration element of the Game Flow. Providing a lot of stimuli from different sources is a criteria that contributes to the concentration element and that in turn contributes to the flow. As the weather is another stimuli we wondered if this element might favor concentration. Another of the elements of the Game Flow is immersion. In what refers to this element players were asked if they felt involved by the game, less aware of what was surrounding them and less worried about everyday life. As the weather surrounds the player, constantly immersing her, eventually this might favor immersion. However, our results regarding concentration (Figure 11 (a)) and immersion (Figure 11 (b)) were quite neutral. The average value for concentration is 3.2 and the average value for immersion is again 3.2. This may be due to the fact that Weather Wizards is a casual game designed to be played during short bursts of time and meant to be easily interrupted in case the player has something else to do [24]. So perhaps Weather Wizards' casual nature didn't inherently favor concentration or immersion.

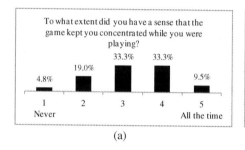
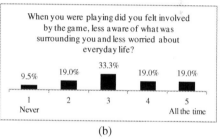

(a)   (b)

Fig. 11. Players' opinion about the (a) concentration and (b) immersion elements of Game Flow

In the survey players were asked how the game could be better, what they liked and what they didn't like. 28.6% of the players wanted better graphics. Conversely, 14.3% of the players liked the game's graphics and praised its simplicity. 23.8% of the players wanted more interactive combats and demanded features such as friends' lists, so that they could track their progress and challenge them, exchange of messages between wizards or different privileges based on the player's real location. 42.9% of the players praised the innovation, originality or idea behind the game. 9.5% of the players mentioned the masters and lackeys functionality (Figure 5) as good way for new players to more easily attain visibility and rise in the game's hierarchy (Figure 6 (b)). Experience is cumulative over time, so it is more difficult for a new player to surpass players that have been in the game for longer. Lackeys, in contrast, are relatively easier to steal.

Our results indicate that real time weather data has potential to contribute positively to player enjoyment in a game, but there are risks associated with it [25]. Weather data providers may crash or may not scale appropriately if the number of players increases. Furthermore, if one opts for a paid solution weather data will become an extra cost. Inaccuracy problems may also surface as the weather data supplied by the provider may be wrong. However, there may be one way to avoid this external dependency. The application Weddar [26] may have found the solution. Weddar is a weather report service powered by its own users. It is not a game, but the strategy that they used may be the way out for games not to become dependent from an external, possibly paid, solution. Of course, there can be some inaccuracy in this sort of approach, but weather data providers may also suffer from some form of inaccuracy. So this may well be a possibility worth considering.

4   Conclusions and Future Work

In this work, the contribution of real time weather data to the player enjoyment was analyzed. To this effect we created a game, Weather Wizards, where the weather is central to the gameplay and conducted a survey to the players. 71.5% of the players considered that using real weather data was fun and 57.2% of them felt that the use of real weather made them feel that the game was dependent from the real world. When asked if they would prefer using real weather data or randomly generated weather data 86% of the users preferred real weather data and only 14% would opt for randomly generated weather data. Our results therefore indicate that real time weather data can contribute positively to player enjoyment.

In what refers to the concentration and immersion elements of the Game Flow, our results were only slightly positive, possibly because Weather Wizards is a casual game, built to be played for short amounts of time. In a short amount of time it is difficult for a player to feel completely immersed and detached from the real world.

Our survey was conducted in a limited population, and the respondent rate might eventually have affected the outcome, but the user results about the use of real weather data are encouraging so we believe there are still many opportunities to explore in what refers to the combination of weather and games.

As future work we plan to port this application to other devices in order to augment the number of potential players and run more user tests. We also plan to offer the choice of different skins for the game because even though several users complimented the aesthetics and simplicity of the game, others would prefer a more elaborate design.

Acknowledgements. The authors thank everyone at IMG-CITI and to everybody who helped us test the game. This work was partly funded by FCT/MCTES, through grant SFRH/BD/61085/2009, and by Centro de Informática e Tecnologias da Informação (CITI/FCT/UNL) - 2011-2012 through grant PEst-OE/EEI/UI0527/2011.

References

1. Walther, B.K.: Atomic actions - molecular experience: Theory of Pervasive Gaming. Computers in Entertainment 3, 4 (2005)
2. Sharkrunners HQ: Sharkrunners: Shark Week: Discovery Channel,
   http://dsc.discovery.com/convergence/sharkweek/shark-runners/shark-runners-hq.html

3. boktai - The Sun is in Your Hand, `http://www.konami.jp/gs/game/boktai/english/game_index.html`

4. Adaptronic Games, Pervasive Games: Theory and Design, `http://pervasivegames.wordpress.com/2009/04/09/adaptronic-games/`

5. Microsoft's Peter Molyneux | GamesIndustry International, `http://www.gamesindustry.biz/articles/microsofts-peter-molyneux-interview?page=2`

6. Lund, K., Coulton, P., Wilson, A.: Participation inequality in mobile location games. In: Proceedings of the 8th International Conference on Advances in Computer Entertainment Technology - ACE 2011. ACM Press, New York (2011)

7. Sheldon, J., Perry, J., Klopfer, E., Ong, J., Chen, V.H.-H., Tzuo, P.W., Rosenheck, L.: Weatherlings: a new approach to student learning using web-based mobile games. In: Proceedings of the Fifth International Conference on the Foundations of Digital Games - FDG 2010, pp. 203–208. ACM Press, New York (2010)

8. Paavilainen, J., Korhonen, H.: Player perception of context information utilization in pervasive mobile games. Breaking New Ground: Innovation in Games, Play, Practice and Theory. (2009)

9. Laine, T.H., Sedano, C.I., Sutinen, E., Joy, M.: Viable and portable architecture for pervasive learning spaces. In: Proceedings of the 9th International Conference on Mobile and Ubiquitous Multimedia - MUM 2010, pp. 1–10. ACM Press, New York (2010)

10. Broll, W., Ohlenburg, J., Lindt, I., Herbst, I., Braun, A.-K.: Meeting technology challenges of pervasive augmented reality games. In: Proceedings of 5th ACM SIGCOMM Workshop on Network and System Support for Games, NetGames 2006 (2006)

11. Krikke, J.: Samurai Romanesque, J2ME, and the battle for mobile cyberspace. IEEE Computer Graphics and Applications 23, 16–23 (2003)

12. Weather - FlightGear wiki, `http://wiki.flightgear.org/Weather`

13. The Weather Channel and Skyworks Technologies Launch the First Online Games Featuring Real-Time Weather!, `http://press.weather.com/press_archive_detail.asp?id=99`

14. Yongyuth, P., Prada, R., Nakasone, A., Kawtrakul, A., Prendinger, H.: AgriVillage: 3D multi-language internet game for fostering agriculture environmental awareness. In: Proceedings of the International Conference on Management of Emergent Digital EcoSystems, pp. 145–152. ACM, New York (2010)

15. Harteveld, C., Guimarães, R., Mayer, I., Bidarra, R.: Balancing Pedagogy, Game and Reality Components Within a Unique Serious Game for Training Levee Inspection. In: Hui, K.-c., Pan, Z., Chung, R.C.-k., Wang, C.C.L., Jin, X., Göbel, S., Li, E.C.-L. (eds.) EDUTAINMENT 2007. LNCS, vol. 4469, pp. 128–139. Springer, Heidelberg (2007)

16. Reis, S., Correia, N.: Engaging the Players with the Use of Real-Time Weather Data. In: Proceedings of the 4º Science and Videogames Conference - 2011, Portuguese Society for Videogames Science (2011)

17. Reis, S., Romão, T., Correia, N.: Pervasive play for everyone using the weather. In: ACE 2010 Proceedings of the 7th International Conference on Advances in Computer Entertainment Technology, pp. 104–105. ACM (2010)

18. Weather Wizards - Android Apps on Google Play, `https://play.google.com/store/apps/details?id=com.weatherwizards`

19. Weather API: Weather Underground, `http://www.wunderground.com/weather/api/`

20. The Google Geocoding API - Google Maps API Web Services - Google Developers, `https://developers.google.com/maps/documentation/geocoding/`.

21. Cramer, H., Rost, M., Belloni, N., Bentley, F., Chincholle, D.: Research in the large. using app stores, markets, and other wide distribution channels in Ubicomp research. In: Proceedings of the 12th ACM International Conference Adjunct Papers on Ubiquitous Computing - Ubicomp 2010, pp. 511–514. ACM Press, New York (2010)
22. Sweetser, P., Wyeth, P.: GameFlow: a model for evaluating player enjoyment in games. Comput. Entertain. 3, 3 (2005)
23. Nakamura, J., Csikszentmihalyi, M.: The concept of flow. In: Handbook of Positive Psychology. Oxford University Press (2002)
24. Rohrl, D.: 2008-2009 Casual Games White Paper. IGDA (2008)
25. Becam, A., Nenonen, V.: Designing and Creating Environment Aware Games. In: 5th IEEE Consumer Communications and Networking Conference, CCNC 2008, pp. 1045–1049 (2008)
26. Weddar - How does it feel?, http://www.weddar.com/

fAARS:
A Platform for Location-Aware Trans-reality Games

Lucio Gutierrez, Eleni Stroulia, and Ioanis Nikolaidis

Computing Science Department, University of Alberta, Edmonton, AB T6G 2E8, Canada
{lucio,stroulia,nikolaidis}@ualberta.ca

Abstract. Users today can easily and intuitively record their real-world experiences through mobile devices, and commodity virtual worlds enable users from around the world to socialize in the context of realistic environments where they simulate real-world activities. This synergy of technological advances makes the design and implementation of *trans-reality games,* blending the boundaries of the real and virtual worlds, a compelling software-engineering problem. In this paper, we describe fAARS, a platform for developing and deploying trans-reality games that cut across the real and parallel virtual worlds, offering users a range of game-play modalities. We place fAARS in the context of recent related work, and we demonstrate its capabilities by discussing two different games developed on it, one with three different variants.

Keywords: Game platform, trans-reality games, virtual worlds, mobile games.

1   Introduction

Location-based games are a type of pervasive games that use the physical space of our entire world as a game board [8]. Their implementation relies on special-purpose middleware that integrates the players' smart-phones so that they can share information about their location, surroundings and actions. The players' game experience can be further enhanced with parallel virtual worlds, so that they can experience the game in the real world and in alternate realities, possibly at the same time. This technological convergence, on one hand, and the pervasiveness of the "gamification" concept across many aspects of our activities today, on the other, has brought to the forefront a new breed of pervasive games called "trans-reality games". This term refers to a relatively new, yet increasingly interesting, class of games, played using mobile devices indoor, outdoor and in virtual worlds. Trans-reality games were first conceptualized by Lindley in 2004. This type of games can be deployed and played in "natural" neighborhoods, such as a campus, a city, or a broader geographical area. Game players interact with the games (a) in the real world through location-specific clues communicated to them through smart-phones that "augment reality" and are aware of each other's locations using GPS or QR codes, and (b) in (possibly multiple) parallel virtual world(s), which represent alternate reality(ies) that reflect the real world in some dimensions and extend it in others.

The fAARS (for Augmented Alternate Reality Services) platform supports the implementation and deployment of trans-reality games in the virtual treasure-hunt and

M. Herrlich, R. Malaka, and M. Masuch (Eds.): ICEC 2012, LNCS 7522, pp. 185–192, 2012.

role-playing style. It consists of a set of components, flexibly integrated with its event-driven game engine, through RESTful APIs. So far, we have developed two different trans-reality games using the fAARS platform. The first game was the "Human Geometric Orientation" game. Through this game, players in a virtual world participate in an experiment, designed to study human orientation mechanisms. The second game, "Outbreak: Safety First", is a "serious game" designed to educate health-science students in precautionary procedures for avoiding nosocomial infections, and can be played in three different game-play modalities.

In the rest of this paper we discuss our work and experience to date. In section 2, we review the background for our work, by reviewing recent trans-reality games and existing platforms for location-aware games. In section 3, the design and implementation of fAARS and its constituent components are fully described. In section 4, we report on our evaluation of the platform through the development of two separate games. Finally, in section 5, we conclude with the contribution of our work.

2   Trans-reality Games and Pervasive-Game Platforms

The "pervasive games" heading includes a broad range of games that integrate ubiquitous technology with physical spaces to provide a gaming experience. Montola [9] introduced a conceptual framework for analyzing the spatial, social, and temporal features of pervasive games, leading to a classification of these games into six types. *Mixed-reality games* are played in physical spaces where virtual and physical components co-exist. *Trans-reality games* are played in physical and virtual spaces at the same time, with the actions of the player avatars in the virtual world affecting the game play in the real world and vice versa. *Adaptronic games* are played in a virtual world but react to real-world events. *Crossmedia games* involve different types of pervasive technologies. *Alternate-reality games* create the illusion that game-play events should be considered "real", thus creating an alternate reality where players act according to hidden clues. Finally, in R*eality games*, everything that happens in the game is real and can have consequences on the real life of players.

Trans-reality games are a particularly interesting and challenging class of pervasive games. "ARQuake" [11] was one of the first outdoor/indoor augmented-reality location-aware games based on the desktop game Quake. Two years later, "Human Pac-man" [4] was the first outdoor augmented-reality game to blend the real and virtual dimensions. Both games required players to wear their particular versions of cumbersome equipment. In 2005, "Magic Land" [12] blended 3D avatars of real players with 3D computer-generated animations, fusing the real and the virtual worlds in a novel way. Between 2004 and 2006, trans-reality games, such as "Can you see me now?" [1], "Uncle Roy All Around You" [2], and "I Like Frank" [3], demonstrated the use of mobile devices in real-world playgrounds blurred with virtual worlds, with players in both worlds advancing the game, although the actions allowed to players in the virtual world were very limited. These games were developed on special-purpose hardware and software technologies, with no reuse potential. Furthermore, in the above trans-reality games, virtual worlds have been used primarily as an information resource, and there is still substantial work to be done towards the comprehensive integration of virtual- and real-world game-play.

Table 1. Pervasive-Games Platforms

PLATFORM	Indoors	Outdoors	Individual	Teams	Map	Augmented Browser	Raw Game Data	Treasure Hunt	RPG	Capture-the-flag	Peer-to-peer	Client-server	Game Authoring
fAR-Play [6]	√	√	√			√	√	√				√	√
SCVNGR - www.scvngr.com		√	√		√		√	√				√	√
MUPE [13]		√	√				√	√	√		√	√	
Mobile Chase [5]		√	√				√	√				√	
FRAP [14]		√		√	√		√	√		√		√	
Wherigo - www.wherigo.com		√	√		√		√	√				√	√
PCAFPEA [10]		√	√		√	√	√	√			√	√	

As fAARS is on the overlap between trans-reality and location-aware mobile games, we review above the features of some important platforms for location-aware games. The comparison of the features of these platforms is summarized in **Table 1.** As it can be seen in the table, a few of the platforms support indoors and outdoors game-play but none support virtual worlds; thus, they are not able to support trans-reality games. Most are tailored to individual game-play, except from FRAP that also supports teams. Most augment the players' game-play experience with game-related content; some include an augmented-reality browser that superimposes this content on the image that players see through their cameras, or on a map where they can see their (and other players') location(s). All support treasure-hunt games; Mupe also supports role-playing games and FRAP supports capture-the-flag games. All support communication between players through the game engine; Mupe and PCFPA also support peer-to-peer interactions of players in close proximity to each other. Finally, most of the platforms offer some game-authoring tools.

3   The fAARS Software Architecture

fAARS was conceived as a new-generation pervasive-game platform, extending the space of the game play from the real world (indoors and outdoors) to parallel virtual world(s) in order to support location-aware trans-reality games. In these games (a) the real-world space and locations (and any information associated with them) are mapped to the virtual world; (b) the movement and actions of the real-world players is reflected through their avatars in the virtual world; (c) the movement and actions of the virtual-world players is communicated to real-world players through their smart phones; and (d) in addition to real-world and virtual-world players, non-playing characters, controlled by a simulation engine, can also change the game state. fAARS supports the deployment of trans-reality games in the virtual treasure-hunt and role-playing game styles. fAARS integrates OpenSim (http://opensimulator.org/) as the virtual-world game-play environment and considers two types of mappings between the real- and virtual-world spaces. In the "parallel worlds" mapping, the virtual-world setting mimics the real-world setting and the coordinates of every location in the real-world playground are transformed to a pair of virtual-world coordinates. In the "points-of-interest" mapping, the virtual world may represent a conceptually different metaphor from the real world, and only specific points of interest may be mapped across the two. In this case, the players' locations can only be reflected across the two worlds when the players are close to any of the pre-defined points of interest.

fAARS supports three different game-play modalities [7]. In the *Dormant* modality, players play the game in the real world using smart-phones. In the *Dreaming* modality, players play the game in the virtual world. Finally, in the *Astral-projection* modality, players choose to play in the virtual world or in the real world using smart-phones; in the latter case, the real-world players' avatars interact with other players and objects in the virtual world at the same time.

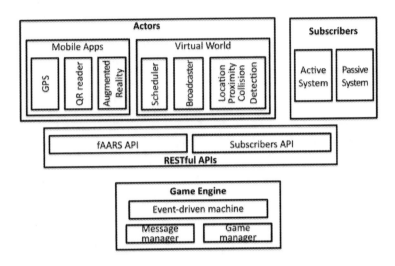

Fig. 1. The fAARS Platform Software Architecture

As shown in Fig. 1. , the fAARS platform consists of two main components: (a) the *Actors* (and their devices) corresponding to the real-world and virtual-world players; and (b) the *Game Engine*, which is responsible for recognizing the *Actors'* actions and inferring the next game state based on the game rules. The *Actors* access the game engine through the *fAARS API*. Furthermore, external components (i.e., Subscribers) can be integrated with the *Game Engine* through the *Subscribers API*. The fAARS platform is implemented according to the Event-Driven SOA (Service Oriented Architecture) style.

The Actors: In fAARS, every player in the real and virtual worlds is represented as an *Actor*. In the real world, *Actors* interact with the game using a mobile application running on a smart-phone. The mobile application senses the *Actors'* location and actions, using the smart-phone GPS and a built-in QR-code reader. In the virtual world, players have the same cross-platform application running on a HUD (Heads-Up Display). The HUD senses the virtual-world through collision, proximity, and location detectors. The virtual world also provides a *Scheduler* and a *Broadcaster*.

The former supports the communication between the virtual world and the game engine, through a XML-RPC port, and maintains a set of global parameters related to the virtual-world game. The *Broadcaster* maintains a list of the active virtual-world objects and forwards them relevant communications from the *Game Engine*.

The Game Engine is responsible for maintaining and advancing the state of the *game*; it receives *Events* from the *Actors*, processes the game rules and accordingly updates the state of the game, and notifies the players and registered *Subscribers*. The *Game Engine* consists of (a) the *Event-driven Machine*, (b) the *Message Manager*, and (c) the *Game Manager*. The *Message Manager* receives *Actor*-generated events and forwards them to the *Event-driven Machine,* which communicates with the *Game Manager* to query the fAARS database for the relevant game rules[1]. Based on the rules, the *Event-driven Machine* updates the state of the virtual world and the state of the *Actors* and notifies the *Subscribers* about *Events* of interest. The *Message Manager* notifies the *Actors* as necessary and updates the cross-platform mobile applications and the virtual-world HUDs, without requiring players to explicitly request updates from the *Game Engine*.

The Subscribers RESTful Interface: fAARS provides a REST service that allows external systems to observe a game and to provide further downstream functionality to fAARS games, as if they were part of the platform. As shown in Figure 1, *Subscribers* can be either Active or Passive. Active subscribers can push events to the *Game Engine* (through the *pushEvents* API) where passive systems are only notified about *Events* (through the *registerObserver* API).

The fAARS RESTful API is composed of thirty APIs, which provide access to functionality of different internal pieces of fAARS, specifically to the internal pieces of the *Game Engine* as depicted in Figure 1. The APIs are divided in four categories: a) event-driven machine (push events: 2 APIs), b) game manager (query the game state: 16 APIs), c) message manager (send and receive messages: 2 APIs), and d) virtual world (update the virtual world: 10 APIs).

4   Two Games on the fAARS Platform

We have validated the usefulness and generality of fAARS by developing two games with it.

The "Human Geometric Orientation" Game (HGO): Systematically examining whether and how each geometrical property impacts animals and humans' orientation implies the need to "build" environments in a controlled manner with their properties systematically varied. This is practically impossible and this is why our psychology colleagues decided to conduct their study by developing a fAARS game. In this game, players were trained to locate two geometrically equivalent corners in a number of parallelogram-shaped rooms in a first-person navigable virtual world. With the HGO

---

[1] Note that, as of today, fAARS does not offer an authoring environment; therefore, the game rules have to be stored directly in the database by someone familiar with the fAARS database design.

game, the researchers could systematically specify the types of room shapes they wanted, and we were able to systematically construct them in the virtual world using the OpenSim building tools. Of course, it was impossible to construct parallel real-world settings; therefore, the HGO game was played only in the virtual world, in the so-called *Dreaming modality*, with players logging in the virtual world and interacting with the room corners to generate virtual-world *Events*.

Referring to Fig. 1. , the fAARS components used for the HGO game are the virtual world, the game engine, and an external system as an active subscriber.

- A total of 99 *Actor* instances (one for each subject) with unique IDs were created to allow participants to interact with the corners in each of the rooms in the virtual world. The room corners were also represented as *Actor* instances, in order to rely on the virtual-world collision detection for generating corner-choice events
- The HGO *game engine* has a single rule that upon recognizing a corner-choice event, it increases the score of the *Actor,* if the corner choice was correct.
- The *Virtual World* was the setting of the game with rooms constructed manually in a systematic manner and the corners associated with invisible *Actors*.
- There is a single *active event subscriber* that keeps track of the number of tries of every *Actor* for each of the rooms in the virtual world, and updates the location of the *Actor* instances based on the number of tries.

The "Outbreak: Safety First" Game (Outbreak): The second game developed on fAARS, "Outbreak: Safety First", was designed as a learning activity for medical students in an epidemiology course. The game narrative places the players in a hospital where they have to visit a number of patients. As they move from one patient to another they have to avoid infectious viruses and to answer questions. At the patients' rooms, they have to follow appropriate precautionary procedures to protect themselves from infections, depending on the patient symptoms.

Taking full advantage of the fAARS functionalities, this game was deployed in three different variants. The first variant was played in the real world only, in a teaching-hospital ward. Players have to scan QR codes to see the symptoms of the simulated patients they visit, to select the appropriate gear to don, to answer questions, and to get treated if they were infected. As the game evolves, players "get infected" through actions dictated by the game (scanning QR codes attached on infected landmarks) or through the exposure of their avatars to virtual viruses in the simulation running in the virtual world. When this happens, they are informed through a message to their mobile device, at which point, they have to choose appropriate measures to protect themselves and the patients. The viruses, their infection cycle, their contagion to patients and players are controlled through a simple simulation in the virtual world, setup in a parallel mapping to the real world. This type of game play represents the so-called *Astral-projection modality,* where virtual- and real-world players can interact with each other in any world, and activities are reflected in both worlds.

The other two game *Dreaming modality* variants were deployed in a virtual world, as desktop video games. The first one uses the virtual world as a clickable 2D map (virtual 2D version) of a Pacman board, on which players and viruses interact with each other. The third game variant takes place in a 3D virtual world, where the virtual space configuration is similar to the ward of the mobile version, and players have a first-person view in a navigable virtual world.

The first game variant uses all the fAARS components, including two external systems as active subscribers. The other two game variants use the virtual-world actors, the game engine, and the same two external systems as active subscribers (similar to the HGO game). Let us now review the development process for the Outbreak game.

- We created *Actor* instances for each of our student participants; some were real-world Actors (for the first game variant) and some were virtual-world Actors (for the other two variants). In addition, a number of *Actors* acting as NPCs (Non-player Characters) were deployed to represent the virtual-world viruses.

- The Outbreak *game engine* has many more rules than the HGO game that control the interactions of *Actors* with the QR codes representing questions, the QR codes outside the patients' rooms, and the collision with viruses. The *Event* types used to define the *ECA* rules of the game ware the *decodeQR* and *onCollision* Events.

- The *virtual world* was an essential component for all three versions of this game. In the *Astral Projection* modality, the virtual world is used as an extension of the real world, where all *Actor* instances can be infected by *NPCs* representing viruses flying around in the game. In the *Dreaming* modality, it is in the virtual world where the interactions among all *Actors* and *NPCs* happen during game-play.

- There were two *event subscribers* in this game that provided further downstream functionalities for all three versions of the game. The first was a repository of questions, which allowed players to increase their score if they correctly answered a question. The second was a mobility controller that moves the virus *NPCs* in the virtual world in a pseudo-random fashion.

5   Conclusions

The development of fAARS was motivated by our realization that, with the increased maturity and adoption of mobile and virtual-world platforms and momentum of the *"gamification"* paradigm in education there is a great opportunity for trans-reality games. The fAARS platform supports a specific style of trans-reality games, grounded on a complex spatial metaphor and following the virtual treasure-hunt and RPG styles. The fAARS platform extends the state-of-the-art in pervasive location-aware gaming platforms in the following ways.

fAARS is the only platform that enables the deployment of location-aware games in a virtual world, as an extension of the physical indoors/outdoors playground. The virtual-world playground may "parallel" the real world (with all real-world and virtual-world coordinates mapped through a bi-directional function) or it may communicate a completely different metaphor to the game story (mapping only interesting locations across the worlds). fAARS supports peer-to-peer interactions among players in the virtual world. Mimicking the functionality of NFC, a special-purpose software device in the virtual world recognizes player proximity. This event can be used by the game story to notify the players and give them opportunities to advance the game play. Finally, fAARS enables a variety of game play combinations in the real and the virtual world. The two example games discussed in Section 4 demonstrate how fAARS can be used to develop real-world only games (like the platforms discussed in Section 2.), or virtual-world only games, or true trans-reality games.

References

1. Benford, S., Crabtree, A., Flintham, M., Drozd, A., Anastasi, R., Paxton, M., Tandavanitj, N., Adams, M., Row-Farr, J.: Can you see me now? ACM Trans. Comput.-Hum. Interact. 13, 100–133 (2006)
2. Benford, S., Flintham, M., Drozd, A., Anastasi, R., Rowland, D., Tandavanitj, N., Adams, M., Row-Farr, J., Oldroyd, A., Sutton, J.: Uncle Roy All Around You: Implicating the City in a Location-Based Performance. In: Proc. Advances in Computer Entertainment (ACE 2004), ACM Press (2004)
3. Blast Theory (n.d.). I like Frank, http://www.blasttheory.co.uk/bt/work_ilikefrank.html (retrieved April 1, 2012)
4. Cheok, A.D., Goh, K.H., Liu, W., Farbiz, F., Fong, S.W., Teo, S.L., Li, Y., Yang, X.: Human pacman: a mobile, wide-area entertainment system based on physical, social, and ubiquitous computing. Personal Ubiquitous Comput. 8 8, 71–81 (2004)
5. Fetter, M., Etz, M., Blechschmied, H.: Mobile chase–towards a framework for location-based gaming. In: GRAPP (AS/IE), INSTICC–Institute for Systems and Technologies of Information, Control and Communication, pp. 98–105 (2007)
6. Gutierrez, L., Nikolaidis, I., Stroulia, E., Gouglas, S., Rockwell, G., Boechler, P., Carbonaro, M., King, S.: far-play: A framework to develop augmented/alternate reality games. In: IEEE PerCom Workshops, pp. 531–536 (2011)
7. Lindley, C.A.: Game space design foundations for trans-reality games. In: Proceedings of the 2005 ACM SIGCHI International Conference on Advances in Computer Entertainment Technology, ACE 2005, pp. 397–404. ACM, New York (2005)
8. Magerkurth, C., Cheok, A.D., Mandryk, R.L., Nilsen, T.: Pervasive games: Bringing computer entertainment back to the real world. ACM Computers in Entertainment 3(3), Article 4A (2005)
9. Montola, M.: Exploring the Edge of the Magic Circle. Defining Pervasive Games. In: Proc. of Digital Experience: Design, Aestethics, Practice Conference, Copenhagen (2005)
10. Papakonstantinou, S., Brujic-Okretic, V.: Prototyping a context-aware framework for pervasive entertainment applications. In: Proceedings of the 2009 Conference in Games and Virtual Worlds for Serious Applications, VS-GAMES 2009, pp. 84–91. IEEE Computer Society, Washington, DC (2009)
11. Piekarski, W., Thomas, B.: Arquake: the outdoor augmented reality gaming system. Commun. ACM 45, 36–38 (2002)
12. Qui, T.C.T., Nguyen, T.H.D., Mallawaarachchi, A., Xu, K., Liu, W., Lee, S.P., Zhou, Z.Y., Teo, S.L., Teo, H.S., Thang, L.N., Li, Y., Cheok, A.D., Kato, H.: Magic land: live 3d human capture mixed reality interactive system. In: CHI 2005 Extended Abstracts on Human Factors in Computing Systems, CHI EA 2005, pp. 1142–1143. ACM, New York (2005)
13. Suomela, R., Räsänen, E., Koivisto, A., Mattila, J.: Open-Source Game Development with the Multi-user Publishing Environment (MUPE) Application Platform. In: Rauterberg, M. (ed.) ICEC 2004. LNCS, vol. 3166, pp. 308–320. Springer, Heidelberg (2004)
14. Tutzschke, J.-P., Zukunft, O.: Frap: a framework for pervasive games. In: Proceedings of the 1st ACM SIGCHI Symposium on Engineering Interactive Computing Systems, EICS 2009, pp. 133–142. ACM, New York (2009)

How to Analyse Therapeutic Games:
The Player / Game / Therapy Model

Stéphanie Mader*, Stéphane Natkin, and Guillaume Levieux

C.E.D.R.I.C. / C.N.A.M.,
292 Rue Saint Martin, 75003 Paris, France
{stephanie.mader,stephane.natkin,guillaume.levieux}@cnam.fr
http://cedric.cnam.fr

Abstract. In this paper, we present a new model to analyse therapeutic games. The goal of the model is to describe and analyse the relations between the three aspects of a therapeutic game: the player, the game, and the therapy. The model is intended to game designers. It is a tool to improve the communication between health experts and game designers, and to evaluate the game design coherency of therapeutic games. It also helps to analyse existing games to discover relevant features. The model is built with respect to existing serious game definitions and taxonomies, medical definitions, motivation theory, and game theory. We describe how the model was used to design *le village aux oiseaux*, a therapeutic game which goal is to train people with attention disabilities. In the last section, we present the results of analysis done with our model and discuss the model limits.

Keywords: video games, evaluation, analysis, model, game design, serious games, therapeutic.

1   Introduction

"*Game design is the process by which a game designer creates a game, to be encountered by a player, from which meaningful play emerges*" [29]. Salen and Zimmerman's definition emphasizes that a game can not be dissociated from its player. Neither the player and its relation to the game, nor games fundamentals like gameplay, feedbacks, or goals are stressed in existing definitions of serious game. In this paper, we present a new analysis model for therapeutic games. This model is intended to game designer. They can use the model to evaluate the coherency of their design regarding the relation that bounds the three aspects of a therapeutic game: the therapy, the game, and the player. The goal of the model is also to facilitate the communication between game designers and health experts. Finally, the model can be used to analyse existing therapeutic games to better understand why some of them are efficient while others are not.

* Stéphanie Mader gratefully acknowledges the financial support of the Swiss National Science Foundation (SNF).

M. Herrlich, R. Malaka, and M. Masuch (Eds.): ICEC 2012, LNCS 7522, pp. 193–206, 2012.

First, we present how we built the model with respect to existing serious game definitions and taxonomies, medical definitions, motivation theories and game theories. Then, we present our model and explain how it was used during the design of *le village aux oiseaux*. After that, we present interesting results of analyses made with the model. Finally, we discuss our work and present the next steps of our research.

2   Background

2.1   Serious Games

According to Sawyer and Smith, the definition of serious game has evolved [30]. Old definitions were narrow, they restricted serious games to certain game genres (i.e. simulation-based game) and application fields (e.g. government, education). New definitions are more general, they include all game genres and application fields. Although these definitions are numerous [7,8,11,35], we have identified two main common aspects: a serious game has a purpose beyond entertainment, and the main objective of this combination (serious and game) is to use the *attractive shapes* of the game to serve the serious purpose. Many other authors also consider that enhancing the user's motivation is the main advantage of serious games over other media [2,6,10,26]. However, other aspects of serious games are still under discussion. For our research, we use the definition of Guardiola et al.: "*A serious game is a rule-based formal system with a variable and quantifiable outcome, where different outcomes are assigned different values, the player exerts effort in order to influence the outcome, the player feels attached to the outcome. But a serious game is combined with a defined real life objective.*"[1] [11]. This definition is based upon the classical game definition of Juul [14]. According to Guardiola et al., the main difference between a video game and a serious game is that the designer of a serious game try to have an impact on *real life*. Thus, the *real life* consequences, that are optional and negotiable as stated by Juul, become more controlled by the designer in a serious game. If this serious purpose is what differentiate a video game and a serious game, according to existing taxonomies, the serious purpose is also what differentiate a serious game from another one.

Sawyer and Smith propose several taxonomies for serious games [30]. Based on market and purpose, their taxonomy split serious games into categories like Games for Education or Game for Health. Then, for each of these categories, Sawyer and Smith propose a specific taxonomy. The taxonomy of Games for Health has two parameters: *function* (preventative, therapeutic, assessment, educational, informatics) and *public* (personal, professional practice, research / academia, public health). Djaouti and Alvarez built their own classification

---

[1] "*un jeu utile est un système dynamique formel dont le comportement, délimité par des règles, produit des conséquences variables et des effets quantifiables. Le joueur doit avoir la sensation que ses actions influencent de façon contrôlée le comportement du jeu. Il doit être émotionnellement attaché aux résultats observés. Mais le jeu utile est associé à un objectif défini de la vie réelle*"

upon Sawyer and Smith's taxonomies [1, 7]. Djaouti and Alvarez classification of Games for Health is a four-parameter model: *gameplay, purpose, function, and public*. *Function* and *public* parameters are similar to Sawyer and Smith's, except that *therapeutic* becomes a subitem of the broader function *care*. The *purpose* only contains three items: broadcast a message (which can be informative, persuasive, etc.), provide a training, enhance data sharing. Djaouti and Alvarez's work provides information on game features. Their *gameplay* parameter makes the difference between *Ludus* and *Païda* based on the presence or not of explicit goals. Moreover, they work on a general serious game classification which uses their gameplay bricks taxonomy along with game genres and themes keywords [21] [8].

With the help of these taxonomies, we identified that therapeutic games are serious games which are classified as Games for Health. Their therapeutic function is what makes them different from other Games for Health. Although we did not found a classification specific to therapeutic games, the classification of Alvarez and Djaouti helps to differentiate therapeutic games. Such classification is useful. First, it deepens our understanding of what therapeutic games can achieve. Second, it helps to find similar therapeutic games. Finally, it makes possible to delimit the scope of a therapeutic game during the design steps. Thus, we use this classification to study therapeutic games in the next section.

2.2   Therapeutic Games

McGraw-Hill Concise Dictionary of Modern Medicine[2] proposes this definition of a therapy: "*A general term for any form of management of a particular condition; treatment intended and expected to alleviate a disease or disorder; any technique of recovery, which may be medical, psychiatric, or psychological.*" The dictionary also proposes a list of more than two hundreds different therapies. Some of them are very general (e.g. Physical therapy), while others are very specific (e.g. Nicotine replacement therapy). But game designers are seldom medical experts. Thus, it would not be useful for them to classify therapy from a medical standpoint. However, we have to acknowledge the wide scope of possible therapeutic protocol and define a classification useful for game designers.

We have analysed existing therapeutic games and identified that, while some of them are directly therapeutic, others are indirectly therapeutic. For example, the game Brick 'a' break described in Burke et al. is a direct therapeutic games [3, 4]. The game activity is the rehabilitation protocol. Brick 'a' break improves the particular condition of having a loss of motor control in upper limb after a stroke. Equally, playing Virtual Iraq is what directly alleviate or suppress the post traumatic stress of soldiers [27]. Also, *le village aux oiseaux* aims to reduce the effects due to the disease Alzheimer by training the patient's attentional network.

On contrary, indirect therapies are in themselves not sufficient to improve the particular conditions of a patient. Instead, they improve the patient behaviour,

---

[2] © 2002 by The McGraw-Hill Companies, Inc.

mood, or observance. For example, RE-Mission is a game for patients having a cancer [15]. The game provides knowledge on the disease, its treatment, as well as the means to alleviate the adverse effects. As a result, the patients become more observant with their therapy protocol (i.e. they take more regularly their oral chemotherapy, along with drugs to alleviate the adverse effects). This change in the patient's behaviour make the main therapy more efficient.

Other indirect therapeutic games do not target the patient, but the care giver work, the scientific research or the patient's relatives. For instance, SnowWorld is a virtual reality game that try to overload the attentional network of highly-burned patients. The objective is to alleviate the patient's pain during the bandage change in order to facilitates the care giver's work [12]. FoldIt and Phylo are games that help the scientific research to advance on therapeutics by using the computing power of mankind [17] [16]. These games aims the gathering of knowledge that could improve the development of therapy. Finally, other therapeutic games target the patient's relatives. For instance, Elude helps the patient's relatives to understand what it means to be depressive [31]. These games have an indirect therapeutic effect by engaging the relatives in the recovery process.

We have classified these therapeutic games according with Alvarez and Djaouti's *public* and *purpose* parameters.

Name	Public	Purpose
Brick 'a' break	Patient / Direct	Provide a training
Virtual Iraq	Patient / Direct	Provide a training
Le Village aux Oiseaux	Patient / Direct	Provide a training
RE-Mission	Patient / Indirect	Broadcast a message
FoldIt / Phylo	Everyone / Indirect	Improve data sharing
Elude	Patient's relatives / Indirect	Broadcast a message

Fig. 1. Classification of some therapeutic games

These different therapeutic uses of games do not require the same design methods. For example, games like RE-Mission or Elude are, from a game design standpoint, similar to Games for Education. They can be designed with existing methods, see [24] or [34] for examples. Also, FoldIt and Phylo are defined as Games for Research, they require a specific design process which is different from, for example, the game design process of *le village aux oiseaux* or Virtual Iraq. Also, we did not classify SnowWorld. The game has a direct therapeutic effect (i.e. it alleviates temporary the patient's pain) and an indirect therapeutic effect (i.e. it facilitates the care giver's work). But, none of these effects are precisely described with the existing items of Djaouti and Alvarez's *purpose* parameter. As our objective is to improve the design efficiency, we prefer to treat games like SnowWorld as special case, instead of describing them imprecisely. In fact, the most relevant *purpose* item is the broadcast of a persuasive message. But the design of persuasive game seems not to be the same as the design required to create a game like SnowWorld. The analyses of these therapeutic games reveal that they require very different design process. Thus, we decided to limit the scope of the first version of our model to therapeutic games which provide a training that improve directly the patient condition.

Most of these therapeutic games have been evaluated and have a proven medical efficiency. The fact they are played could indicate that they are good games, but they can also be played only for their therapeutic efficiency (i.e. without pleasure). As we advocate that therapeutic games have to be good games, we study why games are motivating in the next section.

2.3   Game

As motivation is the most expected effect of a game in the context of a therapy, the model emphasizes motivational aspects of games. First, we compare play and therapeutic activities regarding motivation theory. Then, we examine game theory with regards to their relation to the player motivation.

Ryan and Deci classify motivation quality as follows: amotivation (i.e. when there is no motivation), extrinsic motivation (i.e. when the activity is done to obtain a separable outcome), and intrinsic motivation (i.e. when the activity is done for the activity itself) [28]. They split extrinsic motivation into four subcategories, depending on the level of internalization (i.e. the process of taking in a value or a regulation) and integration (i.e. transformation of the value or regulation to fully integrate the sense of self) one's made of the activity. Also, Ryan and Deci stated that *"intrinsic motivation exists in the nexus between a person and a task"*.

However, Csikszentmihalyi's flow theory explains that some activities can more easily elicit intrinsic motivation [5]. Because games are designed to be pleasurable and interesting activities, games are very powerful to create and foster motivation of their players. Generally, games are played for the sake of playing them. On the contrary, therapeutic activities are designed to maximise their efficiency. Patients engage in therapy for an identified separable outcome: health recovery. Ryan and Deci describe a similar issue in education: *"Given that many of the educational activities prescribed in schools are not designed to be intrinsically interesting, a central question concerns how to motivate students to value and self-regulate such activities, and without external pressure, to carry them out on their own."* But, according to Ryan and Deci, an activity started for a separable outcome can become a self-determined activity if the person finds the activity sufficiently interesting. We emphasize this and recommend to make a therapeutic game as interesting and fun as possible to smooth out the medical aspect. Doing so should maximise the patient's motivation. As a result, we have now to understand which game features enhance the player motivation.

There exists numerous models of what makes a good video game [6, 18, 19, 23, 25, 33]. These models encompass many aspect of video game enjoyment: for instance having an adapted level of challenge, as well as fostering social connectedness or having a high level of fantasy. In this paper, we propose a model for game designers, and moreover, designers of therapeutic games. We will thus extract the very common and core features of these models, and especially the features related to the very basis of the game designer's work.

Two features seems to be present in many models and are fundamental to the game designer's work: *challenge* and *variability*. Challenge is common to all of the pre-cited models. Malone defines challenges as the fact that the player is uncertain to reach his goals. This is why games have a certain difficulty level: the outcome of the game depends on the player inputs, and not any input may lead the player to his goal. To analyse the challenge level of a game, we may consider different kinds of difficulty that a game may rely on. For instance, Levieux proposes to distinguish between sensitive, logical and motor difficulty to better analyse the challenge level of a task [20]. These kinds of difficulty are particularly relevant for therapeutic games. For instance, patients having low motor abilities can have standard logical abilities.

Variability is common to [6,18,23,33]. In his model, Malone presents variability as the *curiosity* level. It may be sensitive curiosity, that is, the variability of the representation, or the cognitive curiosity, which corresponds to how much information the player can learn when playing a game. Also Vorderer et al explains that a game should propose many choices to the player [33], Ralph Koster that we enjoy learning patterns in games [18], and Denis and Jouvelot that game designers must *derail the gameplay* to create alternatives for the player [6].

Challenge and variability aspects are tightly related to the design of a therapeutic game. If we want to keep the player motivated, we have to inform him on his progression towards the goal. Another basis is to adapt the challenge level, if we don't want to create anxiety or boredom, or even let the player reach a flow state [5]. And if we want to keep the player motivated in the long run, we must provide enough variability. It is not enough to give the player the same task with an adapted difficulty level, we must also make him learn new patterns, gather new informations, explore the consequences of making different choices.

2.4   Le village aux oiseaux

The model presented in this paper has been built during the design of *Le village aux oiseaux*. *Le village au oiseaux* is born from a partnership between four companies (Tekneo, Seaside Agency, SpirOps, Neofactory) and two research laboratories (CEDRIC[3], INSERM [4]). *Le village au oiseaux* targets patients suffering from the Alzheimer disease. The game stimulates the patient's attention to slow down the cognitive decline due to the disease. *Le village au oiseaux* is designed to be a full-featured game providing a game world, a story and different gameplay activities. The player takes the role of a photograph that will help the inhabitants of a little town to avoid their town's destruction. The player's mission is to take pictures of rare birds. After the model presentation, we explain how the model has proven useful during the design process of *le village aux oiseaux*.

---

[3] Center for Research in Computer Science and Telecommunications.

[4] National Institute for Health and Medical Research.

3   Therapeutic Game Model

As seen in section 2.2, a therapy targets a *particular condition* which can be a disease, a disorder or a function to recover. Thus, the context of use and the patient's condition are mandatory parameters to define a therapeutic game. A game is not therapeutic *de facto*, the therapeutic function emerges from the relation between the player and the game. To illustrate this fact, a good example is Active Music Therapy which uses music as a mediation mean [2]. Most of the time, playing music is not a therapeutic activity, but within the specific context of psychotherapy, playing music becomes therapeutic.

Moreover, games are designed to please a specific audience. In consequence, a strong understanding of the therapy, the player, the game, and their underlying relations is necessary to design a therapeutic games. This is the main reason why our analysis model is built around these three aspects: player, game, and therapy. In the following section, we explain the scope of the model and our global goals. Then, we study what is important for each aspects of our analysis model. As these aspects have been thought to be analysed quite independently, the relation between each aspect can be examined to find design inconsistencies. Our analysis model is a list of items to look at for each aspect. To help the game designer to understand which information are relevant, the items proposes examples or questions the analysis has to answer.

3.1   Model Objectives

As seen in section 2.2, we decided to limit the scope of our model to therapeutic games which are directly therapeutic, target the patient, and provide a training which can be cognitive or motor. Our model goal is two-fold. First, with our model, we can analyse existing therapeutic games to find their interesting features. Second, the model should facilitate the game designer's work during the design process. At the beginning, the model tells the game designer which information he has to gather, especially medical information. Knowing which information is necessary should improve the communication between game designers and health experts. Then, along the design and development of a therapeutic game, the model helps to examine the coherency of the game design choices. For example, an as-fast-as-you-can scoring system is not a coherent design choice for a game that train fine motor control. In this context, such scoring system could even be harmful for the patient. The model helps to reveal these kind of design inconsistencies. More broadly, the objective of the model is to find the therapeutic constraints. By doing so, the game designer is aware of which game features he has to design very carefully (i.e. which part of the game design is strongly constrained by the therapy). Also, the game designer knows on which game features he can be more creative to provide a pleasurable and interesting game.

3.2   Therapy

As stated before, the therapeutic function emerges from the relation between the player and the therapy. As a result, the most important element of a therapy is what the therapy can improve. Also, the definition of therapy states *intended and expected*. As a therapy is a medical practice we advocate that this expectation is based on a scientific evaluation of efficiency. However, scientific evaluation is not possible from the very start of the development (i.e. during the conceptual step). During the development, evaluation can be done on prototypes but will generally not be sufficient. When the development is finished, long-term benefits evaluations can start. These facts reveal that being clear-cut on scientific proof of efficiency could be harmful to our model, it would exclude not yet finished therapeutic games. As our model is intended to help the game designer during the design process, we want to propose a smoother approach. So, our model defines in-development game as *te be evaluated*. However, we want to know if these games are founded on existing scientific evidences (e.g. similar positive effects proven in similar games). Nevertheless, a minimal assessment of efficiency is necessary. Games that have been negatively or not evaluated after their completion are thus determined as not therapeutic by our model.

- **Expected short-term therapeutic value:** e.g. burning calories, improving attentional network
- **Expected long-term therapeutic value:** e.g. definitive recovery, life-long supporting therapy
- **Scientific proof of efficiency:** e.g. long-term effects demonstrated, to be evaluated, discussed
- **Scientific references:** Do similar useful games features have been scientifically evaluated in other games?

3.3   Player

Understanding the player is an important aspect of game design. Thus, numerous studies, either academical or industrial, have been conduced to analyse the player and understand what he likes while playing. But, as stated by Ijsselsteijn et al. [13], while information are numerous about usual targets of video games, there is a lack of information on specific population (e.g. seniors). Although there exists numerous usability guidelines for these population, these guidelines are not informative on what, for example, seniors enjoy while playing or which game genres they prefer. As a result, our player model is limited to demographic information and health condition. For the game designer, the most important is to understand what the target is able to do and learn regarding its health condition. Demographic information serves to know player preferences and interests, as well as knowing which usability guidelines to follow. Also, we advice game designer to create *personas*[5] of their targeted players. It gives guidance while designing by determining the *extreme profiles*: a senior who never used a

---

[5] A persona is a description of an imaginary person which represents an entire group.

computer, while another one is fond of new technologies. Using these *extreme profiles* can make the game designer aware of the wide range of different individuals the game should be able to entertain. It also reveals potential usability issues. Finally, we believe that game designers has to gather more information on the target's interests if these information are not available. For example, the game designer can conduce early playtests with similar games as we explained in another article [22].

- **Age range**
- **Gender**
- **Particular conditions:** e.g. early states of the Alzheimer disease, motor control loss in upper limb
- **Abilities:** Regarding their age and particular conditions, which are the knowledge and abilities (i.e. motor control and cognitive functions) of the player? Are they likely to present other particular conditions?

3.4   Game

As seen in section 2.3, numerous approach exists on what makes a good game, but we have identified that challenge and variability were very common and important. Thus, we propose to analyse the gameplay of therapeutic games from the challenge (goals, feedbacks, scores, and difficulty) and variability perspectives. Also, information about the input and output systems are relevant elements while designing a game. As some games are recognised to provide positive side-effects, the model asks if the game has features which are known to create positive side-effects (e.g. some games are known to improve the mood or self-esteem of their players).

- **Input system:** How does the player interact with the game?
- **Output system:** How does the game convey information?
- **Goals:** Are there appealing goals? Are they short, mid or long-term goals?
- **Feedbacks:** Which means are used to communicate with the player? Are they informative on the player performance or progression?
- **Score:** What does the score mean? (e.g. player performance, player progression, health improvement) Is the score informative on the progression towards mid or long-term therapeutic goals?
- **Difficulty:** How is the difficulty level chosen? (e.g. adaptive, manually chosen by the player, manually chosen by another person) If adaptive, how does it work? Which parameters of the game are modified by the difficulty level?
- **Variability:** Does the game propose enough variability? (e.g. the player is always doing the same sequence of actions, the player learns regularly to master new patterns, the player can choose his own path within the game, the player has to create new strategies to progress)
- **Usability:** What are the minimal abilities and knowledge necessary to play the game? Does the game features tutorials and explanations?

- **Expected positive side-effect:** What can the game provide to the player that is not part of the therapy itself?
- **Reported serious uses:** Have the game or analysed features been used for another serious purpose?

3.5   Underlying Relations

The most important part of the analysis process is to validate the design coherency. This coherency is examined by evaluating the relation between each aspects of a therapeutic game: the player, the game, and the therapy. Moreover, each aspect of our model has been thought to be independent. So, the model is useful to evaluate an entertainment game: finding its motivational features, existing serious uses, and possible positive effects.

- **Player / Therapy:** Does the player have a particular condition that can be improved by the therapy?
- **Game / Therapy:** What is the context of play? (e.g. at home, with a therapist) What is the place of the game within this context? Which game features are therapeutic? (e.g. the gameplay) Which game features are only motivational means?
- **Player / Game:** Is the player able to play the game? Is the game enjoyable for the player? Is the game safe for the patient's health?

3.6   Le village aux oiseaux

Le village aux oiseaux has been inspired by a scientific study of Green and Bavelier. This study proves that action games, particularly first person shooter (FPS), improve the attention network of their players [9]. *Le village aux oiseaux* uses these intrinsic effects of FPS to smooth the cognitive decline of patients suffering from the Alzheimer's disease. At the beginning of the project, we had information about the game genre and the player demographic information. However, with the model, we knew that we lacked information about our player's abilities, as well as which features of FPS games are effectively training the attention network. Here, to illustrate how our model can work while designing a therapeutic game, we explain two main design decisions the model helped us to make.

First, the analysis of the player-game relation makes clear from the very start that it would not be possible for seniors to play a standard FPS. These games require a strong ability to move in a virtual 3D space. We assumed that starting a therapeutic game by having to learn a difficult ability would alienate our players. So, we decided that *Le village aux oiseaux* would be a rail shooter (i.e. the player movement are automated and he can focus on the aim and shot activity), and that the player will aim with a natural controller (i.e. similar to the Nintendo's wiimote). However, we had no data to prove that seniors may enjoy a game were they have to aim and shoot with a natural controller. In consequence, we conduced early playtests with similar games to be sure that seniors will enjoy the game we were designing. These playtests and results have been detailed in another article [22].

Second, as the gameplay was the therapeutic part of the game, it was really important to know better what was therapeutic in it. This aspect required to exchange with health experts. To sum up, the main concept that health experts make us understand was that if the player can use his memory (i.e. instead of processing the game environment) the therapeutic gameplay fails at training the attention. But, challenge and scoring system of rail shooters are strongly tied to the memorisation of the game sequences. The long-term player's objective is to perform each sequence perfectly. We changed this aspect of the game to make it therapeutic. This is why *le village aux oiseaux* features adaptive levels, in which the birds act differently each time. We knew that this change had consequences on the long-term motivation provided by the game. With adaptive levels, the player can't dedicate himself to perform perfectly the game sequences. So, to compensate the loss of these long-term goals and strengthen the patient's motivation, we had to design other features (e.g. storyline, collection of pictures, rare birds to discover).

In conclusion, the model helped us to find design inconsistencies. It also revealed the consequences of each game design change and helped us to design more efficiently.

4   Discussion

So far, we used our model to analyse five entertainment games and therapeutic games. From these analyses, we draw some early conclusions on the model usefulness. First, the model can be used to determine if a particular use of a game is therapeutic or not. For instance, Brain Age has some proven effects on the brain (e.g. memory improvement). But Brain Age is not therapeutic, because it does not target any particular medical conditions. Equally, the game Ico has been designed for entertainment. Within the specific context of a psychotherapy, Ico can be used as a mediation tool with children having a particular psychology condition [32]. This specific use of Ico is therapeutic. With our model, we can analyse Ico has an entertainment game, but we can also analyse the specific therapeutic use of ICO. Finally, using the model is efficient to find similarities and differences between an entertainment game and a therapeutic games. For example, Dance Dance Revolution and Dance Town feature the same gameplay. Dance Dance Revolution (DDR) is an entertainment rhythm game where the player has to step on buttons according to arrow patterns displayed on a screen. DDR targets adolescents and young adults. On the contrary, Dance Town targets seniors to improve their coordination and balance. We have found that Dance Town features three main adaptations: more protection around the dance pad, songs and visuals that please the seniors, and easier arrow patterns (both in rythm and complexity). These adaptations aims to make the game playable for seniors, but also pleasurable by featuring, for instance, songs they like. In conclusion, the effect of improving coordination and balance is already present in the original DDR, game designers of Dance Town have mainly adapted DDR for the specific target.

However, we have also found weaknesses in our model. First, the model asks the game designer to write full-text description for each items. This is very useful and usable for game designers, but not very efficient to conduce automated meta-analyses. Also, we limited the quantity of items in each aspects trying to keep only essential ones. We have now to conduce more analyses to be sure that these items are sufficient. We think that analysing more games like Virtual Iraq could reveal other essential game features (e.g. environment, story).

The next step of our research will be the development of a tool. This tool has the objective to facilitate the use of our model. Also, it will help to structure data in order to conduce meta-analyses later. After that, we will analyse numerous existing therapeutic games to better understand how they are designed and how the relations between the player, the game, and the therapy work. This analysis model and the building of more knowledge is the first step of our research, our final objective is to provide methods to design therapeutic games more efficiently.

5   Conclusion

In this paper, we have presented how we built an analysis model for therapeutic games. The model proposes to analyse separately each aspect of a therapeutic games: the player, the game, and the therapy. The objective of the model is to help a game designer while designing a therapeutic games: gathering information with medical experts, examining the game design coherency by analysing the relations between each aspect, evaluating the game efficiency regarding the two objectives of a therapeutic game (i.e. being therapeutic and motivating), and analysing similar games to find their interesting features and how they work regarding therapeutic activity.

During the design of le village aux oiseaux, the model has proven useful. It helped us to make design decision and predict consequences of game design changes. Also, by conducing some analyses, we have found that our model was able to deepen our knowledge on therapeutic games. Separating the three aspects of therapeutic games (i.e. player, game, and therapy), to then analyse their relations has been powerful to understand how therapeutic games work. Also, we have used our model to make comparison between similar games to better understand the effects of certain games features. However, we need a tool to improve the analysis model usability and to obtain structured data on therapeutic games. The development of this tool is the next step of our research, then we will deepen even more our knowledge on therapeutic games. Finally, our objective is to build design methods alongside this analysis model.

References

1. Alvarez, J., Djaouti, D.: Une taxinomie des serious games dédiés au secteur de la santé. Revue de l'Electricité et de l'Electronique, Société de l'Electricité, de l'Electronique et des Technologies de l'Information et de la Communication (SEE) 11, 91–102 (2008)
2. Benveniste, S., Jouvelot, P., Lecourt, E., Michel, R.: Designing wiimprovisation for mediation in group music therapy with children suffering from behavioral disorders. In: Proceedings of the 8th International Conference on Interaction Design and Children, IDC 2009, pp. 18–26. ACM, New York (2009)
3. Burke, J.W., McNeill, M.D.J., Charles, D.K., Morrow, P.J., Crosbie, J.H., McDonough, S.M.: Optimising engagement for stroke rehabilitation using serious games. Vis. Comput. 25, 1085–1099 (2009)
4. Burke, J.W., McNeill, M.D.J., Charles, D.K., Morrow, P.J., Crosbie, J.H., McDonough, S.M.: Augmented reality games for upper-limb stroke rehabilitation. In: Proceedings of the 2010 Second International Conference on Games and Virtual Worlds for Serious Applications, VS-GAMES 2010, pp. 75–78. IEEE Computer Society, Washington, DC (2010)
5. Csikszentmihalyi, M.: Flow: The Psychology of Optimal Experience. Harper Perennial (March 1991)
6. Denis, G., Jouvelot, P.: Motivation-driven educational game design: Applying best practices to music education. In: Proc. Int. Conf. on Advances in Computer Entertainment Technology, pp. 462–465. ACM Press (2005)
7. Djaouti, D.: Serious Game Design Considérations théoriques et techniques sur la création de jeux vidéo á vocation utilitaire. PhD thesis, Université Toulouse III Paul Sabatier (UT3 Paul Sabatier) (2011)
8. Djaouti, D., Alvarez, J., Ghassempouri, R., Jessel, J.P., Methel, G.: Towards a classification of video games. In: Artificial and Ambient Intelligence convention (Artificial Societies for Ambient Intelligence) (2007)
9. Green, C.S., Bavelier, D.: Action video game modifies visual selective attention. Nature 423(6939), 534–537 (2003)
10. Greitzer, F.L., Kuchar, O.A., Huston, K.: Cognitive science implications for enhancing training effectiveness in a serious gaming context. J. Educ. Resour. Comput. 7 (November 2007)
11. Guardiola, E., Natkin, S., Soriano, D., Loarer, E., Vrignaud, P.: Du jeu utile au jeu sérieux (serious game). Hermés 62, 87–93 (in press, 2012)
12. Hoffman, H.G., Doctor, J.N., Patterson, D.R., Carrougher, G.J., Furness, T.A.: Virtual reality as an adjunctive pain control during burn wound care in adolescent patients. Pain (85), 305–309 (2000)
13. Ijsselsteijn, W., Nap, H.H., de Kort, Y., Poels, K.: Digital game design for elderly users. In: Proceedings of the 2007 Conference on Future Play, Future Play 2007, pp. 17–22. ACM, New York (2007)
14. Juul, J.: In: The Game, the Player, the World: Looking for a Heart of Gameness, vol. 120, pp. 30–45. Utrecht University (2003)
15. Kato, P.M., Cole, S.W., Bradlyn, A.S., Pollock, B.H.: A video game improves behavioral outcomes in adolescents and young adults with cancer: A randomized trial. Pediatrics 122(2), e305–e317 (2008)
16. Kawrykow, A., Roumanis, G., Kam, A., Kwak, D., Leung, C., Wu, C., Zarour, E., Sarmenta, L., Blanchette, M., Waldispühl, J.: Phylo: A citizen science approach for improving multiple sequence alignment. PLoS ONE 7(3), e31362 (2012)

17. Khatib, F., Cooper, S., Tyka, M., Xu, K., Makedon, I., Popović, Z., Baker, D., Players, F.: Algorithm discovery by protein folding game players. Proceedings of the National Academy of Sciences 108(47), 18949–18953 (2011)
18. Koster, R.: A Theory of Fun for Game Design. Paraglyph Press, Scottsdale (2005)
19. Lazzaro, N.: Why we play games: Four keys to more emotion without story. In: Game Developers Conference (March 2004)
20. Levieux, G.: Mesure de la difficulté dans les jeux vidéo. PhD thesis, Conservatoire National des Arts et Métiers (2011)
21. Ludoscience: Serious game classification, http://serious.gameclassification.com (last access June 08, 2011)
22. Mader, S., Dupire, J., Guardiola, E., Natkin, S.: Conception de jeux thérapeutiques pour seniors: l'exemple du village aux oiseaux. In: Handicap 2012, Paris (June 2012)
23. Malone, T.W.: What makes things fun to learn? heuristics for designing instructional computer games. In: SIGSMALL 1980: Proceedings of the 3rd ACM SIGSMALL Symposium and the first SIGPC Symposium on Small Systems, pp. 162–169. ACM, New York (1980)
24. Marne, B., Huynh Kim Bang, B., Labat, J.M.: Articuler motivation et apprentissage grâce aux facettes du jeu sérieux. In: Environnements Informatiques Pour l'Apprentissage Humain, pp. 69–80 (May 2011) ISBN: 978-2-87325-061-4
25. McGonigal, J.: Reality is broken. Penguin Books, New York (2011)
26. Prensky, M.: Digital game-based learning. Comput. Entertain. 1, 21 (2003)
27. Rizzo, A., Difede, J., Rothbaum, B., Reger, G., Spitalnick, J., Cukor, J., Mclay, R., et al.: Development and early evaluation of the virtual iraq/afghanistan exposure therapy system for combat-related ptsd. Annals of the New York Academy of Sciences 1208(1), 114–125 (2010)
28. Ryan, R.M., Deci, E.L.: Intrinsic and extrinsic motivations: Classic definitions and new directions. Contemporary Educational Psychology 25(1), 54–67 (2000)
29. Salen, K., Zimmerman, E.: Rules of Play: Game Design Fundamentals. The MIT Press (October 2003)
30. Sawyer, B., Smith, P.: Serious game taxonomy. In: The Serious Games Summit @ GDC (2008)
31. Singapore MIT GAMBIT Game Lab: Elude, http://gambit.mit.edu/loadgame/elude.php (last access March 29, 2012)
32. Stora, M.: Histoire d'un atelier jeu vidéo: " ico ", un conte de fée interactif pour des enfants en manque d'interactions (2008), http://www.omnsh.org/spip.php?article84 (last access June 08, 2011)
33. Vorderer, P., Hartmann, T., Klimmt, C.: Explaining the enjoyment of playing video games: the role of competition. In: ICEC 2003: Proceedings of the Second International Conference on Entertainment Computing, Pittsburgh, PA, USA, Carnegie Mellon University, pp. 1–9 (2003)
34. Wei, T., Li, Y.: Design of Educational Game: A Literature Review. In: Pan, Z., Cheok, A.D., Müller, W., Zhang, X., Wong, K. (eds.) Transactions on Edutainment IV. LNCS, vol. 6250, pp. 266–276. Springer, Heidelberg (2010)
35. Zyda, M.: From visual simulation to virtual reality to games. Computer 38(9), 25–32 (2005)

Game-Based Trust

Sebastian Matyas[1,2], Daishi Kato[2], Takao Shime[2],
Kazuo Kunieda[3], and Keiji Yamada[2]

[1] Japanese Society for the Promotion of Science Fellow
[2] NEC C&C Innovation Initiative,
[3] NEC Capital Solutions Limited,
8916-47, Takayama-cho, Ikoma, Nara, 630-0101, Japan
smatyas7@googlemail.com,
daishi@cb.jp.nec.com, t-shime@ce.jp.nec.com,
k-kunieda@ak.jp.nec.com, kg-yamada@cp.jp.nec.com

Abstract. Trust stands at the beginning of every meaningful interaction between members of any kind of community – be it in the real world or in a
virtual one. But how could an application look like that helps to create or even
foster the interpersonal trust of its users? We developed a game – *Kokochi* –
with the goal to positively affect the interpersonal trust level of its players. We
evaluated *Kokochi* in two case studies and compared the results with a control
group that didn´t play the game. We could show that playing the game – featuring three unique game elements to enhance trust: disclosure of personal information (emotional statements), collaborations (face-to-face) and showing
goodwill towards other players (virtual hugging) – resulted in an (significant)
higher interpersonal trust level of the subjects after the game than they had
before.

Keywords: Emotion, Trust, Location-based gaming, Collaboration.

1   Introduction

For several decades researchers have discussed about the various definitions of trust
and depending on the research field (Psychology, Social Sciences, Computer Sciences
– especially MAS (Multi-Agent-Systems) and virtual communities – or others) they
associated various properties with the term "trust". For an overview on these properties of trust see e.g. the works of Kramer (1999), Marsh (1994) and Goldbeck (2005,
2006). Although certainly not complete the following properties are the most noted
ones: Social uncertainty[1], Commitment (Dellarocas, 2003)[1], Goodwill/Benign intent[1,2], Reputation[1], Consistency[1] (Past experience/interaction), Delegation[2] (Castelfranchi and Falcone, 1998), Attitude/Mood/Optimism[2] (Jones, 1996) and Confidence
(Golembiewski and McConkie 1975).

---

[1] Yamagishi and Yamagishi (1994); Yamagishi, Cook, Watabe (1998).
[2] Subsumed under the term "emotion".

M. Herrlich, R. Malaka, and M. Masuch (Eds.): ICEC 2012, LNCS 7522, pp. 207–220, 2012.
© IFIP International Federation for Information Processing 2012

But how could an application look like that helps to create or even foster the inter-personal trust of its users? Which kinds of features are appropriate to help realizing one or more of the above mentioned properties of trust?

Fig. 1. (top row): Intro, Log in, **Home** and Timeline screen; (bottom row): Map, **Ritual**, Community Tree and Player ranking screen

It is a well accepted fact that games can be used to motivate people to take part in various kinds of activities they otherwise would be more reluctant to do - for example to do sport activities (Mueller et al. 2007), to look after one's health (Anderson et al. 2007), learning (Johnson 2010) or even to work for free (like labeling photos on the web or map the world, Ahn and Dabbish 2008). The first two practices are used in the research of serious gaming while the later one is featured in the human computation (Ahn and Dabbish 2008) and volunteered geographic information (VGI) (Goodchild 2007) field.

We use the motivational ability of a location-based game to foster interpersonal trust in a real-world community of players. Therefore we present the game Kokochi (Figure 1 shows screenshots of our current build) that implements unique game elements to realize three of the above mentioned properties – social uncertainty, commitment and goodwill:

- disclosure of personal information (emotion statements) – **Home** screen (Fig. 1)
- collaborations (face-to-face) – **Ritual** screen (Fig. 1)
- showing goodwill towards other players (virtual hugging) – **Home** screen (Fig. 1)

Kokochi is both a collaborative and competitive game experience that significantly affects the interpersonal trust level of its players.

The rest of the paper is structured as follows: In the next section we will outline the related work with regard to trust in general and some of its properties that were already used in game-like applications. Section 3 introduces our Kokochi game and its trust fostering game elements. We evaluated our game in two case studies - described in section 4 – which results in a significant rise of the interpersonal trust level of its participants. In the last section we discuss this result and give an outlook on further studies.

2   Related Work: Collaboration, Trust, Emotions

According to the uncertainty reduction theory (URT) after Berger and Calabrese (1975) – see also Blanchard and Markus (2004) and Virtanen and Malinen (2008) – one of the aims in every interpersonal interaction is to get to know as much personal traits of your interaction partner as possible. This personal identity disclosure leads to more trust and communication between them. As there are numerous personal traits that one can disclose to other people we were looking at those that are especially suitable for a game-based experience.

Emotions are an essential part of every game-based experience. Research topics like immersion (Carrigy 2010) and game-flow (Jegers 2007) are well established in the game research community. And everyone that has played a game with friends or strangers over the internet or in a living room can tell some funny, angry, sad or happy stories that happened while playing the game. Our idea is to let players communicate their emotions during game play as one part of their personality.

From the literature (Lount 2010) it is known that emotions, or moods (sometimes there is no clear distinction between the two), can have a significant effect on the judgments we make about other people. Two main models are extensively investigated in this context. On the one hand we have the Mood-Congruent model (Mayer et al. 1992) that simple says that your judgments are influenced in the direction of your current mood state. So if you are in a positive (negative) mood your judgment will also be more positive (negative) too. On the other hand we have the Accommodation–Assimilation model (Bless and Fiedler, 2006) that makes the point that under a positive mood people are more sensible about clues that either supports a positive or negative judgment of other persons, leading to more or less trust. In either way there seems to be a positive correlation between mood and how you judge respectively trust other people. So far neither the Mood-Congruent nor the Accommodation–Assimilation model has been used in a real-world application.

The works of George and Brief (1992) and others have shown one interesting way to get people into a positive mood and that is by getting them to do some good task. They look especially into tasks for the public good where there is no monetary gain to be achieved. One prominent example is donating money to a non-profit organization or community service. In correspondence with the above mentioned mood-trust models this could lead to some promising applications as we will see in this paper.

Bernhaupt et al. (2007) and Church, Hoggan and Oliver (2010) are two of the more recent examples that uses emotions in their research. The first one is a game-like application where the emotional states of office workers are detected via facial expression recognition. The more positive expressions of a player are recorded the faster he lets a virtual flower grow. The player who first lets his flower fully grow wins the game. The authors report that this kind of game can increase for example communication between the players.

In the later one the authors present *MobiMood*, an iPhone app, that lets its users share their current emotional state. To do this they simple have to select one of the predefined emotions in the app or create a new one and send it to all the other users of the app. In addition the location where the emotion was experienced is shared as well. Though the study was more focused on design principles one interesting result was that it enhanced the communication between the users also outside of the application itself. The connection to interpersonal trust was not analyzed.

Research on trust in virtual teams e.g. by Jarvenpaa and Leidner (1999) focuses more on what kind of effect trust has on the successful outcome of a project. Our focus is to identify game elements that can help to foster interpersonal trust. In the same context Lionel et al. (2009) investigate the occurrences of "swift trust" in virtual teams but don´t propose any specific techniques to build up trust in such teams.

3   *Kokochi*: Emotion-Based Collaboration Game

Our game *Kokochi* is both a collaborative and competitive game experience. The background story tells about a cherry blossom tree that once blossomed throughout the whole year and kept the community of the players save from evil. But because the people living in the community stopped to share their emotional state with each other the tree withered and lost its protective power.

Fig. 2. The four possible states of the cherry blossom tree in Kokochi; when the last state is reached the game ends

The collaborative goal of Kokochi is now to help the communities cherry blossom tree to fully blossom again. The players can achieve this goal by successfully performing a ritual with at least one other player in the game. In order to perform a successful ritual at least one of the collaborative players has to have a specific combination of emotions that is unknown to them before they start a ritual. The game ends when the last of four blossom states is reached - Figure 2 shows all possible blossom states of the cherry blossom tree in the game. The number of cherry blossom states in our study has been chosen to make the game evenly paced. The one player that helps most to restore the power of the tree gains a free wish from him (see also[3] for the corresponding comic strip).

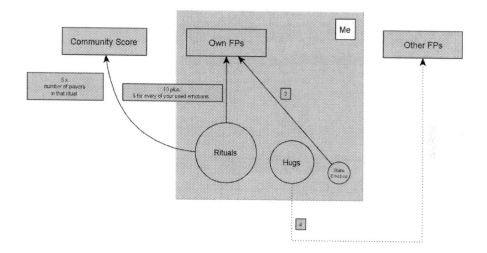

Fig. 3. Scores in *Kokochi* (FPs = Flower Points)

To achieve this competitive goal of *Kokochi* a players needs to have the most Flower Points (FPs) when the cherry blossom tree reaches its fourth blossom state. A player gains FPs by stating emotions (2 FPs) by getting hugged by other players (4 FPs) and by successfully performing rituals with other players (10 + 5 FPs for every emotion of a player that is used to fulfill the required emotion combination) - see Figure 3 for a structured overview of the point allocation for each game activity. The specific point counts were chosen so that a game of Kokochi would last – depending of the number collaborations between the players – on average around a week.

Consequently the game features two kinds of scores one for each goal. The community score keeps track of the progress of all players in the game – the collaborative game part – and the FPs keep track of the progress of an individual player – the competitive game part. Players have to keep both scores in mind when they play the game as they don´t want to end the game by contributing to the community score before their individual score is high enough. This leads to some interesting game design decisions that we will discuss in the following when we look into the individual game elements of *Kokochi*.

The game itself is realized as a HTM5 web-application and therefore runs on any kind of mobile device.

---

[3] http://81.20.134.106/ moodGame/m.kokochi.html

3.1   Stating Emotions and Virtual Hugs

The game features 28 predefined emotions organized in four distinguish categories – excited, relaxed, depressed and frustrated. All emotions are taken from Russell (1980). Players can state any emotion freely throughout the game. As emotions can change rather quickly – according to the literature they normally last no longer than 15 minutes – we made it possible that a player can state up to three emotions during a period of 20 minutes. During these 20 minutes any combination of emotion statements is possible, the player can even state three identical emotions to emphasize in some way the strength of her emotion. Figure 4 shows that stating an emotion is simple done by pressing a button.

But the 20 minute time restriction also serves as a soft cheating prevention mechanism. Because we have no way to verify if players truly state their emotion the players could just state continuously any kind of emotion and gather FPs very quickly in this way. With the time constraint a player has at least to wait the full 20 minutes until she can state three fresh emotions and there is a clear limit to the number of FPs one can achieve in this way.

Another anti-cheating measurement is the relatively low amount of FPs an emotion statements earns a player (2 FPs). He would have to state emotions for more than half an hour for example to make up for only one ritual that another player could perform in the same time frame. These measurements together with the way rituals are performed should make it very unattractive for a player to falsely state his emotions.

Fig. 4. Stating emotions (left) and hugging (right)

Every player can give any other player a virtual hug in the game. As stated in the introduction these virtual hugs should give the players the opportunity to show good-will towards the other players to rise their and the other players mood within the game in the long term. Consequently hugging another player is not only a nice gesture like for example the *like*-button in Facebook[4] but also bears additional meaning: the hugged player receives four FPs for free.

Again this could be potentially be misused by pairs or groups of players who hug each other continuously during the game. That is why each player can only send ten hugs to another player during a period of 24 hours.

For both, emotion statements and hugs, the GPS coordinate was recorded. This way a player can see where each of the above described game actions took place by selecting the Map screen of *Kokochi*.

3.2   Performing Rituals

Rituals are the only way to actually finish the game. A ritual can be performed by two or more players. To perform a ritual they have to select their ritual partners on the ritual page in *Kokochi* and then press the start button – see Figure 5. The game internally then randomly builds an emotion pattern. If the players have stated the emotions that the game chose for the pattern any time before the collaboration they succeed in performing the ritual and get their FPs as well as let the cherry blossom tree grow through the community score. The players only know about the composition of the generated emotion pattern after the ritual is performed. If the ritual was successful the players lose the emotions used for that ritual so that they have to state that emotion again before they can use them in another ritual.

Fig. 5. (left to right): Player 4s ritual screen, Player 3s ritual screen, Ritual successful message

Once again cheating is the main reason to keep the pattern information hidden from the players. Our goal here was to not give the players any motivation to just state the emotions needed to successfully perform a ritual but let them state their true emotions.

The emotion pattern changes with every ritual – that is how many emotions are needed in total, the type of emotion that is needed and how many of each individual

---

[4] www.facebook.de

emotion the players need. Figure 5 shows an example of a successful ritual. Here player 3 and 4 want to collaborate and perform a ritual together. So they meet face-to-face, select one another on the list of players and then start the ritual. Note that *Koko-chi* features no communication function like chatting or email on purpose to make the players talk to each other face-to-face to initiate the ritual in the first place. In our example the game generated the pattern (**Sleepy, Happy**). The (**1,1**) shows that both emotions are only need a single time. Now one of the players needs to have stated either **Sleepy** or **Happy** or both sometime before this ritual took place in order to make in successful.

From the literature (Matyas et al., 2009, and Bell et al., 2006) we know that if players fall behind on a leader board too much they become uninterested in a game very fast. *Kokochi* tries to solve this problem with how the emotion pattern is generated by the game.

First of all in the early stages of the game – also depending on how many emotions the players already stated at the point in time they perform a ritual – every ritual succeeds. This is done to not let the players lose their interest early in the game. Secondly the emotion pattern is constructed by the game so that – if it is possible – more emotions of the lower ranked player are used for the pattern as from the higher ranked player in such collaboration. In this way the lower ranked player always gets more points out of a successful ritual. Therefore the lower ranked players have an incentive to perform rituals with higher ranked players and the higher ranked players need to perform rituals either way to finish the game and win.

As for emotion statements and hugs, the GPS coordinate for successful rituals are recorded and visualized on the Map screen of *Kokochi*.

4   Fostering Trust with *Kokochi*

To evaluate *Kokochi* and its trust fostering abilities we conducted two case studies in February/March of 2012. One 3-week case study with 11 members of our laboratory (the CCIL[5]) consisting of 9 male and 2 female players was carried out. Furthermore a 3-day study took place with 6 NAIST university[6] students – 5 male and 1 female players. The age average for the CCIL study was 34,8 and for the NAIST study 29,5. The participants in the former study were all Japanese researchers and in the later international computer science PhD students.

At the start of each study the trust score of each participant was recorded using Rottens (1967) interpersonal trust questionnaire - reprinted in Robinson et al. (1991) It contains of 25 questions and results in a numeric trust value (ranging from 25 to 125 points). The same questionnaire was used at the end of each study to evaluate the change in the trust scores for the players. Additionally all players filled out a general game-related questionnaire after the study that we designed for these studies.

---

[5] http://www.nec.co.jp/rd/en/ccil/
[6] http://www.naist.jp/index_j.html

4.1   Case Study Results

We used a One-Way ANOVA test (using R^7 as our statistic software) to verify if the recorded trust levels of the participants changed significantly. See Figure 6 for the boxplot of the individual trust scores of the participants before (base) and after (post) the game for the CCIL (1) and the NAIST (2) study.

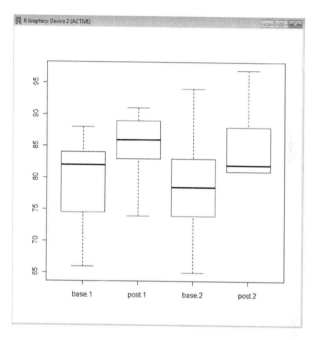

Fig. 6. Trust values before (pre) and after (post) the CCIL Kokochi (1) and the NAIST (2) game (n=11 for base-Group and n=9 for post-Group in the CCIL study and n=6 for base/post-Group)

Table 1. ANOVA result of CCIL game (left) and the NAIST game (right)

	Df	Sum Sq	Mean Sq	F value	Pr(>F)		Df	Sum Sq	Mean Sq	F value	Pr(>F)
Group	1	158.38	158.38	3.9507	**0.06228** .	Group	1	120.333	120.333	8.1674	**0.03549** *
Residuals	18	721.62	40.09			Residuals	5	73.667	14.733		

Signif. codes: 0 '***' 0.001 '**' 0.01 '*' **0.05** '.' **0.1** ' ' 1

---

[7] http://www.r-project.org/

The One-Way ANOVA analysis shows a significant rise in trust scores for the players in the CCIL study (where only the Group average of the trust values was evaluated – Group, p=0.06228, left side Table 1) and in the NAIST study (where the individual trust levels where evaluated - Subject:Group, p=0.03549, right side Table 1). For the CCIL study we were only interested in the general effect.

Additionally we evaluated both studies in a combined analysis (taking the study as a factor into account in the ANOVA analysis – labeled as "Experiment" in Table 2).

As the boxplot (left side of Figure 7) and the ANOVA results show the combination of the studies further improves the p-value (p=0.02585) of the analysis – the non-significant factor "Experiment" allows us to combine the two studies in the first place.

Table 2. ANOVA result of the combined studies

	Df	Sum Sq	Mean Sq	F value	Pr(>F)
Group	1	277.21	277.208	5.5391	**0.02585** *
Experiment	1	0.65	0.654	0.0131	**0.90982**
Group:Experiment	1	0.86	0.856	0.0171	**0.89691**
Residuals	28	1401.28	50.046		

Signif. codes: 0 '***' 0.001 '**' 0.01 '*' **0.05** '.' 0.1 ' ' 1

To verify that the increase in the trust level of the players of *Kokochi* didn´t result from influences outside of the game experience we had a control group fill out the identical trust questionnaire during a two week period in the same time frame as the two studies took place. See the right side of Figure 7 for the boxplot. In the control group half of the participants resided inside of Japan (at the CCIL laboratory) and half were staying outside of Japan (in Bamberg, Germany) – all of them were non-Japanese. The age average was 34,8. The ANOVA results show that there was no significant effect measurable outside the game experience that may had caused the trust fostering effect of *Kokochi* (p=0.488, see Table 3).

Table 3. ANOVA result of the control group

	Df	Sum Sq	Mean Sq	F value	Pr(>F)
Group	1	64.0	64.00	0.5074	**0.488**
Residuals	14	1765.8	126.12		

Signif. codes: 0 '***' 0.001 '**' 0.01 '*' 0.05 '.' 0.1 ' ' 1

4.2   Discussion

For the presented results three factors have to be taken into account. As it is not unusual in case studies in the computer science field both studies are biased towards male participants. Taken individually the number of participants in both studies was on the lower end of the spectrum to be able to generalize the presented findings.

Taken together we think the number of participants is sufficient. The validity of the control group is limited as half of the participants did not reside in the same geographic region as the participants of the main studies.

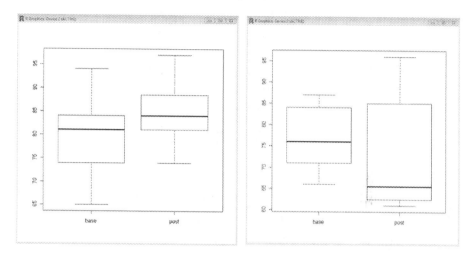

Fig. 7. Left: Trust values of the combined study (base n=17 and post n= 15); *Right:* Trust values of the control group (n=8)

In addition to the trust questionnaire a general game-related questionnaire was filled out by the players after the game and also semi-structured interviews were conducted with the NAIST game participants. Also different kind of log data was recorded and reviewed with a custom-build viewer[8].

One example can be seen in Figure 8 were we illustrate the temporal flow of the CCIL game with respect to the number of hugs, performed rituals and stated emotions. What the trend line indicates is that the number of emotions stated during the game period increases. We take that as an indicator that the game remained interesting for the players till the end and that it gave a sufficient motivation to the players to state their emotion with it. The same is true for the number of hugs. Looking at the raw numbers one can see that hugging was nearly as popular as stating emotions. This is even more surprising as hugging someone gives the players no immediate advantage in the game itself – also no misuse of the hugging feature was observed as discussed in section 3.1. In this context players agreed (11 out of 14) that getting hugged made them feel good but only four (with four neutral on this subject) agreed with the fact that hugging another player made them feel good. We suspect that the mood leveling of hugging is more subtle than the immediate feeling you have when getting hugged.

---

[8] http://81.20.134.106/moodGame_jp/map.html

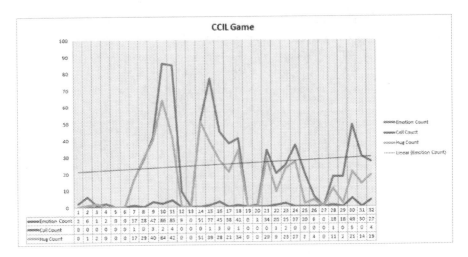

Fig. 8. Flow of the CCIL game: Number of hugs, performed rituals and number of stated emotions per day

5   Conclusions and Outlook

In this paper we presented the (location-based) game *Kokochi* that affects the trust level of its players in a positive way through the implementation of three unique game elements: emotion statements, hugging and rituals. As we have shown with the results of two case studies, playing the game results in a significant raise in the players interpersonal trust.

In our further research we will address the limitations of the presented studies, the number of participants, the bias towards male players and the construction of the control group. We also want to look into a more meaningful usage of the recorded GPS data within the game experience. Another interesting line of research could be to compare our presented emotion-based approach with more traditional forms of team building or sport activities in general.

With the help of more detailed studies we want to evaluate how each of the three used game elements contributed to the enhanced trust scores individually. Furthermore despite the methods we implemented in the current version of *Kokochi* cheating remains – especially in the emotion statement part – one of the biggest concerns with regard to a real-world usage of this kind of gameful trust building application. Here the answers of the post-game interviews give a first hint – namely to separate the emotion stating part from the rest of the game experience. That means that stating emotions themselves doesn't earn a player FPs. Players reported that they would nevertheless state their emotions in such a constellation. They especially liked the act that they could see the emotions statements of the other players.

Acknowledgments. We want to thank Prof. Kato, Prof. Shibata and Prof. Nakamura from NAIST University for their help in the second case study. We also would like to thank Mariana Irigaray for the art work in *Kokochi*. This work was supported by the JSPS[9] scholarship program.

References

1. Anderson, I., Maitland, J., Sherwood, S., Barkhuus, L., Chalmers, M., Hall, M., Brown, B., Muller, H.: Shakra: Tracking and sharing daily activity levels with unaugmented mobile phones. Mob. Netw. Appl. 12(2-3), 185–199 (2007)
2. Berger, C.R., Calabrese, R.J.: Some Explorations in Initial Interaction and Beyond: Toward a Developmental Theory of Interpersonal Communication. Human Communication Research 1(2), 99–112 (1975)
3. Bell, M., Chalmers, M., Barkhuus, L., Hall, M., Sherwood, S., Tennent, P., Brown, B., Rowland, D., Benford, S., Capra, M., Hampshire, A.: Interweaving mobile games with everyday life. In: Grinter, R., Rodden, T., Aoki, P., Cutrell, E., Jeffries, R., Olson, G. (eds.) Proceedings of the SIGCHI Conference on Human Factors in Computing Systems (CHI 2006), pp. 417–426. ACM, New York (2006)
4. Bless, H., Fiedler, K.: Mood and the regulation of information processing and behavior. Affect in social thinking and behavior. In: Affect in Social Thinking and Behavior, pp. 65–84 (2006)
5. Blanchard, A.L., Markus, M.L.: The Experienced "Sense" of a Virtual Community: Characteristics and Processes. The DATA BASE for Advances in Information Systems 35(1), 65–79 (2004)
6. Castelfranchi, C., Falcone, R.: Principles of Trust for MAS: Cognitive Anatomy, Social Importance, and Quantification. In: Multi Agent Systems 1998, pp. 72–79 (1998) IEEE 0-8186-8500-X
7. Church, K., Hoggan, E., Oliver, N.: A study of mobile mood awareness and communication through MobiMood. In: NordiCHI 2010, pp. 128–137 (2010) ACM 978-1-60558-934-3
8. Carrigy, T., Naliuka, K., Paterson, N., Haahr, M.: Design and evaluation of player experience of a location-based mobile game. In: Proceedings of the 6th Nordic Conference on Human-Computer Interaction: Extending Boundaries (NordiCHI 2010), pp. 92–101. ACM, New York (2010)
9. Dellarocas, C.: The Digitization of Word of Mouth - Promise and Challenges of Online Feedback Mechanisms. Management Science 49(10), 1407–1424 (2003)
10. Golbeck, J.A.: Computing and Applying Trust in Web-Based Social Networks. PhD thesis. Faculty of the Graduate School of the University of Maryland (2005)
11. Golbeck, J.A.: Trust on the World Wide Web: A Survey. Foundations and Trends in Web Science 1(2), 131–197 (2006)
12. George, M.J., Brief, P.A.: Feeling Good-Doing Good: A Conceptual Analysis of the Mood at Work-Organizational Spontaneity Relationship. Psychological Bulletin 112(2), 310–329 (1992)
13. Golembiewski, R.T., McConkie, M.: The Centrality of Interpersonal Trust in Group Processes. In: Cooper, C.L. (ed.) Theories of Group Processes, ch. 7, pp. 131–185. Wiley (1975)

---

[9] http://www.jsps.go.jp/english/e-fellow/

14. Goodchild, M.F.: Citizens as Voluntary Sensors: Spatial Data Infrastructure in the World of Web 2.0. International Journal of Spatial Data Infrastructures Research 2, 24–32 (2007) ISSN: 17250463
15. Jones, K.: Trust as an Affective Attitude. Ethics 107(1), S.4–S.25 (1996)
16. Johnson, W.L.: Serious Use of a Serious Game for Language Learning. Int. J. Artif. Intell. Ed. 20(2), 175–195 (2010)
17. Jegers, K.: Pervasive game flow: understanding player enjoyment in pervasive gaming. Comput. Entertain. 5(1), Article 9 (January 2007)
18. Jarvenpaa, S.L., Leidner, D.E.: Communication and Trust in Global Virtual Teams. Organization Science 10(6), 791–815 (1999)
19. Kramer, R.M.: Trust and Distrust in Organizations: Emerging Perspectives, Enduring Questions. Annu. Rev. Psychol. 50, 569–598 (1999)
20. Robert Jr., L., Denis, A., Hung, Y.-T.: Individual Swift Trust and Knowledge-Based Trust in Face-to-Face and Virtual Team Members. J. Manage. Inf. Syst. 26(2), 241–279 (2009)
21. Lount, R.B.: The impact of positive mood on trust in interpersonal and intergroup interactions. Journal of Personality and Social Psychology 98(3), 420–433 (2010)
22. Marsh, S.P.: Formalising Trust as a Computational Concept. PhD thesis. University of Stirling, Stirling. Department of Computing Science and Mathematics (1994)
23. Matyas, S., Matyas, C., Mitarai, H., Kamata, M., Kiefer, P., Schlieder, C.: Designing Location-based Mobile Games – The CityExplorer Case Study. In: de Souza e Silva, A., Sutko, D.M. (eds.) Digital Cityscapes: Merging Digital and Urban Playspaces, vol. 6, pp. 187–203. Peter Lang Publishers, NY (2009) ISBN 978-1-4331-0532-6
24. Mayer, J.D., Gaschke, Y.N., Braverman, D.L., Evans, T.W.: Mood-Congruent Judgment Is a General Effect. Journal of Personality and Social Psychology 63(1), 119–132 (1992)
25. Mueller, F., Stevens, G., Thorogood, A., O'Brien, S., Wulf, V.: Sports over a Distance. Personal Ubiquitous Comput. 11(8), 633–645 (2007)
26. Robinson, J.P., Wrightsman, L.S., Andrews, F.M.: Measures of personality and social psychological attitudes: Academic Pr. Inc. (Measures of Social Psychological Attitudes, 1) (1991)
27. Bernhaupt, R., Boldt, A., Mirlacher, T., Wilfinger, D., Tscheligi, M.: Using emotion in games: emotional flowers. In: Proceedings of the International Conference on Advances in Computer Entertainment Technology (ACE 2007), pp. 41–48. ACM, New York (2007)
28. Russell, J.A.: A circumplex model of affect. Journal of Personality and Social Psychology 39(6), 1161–1178 (1980)
29. Virtanen, T., Malinen, S.: Supporting the Sense of Locality with Online Communities. In: MindTrek 2008, pp. 145–149 (2008) ACM 978-1-60558-197-2/08/10
30. von Ahn, L., Dabbish, L.: Designing games with a purpose. Commun. ACM 51(8), 58–67 (2008)
31. Yamagishi, M.: Trust and commitment in the United States and Japan. Motivation and Emotion 18(2), 129–166 (1994)
32. Yamagishi, T., Cook, K.S., Watabe, M.: Uncertainty, Trust, and Commitment Formation in the United States and Japan. Am. J. Sociol. 104(1), 165–194 (1998)

Design of Tangible Games
for Children Undergoing Occupational
and Physical Therapy

Robby. van Delden[1], Pauline Aarts[2], and Betsy van Dijk[1]

[1] Human Media Interaction, University of Twente, Enschede, The Netherlands
P.O. Box 217, 7500 AE, Enschede, The Netherlands
{r.w.vandelden,e.m.a.g.vandijk}@utwente.nl
[2] Department of Paediatric Rehabilitation, Sint Maartenskliniek,
Hengstdal 3, 6574 NA Ubbergen (near Nijmegen), The Netherlands
p.aarts@maartenskliniek.nl

Abstract. Games can offer an entertaining alternative to repetitive tasks. In this paper, we propose the use of tangible interactive games for the repetitive training of upper limbs in the therapy of children with Cerebral Palsy (CP). We obtained promising results. The total of four created games succeeded in triggering all the to-be-trained movements properly and in a motivating and entertaining way. A physical quiz game was especially successful as children kept on playing the game making the proper movements without additional encouragement or instructions of the therapists or researchers. These results indicate that in this kind of occupational or physical therapy, there is additional value in using tangible interactive games. Furthermore, the research shows the importance of including the therapists in the design of games and we report on several ways to achieve that.

Keywords: Participatory design, games for therapy, tangible games, special user groups, children, cerebral palsy.

1 Introduction

Hitting a button for almost a thousand times does not sound like much fun. However, over the last three decades children have had fun doing this in the form of computer games. Most forms of physical therapy for children are also repetitive in nature, especially for children with unilateral Cerebral Palsy (CP). Unilateral CP is a disorder of posture and/or motor function due to brain damage in the first year of life. In the unilateral type of CP, the right or left side of the body is affected. Therapy for CP children can be effective but can also be boring at times because of this repetitive nature [1]. Using interactive games could reasonably be expected to help in bringing additional motivation and so more enjoyable therapy.

The *TagTiles* platform can be used for creating such interactive games with tangibles; it is a system that can automatically localise multiple objects on its

M. Herrlich, R. Malaka, and M. Masuch (Eds.): ICEC 2012, LNCS 7522, pp. 221–234, 2012.
© IFIP International Federation for Information Processing 2012

surface by using RFID tags. This system gives feedback with full colour LEDs and with playing sounds. In previous research, *TagTiles* games were created for therapy for CP patients [15]. However, these games were not implemented as the proper movements were not triggered enough and compensating movements were observed too often. Nonetheless, the use of entertaining interactive tangible games built for the *TagTiles* system was promising according to the therapists. That new games for the *TagTiles* system were not developed earlier by therapists themselves is probably due to a lack of time, effort and know-how from therapists to develop games that are suitable [13].

Children with unilateral CP are inclined to make compensating movements. In other words, they prevent certain movements that are hard for them and thereby further diminish their capability of performing these movements. Therapy especially focuses on training the fine motor skills of the upper body. Therapists have a good insight in how to trigger the correct movements and what the preferences are of the children. We thus chose to use a participatory design approach. At the same time, we had to keep in mind that there is limited time available for non-therapy activities by the therapists and children [13].

These children may also suffer from forms of mental retardation and low self-esteem. Although several guidelines for developing motivating games exist (e.g. [16]), they do not explicitly take into account the special needs of these children. Thus, during this research we looked into the use of sounds and evaluated and compared different versions of tangible games for therapy along the dimensions of challenge and interpersonal competition.

In related work, several attempts of using interactive games in therapy are reported and results seem promising [2,5,7,9]. However, to our knowledge there are no successful and well-tested implementations of interactive tangible games for physical therapy of CP patients focusing on the upper limbs. This was a main motivator for our research.

Over one and a half years of research, several design tools and techniques were used to deal effectively with this challenge. We used a participatory design approach, incorporating the therapists knowledge and the children's interests. This was done in two main rounds of development leading to four basic games. The games were evaluated in a mainly qualitative way with a total of seven therapists and eighteen different children undergoing therapy.

The remainder of this paper is structured as follows. In the following section, we summarise related work on motivating games and games for therapy. Section 3 describes the methodology and test setup. Section 4 describes the games developed. This is followed in Section 5 with the results. The paper concludes with a discussion and proposals for future work.

2   Motivation and Games for Physical Therapy

Adding motivation and turning cumbersome activities into fun and engaging tasks for children is challenging. Malone and Lepper pioneered research in this field [16]. They worked on fun and motivation in educational computer games.

We will only mention some of their findings as their work has already been analysed, rewritten and complemented several times (e.g. [12,17]).

Their analysis resulted in four individual criteria: Challenge, Curiosity, Fantasy and Control. Three interpersonal criteria were also stated: Cooperation, Competition and Recognition (meaning appreciation). These aspects still seem to cover the most important aspects of what makes games fun and can be found in one way or another in most of the recently developed frameworks (e.g. [14]).

TagTiles has been targeted as a platform for therapy before by Li et al. [15]. They developed three games for *TagTiles*. Results were promising but they overestimated the physical abilities of the children and the games lacked the capability to withstand possible compensations by the children to circumvent the to-be-trained movements. This mainly involves circumventing difficult movements. For example, using their non-affected arm to grab something or bending their affected wrist downward (palmar) to an extreme extent. However, *"All participants said they enjoyed playing the game"* and *"Therapists were happy to observe children engage in the desired movements spontaneously, something that they said was not common in their standard therapy sessions."* [15, p190].

Getting games to be used in therapy also requires incorporating the context and therapist's view. Applicable requirements and effective methodology for this context can be found in [2]. Based on observation of therapy and a small-scale implementation, the following was emphasised: the importance of limited preparation and start up time, adaptability and adaptivity, simplicity and (where possible) automated logging.

Several studies underline that using interactive video games for therapy and rehabilitation can be useful [9]. For instance, playing the basic games on the *Wii* had a positive result in motor function of the legs, such as increased gait distance and increased postural control of a 13-year old CP patient suffering from double leg impairment [7]. Another small-scale study of four children using a camera-based input virtual reality application for two weeks, showed it is also possible to improve "reaching kinematics" of children with CP by using games [5]. The therapy of our target group mainly focused on training fine motor skills, such as improving their grasps and learning new grasps. Thus, instead of using a camera-based input they might benefit more from using tangibles.

3   Test Setup and Methodology

A case study was done in collaboration with the Sint Maartenskliniek (Nijmegen, the Netherlands), a hospital that specialises in posture and movement. This hospital offers specialised therapy for children between two and a half and eight years old with mild forms of unilateral CP. The therapy focuses on improving their affected hand and arm coordination and functioning. It consists of playful exercises such as playing board games and singing songs. During these exercises, they repetitively move their hands and arms. An example of such a therapy is the one called *Pirate Group*, in which the context of pirates is used to engage the children in the therapy. This is a type of modified Constraint Induced Movement

Therapy combined with Bimanual Training intervention (mCIMT-BiT); children are forced to use their affected arm in the first few weeks, but later on they are allowed to use both hands in order to train their coordination. For further details of the therapy, please refer to [1].

As understanding both the therapy and the target group requires detailed knowledge, we chose to use a participatory design method. We implemented this throughout the design process: in gathering requirements, during the generation and development of concepts and finally in the evaluations. This was done in an iterative fashion in two main design rounds. The first round contained five sub-iterations and we made small changes to the games in each sub-iteration. In this first round of development we investigated several game dynamics using three games, whereas the second round focused more on therapists' and children's experiences.

We included spoken instructions in all games. The games made use of logging functionality to automatically record the time needed to finish a game. After the children finished the games, we asked them some questions, e.g. *"Which game would you like to play again?"*. We also asked therapists for their feedback, focusing on movements and applicability. Below we will further explain the methodology used, and describe both the participants and the setting. In the next section, the games created will be described.

3.1 First Round

In the first sub-iteration we started with listening closely to the therapists to get to know the therapy, the target group and to assemble the requirements for the games. To this end, we held several interviews and informal discussions with four different therapists. In addition, an observational study was done by actively participating in two therapy sessions of one single group of five children with CP. To aid understanding of the therapists and to make communication easier, we did a literature review on CP. During the observational sessions, we witnessed the interests of the children closely and recorded these by taking notes. These interests were then used as basis for the first three games. These games were designed using a mixture and adaptation of design techniques involving physically acting out movements, combined with the use of objects lying around [3,4,8]: we were able to generate three games by repetitively acting out the to-be-trained movements. By using body movements, we tried to reduce the gap between creating games and triggering the proper movements. For further details about this methodology, please refer to [6]. We programmed the games using the SDK for *TagTiles* [10]. We finished the first sub-iteration by showing a video prototype to one of the therapists.

In the second sub-iteration we tested the games informally on ten non-CP participants, mainly to find bugs and to improve game play. These tests were done in a home setting.

The third sub-iteration consisted of an evaluation with end users to test the suitability of the games and the triggered movements. We did the tests of the third sub-iteration in a classroom-like environment, containing one or two therapists, one researcher and one or two participants. Six children participated: three boys and three girls, all between four and six years old.

The fourth sub-iteration consisted of an in-subject test with four children. We used this evaluation to gain more insight into three game variables: sound, challenge and inter-personal competition, with a focus on the latter two. Because of the target group's reduced self-image it is important to choose the proper level of challenge which could help to increase their feeling of competence. Competition and cooperation are also relevant to that feeling. However, using one *TagTiles* system with two children at a time is impractical. In that case, the interactive space is too small to effectively train movements and using a turn-taking approach will reduce effectiveness of therapy as intensity is an important factor. Competition is also stimulated by adding a scoring system [16]. The children played two variants of two games to analyse the effect of challenge and competition; these versions and the results will be described in Section 5. They played the "A-versions" in the first session and the "B-versions" in the second session or vice versa. The participants of this fourth sub-iteration did their tests in a small room with one participant, one therapist per child and a researcher present. The children were one 8 year old boy and three girls, two of 9 and one of 8.

In the fifth sub-iteration, another group of children tested the games. The participants of the fifth sub-iteration used the same setting. The five children were an 8 year old girl, a 5 year old boy and girl, a $2^{1/2}$ and a 3 year old girl. They played only one version of the game.

3.2   Second Round

We started the second round with a more thorough cooperative design session, to better include the therapists also during the creation process. During this session, two therapists developed several ideas using two design techniques in less than an hour. This design session was done with a physiotherapist and an occupational therapist in one of their offices.

The first design technique used is interaction relabelling [8]. In this technique, interactions of an object are translated to a new object, or in our case translated to a tangible game. Based on a first test session, with three other participants (non-therapists), it was decided to make use of objects with a mechanical character to efficiently trigger creativity. We used a stapler, a multi-head screwdriver, a Rubik's Cube and a small plastic box with a magnetic fastening. Participants were told to take the first prop in their hands and explain how they would use this. Based on this explanation they had to come up with ways to alter this into a game, training the wanted movements.

The second technique was a shortened version of Systematic Inventive Thinking (SIT). SIT is a way to alter a product, or to overcome a problem, by using effective often reoccurring thinking patterns [11]. SIT consists of the following steps:

- identifying the components of the idea/product,
- applying one of the thinking patterns, namely division, multiplication, subtraction, (task) unification or (change of) attribute dependency,

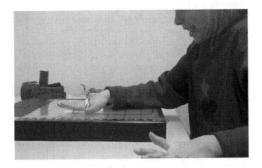

Fig. 1. A nine year old girl laughing while playing the hitting game

- visualising this solution,
- foreseeing whether it will fulfil the (new) needs.

For both techniques, a small explanatory presentation of 5 minutes was given to the therapists just before using the technique. Interaction relabelling was used for 20 minutes to create ideas followed by 25 minutes of SIT to further develop some of those ideas. Based on the outcome of this session, one game was created, incorporating the input of the therapists.

This game was tested by observing children playing the game. Three children participated: two 8 year old boys with reasonable hand and arm functionality and one 8 year old girl with more limited capabilities. The classroom setting of the second sub-iteration in the first round was used again. Children had to play the game for 15 to 30 minutes until a good image of the interaction was formed by direct observations. Following the gameplay, two therapists were interviewed. This included one therapist that observed all the three participants playing. The other therapist, who also participated in the design session, observed only two of the participants.

4   Games

Three games were created in the first round: a hitting game, an animal game and a boat shooting game. In the second round, a quiz game was developed. The games, the movements they trigger and the origin of the used themes will be described in this section.

4.1   Hitting Game

The hitting game is a simple game based on triggering rotation of the hand backwards. Children have to wear two hook and loop fastener strips for sensing purposes, one fastened around the wrist and one around the palm of the hand; see Fig. 1. One of the squares is lit yellow for about two seconds and then 'jumps' to the next square. While keeping their arm on the board they have to raise their palm and then hit the lighted square in time. On hitting the square, one of ten

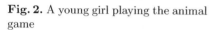

Fig. 2. A young girl playing the animal game

Fig. 3. The final version of the tangibles used for the boat shooting game

'funny' sounds is played and a point is awarded. If the wrist is raised while hitting, this is indicated by playing a spoken text. Once 16 points are achieved the game is won and the border of the board flashes green for several seconds.

4.2 Animal Game

During the observations, children were seen to enjoy making animal sounds and listening to how others made animal sounds. This was used as the inspiration for the animal game; see Fig. 2. In this game, the name of a colour is played, e.g. *"Brown"*, then the child has to pick a miniature animal and place it on the board at the square lit in this colour. On placing the proper animal, either an indication that the child performed well is played, for example *"Well done, a dog"* or an animal sound is played. All the animals have to be placed and removed from the board to finish a round; the game consists of two rounds. If a child takes too long to place the animal, e.g. when losing concentration, a reminder is given *"Which animal is brown?"*. This is followed by indicating the right animal after some seconds with *"The doggy is brown"*. When a child places the wrong animal, this is also stated: *"That is not the right animal"*. The game requires extension of the elbow and trains several grasps. We tried to pick the right variety of shapes and weight to trigger several grasps and to reduce the possibility of compensating movements.

4.3 Boat Shooting Game

Fitting the topic of the *Pirate group*, this game involves rotating a boat to shoot incoming targets. In the game created, targets slowly move down and a pirate boat has to be turned into the direction of the target; see Fig. 3. Aiming in the right direction results in destroying the target and one of two explosion sounds being played. The rotation of the boat requires rotating the hand backwards. To make this boat game playable for children with very limited ability to move their hand backwards, the board was rotated between 0 and 45 degrees, depending on the maximum angle the child showed to be able to manage.

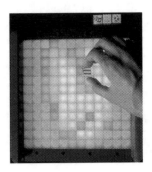

Fig. 4. Hearing the answers in the "Ik hou van Holland" game: tumbling a block, targets a passive form of rotating the hand backwards

Fig. 5. The start of the "Ik hou van Holland" game. Placement of a wooden cube to select a category which triggers the shown "pincher grasp"

4.4 Quiz Game

This game is based on answering multiple choice questions. It is implemented on a newer version of *TagTiles*; see Fig. 4. To answer the questions, several actions have to be performed, that trigger several movements. The game consists of: picking a category, getting a random question, hearing the options, choosing an answer, loading this answer and then hearing if it is correct or not. With the selection of actions and objects we tried to minimise compensating movements. The group from which three participants were selected in the evaluation of this game participated in (mCIMT-BiT) therapy with "Ik hou van Holland" as a metaphor. This is a Dutch TV-show in which Dutch TV personalities answer questions about Dutch habits, songs and personalities.

The game created starts with the intro tune and shows a tulip symbol. A category of questions has to be selected using a small wooden cube; see Fig. 5. This action requires a correct grasp of a small object triggering the pincher grasp; see Fig. 5.

An instruction is played to tip a question tag onto the board from the question box. The tipping movement triggers rotating the arm inwards and triggers outward rotation when placing it on the table again.

Four multiple choice answers can be heard by rotating a block over the board. This triggers rotating the hand backwards; see Fig. 4. An instruction is given to select the correct answer by placing an answer disc onto the board. This action also triggers the pincher grasp.

The user is instructed to load the answer. The answer has to be put into a tube. The user is then instructed to throw the 'answer' on the board. If the answer is wrong, the game proceeds again from hearing the question. If a question has been answered incorrectly for the second time or the correct answer is given, then the game starts again with selecting the category.

When all questions from a category are answered and this category is chosen, the user is instructed to select another category. If this happens, then the score is shown on the board. At the start of the game, the therapist or user can select the number of questions that have to be answered ranging from 5-12. When all answers from one category and the total number of questions are answered, the user hears that he or she did very well to answer all these questions correctly. This is followed by 20 seconds of the Queen song *"We are the champions"*.

5   Evaluation and Results

Several evaluations have been done throughout the research. The most important of these will be described in this section. We have little to say about the use of a video prototype of a preliminary version in the first iteration. It was useful as it did not require fitting in a co-located meeting in a tight schedule. Also, it gave an early indication of whether the games would work. As for the second sub-iteration: testing with non-CP participants we found bugs and made improvements without 'bothering' children or therapists. Nine changes were incorporated as a result of these tests.

5.1   Game Design Variables

We researched three game design variables: sound, competition and challenge. We used an in-subject test in the fourth sub-iteration for the latter two.

Sound. In the third sub-iteration, we let some of the children play the hitting game without sound. We used direct observations of a researcher and therapists. Not having sound reduced the clarity of feedback and the entertainment drastically, thus in the forth and fifth sub-iterations we only used the version with sound. Analysis of videos taken in the fourth sub-iteration showed that three of the four children grinned upon hearing the first or second sound in the hitting game; see Fig. 1. Including the video analysis of the fifth sub-iteration of the first round as well, six out of nine children grinned or smiled as soon as they heard the first or second sound.

Competition. We compared two versions of the animal game to evaluate influence of competition. In the "A-version" of the animal game we introduced a competitive objective in two ways: (1) we instructed the children to finish as quickly as possible and to make as few mistakes as possible, (2) we introduced feedback on high scores after finishing the first and the second round of a game. In the "B-version" we excluded both forms of competition. The participants of the fourth sub-iteration did not give clear responses after hearing their results. The first participant sighed deeply and moved with her chair from left to right. The third participant stated he found the animal game too simplistic. We had expected that the encouragement would result in significantly faster finishing of the second round of the animal game. However, such an effect could not be observed.

Challenge. We compared two versions of the boat game. The "A-version" with a higher level of challenge by targets coming down faster after each hit. The game also goes into a *game over* state when a target reaches the bottom of the board. The "B-version" did not have such an increase of speed or game over state. Two of the girls of the fourth sub-iteration smiled after losing the "A-version". In the interview, they both stated they disliked the game (both versions), they disliked that it was so difficult to aim in the required direction. One girl laughed after winning the pirate boat game after having lost the altered version during her previous session. One boy had some difficulty playing the game mainly due to the version of the tangible boat used. He could not finish it on his own and showed no clear reaction after losing the game. The challenge in the boat game was high, both handling the tangible object and aiming it in time, so all participants of the fourth sub-iteration lost the altered game. No clear indications of difference in perceived entertainment value was seen between the two versions of the game.

5.2   Use of SIT and Interaction Relabelling

Using interaction relabelling resulted in generating eight ideas. From these ideas, four were chosen in conjunction with the therapists to further develop, each using one or two randomly selected thinking patterns. Applying and understanding the thinking patterns was found to be more difficult than using interaction relabelling. The SIT-session nonetheless resulted in ten simple alterations. We implemented these proposed game elements and movement-object combinations in the quiz game.

5.3   Age Dependency

Based on the fourth sub-iteration (in-subject tests) and the fifth sub-iteration combined, taking everyone's first attempt and using an independent samples one-tailed t-test we could see a clear age difference in completion time for the animal game ($p < 0.001$) and the hitting game ($p < 0.001$) between 2-3 year olds(n=2) and 5-9 year olds (n=7). For the hitting game, there was also a significant difference between 5 and 8-9 year olds and between 2-5 and 8-9 year olds(both $p < 0.05$)).

The second youngest child needed help in hitting the first target in the hitting game. In the animal game, someone had to put the correct animal in her hand and she needed additional instructions from the therapists. The pirate game was played together with the therapist but even in this way she could not understand it enough to play the game. Similar problems occurred with the youngest child. She often had to be directed towards where the target was in order to keep her attention on the game. During the animal game, the animals either had to be pointed out or handed to her. Several times she had a difficult time placing the animal upright on its pedestal.

The second youngest child showed clear use of the unwanted extreme (palmar) flexing of the wrist when placing some of the animals. However, the youngest did perform a proper grasp and placement by herself, see Fig. 2.

5.4   Liking, Triggered Movements and Compensating Movements

Responses from the children were quite positive. In the first round, one of the children of the third sub-iteration even spontaneously mentioned she would like to have the game at home. In the fourth and fifth sub-iterations, the hitting game and animal game were the most preferred (both 4 times). The youngest participant preferred the boat game. After being encourage by a therapist, she acknowledged this was because she liked the attractive tangible object. The therapists especially liked the animal game.

The children in the second round were positive about the quiz game. One of the boys, even without encouragement, kept on playing. Both boys replied that they would like to play the game again. The girl stated she did like the game more than other exercises she had done in therapy thus far. One of the participants found the questions a little too hard, though another did not mind that he did not know all the answers.

According to the three therapists present during tests in the first round, all targeted movements with the exception of rotating the arm outward were triggered. Turning the arm outward was triggered later on in the quiz game, for instance by putting the answer tube next to the board. In the discussion, both therapists concluded that especially the children with better arm-functions made the proper movements. Some forms of compensation were seen. For example, in the first sub-iteration a child moved the boat to the targets instead of turning it. In the boat game, extreme (palmar) flexing of the wrist was also seen. We fixed the boat to an axis in the latest version of the boat game to prevent these things from happening; see Fig. 3. With loosening or tightening the axis we could also adjust to the strength of the child. The animal game was mainly used as intended with a minimum of compensation, except for the second youngest child. In the quiz game, another girl –being slightly less capable– made more compensating movements than the two boys. For instance, she had to be reminded several times to perform the actions with her affected arm. Also, instead of turning the answer block she tumbled it by gently hitting it.

One of the therapists liked the feature that multiple movements were triggered in one game, especially if the game could be adapted to the player's personal functioning, for example by skipping parts of the game. The newer version of *TagTiles* was also liked, as it did not need an external laptop. This made it more mobile and reduced preparation time.

6   Discussion

Based on our research findings, we can draw several conclusions and make proposals for future research. Our findings can be very useful for future research in the field of tangible games, serious gaming for physical therapy and in general for designing interactive systems for people with specific needs.

6.1   Methodology

We found that design techniques with acting out of movements were very applicable for designing physical therapy games. It certainly seemed to reduce the gap between training movements and developing a game. The relabelling in the participatory design session of the second round seemed useful and also very applicable. However, SIT seemed to need some more time to comprehend and use efficiently. Children, especially those with special needs such as children with CP, form a diverse and hard to reach target group. This makes it difficult to do proper research. We found that one should be very careful in generalising for instance the capabilities of the children.

6.2   Utilisation of Traditional Game Variables for CP Therapy

Sound brings additional fun to games. Increasing challenge to the extend that one sometimes loses a game, might add extra motivation and feelings of fulfilment and capability when in the next attempt one does win. For instance, one girl showed a very enthusiastic response winning after losing first. Losing a game did not lead to extreme reactions like crying. Our addition of an inter/intra-personal competition feature by using high scores did not lead to noticeable effects in our tests.

6.3   Using Tangibles for Occupational and Physical Therapy

We found significant differences in the target group, for instance between age groups, hence we think it is essential to make games adaptable. We did some tests in which therapists could change settings in a GUI, such as timings and which animals to use, but the results were inconclusive. Based on interviews we came to the conclusion that if one instead uses a purely adaptive system, it might fail on some occasions. A system will have a hard time recognising the difference between lost attention (so a possible lack of challenge) and low capabilities (so too challenging). One solution is an adaptable adaptive system: one that can automatically change the game within the limits of a specific user.

We succeeded in creating an entertaining set of games that can bring additional motivation and fun in the context of occupational and/or physical therapy for children with CP. The games succeeded in training the correct movements related to goal-directed activities. Especially the fourth game, being a physical quiz created for the latest version of *TagTiles*, seems very promising. The children kept on playing the game, mainly making the proper movements without additional encouragement by or instructions from the therapists or researcher. However, some compensation still occurred, such as the tendency to grab objects with the non-affected hand during the quiz game and (palmar) flexing of the wrist too far in both the animal game and the boat game.

This kind of compensating movements remains a problem especially if one prefers partially unsupervised therapy. According to one of the therapists, a more mechanical device strictly guiding the movements might be more suitable for children with more limited physical capabilities, as compensating movements can be inhibited in such a device to a larger extent. On the downside such approaches usually require additional setup time and have higher costs. Using other less or non-tangible interaction techniques, such as the Kinect or Wii, might be more suitable for detecting and training some movements [5], for instance for the turning of the underarm outwards. Even if a child cannot grasp an object, it can still benefit from training other kinds of movements but might not manage with tangibles alone. However, using tangibles can trigger training of grasps quite well –as demonstrated in our research.

6.4   Future Work

Ongoing research by the consortium called Wikitherapist will further investigate the opportunities and limitations of using the *TagTiles* platform in combination with end-user development for occupational and physical therapy purposes. More quantitative measures about improvement in motor function using tangible games in therapy could help to encourage more widespread use. An interesting observation was the enjoyment in destroying virtual things. This was both stated in interviews and seen in observations. Although much research has been done on the effects of violence in games, we only found a limited amount of research investigating the link between fun and destroying virtual things. During several iterations, we found and solved both major and minor problems. However, we succeeded in triggering the correct movements and increasing motivation. It is considered worthwhile to further improve the quiz game with adaptability, adaptivity and incorporating additional game development principles, so as to make it an even more suitable and entertaining activity to use in occupational and physical therapy.

Acknowledgments. This publication was supported by the Dutch national program COMMIT. Intellident sponsored us with several RFID tags. Many thanks go out to: Julia Garde and Ronald Poppe for the pleasant discussions and their useful input, to the therapists of the Sint Maartenskliniek and to Serious Toys for providing information, help and the *TagTiles* used for this research.

References

1. Aarts, P.B., Jongerius, P.H., Geerdink, Y.A., van Limbeek, J., Geurts, A.C.: Effectiveness of modified constraint-induced movement therapy in children with unilateral spastic cerebral palsy: a randomized controlled trial. Neurorehabilitation and Neural Repair 24(6), 509–518 (2010)
2. Annema, J.H., Verstraete, M., Vanden Abeele, V., Desmet, S., Geerts, D.: Videogames in therapy: a therapist's perspective. In: Proceedings of the 3rd International Conference on Fun and Games, pp. 94–98. ACM, New York (2010)
3. Burns, C., Dishman, E., Verplank, W., Lassiter, B.: Actors, hairdos & videotape-informance design. In: Conference Companion on Human Factors in Computing Systems, CHI 1994, pp. 119–120. ACM, New York (1994)

4. Buur, J., Jensen, M.V., Djajadiningrat, T.: Hands-only scenarios and video action walls: novel methods for tangible user interaction design. In: Proceedings of the 5th Conference on Designing Interactive Systems: Processes, Practices, Methods, and Techniques, DIS 2004, pp. 185–192. ACM, New York (2004)
5. Chen, Y.P., Kang, L.J., Chuang, T.Y., Doong, J.L., Lee, S.J., Tsai, M.W., Jeng, S.F., Sung, W.H.: Use of virtual reality to improve upper-extremity control in children with cerebral palsy: a single-subject design. Physical Therapy 87(11), 1441–1457 (2007)
6. van Delden, R.W.: Design of therapeutic TagTile games for children with unilateral spastic cerebral paresis. Master's thesis, University of Twente, the Netherlands (September 2011)
7. Deutsch, J.E., Borbely, M., Filler, J., Huhn, K., Guarrera-Bowlby, P.: Use of a low-cost, commercially available gaming console (Wii) for rehabilitation of an adolescent with cerebral palsy. Physical Therapy 88(10), 1196–1207 (2008)
8. Djajadiningrat, J.P., Gaver, W.W., Fres, J.W.: Interaction relabelling and extreme characters: methods for exploring aesthetic interactions. In: Proceedings of the 3rd Conference on Designing Interactive Systems: Processes, Practices, Methods, and Techniques, DIS 2000, pp. 66–71. ACM, New York (2000)
9. Griffiths, M.: The therapeutic use of videogames in childhood and adolescence. Clinical Child Psychology and Psychiatry 8, 547–554 (2003)
10. van Herk, R., Verhaegh, J., Fontijn, W.F.: Espranto sdk: an adaptive programming environment for tangible applications. In: Proceedings of the 27th International Conference on Human Factors in Computing Systems, CHI 2009, pp. 849–858. ACM, New York (2009)
11. Horowitz, R., Maimon, O.: Creative design methodology and the sit method. In: Proceedings of DETC 1997: 1997 ASME Design Engineering Technical Conference, pp. 14–17 (1997)
12. Kannetis, T., Potamianos, A.: Towards adapting fantasy, curiosity and challenge in multimodal dialogue systems for preschoolers. In: Proceedings of the 2009 International Conference on Multimodal Interfaces, ICMI-MLMI 2009, pp. 39–46. ACM, New York (2009)
13. Kierkegaard, P., Markopoulos, P.: From Top to Bottom: End User Development, Motivation, Creativity and Organisational Support. In: Costabile, M., Dittrich, Y., Fischer, G., Piccinno, A. (eds.) IS-EUD 2011. LNCS, vol. 6654, pp. 307–312. Springer, Heidelberg (2011)
14. Korhonen, H., Montola, M., Arrasvuori, J.: Understanding playful user experience through digital games. In: Guenand, A. (ed.) Proceedings of the 4th International Conference on Designing Pleasurable Products and Interfaces, DPPI 2009, pp. 274–285 (2009)
15. Li, Y., Fontijn, W., Markopoulos, P.: A Tangible Tabletop Game Supporting Therapy of Children with Cerebral Palsy. In: Markopoulos, P., de Ruyter, B., IJsselsteijn, W.A., Rowland, D. (eds.) Fun and Games 2008. LNCS, vol. 5294, pp. 182–193. Springer, Heidelberg (2008)
16. Malone, T.W., Lepper, M.R.: Making learning fun: A taxonomy of intrinsic motivations for learning. In: Snow, R.E., Farr, M.J. (eds.) Aptitude Learning and Instruction: III Conative and Affective Process Analyses, vol. 3, pp. 223–253. Lawrence Erlbaum Associates, Hilsdale (1987)
17. Moon, H.K., Baek, Y.K.: Exploring variables affecting player's intrinsic motivation in educational games. In: Proceedings of the 17th International Conference on Computers in Education, pp. 718–722 (2009)

Game Design for Older Adults: Effects of Age-Related Changes on Structural Elements of Digital Games

Kathrin Maria Gerling[1], Frank Paul Schulte[2], Jan Smeddinck[3], and Maic Masuch[2]

[1] University of Saskatchewan, 110 Science Place,
Saskatoon SK S7N 5C9, Canada
kathrin.gerling@acm.org
[2] University of Duisburg-Essen, Forsthausweg 2,
47057 Duisburg, Germany
{frank.schulte,maic.masuch}@uni-due.de
[3] University of Bremen, Bibliothekstraße 1,
28359 Bremen, Germany
smeddinck@tzi.de

Abstract. Recent studies report various positive effects on elderly persons playing digital games. Yet, games are rarely designed with an elderly user group in mind. In this paper, this issue is addressed by providing an overview of common age-related changes followed by a summary of game design considerations for senior audiences. The impact of age on game design is discussed based on an analysis of the most important structural elements of games. The analysis shows that age-related changes in users' cognitive and physical abilities affect the use of games on multiple levels, making the complexity of games and interrelations between different game mechanics a crucial factor when designing for older adults.

Keywords: Game design, older adults, accessibility, design recommendations.

1 Introduction

Engaging with digital games has a positive impact on the emotional and physical well-being of elderly in nursing homes as recent research suggests [10]. However, many commercially available gaming products are not suitable for elderly persons [7]. Apart from the development of therapeutic applications and serious games, a structured approach to digital game design for an elderly audience based on age-related changes and impairments has rarely been the subject of academic work [11]. Understanding both chances and challenges of an elderly target audience is vital, if senior citizens are to be addressed by and engaged in video games [9]. Core aspects that might foster or hinder the engagement of seniors in the use of video games as leisure activity must be identified. This paper provides an overview of age-related changes and diseases and discusses existing approaches towards game design for senior citizens, which are extended based on a structural analysis of digital games.

M. Herrlich, R. Malaka, and M. Masuch (Eds.): ICEC 2012, LNCS 7522, pp. 235–242, 2012.
© IFIP International Federation for Information Processing 2012

2   Game Design for Older Adults

This section summarizes age-related needs and changes that are caused by regular aging processes and provides an overview of game design recommendations to foster the creation of accessible games for older adults.

2.1   Common Age-Related Changes Among Senior Citizens

From a biopsychological perspective, aging affects the quality of life on various levels. Besides sensory decrements in vision and hearing [7], older adults often experience:

- Cognitive impairments, which affect problem solving skills, information processing [2, 6] and result in a reduced attention span when working on complex tasks [2, 3].
- A decline of motor skills, which includes a decrease in fine motor skills, changes in posture and balance [2], and negatively affect motor learning [2, 3].
- Chronic illnesses, which range from arthritis to severe heart conditions, and which have an impact on the physical abilities and mobility of senior citizens [3].

Older adults living in full-care nursing homes are most likely to be severely influenced by age-related impairments [3]. Additional diseases may lead to more physical impairments in late life. Generally speaking, age-related changes limit the patient's possibilities of participating in regular leisure activities and lead to special requirements for the design of interactive entertainment systems.

2.2   Game Design Considerations

In the early 80s, Weisman introduced video games to institutionalized older adults [15]: Based on observations, he claims that games with an adaptable level of difficulty are advantageous because they support individual preferences and sensomotor abilities best. The use of large and well-defined visual symbols and clear auditory feedback is recommended to address visual and auditory impairments. Almost 25 years later, Ijsselsteijn et al. [9] identify the decline of visual and auditory abilities as well as a loss of sensomotor skills as most important age-related impairments, which influence the use and reception of digital games by senior citizens. They suggest visually adjustable games (e.g. regarding the font- and window-size, colors and contrast) that deliver multimodal feedback relying on more than one communication channel and feature user interfaces that are of low complexity. Flores et al. [4] include the design of appropriate cognitive challenges, which have the potential of keeping the interest of older adults. Based on findings from the *ElderGames* project, usability criteria for advanced technologies for the elderly were compiled [6]. They include a reduction of steps necessary to complete tasks, a reduction of the cognitive load, the availability of immediate feedback and the adaptation of digital systems to the users' goals. Additionally, the importance of system consistency and fault tolerance is highlighted.

Furthermore, when designing entertainment systems for senior citizens, it seems important to consider the impact of game content, genres and benefits from playing digital games. Ijsselsteijn et al. [9] identified games for relaxation and entertainment, games which support social activities, games to sharpen one's mind, and exertion games as suitable game types. Flores et al. [4] highlight the creation of meaningful play through learning objectives and social play. Results from the ElderGames project suggest that elderly players have a preference for simplistic puzzle and quiz games, which may have a positive impact on daily life [9, 13]. De Schutter and Vanden Abeele [13] identified connecting players, cultivating skills and contributing to society as important aspects of digital games for older adults. In terms of game features, the social aspect of games is frequently addressed by the recommendation of a multiplayer mode. A large amount of senior citizens engages in games as active non-players who watch others play, cheer and comment on in-game situations [14].

The guidelines and design recommendations presented within this section cover the issue of aging and game design on a formal level and primarily address usability and accessibility issues. The majority of guidelines focuses on the impact of age-related changes and impairments on interface design and includes detailed recommendations for designers. However, those design guidelines that address game features and genres only discuss game design issues on a meta-level (e.g. in terms of genre recommendations) and do not give detailed information on the impact of age on structural elements of games.

3   Structural Models of Games

This section provides an overview of two theoretical approaches to a formal description of digital games by Adams [1] and Fullerton [5]. For an overview of the development of the definition of games cf. Salen and Zimmerman [12].

Fullerton's [5] formal elements of games include *players, objectives, procedures, rules, resources, conflict, boundaries* and an *outcome*. Adams' [1] structured approach towards the key components of video games primarily focuses on the interaction between *core game mechanics* and the *user interface*. Core mechanics include in-game resources, further attributes as well as general mechanics [1]. The *user interface* acts as a broker between core mechanics and the player. Because of the strong focus on interface design and its relation with game mechanics, Adams' model offers the opportunity of combining interface-related design guidelines with complex criteria derived from age-related needs and requirements which are expected to map on the complexity of digital games. In contrast, Fullerton provides a broad approach towards the structure of games that covers relevant areas of game design.

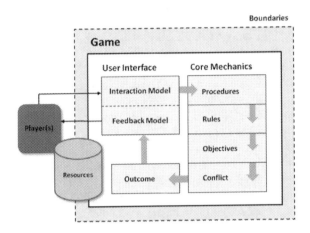

Fig. 1. The extended model of digital games (based on Adams and Fullerton)

3.1   Creation of an Extended Model

Both Adams and Fullerton refer to games as complex systems that feature different sets of mechanics to create a unique user experience. These mechanics are affected by user input. According to Adams, the interaction model turns user input into actions, which may be interpreted by the core mechanics of the game [1]. Fullerton refers to actions as a part of procedures that are deeply rooted within the rules of the game, but does not define the precise relationship between user interface and game mechanics. Additionally, her concept of procedures includes both player actions and system procedures, which incorporate complex methods of play [5]. While Fullerton suggests that the outcome of the game affects the player and determines whether the conflict was successfully resolved, Adams states that new challenges may be presented to the player via the user interface. Because Fullerton does not give detailed information regarding the relationship between game mechanics and the user interface, Adams' model offers the possibility of extending her definition. Other than that, Adams' definition of core mechanics is not as precise as Fullerton's description of the structure of games. In the extended model, Adams' camera model is referred to as feedback model, including visual, haptic and auditory output. Figure 1 shows a combination of the approaches.

3.2   Effects of Age-Related Changes on Structural Models of Games

Based on the joint model, the relevance of age-related changes and age-associated diseases in the context of game design can be analyzed with a focus on the impact of age on the structural elements of games.

Players and Resources. When designing for today's senior audience, game designers have to create games for a target group with – at least nowadays – very limited gaming experience. Since research has shown that elderly persons enjoy both engaging in active play as well as following games as spectators and commenting on other *players*, designers should address the needs of those audience participants, e.g. by offering interesting visual sceneries, or fostering competition similar to sports events. Depending on the context of play, different competition types seem appropriate for elderly persons. "Local team versus game" competitions offer the opportunity of engaging groups of senior citizens in play, online multiplayer functionality offers the possibility of experiencing competition or cooperation to senior citizens who live an independent life. *Resources* are another important aspect that should be considered. The attention span of the player may be a relevant resource: When games require elaborate decision making or quick reactions, changes in short-term memory might affect the player's ability to recall in-game information at a later point. Sensorimotor skills are an important resource if certain game mechanics include complex interaction paradigms or repetitive user input and time-critical player feedback. Generally, the availability of in-game resources should not be as restrictive as for a younger audience and ideally be individually adjustable.

User Interface. The use of input devices may also be limited due to age-related changes in motor skills. While active senior citizens may still be able to use regular game pads, institutionalized older adults may experience difficulties in holding the controller in their hands while pressing small buttons. Furthermore, the complexity of input sequences should be significantly reduced for an elderly audience to account for decrements of cognitive abilities, especially attention processes and short-term memory. In this context, possible difficulties with parallel player input (e.g. moving a haptic device and pressing a button at a certain point of time or performing complex point-and-click operations) should be considered. Additionally, the graphical user interface has to be adjusted to meet the needs of elderly persons (e.g. with regard to visual game element size, font size, high contrast, etc.) when designing the feedback model which presents the game to the player, for instance via visual, auditory or haptic output.

Core Mechanics. Core mechanics describe internal processes and requirements of digital games. They consist of *procedures*, *rules*, *objectives* and *conflict* and define both challenges of and players' interactions with the game. Certain aspects of core mechanics (e.g. limitations caused by rules) have to be learned in order to master a game. Decrements in memory and elderly persons' attention span affect information processing from short-term to procedural memory. Thus, the ability of learning how to play a game is limited, and learning processes take more time if the player is affected.

In-game actions available to the player – procedures – should be easy to understand and ideally incorporate metaphors of daily life to facilitate learning processes. Additionally, designers should avoid parallel input and quick sequential reactions to lower the player's cognitive load and account for changes in sensorimotor abilities. Rules should be easy to understand to facilitate the player's entry into game play. In this context, elderly players may need additional and more detailed information to understand restrictions and requirements of digital games due to their lack of gaming experience. Objectives have to be more clearly defined and communicated to the elderly player. Since objectives have an impact on the overall direction on the game, it is not only important to account for age-related changes, but also to consider suitable game genres and features.

Outcome. Because age-related impairments are likely to reduce the player's ability to master games in comparison to a younger audience, it is important to consider the effects of impairments when defining the *outcome* of the game. Adjustable limits for the internal assessment of player success offer the possibility of providing the user with feedback which is based on his or her individual skills.

4   Application of the Model

Based on the evaluation results [8] and observations during the design process of *SilverPromenade*, a game specifically addressing older adults, we discuss the applicability of the extended model of digital games in game design for senior citizens and potential extensions and future use-cases.

When creating the game design concept for SilverPromenade, we applied the extended model of digital games at an early stage of the development process. First, we created a general vision outline of the game concept. Second, we redefined single aspects using the list of structural elements and the associated recommendations regarding the impact of age. The model helped shape our game design document and provided a foundation for the more detailed analysis of certain game design decisions, the discussion of design alternatives and the integration of suitable game mechanics, e.g. the inclusion of the three different player roles to accommodate different abilities. Finally, when preparing the evaluation of the SilverPromenade, the model could be used to draw attention to important aspects of the game and provided a foundation for observations during the study. On a general level, the extended model of digital games with a focus on age-related changes provides a structure for designers to consider important issues associated with senior audiences during the design process. Its broad approach can help them to encompass basic needs of older adults and foster the creation of accessible games; the model embraces a wide range of game design elements supporting the systematic examination of the impact of ageing on the interaction with video games. In contrast to previous work on game design recommendations for elderly persons, the model accounts for the connection of interface and game design by linking the effects of core mechanics as well as the interaction and feedback model. Recognizing interrelations between user interfaces and game mechanics is also important when considering the growing popularity of motion-based games, in which interaction paradigms are frequently matched with game mechanics and which hold the promise of fostering physical activity.

Limitations of the Model. Even when accounting for common age-related changes, older adults represent a heterogeneous target audience, thus general player abilities are difficult to capture. The evaluation of SilverPromenade showed that although our model covers the most important issues of game design for elderly, it lacks individual details that are difficult to integrate. To solve this issue, we suggest a user-centered design process which allows for user-testing at an early stage for further adjustments. Additionally, the current version of the model accounts for technical and structural aspects of game design only. In order to fully grasp the interaction between players and the game, the aspect of user experience needs to be examined and integrated into the existing approach. This is especially interesting when designing for a senior audience as only little research focused on the game experience of elderly players. Another opportunity which has not been explored and that could be examined based on structural considerations is the design of narrative and dramatic elements in video games. Generally speaking, the model presented in this paper provides a broad overview of common age-related issues as a starting point for further considerations. Individual adjustments have to be made based on an analysis of the particular target audience and application context to ensure the accessibility.

5   Conclusion and Future Work

In this paper, the impact of prevalent age-related impairments among senior citizens on structural elements of video games was discussed based on a joint model of digital games featuring the work of Adams [1] and Fullerton [5], which was then evaluated through the design of SilverPromenade [8]. The analysis showed that cognitive and sensory decrements as well as age-associated diseases affect various aspects regarding the use of digital games and have to be considered when designing for older adult players. While sensory decrements mostly affect the design of the user interface and appropriate design considerations have been presented by many authors, cognitive impairments and the lack of gaming experience among today's elderly population are an important factor when designing game mechanics. In this context, the analysis has shown that the complexity of digital games and interrelations between different mechanics are a crucial factor when designing for older adults: On the one hand, elderly players have to be provided with sufficient information to be able to interact with the game adequately. On the other hand, core mechanics of the game have to be simplistic and easy to learn in order to reduce the cognitive load of an elderly audience. A structured analysis of digital games and their interrelation with age-related changes helps fostering the integration of concerns regarding the target audience early in the development process. It may also help to guide designers even if they have no prior experience in working with elderly. Future work includes the further verification of the feasibility of design recommendations based on the structural approach towards digital games presented in this paper. We aim to examine the usage of our model beyond academic game development to gain further insights into the applicability of our work in an industry context.

References

[1]   Adams, E.: Fundamentals of Game Design. New Riders Publishing, Berkeley (2010)
[2]   Birren, J.E., Schaie, K.W.: Handbook of the Psychology of Aging. Academic Press, San Diego (2001)

[3] Czaja, S.J., Lee, C.C.: Information Technology and Older Adults. In: Sears, A., Jacko, J.A. (eds.) The Human-Computer Interaction Handbook. Lawrence Erlbaum Associates, New York and London (2006)

[4] Flores, E., Tobon, G., Cavallaro, E., Cavallaro, F.I., Perry, J.C., Keller, T.: Improving patient motivation in game development for motor deficit rehabilitation. In: Proceedings of ACE 2008, Yokohama, Japan (2008)

[5] Fullerton, T.: Game Design Workshop, Second Edition: A Playcentric Approach to Creating Innovative Games. Morgan Kaufmann Publishers, Burlington (2008)

[6] Gamberini, L., Alcaniz, M., Barresi, G., Fabregat, M., Ibanez, F., Prontu, L.: Cognition, technology and games for the elderly: An introduction to ELDERGAMES Project. PsychNology Journal 4(3), 285–308 (2006)

[7] Gerling, K.M., Schild, J., Masuch, M.: Exergame Design for Elderly Users: The Case Study of SilverBalance. In: Proceedings of ACE 2010, Taipei, Taiwan (2010)

[8] Gerling, K.M., Schulte, F.P., Masuch, M.: Designing and Evaluating Digital Games for Older adults. In: Proceedings of ACE 2011, Lisbon, Portugal (2011)

[9] Ijsselsteijn, W., Nap, H.H., de Kort, Y.: Digital Game Design for Elderly Users. In: Proceedings of FuturePlay 2007, Toronto, Canada (2007)

[10] Jung, Y., Li, K.J., Janissa, N.S., Gladys, W.L.C., Lee, K.M.: Games for a Better Life: Effects of Playing Wii Games on the Well-Being of Seniors in a Long-Term Care Facility. In: Proceedings of IE 2009, Sydney, Australia (2009)

[11] Nap, H.H., de Kort, Y.A.W., IJsselsteijn, W.A.: Senior gamers: preferences, motivations and needs. Gerontechnology 8(4), 247–262 (2009)

[12] Salen, K., Zimmerman, E.: Rules of Play: Game Design Fundamentals. MIT Press, Cambridge (2004)

[13] De Schutter, B., Vanden Abeele, V.: Meaningful Play in Elderly Life. In: Proceedings of the 58th Annual Conference of the ICA, Montreal, Canada (2008)

[14] Shim, N., Baecker, R., Birnhotz, J., Moffatt, K.: TableTalk Poker: An Online Social Gaming Environment for Seniors. In: Proc. of FuturePlay 2010 (2010)

[15] Weisman, S.: Computer Games for the Frail Elderly. Gerontologist 23(4), 361–363 (1983)

The Effect of Closely-Coupled Interaction on Player Experience in Casual Games

Anastasiia Beznosyk, Peter Quax, Wim Lamotte, and Karin Coninx

Hasselt University - tUL - IBBT
Expertise Centre for Digital Media
Wetenschapspark 2
3590 Diepenbeek, Belgium

Abstract. This paper presents a study investigating cooperation between players in casual games. Although widely used in co-located or asynchronous settings, cooperative gameplay elements are not popular in networked synchronous casual games. In our study, we have analyzed different types of cooperation between players in casual games. Each of these is based on a certain cooperative game design pattern, and can be classified as either closely- or loosely-coupled. Six game patterns have been selected and an equal number of games developed, each targeting one pattern. By means of a user experiment we have investigated which cooperation types fit most of the criteria that define casual games. More specifically, we have focused on the applicability of close coupling between players. Based on the games used in the experiment, most patterns with closely-coupled interaction have shown an overall higher user evaluation than loosely-coupled, satisfying criteria of casual games. These results indicate that introducing close coupling in the casual games under consideration is a potential way to increase the player experience.

Keywords: casual games, cooperative game patterns, closely-coupled interaction, loosely-coupled interaction.

1 Introduction and Related Work

Over the last decade, casual games have become one of the most popular game type played over the Internet. These video games, targeted at a mass audience of casual gamers, attract because of their gameplay simplicity, a short play time and a minimum of required commitments to progress in a game [1]. Additional popularity of casual games is caused by the rise of social networks (e.g. Facebook) and the availability of various game consoles (e.g. Wii) and mobile devices (e.g. smartphones, tablets) that allow competition and cooperation among friends [2,3]. Studies on digital games have shown that social characteristics of play settings have a strong impact on players' in-game experience [4].

Leaving competitive casual games out of the scope of this paper, our work focuses on cooperation in casual games. While intensively addressed in hardcore gaming (where gamers prefer to take significant time and develop their skill level,

M. Herrlich, R. Malaka, and M. Masuch (Eds.): ICEC 2012, LNCS 7522, pp. 243–255, 2012.
© IFIP International Federation for Information Processing 2012

like in role-playing games), cooperation has not been widely investigated in the context of casual games. Here, most existing works focus on asynchronous interaction [5], where simultaneous play is not required. This type of collaboration is widely used for games on social networks (FarmVille[1] or CityVille[2]). With the increased use of social games the game producers started to utilize this type of play [6], allowing players to play a game in sequence and break whenever is needed to "accommodate real life necessities". Casual games with synchronous collaboration appear to be mainly co-located. Players share the same screen and can naturally communicate and see each other. Games like Rock Band[3] and Mario Bros. Wii[4] are successful examples of synchronous cooperative casual games.

In most cases, games played over distance, which employ synchronous features, are limited to communication such as different forms of chats [7]. Existing cooperative games that can be played remotely, are mainly based on loosely-coupled interaction (e.g. achieving a shared goal) without direct players' influence on each other. To our knowledge, closely-coupled collaboration, where one player's actions are directly influenced by the other(s), remains limited in existing casual games. One of the possible reasons for that can be a necessity to actively communicate and coordinate actions when tightly collaborating. Casual games are characterized by short game sessions oppositely to hardcore games, which take a substantial amount of time. Therefore, providing rich voice communication in casual games may become cumbersome for game developers or players might not want to be heard (e.g. playing during breaks at work).

We investigate the application of synchronous cooperation in remote casual games where no communication exists between players. By analyzing different types of cooperation (based on cooperative game patterns [8]), we aim to study the effect of closely-coupled collaboration on player experience in casual games through a comparison with loosely-coupled interaction.

1.1   Cooperative Patterns

Patterns in game design have been widely investigated [9,10,11]. Game patterns are descriptions of reoccurring interaction, that depict how game components are used by players to affect various aspects of gameplay [11]. Since cooperation became an integral part of many multiplayer games and virtual communities, defining and analyzing effective cooperative patterns are the primarily goals in game design studies [8,12].

The authors of [13] define collaboration patterns for knowledge sharing in Second Life[5] based on the purpose of interaction (e.g. virtual meeting, design studio). Interaction patterns in massive multiplayer games (based on the

---

[1] www.facebook.com/farmville

[2] www.facebook.com/cityville

[3] www.rockband.com

[4] www.mariobroswii.com

[5] www.secondlife.com

example of Star War Galaxies[6]) are investigated by Ducheneaut et al. in [14]. Here the authors focus on the social aspects of interaction (verbal and non-verbal communication between players). Such cooperative patterns as turn-taking and enforced collaboration are studied by Goh et al. [15].

Studies presented in [8,12,16] investigate cooperative patterns based on existing games. In [16], Zagal et al. explore cooperative patterns within traditional board games, and summarize observations that can be applied to computer games. Work presented by Rocha et al. [12] introduces a list of cooperative patterns based on the analysis of numerous commercial computer games available on the market. This list is considerably extended by El-Nasr et al. [8] by analyzing more recent games that support some form of collaboration between players. Here, the authors also investigate which pattern triggers which event (e.g. laughing, discussions, waiting for other players, etc.) during the shared gameplay.

Although cooperative patterns have been widely analyzed [16,12,8], these works always assume presence of communication between players or even an ability to see each other. Oppositely to the existing studies, our work focuses on collaboration in games where communication is not supported and players are remotely located. When considering interaction over distance, especially when no communication is allowed, additional challenges are present when trying to maintain the same level of player experience. Games based on the same cooperative patterns can result in an entirely different experience when considered in a non-collocated setup. Moreover, for our research a consistent game design is utilized to provide players with an equal perception of the game world while highlighting the impact of each interaction pattern. Most previous works are based on the existing games, where the same patterns are evaluated in different games that may influence player experience. Therefore, we find it crucial to investigate how interaction between players can be improved based on introducing different cooperative patterns in order to compensate a possible negative effect due to a lack of communication. We believe, knowing this may help game developers improve player interaction in cooperative multiplayer casual games.

2   Experiment

In order to analyze synchronous cooperation in remote casual games, an experiment was conducted. During the experiment pairs of participants had to evaluate six games, each based on one of the cooperative patterns. A selection of patterns (selected from the list presented in [8]) was made based on their popularity and the frequency of appearance in existing multiplayer games. Based on the coupling between players, we grouped the selected patterns either in closely- or loosely-coupled type of interaction. Our previous studies have shown a positive player reaction towards closely-coupled collaboration in comparison with loosely-coupled when accomplishing game-like tasks in a 3D virtual environment [17]. In our current work, we investigate whether closely-coupled interaction can be

---

[6] www.soe.com

beneficial for casual game design by providing players with a better experience than loose coupling. In order to decide upon the suitability of the cooperation type in the context of casual games, each game was analyzed based on five criteria: excitement, engagement, challenge, understandability and replay value (further referred as replayability).

2.1   Participants

We recruited thirty-six unpaid volunteers (thirty-one males and five females) to participate in the experiment. The average age of participants was 28 years old, from 21 to 38 years. Most of them had a computer science background and were recruited among university staff and students. According to self evaluation, the average player experience with any type of casual games was 3.19 on a scale from 1 (never played) to 5 (played a lot).

2.2   Apparatus

During the experiment two players were located in neighboring rooms separated by a hallway. Each player used a 15.4" laptop connected over a LAN. One of the laptops was a HP Compaq 8510p (Intel Core 2 Duo T8100, 2.1 GHz, 3 GB with ATI Mobile Radeon HD2600 graphic adapter) and the other was a Dell Latitude E6510 (Intel Core i3 M370, 2.4 GHz, 2 GB with NVIDIA NVS 3100M). A separate external keyboard was attached to each laptop for a more comfortable input. No communication was possible between the two players. One observer was present in each room and sat beside the participant.

2.3   Developed Cooperative Casual Games

Six custom games were created for the experiment, each adopting one of the selected cooperative game patterns. Based on the coupling between players, we classified each game into one of two categories: closely- or loosely-coupled. If a game requires a lot of waiting or if the actions of one player directly affect the other player, it was categorized as the first type. The games that do not require tight collaboration between players and allow more independent performance were assigned to the second type.

For every game, a similar 3D virtual environment (Fig. 1) was developed, which consists of several islands (a rectangular area, on which all game elements are located). Players are represented by alien-like avatars used from Unity 3D tutorial[7]. To distinguish the two avatars in the virtual environment, one is colored in a light blue color, while the other avatar is brown. Players are able to navigate freely in the environment and are not forced to stay together. They have to collect different objects by running over them. Some of the objects are located on higher platforms not directly reachable by the players. Therefore, they have to

---

[7] available online at
http://unity3d.com/support/resources/tutorials/3d-platform-game

use the jumping pads that help a player to jump higher to collect certain items. In order to get on a different island players need to jump across the abyss. If one of the players falls off the island the team loses one life. In all games players have five lives. After a fall, the player reappears at one of the respawn points. A group score is calculated and analyzed to measure the successfulness of the game completion. All closely-coupled games have equal conditions: players need to pick up 75 objects within 7 minutes. Loosely-coupled games are not designed equally and their play conditions are described further individually. The duration of loosely-coupled games is limited to 5 minutes. The game continues until one of the following conditions is met: (1) players collect all required objects; (2) players lose all their lives; (3) the time runs out.

Fig. 1. An example of the game scene

A *limited resources* pattern is adopted for closely-coupled **Game 1**. Two players have to collect items, but are able to store a maximum of 10 items at the same time. Once both players reach the maximum amount of items, they can collect the following 10 objects. If one of the players collects 10 objects he/she has to wait for the other player and cannot pick up new items in the meantime.

A *complementary* pattern is used in closely-coupled **Game 2**, which implies that players have a different role to complement each others' activities within the game. During this game two roles are introduced. One player moves the jumping pad around the island while not being able to jump, and the other player uses it for jumping to reach objects located on higher platforms. There is only one jumping pad on each island. The roles are assigned randomly when players start the game.

An *interaction with the same object* pattern is followed in closely-coupled **Game 3**. In this game players have to move the jumping pad simultaneously. As soon as one of the players selects the jumping pad to move, the other player receives a message on his/her screen that the pad is selected and he/she is needed to help moving it. However, it does not indicate the location where the player has to be in order to help his/her teammate. When selected by two players, the jumping pad can be moved when both players walk in the same direction. Both players can use it for jumping. Similar to game 2, there is only one jumping pad on each island.

Loosely-coupled **Game 4** utilizes a *shared puzzles* pattern. Here, the focus is to collect 10 special objects: each contains a heart with a letter on one side. Once all 10 special objects and therefore 10 letters are found, players need to use them to formulate a word containing all the letters, and put them in a designated window. The game succeeds when the word is entered correctly. Players do not see what words are entered by their partners while guessing. Once the correct solution is given by one player, the other one can also see it in his/her window.

An *abilities that can be used on other players* pattern is used in loosely-coupled **Game 5**. In this game, players have to collect two types of objects: hearts and weapons. Each one is assigned to one player. They can see only one type which is randomly assigned on starting the game. Every time a player collects his/her 10 items, he/she gets the ability to see the partner's objects for about twenty seconds, and is able to collect them as well. The goal of the game is to collect 150 objects together, where every player has at least 50 objects of own type, and 15 objects of the partner's type.

A *shared goals* pattern is utilized in loosely-coupled **Game 6**. The collaboration is reduced to a shared goal of collecting 115 objects while acting independent from the partner.

2.4   Procedure

During the experiment, participant pairs completed consequentially six sessions, each corresponded to one of the casual games described earlier. In each game the player had to collaborate with his/her partner who was located in a different room. Like in many online games, players were coupled anonymously and, therefore, did not know who their partner was. Any form of communication (voice chat, text chat, pop-up messages, etc.) was avoided. Pop-up windows were used only in one game to support some basic level of awareness between two players. Before the actual experiment, a pilot test was performed to check the playability of every game.

Before the experiment, participants read a brief introduction and conducted a five-minute trial to familiarize themselves with the gaming environment and controls. In addition, written rules were given, in which both the goal and the way of interacting with the partner were explained. After each game, players were asked to evaluate the subjective perception of their experience. Based on the way they interact with the partner, they were asked to quantify the level of their excitement and engagement. Additionally, they evaluated how challenging and easy to understand each game was. Finally, they provided information regarding game replayability. For evaluation purposes, a visual analogue scale (VAS) was used. The participants marked on the 10 cm line the point that they felt represented their perception of the current state from *not at all* to *very much*.

Also, the behavior of each player was observed and analyzed afterwards. It took approximately 60 minutes for each pair to complete the actual experiment.

2.5 Design

During the experiment, a within-subject design was used. The independent variable was the game type with six conditions. All participants, in pairs, had to complete six sessions testing every game type. The order of the conditions was counterbalanced using a balanced Latin square design. The dependent variables were excitement, engagement, challenge, understandability and replayability, so different components of a subjective evaluation of each game type. These were collected after each session through a questionnaire.

2.6 Hypotheses

To analyze six cooperative games from the perspective of their applicability for casual gaming, and more specifically to investigate the potential of closely-coupled games, we compare them based on five different criteria. While some of these criteria are chosen based on general requirements for computer games (excitement, engagement, challenge), the others represent characteristics more specific for casual games (understandability and replayability).

We state five hypotheses that apply to the games evaluated in our study. We want to see whether closely-coupled interaction, integrated in our games, can be of any advantage for casual gaming when compared to loose coupling. To check this assumption the following hypotheses are formulated with respect to the casual games criteria:

H1: each closely-coupled game provides higher excitement than each of the loosely-coupled games evaluated in the experiment;

H2: each closely-coupled game provides higher engagement than each of the loosely-coupled games evaluated in the experiment;

H3: each closely-coupled game provides more challenges than each of the loosely-coupled games evaluated in the experiment without any negative impact on player excitement;

H4: each closely-coupled game does not provide additional difficulty to understand the interaction between players in the game when compared to each of the loosely-coupled games evaluated in the experiment;

H5: each closely-coupled game provides a higher level of replayability than each of the loosely-coupled games evaluated in the experiment.

3 Results

This section presents the results of our study. Firstly, analysis of the six games is reported based on five criteria: excitement, engagement, challenge, understandability and replayability. Secondly, we examine player experience based on the observations done during the experiment.

3.1 Subjective Player Evaluation

During the experiment the six games were compared based on five criteria: excitement, engagement, challenge, understandability and replayability. Fig. 2 represents the averages and standard deviations of each criterion for every game based on the subjective player evaluation.

Although the games evaluated in the experiment share a lot of similar features like the graphics and in-game tasks (e.g. navigation, jumping, collecting objects), the interaction between players has been designed differently. Therefore, we check the hypotheses, presented in the previous section, separately for each closely-coupled pattern. By doing so we identify the closely-coupled patterns that improve casual gaming experience when compared with the loosely-coupled patterns. Table 1 summarizes the decision upon each hypothesis (accepted or rejected).

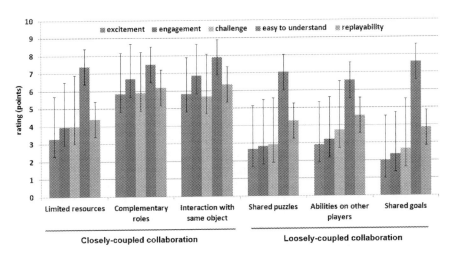

Fig. 2. Subjective player evaluation of the games

First of all, we analyzed player *excitement* in every game. From Fig. 2 we observe that closely-coupled games support a higher level of excitement. Repeated measures ANOVA with a Greenhouse-Geisser correction has shown a significant difference between the six games ($F(3.72, 130.34) = 28.72$, $p < 0.01$). A Bonferroni post-hoc test revealed that games 2 and 3 were found significantly more exciting ($p < 0.01$) than any of loosely-coupled games. Although game 1 showed an increase of player excitement when compared to the loosely-coupled games, the difference was not significant.

We have also discovered that not all closely-coupled games used in the experiment were equally exciting, as a significant difference existed among them. In particular, game 1 was found to be significantly less exiting ($p < 0.01$) than the other two closely-coupled games. One of the possible explanations for this could be the different nature of the in-game activities. Games 2 and 3 were the only ones where players had to move the jumping pad, which was not necessary in the other games.

Table 1. Hypotheses check for the closely-coupled games evaluated in the experiment

Pattern type	Hypothesis confirmed?				
	H1 excitement	**H2** engagement	**H3** challenge	**H4** understandability	**H5** replayability
Limited resources	No	No	No	Yes	No
Complementary roles	Yes	Yes	Yes	Yes	Yes
Interaction with same object	Yes	Yes	Yes	Yes	Yes

The second important characteristic is a high level of player *engagement* with a game. We asked players to evaluate how engaging they found cooperation in every game. Performed repeated measures ANOVA with a Greenhouse-Geisser correction has shown that not all games were similarly engaging ($F(3.75, 131.22)$ $= 36.54$, $p < 0.01$). Again we observed that games 2 and 3 obtained the highest points based on the players ratings. These two games were significantly more engaging than all loosely-coupled games ($p < 0.01$). Though being evaluated higher than the loosely-coupled games, game 1 did not significantly differ from them.

The next step was to analyze how *challenging* interaction between players in each game was. All games, except games 2 and 3, received a relatively low rating (on average for each game below 4 on the 0 to 10 scale). We found a significant difference among the six games ($F(5,175) = 13.54$, $p < 0.01$). Both games 2 and 3 have shown to be more challenging than other games considered in the study ($p < 0.01$).

As additional challenges may decrease player enjoyment while playing a game, we investigated whether any negative influence existed in our case. This was particularly important for closely-coupled games, as this type of interaction was found to be more challenging. For each game, we checked the correlation between level of challenge and player excitement. Every of the six games has shown a significant positive correlation between these two parameters, indicating that in fact additional challenges, caused by the interaction between players in cooperative games, result in a higher enjoyment. This confirmed that more challenging closely-coupled games did not negatively impact player excitement.

The following criterion evaluated by players was *understandability*. As casual games imply easy understandable rules that do not require much experience, it is important that the way of interaction introduced in cooperative gaming does not decrease this understandability. All games have shown a high level of comprehension, without a significant difference across the six games ($F(4.11, 143.87) = 2.18$, $p > 0.05$).

The last characteristic rated by players was replay value or *replayability* of the game. For casual games, it is a paramount characteristic that guarantees that people will be willing to play the same game again in the future without getting bored very quickly. Repeated measures ANOVA with a Greenhouse-Geisser correction has shown that the six games were not equal in this characteristic ($F(3.45, 120.72) = 9.97$, $p < 0.01$). Based on a Bonferroni post-hoc test, the games of the closely-coupled group have shown a higher player preference to replay the games again with a similar type of interaction between players ($p < 0.01$). The highest values were obtained for games 2 and 3, showing a significantly higher level of replay value in comparison with all loosely-coupled games.

The obtained results have shown the difference among closely-coupled games, explained earlier in this section. As can be seen from Table 1, only one hypothesis was confirmed for game 1. At the same time, games 2 and 3 were evaluated similarly based on all criteria due to the design resemblance between these two games. Every hypothesis was confirmed for games 2 and 3, indicating their high potential for casual game design.

3.2 Observations of Players' Behaviour

Besides the subjective player evaluation, we analyzed player experience based on the observations done during the experiment. We present these observations under three categories: players' emotions, performance and communication. For the latter, we consider different remarks that the participants gave about the communication component in cooperative games, as well as their attempts to communicate with the other player through the in-game actions.

Players' Emotions. Although several players were quite concentrated while playing, almost all of them showed a lot of positive emotions (smiling and laughing). In particular, this occurred when the player encountered his/her partner's avatar. Players were free to navigate in the environment, and therefore, could lose each other in the 3D world. This happened mainly during loosely-coupled games, where players did not stay together most of the time and rarely met each other. The positive reaction appeared also when the players were in each others' way, making the game a bit competitive by preventing the partner to pick up his/her objects directly. When being alone in the scene, players showed to be less emotional and were more focused on the task. They indicated that the loosely-coupled games appeared to be more competitive than cooperative, with the goal of collecting more objects than the partner. Therefore, participants were focused on the task of getting more objects. Because most positive emotions were caused by (successful or not) interaction with another game character, loosely-coupled games resulted in less smiling or laughing than closely-coupled ones. One of the most 'emotional' games was game 3, as it required almost constant interaction with a shared object and, thus, with the other player. Due to its nature, this game caused a lot of excitement among players. Positive emotions were not only caused by a successful play, but also, for example, while trying to move the same object in different directions.

Performance. Observing player performance revealed the following aspects of cooperative interaction. In case of closely-coupled interaction, players tended to follow their partners all the time, in case help would be necessary during the game (mainly in games 2 and 3; but this also occasionally occurred in other games). If, for some reason, they lost each other in the environment, we observed players trying to find their partner as soon as possible, especially when they were waiting and could not proceed further without their help. As there was no communication, players tried to take into account all visual information in order to adjust their actions to partner's performance and help the partner. For example in game 2, once a player saw that his/her partner experienced difficulties in reaching objects on higher platforms, he/she immediately adjusted the position of the jumping pad. In loosely-coupled games players were free to decide whether or not they preferred to be alone or stay together with the other player. In contrast with this situation, closely-coupled games forced both players to be together or to wait for each other most of the time. We observed that a player acting extremely slow, made the experience of the other player less enjoyable.

Communication. During the experiment players were not allowed to communicate in any form. They learned from the game rules what they had to do, but could not discuss strategy or ask for help. Nevertheless, some of the players indicated that they were not affected too much by the absence of communication. In fact, they pointed out that the absence of communication made the game more challenging, and thus, more interesting and entertaining. They stated that information, they obtained from rules and what they observed on the screen, was sufficient for a successful gameplay. Based on the observations, we concluded that this was mainly typical for the evaluated closely-coupled games, as players were together most of the time and were aware of each others' actions. Here, it was not required to search for another player, making the need of communication less strong. In loosely-coupled games, players were not always sharing the same area of the virtual world and, therefore, they were not always aware about the partner's actions.

While observing participants, we noticed frequent occurrence of "communication with the screen". Players tried to explain their partners what they had to do, yet knowing that their messages could not be heard. Being not able to talk, players tried to find out ways in which they could assist their partners when it was obvious that he/she experienced difficulties. One of the solutions, we observed, was an attempt to 'communicate' an advice by moving his/her own avatar in front of the other player. By his/her own action, a 'better' player showed where the other one had to be for an easier accomplishment of the task.

Most games were played successfully under the given conditions of the remote setup without communication. However, half of the participants stated that the presence of communication would increase their performance. Although it was not proven by letting them play with communication, players pointed out that an ability to talk (either via text messages or voice) would make them more efficient. In particular, they mentioned an advantage of communication in order to divide areas for objects search. It was often the case that players lost a lot of time by going to the areas, where their partner had already harvested all objects. In general, participants expressed a strong wish for being able to talk with the other player even when it was not absolutely necessary for the game. For instance, if the strategy or in-game tasks were clear without actual communication, players still wanted to talk in order to make fun of each other and joke together.

4   Conclusion

In this paper we presented a study investigating synchronous cooperation in remote casual games where no communication existed between players. We analyzed six different types of cooperation (based on cooperative game patterns), each being either closely- or loosely-coupled. It has been shown that introducing closely-coupled interaction in casual games leads to a better player experience. We have observed that two of the three evaluated closely-coupled games introduced a higher level of player excitement, engagement and replayability without additional learning difficulties. In particular, games 2 (complementary roles pattern) and 3 (interaction with the same object pattern) satisfied all 5 criteria considered in the study, showing the advantage over the loosely-coupled games evaluated in the experiment.

Although we have seen player preference towards closely-coupled interaction in games, not all closely-coupled games were evaluated equally. Due to the possibility to design closely-coupled tasks differently, we realize the impact of game design on player evaluation. From the results, we observed that the design of games 2 and 3 differs more from the one of game 1 (limited resources pattern) than from each other.

With this study we have made the first attempt to evaluate cooperative game patterns in remote setup where any form of communication was not supported. Comparing results of our study with the existing works allows us to draw conclusions about an impact of the setup on the player experience [18]. In particular, findings reported in [8] showed a higher contribution of several loosely-coupled patterns to the overall player experience (e.g. shared puzzles), while in our case close coupling was more preferred among players. We believe that such difference between remote and co-located setups is caused by the inability to talk.

Based on these findings, we can conclude that integration of closely-coupled interaction together with an appropriate game design has great potential for casual gaming. This triggers further research to confirm the obtained findings and generalize them to other games. By doing so it is possible define ways of making closely-coupled interaction more interesting for cooperative casual games among distributed players.

Acknowledgments. The research described in this paper is directly funded by Hasselt University through the BOF framework. The authors would like to thank Tom De Weyer for his assistance with the implementation and all participants who contributed to this research by taking part in the experiment.

References

1. The Nielsen Company: Insights on casual games: analysis of casual games for the PC (2009), http://blog.nielsen.com/nielsenwire/wp-content/uploads/2009/09/GamerReport.pdf
2. Li, K.A., Counts, S.: Exploring social interactions and attributes of casual multiplayer mobile gaming. In: Proc. Mobility 2007, pp. 696–703. ACM (2007)
3. Mueller, F.'., Gibbs, M.R.: Evaluating a distributed physical leisure game for three players. In: Proc. OZCHI 2007, pp. 143–150. ACM (2007)
4. Gajadhar, B., Nap, H., de Kort, Y., IJsselsteijn, W.: Let's sweep some mines together: Social interaction & competition in casual games. In: Proc. Fun and Games 2010, pp. 19–30 (2010)
5. Bogost, I.: Asynchronous multiplay: Futures for casual multiplayer experience. In: Proc. Other Players Conference 2004 (2004), http://www.bogost.com/downloads/i.%20bogost%20-%20asynchronous%20multiplay.pdf
6. Di Loreto, I., Gouaich, A.: Social casual games success is not so casual (2010), http://hal.archives-ouvertes.fr/lirmm-00486934
7. Ricchetti, M.: What makes social games social? (2002), http://www.gamasutra.com/view/feature/6735
8. El-Nasr, M.S., Aghabeigi, B., Milam, D., Erfani, M., Lameman, B., Maygoli, H., Mah, S.: Understanding and evaluating cooperative games. In: Proc. CHI 2010, pp. 253–262. ACM (2010)
9. McGee, K.: Patterns and computer game design innovation. In: Proc. IE 2007, RMIT University, pp. 16:1–16:8 (2007)
10. Kreimeier, B.: The case for game design patterns (2002), http://www.gamasutra.com/view/feature/4261
11. Björk, S., Holopainen, J.: Patterns in Game Design (Game Development Series). Charles River Media, Inc. (2004)
12. Rocha, J.B., Mascarenhas, S.P.R.: Game mechanics for cooperative games. In: ZDN Digital Game, pp. 73–80 (2008)
13. Schmeil, A., Eppler, M.J.: Knowledge sharing and collaborative learning in Second Life: a classification of virtual 3D group interaction scripts. Journal of Universal Computer Science 14, 665–677 (2009)
14. Ducheneaut, N., Moore, R.J.: The social side of gaming: a study of interaction patterns in a massively multiplayer online game. In: Proc. CSCW 2004, pp. 360–369. ACM (2004)
15. Goh, W.B., Fitriani, Ting, L.G., Shou, W., Goh, C.F., Menon, M., Tan, J., Cohen, L.G.: Potential challenges in collaborative game design for inclusive settings (2011), http://www.dfki.de/educationchi2011/
16. Zagal, J.P., Rick, J., Hsi, I.: Collaborative games: lessons learned from board games. Simulation and Gaming 37(1), 24–40 (2006)
17. Beznosyk, A., Quax, P., Coninx, K., Lamotte, W.: The influence of cooperative game design patterns for remote play on player experience. In: Proc. APCHI 2012. ACM (2012)
18. Beznosyk, A., Quax, P., Coninx, K., Lamotte, W.: User enjoyment and performance in collaborative and cooperative games in shared 3d virtual environments. In: Proc. GRAPP 2011, pp. 302–307 (2011)

Leisure Food: Derive Social and Cultural Entertainment through Physical Interaction with Food

Jun Wei* and Ryohei Nakatsu

Keio-NUS CUTE Center, IDM Institute,
NGS, National University of Singapore, Singapore
{weijun24,elenr}@nus.edu.sg

Abstract. Food is not simply a source of nutrition, but also a symbolic medium for social bonds and entertainment. Beyond this, food is common artefact across cultures, embedded with internal cultural value and identity. This paper presents the notion of "Leisure Food", which explores the roles of mundane food in deriving social and cultural entertainment from people's interaction with physical food. We focus on the application of culturally based food experiences as a gateway for enriched and profound entertainment, through maximizing the physical, social and cultural affordances of food using technologies. From this notion, we developed two prototypes based on the positive interactions that people have as they eat and prepare food in their everyday lives and also extend them to remote situations. The preliminary user study demonstrates that these two prototypes can enhance the level of social engagement and culture recollection experience through the new designed forms of physical food-mediated interaction, which verified the proposed features regarding "Leisure Food".

Keywords: Food-mediated interaction, social entertainment, culture recollection, user experience.

1 Introduction

Entertainment, defined as occasions for creating pleasure, is so pervasive and influential in the contemporary society and adds a key dimension to the lifestyle and sense of self-satisfaction of human beings. Yet the term of entertainment is currently narrowly defined within computer-based technologies and interactive media experiences.

Essentially, entertainment is based upon providing pleasure by stimulating physical and emotional arousal [1]. It is multifaceted, besides relying heavily on today's electronic devices for fun and excitement, we also need physical interaction to go beyond the barrier created by the pure digital content. One of the great

---

* This research is supported by the Singapore National Research Foundation under its International Research Centre @ Singapore Funding Initiative and administered by the IDM Programme Office.

M. Herrlich, R. Malaka, and M. Masuch (Eds.): ICEC 2012, LNCS 7522, pp. 256–269, 2012.

affordances of physical artefacts is the tangibility, which conveys emotional importance beyond the excessive information. Social and physical interactions are the new paradigms that outline a vision for the next generation of entertainment systems [2].

Beyond this, we consider culture as another important dimension for entertainment. As Stromberg indicated, "entertainment is a cultural system through which commitment to certain values is generated" [1]. The culture we discuss here is not the high-level artistic culture, but the civilian culture that has been interwoven with and reflected in people's everyday life, and conveyed through the certain ways people communicate with each other and conduct their activities. Culture activities can serve as a source not only for new interaction metaphors, but further, for entertainment as well.

Therefore, after broadening our understanding of what entertainment involves in everyday experiences, we locate special concentration on the sociable, emotional and cultural aspects. The socio-cultural context is part of the user experience, as suggested by Alben's definition of user experience [3]. We believe these two features can lead to a different level of entertainment, triggering more "thick" and profound experience.

On the other hand, as we may noticed, entertainment is so woven into the fabric of current everyday life that most of the emerging devices have some playful functions inside, or are created just for entertainment, such as the smart phones, tablets, or the ambient displays for games, while the potentials of our traditional surrounding artefacts have been somewhat neglected.

In the everyday household and community life, food is often at the center of social interaction, entertainment and cultural expression. As Finkelstein proposed, "The idea of food as a source of amusement has been parallel to the experience of eating since gastronomy began" [4]. One important perception of food is the enjoyment of eating and socializing at the same time. People enjoy their food, relish the practice of making it, and above all celebrate the sharing of it [5]. What's more, food is also considered as the ultimate embodiment of human culture. Special foods or significant eating events are often imbued with core social values [6].

People are familiar with food, and food in itself encompasses a variety of characteristics that can be utilized to communicate emotional feelings, such as the food texture, shape, pattern, colour, even smell and taste. For example, the aroma of baked bread, fresh coffee, and the sensation of chocolate melting in the mouth, can often evoke a sense of comfort and contribute to the eating pleasure. Given the diversity of role that food plays in everyday life, together with its social and cultural impact, we present the notion of "Leisure Food". The core concept is to seek ways to utilize the unique potentials of food and create new channels to derive increased social and cultural entertainment from the physical food interactions.

With the pursuit of deeper emotional feeling through resonance with people's social and cultural experiences, this research looks into interesting human activities that can serve as the basis for deriving new food entertainment ideas.

We then designed and implemented two prototypes based on the notion, and also conducted a preliminary user study to obtain users' perception and experience regarding the prototypes, so as to evaluate the effectiveness of the prototypes and also to validate the proposed notion. The contribution of this paper is its exploration into the potential space to derive entertainment in the area of human-food-human interaction, by extending and multiplexing individuals' current experiences and interactions around food.

The remaining paper is organized as follows. Section 2 introduces the social and cultural framing of entertainment and the background for "Leisure Food" paradigm, followed by the works related to food interaction for entertainment. Section 3 describes the two prototyped systems we designed for food eating and cooking respectively, and section 4 presents the results and discussion from a user study. Finally, section 5 concludes the research theories and proposes future works towards pleasurable human experience over food.

2   Background and Related Works

Entertainment is one of the essential elements in human society. Entertainment computing has been traditionally associated with interactive entertainment media and game playing. The rapid development of digital technology promotes the "high technologification" of various entertainments and alters our concepts of entertainment mode, thereby giving birth to the digital entertainment [7]. However, it can take various styles, not limited to film, game, music, theme parks and other established forms of entertainment industries. Entertainment includes "fun" in our everyday life activities, from meeting friends to relaxing at hot spas [8].

Entertainment as an end-product is amusing; as a tool it is powerful. With powerful functionality, it is being applied to all aspects of life from learning, training, designing, communicating and collaborating everywhere. One of the main explorations will be to examine how new forms of mediated interaction can lead to radical new forms of technology and art for entertainment computing [9].

2.1   Social and Cultural Dimensions

All forms of entertainment are having levels of interactivity added to them [10]. An important feature of entertainment is the ability to socialize, by extending the concepts of social networking with novel interactive entertainment concepts. Sociability allows people to assemble based on common interest and personal affinities, creating alternate forms of community.

On the other hand, the arrival of new media strongly influences the forms and content of entertainment. Although it decreases the gap of entertainment styles between people in different areas, at the same time, it causes the losing of local features of traditional cultures, the internal core of various entertainments for different cultures. The entertainment realm keeps on evolving rapidly, but there is still something that keeps constant and cherished by most human beings:

the culture. Culture is the product of ongoing symbolic human activities that is old and pervasive as human society itself. Entertainment, by contrast, is now primarily connected with the various forms of digital visual pleasures provided by the mass media technology. Bringing culture and entertainment together would make the entertainment experience more unique, meaningful and evoking.

From this point, entertainment can be sustained by the unique aspects of the culture contexts, and makes the experience more meaningful and long-lasting. The cultural background largely depends how we interpret the interactions with others, especially the non-verbal interactions. This cultural dependency allows for a much richer experience to be rendered. This is thanks to the complexity and depth of the semantics involved and the user familiarity with them. There is also the advantage of higher bandwidth of information at the interfaces as symbolic meanings and implicit knowledge can be used. The interface is not limited to explicit messages and meanings anymore. The cultural contexts within entertainment provide spiritual pleasure for human beings [11]. Cultural entertainment as the occasions for pleasure is therefore dependent on the shift from sensations to emotions.

Considering contemporary society's fascination with entertainment, we think it is very necessary to explore enriched entertainment styles from everyday life, which highlight the social and cultural grounding of interactive entertainment.

2.2   Food: A Significant Facilitator of Entertainment

There are various reasons why food can be a promising medium to explore in the social and cultural contexts of entertainment. Except for providing basic nutrients, food is also considered as a symbolic medium with internal emotional attachments to express and trigger positive feelings. Food can alleviate depression and provide comfort, and eating in itself can serve as a very relaxing, stress-relieving activity. Eating and drinking are modes of entertainment for human beings; humans get pleasure out of gustatory information obtained from food.

Furthermore, we believe food is one of best and most enjoyable social networking platforms - individuals interact through and around it. Food is the glue that bonds people connected to their family, friends and neighbourhoods on the occasions like family dinner, parties, and get-together. Pleasure and family connectedness are included among the several positive aspects of people's interaction with food [5]. Food has also been used as a metaphor to represent culture and identity, the nostalgic longing and consumption of particular food items sustain one's sense of cultural, familial and self-identity. Most of us would admit that, "One way of exploring a culture is through their food and cultural food practices. For example, serving food is considered as typical and representative of the politeness and hospitality in Asia. These viewpoints verify the potential of augmenting food as a novel but intuitive medium to provide enhanced social interaction and playful cultural experience.

Over the years, interaction designers have recently begun to explore the area of human-food-interaction and its implications for design. These explorations have ranged from positive social concepts around human-food interaction and how technology can create new kinds of engagements [12,13]. Some existing intersections between food and technology mainly take the form of food social network sites, online cooking and farming games, and restaurant recommender or ratings applications. Parallel to this, there have also been some explorations towards playful interaction design on the actual food and food-related activities. "Mamagoto" [14] is an interactive and context-aware dining system which encourages small children to "play" with food, using their curiosity towards food to expand their sensory experience while eating. DinnerWare [15] is an exploration of eating as a medium for computation and aesthetic expression. It consists of a dining service electronically equipped to react to the properties of the food and respond to a user's gestures. Gamelunch [16], a sonically augmented dining table, maps the usual dining actions like cutting and slicing onto physically-based sound synthesis. MetaCookie [17] realized "Pseudo-gustatory" display that represents the desired flavors of cookie by means of a cross-modal effect elicited by visual and olfactory augmented reality. EaTheremin is a fork-type device that enables users to play various sounds by eating foods, which changes the act of eating into practical daily entertainment [18]. Playful Tray [19] is embedded with an interactive game play over a weight-sensitive tray surface, and uses children's eating actions as game inputs for reducing their poor eating behaviours.

These works augmented the affordances of actual food by embedding various sensors and actuators over food or tableware. However, they mainly concentrate on the personal human-food interaction, instead of human-to-human interaction mediated by food. Furthermore, none of these studies has looked closely at the manipulation and interaction process around food, and what aspects of this interactive and collaborative process could yield insights into the design of technology and everyday rituals. Different from this, we explore how technology can be designed to shape and enrich the way people interact with food and further enhance the social and cultural food experiences.

Food is not simply a source of nutrition, but is also central to the production of community life, a site for personal and shared reflection and story-telling [20], a medium for social interaction and a symbol of personal identity. Food preparation and sharing in particular provide opportunities to support the creative, sensory, aesthetic and social nature of human-food-human interaction. Furthermore, food related behaviours, such as shared meals, food creation, food preparation and so on, can all be considered to form an integral part of social and personal wellbeing. Could food interaction design also be an important and useful metaphor for the future practice of user experience itself [21]?

Rather than the external playfulness and fantasies, we explore new interaction styles into the wider implications (human, social, cultural, and ethical) of experiences and try to apply it onto food. Extending the growing literature in this area, we look to expand the range of food experience by examining the in-depth roles of food in supporting positive physical and emotional responses, with a focus on the social and situated nature of food interactions, the internal physicality, sociability and cultural recollection.

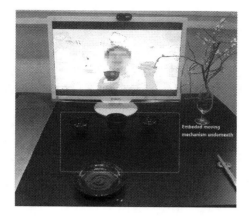

Fig. 1. Overview of the ServeDish Table in dining scenario

3   Prototypes towards "Leisure Food"

The domain of entertainment is much broader than just games and leisure activities; entertainment can also take forms in our everyday activities in an interactive and playful way, and designing for this kind of playfulness involves creating objects that elicit a playful approach and provide enjoyable experiences [22]. To design for meaningful and positive interactions, it is essential to identify daily food practices and the opportunities for the design of technology to support such practice. To do this, we need to fully understand the role of technologies to support human-food interactions in social settings.

Towards the "Leisure Food" paradigm, we rely on the cultural understanding of human activities to create expressive interactions and entertainment. The various ways that people find pleasure in food can all serve as springboards for technological designs that reflect or augment the ways to provide new hedonic food experiences for people. In general, food consumption involves many sensory and aesthetic experiences such as cooking meals, sharing and eating food. In this section, we present two prototypes that draw from people's routine activities with food, encourage them with interactive technologies and extend them to remote situations to achieve the shared entertainment experience.

3.1   ServeDish Table: Enlighten Eating Culture

Eating food together is always compelling to people, it creates a warm atmosphere that keeps people happy, occupied and entertained. Considering one of the positive aspects about food interaction while eating together, we developed ServeDish Table to mimic the mutual food serving activity in dining situation to provide the warm feelings of pleasure and intimacy, even if people are physically apart. In many Asian cultures, serving food is a conventional dining etiquette to show respect, love and care to family members and guests as well. This tradition has been deemed as a kind of spontaneous activity in our culture, something

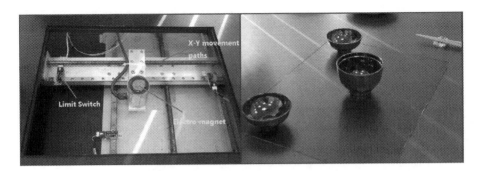

Fig. 2. (Left)Mechanism of ServeDish Table (Right)Actual snapshot when serving dish remotely

that we regularly and unconsciously engage in. Using this system, we attempt to bring back this ritual dinner etiquette and derive emotional pleasure from this physical interaction via food and tableware, even when people fail to share the same dining table.

This prototype includes the visual interface part and the execution mechanism. The visual interface can be a TV monitor embedded with a video camera and Kinect Sensor [23] to track the user's hand movement and achieves gesture-based on-screen menu selection. This function allows the user on one side to easily select one dish, and then the signal would be transmitted to the remote location, triggering the corresponding mechanism to execute the food serving on the other side. Figure 1 is an overview of this system in the dining scenario.

To achieve the remote food serving, we designed the execution mechanism and embedded it into the normal dining table. The mechanism applies the basic principle of magnetic attraction, combined with two-axis linear movement structure, as shown in figure 2 (Left). Permanent magnets are attached on the bottom of the tableware, including bowls and plates. By controlling the movement of electro-magnet component underneath, we can control the movement of the dishes on the table. We chose to use magnets because they are simple to implement, easy to control, and require no wires. When the master controller receives the activation signal, the motors and magnets are activated accordingly to execute the remote moving of dishes on the table surface. Figure 2 (Right) is a screenshot of the actual food serving when user selects one dish.

Using two connected systems in different locations, people can initiate the remote mechanism through gesture interaction with the visual interface to choose one dish to serve, thus to carry out the remote interaction in a physical way. When user on the other side selects one of the dish icons from the screen, let's say, serving rice dish on their partner's table, the electro-magnet will move directly to the position of that dish, activate the magnet, and drag the rice smoothly towards the user on the table surface.

Although different from the actual food serving face-to-face, this simulated activity on physical dish during eating provides a new channel for playful interaction using food. Furthermore, we believe the actual movement of dishes can create a feeling of "magic moving", surprising and delighting the receiver, and evoke increased cheering and comforting emotions. Through rethinking how we approach everyday food behaviours, we propose this design of interactive system to engage individuals' socio-cultural reflection on food practices. Although it is not like the common amusement we get from games or movies, the interactivity and cultural retrospective can convey more delicate human emotions and stronger feeling of warmth, which comes in accordance with our theme of "Leisure Food".

3.2 Food Messaging: Playful and Customized Cooking for Expression

In addition for eating, food as gifts are also culturally appropriated and encouraged, especially during festivals, anniversaries and celebrations, for example, sending the specially-designed food with personal messages. Cooking and sharing food are important activities to enhance the relationship and intimacy, transmitting warm feelings among people. We would all agree that eating is a form of entertainment experience, so as the cooking process. What about cooking or eating the customized food with special messages inside? As a reproduction and extension of the social fun around food creation and gifting, we developed this food messaging system, which transformed the normal messaging process into a new channel for meaningful and emotional expressions using organic food.

Although it is now almost effortless to send Short Message Service (SMS), digital photos or gift, these intangible messages miss out the physical and emotional sense of care. Instead, imagine sending an edible "Hello" to your remote family members by displaying it on a cake in their kitchen. Food Messaging achieves this by reproducing the digital greetings (i.e. Messages and gift) using edible food materials, which makes tangible the digital messages, creating personalized expressions and gifting in edible format.

To allow the real-time design, transmission, and crafting of self-designed pattern, the system consists of the application software on the mobile side and the food crafting mechanism. User's finger movement is tracked in real time, and the detected pattern is sent to the mechanism via the server in between, then the synchronous crafting is done in three dimensions with multiple flavors using accurate step-motor control and triple-syringed food material injection, through a layer-by-layer printing process. The crafting process, including the motor movements and food materials change, is controlled precisely in accordance with the user's input design. Figure 3 gives an overview of the system structure.

The input interface is designed as an easy-to-use mobile application that allows users to create their preferred food patterns virtually. User can compose their unique messages or patterns by scrawling and writing on the touch screen. They can also change the shapes, colors, text, and even taste of the messages, by tapping on different food materials during the design. Accordingly, the system is designed to craft with multiple food materials, the purpose is not only to make the food messages colorful visually and more tasty, but also enable the creation of contextual messages with changed color, smell and flavor, to represent

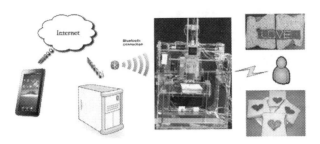

Fig. 3. System design of the Food Messaging prototype

different emotions or feelings. User can also compose different patterns for different layers, thus to construct the 3-dimensional food with changed taste in each layer. When people are drawing on the screen, their fingers' movements are tracked, and then the detected design is divided into a series of segments, each tagged with their direction and length. When user pressed the "print" button, all the data would be transmitted to the master board of the food crafting mechanism, to indicate the movement route in each axis, thus to exert the crafting process accurately.

The food crafting mechanism functions as the output of the user's input design. Controlled by the master board, this mechanism is supposed to craft the corresponding pattern received from the design interface with real edible food. For accurate food crafting, we employ the motor-controlled syringe injection on a 3-axis robotic carriage. Basically, the model is designed to use 3-degree freedom robotic carriage to move the food depositing component along the x and y axis, and the platform up and down to form the z coordinate of the system. The accurate and smooth movement of each axis is achieved through lead-screw coupling powered by step motor, controlled by the microchip from the master board. Through balancing the coordinate movement of syringe position and food extrusion, the mechanism is able to form any designed shape using different food materials.

When receiving the interpreted data of user's design, the step motors would start accordingly to move the robotic carriage. Simultaneously, the robotic carriage moves the attached food depositing component along the x and y axis to complete one layer. When finishing the top layer, the platform will move down a certain distance to continue with the next layer. Material change is achieved by rotation of depositing syringe to a certain degree. Through this layer-by-layer crafting, a piece of 3-dimensional physical food can be constructed. Using this system, people can creatively compose their message-embedded food, and transmit it to remote loved ones as a unique gift, showing greetings and care in a physical format. It is an innovative way of customized cooking and social interaction through food, also conveying love and care physically to remote people.

Messaging and gifting through food demonstrates a subtlety and courtesy that messaging through digital devices sometimes lacks. Compared with plain

Fig. 4. Examples from interaction with the Food Messaging prototype

text, or digital message like SMS or twitter, expression through organic food can convey a stronger sense of emotional warmth and connectedness. It is more than simply saying "I love you" or "I miss you", it is a physical embodiment of care and affection of one person to others [24], not only visually, but also with smell and taste. Food here is the multisensory medium for remote communication and entertainment, and each flavor can be translated into a corresponding emotional state or special experience from one's memory. This flavor-changed eating experience of food acts as a meaningful way for emotional expression.

This prototype provides an alternative approach of engaging with food. By sending routine, social touch messages, such as birthday greetings, good luck messages and other general expressions of affection, people actually involve themselves into the creative and personalized cooking process. The richness of entertainment experience can be much increased and intensified by this playful and interactive way of personalized food creation and expression. Rather than focusing on the information transmission, it emphasizes more on the enriched food experience, which engages people into the social communication and entertainment over food, in a playful and meaningful way. It enhances the engagement to connect digital playfulness to active participation in the target activity of cooking and eating.

4   Evaluation and Discussion

To investigate the actual effectiveness of the working prototypes, we conducted the preliminary user study to see whether they reach the intention of proposed "Leisure Food" theme, and get a deeper understanding of the user perception.

We recruited 29 volunteers (17 male and 12 female) from the general public, aged from 20 to 40 years old. They are from different countries, like China, India, Japan, Sri Lanka, Korea, and Spain also. After explaining the general concept of the two systems and how to use them, we asked every user to use each system for about 5 minutes (We did not apply the remote setting, so that user can activate the system and see the output at the same location). Then we use the questionnaire to elicit their responses about what they think and feel about the systems, in terms of level of engagement and evoked cultural recalling. The participants were given the questionnaire right after their usage both systems.

Regarding the questionnaire, we use the Likert Scales [25], a series of statement to which the respondents rate their level of agreement on a 5-point scale. The rankings from 1 to 5 indicate from "Strongly Disagree" to "Strongly Agree". In this study, we focused on the two attributes for the users to evaluate: 1. The system increases the engagement experience; 2. The system supports the cultural recollection experience. The participants were required to rate their agreement on these two statements regarding each prototype.

What's more, to avoid the "social desirability bias" [25], we collect the post-test data in a way that the evaluator did not see the responses until the participant has left, and we also made the survey itself anonymous to elicit more honest reactions. Data collected in the survey are expressed by histogram in percentage.

Regarding the engagement experience of the ServeDish Table, we got very positive ratings from the users. Participants reported a mean value of 4.11 (SD=0.557), indicating the level between "Agree" and "Strongly Agree". As shown in figure 5 (Left), a great majority of participants admitted that the interaction of serving dish remotely can enhance their engagement experience while eating, except for 10% of people who rated neutral on this statement.

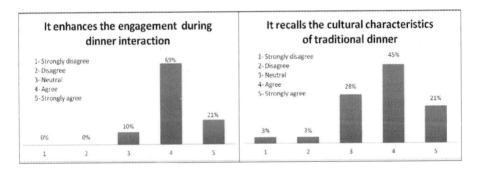

Fig. 5. Users' feedback regarding the interaction experience with ServeDish Table

The ratings on the cultural experience through this prototype are slightly different from the engagement aspect. Participants reported a mean value of 3.76 (SD=0.951), somewhere between neutral and agree. The responses are generally lower and more varied on this attribute than the engagement aspect, probably because people from different backgrounds have different awareness and perception levels regarding this dining culture. People grown up in western lifestyle (e.g. Spain) may have no idea about this etiquette and feel less engaged, so it would be more difficult for them to understand the underlying grounding in culture that reflected from the physical manipulation of dishes from another person.

As for the engagement level triggered by the Food Messaging system, participants reported an average value of 4.11, similar with the ServeDish Table but with larger variance (SD=0.860), having more people rated "Strongly Agree" for this prototype (figure 6). From this, we can tell that participants would be more motivated and delighted to be creative in the sending of playful and inventive messages through this system than would be the case if they were sending content to a mobile phone. On the other hand, the level of culture recollection was rated lower. They reported a mean value of 3.448 (SD=0.948) regarding the cultural experience, 42% rated as "Agree" and 10% rated "Strongly Agree".

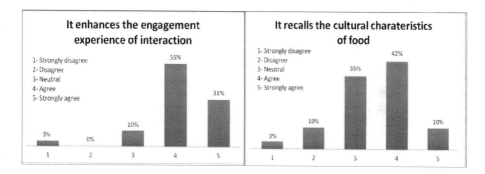

Fig. 6. Users' feedback regarding the interaction experience with Food Messaging

This preliminary study provides a snapshot into the users' perception of the two systems. Users' overall reactions were quite positive. They found the prototypes really provide more enjoyment for food cooking and eating, and they were a pleasure to use. As one user reported, "I am really surprised when the bowl begins moving towards me, and it makes me feel much more excited when eating". Similarly, another user mentioned, "It was really great to see my drawings actually been printed out on a piece of bread, and I am sure my Mum would be happy to receive it." However, they also expressed some concerns about the prototypes, for example, the set up of the system, the noise from the motors, and cleaning issues, all of which are of great help for the further improvements.

This evaluation has demonstrated that both of these two prototypes achieve the increased entertainment experience with cultural recollection in a certain degree. In comparison, users gave higher ratings on the engagement aspect than the cultural feeling experience regarding both prototypes. Although these two prototypes basically achieve the two proposed affordances of "Leisure Food", this slight difference indicated us the necessity to explore further into the grounding culture of food interaction, so as to gain more insights on how to reflect and highlight the culture embodiment through these food interactions.

Towards enriched hedonic experience of food interaction, we need to understand more about the positive aspects of the human experience with food. It is at this point that we can begin to design for "Leisure Food"; using technologies to reconstruct and augment the usual way that people interact with foods.

5 Conclusion

Entertainment is now a key driver in the development of technology. In this paper, we leverage on the rich potentials of food and propose the notion of "Leisure Food", as a paradigm to empower food with technology towards enhanced social and cultural entertainment. "Leisure Food" aims to expand the human-food interaction and create technologies or applications that embrace the positive, and delightful aspects of food practices as social and cultural experience.

Whether noticed or not, the practice around food is actually about food and also what people consider as significant in the process of cooking and eating food. This notion relies on people's customary social manipulations and culturally responsive activity with food, and then extends them to remote situations to achieve enriched shared entertainment. We describe how studying the positive aspects of people's interactions with food can lead to designing very different types of entertainment technologies. The two examples in this paper are some of the ways that we can think about the positive ways that people interact with each other through food, the food sharing and serving while eating together, and the creativity expression and symbolic gifting through cooking.

As we move on to explore and create "Leisure Food", it is important to draw from and embrace the deep and wide cultural repository of human experiences with food, discover the significant values human have towards food and then take a closer look at how to harness such values to enhance the enjoyable aspects of food entertainment. Humanity possesses a rich pool of cultural experiences which can contribute fundamental resources to the embodied interaction design [26], and to the entertainment as well. It is necessary to develop a better understanding about how to go beyond the amusement from mass media and into encouraging positive experience. We hope the future research can explore further to design embodied interaction based on cultural practice, thus to derive social and cultural entertainment out of human's internal values and identities.

Acknowledgments. We thank our colleagues from Keio-NUS CUTE Center of National University of Singapore, who helped in the building of the prototypes.

References

1. Stromberg, P.: Person and Community in the Culture of Entertainment. Pastoral Psychology, 1–8 (2010)
2. Cheok, A.D., et al.: Social and physical interactive paradigms for mixed-reality entertainment. Comput. Entertain. 4(2), 5 (2006)
3. Alben, L.: Quality of experience: defining the criteria for effective interaction design. Interactions 3(3), 11–15 (1996)
4. Finkelstein, J.: The Taste of Boredom: McDonaldization and Australian Food Culture. American Behavioral Scientist 47(2), 187–200 (2003)
5. Grimes, A., Harper, R.: Celebratory technology: new directions for food research in HCI. In: Proceeding of CHI 2008, pp. 467–476. ACM, Florence (2008)
6. Quandt, S.A., et al.: The social and nutritional meaning of food sharing among older rural adults. Journal of Aging Studies 15(2), 145–162 (2001)

7. Jin, Z.: Global Technological Change: From Hard Technology to Soft Technology - Second Edition. Intellect Ltd. (2011)
8. Shedroff, N.: Experience Design 1. New Riders Press, New Riders (2001)
9. Cheok, A.D.: Art and Technology of Entertainment Computing and Communication. In: Advances in Interactive New Media for Entertainment Computing, pp. 1–18. Springer (2010)
10. Lampel, J., Shamsie, J., Lant, T.K.: The business of culture: strategic perspectives on entertainment and media. Lawrence Erlbaum Assoicates (2006)
11. Salem, B., Rauterberg, M., Nakatsu, R.: Kansei Mediated Entertainment. In: Harper, R., Rauterberg, M., Combetto, M. (eds.) ICEC 2006. LNCS, vol. 4161, pp. 103–116. Springer, Heidelberg (2006)
12. Hirsch, T., et al.: Making food, producing sustainability. In: Proceedings of the CHI 2010 Extended Abstracts, pp. 3147–3150. ACM, Atlanta (2010)
13. Bell, G., Kaye, J.: Designing Technology for Domestic Spaces: A Kitchen Manifesto. Gastronomica 2(2), 46–62 (2002)
14. Arakawa, T., Inakage, M.: Mamagoto: "playing" with food. In: ACM SIGGRAPH 2007 Posters, p. 161. ACM, San Diego (2007)
15. Coelho, M.: DinnerWare: why playing with food should be encouraged. In: Proceedings of the CHI 2009 Extended Abstracts on Human Factors in Computing Systems, pp. 3505–3506. ACM, Boston (2009)
16. Polotti, P., et al.: Gamelunch: forging a dining experience through sound. In: CHI 2008 Extended Abstracts on Human Factors in Computing Systems, pp. 2281–2286. ACM, Florence (2008)
17. Narumi, T., Nishizaka, S., Kajinami, T., Tanikawa, T., Hirose, M.: Augmented reality flavors: gustatory display based on edible marker and cross-modal interaction. In: Proceedings of CHI 2011, pp. 93–102 (2011)
18. Kadomura, Nakamori, R., Tsukada, K., Siio, I.: EaTheremin. In: SIGGRAPH Asia 2011 Emerging Technologies on - SA 2011, p. 1. ACM Press (2011)
19. Lo, J.-L., Lin, T.-y., Chu, H.-h., Chou, H.-C., Chen, J.-h., Hsu, J.Y.-j., Huang, P.: Playful Tray: Adopting Ubicomp and Persuasive Techniques into Play-Based Occupational Therapy for Reducing Poor Eating Behavior in Young Children. In: Krumm, J., Abowd, G.D., Seneviratne, A., Strang, T., et al. (eds.) UbiComp 2007. LNCS, vol. 4717, pp. 38–55. Springer, Heidelberg (2007)
20. Bh, M.T., et al.: 4Photos: a collaborative photo sharing experience. In: Proceedings of the 6th Nordic Conference on Human-Computer Interaction: Extending Boundaries, pp. 52–61. ACM, Reykjavik (2010)
21. Venkatacharya, P.S., et al.: What can user experience learn from food design? In: Proceedings of the 27th International Conference Extended Abstracts on Human Factors in Computing Systems, pp. 3287–3292. ACM, Boston (2009)
22. Lucero, A., Arrasvuori, J.: PLEX Cards: a source of inspiration when designing for playfulness. In: Proceedings of the 3rd International Conference on Fun and Games, pp. 28–37. ACM, Leuven (2010)
23. Microsoft Xbox Kinect, http://www.xbox.com/kinect
24. Perry, M., Rachovides, D.: Entertaining Situated Messaging at Home. Comput. Supported Coop. Work 16(1-2), 99–128 (2007)
25. Tullis, T., Albert, B.: Chapter 6 - Self-Reported Metrics. In: Measuring the User Experience, pp. 123–166. Morgan Kaufmann, San Francisco (2008)
26. Lindtner, S., Anderson, K., Dourish, P.: Cultural appropriation: information technologies as sites of transnational imagination. In: Proceedings of CSCW 2012, pp. 77–86. ACM (2012)

A Method for Measuring the Creative Potential
of Computer Games

Wilawan Inchamnan, Peta Wyeth, Daniel Johnson, and David Conroy

Electrical Engineering and Computer Science, Queensland University of Technology, Australia
{w.inchamnan,dj.conroy}@student.qut.edu.au,
{peta.wyeth,dm.johnson}@qut.edu.au,

Abstract. This paper describes a method for measuring the creative potential of computer games. The research approach applies a behavioral and verbal protocol to analyze the factors that influence the creative processes used by people as they play computer games from the puzzle genre. Creative potential is measured by examining task motivation and domain-relevant and creativity-relevant skills. This paper focuses on the reliability of the factors used for measurement, determining those factors that are more strongly related to creativity. The findings show that creative potential may be determined by examining the relationship between skills required and the effect of intrinsic motivation within game play activities.

Keywords: Creative potential, Computer game, Creative measurement, Task motivation, Domain-relevant skill, Creativity-relevant skill, Behavioral assessment.

1 Introduction

Creative thinking processes are vital in helping people solve problems [23]. Digital simulations and games may play a significant role in facilitating exploration and creative problem solving. Although there are educational computer games that have been designed to support cognitive and creative activity [5], there is limited research to date research on how to measure the potential of a computer game to facilitate creative processes.

Assessing creative potential requires a focus on how and why an individual responds to activities [17]. However, no studies have been conducted to determine the specific interactions that occur during gameplay that support creative processes. Previous research studies have not applied coherent theories of creativity assessment to the domain of computer games. To understand the creative potential of games, criteria related to creativity activity must be clearly stated and readily translated into assessment [1].

A primary goal of this study is the development of a method for measuring the creative potential of computer games. Previous research has examined computer game play in relation to personal creative traits [8]. Our research is particularly interested in creative *process*, rather than the creative attributes of a person (i.e. [29]) or creative

M. Herrlich, R. Malaka, and M. Masuch (Eds.): ICEC 2012, LNCS 7522, pp. 270–283, 2012.
© IFIP International Federation for Information Processing 2012

product. The study forms part of a program of research designed to better understand the creative processes that people engage in while playing computer games. The measurement method described in this paper has been adapted from an existing theory of creative assessment [23] and its reliability for creative assessment within the computer game context is investigated. The method developed focuses on the componential framework of creativity that includes three major components: domain-relevant skills, creativity-relevant skills and task motivation [1]. To examine the creative process potential of computer games using this comprehensive assessment technique, we have adapted the existing behavior and verbal protocol developed by Ruscio et al. [23], which has been used previously for assessing a range of creative activities. The measurement method is designed to explore the relationship between task motivation, domain relevant skills and creativity relevant skills within a particular activity.

2   Creative Potential of Computer Games

Creativity involves problem discovery, goal identification and engagement in heuristic activity [7],[13]. Creative problem solving is constructed using a certain set of goals, paths, and available conditions [31]. It involves sensitivity to problems and a sense of curiosity, as individuals find problems, manage discrepancies and discover answers to things they do not understand [15]. The process of becoming sensitive to problems and identifying deficiencies, missing elements and gaps in knowledge has been recognized as core to creative process [29]. It involves thinkers grasping the essential features of the problem and understanding how these features relate to the final solution [32].

Divergent and convergent thinking are core elements of the creative process. Divergent thinking is important for idea generation [3], and necessary to produce many alternative solutions to the problem [14]. Creative ideas result from the novel combination of two or more ideas that have been freed from their normal links [27]. Convergent thinking as a creative process occurs in the idea validation stage [3]. It allows an individual to select the correct way to approach the task at hand [28], with the ability to select a single response from a series of alternatives [9]. Based on the review of the literature, creative potential for this study is defined in terms of:

- Sensitivity to problems;
- The process of finding appropriate solutions through the exploration of multiple paths;
- Motivations of curiosity, discrepancies and gaps in knowledge to drive the creative problem solving process; and
- The process of evaluating solutions and settling on the most appropriate for the given problem space.

Computer games have contributed to the practice of enhancing problem-based learning processes. The experiences that occur in computer games may enhance creative processes [33]. Games support the development of critical thinking through visualization, experimentation and creativity [4]. Game elements may provide a problem solving experience as players break down tasks, engage meta-cognitive skills and think critically [30]. Games offer an opportunity to explore new ideas and actions through the diverse gameplay opportunities generated by communities of players. . Game experiences that are active and provide intrinsic motivation have great potential to support creative processes [20].

The componential model of creativity describes the ways in which we enter into stages of the creative activity. The componential framework of creativity has problem solving at its core and includes three major components: domain-relevant skills, creativity-relevant skills and task motivation [1]. As people solve problems they generate response possibilities from an array of available pathways and explore the environment to determine the best solution. Domain knowledge plays an important part in generation of an acceptable solution. Engaging in playful activities or fantasy can have a positive effect that influences the active engagement of creativity-relevant processes [3]. Creative-relevant skills influence the quality of the ideas produced and task motivation influences the quantity of ideas [1],[2],[3]. The three components are crucial characteristics of a creative process. We propose that the creative potential of computer games may be measured using these three major components.

3   Assessing Creative Potential of Computer Games

Designing an assessment lens for creative processes requires analysis and interpretation of exiting measures. Behavioral assessment allows for analysis of creativity from a divergent thinking and convergent thinking perspective. The measurement can be used in the identification and development of creative potential [26]. The method we consider focuses on behavioral observation and verbal protocol analysis during creative activity [23],[17]. Measurement of creative potential involves examining the relationship between tasks, from both a domain skill and creative skill perspective, and the effect of intrinsic motivation [23]. It has been used previously to measure creativity in structure building activities, collage making and poem writing. The research yielded a specification of particular task behaviors that strongly predict creativity. In addition, analysis of the verbal protocol yielded process measures that were strongly related to creativity [23].

3.1   Task Motivation

Task motivation accounts for motivation variables that encourage an individual's approach to a given task. This component is responsible for initiating and sustaining the creative process [1]. Research has demonstrated creativity is most likely to appear when a person is intrinsically motivated [3]. Task motivation includes two elements: traits that determine an individual's baseline attitude toward the task, and the individual's perceptions of a task and/or reasons for undertaking it in a given instance. Task motivation is specific to a particular task, influenced by baseline attitude toward the task and a person's own interest [6]. It is an important component of creative thinking, especially during the problem presentation stage and during response generation of the process. Task motivation may determine the difference between what an individual can do and what he/she will do [3]. It is assessed through an examination of social-environmental influences; that is the intrinsic and extrinsic factors that support autonomy, competence, control, and task involvement [3]. In a computer game context, intrinsic needs such as competence, autonomy, and relatedness are the core motivational dynamics that operate across the interactivity between the game and the player [21].

The model proposed by Ruscio et al. [23] identifies task motivation as a measure of involvement in tasks. Behaviors such as set breaking, task pace, exploration, enjoyment, and concentration are identified as the ways in which intrinsic motivation manifests itself within the creative process. We have taken these behaviors [23] and modified them for gaming environments in order to assess task motivation within computer games. The creative game potential measures, in terms of task motivation, are:

- Involvement (A1): Work on solving the problem
  - Item 1: Participant works on solving problems within the game (L^1).

- Stability (A2): Refining the integrity or stability of a problem solution within the game
  - Item 4: Participant can work on refining the integrity or stability of a problem solution within the game (L).

- Set breaking (A3): Manipulates materials; uses or attaches them in new ways
  - Item 5: In-game objects and materials are able to be readily manipulated (L).
  - Item 6: In-game objects and materials can be used in different ways (L).

- Pace (A4): Speed at which participant works on tasks/challenges; a slow to fast gradient of working rate
  - Item 7: The speed at which participant is required to interact within the game progresses from a slow to fast gradient of working rate (L).

- Planning (A5): Organizes material; establishes an idea, order to build in, steps to take
  - Item 8: Planning is an important part of game play (L).
  - Item 9: Participant can organize materials within the game (L).
  - Item 10: Participant is able to establish ideas within the game (L).
  - Item 11: Participant can plan the order of actions and steps to take within the game (L).

- Playfulness (A6): Engaging in tasks in curious manner; trying out ideas in a carefree way
  - Item 12: Participant can engage in game tasks in a curious manner (L).
  - Item 13: The game provides opportunities to try out ideas in a carefree way (L).

- Exploration (A7): Curious, or playful testing out of ideas
  - Item 14: Curiosity during game exploration is encouraged (L).
  - Item 15: The game encourages playful testing out of ideas (L).

---

[1] Within notation in the factors, (L) refers to Likert scale measures, (F) refers to frequency measures and (-) refers to reverse coded items.

- Enjoyment (A8): Having a good time, finding pleasure in the task / challenge
  - Item 16: The game allows players to have a good time (L).
  - Item 17: Game play tasks are pleasurable (L).
- Concentration (A9): Focused on the task; not distracted
  - Item 2: There is minimal distraction from solving problems in the game (L).
  - Item 3: Participant becomes focused on the tasks in the game (L).

3.2   Domain-Relevant Skills

Domain-relevant skills form the basis from which any performance must proceed. This component incorporates factual knowledge, technical skills and special talents in a particular domain. The information, skills and talents that an individual brings to a task influence the creative preparation process. Domain-relevant skills define the set of possible responses available to a person [3]. Any problem domain consists of a unique set of rules and practices [31] and this knowledge allows people to identify various strategies for conducting information analysis. Domain-relevant skills provide the material drawn on during operations that determine problem-solving pathways. They also provide the criteria that will be used to assess the response possibilities [1], which are then synthesized to form a judgment [23]. Knowledge of a particular domain influences the evaluation process [6]. The process includes familiarity with and factual knowledge of the domain in question: facts, principles, and opinions within the problem-solving domain [23].

Domain-relevant skills determine the initial set of pathways to search for a solution and the ability to verify an acceptable solution [1]. Domain-relevant skills are driven by task motivation and task motivation, in turn, is increased by a positive environment and earlier success in tasks [1]. From a gaming perspective, domain-relevant skills can be evaluated through examining how well the player understands the game domain. Understanding of the game's goals and sub-goals at a particular point and the actions available to achieve these goals is important domain knowledge. Domain-relevant skills can be assessed through examination of factual knowledge of the domain in question and the technical skills demonstrated.

The measures identified by Ruscio et al. [23] as predictors of creativity are assuredness, difficulty (-) and exhibited uncertainty (-). These process factors have been adapted to formulate creative game potential measures in terms of domain-relevant skills in the context of computer game play. They include:

- Exhibited uncertainty (-) (B1): Self-initiated backtracks by using intentionally moves to previous locations or revisits a particular game task / challenge.
  - Item 25: Participant reverses or undoes steps/actions performed in the game (F).
- Assuredness (B2): Confidence: certainty of ability to complete task; assuredness in going about the task; not doubtful, timid, or anxious. Pace and the speed at which particular task /challenge are addressed; a slow to fast gradient of playing rate. Difficulty solving problems encountered, trouble interacting with game elements.
  - Item 18: The game allows participant to feel assured in going about required tasks (L).
  - Item 19: Participant feels certain about his/her ability to complete tasks in the game (L).

- Item 20: There is no doubt about what participant is required to do during the game (L).
- Item 21: Participant doesn't feel anxious or timid playing the game (L).
- Item 22: Participant encounters problems playing the game (L).
- Item 23: It was difficult to complete tasks in the game (L).
- Item 24: It was difficult to work with the objects/resources in the game (L).

- **Difficulty (-) (B3):** Problem with self: uncertainty, self-doubt, negative statements about ability or mood. Negative exclamations by using usually one word, can be two or three; curses or otherwise sharply negative statements.

  - Item 26: Participant feels uncertain completing tasks in the game (F).
  - Item 27: Participant has feelings of self-doubt while playing the game (F).
  - Item 28: Participant produces negative statements about his/her ability as participants play the game (F).
  - Item 29: Participant produces negative exclamations (e.g. curses) while playing the game (F).

3.3   Creativity-Relevant Skills

Creativity-relevant skills include cognitive style as well as the application of heuristics for the exploration of new concepts [1]. These factors influence the response generation process. Heuristic thinking is a skill that relies on a person's intellectual and emotional comfort with a situation. Differences in cognitive style result in different behaviors individuals apply when they gather and evaluate information [16]. Creativity-relevant skills act as an executive controller that influences the way in which the search for responses proceeds [1]. Creativity-relevant skills include the ability to concentrate for the long periods of time [6]. The relevant characteristics that are commonly reported as correlates of creative people include self-discipline, an ability to delay gratification, perseverance, and absence of conformity [6]. Problem solvers automatically activate areas of knowledge that are associated with the past problem solving experience and relevant knowledge [25]. This component of creative thinking includes the ability to break away for standard thinking, approaches and solutions during problem solving. Individuals can gain experience from idea generation that may inform their own strategies for creative thinking processes [3]. Creativity-relevant skills influence the quality of the ideas produced [1].

Creativity-relevant skills are measured through the specific process factors of concrete focus (-), concept identification, wide focus and striving [23]. These have been adapted for the gameplay context. The creative game potential measures, in terms of creativity-relevant skills, are:

- **Wide focus (C1):** Goal statements: Something that cannot be done in one step, future oriented; restatement of problem given, self-imposed goal, statement dealing with a desired final goal, etc. Irrelevant to task: Anything not related to performing the task / challenge.
  - Item 33: The current problem that needs to be solved in the game requires more than one step (F).
  - Item 34: The current problem in the game is future oriented (F).
  - Item 35: Participant restates the problem presented by the game (F).
  - Item 36: Participant is able to develop his/her own goals within the game (F).
  - Item 37: Participant is performing actions not related to game tasks/goals (F).

- Striving (C2): Difficulty: encountering problems or obstacles to completing some or all of the tasks/challenges. Transitions: Movement to new area of action; includes place holding utterance. Question how: Questioning how or what to do; what is currently being done. Repeat something: Repeats instructions, words or concepts presented in the game: Exclamations: based on positive or negative outcomes.
  - Item 30: Participant encountered problems while completing tasks in the game (L).
  - Item 31: Participant encountered obstacles while completing tasks in the game (L).
  - Item 32: Participant questions what to do at particular stages in the game (L).
  - Item 38: Participant transitions to a new topic area or action in the game (F).
  - Item 39: Participant questioned how to complete tasks in the game (F).
  - Item 40: Participant questions his/her current actions in the game (F).
  - Item 41: Participant repeats instructions, words or concepts presented in the game (F).
  - Item 42: Participant makes exclamations, as a positive or negative outburst (F).
- Concrete focus (-) (C3): Talks about task: statements of like or dislike about the task. Describes game elements: statement about texture, color, or other attributes of elements, naming game elements.
  - Item 43: Participant makes statements of like or dislike about game tasks (F).
  - Item 44: Participant talks about the qualities of the materials, objects or attributes of the game world (F).
- Concept identification (C4): Analogies: Description or statement containing an analogy or metaphor. Aha: Eureka-type statements; abrupt change in activity. Transitions: movement to new action; includes place holding utterances.
  - Item 45: Participant describes action/tasks/goals in terms of analogies or metaphors (F).
  - Item 46: Participant had eureka-type moments in the game (F).
  - Item 47: Participant has an abrupt change in activity designed to help complete a task (F).

4   Research Design

This study assesses a method for measuring creativity. The methodological contribution of the study is the demonstration that creative behaviors and processes that occur during gameplay can be examined using behavioral observation techniques and verbal protocol analysis. Behavioral observation techniques and verbal protocol analysis may be applied to identify and quantify predictors of creativity [23].

The data gathered analyzes the relationship between the components of creativity, through the creative game potential measures outlined in section 3. Game task behaviors and verbalizations were coded to obtain empirical indices of the assessed factors: task motivation, domain-relevant skills and creativity-relevant skills. The observations constitute evidence of game activities that have a positive impact on creative potential.

4.1   Participants

Seven participants (1 female) participated in the study. They had an average age of 22, and ages ranged from 18 to 34. Six of the participants were native English speakers. Seventy-one percent indicated that they played games daily, and 28.6% showed that they played games several times a week.

4.2   Procedure

Participation in the study involved being observed while playing three selected games: Portal 2, Braid and I-Fluid. Participants played approximately 45 minutes in total and completed a brief questionnaire on completion of each game. They played each game for 15 minutes. To examine the creative process, participants were video recorded while playing the games and a subset of players were asked to think aloud as they participated. Two researchers gathered data through behavioral and verbal coding techniques. Behavioral coding involves watching video and coding of the behaviors that occurred during game task performance. A video coding scheme was used to capture the type and frequency of observable behaviors and participant verbalizations. Video coding was completed for each of the participants, for each of the games, resulting in 21 data sets.

Coders practiced rating on pilot video records captured before the study was conducted. The researchers individually observed the game play of two people playing the three games used for the study. This resulted in 6 data sets that were examined using the Coefficient of Variation that compares variability. A data set which was collected consistently had a Coefficient of Variance of less than 20%. Three items were refined to yield improvements in coding reliability.

4.3   Materials

Game related behavior was used to assess participants' level of creativity during various game activities on a seven-point Likert scale ranging from 1 (low) to 7 (high), and through the use of a frequency tally. Seventeen items related to task motivation (e.g., "Participant works on solving problems within the game."). The items were grouped within nine variables (see section 3.1): Involvement (A1), Stability (A2), Set breaking (A3), Pace (A4), Planning (A5), Playfulness (A6), Exploration (A7), Enjoyment (A8), and Concentration (A9). All task motivation items are assessed using 7-point Likert scales.

Twelve items were included to analyze domain-relevant skill factors (e.g., "Participant feels certain about his/her ability to complete tasks in the game"). The items were grouped into 3 variables (see section 3.2): Exhibited uncertainty (B1), Assuredness (B2), and Difficult (B3). Seven items are assessed using a 7-point Likert scales and data for five items is captured as frequency counts.

Eighteen items were designed to measure creativity-relevant skills (e.g., "Participant is able to develop his/her own goals within the game"). The items were grouped into four variables (see section 3.3): Wide focus (C1), Striving (C2), Concrete focus

(C3), and Concept identification (C4). Only three items are assessed using a 7-point Likert scales. Fifteen items are assessed using frequency counts.

In order to make all items comparable to the other items, nine negative items (22, 23, 24, 25, 26, 27, 28, 29, and 44) are reverse-scored. To make each variable contribute equally to the mean, values of frequency items are standardized [19].

5   Results

The analyses involved three measures: (A) task motivation factors, (B) domain-relevant skill factors and (C) creativity-relevant skill factors. The internal reliability of all creative game potential measures was acceptable (α = .78). Differences across the three components being measured were examined using Cronbach's Alpha to determine internal reliability within each [11].

5.1   Task Motivation Factors

Cronbach's alpha for task motivation measures is .88, suggesting that A1 to A9 (17 items for task motivation) have relatively high internal consistency. Results indicate that removal of A9, item 3 would lead to a small improvement in Cronbach's alpha (α = .89). Correlation for item 3 was low (α = .057) and as a result the concentration factor included in item 3 (A9) should be reconsidered and potentially removed as a task motivation measure.

5.2   Domain-Relevant Skill Factors

The data shows an alpha coefficient of .79 for domain-relevant skill measures, suggesting that the 12 items have relatively high internal consistency. Item 22 (B2) and 25 (B1) have item-total correlation values of less than .2 [11] (α = -.59 and α = -.02 respectively). Analysis indicates that removal of these items leads to an improvement in Cronbach's alpha (α = .89) and a highly reliable 10-item measure of domain relevant skills.

5.3   Creativity-Relevant Skill Factors

The data for creativity relevant skill factors produces an alpha coefficient of .75, suggesting that 18 items have relatively high internal consistency. The item-total correlation values for items 30, 33, 34, 36, 41, 44 are low (α < .2) [11]. Items 33, 34 and 36 are wide focus items (C1), 30 and 41 are striving items (C2) and item 44 relates to concrete focus (C3). The removal of these items leads to an improvement in Cronbach's alpha to .81. This results in a highly reliable 12-item measurement of creativity-relevant skills.

6   Discussion

This paper examines a method for measurement the creative potential of puzzle-based computer games. Analysis of our adapted measurement items demonstrates that internal reliability within each component is satisfactory. Low item-total correlations for some items indicated areas for improvement.

The observation analysis used in this study identified good reliability for the 17 task motivation factors. However, item 3 is flagged as having low item-total correlation. This item is one of two concentration items (A9) designed to examine the level of a player's focus in the game. In the study, the item is phrased as "Participant becomes focused on the tasks in the game". This item has strong face validity as reflection player concentration within the game. Given the high initial alpha value and the minor improvement that results from removing item 3 (.88 to .89), we decided to keep this item. It is anticipated that improvement may be achieved with a slight rewording of the item to "Participant is focused on tasks in the game" to capture the present state of the player activity rather than an emerging behavior. The seventeen factors within categories A1 to A9 that we have identified as reliable measures in terms of task motivation are included in Fig 1.

The study data analysis resulted in acceptable reliability for the 12 domain relevant skill factors. The sole exhibited uncertainty (C1) factor had low item-total correlation. This item, "participant reverses or undoes steps/actions performed in the game", was designed to reflect uncertainty in participant behavior, yet it does so through an activity or path that is unavailable in many game experiences. Many of the rule structures and challenges embedded in games emerge through players not being able to change decisions or reverse actions or steps. Given this consideration, it is logical to remove this item. Other items relating to difficulty (B3) capture the concept of uncertainty in a way that is more appropriate in a gaming context (e.g. player feels uncertain completing tasks in the game). Analysis indicated that alpha value improvement would result from the removal of an assuredness (B2) item. This item, "participant encounters problems as he/she plays the game", is phrased in the reverse and is designed to demonstrate player assuredness. Once again, this item suffers in its translation to a gaming context. All games are designed around the idea of encountering problems and are underpinned by this notion of challenge. The notion of assuredness is better captured in the more specific items related to ability and issues with completing tasks (e.g. it was difficult to complete tasks in the game (-). Removal of these two items results in good reliability for measuring domain skills. The 10 factors within categories B2 and B3 that have been identified as reliable measures in terms of domain-relevant skill are included in Fig 1.

Analysis of study data revealed acceptable reliability for the 18 creativity skill factors used in the study. However, low item-total correlation was identified across six items. Three of these items related to wide focus (C1: item 33, item 34, and item 36).

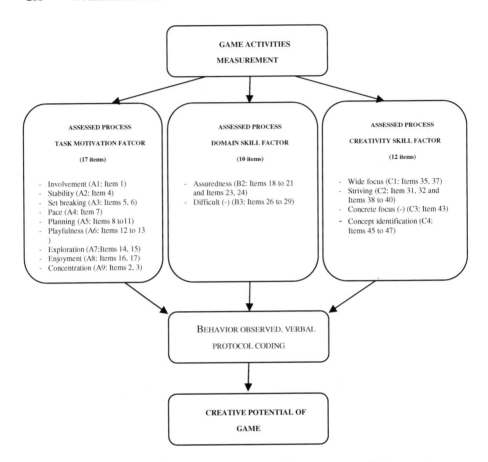

Fig. 1. . A model of process factors for creative potential measurement within computer games (based on [23])

This result may be interpreted as being related to the context of gameplay generally and the puzzle game genre more specifically. Games create environments where each atomic challenge is stand-alone and is addressed that way by a player. While one problem may link to another they tend not to be interdependent. Puzzle games focus on logical and conceptual challenges and they are not generally the type of experiences where players develop their own goals. One other item that was removed to improve internal validity related to striving (C2) in terms of difficulty and problems encountered. The need to remove this item may arise from issues surrounding the notion of encountering problems discussed earlier. It may also be attributable to the items approaching the concept of striving from a difficulty point of view. Striving factors that were focused on the positive, for example achievement and questioning, had the strongest item-total correlations.

The final two items remove related to verbalization. From a concrete focus (C3) perspective, the item looked at verbalization around qualities of materials and objects in the game. This is an item that required a reversal of coded values, as creative processes are shown to be potentially restricted when people think about the concrete aspects of the materials they engage with [23]. We speculate that the very concrete nature of a game world, filled with interesting and perhaps unfamiliar items and objects, leads to player verbalization. The other verbalization related to striving (C2) in terms of repeating instructions, words or concepts presented in the game. Within games, and puzzle games specifically, instructions are kept to a minimum and concepts encountered are centered on visual synthesis and interpretation. This might explain the improvement that would result with the removal of this item. The 12 factors within categories C1-C4 that have been identified as reliable measures in terms of creativity-relevant skill are included in Fig 1.

The conceptual method that was employed to assess creativity is illustrated in Fig 1. The internal reliability of the 39 items remaining as measures of creative game potential is acceptable ($\alpha = .791$). In addition, the quality of the data and the resulting interpretations demonstrates their potential effectiveness in assessing each of the components of creativity. The creative potential prediction involves the relationship between task creativity within a knowledge domain and the effect of intrinsic motivation on the process. We have measured this creativity within a computer game context through behavior assessment and verbal protocol techniques. Data collected has resulted in a reliable measure of the creative potential of puzzle games that includes 12 items within the creativity-relevant skills factor, 10 items within the domain-relevant skills factor and 17 items within the task motivation factor.

7   Conclusions and Future Research

The research presented in this paper demonstrates that existing measures and techniques can be successfully adapted for use in assessing the creative processes that occur within gameplay experiences. It has identifying the key specific components of computer game experiences that may be measured to assess a game's potential for supporting creative activity. Creativity can be measured by examining domain-relevant and creativity-relevant skills as well as task motivation during game play. In future, this understanding of the ways in which games facilitate creative thinking will be used to create a framework for designing new gaming experiences. The framework will identify crucial characteristics of the creative process that emerge throughout the process of playing games and map elements of computer games to components of the creative process.

While present research has focused on the puzzle game genre and our current results cannot be extrapolated beyond this genre, future work will explore creativity in the gameplay process more generally. The knowledge generated through this research will assist in adding a new and helpful educational dimension to either educational or traditional commercial games. The design framework produced will guide game designers in the creation of games to facilitate people's creative thinking skills.

References

1. Amabile, T.M.: The social psychology of creativity: A componential conceptualization. Journal of personality and social psychology 45, 357 (1983)
2. Amabile, T.M.: How work environments affect creativity. Paper Presented at the IEEE International Conference on Systems, Man and Cybernetics, Conference Proceedings, vol. 1, pp. 50–55. IEEE (1989)
3. Amabile, T.M.: Creativity in Context. Boulder, Colorado. Westview Press Inc. (1996)
4. Amory, A.: Game object model version II: a theoretical framework for educational game development. Educational Technology Research and Development 55, 51–77 (2007)
5. Amory, A., Seagram, R.: Educational game models: conceptualization and evaluation. South African Journal of Higher Education 17, 206–217 (2003)
6. Brown, R.T.: Creativity: What are we to measure? (1989)
7. Campbell, D.T.: Blind variation and selective retentions in creative thought as in other knowledge processes. Psychological Review 67, 380 (1960)
8. Catala, A., Jaen, J., Van Dijk, B., Jordà, S.: Exploring tabletops as an effective tool to foster creativity traits, pp. 143–150. ACM (2012)
9. Clark, C.M., Veldman, D.J., Thorpe, J.S.: Convergent and divergent thinking abilities of talented adolescents. Journal of Educational Psychology 56, 157 (1965)
10. El-Murad, J., West, D.C.: The definition and measurement of creativity: what do we know? Journal of Advertising Research 44, 188–201 (2004)
11. Everitt, B., Skrondal, A., Books24X7, I. :The Cambridge dictionary of statistics, vol. 4. Cambridge University Press, Cambridge (2002)
12. Finke, R.A., Ward, T.B., Smith, S.M.: Creative cognition: Theory, research, and applications. MIT Press, Cambridge (1992)
13. Getzels, J.W., Csikszentmihalyi, M.: The creative vision: A longitudinal study of problem finding in art. Wiley, New York (1972)
14. Gordon, W.J.J.: Synectics, the Development of Creative Capacity. Collier, New York (1961)
15. Guilford, J.P.: Creativity. American Psychologist 5, 444–454 (1950)
16. Gutierrez, O., Greenberg, E.: Creative problem solving in the specification of information requirements. Systemic Practice and Action Research 6, 647–667 (1993)
17. Kaufman, J.C., Kaufman, S.B., Lichtenberger, E.O.: Finding Creative Potential on Intelligence Tests via Divergent Production. Canadian Journal of School Psychology 26, 83–106 (2011)
18. Mumford, D., Fogarty, J., Kirwan, F.C.: Geometric invariant theory. Springer (1994)
19. Myers, J.L., Well, A.: Research design and statistical analysis, vol. 1. Lawrence Erlbaum (2003)
20. Paras, B., Bizzocchi, J.: Game, motivation, and effective learning: An integrated model for educational game design (2005)
21. Rigby, S., Ryan, R.: Glued to Games: How Video Games Draw Us in and Hold Us Spellbound. Praeger Publishers (2011)
22. Runco, M.A.: Problem finding, problem solving, and creativity. Ablex Publishing Corporation (1994)
23. Ruscio, J., Whitney, D.M., Amabile, T.M.: Looking inside the fishbowl of creativity: Verbal and behavioral predictors of creative performance. Creativity Research Journal 11, 243–263 (1998)
24. Ryan, R.M., Rigby, C.S., Przybylski, A.: The motivational pull of video games: A self-determination theory approach. Motivation and Emotion 30, 344–360 (2006)

25. Santanen, E.L., Briggs, R.O., de Devreede, G.J.: Toward an understanding of creative solution generation, pp. 2899–2908. IEEE (2002)
26. Schaefer, C.E.: The prediction of creative achievement from a biographical inventory. Educational and Psychological Measurement 29, 431 (1969)
27. Spearman, C.E.: Creative mind. D. Appleton and company (1930)
28. Sviderskaya, N.: The EEG spatial pattern and psychophysiological characteristics of divergent and convergent thinking in humans. Human Physiology 37, 31–38 (2011)
29. Torrance, E.P.: Gifted children in the classroom. Macmillan, New York (1965)
30. Turcsányi-Szabó, M., Bedő, A., PluháR, Z.: Case study of a TeaM challenge game—e-PBL revisited. Education and Information Technologies 11, 341–355 (2006)
31. Wang, Y.: On cognitive foundations of creativity and the cognitive process of creation, pp. 104–113. IEEE (2008)
32. Wertheimer, M.: Productive Thinking. University of Chicago Press, Chicago (1945)
33. Yee Leng, E., Zah Bte Wan Ali, W., Baki, R.: Computer games development experience and appreciative learning approach for creative process enhancement. Computers & Education 55, 1131–1144 (2010)

Similarity in Visual Designs: Effects on Workload and Performance in a Railed-Shooter Game

David Milam[1], Magy Seif El-Nasr[2], Lyn Bartram[1],
Bardia Aghabeigi[1], and Perry Tan[1]

[1] School of Interactive Arts + Technology (SIAT), Simon Fraser University Surrey
250 -13450 102 Avenue, Surrey BC V3T 0A3 Canada
{david_milam,lyn,baa17,pta13}@sfu.ca
[2] Northeastern University,
Colleges of Computer and Information Sciences, Arts, Media and Design,
Boston, MA, 02115 USA, 1 617.373.3982
magy@neu.edu

Abstract. Games are a popular form of digital entertainment and one elusive question is how complex visual designs affect the player experience. We address one aspect of this topic in terms of similarity of visual features, explored both as an organizing principle in Gestalt psychology and as a theory in visual attention. To address this issue, we developed a 3D railed shooter game with adjustable visual features of size, speed, and density of targets and non-targets. Based on these features we evaluate 105 player's performance in 4 visual conditions. In addition, we employ a cognitive workload assessment as a means to understand the perceived demands on players. Results show effects of expertise on performance and cognitive workload, per visual condition. Our methods and implications on game design are discussed.

Keywords: Game Design, Visual Design, Cognitive Load, User Research.

1 Introduction

3D video games engulf users in sensory rich environments made possible through the visual design. The visual design helps distinguish the importance of elements among less important elements. Often without our awareness, activities, such as searching for artifacts or shooting enemies are comprised of visual search tasks. Visual search tasks require both perception of the environment and attention to elements with expressive features. This work considers visual search in situations, where the environment is too busy or contains many features at once causing a player to misperceive what is important. This disruption can lead to mistakes or a *breakdown in performance* [1]. Game designers remedy this problem by making game elements tied to goals clearly visible [2] and allude to the player's focus of attention [3, 4]. However, these works have not been empirically validated and are disconnected from a formal theory of attention. The goal of this paper is to apply a theory of visual attention to visual game elements and then analyze differences in players' performance and perception. We argue that this approach can improve game difficulty settings and accessibility.

M. Herrlich, R. Malaka, and M. Masuch (Eds.): ICEC 2012, LNCS 7522, pp. 284–291, 2012.

Researchers within the fields of attention and perception proposed different theories through controlled experiments. Among the most foundational are *feature integration* [5] and *guided search* [6], whereby bottom-up (stimuli driven) and top-down (goal driven) approaches work in parallel in a given search task. Tests such as these are comprised of target and non-target elements combined with expressive features, such as color, shape, and motion. Attention researchers tested expert gamers and non-gamers in these tests [7], and found the experts have greater attentional resources than novices in spatial attention acuity, such as peripheral vision. Researchers in game approachability [8] reached similar conclusions, that inexperienced players perceive and perform differently in the face of challenge. While these insights are not surprising, the take away design lessons are not clear since the experiments either occur outside the context of a game or do not consider the visual relationships between elements in sufficient detail.

Visual search in sensory rich 3D games is complex due to the continuous change of visual stimuli, such as player's viewpoint and presentation of elements, over time. Gestalt organizational principles [9] support one well known approach to perceptually characterize this kind of complexity. The principles include proximity, similarity, common fate, continuity, and closure. Regardless of the underlining goal, the principles only consider visual relationships between element groups and the background.

We focus on *similarity*, defined as the degree of similarity between target and non-target elements sharing a common feature. Similarity is also chosen due to its application as a theory in attention [10], whereby a target search task decreases in efficiency and increases in reaction time as the non-targets become similar or dissimilar in appearance to targets. In this effort, we evaluate 4 experimental visual conditions according to the theory in a simple game called EMOS (*Expressive MOtion Shooter*). Only the presentation of target or non-target elements change, specifically speed, size, and density. Our research question is based on an analysis of players' play performance and self report between novice and expert players.

- **RQ1:** What design variables (speed, size, and density) applied to game target and non-target elements, tested in 4 different conditions (produced based on designers' choices), produce performance differences perceived and actual? Based on previous work, we know that expertise will have an effect on both performance measurements, thus we also look at expertise as a factor.

The previous work section introduces relevant work in visual attention and game user research methods. This is followed by our methodology including the experimental railed-shooter game developed, definition of visual conditions, and analysis procedure. Results are organized respective to each experimental condition.

2   Relevant Work

Many empirical approaches investigated visual design in games, such as dynamic lighting [11], color [12], and visual cues [13–15], to influence emotion or performance. To our knowledge, with the exception of our work [16], no one addressed multiple elements in motion within the context of a game. Within the field of visual perception, there is abundant research on the expressive properties of motion including *speed*, *shape* (the path a motion follows), *phase* (periodic motion), *flicker* (flashes), *smoothness,* and *direction* [16, 17]. For instance, many of these properties are found to influence affective impressions, such as valence, comfort, urgency, and intensity [17]. Another work evaluated the similarity of properties [18], specifically direction of motion and density of targets, on visual search.. Results found that reaction time increases not only with a higher density of targets, but also due to specific patterns of motion between target and non-target elements. The limitation with this work is that it is not situated within the context of a game. For instance, the random ordering removes any coherent escalation of difficulty, lack of task reward, or visual feedback, which is common in a game. We addressed these limitations in EMOS.

Game user research is a growing network of industry and academic groups [19, 20] with the goal to improve the play experience. Methods, such as triangulation and heuristic evaluation, have been applied to identify performance breakdowns. Triangulation methods include multiple data sources, such as the player's performance [20, 21] and attitudinal questionnaires [22, 23]. The most common metrics include time on task, task success, errors, and learnability (performance change over time) [20]. Others applied heuristic evaluation [8] to improve games for inexperienced players. For instance, game approachability principles [8] incorporate the player's self-efficacy [24] beliefs since the same level of challenge can be interpreted positively or negatively depending on expertise. These methods allow designers to gain in depth understanding *why* players feel the way they do, so corrective action can be taken.

3   Methodology

3.1   EMOS Railed Shooter Game

We investigate the impact of visual features on users' performance in the EMOS railed shooter game, developed in the Unity™ engine. Only one button is used to point and shoot. Additionally, there is no punishment as levels auto advance after 11 or 13 seconds. Like the perceptual tests, EMOS is comprised of 6 game elements; 2 types of targets, 2 non-targets, and 2 types of visual feedback. *Speed*, *size*, and *density* variables attach to the targets and ambient non-targets. The boss targets (TB) restrict advancement through levels and the minions (TM) increase the score. The non-target elements include ambient (NTA) and background ring (NTR) distractor elements. The ambient non-targets are the same color as boss targets, but do not contribute to the score or advance levels. The non-target rings rotate and are only variable by *speed*. Their purpose is to convey an illusion of camera movement. Finally, visual feedback for each shot fired (NTS) and on target explosions (NTE) is adjustable by *size*.

The game elements are abstract since we did not want the art-style to inform a strategy. To this extent, we also used simple geometric shapes, monochromatic color, basic sound effects, and periodic motion trajectories to the elements. Figure 1 shows an example of the game and how elements can visually change. The left image has small targets and many small ambient non-targets, while the targets on the right are larger with fewer ambient non-targets. In these levels, the boss and minion targets and ambient non-targets move along a circular trajectory (yellow arrow).

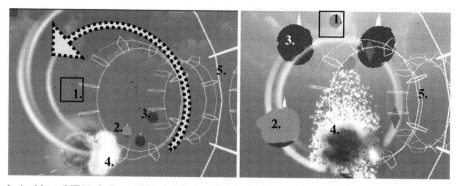

1. Ambient (NTA) 2. Boss (TB) 3. Minion (TM) 4.Visual feedback (NTE) 5. Rings (NTR)

Fig. 1. Adjustable visual balance (top and bottom)

3.2   Visual Conditions

In our previous work [25], 8 expert game designers manipulated the variables: *speed, size,* and *density,* associated to target and non-target elements, in a toolset to manipulate the design of EMOS. Designers identified suitable designs for novice, intermediate, and expert levels. We then developed patterns from these designs. The study described in [26] discusses in depth the methodology, the study and the results. For the study presented here we will assume that the patterns used to construct the 4 conditions for the experiment are valid designs confirmed by eight expert game designers. We thus describe the 4 conditions here. Condition 1 is designed for intermediate difficulty level, and conditions 2-4 are designed for expert difficulty level. To preserve ecological validity as a game (as this is how designers indicated the design should proceed), condition 1 is played first by all players, followed by a random assignment to one of the expert difficulty conditions.

Due to the amount of elements that could change using the toolset, all four conditions modify *multiple* elements once. This approach is different from traditional perception experiments, which typically change one variable at a time. However, these conditions are more in sync with how designers approach level design. Designers typically change many elements between play tests. Therefore, to produce valid design lessons, the conditions need to adhere to designers' philosophy of how they typically manipulate the designs. The conditions produced are:

- **Condition 1: Increase T Density, Increase NT Speed:** Increases the density of targets, speed of targets, ambient, and ring non-targets. Boss and minion target density increases from 1 to 3, and 3 to 5, respectively. Target size is 3.5 times larger than the ambient non-target size. Target and ambient non-target speed increase 14% and 19% respectively, and ring speed increase 52%.
- **Condition 2: Increase T Density and Increase in NTR Speed:** Similar to condition 1 except target speed is held constant since fast speeds will be physically harder to shoot for novice players. Boss and minion target density starts from 2 and 4 respectively and end with 3 and 7, respectively. Non-target ring speed is *twice* the speed in comparison to condition 1.

- **Condition 3: Increase similarity between T NT Size by Decreasing T Size:** Target and ambient non-target size become more similar with all remaining values are held constant. Target size decreases 24% respective to condition 1 and is now only 12% larger in comparison to the ambient non-target size.
- **Condition 4: Increase NT Density, NTE Size, and NTS Size:** Increases the ambient non-target density, visual feedback explosion and sparks size. In comparison to condition 1, the ambient density is 2.5 times higher, explosion size is 2 times larger, and sparks size is 28% larger.

3.3   Data Collection, Analysis, and Study Design

We collected 3 game metrics per level: level time (seconds), number of mouse clicks (#), and enemies shot (#). From these metrics, we generate the mean and rate of change, based on the slope of the linear regression line through data points in the known y axis (performance metric) and the known x axis (across 5 levels in each condition). Also, we administered two post-play surveys: 1) the task load index as a measure cognitive workload [26], and 2) five questions gauging gaming habits [22] as a basis for expertise. The workload survey contains questions regarding: mental demand (defined as following the target and ignoring distractions), physical demand (moving and clicking the mouse), temporal demand (feeling hurried or rushed), effort, success, and frustration. Each question is rated on a 7-point Likert scale (1=lowest and 7=highest). A response to an expertise questionnaire was also collected through surveys at the end so as not to bias participants [27]. The questionnaire gauged expertise based on the types and time spent playing games on a weekly basis. Players are novice if they play less than the average, prefer casual games, and non 3D genres.

4   Results

All analysis are within conditions, where expertise is evaluated in relationship to the independent variables (metrics and self report) using T-tests. Due to space limitations, we present values for statistically significant results only. The 105 participants include 48 females, 57 males, 55 experts, and 55 novices with an average age of 22.

- **Condition 1: Increase T Density, Increase NT Speed:** Mental, temporal, and effort are rated higher for the novice player in comparison to experts (p < .001, .004, and 002 respectively). Conversely success is perceived at a higher rate (p < .019) for expert players (mean rating is 5.4 vs. 4.9). Regarding performance, experts completed levels on average 28% faster with a lower rate of change (p < .001 and .007). Experts also fired 19% fewer shots with a lower rate of change (p < .004 and .005). As expected, experts perceived higher success in comparison to novices, and novices perceived higher cognitive load than experts. These perceptions suggest that even the intermediate difficulty was not as easy as we thought and may be problematic for novices. This is an important baseline.

- **Condition 2: Increase T Density and Increase in NTR Speed:** 20 experts and 15 novices. The success rating was perceived higher for experts ($p < 0.029$) in comparison to novices (mean 4.1 and 3.5 respectively), even though no significant change in performance was found within the condition. Thus, even though novices demonstrated improved performance from condition 1, and their performance was comparable to experts, they did not perceive high success rates in comparison to experts. In comparison to condition 1, all subjects improved performance, increased the enemies shot rate, while the level time and shots fired rate decreased.

- **Condition 3: Increase similarity between T NT Size by Decreasing T Size:** of 19 experts and 16 novices. No difference in self report ratings were found, even though on average experts finished levels 16% faster and shot 29% more enemies ($p < 0.004$ for both) in comparison to novices. In comparison to condition 1, all mean performance values increased, except for the enemies shot, which decreased for novices and remained constant for the expert players.

- **Condition 4: Increase NT Density, NTE Size, and NTS Size:** 16 experts and 19 novices. Success is perceived again higher for the expert ($p < 0.005$) in comparison to the novice player (mean 5.5 and 4.2 respectively) even though no significant change in performance was found within the condition. One possible explanation is that the large visual feedback size was perceived to be a higher reward even though the rules never change.

5   Discussion

Supported by a theory of stimuli similarity [10] in an experimental game, these findings are based on a definition of visual features attached to target and non-target, elements. In regard to the research question, we found that most differences in self reports and performance occur in the intermediate difficulty condition 1, rather than the more difficult conditions 2-4. This finding not only underscores the importance of training and preparation, but also sets a baseline in the perception of performance for the difficult levels that follow. Within conditions 2 and 4, novices demonstrated *improved* performance on par with expert players, yet report less success in comparison to experts. For novice players, feelings of success are dampened by the higher mental, temporal, and effort ratings in condition 1. In contrast, expert players report high success as a response to increased density of targets in condition 2, or the increased non-target visual feedback explosion size in condition 4. Within condition 3 by contrast, performance differences are found, yet no difference in self report ratings are found.

6   Conclusion and Future Work

This work investigated intermediate and complex visual designs informed by the similarity theory of visual attention, in an experimental railed shooter game. Our analysis found effects of expertise on performance and self report of performance in the intermediate difficulty condition. The same analysis in the complex visual settings found consistent *disagreement* in performance and perception of performance. Expert players report higher success in response to an increased density of targets or size of visual feedback, even though no performance differences are found. By contrast, no self report differences are found in the condition with an actual performance difference. Our contribution lies in the discussion of these results as well as the methods used to uncover them. Our future work incorporates pupillometry (pupil size) metrics as a continuous physiological metric and identifies additional implications on design.

Acknowledgements. This research is supported by the Natural Sciences and Engineering Research Council of Canada and Graphics, Animation, and New Media Network (GRAND).

References

1. Ryan, W., Siegel, M.A.: Evaluating Interactive Entertainment using Breakdown: Understanding Embodied Learning in Video Games. Breaking New Ground: Innovation in Games, Play, Practice and Theory. DIGRA, West London (2009)
2. Smith, R.: Helping Your Players Feel Smart: Puzzles as User Interface. In: Game Developers Conference, San Francisco, CA (2009)
3. Lemarchand, R.: Attention NOT Immersion: Making your games better with psychology and playtesting, the Uncharted Way. In: Game Developers Conference, San Francisco, CA (2012)
4. Björk, S., Holopainen, J.: Games and Design Patterns. In: Zimmerman, E., Salen, K. (eds.) The Game Design Reader. MIT Press, Cambridge (2006)
5. Treisman, A.M., Gelade, G.: A feature-integration theory of attention. Cognitive Psychology 12, 97–136 (1980)
6. Wolf, J.: Guided Search 2.0: A revised model of visual search. Psychonomic Bulletin & Review 1, 202–238 (1994)
7. Green, S., Bavelier, D.: Effect of Action Video Games on the Spatial Distribution of Visuospatial Attention. Journal of Experimental Psychology: Human Perception and Performance 32, 1465–1478 (2006)
8. Desurvire, H., Wiberg, C.: User Experience Design for Inexperienced Gamers: GAP - Game Approachability Principles. In: Evaluating User Experiences in Games. Springer, London (2010)
9. Wertheimer, M.: Untersuchen zur lehre von der Gestalt (Laws of Organization in Perceptual Forms). Psychologische Forschung (Psychological Research) 4, 301–350 (1923)
10. Duncan, J., Humphreys, G.W.: Visual search and stimulus similarity. Psychological Review 96, 433–458 (1989)
11. Seif El-Nasr, M., Vasilakos, T., Rao, C., Joseph, Z.: Dynamic Intelligent Lighting for Directing Visual Attention in Interactive 3D Scenes. IEEE Transactions on Computational Intelligence and AI in Games 1 (2009)
12. Niedenthal, S.: Complicated Shadows: The Aesthetic Significance of Simulated Illumination in Digital Games (2009)
13. Hoeg, T.: The Invisible Hand: Using Level Design Elements to Manipulate Player Choice (2008)
14. Milam, D., Seif El-Nasr, M.: Analysis of Level Design "Push & Pull" within 21 games. In: Foundations of Digital Games. ACM, Monterey (2010)

15. Samarinas, A.: Illuminating Minotaur's Lair: Light Design and Navigation in Gameworlds (2009)
16. Bartram, L., Ware, C.: Filtering and Brushing with Motion. Information Visualization 1, 66–79 (2002)
17. Lockyer, M., Bartram, L., Riecke, B.: Simple Motion Textures for Ambient Affect. In: Computational Aesthetics. ACM, Vancouver (2011)
18. Kingstone, A., Bischof, W.F.: Perceptual grouping and motion coherence in visual search. Psychological Science 10, 151–156 (1999)
19. Isbister, K., Schaffer, N. (eds.): Game Usability: Advice from the Experts for Advancing the Player Experience. Morgan Kaufmann, San Francisco (2008)
20. Tullis, T., Albert, B.: Measuring the User Experience: Collecting Analyzing, and Presenting Usability Metrics. Morgan Kaufmann, Burlington (2008)
21. Pagulayan, R., Keeker, K., Thomas, F., Wixon, D., Romero, R.: User Centered Design in Games. In: Sears, A., Jacko, J. (eds.) Human-Computer Interaction Handbook: Fundamentals, Evolving Technologies, and Emerging Applications. Lawrence Erlbaum Associates, New York (2008)
22. Erfani, M., Seif El-Nasr, M., Riecke, B.E.: The Effect of Previous Gaming Experience on Game Play Performance. Presented at the International Conference on Advances in Computer Entertainment Technology (2010)
23. IJsselsteijn, W., Poels, K., de Kort, Y.A.W.: The Game Experience Questionnaire: Development of a self-report measure to assess player experiences of digital games. In: Fun of Gaming (FUGA) Workshop (2008)
24. Klimmt, C., Hartmann, T.: Effectance, self-efficacy, and the motivation to play video games. In: Vorderer, P., Bryant, J. (eds.) Playing Video Games: Motives, Responses, and Consequences, pp. 132–145. Lawrence Erlbaum Associates, Mahwah (2006)
25. Milam, D., Seif El-Nasr, M., Bartram, L., Lockyer, M., Feng, C., Tan, P.: Toolset to explore visual motion designs in a video game. In: SIGCHI, Play Experience Workshop, Austin, TX (2012)
26. Hart, S.G., Staveland, L.E.: Development of NASA-TLX (Task Load Index): Results of empirical and theoretical research. In: Hancock, A., Meshkati, N. (eds.) Human Mental Workload. North Holland Press, Amsterdam (1988)
27. Boot, W., Blakely, D., Simons, D.J.: Do action video games improve perception and cognition? Frontiers in Psychology 2 (2001)

A Hybrid GPU Rasterized and Ray Traced Rendering Pipeline for Real Time Rendering of Per Pixel Effects

Thales Luis Sabino[1], Paulo Andrade[1], Esteban Walter Gonzales Clua[1], Anselmo Montenegro[1], and Paulo Pagliosa[2]

[1] Universidade Federal Fluminense, Niterói - Rio de Janeiro, Brazil
{tsabino,pandrade,esteban,anselmo}@ic.uff.br
[2] Universidade Federal do Mato Grosso do Sul,
Campo Grande - Mato Grosso do Sul, Brazil
pagliosa@facom.ufmt.br

Abstract. Rendering in 3D games typically uses rasterization approaches in order to guarantee interactive frame rates, since ray tracing, a superior method for rendering photorealistic images, has greater computational cost. With the advent of massively parallel processors in the form of GPUs, parallelized ray tracing have been investigated as an alternative to rasterization techniques. While many works present parallelization methods for the classical ray tracing algorithm, in order to achieve interactive, or even real time ray tracing rendering, we present a rasterized and ray traced hybrid technique, completely done in GPU. While a deferred render model determines the colors of primary rays, a ray tracing phase compute other effects such as specular reflection and transparency, in order to achieve effects that are not easily obtained with rasterization. We also present a heuristic approach that select a subset of relevant objects to be ray traced, avoiding traversing rays for objects that might not have a significant contribution to the real time experience. This selection is capable of maintaining the real time requirement of games, while offering superior visual effects.

Keywords: ray tracing, rasterization, OptiX, CUDA, GPU, hybrid rendering, OpenGL, GLSL, real-time, global illumination effects, deferred shading.

1 Introduction

In the computer graphics field, it is a common belief that raster techniques are better suitable for real-time rendering while ray tracing is a superior technique to create photorealistic static images, due to the ray tracing processing cost. Recent Graphics Processing Units (GPUs) can also work as general-purpose massively parallel processors [1], promoting the possibility of Real-Time Ray Tracing (RTRT) implementations using GPUs as an alternative to raster based approaches due to its parallel nature by its concept [2]. Many works explore the

M. Herrlich, R. Malaka, and M. Masuch (Eds.): ICEC 2012, LNCS 7522, pp. 292–305, 2012.

possibility to accelerate ray tracing in order to make it a real-time process with GPU only or hybrid CPU and GPU approaches. However, results of different investigations indicate that RTRT remains a challenging computational task [3–6], suitable only with specific conditions and constraints.

Offline renderers accurately simulate the way light interact with surfaces. Since the simulation of every beam of light in a 3D space is impractical, other approaches were developed to simulate the way light works. One of these approaches is the Backward Ray Tracing, where rays are launched from the camera position to different parts of the 3D space. Depending on the characteristics of the surfaces of the objects hit by the rays, secondary rays may be recursively generated. These secondary rays can be used to model many light effects such as soft shadows, mirror and diffuse reflection, depth of field, motion blur, refraction, transparency, among others.

RTRT is a hard computational task, not only because each pixel in the image must be calculated separately, but also because the final color of a single pixel can be affected by more than one recursive ray. Another consideration is that ray tracing algorithms waste from 75% to 95% of its execution time calculating intersection points between rays and objects [7].

In this paper, we describe an improvement of the graphics pipeline, by creating a hybrid ray trace and raster rendering process. In this method, the deferred rendering process is used to calculate the primary rays collision, while the secondary rays use a ray tracing approach to obtain shadow, reflection and refraction effects. This approach vastly improves ray tracing performance, not only because we avoid many unnecessary traditional ray tracing tasks, but also because we guarantee that a complete image will be available to show in a demanded time, even if there is not enough time to finish all the effects calculations. We also developed an efficient and customized data structure to manage part of the geometry inside the GPU memory and a heuristic approach that adequately chooses a subset of objects to generate visual effects using secondary rays.

This proposal differs from most related works, since the goal is not entirely replace the graphics pipeline by a ray tracing only approach. This work use GPU ray tracing only for a set of objects, seeking for those that will have more visual impact for each frame generated. The main focus is to render complex scenes in real-time using raster techniques and get the refined best visual look including algorithms that simulate global illumination effects. Since most global illumination effects are better simulated using ray tracing techniques, one approach proposes to combine these two techniques in the same rendering pipeline. This paper presents and discusses strategies applied to develop a real-time hybrid GPU-only ray tracer, that uses raster techniques to improve the performance of a ray tracer and a smart strategy for prioritizing regions and objects that will receive the ray tracing light effects.

This paper is organized as following: after a brief introduction we present different hybrid CPU and GPU raytracing approaches in Section 2, then we present a hybrid ray tracing model, detailing the composition methods in Section 3. Section 4 presents and discusses our heuristic approach for prioritizing regions and objects for the ray tracing phase. In Section 7 we present implementation details, followed by the results, comparisons and discussions, in session 8. Finally, we conclude the work and state future proposals in Section 9.

2   Related Work

The concept of a hybrid Real-Time Raster and Ray Tracer renderer is not new. Beck et al [8] proposes a CPU-GPU Real-Time Ray-Tracing Framework and Bikker [9] developed a Real-Time Path Tracer called Brigade, which divides the rendering task seamlessly over both GPU and CPU available cores. Brigade aims the production of *proof-of-concept* games that use path tracing as the primary rendering algorithm.

Beck [8] proposal spread the traditional stages of ray tracing in independent tasks for the GPU and CPU. These render tasks can be summarized into three GPU render passes: a shadow map generation pass, a geometry identification pass and a blur pass. In the geometry identification pass, the triangle numbers are encoded as RGB colors in a framebuffer and the result of the shadow map pass is blurred inside the alpha channel, in the same framebuffer. The CPU receives the framebuffer for reflection and refraction generation pass using a ray tracing algorithm. Finally it is applied a phong shading pass that also merges the results of the other passes.

NVIDIA's OptiX [10] is a general purpose ray tracing engine targeting both NVIDIA's GPUs and general-purpose hardware in the current version. OptiX architecture offers a low level ray tracing engine, a programmable ray tracing pipeline with a shader language based on CUDA C/C++, a domain-specific compiler and a scene-graph based representation. OptiX is a GPU only solution with remarkably good results for interactive ray tracing.

Pawel Bak [11] implements a Real-Time Ray Tracer using DirectX 11 and HLSL. Similar to Beck's work [8], his approach also uses rasterization in order to achieve the best possible performance for primary hits but uses DirectX 11 and HLSL instead of OpenGL and GLSL.

Chen [12] presented a hybrid GPU/CPU ray tracer renderer, where a Z-buffered rasterization is performed to determine the visible triangles at the same time that primary rays intersections are determined. The CPU reads the data back in order to trace secondary rays.

Finally, Hachisuka [5] surveyed several ray-tracing algorithms for graphics hardware. The author concludes that although the ray tracing method seems to be extremely well studied and their parallel nature can be understand easily, many issues need to be solved to implement it efficiently. Some of the issues were presented, such as data retention, the requirement of graphics hardware to perform the same computation over several pixels and their stack-based characteristic. His work classifies different approaches based on their features. Additionally, these algorithms are compared considering their bottlenecks and possible improvements are also discussed.

3   Hybrid GPU Ray Tracing

Most works about hybrid ray tracing techniques tries to balance the workload between GPU and CPU in order to achieve maximum performance of both parts. Using modern graphics hardware and APIs that allows efficient use of rendering techniques such as Multiple Render Targets (MRT) and Deferred Shading [13], it is possible to use the traditional raster pipeline as the first stage of a complete ray tracing pipeline: the generation and intersection of primary rays.

3.1   Primary Rays Generation and Intersection with Deferred Shading

Deering [13] introduced the idea of deferred shading. Although the article never uses the term "deferred", it introduces a key concept; each pixel is shaded only once after depth resolution. The term *deferred shading* was adopted later, and its usage in real-time rendering applications, mainly video-games, became mainstream since 2008.

The basic idea behind deferred shading is to perform all visibility tests before performing any lighting computations. In traditional GPU rendering, the Z-buffer normally shades as it goes. This process can be inefficient, as a single pixel often generates more than one fragment. A rough front-to-back sort of objects can help to avoid this problem, but deferred shading perfectly solves it, and also solves light/material combination issues [14].

Deferred Shading takes advantage of a structure called G-Buffer [15]. This structure is filled with geometric data, using the presented geometry pass. Values saved includes the z-depth, normal, texture coordinates and material parameters. These values are saved to Multiple Render Targets accessed by the pixel shader program.

The values stored into G-Buffers depend on the application. For this work, we store the following per-pixel values, one for each target: position, normal, z-depth, albedo color and specular color. These values are used later in the lighting stage of deferred shading (see Figure 1). For information about deferred shading implementation in this work, please refer to Section 7.

Although the information stored in the G-Buffer is enough to determine the origin and direction of shadow rays, it is not possible to establish the need for tracing reflection and refraction rays only with geometry data. The G-Buffer is extended with one more render target that stores optical properties of each pixel. Reflectivity, index of refraction, opacity and specular exponent are included in this target.

Deferred shading does have some drawbacks. The video memory requirements and fill rate costs for the G-Buffers are significant. One of the most significant technical limitations is in the process of antialiasing and transparency. Antialiasing is not performed and stored for rendered surfaces. To overcome this limitation, antialiasing image-based techniques such as Shishkovtosov edge-detection method [16] and, more recently, Morphological Antialiasing [17] can be employed for better image quality.

Fig. 1. The six textures generated by the geometry pass: (a) position, (b) normal, (c) z-depth, (d) diffuse or albedo color, (e) specular color and (f) encoded optical properties. (g) is the image produced after the lighting stage.

3.2 Selective Global Illumination Effects

In ray tracing, secondary rays are used to produce global illumination effects. Once primary rays are handled, shadows rays need to be traced from the hit point through the scene in the direction of light sources. Shadow maps present some advantages over ray traced shadows, including avoiding the knowledge of the scene geometry and automatic adjustment over geometry changes on GPU. On the other hand it requires a large amount of memory in order to avoid aliasing, and the scene must be rendered once per light source. Precise shadows resulting from the shadow map technique require a large amount of memory in order to avoid aliasing [18].

The G-Buffer produced by the deferred rendering stage contains information about *optical properties* of the underlying material of each pixel. The render target represented by Figure 1(f) is used to determine the need for tracing reflection/refraction rays. It is composed by reflectivity, index of refraction, specular exponent and opacity, respectively. The Armadillo was highlighted meaning that rays only need to be traced from its surface through the scene. Since it is composed by a refractive material, we are able to avoid trace of unnecessary rays in places where the material is neither refractive nor reflective.

At this point, the ray tracing algorithm can follow its own path. Any secondary ray generated will be traced against scene in order to produce other global illumination effects, such as reflections and refractions. The result of this stage can be understood as the generation of a ray trace effects layer. This effects layer will be blended to the image already generated, in order to improve its visual quality with global illumination effects.

4   Ray Tracing Heuristic for Real Time Rasterization Pipelines

In order to improve the performance of a hybrid ray tracer for real time applications, we propose a heuristic to dynamically select relevant objects to trace.
The selected objects are ray traced for effects in a predefined and fixed time
constraint. The heuristic is capable of selecting the most relevant objects in a
scene and still maintain the expected frame rate. We define relevant objects as
those that better contribute to the visual experience at a specific frame.

The idea of ray tracing a subset of objects and still have an improved experience in real time applications is based on the real world observation that when
the perceived image constantly changes, as when we drive a car or walk, many
elements are ignored by our conscious mind. This simple fact is the motivation
of the development of warning signs, as the ones we see in highways to call our
attention for relevant information. It is a fact that our attention is more focused
in near objects, and objects directly in front of our field of view. Considering this
observation, a simple heuristic would be to *trace the objects near the observer,
and in front of his/her field of view.* Unfortunately, this simple heuristic is not
capable of guaranteeing performance, also, not all objects improve in visual quality when using ray tracing instead of rasterization. The decision of what objects
deserve to be ray traced is an environment designer decision since no technology
can substitute the artist's eye. The heuristic tries to select the best candidates
to ray trace, using some predefined information.

4.1   Pre-production Phase

The first step happens during the scene design. This step is the selection of a
group of objects that are candidates to ray trace for a given environment. For
every object chosen, it is also necessary to define the kind of secondary rays that
should be generated after the first hit (primary ray). In this work, we considered
three different light effects to be ray traced if possible: reflection, refraction and
shadows for high detailed objects.

The initial cost of the object is defined by its initial visibility (V), and the estimated number of secondary rays needed to represent the object light effect (Q).
Visibility is defined by Equation 1 and Object cost (C) is defined by Equation 2.
Visibility is defined by the average area initially visible of the object (A) times
the 2D projected distance of the object considering the center of the projection
(P) divided by the distance (D) of the object from the observer. The farthest
the object, less visible it is, considering its area. Also, the farther the object is
from the center of the 2D projection of the visible space, less relevant it is for
the final image. P is a value in the range $[0, 1]$, where one is the exact center of
the scene, and 0 means the object is outside the field of view. Both equations
are simplifications of the complete formulation.

$$V = \frac{A \times P}{D} \tag{1}$$

$$C = V \times Q \tag{2}$$

Finally, every object has a relevance factor R defined by the fact that it was selected S before to be traced. We call as S a binary value of 0 (previously unselected) or 1 (previously selected), times a constant that represents the importance I of the render of previous rendered objects (defined by the application. Equation 3 represents relevance for our heuristic.

$$R = S \times I + V \tag{3}$$

All the tree equations are calculated for all the objects, frame by frame, in order to update the scene graph.

4.2 Selection Graph

When the GPU loads the information necessary to render the objects selected for ray tracing in its memory, a directed graph with information of the objects is built for the ray trace phase. Since the GPU is a massive parallel processor, the number of initial objects to be traced is proportional to the number of Stream Processors of the GPU architecture. The graph is a directed graph, where every node represents an object. A node points to another whose cost (C) is smaller than the actual node but equal or higher than the cost of all other nodes. Also, every node points to all N other nodes that are more relevant but not selected yet to be ray traced. The N pointers in every node are ordered considering their relevance. When an object finishes rendering, the graph is traversed in order to find the node whose rendering cost is less than the cost required to render it, considering the time still available for the ray tracing phase. If the node points to other node more relevant node, this one is selected to be ray traced, and the graph is updated. Figure 2 presents the graph structure. Red circles are the first nodes selected because of their relevance, and the gray circles are nodes that will still be selected. Black arrows represent the nodes order according to their cost (C) and the blue dashed arrows represent the N more relevant nodes (R) than the selected node, and with less cost.

Table 1. Cost and Relevance for the Selection Graph represented in Figure 2

Node	1	2	3	4	5	6	7	8	9	10	11	12	13	14	15	16	17	18	19	20	21	22
C	-	-	-	-	-	-	-	-	20	19	18	17	16	15	**14**	**14**	13	12	11	10	**9**	**9**
R	-	-	-	-	-	-	-	-	22	21	18	30	31	32	28	27	9	29	1	20	4	3

4.3 Object Selection and Graph Rebuild

When the render of the first object is finished, the next one must be selected according to the time left to render. The selection graph is traveled until a node with an estimated cost less than the cost left to render is achieved. In this node,

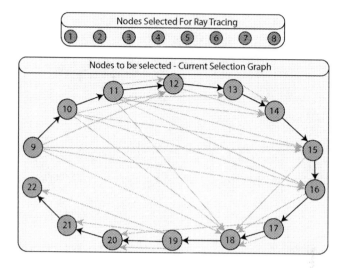

Fig. 2. Selection Graph

it is verified if it points to another node less relevant. If so, this node is also verified for relevance, until the most relevant node is found. When the node is selected to render, it is also moved to another graph, under construction for the next frame. Using the information provided by render engine, this node and all the nodes with cost higher than the cost used to find the first node are inserted into the new graph and the graph is properly updated.

The current graph is also updated if the selected node is not at the node that was selected only according to its cost. If no time is left to render any object, this time is used to move all the nodes not selected to the new graph. Figure 3 represent the selection of a new node to render and the new future selection graph. Considering that the time left to render allows just a node with cost 18 or less to be selected, nodes 9 and 10 are removed from the selection graph and will be moved to the new graph, in construction. Since node 11 has cost 18 but is not the most relevant, node 14 is selected and the corresponding object is ray traced.

5   Final Scene Composition

This step consists in assembling the final image that will be displayed. This process is done by a blend operation between the rasterized image and the ray traced image. The weights for this blend are relative to the desired amount of ray tracing effects desired for the final image. At this point, the frame buffer contains two color attachments, the first one generated by the raster stage and the second one filled by the ray tracer stage.

The simplest approach to generate the final image, given a filled framebuffer, is to superimpose the ray traced image with the rasterized image. This can be

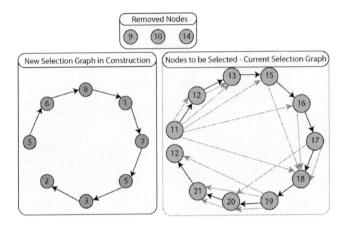

Fig. 3. Current Selection Graph and the Future Selection Graph in Construction

easily accomplished with a shader program adding another light-weight render pass to the process, since we only need to render a screen-size quadrilateral primitive. Note that a simple superimposing of the ray traced image with the rasterized one will not present additional problems since only pixels that were shaded using the ray-tracing engine are visible.

6   Hybrid Pipeline Overview

In previous sections we described the stages that compose our hybrid raster/ray tracer pipeline. In this Section, we present an overview of the complete pipeline.

In order to illustrate the process, we use a simple scene composed of three textured objects and one point light. This scene is composed by 4,746 vertices and 9,470 faces. Figure 4 shows the five stages of our proposed pipeline:

- **Deferred rendering and primary Rays resolution:** Stage 4(a) consists in rendering the scene using a deferred rendering technique resulting in a filled G-Buffer. The obtained G-Buffer contains information about visible fragments, and it can be seen as a primary ray resolution stage of a traditional ray tracer. The result image of this stage has the edge-detection antialiasing algorithm applied [16].
- **Shadows:** With data extracted from the G-Buffer, shadow rays are generated for valid hit points. In Figure 4, invalid hit points are those that must be shaded using the sky color or environment map, being such pixels the blue ones of Figure 4(a). The shadow pass result is presented in Figure 4(b).
- **Reflections and refractions:** Stage 4(c) follows the ray tracing algorithm in order to calculate reflection and refractions. For this example, we use reflections on the ground to illustrate an application of such effect.

- **Final Composing:** The final composing stage 4(d) is responsible for blending images generated at stages 4(a) and 4(c). We compose this scene using a shader program to draw the ray tracing effects layer with an OpenGL blending operation. The amount of ray traced effects on the final image may also be configured.

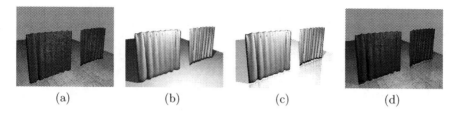

(a)   (b)   (c)   (d)

Fig. 4. Overview of our hybrid rendering raster/ray tracing pipeline. The first stage *(a)* consists in rendering the scene using a deferred rendering technique resulting in a filled G-Buffer and a basic rendered image. Stage (b) traces shadow rays. Stage (c) is responsible for tracing and shading secondary rays. In this example, the ground is made of a reflective material. Finally, stage (e) is responsible for blending images generated at stages (c) and (a).

7   Implementation Details

In this section, we give more details of our implementation concerning efficiency and robustness. This system was implemented using C++ as the main language. The *Open Asset Import Library* was used in order to read common scene file formats. The *Free Image Project* was used to read texture images. We use GLSL as the shading language on the primary rays resolution stage and for rendering purposes. The NVIDIA OptiX engine was adopted to trace and shade secondary rays, due to its practicability in terms of freedom on building the ray tracing pipeline and hiding GPU hardware details when writing ray tracing shaders. Besides the advantages of being a generic ray tracer engine, its bond to OpenGL for reading and writing graphic resources is straightforward.

The geometry stage of deferred shading implements a perspective projection camera, and it is responsible for feeding the G-Buffer with information to be used in the next stages. All subsequent stages operate in image-space and work with an orthographic projection camera using the screen resolution dimensions. The lighting stage receives as input the contents of the G-Buffer as well as light sources information and it accumulates lighting effects into a full resolution P-Buffer (pixel buffer). Table 2 shows the configuration adopted in the implementation of the deferred shading technique.

Table 2. Configuration properties of the G and P-Buffers

Storage Options for G-Buffer		
Target	*Format*	*Type*
Position	GL_RGBA32F[1]	GL_FLOAT
Normal	GL_RGBA8	GL_UNSIGNED_BYTE
Depth	GL_DC24[2]	GL_DC[2]
Albedo	GL_RGBA8	GL_UNSIGNED_BYTE
Specular	GL_RGBA8	GL_UNSIGNED_BYTE
Optical props	GL_RGBA32F[1]	GL_FLOAT
Antialias	GL_RGBA8	GL_UNSIGNED_BYTE
Destination	GL_RGBA8	GL_UNSIGNED_BYTE

8   Results

In this section, we present the results in terms of performance comparing our hybrid approach with a pure GPU ray tracer as well as a comparisson with Brigade Real-Time Path Tracer. The difference between the pure GPU ray tracer implementation and our hybrid implementation is that, instead of using the G-Buffer information, primary rays are generated by the camera. In the pure GPU ray tracer implementation, OpenGL render is disabled.

We conduct the tests in a desktop system equipped with an AMD Phenom II X4 965 3.4GHz, 16GB of RAM and a NVIDIA GeForce GTX570. As operating system, we use the 64bits version of Windows 7 Professional.

Table 3 summarizes the results in terms of performance with the measurements based on frames per second (FPS) for each scene. All scenes were rendered with resolution 1280x720 pixels.

Table 3. Performance comparison between our hybrid render and a pure ray tracer implementation. The times are expressed in milliseconds.

Performance comparison in milisseconds (ms)						
Scene	*Vertices*	*Triangles*	**DR**[3]	**RT**[4]	**Hybrid**	**Gain**
Armadillo (Fig. 5(c))	193737	380655	3,134	25,112	18,518	1,35
Sponza (Fig. 5(a))	145173	262187	2,227	66,667	34,482	1,93
Sponza Simplified	48556	90349	1,666	33,334	25	1,33
Showcase (Fig 5(b))	112603	224440	2,336	40	23,255	1,72

---

[1] GL_RGBA32F was chosen because of the need to store the coordinates in view-space in the position buffer and values that lies outside the rage [0, 1] for the Optical Properties buffer.

[2] GL_DC is the abbreviation for GL_DEPTH_COMPONENT.

[3] DT stands for *Deferred Rendering Time*. It is the time our implementation spends with the rasterization stage.

[4] RT stands for *Ray tracing Time*. It represents the time necessary to render the scene with a ray tracing-only renderer.

As one can see in Table 3, our hybrid implementation was able to achieve a higher frame rate than a pure ray tracer implementation. It is easy to notice that both the Armadillo Scene and the Showcase Scene got a bigger difference than the Sponza Scene. This is because Armadillo and Showcase are open environments, which means that more rays are likely to escape avoiding extra computation. Since Sponza Scene is a closed scene, the method tends to spend more time when tracing both primary and secondary rays.

The comparison with Brigade was made with the Dining Room scene. It is available as a demo in Brigade Homepage [19]. Table 4 shows the results.

We expect to reduce the time of our approach using OptiX support for mipmaps, since coalesced memory access in GPU is one of the keys to achieve real-time frame rates.

Table 4. Performance comparison between our hybrid render and Brigade. The times are expressed in milliseconds.

Performance comparison in milisseconds (ms)				
Scene	Vertices	Triangles	**Brigade**	**Hybrid**
Dining Room (Fig. 5(d))	386541	224954	76,920	28,283

(a)   (b)   (c)   (d)

Fig. 5. Images rendered with our hybrid ray tracer implementation. *(a)* Sponza Atrium Scene. This scene highlights the real-time reflection and refractions effects. *(b)* Showcase Scene. In this scene we highlight the colored shadows of transparent objects. *(c)* Armadillo Scene. This is demonstration of a refractive material applied to a model. *(d)* Dining Room Scene. All images have a resolution of 1280x720 pixels.

9   Conclusion

We have described a ray tracer approach with primary ray hits using traditional graphics pipeline, taking advantage of the depth-buffer algorithm implemented on hardware and the data stored in the G-Buffer generated with deferred shading strategy. It was presented a way to avoid merging the scene geometry into a single mesh. We also present the details regarding implementation on how to use the same geometry on OpenGL and OptiX contexts as well as the removal of the common bottleneck of data transfer between GPU and CPU.

We present results in terms of performance for different scenes and show that our hybrid approach can accelerate ray tracing by turning the primary rays resolution stage into a render task. We highlight the fact that our system was built so that existing shaders are not modified taking advantage of the graphic effects created so far. The heuristic approach guarantees that we process the most important objects with ray tracing and guarantees that the real time constraint is being maintained, something that is fundamental for virtual reality applications.

As future works, we propose the development of new heuristics to find the best elements where to apply ray tracer effects. We also want to compare the use of shadow maps with ray traced shadows in terms of performance and visual quality within our hybrid pipeline. This may drastically reduce the number of rays that need to be traced. At the primary rays resolution stage, we propose a generation and compaction of a list of valid rays. Also, we want to incorporate animations in our implementations in order to evaluate the performance of rebuilding the acceleration data structures on the fly.

Considering the pre-production phase, where the objects are selected to be ray traced, one strategy not explored in our work is to have more than one model to represent the same object, using discreet level of detail approach. The artist could create, for example, tree objects, one highly detailed, one with medium detail and a simplest one. The level of detail does not need to be only in the geometry, but also in the effects characteristics. A translucent object, for instance, could have different diffuse characteristics, proportionately reducing the work necessary to ray trace.

One of the advantages of ray tracing over raster techniques is its natural way of using parametric surfaces. Implicit representation of surfaces requires only the storage of its associated parameters and ray intersection algorithms are faster when dealing with parametric equations. Also, due to the complexity of incorporation in raster systems, in future, we want to incorporate implicit surfaces in our hybrid approach. When computing the first hit stage, the object could be approximated with a low resolution polygonal mesh and then, the ray tracing stage will be responsible for global illumination effects applied on the accurate implicit representation.

As stated, ray tracing is a technique capable of high quality image synthesis. Across with the more efficient implementations, along with the advance of computational hardware, at future it will be possible to simulate effects only reliable in offline rendering. At the future, we may see global illumination effects applied in real-time at high frame rates inside game and visualization environments.

Acknowledgment. The authors would like to thank Leandro Fernandes for his help with shader programs, NVIDIA and people that spent a little of time discussing OptiX and CUDA related subjects in the web forum and CNPq for the financial support of this work. We also thank Crytek for proving a renewed Sponza scene suitable for testing on modern graphics cards.

References

1. Kirk, D.B., Hwu, W.M.W.: Programming Massively Parallel Processors: A Hands-on Approach, 1st edn. Morgan Kaufmann Publishers Inc., San Francisco (2010)

2. Bigler, J., Stephens, A., Parker, S.G.: Design for parallel interactive ray tracing systems. In: IEEE Symposium on Interactive Ray Tracing 2006, pp. 187–196 (September 2006)
3. Aila, T., Laine, S.: Understanding the efficiency of ray traversal on gpus. In: Proc. High-Performance Graphics 2009, pp. 145–149 (2009)
4. Lauterbach, C., Garland, M., Sengupta, S., Luebke, D., Manocha, D.: Fast BVH Construction on GPUs. Computer Graphics Forum 28(2), 375–384
5. Hachisuka, T.: Ray tracing on graphics hardware. Technical report, University of California at San Diego (2009)
6. Heirich, A., Arvo, J.: A competitive analysis of load balancing strategies for parallel ray tracing. The Journal of Supercomputing 12, 57–68 (1998), doi:10.1023/A:1007977326603
7. Whitted, T.: An improved illumination model for shaded display. Commun. ACM 23, 343–349 (1980)
8. Beck, S., Bernstein, A., Danch, D., Frohlich, B.: Cpu-gpu hybrid real time ray tracing framework (2005)
9. Bikker, J.: Real-time ray tracing through the eyes of a game developer. In: Proceedings of the 2007 IEEE Symposium on Interactive Ray Tracing, pp. 1–10. IEEE Computer Society, Washington, DC (2007)
10. Parker, S.G., Bigler, J., Dietrich, A., Friedrich, H., Hoberock, J., Luebke, D., McAllister, D., McGuire, M., Morley, K., Robison, A., Stich, M.: Optix: A general purpose ray tracing engine. ACM Transactions on Graphics (August 2010)
11. Bak, P.: Real time ray tracing. Master's thesis, IMM, DTU (2010)
12. Chen, C.C., Liu, D.S.M.: Use of hardware z-buffered rasterization to accelerate ray tracing. In: Proceedings of the 2007 ACM Symposium on Applied Computing, SAC 2007, pp. 1046–1050. ACM, New York (2007)
13. Deering, M., Winner, S., Schediwy, B., Duffy, C., Hunt, N.: The triangle processor and normal vector shader: a vlsi system for high performance graphics, pp. 21–30. ACM, New York (1988)
14. Akenine-Möller, T., Haines, E., Hoffman, N.: Real-Time Rendering, 3rd edn. A. K. Peters, Ltd., Natick (2008)
15. Saito, T., Takahashi, T.: Comprehensible rendering of 3-d shapes. SIGGRAPH Comput. Graph. 24(4), 197–206 (1990)
16. Shishkovtov, O.: Deffered shading in s.t.a.l.k.e.r. GPU Gems 2 2, 143–166 (2005)
17. Reshetov, A.: Morphological antialiasing. In: Proceedings of the 2009 ACM Symposium on High Performance Graphics (2009)
18. Williams, L.: Casting curved shadows on curved surfaces. In: Computer Graphics (SIGGRAPH 1978 Proceedings), pp. 270–274 (1978)
19. Bikker, J.: Brigade: Real-time path tracer. Webpage (April 2012)

A Parallel Fipa Architecture Based on GPU for Games and Real Time Simulations

Luiz Guilherme Oliveira dos Santos[1], Esteban Walter Gonzales Clua[1],
and Flávia Cristina Bernardini[2]

[1] Universidade Federal Fluminense — UFF
Instituto de Computação — IC
MediaLab
Niterói - RJ, Brasil
[2] Universidade Federal Fluminense — UFF
Instituto de Ciência e Tecnologia — ICT
LabIDeS — Laboratório de Inovação no Desenvolvimento de Sistemas
Rio das Ostras - RJ, Brasil

Abstract. The dynamic nature and common use of agents and agent paradigm motives the investigation on standardization of multi-agent systems (MAS). The main property of a MAS is to allow the sub-problems related to a constraint satisfaction issues to be subcontracted to different problem solving agents with their own interests and goals, being FIPA one of the most commonly collection of standards used nowadays. When dealing with a huge set of agents for real time applications, such as games and virtual reality solutions, it is hard to compute a massive crowd of agents due the computational restrictions in CPU. With the advent of parallel GPU architectures and the possibility to run general algorithms inside it, it became possible to model such massive applications. In this work we propose a novel standardization of agent applications based on FIPA using GPU architectures, making possible the modelling of more complex crowd behaviours. The obtained results in our simulations were very promising and show that GPUs may be a choice for massively agents applications. We also present restrictions and cases where GPU based agents may not be a good choice.

1 Introduction

A multi-agent system — MAS — has the interesting property to allow modeling subdivisions of the constraint satisfaction problem to individual and different agents specifications, with their own interests and goals. Furthermore, domains with multiple agents of any type, including autonomous vehicles [6] and human-agents massively used in game development, are generally solved with this approach.

The dynamic nature of agent distribution motivates research by groups working on the standardization of dynamic collaborative MAS. Mendez [5] describes each model of MAS proposed by these groups, and concludes that "The architecture models open environments composed of logically distributed areas where

M. Herrlich, R. Malaka, and M. Masuch (Eds.): ICEC 2012, LNCS 7522, pp. 306–317, 2012.

agents exist. The basic agents in this architecture are minimal agents, local area coordinators, yellow page servers, and cooperation domain servers". One of these models, used in this work, is Foundation for Intelligent Physical Agents (FIPA).

The main concept of a MAS is to simulate real world environments and interactions, composed by many entities, *e.g.* a building full of people during an emergency evacuation, a bee community, biological interactions between cells or enzymes, and so on. In applications such as games and simulation, the creation of many individuals with different behaviors and/or objectives became widespread. There are several approaches that explore this dynamic property [17,12,18,15], but when dealing with video-games and interactive applications, there are many computational restrictions that must be carefully analysed, since their computation can be expensive. Most of previous work explore the hardware limitations to create bigger crowds [16,2]. Others explore some of the problems related to the simulation itself just like collisions [7], Path-Planning [29], many behaviors [22] and so on. The biggest problem is that a crowd simulation leads to a huge amount of computing data, and it is hard to make it real time. Researches like [10] explore a different hardware models to improve its results and create many agents as possible.

Since 2006, the use of graphics processing units paradigm (GPUs) became not only a new research area, but it is being used inside many applications and operational systems to escape from performances bottlenecks. When GPUs became cheaper and fully programmable, many researchers are exploring this power in order to create more agents with improved behaviours, according to its limitations [3,24]. However, mapping agent behaviors to GPU architectures is not trivial, given the GPU restrictions and the complexity of Artificial Intelligence algorithms. Many heuristics of this field try to avoid $O(n^2)$ complexity using different and complex structures and decision trees. Although these AI algorithms gives good results to a single number of agents, hardly they achieve a good scalability [25].

Unlike other researches, we believe that a standardization of this process of creating agents in GPU architectures is necessary not only to improve the actual implementations, but also to make easier to game developers. This work is a continuation of previous work [19,20] where it has been exposed a mapping process using a wide spread framework to program FIPA agents called JADE [1] to GPU Computing.

The purpose of this work is to present a novel and efficient architecture to autonomous agents using GPU Computing paradigm. We describe how a MAS is usually implemented following the FIPA model, and we develop a new paradigm to implement a MAS in GPU Computing based architectures. We also present a case study where we show how to map a typical MAS problem to GPU Computing based architecture.

This paper is organized as follows: Section 2 presents FIPA patterns and gives an overall about its usage and implications. Section 3 shows the architecture we are proposing, and gives a study case. Section 4 analyses the implementation and performance results. Finally, Section 5 concludes this work and describes future work.

2   FIPA

Agents can be based on two different architectures: logic- and reactive-based [5]. The former is based on knowledge systems, in which the programmer has to represent the complete environment and create rules to manipulate the agent according to reasoning mechanisms. The latter is generally based in a decision-making behavior. Unlike the logic-based method, the reactive doesn't need a reasoning system, but only the modeling of a communication with the environment data, in order to receive some sort of information, and acting according to the observed data.

FIPA stands for *Foundation For Intelligent Physical Agents* [4] and it is a non-profit organization, which develops patterns to create applications using agent-based approaches. This organization, founded in 1996, is composed from both academic and industry members since its creation. These agent-based approaches are widely used by academic and industrial computing solutions. Other patters such as MASIF(Mobile Agent System Interoperability Facility)[9], are used to specific applications, and are not so generic as FIPA.

During the evolution of FIPA, two main concepts has being developed: the FIPA-ACL (for communications purposes) and the Agent Management Framework. FIPA-ACL is the communication standard among agents based on the 90's internet patterns such as OMG, DCE W3C and GGF. The Agent Management Framework focus on how to create, operate and manipulate the agents. It defines the creation, registration, location, communication and operation process of the agents. In this paper, our efforts lies on the management of these agents.

FIPA stands that there is an abstract layer where all the agents have services provided to them and the programmer could develop application on the top layer of this architecture. On the other hand, all the agents are autonomous, they act like a peer-to-peer application and there must be a top application that controls their execution called Container. The container has an Agent Description of the agents inside it and has the authority to start the agents and control the agent's environment. This paradigm is called *Agent Oriented Programming — AOP*. Figure 1 shows at a top level the architecture of a system implemented according to AOP approach. There are many frameworks, platforms and applications based on AOP approach, such as JADE [1], FLUX [23] and JACK [28]. Nowadays, its use is as variable as possible, for instance: "robots" that search pieces of information in websites, media-oriented services[8] , evacuation and massive people simulations [26], and so on.

3   A GPU Based Architecture for Massive FIPA Based Agents

In this work we propose a novel FIPA based architecture using AOP paradigm for a massively concurrent agents application. As discussed in introduction, mapping an agent-based architecture to a SIMD paradigm, on which GPU is based, is not trivial and new structures must be proposed and developed. To test how works our general architecture, we implemented a simple agent system that behaviors based on a traditional A* path-finding algorithm, described in Subsection 3.3. Our objective in our experiments is analyze how scalable are the problems implemented using AOP paradigm on GPU architecture. So, due to lack of performance on GPU when processes execution demands high volume of communication, we avoided data communication among the agents. Results and tests using our proposed architecture to implement our MAS with the chosen agent behavior are presented and discussed in Section 4.

3.1   The GPU FIPA Architecture

Since FIPA is an Agent Oriented programming pattern, the main actor we have in our architecture is the agent. A simple agent life cycle in this architecture is illustrated in Algorithm 1.

Algoritm 1. Life Cycle of a Generic Agent

Require: *Evironment*: Agent's world.
Require: *State*: Agent's Initial State.
 1: Load all initial variables;
 2: **while** (Agent's conditions to stop are not valid) **do**
 3:    Execute Agent's Behavior;
 4:    Interact with the *Environment*;
 5:    Change Agent's *State*;
 6: **end while**

The main controller of the agents is called a Container. It is possible to have one or more containers in an application and different types of agents within this container. One or more containers can also share the same environment. Generally, there is a Main Container to control all the other containers.

In the model we follow the agent is not directly implemented, but it has many descriptions that help the controller of these agents to know how to stop them and maintain its autonomy. Figure 1 shows how the role of both container and agent description during the execution and the relationship between them.

Each agent description dictates how the agent must be executed and what are the conditions to make the agent stop. This has to be implemented on the functions action and done respectively. In a CPU implementation these descriptions are inside the agents description, different from the GPU, that we need to put these in a separated file that goes there because of GPU compiler restrictions, as shown in Figure 2.

3.2   Kernel Structure

In a typical CPU approach the agent live along all the cycle, with the agent description for convenience. Another possible approach is to create a Behavior

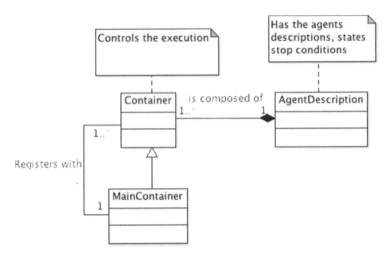

Fig. 1. Top Level Agent Oriented Programming Architecture

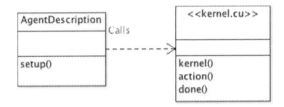

Fig. 2. Description of how a kernel is linked to the solution and called

class that maps the agent's algorithm and improve the liability of the code. Since every agent has an autonomous execution and the GPU architecture follows a SIMD paradigm, it is necessary that each agent has the knowledge of his own code and data. Each agent is mapped to CUDA as threads, but not all agent's data will be processed inside the kernel, as shown in Figure 2, where method setup from AgentDescriptor class calls the kernel method in «kernel.cu». Methods action and done are called only inside the kernel («kernel.cu»).

Since the number of agents is variable, the kernel algorithm needs to be suitable to many different configurations. GPUs restrict the number of threads and blocks to be power of 2. For instance, if there are 1000 agents inside a simulation, there will be 1024 threads divided in blocks. In Algorithm 2 we see how this is done. If an agent has a Unique ID (UID) greater than the maximum number of agents, this agent will be idle. Since every agent is mapped into a thread, the UID can be easily achieved by a simple arithmetic using descriptors of the dimension of the block, ID of the block and ID of the thread.

To calculate the number of threads and blocks used, we use the following equations:

$$N_T = 2^{\left\lceil \frac{\log\left(N_A\right)}{\log 2} \right\rceil} \tag{1}$$

Algoritm 2. Kernel

Require: *World*: Agent's world.
Require: *State*: Initial Position of the Agent.
Require: *NumberofAgents*: Max number of agents used.
 1: $UID = (BlockIndex \times BlockID) + ThreadID$;
 2: **if** $(UID < NumberofAgents)$ **then**
 3:    **while** (Agent's not in final position) **do**
 4:       $State = $ NextState($State, World$);
 5:    **end while**
 6: **end if**

$$N_B = \frac{N_T}{N_W} \tag{2}$$

$$N_{TpB} = \frac{N_T}{N_B} \tag{3}$$

where:

N_A is the number of agents in a simulation;
N_T is the real number of threads that is going to be executed;
N_B is the number of blocks created;
N_W is the number of threads in a warp[1]. It is given by the GPU specification;
N_{TpB} is the number of threads per block. The total amount of threads is given
   by $N_B \times N_TpB$.

These equations minimize the number of warps, improves the scalability and
calculates the blocks and threads in power of 2. If the number of blocks or the
number of threads per blocks is higher than the maximum of the GPU we relax
the second equation and allows more warps per blocks.

Using an heterogeneous programming paradigm, the Agent Descriptor has to
configure and call a kernel one or more times, depending on the solution provided.
When GPU is used, the Descriptor also makes the memory copies from CPU to
GPU and vice versa. It has also to make the kernel configuration and the GPU
deallocation. The agent behavior will be incorporated by the kernel itself and
will be specific for each kind of actions. In our platform we develop a pathfinding
agent, typically found in many crowd behavior games.

4   Test Case — Pathfinding Agents

The A* algorithm [13] is a search algorithm that uses a minimum cost heuristic
and dynamic programming techniques. Different from other GPU implementations of this algorithm [3,27], we used the traditional heuristic of A*, defined

---

[1] Each thread is executed by a single core, and each block of threads in a Stream
   Multiprocessor(SM), which consist of array of cores. Warp is each subset of threads
   running in parallel in each block. The programmer does not have control of these
   warps swaps, being completely scheduled by the GPU itself.

by Equation 4, where $g(n)$ evaluates the sum of costs from the beginning node to the node n, and $h(n)$ is the distance between the node n and the objective node. We based our implementation on [11]. Algorithm 2 shows how is the kernel implementation. Not that if on line 3 restricts the number of agents inside the kernel, as explained in Section 3.2.

$$f(n) = g(n) + h(n) \qquad (4)$$

A*'s Complexity: In best case, A*'s complexity is $O(N)$, where the algorithm finds the path directly to the objective node, where N is the number of nodes between the base node and the objective node. On worst case the algorithm is $O(b^N)$, where b is a partition factor. The complexity of A* depends directly of the heuristic function used, tending to be exponential if the function is too precise [21]. The average complexity is $O(N \exp (C\phi(N)))$, where $\phi(N) = log(N)^k$ [14].

For simplicity, this test case has no obstacles and the agents are located into a two dimension map. The class diagram shown in Figure 3 shows the structure of an oriented object implementation of an agent description on the CPU. Figure 4 illustrates the class diagram of an agent description that uses a GPU to process part of its information. The kernel is placed in a separated file as a library, and executes the behavior of an agent. All the other settings are in myAgent class,

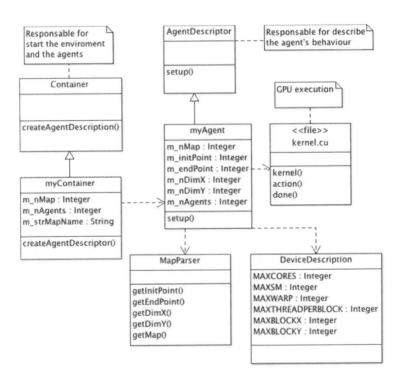

Fig. 3. Basic Class Diagram using the CPU

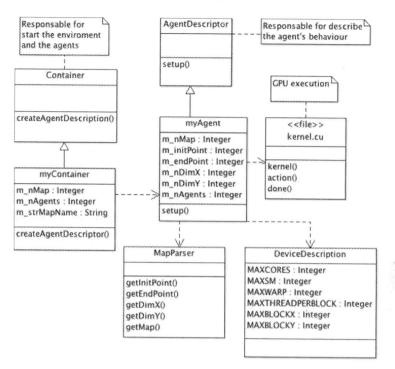

Fig. 4. Basic Class Diagram for the Agent Pathfiding on GPU

that is triggered by the setup function. Note that Figure 4 shows how our GPU FIPA Architecture is used to model a MAS.

Performance Analysis: We want to verify the scalability of the application: the execution times maintain when we change the number of agents? We used an Intel Core i7 3.07GHz and 8GB DDR3 memory for the CPU, and a GeForce GTX 580 with 512 CUDA cores, 1544MHz for each core and 1536MB GDDR5 memory for the GPU tests. All the test case scenarios (Test Scn.) in Table 1 were performed 10 times in a CentOS 6 operational system. The map has a fixed 1000×1000 dimension[2]. Note that the columns N_A (number of agents in a simulation), N_B (number of blocks created) and N_{TpB} (number of threads per block) are used for GPU configuration calculated by Equations 1, 2 and 3.

Table 2 shows the mean and standard deviation of the 10 times measured on executions. We can observe that, as the number of agents grows (T_1 to T_6), the GPU maintains the scalability, loosing time only when the number of warps grows. However, these still are good times for a realtime simulation. On the other hand, the CPU times increase linearly as the number of agents grows. To a better perception of the time increase on GPU implementation, Figure 5 shows the evolution of the time execution when increasing the number of agents. It is

---

[2] This size of map is considered a large one.

Table 1. Test Scenarios performed

Test Number	N_A	N_B	N_{TpB}
T_0	10^0	1	1
T_1	10^1	1	16
T_2	10^2	4	32
T_3	10^3	32	32
T_4	10^4	512	32
T_5	10^5	1024	128
T_6	10^6	1024	1024

Table 2. Algorithms performance on both CPU and GPU

Test Number	CPU		GPU	
	Mean Time(s)	Standard Deviation(s)	Mean Time(s)	Standard Deviation(s)
T_0	0,000027	0,000004	0,102781	0,001090
T_1	0,000240	0,000005	0,103334	0,000914
T_2	0,002377	0,000006	0,104765	0,003214
T_3	0,024976	0,000911	0,105510	0,004830
T_4	0,235692	0,000077	0,107930	0,008282
T_5	2,360808	0,003434	0,108138	0,005976
T_6	23,562007	0,000502	0,119523	0,001940

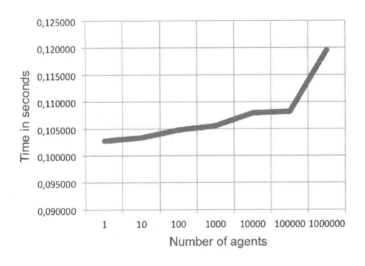

Fig. 5. Test Scenarios Results Chart

possible to see that there are perceptual changes when more warps per blocks are required, specially from 10^5 to 10^6 agents.

Restrictions of the Architecture: The proposed architecture follows some of the agent management patterns defined by FIPA and can be easily reproduced and adapted by some modifications. Though, there is still many restrictions implemented in our architecture regarding to implement heterogeneous agents with heterogeneous behaviors and agent communications. These restrictions exist due to the SIMD paradigm of the GPU, where is not recommended to create different branches inside one kernel just to solve these problems. One good solution could be multiple kernel calls, but nowadays we do not have control of how much of the GPU capacity will be allocated to each concurrent kernel. So it is hard to distribute the kernel calls correctly and smoothly. For this reason, our solution is focused for programmers that want to create FIPA agents with few communication and few heterogeneity among them. Another good point of it is to reproduce innumerable problems with the same pattern, only changing a few lines, increasing the productivity and the liability of the code, which is a big issue when dealing with game engines.

5 Conclusion and Future Work

Agent oriented paradigm has been largely used in game development, but almost all approaches implement them in a CPU architecture. While CPU's approaches allows generic and complex agent behavior solutions, it is shown that a huge amount of agents may be impracticable for interative frame rates. In this paper we present a novel and efficient multi-agent architecture for a GPU programming paradigm, allowing up to two orders of magnitudes of agents in interative frame rates.

In the future, this works aims to determinate how to use GPU computing inside AOP paradigm. With the evolution of this work, we intend to create an abstraction layer to turn possible to create agents directly in GPU. This aims to facilitate the developer to not have to learn GPU's architecture, increasing the productivity process in applications that require massive use of agents.

We believe that along with the development of the GPU Computing, the restrictions in creating agents that we've shown will sightly decrease during the time. However, its scalability and massiveness nature will be maintained. For future work we intend to evolve the standardization of this architecture solving some of the restrictions we've found, such as communications and execution of heterogeneous agents in a more complex environment. We also intend to accept in our architecture more behaviors to agents, with the possibility to explore kernel capabilities of the GPU. This functionality will allow to different behaviors be treated in parallel.

References

1. Bellifemine, F., Caire, G., Greenwood, D.: Developing multi-agent systems with JADE. Wiley Series in Agent Technology (2007)
2. van den Berg, J., Patil, S., Sewall, J., Manocha, D., Lin, M.: Interactive navigation of multiple agents in crowded environments. In: Proceedings of the 2008 Symposium on Interactive 3D Graphics and Games, I3D 2008, pp. 139–147. ACM (2008), http://doi.acm.org/10.1145/1342250.1342272
3. Bleiweiss, A.: Gpu accelerated pathfinding. In: Proceedings of the 23rd ACM SIGGRAPH/EUROGRAPHICS Symposium on Graphics Hardware, pp. 65–74. NVidia (2008)
4. FIPA: Foundation for intelligent physical agents (2012), http://fipa.org/
5. Flores-Mendez, R.: Towards a standardization of multi-agent system frameworks. ACM Crossroads Magazine (1999), http://www.acm.org/crossroads/xrds5-4/multiagent.html
6. Franklin, S., Graesser, A.: Is it an Agent or Just a Program? a Taxonomy for Autonomous Agents. In: Jennings, N.R., Wooldridge, M.J., Müller, J.P. (eds.) ECAI-WS 1996 and ATAL 1996. LNCS (LNAI), vol. 1193, pp. 21–35. Springer, Heidelberg (1997)
7. Guy, S.J., Chhugani, J., Kim, C., Satish, N., Lin, M., Manocha, D., Dubey, P.: Clearpath: highly parallel collision avoidance for multi-agent simulation. In: Proceedings of the 2009 ACM SIGGRAPH/Eurographics Symposium on Computer Animation, SCA 2009, pp. 177–187. ACM (2009), http://doi.acm.org/10.1145/1599470.1599494
8. Han, S.W., Kim, J.: Preparing experiments with media-oriented service composition for future internet. In: Proceedings of the 5th International Conference on Future Internet Technologies, CFI 2010, pp. 73–78. ACM, New York (2010), http://doi.acm.org/10.1145/1853079.1853099
9. Islam, N., Mallah, G.A., Shaikh, Z.A.: Fipa and masif standards: a comparative study and strategies for integration. In: Proceedings of the 2010 National Software Engineering Conference, NSEC 2010, pp. 7:1–7:6. ACM, New York (2010), http://doi.acm.org/10.1145/1890810.1890817
10. Lamarche, F., Donikian, S.: Crowd of virtual humans: a new approach for real time navigation in complex and structured environments. Computer Graphics Forum 23, 509–518 (2004)
11. Lester, P.: A* for beginners (2004), http://www.policyalmanac.org/games/aStarTutorial.htm
12. Musse, S.R., Thalmann, D.: Hierarchical model for real time simulation of virtual human crowds. IEEE Transactions on Visualization and Computer Graphics 7, 152–164 (2001)
13. Nilson, N.J.: Problem-solving methods in Artificial Intelligence. McGraw-Hill (1971)
14. Pearl, J.: Heuristics: Intelligent Search Strategies for Computer Problem Solving. Addison-Wesley (1984)
15. Pelechano, N., Allbeck, J.M., Badler, N.I.: Controlling individual agents in high-density crowd simulation. In: Proceedings of the 2007 ACM SIGGRAPH/Eurographics Symposium on Computer Animation, SCA 2007, Aire-la-Ville, Switzerland, Switzerland. Eurographics Association (2007), http://dl.acm.org/citation.cfm?id=1272690.1272705

16. Reynolds, C.: Big fast crowds on ps3. In: Proceedings of the 2006 ACM SIG-GRAPH Symposium on Videogames, Sandbox 2006, pp. 113–121. ACM (2006), http://doi.acm.org/10.1145/1183316.1183333
17. Reynolds, C.W.: Flocks, herds, and schools: A distributed behavioral model. In: ACM SIGGRAPH 1987 Conference Proceedings, vol. 21, pp. 25–34 (1987)
18. Musse, S.R., Thalmann, D.: A model of human crowd behavior: Group inter-relationship and collision detection analysis. In: Workshop Computer Animation and Simulation of Eurographics, pp. 39–52 (1997)
19. dos Santos, L.G.O., Bernardini, F.C., Clua, E.G., da Costa, L.C., Passos, E.: Mapping multi-agent systems based on fipa specification to gpu architectures. In: 3^a Conferencia Anual em Ciencia e Arte dos Videojogos, pp. 109–118. Instituto Superior Tecnico, Taguspark (2010)
20. dos Santos, L.G.O., Bernardini, F.C., Clua, E.G., da Costa, L.C., Passos, E.: Mapping a path-fiding multiagent system based on fipa specification to gpu architectures. In: X Simposio Brasileiro de Games e Entretenimento Digital (2011)
21. Stefik, M.: Introducing to Knowledge Systems. Morgan Kaufmann (1995)
22. Sung, M., Gleicher, M., Chenney, S.: Scalable behaviors for crowd simulation. In: Eurographics 2004 (2004)
23. Thielscher, M.: Flux: A logic programming method for reasoning agents. Theory and Practice of Logic Programming 5, 533–565 (2005)
24. Torchelsen, R.P., Scheidegger, L.F., Oliveira, G.N., Bastos, R., Comba, J.L.D.: Real-time multi-agent path planning on arbitrary surfaces. In: Proceedings of the 2010 ACM SIGGRAPH Symposium on Interactive 3D Graphics and Games, I3D 2010, pp. 47–54. ACM (2010), http://doi.acm.org/10.1145/1730804.1730813
25. Turner, P.J., Jennings, N.R.: Improving the Scalability of Multi-agent Systems. In: Wagner, T.A., Rana, O.F. (eds.) AA-WS 2000. LNCS (LNAI), vol. 1887, pp. 246–262. Springer, Heidelberg (2001)
26. Valckenaers, P., Sauter, J., Sierra, C., Rodriguez-Aguilar, J.A.: Applications and environments for Multi-Agent Systems. Autonomous Agents and Multi-Agent Systems 14(1), 61–85 (2006)
27. Walsh, K., Banerjee, B.: Fast A* with iterative resolution for navigation. International Journal on Artificial Intelligence Tools 19, 101–119 (2010)
28. Winikoff, M.: Jack intelligent agents: An industrial strength platform. In: Multi-Agent Programming, pp. 175–193. Kluwer (2005)
29. Yersin, B., Morini, F., Thalmann, D.: Real-time crowd motion planning: Scalable avoidance and group behavior. Vis. Comput. 24(10), 859–870 (2008), http://dx.doi.org/10.1007/s00371-008-0286-0

Cognitive Agents for Microscopic Traffic Simulations in Virtual Environments

Sven Seele[1], Rainer Herpers[1,2,3], and Christian Bauckhage[4]

[1] Bonn-Rhine-Sieg University of Applied Sciences, 53757 Sankt Augustin, Germany
{sven.seele,rainer.herpers}@brsu.de
[2] University of New Brunswick, Fredericton, E3B 5A3, Canada
[3] York University, Toronto, M3J 1P3, Canada
[4] University of Bonn, 53115 Bonn, Germany
bauckhage@bit.uni-bonn.de

Abstract. Traffic simulations in current open world video games and driving simulators are still limited with respect to the complexity of the behavior of simulated agents. These limitations are typically due to scarce computational resources, but also to the applied methodologies. We suggest adding cognitive components to traffic agents in order to achieve more realistic behavior, such as opting for risky actions or occasionally breaking traffic rules. To achieve this goal, we start by adding a personality profile to each agent, which is based on the "Five Factor Model" from psychology. We test our enhancement on a specific traffic scenario where simplistic behaviors would lead to a complete standstill of traffic. Our results show that the approach resolves critical situations and keeps traffic flowing.

Keywords: virtual environments, multi-agent systems, cognitive agents, traffic simulation.

1 Introduction

Recently, open world games have become very popular, since they allow players to roam freely through large areas and enable a non-linear playing experience. Obviously, this experience also requires virtual worlds to be populated by believable agents. If these simulated agents use means of transportation such as automobiles, simulations of vehicular traffic need to be realistic. However, state-of-the-art traffic simulations for digital games usually only display relatively simple, rule-based behaviors, so they do not mimic the reality of road traffic. This hampers the player's feeling of immersion. In serious games applications, such as driving simulators for road safety education (cf. the FIVIS bicycle simulator system [5]), a lack of realism is in fact harmful.

Our goal is therefore to equip virtual agents with skills and reasoning mechanisms that produce real-world behaviors. With respect to traffic simulations, the critical observation is that, in everyday traffic, rules are frequently broken, either on purpose or because of human error. The aim of simulators, such as in

M. Herrlich, R. Malaka, and M. Masuch (Eds.): ICEC 2012, LNCS 7522, pp. 318–325, 2012.

the FIVIS project, is to teach children to identify and resolve potentially hazardous situations resulting from misconduct. If simulated traffic participants are to be useful for road safety training, they need to have a tendency to make errors and to occasionally defy traffic rules. However, in order for the misbehavior to make sense to an observer, it must be grounded in the momentary circumstances. Hence, the agents must be able to perceive and reason about their environment before making decisions. Unfortunately, current traffic simulations typically rely on scripted or randomized behaviors and therefore rarely produce realistic hazardous situations. In this paper, we therefore investigate the effects of adding psychological profiles to agents.

2   Related Work

Traffic simulations have been researched since the 1930s (see [14] for an exhaustive overview of different approaches). The field is mainly concerned with investigating emergent traffic behaviors in order to plan roads or predict jams. While applications like these require general models of driving behavior, they are not concerned with individual habits or actions of agents. In virtual environments, however, where users directly interact with a simulated world, individual behaviors are a major component of the user's experience.

Traffic simulations for virtual environments are often of limited complexity, typically because of scarce computational resources but also because of the current state of artificial intelligence. In fact, some researchers have criticized the limited character of game AI as one of the major shortcomings of current digital experiences and have focused on providing adaptive game AI using methods such as case-based reasoning or reinforcement learning (see e.g. [2,12,13]).

Research on cognitive architectures naturally influences work on modeling cognitive traffic agents. While there are numerous different paradigms and concepts [1,4,9], ICARUS [10] is an example of a corresponding framework applied to the domain of in-city driving. ICARUS enables an agent to learn how to perform basic driving tasks, for example, aligning itself in a lane or accelerating or decelerating for turns. Similarly, the work in [11] used a cognitive architecture to model erroneous behavior of pilots and drivers. However, it focused on attention mechanisms for assistance systems and did not address decision-making.

Earlier work in [8] presented the concept of a more realistic traffic agent based on psychological personality profiles. Its core is the "Five Factor Model" (FFM) which states that every personality can be defined using only five distinct personality traits (openness, conscientiousness, extraversion, agreeableness, neuroticism) [3,6]. However, the correlation between an agent's personality and its behavior in traffic was not worked out. Nevertheless, the FFM provides an auspicious starting point for the work presented here.

3   Modeling Cognitive Traffic Agents

While the approaches reviewed above apply many interesting concepts, they do not address the problem of modeling *misbehavior*. However, to achieve a realistic

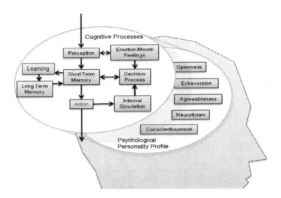

Fig. 1. Cognitive traffic agents for virtual environments could contain the depicted modules from cognitive architecture research. The psychological profile is depicted in a separate layer to indicate that it may influence all cognitive processes.

traffic simulation, agents need to behave and misbehave just as humans do. When they misbehave, they should only do so in situations where it makes sense to an observer, thus ruling out solutions solely based on randomization. We therefore aim to devise agents that are willing to intentionally take certain risks to reach their goals. Choosing risky actions could cause the agent to break traffic rules, which in turn would create potentially dangerous situations for other traffic participants. Our hypothesis is that modeling cognitive processes performed by human drivers and equipping agents with the ability to imitate these processes will result in the desired realistic behavior.

The first important aspect is to model what an artificial traffic participant should be able to perceive of its environment. As human drivers have limited perception, realistic agents need to be equipped with a "perception filter" that controls which information actually reaches the agent. We therefore model the visual field of an agent geometrically within a 3D game engine. Other agents residing within this geometric construct are considered to be perceivable. The concepts of attention selection and attention division presented in [11] can be added in a modular fashion to refine this simple perception model. Figure 1 shows a corresponding example of a cognitive traffic agent. It draws heavily on existing cognitive architectures and features typical elements of this domain, for instance, a short and long-term memory, decision and learning processes, as well as links to the agent's environment in the form of perception and action modules. Additionally, emotions, mood and feelings can influence the current perception/attention of the agent as well as decision-making.

To ground the agent's possible cognitive processes in realistic traffic behavior, we add a psychological component to each agent. The "Five Factor Model", a common method in psychology, is used to classify personalities based on five distinct character traits. Researchers have tried to correlate the model's factors with driving behavior, but according to Herzberg the results show varying success, with conscientiousness being the only trait consistently connected to driving behavior [6]. However, in his studies, Herzberg was able to show a correspondence between driving behavior and personality prototypes. The prototypes are based on trait configurations and three classes are especially prominent: resilient, overcontrolled, and undercontrolled drivers.

To identify a subject's personality, tools like the NEO-Five-Factor Inventory (NEO-FFI) can be used. The NEO-FFI is a questionnaire that assigns scores to the five traits of the FFM [3]. Individuals belonging to the resilient class score low in neuroticism but high for all other traits. *Overcontrollers* score high in neuroticism and conscientiousness, low in extraversion and openness, and average in agreeableness. *Undercontrollers* show high scores in neuroticism and openness, low scores in conscientiousness and agreeableness, and average scores in extraversion. Drivers belonging to the class of *undercontrollers* tend to take more risks and drive more aggressively. On the other hand, *overcontrollers* tend to closely follow traffic rules. *Resilients* are individuals whose behavior lies somewhere in between the other two classes [6].

To test our agent model, we defined a scenario which challenges regular rule-based traffic agents. If agents simultaneously approach an intersection from all sides, the rules of right-hand traffic demand that each agent yields to the one coming from the right. If every traffic participant abided strictly by the rule, a deadlock situation would result, leading to an irresolvable congestive state. To prevent this, drivers in real traffic would communicate – typically through hand signs – who is willing to waive the right of way. Interestingly, one of the participants would thus consciously break a traffic rule but resolve the deadlock.

To determine which traffic agent gives up its right of way in a deadlock situation, we considered the three psychological prototypes. Since *undercontrollers* tend to drive aggressively, they are not likely to give in. This explains the low agreeableness scores of this class. People with high scores in agreeableness usually oblige to other people's needs, tend to avoid confrontation, and adapt their behavior. High agreeableness scores among *resilients* suggest that drivers from this group would probably allow other drivers to pass. One would suspect overcontrolled drivers to do the same, since they are overly careful. Yet, they also strictly adhere to traffic rules and might thus be more reluctant to waive their rights. This is well reflected in the fact that *overcontrollers* score only average in agreeableness. Since *overcontrollers* and *resilients* are more likely to yield than *undercontrollers*, and since *resilients* are more likely to yield than *overcontrollers*, we use a combination of conscientiousness and agreeableness traits to determine which traffic agent waives the right of way in a deadlock situation.

4   Experimental Setup

To investigate the proposed ideas, a model of an uncontrolled intersection with a priority-to-the-right system in effect, was implemented within the Unity 3D engine as shown in Figure 2. The basic system consists of a closed loop of about 1 kilometer of road around a single intersection in the center, i.e. each lane leads to and from the intersection. The system is populated with a specified number

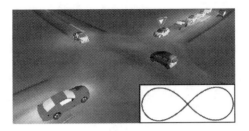

Fig. 2. For evaluation, a closed road system with an uncontrolled four-way intersection was modeled. Colored vehicles represent psychological prototypes: *undercontroller* (red), *overcontroller* (blue), and *resilient* (yellow). In the depicted situation a resilient driver waives its right of way (indicated by a yield sign) allowing the driver on its left to cross the intersection which resolves the deadlock situation.

of traffic agents which follow the road until they reach the intersection. There, they randomly decide whether to go right, left or straight on.

For the basic driving behavior, the intelligent driver model (IDM) was implemented. The IDM is a simple yet complete model for microscopic traffic simulations [7], which considers maximum acceleration, desired velocity or minimum headway. The parameters and their values were chosen according to suggestions in the literature [14]. At the core of the IDM is the calculation of the agent's current acceleration. In a free-flow driving state the agent simply accelerates, based on the given preferences and vehicle characteristics, until it reaches its desired velocity. In the experiment, the desired velocity was set to 30 km/h which typically is the speed limit in areas with priority-to-the-right intersections. If the agent is following another vehicle, a deceleration term based on the difference between the current headway and the desired headway results in adaptations of velocity.

The first part of the experiment was to fill the road network with a specified number of simple, rule-based agents. The agents were randomly distributed across the network and once the simulation started, the time taken to reach a congestive state was measured. For each specified number of agents (15, 20, 25, 30, and 35) fifteen trials were performed.

For the second part of the experiment the rule-based agents were enhanced with a component representing a psychological personality profile. Agents were divided into *overcontrollers*, *undercontrollers*, and *resilients*. Since Herzberg found an approximately even distribution of the three classes amongst drivers [6], we also distributed our simulated traffic agents evenly across personality prototypes. Initial values for agents were set according to the NEO-FFI scores of the respective psychological traits, scaled to a range between -1 and 1.

In a deadlock situation, the personality traits of the agents determine who gives up its right of way. To implement this mechanism, agents were given the ability to perceive the information necessary to detect deadlock situations and to signal their willingness to waive their priority. To test the robustness of the system, several simulations with 35 vehicles were run for 15, 45 and 120 minutes.

5   Results

Assuming an average vehicle length of 4 m, theoretically the maximum capacity of the entire road network corresponds to about 530 vehicles. As expected, deadlock situations occurred for numbers far below this value. The exact moment when a deadlock occurs, depends on the initial vehicle distribution and routing decisions at the intersection. Thus, the fewer number of agents in the system, the higher the chance that a deadlock situation in the system will be delayed. Nevertheless, even at only 3% of maximum capacity (15 vehicles), deadlocks were observed after only 333 seconds on average. At the same time, we also observed two occasions where the simulation continued for 1172 s and 957 s. However, since the median value (216 s) was considerably lower than the average, these cases can be considered as outliers. As illustrated by Figure 3, the time taken to reach a congestive state rapidly decreased as the number of agents in the system increased. An increasing number of vehicles, too, diminished the effect of advantageous routing decisions, since more agents had to wait at the intersection.

Introducing only five additional agents into the simulation decreased the average deadlock-free time by about 3 minutes, while still leaving room for times above the 10-minute mark. However, at 4.7% capacity (25 vehicles), the average and median times fell below one minute, with mean values of 43, 36, and 28 seconds and median values of 46, 36, and 26 seconds for trials with 25, 30, and 35 vehicles respectively. In accordance with the aforementioned observations, the values depicted in Figure 3 also show a decrease in deviations of simulation times as the number of agents increases.

Using our extended model, the simulation was run for three different periods of time. In each of the three trials the traffic never came to a complete standstill. 42 deadlock situations occurred during the 15-minute trial, 116 during the 45-minute trial, and 327 during the 120-minute trial. All situations were resolved allowing the traffic to keep flowing. Figure 4 illustrates a direct comparison of the rule-based agents and our extended model. To achieve comparability between simulations, the random number generator was initialized with identical values,

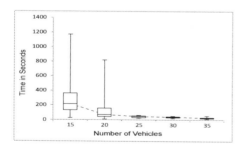

Fig. 3. The box plots depict the times until the simulation of rule-based agents resulted in a deadlock situation at the four-way intersection. For each number of vehicles 15 simulations were run.

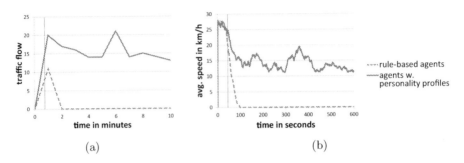

Fig. 4. A comparison of rule-based agents with the extended model using psychological personality profiles. The simulations were run for 10 min. with the first deadlock occurring after 45 sec. (vertical line). The flow (num. of vehicles per min.) was measured at the intersection (a) and the average speed of all vehicles in the simulation (b).

resulting in equal decisions for vehicle distribution and routing. Then the traffic flow at the intersection was measured by counting how many vehicles crossed the intersection in a time interval of one minute. The first deadlock occurred after 45 seconds, but as evident from Figure 4 (a), the flow never reached zero for the enhanced agents. At the same time, the average speed of each vehicle in the simulation was recorded for the duration of the simulation. Figure 4 (b) shows how the average speed continuously decreases after the first occurrence of a deadlock situation for both agent types. However, for the enhanced model the average speed never decreases below 10 km/h.

6   Conclusions and Future Work

In this paper, we discussed the need for more realistic traffic agents in games and simulations. We suggested extending regular, rule-based traffic agents with cognitive components. In particular, in an attempt to equip agents with more realistic behavior, we suggested the addition of psychological profiles based on the "Five Factor Model", dividing agents into three prototypical groups. We evaluated the impact of this extension in a specific traffic situation that cannot be handled by rule-based agents, and we found that our approach is able to seamlessly resolve deadlock situations at uncontrolled intersections.

At the current state of development, the static personality of an agent determines which agent gives up its right of way. In the worst case, this would always be the same agent, forcing it to wait for an extended time to cross the intersection. Currently, we are working towards modifying static personalities by dynamic elements such as emotions, mood and feelings. In this way, frustration levels could be modeled to increase with prolonged waiting times, which would in turn decrease the likelihood of agents giving up their right of way too often. Other improvements concern the agents' perception and the number and complexity of their available actions. However, the most challenging task remains to implement models of internal perception and planning to increase the realism of the agents' overall behavior for traffic simulations in virtual environments.

Acknowledgements. The FIVIS project received additional funding from the Deutsche Gesetzliche Unfallversicherung (grant FP307). The AVeSi project is being funded by the FHprofUnt program of the BMBF (grant 17028X11).

References

1. Anderson, J., Bothell, D., Byrne, M., Douglass, S., Lebiere, C., Quinn, Y.: An integrated theory of the mind. Psychological Review 111, 1036–1060 (2004)
2. Bakkes, S., Spronck, P., van den Herik, J.: Rapid and reliable adaption of video game ai. IEEE Transactions on Compuational Intelligence and AI in Games 2(1), 93–104 (2009)
3. Borkenau, P., Ostendorf, F.: Neo-Fünf-Faktoren Inventar (NEO-FFI) nach Costa und McCrae. Hogrefe, Göttingen (1993)
4. Byrne, M.: Cognitive Architecture. In: Sears, A., Jacko, J.A. (eds.) The Human-Computer Interaction Handbook: Fundamentals, Evolving Technologies and Emerging Applications, pp. 97–117. Lawrence Erlbaum, Mahwah (2003)
5. Herpers, R., Scherfgen, D., Kutz, M., Bongartz, J., Hartmann, U., Schulzyk, O., Boronas, S., Saitov, T., Steiner, H., Reinert, D.: Multimedia Sensory Cue Processing in the FIVIS Simulation Environment. In: Ghinea, G., Andres, F., Gulliver, S. (eds.) Multiple Sensorial Media Advances and Applications: New Developments in MulSeMedia, pp. 217–233. IGI Global (2011)
6. Herzberg, P.: Beyond "accident-proneness": Using Five-Factor Model prototypes to predict driving behavior. J. of Res. in Personality 6(43), 1096–1100 (2009)
7. Kesting, A., Treiber, M.: Agents for traffic simulation. In: Uhrmacher, A.M., Weyns, D. (eds.) Multi-Agent Systems: Simulation and Applications, pp. 325–356. CRC Press, Boca Raton (2009)
8. Kutz, M., Herpers, R.: Urban Traffic Simulation for Games. In: Proc. of the Int. Conf. of Future of Game Design and Technology, pp. 181–185. ACM, New York (2008)
9. Laird, J.: Extending the Soar cognitive architecture. In: Wang, P., Goertzel, B., Franklin, S. (eds.) Proc. of the 2008 Conference on Artificial General Intelligence, pp. 224–235. IOS Press, Amsterdam (2008)
10. Langley, P., Choi, D.: A Unified Cognitive Architecture for Physical Agents. In: Cohn, A. (ed.) Proc. of the National Conf. on AI, pp. 1469–1474. AAAI Press (2006)
11. Lüdtke, A., Weber, L., Osterloh, J.-P., Wortelen, B.: Modeling Pilot and Driver Behavior for Human Error Simulation. In: Duffy, V.G. (ed.) ICDHM 2009. LNCS, vol. 5620, pp. 403–412. Springer, Heidelberg (2009)
12. Sharma, M., Holmes, M., Santamaria, J., Irani, A., Isbell, C., Ram, A.: Transfer learning in real-time strategy games using hybrid CBR/RL. In: Proc. of the 20th Int. Joint Conf. on AI, pp. 1041–1046. Morgan Kaufmann, San Francisco (2007)
13. Thurau, C., Bauckhage, C., Sagerer, G.: Learning Human-Like Movement Behavior for Computer Games. In: Proc. of the Int. Conf. on the Sim. of Adaptive Behavior, pp. 315–323. MIT Press (2004)
14. Treiber, M., Kesting, A.: Verkehrsdynamik- und Simulation. Springer, Heidelberg (2009)

Out of Context Augmented Navfields: Designing Crowd Choreographies

Guillaume Levieux, Stéphane Natkin, and Alexandre Topol

Centre d'Etudes et de Recherches en Informatique du CNAM
Conservatoire National des Arts et Métiers, Paris, France
forename.lastname@cnam.fr

Abstract. This paper presents a way to dynamically influence the shape
and movements of a simulated crowd. We propose a tool and system that
allows to modify a crowd's dynamics in an intuitive, semantically rich
and out of context fashion, while being independent from the global path
finding architecture and having a low computational cost. We follow a
mixed approach where user-specified navigation fields are combined with
steering and global A* pathfinding.

Keywords: crowd, choreography, navfield, simulation.

1 Influencing Crowds Dynamics

Many crowd simulation systems have been developed in the past few years. They
have multiple goals like the study of sociological or psychological principles,
simulation of a crowded building's evacuation, as well as digital entertainment
or military training [1], [2]. These systems use different crowd models, ranging
from fluids [3], particles [4], to basic entities influenced by a simple set of rules
[5] or even autonomous agents with rich decision models [6] [7] [8].

The choice of a crowd simulation model depends on many factors. One of the
biggest trade-off in crowd simulation is computing cost. The more complex an
agent decision is to calculate, the lowest the number of agents can be simulated
in real time. It may always be useful to have the most realistic agents, but the
model has to scale with the number of simulated agents.

Moreover, as Zhou et al stated it, a crowd simulation system needs to be considered from the designer point of view [2] [9]. Having a complex decision system
may lead to more realistic agents, but also make these agents less predictable
and harder to manipulate. Indeed, using autonomous agents leads to a bottom
up architecture, where the crowd's global behavior depends on the many local
decision made by the agents. When a designer wants to influence the crowd's
global dynamics, that is, the global shape and movement pattern of a large group
of agents, we should provide him with a high level tools that directly deals with
these dynamics. Our goal is to propose such a tool.

Our research takes place within the context of the Terra Dynamica project,
in whichF a consortium of industrials and researchers got together to built a

M. Herrlich, R. Malaka, and M. Masuch (Eds.): ICEC 2012, LNCS 7522, pp. 326–332, 2012.

virtual version of Paris city. This simulator has a wide application scope, ranging from urban planning to artistic experiments, and follows an autonomous agents approach. In this project, our goal is to propose a simulation technique that can seamlessly be integrated in an autonomous agent architecture, and let a designer easily influence the shape and moving patterns of a crowd.

Designing tools to control a crowd simulation is a particularly interesting topic. Indeed, the crowd's dynamics emerges from the more and more complex agents behaviour models we set up, but still need simple methods to influence the crowds behaviour, especially in entertainment purposes, where the goal is not to always have a realistic simulation but to reach specific aesthetic goals. Researchers have already proposed such kind of tools. Crowd Brush allow to modify crowd scenes in Real Time [9]. Oshita and Ogiwara's system allows to sketch a crowd's path [10]. ARCrowd allows to control a crowd in real time using augmented reality [11]. Kwon et al systems let the user customize the motion of a group of individuals [12]. Many systems use navfields, that is, grids of direction vectors, to author the navigation of a crowd [13] [14] [3] [15].

Unfortunately, neither of these systems completely addresses our design goals for the Terra Dynamica project, that we describe as follows :

1. **Intuitive**: our representation of the crowds dynamics needs to be easy to author, and represented in the most intuitive way.
2. **Provide a rich semantic** : we do not only want to specify a direction an agent in the crowd should follow, but also allow this direction to be modified within time, or have some stochastic properties.
3. **Out of context**: we want to specify a crowd's dynamic for a group of agents, regardless of the size of the group, of it's absolute location and without knowing the agents that will be involved. That way we can define reusable, generic movements and instantiate them when needed.
4. **Independent**: we want our system to be used in combination with standard A* path finding and state of the art steering. We need it to be activated only when needed, and to be integrated seamlessly in the standard navigation architecture.
5. **Not computationally expensive**: as we use this system in addition with a complex AI system, and as we need to modify the simulation in real time, we need our system to be as light as possible in term of computational cost.

We extend the navfield principle to provide the designer with a more expressive tool. We call these specific navfields "*Out of Context Augmented Navfields (OCANs)*". In the next section, we show how OCANs addresses the needs we have specified in this section.

2   Out of Context Augmented Navfields

We draw inspiration from navfields based systems. Defining a grid of vectors is an intuitive way to represent a crowd's dynamics. Given the right tools, one can paint the vectors on the grid, and easily define the desired movement [15,14].

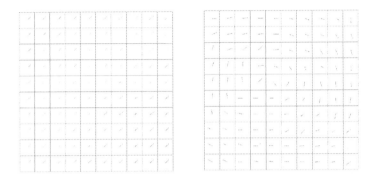

Fig. 1. Two OCANs

The vector field is indeed a nice way to represent a crowd's dynamics, as the information displayed on screen is the resulting movement influence we try to specify. The basic navfield given in fig 1 (left one) could easily be encoded as a mathematical function or a piece of scripted code but we think that the navfield itself is the most intuitive representation to show and manipulate.

We created a GUI tool to define OCANs (fig. 2). The user can easily define an OCAN and edit the various properties that makes OCANs semantically rich. The user can edit the vectors one by one or using a brush. The different tools on the right side of the screen allows to modify the OCAN properties that we define in the reminder of this article. The user can then save all OCAN's in an XML file that will be imported by the choreography manager.

In our system, the user can define a **sequence** of OCANs. Each OCAN in the sequence has a pre-defined life span, and when this lifespan is over, the next OCAN of the sequence is instantiated. Thus, we can define a follow up of

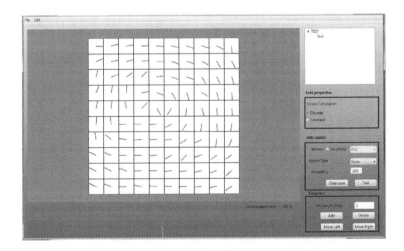

Fig. 2. OCAN's Editor GUI

grids, which allows to define more complex crowd movements. Moreover, each OCAN is annotated by the user. It can be **continuous** or **discrete**, which means that the direction vector given to a specific agent only depends on it's discrete position within the grid. When continuous, the direction vector is the mean of surrounding vectors, weighted by the distance between the location of each cell center and the agent. The user can also assign a **probability** to each cell of the OCAN. That way, and agent will have a given probability to be influenced by the cell, and thus only a portion of the surrounding crowd will be affected. Last, any grid cell can be defined as a **placeholder**. If there is no agent in this cell, the nearest agent in the OCAN will be assigned a direction vector toward the placeholder. That way, it is possible to define formations that the agents within the grid will try to assume, in a best effort way.

OCANs are thus defined out of a specific context. One can define a grid representing a specific crowd movement, and instantiate it later at any location, in real time. Then, it will automatically impact the crowd at this location, influencing their predefined direction vector. We use a specific software component, the choreography manager, that dynamically instantiate OCANs during the simulation, with the desired location, scale and orientation. An OCAN can be instantiated on various requests: for instance a scenario manager can ask for it, or an agent that is a squad leader and want his group to follow a specific dynamic.

However, as OCANs are defined out of a specific context and instantiated on demand, we must be able to integrate them regardless of the navigation algorithm that is used. Our only recommendation is that path planning and steering have to be defined as two different navigation steps. This is very often the case: in video games for instance A* is very often used to generate a global path, while different steering algorithms compute the fine grain movement of the agent [16]. As a result, OCANs will only override the global path finding direction when an agent steps on the grid. The steering mechanism will always be active and let the agent move in a way that is coherent with the other dynamic and static colliders, but it's main direction will be defined by the OCAN. When the agent leaves the OCAN, he will rely again on it's previous path-finding algorithm.

When under an OCAN's influence, the agent's direction is mainly determined by the cell he's in. We thus just have to convert the agent's position in the OCAN's local space to get this vector, defined by a 4*4 matrix, which is a very cheap calculus. If the grid is continuous, the calculation cost is just a bit higher because we compute a weighted sum of the surrounding vertices. The calculation cost is the highest with placeholder cells, because we need to find the closest agent. This process is speeded up by a previous space partitioning [17], allowing to find the closest agents without parsing all of them.

3   Integration Flow

The previous diagram shows more in details how the OCAN system integrates into a standard path finding architecture, as provided by the TerraDynmica

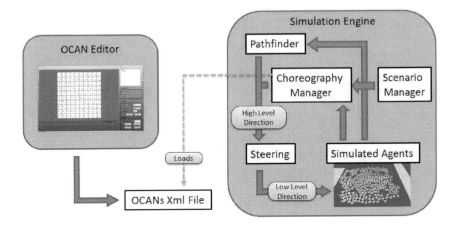

Fig. 3. The OCAN System

simulation engine (fig. 3). Using our dedicated tool, the designer creates sequences of OCANs. Each OCAN sequence is identified by a unique number and stored in a common XML file. When started, the choreography manager, part of the simulation engine, loads the XML file. The simulated agents can go to a desired location using the pathfinding system. The global pathfinding engine will generate a path, that will be filtered by the steering engine to accommodate with local constraints.

But when requested, the choreography engine will instantiate a specific OCAN. It will have the same properties than when designed in the editor, with a specific location and orientation decided at runtime. Many instances of the same OCAN can thus be active at the same time, at different locations. For evey agent whose position is inside one of the instantiated OCANs, global path finding will be replaced by a vector calculated by the choreography manager, based on the current agent position in the OCAN.

As a result, the choregraphy manager, the pathfinder and steering algorithm all work at the same time in an integrated fashion. The OCAN is just a way to by pass the agent decision process with regard to it's current global direction, only where and when needed. For instance, we plan to use OCANs to simulate military tactics in crowd management simulation. Indeed, extract a leader from a civilian crowd responds to a specific choreography : a first sqad runs toward the leader in a triangle shape to penetrate the crowd, expand it's position to make the crowd step back and isolate the leader. Meanwhile, another group follows and catches the leader. Then the first group concentrate again to secure the leader and everybody get back out of the crowd. This kind of choreography can be easily described using a sequence of OCANs, spawned by the squad leader when needed.

4 Conclusion

In this article, we propose a simple way to alter the dynamics of a crowd, using Out of Context Augmented Navfields. As we have shown, such a system can provide an intuitive, semantically rich way to define the shape and movement of a crowd, while having a low computational cost and be integrated in a standard navigation system. The OCAN system place itself between the global path finding algorithm and the local steering algorithm, overriding the global path finding only when needed. As a result, we do not have to take into account the global goal of the agents or the way they avoid obstacles, but just apply a local, smooth influence on their moving dynamics.

The next step of these research is to broadly evaluate the usability of our system, and to enhance it with an even richer semantic.

References

1. Musse, S.R., Ulicny, B., Aubel, A., Thalmann, D.: Groups and crowd simulation. In: ACM SIGGRAPH 2005 Courses. SIGGRAPH 2005. ACM, New York (2005)
2. Zhou, S., Chen, D., Cai, W., Luo, L., Low, M.Y.H., Tian, F., Tay, V.S.-H., Ong, D.W.S., Hamilton, B.D.: Crowd modeling and simulation technologies. ACM Trans. Model. Comput. Simul. 20, 1–20 (2010)
3. Chenney, S.: Flow tiles. In: Proceedings of the 2004 ACM SIGGRAPH/Eurographics Symposium on Computer Animation, SCA 2004, Aire-la-Ville, Switzerland, Switzerland. Eurographics Association, pp. 233–242 (2004)
4. Chen, Y., Wang, Z.: Formation control: A review and a new consideration. In: 2005 IEEE/RSJ International Conference on Intelligent Robots and Systems, pp. 3181–3186 (2005)
5. Helbing, D., Molnar, P.: Social force model for pedestrian dynamics. Physical Review E 51, 4282 (1995)
6. Jiang, H., Xu, W., Mao, T., Li, C., Xia, S., Wang, Z.: A semantic environment model for crowd simulation in multilayered complex environment. In: Proceedings of the 16th ACM Symposium on Virtual Reality Software and Technology, VRST 2009, pp. 191–198. ACM, New York (2009)
7. Shao, W., Terzopoulos, D.: Autonomous pedestrians. In: Proceedings of the 2005 ACM SIGGRAPH/Eurographics Symposium on Computer Animation, pp. 19–28. ACM (2005)
8. Sakuma, T., Mukai, T., Kuriyama, S.: Psychological model for animating crowded pedestrians. Computer Animation and Virtual. Worlds 16, 3–4 (2005)
9. Ulicny, B., de Heras Ciechomski, P., Thalmann, D.: Crowdbrush: interactive authoring of real-time crowd scenes. In: ACM SIGGRAPH 2005 Courses, SIGGRAPH 2005. ACM, New York (2005)
10. Oshita, M., Ogiwara, Y.: Sketch-Based Interface for Crowd Animation. In: Butz, A., Fisher, B., Christie, M., Krüger, A., Olivier, P., Therón, R. (eds.) SG 2009. LNCS, vol. 5531, pp. 253–262. Springer, Heidelberg (2009)
11. Zheng, F., Li, H.: Arcrowd-a tangible interface for interactive crowd simulation. In: 2010 9th IEEE International Symposium on Mixed and Augmented Reality (ISMAR), pp. 287–288 (October 2010)

12. Kwon, T., Lee, K.H., Lee, J., Takahashi, S.: Group motion editing. ACM Trans. Graph. 27, 80:1–80:8 (2008)
13. Jin, X., Wang, C.C.L., Huang, S., Xu, J.: Interactive control of real-time crowd navigation in virtual environment. In: Proceedings of the 2007 ACM Symposium on Virtual Reality Software and Technology, VRST 2007, pp. 109–112. ACM, New York (2007)
14. Patil, S., van den Berg, J., Curtis, S., Lin, M.C., Manocha, D.: Directing crowd simulations using navigation fields. IEEE Transactions on Visualization and Computer Graphics 99(RapidPosts) (2010)
15. Alexander, B.: Flow fields for movement and obstacle avoidance. In: AI Game Programming Wisdom 3. Steve Rabin (2006)
16. Rabin, S.: Movement and Pathfinding. In: AI Game Programming Wisdom 4. Course Technology, Cengage Learning, pp. 59–203 (2008)
17. Reynolds, C.: Big fast crowds on ps3. In: Proceedings of the 2006 ACM SIGGRAPH Symposium on Videogames, pp. 113–121. ACM (2006)

Priority Level Planning in Kriegspiel

Paolo Ciancarini and Andrea Gasparro

Dipartimento di Informatica
University of Bologna, Italy

Abstract. Back in 1950, Shannon introduced planning in board games
like Chess as a selective approach, where the main idea is to select specific
branches of the game tree that satisfy certain conditions. He contrasted
this approach with brute force Minimax-like methods, based on an exhaustive search of the game tree, that aims to select the best path inside
a given search horizon. Historically, the brute force approach won hands
down against planning in complex games such as Chess, as the strongest
Chess programs nowadays all exploit brute force algorithms. However,
planning is still interesting and even necessary in some game-playing domains, for instance based on incomplete information, where there is no
way to evaluate precisely or even build the game tree. In this paper we
describe a technique that produced positive results in Kriegspiel, a variant of Chess played as an incomplete information game. Our main result
is the definition of an algorithm for combining MonteCarlo search with
planning; we tested the algorithm on a strong Kriegspiel program based
on MonteCarlo search, and obtained a clear improvement.

1 Introduction

Partial information games are a challenging domain to study and test decision
making under uncertainty, that is a key concept in game theory and also a
widely studied topic in many economical simulations [4]. For instance, uncertainty can be introduced in perfect information games by making invisible the
opponent moves (as in a war-game referred by an arbiter [9]). This invisibility
usually introduces important changes to any algorithmic playing approach: the
search space size and the related game tree branching usually grow dramatically,
whereas one of the key results in games theory, namely Zermelo's theorem [13],
is no more valid because its assumptions do not apply. More important, these
changes reflect on the effectiveness of playing algorithms which work well for the
standard game [2] but must be completely redefined for its variants based on
partial information.

Kriegspiel, the board game we are focusing on in this paper, is a practical
example of our previous statements: removing most of the information given to a
player about his opponent's moves, increases dramatically the average branching
factor during middle game from 33, that is the Chess branching factor, to 33!,
that is Kriegspiel branching because a player can try its pseudolegal moves in
any order. We remind that the branching factor greatly affects the performances

M. Herrlich, R. Malaka, and M. Masuch (Eds.): ICEC 2012, LNCS 7522, pp. 333–340, 2012.

of Minimax and its derivative algorithms. Hence, the best Kriegspiel artificial player, as described in [6], is not based on Minimax, but on Monte Carlo Tree search instead.

This paper has the following structure: in section 2 we provide a description of Kriegspiel, introducing its rules and most important features, from the point of view of an artificial player. Section 3 contains a description of the state of the art, with special interest to Darkboard, the current world champion of Kriegspiel. Section 4 presents the main topic of this paper, namely our original planning based approach, that we applied to Darkboard to play Kriegspiel, but that can be applied to other playing domains based on partial information and with a large branching factor. In section 5 we present the results obtained by an experimental player, based on the technique we presented, matched against the current world champion program, Darkboard. Finally, in section 6 we summarize and discuss our results, concluding with the future developments we are considering.

2   Kriegspiel

Kriegspiel, or *Blind Chess*, is a chess variant invented by Michael Henry Temple at the end of the XIX century, first played and standardized at the famous London chess club "The Gambit". It can be considered a descendant of an already existent prussian war game, named *Kriegspiele*, invented at the beginning of XIX century for training Prussian army officers. Kriegspiel rules are the same as chess for what concern the goal of the game and piece movement rules, but differently from Chess, there are three main actors involved: the white player, the black player and an umpire.

Each player can see only its pieces, while from the point of view of the umpire, Kriegspiel is just a normal chess game. Being the only one informed on the real state of the board, the umpire is in charge to inform players if the moves they make are legal or they are not. For instance, a move could be illegal because it exposes the king to a check, or because the trajectory to a square is not completely free. If a move is refused by the referee, a player has to chose a different one, that is again evaluated by the umpire, and so on.

Thus, designing a program to play Kriegspiel is very different from designing a program to play Chess, due to information on the game state only partially available. Partial information grows the branching factor, while the space state remains the same of chess, that Shannon estimated at 10^{42} [11]. The reason of the larger branching factor resides in the fact that a Kriegspiel player can try its pseudo-legal moves in any order: if a move is legal then it must stay, else the player must try another move. Thus, all possible permutations of pseudo-legal moves should be enumerated to define the branching factor of Kriegspiel.

This huge increment in the branching factor reflects the fact that in each state a player does not know what is the current position of the opponent's pieces. Hence, an artificial player should somehow keep trace of all the possible configurations of the board, in each different moment of the game. This leads to the need to abstract away different positions, that are indistinguishable from the agent point of view, into a single representation: this is the key idea behind Metapositions, first applied in Shogi [10] and successfully reused in Kriegspiel [1].

The reason why we have chosen Kriegspiel as our domain of study is that it is not yet a fully explored game, with significative differences from Phantom Go and other imperfect information games, as that the nature of Kriegspiel's uncertainty is completely dynamic, making it an interesting environment to simulate different kind of real life tasks.

3   Planning in Board Games: State of the Art

Recent researches in games like Phantom Go and Kriegspiel contributed to focus on a relatively unexplored category of partial information games, derived by well known perfect information games, introducing a concept of invisible moves. This area proved to be a challenging domain for artificial players based on brute force, leading to the development of strategies to handle meta states, with the aim to reduce the space state and the branching. This happened exploring metapositions in in Kriegspiel, as described in [5].

A strategy similar to the one used to play Go proved to be quite effective in Phantom Go, as described in [3], also because of the monotonous decrease of uncertainty that makes progress somehow simpler to handle, in comparison with Kriegspiel.

Until a few years ago, only a few amount of research had been devoted to Monte Carlo in games with dynamic uncertainty, with the notable exceptions of [8], which first studied planning based on MonteCarlo, and [7], which developed a more efficient approach based on a bandit algorithm called UCT (Upper Confidence bounds applied to Trees). We exploited UCT in the development of Darkboard, that is basically a program combining UCT with a node evaluation function [6].

The contributes to the study of Kriegspiel, brought by the experiments conducted developing the artificial player Darkboard, were the most significant progress in the study of the game, involving for the first time the use of metapositions in Kriegspiel, also introducing a Monte Carlo based approach to handle middle-game. Darkboard represents the state of the art in Kriegspiel playing as it is also the current Kriegspiel world champion.

4   Priority Level Planning in Kriegspiel

Kriegspiel is a hard game to play for rational agents: due to the huge branching factor mentioned above, in approaches of Shannon's "Type B", that is brute force, the ability to evaluate different states plays a key role in reducing the search space, that directly reflects on the effectiveness of brute force analysis. Unfortunately, even with the help of Metapositions, this is a very hard task for artificial players, as it involves the ability to understand the "meaning" of a position.

An approach based on planning is a more natural choice to provide an agent with a "human like" understanding of a position. However, planning was not successful in chess-playing programs, as it reduces consistently the speed of states evaluation and, consequently, the horizon of the program. This actually cuts off the possibility to base the evaluation of a state on a long range analysis.

Our approach is then based on a planning technique, meant to predict the evolution of game tree branches, basing only on factors that must be present in the present state. This requires the search of "structural factors" included in each state, that can be associated to a predictable evolution in the long run.

This technique seems to apply perfectly with Kriegspiel, because strategical elements are included in each state. Those elements can be used to form a plan, where a plan is just a sequence of transitions which fit the actual configuration of the board. An example of the strategical elements we are speaking about can be the presence of open files, if heavy pieces are still on the board, etc.

In this paper we focus on the middle-game, as it is the game phase where introducing a priority level planner does not cause any sensible change in move generation's speed. We have built a planner which during middle-game (which starts when the opening phase ends, i.e. when the program exits from its opening book, and ends when the position has no more pawns) splits move generation in two phases: first, it tries to elaborate short term plans, aiming to reach "important" goals which are enough "close", if there are not such goals reachable from the current state, it tries a long term evaluation of each *interesting* candidate transition originated from the current state.

This algorithm requires the definition of two different categories of goals:

Priority Goals. Goals that represent a short term advantage. Examples of short term goals may be piece capture, king safety, etc.

Long Term Goals. Examples of long term goals may be placing our pieces in favorable positions, regrouping pieces in a way that makes easy for them to cooperate, etc. Each goal has a priority that represent its importance. This category includes what a chess player could call strategic or long-term goals.

The goal sets were defined according to standard chess theory. This highlights an advantage of choosing Kriegspiel as our applicative domain: a Kriegspiel planner can benefit from the well known theory of Chess, to identify key factors in a position, as long as it evaluates those factors in his own way, considering the significant differences introduced by partial information.

Our algorithm for move generation includes the following three steps:

EVALUATION. The program evaluates the current board state, searching for priority goals. This task is simplified by Kriegspiel rules, since we identify priority targets thanks to umpire messages informing that a pawn try is available, that a piece has been captured or that one of the player has delivered a check.

SELECTION. If a priority goal is reachable, the goal set includes only the moves that are supposed to lead to the goal, else the agent analyzes each action within two level of depths searching for long term goals.

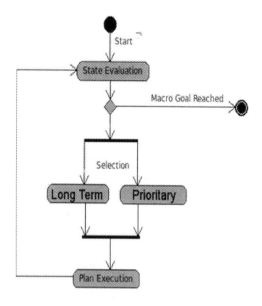

Fig. 1. Activity Diagram representing the move generation process

CONSTRUCTION. The program selects the path with the highest rating. If a priority goal is detected, this unifies with the path to reach this goal.

This description highlights the fundamental importance of long term goals in move generation, as priority goals cover only a small set of possibilities. At the same time, long term goals deal with strategic factors. This technique may be promising in a domain with a clear notion of strategy, as it is the key concept used to predict the quality of a path, without the need to evaluate a large set of states.

This also means that this technique can be applied not only to Kriegspiel, but also to any strategic game with partial information and a large branching factor.

Fig 1 summarizes the process we just described.

The above algorithm contains the key idea of our approach. However, if implemented verbatim it would be be highly ineffective in practice. The reason is that an agent whose move generation relies entirely upon its goal set, when no priority goal is available, is forced to define a huge number of goals to deal with each possible situation. This leads to two different problems: first, it turns out to lack flexibility to handle a complex game like Kriegspiel; second, this does not correspond to what we defined as a long term goal set.

Instead, before searching for long term goals, we execute a one step Monte Carlo analysis to filter moves that have an evaluation below some threshold. After doing so, we execute the steps described above. Nothing changes in handling short term plans, as it does not involve nothing else than an "automatic reaction" to priority goals detection. The modified behavior is shown in Fig 2.

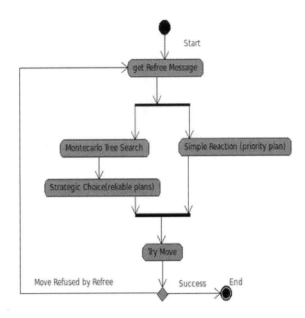

Fig. 2. Activity Diagram representing the move generation in Strategic Darkboard

This second approach offers two advantages. First, it does not force the agent to misrepresent the idea behind the concept of long term goals. The second advantage is that filtering the moves that the planner has to analyze reduces the computational cost dramatically, as it cuts the branching factor, while the brute force method may be limited to a very short depth. Thus, both strategies benefit one of each other.

5   Experimental Results

To evaluate the result obtained introducing a priority level planning in Darkboard, we tested our enhanced player in tournaments against other programs. Those programs were:

- **World Champion** The current world champion version of Darkboard, presented in [6].
- **Random Player** A pseudo-random player, useful to evaluate the behavior of our program against an unpredictable opponent.
- **Strategic Darkboard** The World Champion program enriched with a priority level planner.

Our experiments consisted in tournaments of 20 games between Strategic Darkboard and another program. This is a well known technique, since the first Belle's experiments by Ken Thompson [12].

Table 1. Results of playing experiments

Opponent	Strategic DB	Opponent
World Champion	61%	39%
Random Player	85%	15%

The first series of experiments, consisting in 3 tournaments of 20 games each against the Random Player, confirmed that the random player is not an interesting opponent, as the average result is 85% of success for Strategic Darkboard, where all games that were not won were draws for stalemate (if the opponent king is in check and cannot move a game is draw according to chess rules).

The second series of experiments was far more interesting, consisting in 5 tournaments of 20 games each between Strategic Darkboard and the World Champion: it ended with the average success rate of 61% for Strategic Darkboard. Thus, according to the standard Elo scale, Strategic Darkboard gained a class, compared to Darkboard previous's version.

The table summarizes the results obtained in our tests.

A second set of experiments against human players is currently taking place on the Internet Computer Club (ICC), which hosts the largest Kriegspiel community. The partial results until now indicate a smaller improvement, but it will take some time to collect enough data to drawn some definitive conclusion.

6   Conclusions and Further Developments

One problem when implementing a program for playing an imperfect information game with a high branching factor is the horizon effect. Because of that, planning may be an interesting approach in such a domain, due to the fact that a planner does not analyze the totality of the states, but instead it focusses only on promising branches.

The technique we have proposed is a hybrid between planning and brute force, developed to manage two different aspect: short term game playing, that is based on brute force and somehow does not care about the branching factor, since there is a priority goal reachable inside the horizon of the agent, and long term playing, basing on the notion of strategy.

While experimental results are promising, it is important to remember that this technique relies heavily on the presence of a dense notion of strategy in the application domain, that is a key condition for limiting the depth of the searching algorithm. This limitation however is double edged, since a dense notion of strategy leads to impressing performances as shown by the experiment conducted against the world champion program of Kriegspiel.

A further development will focus on refining the long term goal set; in our experience human players, that currently outperform our Kriegspiel program, orient their game playing according to repetitive strategies: analyzing an already available collection of Kriegspiel games with a pattern recognition algorithm,may lead to identify new goals or even just to update the already existing one ratings, hopefully improving the long term view of the agent, that's the most interesting feature of this technique.

Finally, even if we obtained some interesting results, Strategic Darkboard played with a handicap: in fact, the goal set used by the program is quite limited. Future development will focus on additional strategies to populate the goal set with efficient targets, thus we expect an improvement of the playing strength.

References

1. Bolognesi, A., Ciancarini, P.: Searching over Metapositions in Kriegspiel. In: van den Herik, J., Netanyahu, N. (eds.) 4th Int. Conf. on Computer and Games, RamatGan, Israel (2004)
2. Campbell, M., Marsland, T.: A comparison of minimax tree search algorithms. Artificial Intelligence 20(4), 347–367 (1983)
3. Cazenave, T.: A Phantom-Go Program. In: van den Herik, H.J., Hsu, S.-C., Hsu, T.-s., Donkers, H.H.L.M(J.) (eds.) CG 2005. LNCS, vol. 4250, pp. 120–125. Springer, Heidelberg (2006)
4. Ciancarini, P., DallaLibera, F., Maran, F.: Decision Making under Uncertainty: A Rational Approach to Kriegspiel. In: van den Herik, J., Uiterwijk, J. (eds.) Advances in Computer Chess 8, pp. 277–298. Univ. of Rulimburg (1997)
5. Ciancarini, P., Favini, G.: Representing Kriegspiel States with Metapositions. In: Proc. 20th Int. Joint Conf. on Artificial Intelligence (IJCAI 2007), India, pp. 2450–2455 (January 2007)
6. Ciancarini, P., Favini, G.: Monte Carlo Tree Search in Kriegspiel. Artificial Intelligence 174(11), 670–684 (2010)
7. Kocsis, L., Szepesvári, C.: Bandit Based Monte-Carlo Planning. In: Fürnkranz, J., Scheffer, T., Spiliopoulou, M. (eds.) ECML 2006. LNCS (LNAI), vol. 4212, pp. 282–293. Springer, Heidelberg (2006)
8. Chung, M., Buro, M., Schaeffer, J.: Monte Carlo planning in RTS games. In: Kendall, G., Lucas, S. (eds.) Proc. IEEE Symposium on Computational Intelligence and Games, Colchester, Essex, pp. 117–124. IEEE Computer Society (April 2005)
9. Perla, P.: The Art of Wargaming. Naval Institute Press, Annapolis (1990)
10. Sakuta, M.: Deterministic Solving of Problems with Uncertainty. PhD thesis, Shizuoka University, Japan (2001)
11. Shannon, C.: Programming a computer for playing Chess. Philosophical Magazine (Series 7), 256–275 (1950)
12. Thompson, K.: Computer Chess Strenght. In: Clarke, M. (ed.) Advances in Computer Chess 3, pp. 55–56. Pergamon (1982)
13. Zermelo, E.: On an Application of Set Theory to the Theory of the Game of Chess. In: Proceedings of the Fifth International Congress of Mathematicians, Cambridge, UK, pp. 501–504 (1913)

Writing Real-Time .Net Games in Casanova

Giuseppe Maggiore, Pieter Spronck, Renzo Orsini, Michele Bugliesi,
Enrico Steffinlongo, and Mohamed Abbadi

Università Ca' Foscari Venezia
DAIS - Computer Science
{maggiore,orsini,bugliesi,esteffin,mabbadi}@dais.unive.it
Tilburg University
Tilburg Center for Creative Computing
p.spronck@gmail.com

Abstract. In this paper we show the Casanova language (and its accompanying
design pattern, Rule-Script-Draw) in action by building a series of games with
it. In particular we discuss how Casanova is suitable for making games regardless of their genre: the Game of Life, a shooter game, an adventure game and a
strategy game. We also discuss the difference between Casanova and existing
frameworks.

Keywords: Game development, Casanova, databases, languages, functional
programming, F#.

1   Introduction

There is a growing, substantial interest in research on principled design techniques and
on cost-effective development technologies for game architectures. This is driven by the
diffusion of independent games, an increased need for fast prototyping gameplay mechanics [1], and the need to develop serious or research games [2] for which the same
budget of blockbuster titles cannot be spared. Moreover, as the games market keeps
growing in size [3] this need is further emphasized. Our present endeavor makes a step
along the directions of studying disciplined models for game development.

In this paper we discuss the Casanova language for making games. We do not
present Casanova as such, that being the focus of other papers [5,6,7]. Rather, given
that Casanova exists and works already (albeit under a prototypical implementation),
we study and measure its feasibility when used for making games. We will thus try
and answer the research question *"does Casanova make game development easier?"*
by identifying a series of general, orthogonal activities in game development that we
show built in Casanova, and we will compare our implementation with other languages. We start with a discussion of related work in section 2. We give a first description
of Casanova in section 3. We discuss with detailed examples how to make actual
games with Casanova in section 4. In section 5 we compare Casanova, C# and F#
when used for the games of the preceding section. In sections 6 and 7 we conclude by

M. Herrlich, R. Malaka, and M. Masuch (Eds.): ICEC 2012, LNCS 7522, pp. 341–348, 2012.

discussing some of the extensions that we are planning on adding to Casanova with our future research.

2   Related Work

To build the logic of a game the two most common software architectures are object-oriented hierarchies and component-based systems. In an object-oriented engine the hierarchy is rooted in the Entity class [9]. A component-based system defines each game entity as a composition of components that provide reusable, specific functionality [10]. These two more traditional approaches both suffer from a noticeable shortcoming: they focus exclusively on representing single entities and their update operations in isolation: each entity needs to update itself at each tick of the simulation. This shifts the game focus away from the interactions between entities (collision detection, AI, etc.), from which most of a game complexity comes. Another particularly nasty problem that arises in traditional game development is that of representing long-running behaviors of entities; such behaviors are those processes performed by game entities which last many ticks of the game loop to complete. These behaviors are coded as explicit state machines inside the entities, thereby forcing entities to store spurious data that does not have to do with the entity logical model but rather with the representation of its state machines.

Alternative paradigms have been experimented as part of various research efforts: functional reactive programming (FRP, see [11]), a data-flow approach where values are automatically propagated along a dependency graph that represents the computation; and automatically optimized SQL-queries for games (the SGL language, see [12]). FRP mitigates the problem of representing long-running behaviors, but it offers little else to game development, while SGL focuses exclusively on defining the tick function and not on representing long-running processes.

We have designed Casanova around all these issues: Casanova promotes entities that interact with each other, queries on the game world, long-running behaviors, automated drawing of the game entities, and even consistency of the game world.

3   The Casanova Language

The Casanova language belongs to the ML family (F# in particular, with list comprehensions inspired from the elegant Haskell syntax). Its main design focus is syntactic simplicity, where the language is built around few linguistic primitives that are powerful enough to be combined into many games.

A Casanova game begins with the definition of a series of data structures, which are the world and its entities. The updates of an entity are contained in its rules, a series of methods that take the same name of the field they update at each tick; a rule is invoked automatically for each entity of the game, and it receives as input the current state of world, the current state of the entity being updated, and the time delta between the current frame and the previous frame. All rules do not interfere with each other, can be computed in parallel, and exhibit *transactional* behavior; this avoids temporal inconsistencies where the game world is partially updated. Entities may also have drawable fields such as text, sprites or 3D models; these fields are updated through rules, and at each tick all drawable entities are grouped into *layers* (layers specify a series of draw settings) for drawing.

We could define a hypothetical game world as a series of balls. The world also features a sprite layer, to which renderables will be assigned (Listing 1).

```
type World =   { Sprites    : SpriteLayer
                 Balls      : var<list<Ball>> }
```

Listing 1. A world of balls

Each ball (Listing 2) contains a position and a velocity, in addition to a sprite for drawing. The position is updated by moving it along the velocity, and the sprite position is taken from the entity position:

```
type Ball = {
    Position    : Vector2<m>
    Velocity    : Vector2<m/s>
    Sprite      : DrawableSprite {
    rule Position(world,self,dt) = self.Position + dt * self.Velocity
    rule Sprite.Position(world,self,dt) = self.Position
```

Listing 2. Ball

The initial state of the game features no initial balls and the empty sprite layer. We omit this listing as it is rather straightforward.

We use the main script of the game to create random balls every few seconds (Listing 3).

```
let main world =
  repeat { wait 1.0
           world.Balls.Add … }
```

Listing 3. Spawning balls

4   Making Games with Casanova

To assess the effectiveness of Casanova as a game development language we have undertaken two parallel development initiatives. One such initiative is [13], where we have built a series of small samples that are easy to understand and manipulate; these samples are a series of real-time games, chosen so as to see Casanova in action in different sub-domains of the real-time game genre (possibly the most widespread nowadays). These samples are an asteroid shooter game, an action/adventure game and a strategy game. We will not present the full samples themselves, which are available online. We will now focus on a series of fundamental "development activities" that we believe to be nicely exemplified by our samples; these activities cover some of the most common and important pieces that can be customized, combined and extended into almost any game: *(i)* defining a *player avatar*, handling his input and his shooting; *(ii)* *spawning obstacles* randomly; *(iii)* handling *collisions* between projectiles and obstacles; *(iv)* *active entities* such as bases or buildings that produce units; *(v)* *selection-based input* mechanisms. We show *(i)*, *(ii)*, and *(iii)* from the asteroid shooter in 4.1, and *(iv)* and *(v)* are shown from the RTS game in 4.2. The primitives shown here are just samples, but they can be recombined, modified and reassembled into many new games; we also point the existence of [14], an upcoming (commercial) strategy game that is derived from the RTS sample and that we are building as an ongoing study of how to create non-trivial games with Casanova with this extension process.

4.1   Player Avatar and Shooting Stuff

The asteroid shooter game is a simple shooter game where asteroids fall from the top of the screen towards the bottom and must be shot down by the player.

In this game we will describe how to define: *(i)* the *player avatar*, his movement and shooting; *(ii)* the *spawning of obstacles* such as asteroids; and *(iii)* detection of *collisions* between asteroids and projectiles.

The game world (Listing 4) contains a list of projectiles, asteroids, the cannon, the current score, plus sprite layers for the main scene and the game UI. The game world removes asteroids and projectiles when they exit the screen or collide with each other, and it handles the current score (which is the number of destroyed asteroids).

```
type World = {
    Sprites         : SpriteLayer
    UI              : SpriteLayer
    Asteroids       : var<list<Asteroid>>
    Projectiles     : var<list<Projectile>>
    Cannon          : Cannon }
    rule Asteroids(world,dt) =
        [a | a <- state.Asteroids && a.Colliders.Length = 0 && a.Position.Y < 100.0<m>]
    rule Projectiles(world,dt) =
        [p | p <- state.Projectiles && p.Colliders.Length = 0 && p.Position.Y > 0.0<m>]
```
Listing 4. Asteroids world

The player is represented by a cannon (similarly it might be represented by a moving ship) as an entity that contains a sprite, an angle, and two boolean movement flags set from the input script that determine the variation of the angle and which are reset to false at every tick; the rotation of the sprite is taken from the current angle of the cannon (Listing 5).

```
type Cannon = {
    Sprite          : DrawableSprite
    Angle           : float<rad>
    MoveLeft        : var<bool>
    MoveRight       : var<bool> }
    rule Angle(world,self,dt) =
        self.Angle + if self.MoveLeft then dt elif self.MoveRight then -dt else 0.0<rad>
    rule MoveLeft(world,self,dt) = false
    rule MoveRight(world,self,dt) = false
    rule Sprite.Rotation(world,self,dt) = self.Angle
```
Listing 5. Cannon

The input script that modifies the rotation of the cannon simply checks if the appropriate key is currently pressed, and if so the cannon movement values are set (Listing 6).

```
{ return is_key_down Keys.Left } => { state.Cannon.MoveLeft := true },
{ return is_key_down Keys.Right } => { state.Cannon.MoveRight := true }
```
Listing 6. Cannon movement

Similarly, projectiles are generated (or "spawned", Listing 7) whenever the space key is pressed; contrary to movement, though, after a projectile is spawned the script waits one-tenth of a second to ensure that projectiles are not shot with a frequency of one per frame. It is worth noticing that such a simple activity would require a timer-based event infrastructure that can be quite tedious to write in a traditional language; for example, a timer to wait after the spawning of a projectile would need to be stored, declared, and consulted manually at each tick.

```
{ return is_key_down Keys.Space } => {
    state.Projectiles.Add …
    wait 0.1<s> }
```

Listing 7. Shooting

Asteroids are generated with a simple recursive script that waits a random amount of time and then adds the asteroid to the game world (Listing 8).

```
repeat {
    wait (random(1.0<s>,3.0<s>))
    state.Asteroids.Add …
}
```

Listing 8. Spawning asteroids

Collision detection is simple as well: both asteroids and projectiles compute the list of colliders against themselves; this list is then used in the query shown above in the definition of the game world to cull away asteroids (or projectiles) that are hit by other entities (Listing 9).

```
type Asteroid =
    …
    rule Colliders(world,self,dt) =
        [x | x <- get_colliders world && distance(self.Position, x.Position) < 10.0f]
```

Listing 9. Asteroids collision detection

4.2   Active Map Entities and Selection-Based Input

The strategy game features a series of planets that produce ships, which can then be sent to conquer other planets. In this game we can see: *(iv) active entities*, such as planets, that represent complex components of the game scenario; and *(v)* complex *selection-based input* mechanisms based on the selection of game entities and the interaction with the selected entities. We represent the game world as a series of planets, ships, plus the currently selected planet; the game world also contains sprite layers for rendering the game entities and UI, plus a boolean that allows the game battles to tick at fixed time intervals rather than at each tick of the game (Listing 10).

```
type World = {
    Sprites         : SpriteLayer
    UI              : SpriteLayer
    Planets         : list<Planet>
    Fleets          : var<list<Fleet>>
    TickBattles     : var<bool>
    SourcePlanet    : var<Option<ref<Planet>>> }
rule Fleets(world,dt) =
    [f | f <- self.Fleets && f.Alive && (not(f.Arrived) || f.Fighting)]
```

Listing 10. RTS world

Planets manage the battles in their orbit (which determine the owner of the planet) and ship production; in addition to their other fields, planets store the current owner, the number of allied ships stationed on the planet, and the percentage of production for the next ship; furthermore, a planet maintains a list of the fleets that are targeting itself for attacking or defending it (Listing 11).

```
type Planet = {
    Owner              : Player
    … }
rule Owner(world,self,dt) =
    if self.Armies <= 0 && self.AttackingFleets.Length > 0 then
        self.AttackingFleets[0].Owner
    else self.Owner
…
```

Listing 11. Planet definition

Input scripts manage the selection of a new planet by waiting for a left click of the mouse and then setting the SourcePlanet field of the game world (Listing 12).

```
{ return mouse_clicked_left() } => {
    let mouse = mouse_position()
    let clicked =
        [p | p <- world.Planets && distance(p.Position,mouse) < 10.0 && p.Owner =
Human]
    if clicked <> [] then return Some(clicked.Head)
    else return None } => fun p -> { world.SourcePlanet := Some(p) },
```

Listing 12. Planet selection

Similarly, when the user right clicks if there is an active selection some ships are sent (Listing 13).

```
{ return mouse_clicked_right() && world.SourcePlanet <> None } => {
    let mouse = mouse_position()
    let clicked = [p | p <- world.Planets && distance(p.Position,mouse) < 10.0]
    if clicked <> [] then return Some(clicked.[0],world.SourcePlanet.Value)
    else return None } => fun (source,target) -> { mk_fleet source target }
```

Listing 13. Issuing orders

5   Final Assessment

Assessing the quality of a programming language for a given activity is a daunting task. It is with this in mind that we proceed with offering a series of arguments in answer to our original claim that Casanova is better suited than traditional languages such as C# for real-time game development. Casanova programs are overall much shorter than equivalent C# programs (measured excluding trivial constructs such as constructors or properties), as are all the analyzed snippets. We also include data from the same games implemented in straightforward F# together with our Casanova libraries, which allows retaining most of the advantages of Casanova. The first comparisons that we make can be seen in Figure 1, and is concerned with the surrounding infrastructure, which is all the game code that is not strictly part of the game logic or drawing, and the overall length of the various samples.

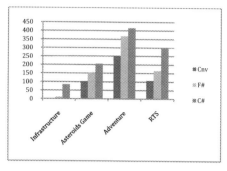

Fig. 1.

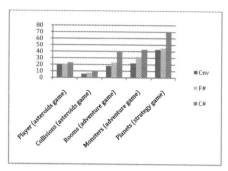

Fig. 2.

In Figure 2 we can see the comparison of the single snippets of game code that we have analyzed. With the data above, we feel it's safe enough to conclude that Casanova allows to express game-related concepts with less verbosity than traditional mainstream languages; specifically, Casanova completely removes the need for boilerplate code to initialize the game (since it is already built-in), and it removes the need to traverse the game world to update and draw each entity (since the framework takes care of evaluating rules and drawing drawable entities). The F# samples fare comparably to Casanova, both in terms of length and code complexity, mostly thanks to the Casanova library that allows the definition of scripts and automated traversal of the game state.

Finally, while we don't have enough data to qualify as a proper user study, we wish to point out the importance of our work in an actual game project, the upcoming strategy game Galaxy Wars [14]. This project is the complete version of the RTS sample discussed in the previous sections. Compared with the RTS sample, Galaxy Wars is much larger (tens of thousands of lines of code), and we have developed it both as a commercial endeavor and as a research test-bed for Casanova, with the aid of a group of Master students in Computer Science.

6   Future Work

We believe our work to have opened exciting new venues of exploration. Casanova started with the goal of making it simpler to build a declarative, easily optimized game logic, with its associated rendering. In addition to completing support for the Casanova language in terms of compiler, development tools, and visual editors, we will: *(i)* design further Casanova components such as menus, networking and audio systems; *(ii)* study a list of query optimizations [16] that could make Casanova more efficient; *(iii)* work on user studies on students and even actual game designers.

7   Conclusions

Game development is a large aspect of modern culture. Games are used for entertainment, education, training and more, and their impact on society is significant. This is driving a need for structured principles and practices for developing games and simulations. Also, reducing the cost and difficulties of making games could greatly benefit development studios with less resources, such as independent-, serious-, and research-game makers. Casanova is a study in the automation and support of the most common game-development activities, in order to allow game developers to put more effort on what really matters (AI, gameplay, shaders, procedural generation, etc.) instead of smaller technicalities.

While Casanova is still in its early stages, we have used it extensively and with good results in a real game [14], and we are certain that with further work the benefits of this approach will become much more apparent.

References

1. Fullerton, T., Swain, C., Hoffman, S.: Game design workshop: a playcentric approach to creating innovative games. Morgan Kaufman (2008)
2. Ritterfeld, U., Cody, M., Vorderer, P.: Serious Games: Mechanisms and Effects (2009)
3. Entertainment Software Association: Industry Facts (2010)
4. Buckland, M.: Programming Game AI by Example, Sudbury, MA (2004)
5. Giuseppe Maggiore, M.: Monadic Scripting in F# for Computer Games, Oslo, Norway (2011)
6. Maggiore, G., Spanò, A., Orsini, R., Costantini, G., Bugliesi, M., Abbadi, M.: Designing Casanova: A Language for Games. In: van den Herik, H.J., Plaat, A. (eds.) ACG 2011. LNCS, vol. 7168, pp. 320–332. Springer, Heidelberg (2012)
7. Maggiore, G., Bugliesi, M., Orsini, R.: Casanova Papers. In: Casanova project page, http://casanova.codeplex.com/wikipage?title=Papers (accessed 2011)
8. DeLoura, M.: The Engine Survey. In: Gamasutra, http://www.gamasutra.com/blogs/MarkDeLoura/20090316/903/The_Engine_Survey_Technology_Results.php (accessed 2009)
9. Ampatzoglou, A., Chatzigeorgiou, A.: Evaluation of object-oriented design patterns in game development. Journal of Information and Software Technology 49 (2007)
10. Folmer, E.: Component Based Game Development – A Solution to Escalating Costs and Expanding Deadlines? In: Schmidt, H.W., Crnković, I., Heineman, G.T., Stafford, J.A. (eds.) CBSE 2007. LNCS, vol. 4608, pp. 66–73. Springer, Heidelberg (2007)
11. Conal, E., Hudak, P.: Functional reactive animation. In: International Conference on Functional Programming (ICFP), pp. 263–273 (1997)
12. Walker White, A.: Scaling games to epic proportions. In: Proceedings of the 2007 ACM SIGMOD International Conference on Management of Data (SIGMOD), New York, NY, USA, pp. 31–42 (2007)
13. Maggiore, G.: Casanova project page (2011), http://casanova.codeplex.com/
14. Maggiore, G.: Galaxy Wars Project Page (2010), http://vsteam2010.codeplex.com, http://galaxywars.vsteam.org
15. Zhao, R., Szafron, D.: Generating Believable Virtual Characters Using Behavior Capture and Hidden Markov Models. In: van den Herik, H.J., Plaat, A. (eds.) ACG 2011. LNCS, vol. 7168, pp. 342–353. Springer, Heidelberg (2012)
16. Garcia-molina, H., Ullman, J., Widom, J.: Database System Implementation (1999)

An Analysis of Player Strategies and Performance in Audio Puzzles

Jaime Carvalho, Luís Duarte, and Luís Carriço

LaSIGE & Department of Informatics, University of Lisbon
Edifício C6, Campo-Grande, 1749-016 Lisboa
{jcarvalho,lduarte}@lasige.di.fc.ul.pt, lmc@di.fc.ul.pt

Abstract. This paper presents the design of a puzzle game for the Android plat-form also shows a study on puzzle solving strategies across different interaction modalities and showcases a player performance analysis in each identified strategy. Solving puzzles is among the oldest challenges and entertainment activities available to us. However, despite major technological advances, the design of such games has never provided individuals with challenges beyond visual puzzles. We capitalized on this opportunity to tackle the design of puzzles which go beyond visual cues, utilizing sound and vibration feedback as well to offer a fresh challenge to players. Along with the design of this game, our research focused on analyzing puzzle solving strategies applied by users. In particular, this paper details a study in which we analyzed if players apply the same strategy to solve a visual and a audio puzzle. Complementing the strategies analysis on the audio mode, we also present a comparative analysis regarding performance metrics such as completion time, number of moves for completion and the attained score. Results point that players often opt to solve prominent areas first, leaving more abstract zones to the end, independently from the interaction modality involved. Performance analysis tells us that there are suitable strategies to maximize different performance metrics.

Keywords: Audio Puzzles, Puzzle Games, Play Strategy.

1 Motivation

Videogames can be used for various ends, ranging from personal entertainment [2][17], as a catalyst for social interaction [12], as a support tool for teaching and learning process [18] or as an experimental platform for new technologies or design concepts [11]. In the education domain, games are of particular importance for students to develop learning skills which allow them to easily create abstractions of concepts or algorithms [10]. In particular, puzzle games have yielded positive results in such learning process. There are various examples of the usage of puzzle games in distinct areas. Hill [5], Levitin [9][10] and Ross [15] have defended utilizing puzzles and games in general as a motivating factor for a diversity of courses. Ginat [4] has also explored the usage of puzzle games as a catalyst for students in learning environments. Outside the education domain, there has been a deployment of a puzzle

M. Herrlich, R. Malaka, and M. Masuch (Eds.): ICEC 2012, LNCS 7522, pp. 349–362, 2012.

game to foster communication and collaboration between children with autism spectrum disorder [1]. All these examples are elucidative of the importance of games in general, and in particular puzzle games, for a diversity of domains, improving aspects of people's lives.

In the entertainment domain, and with the proliferation of various types of mobile devices [3], videogames are currently widespread across different platforms [11][12][16]. Furthermore, given the increased computational power [7] and number of features present in modern mobile devices, developers are recurring to different modalities [14] to provide players with alternative challenges which would not have been possible before [6]. Yet, one game type which still lacks proper support is puzzle games. There are a few examples of puzzle games which go beyond the visual version [2], but they are either too simplistic, or are yet to explore the full potential of modern smartphones to provide players with adequate challenges, specifically with puzzle representations which go beyond the traditional figure jigsaw puzzle.

Given the lack of multimodal versions of puzzle games for mobile devices, we envisioned and developed a Multimodal Puzzle Game which allows players to tackle visual or audio puzzles. The game was developed for Android platforms and allows for the full customization of the puzzle challenge, ranging from number of pieces, to help types as well as allowing the selection of any picture or song present in the user's personal library to be a puzzle. Taking inspiration from different puzzle learning strategies and learning environments, we designed a study which aimed at assessing if players use similar strategies for solving multimodal puzzles. In particular we wanted to determine if users tend to prioritize particular puzzle pieces or if they solved the puzzle in the order the pieces are presented to them. Upon identifying a set of solving strategies, we proceeded to a comparative analysis attempting to determine the best approach according to three different metrics: completion time, number of moves for completion and player score. Results provide a clear conclusion as to which strategies yield the best results. The paper is organized as follows: we start by presenting the multimodal puzzle game and all of its features; then we detail our study, present the results o both the identified strategies and on player performance; after, we discuss our findings, draw final conclusions and unveil some of our future research directions.

2   Multimodal Puzzle Game

The Multimodal Puzzle Game as its name implies is an application developed for Android platforms which allows users to solve puzzles across different modalities. While puzzle solving games are moderately popular, the available solutions are still rooted to solving visual jigsaw puzzles, the original concept of the physical counterpart of this game. As such, we envisioned a multimodal puzzle game which allows players to not only tackle on picture puzzles, but also on musical ones, in which the main goal is to place segments of a musical piece in the correct order.

The multimodal puzzle game possesses a small selection of features which need to be addressed in detail to fully comprehend the contents of the game, namely the available game modes, configurable options and the game's interface.

2.1   Game Modes

The Multimodal Puzzle Game comprises two game modes: a visual one and an audio mode. The visual mode takes inspiration from traditional physical puzzles in which individuals are required to reconstruct a picture by putting pieces in the appropriate positions. The audio mode has not been so thoroughly explored in both research and videogame industry. In this case it provides a challenge to reconstruct a fragmented song by putting each individual segment in the correct order.

Visual Mode. In visual mode, all image puzzles are square shaped (a limitation to accommodate playing in smartphones). This means puzzles will have n^2 number of pieces, where 'n' is a value configured by the player corresponding to the number of pieces per line. The game provides two approaches towards the visual mode:

- Players can take the challenge of one of three pre-loaded images which come with the game (**Fig. 1**). These images were created specifically for the Multimodal Puzzle, serving as a default challenge for players.

Fig. 1. Default images used for the visual mode puzzle

- The second approach stems from a feature included in the game which allows users to browse images stored in the device. The implication is that players can select any image they desire to solve as a puzzle, effectively broadening the horizon of possible new challenges for the players. If the player picks a non-square shape image, the game stretches the image accordingly to fit the playing area.

Audio Mode. The goal of this game mode is for players to correctly order a musical piece which was divided in a configurable number of segments (n^2, similarly to the visual puzzle). Each segment is approximately one second long. Similarly to the visual mode, players have two different approaches to play the music puzzle:

- Players can tackle one of three default songs, specifically created for the game. The song contains a repeating calm beat (**Fig. 2**) which is interrupted by the initial excerpt (first 6 seconds) of Beethoven's 5th Symphony (**Fig. 3**). The three songs are variations of each other, differing between them in the instant in which the 5th's excerpt is introduced (in the first variation it is introduced at the 2nd second, in the second variation at the 6th second and in the third variation at the 9th second).

Fig. 2. Beat excerpt created for the default audio puzzle

- Alternatively, players can select any song they have stored in their smartphone and load it to the game in order to complete it as a puzzle. The game automatically segments the song in n^2 pieces and then shuffles them. If the player picks a song which is not long enough for the number of pieces established for the puzzle, the game prompts the player if he / she desires to change the puzzle length to a more appropriate one, or if he / she desires to pick a new song. If the song is longer than the available puzzle length (the typical scenario) the initial part of the song is selected to feature in the puzzle.

Fig. 3. Beethoven's 5th Symphony initial segment

2.2 Help Type

During the course of the game, players have two help types at their disposal: individual and global. In individual mode, players are able to tap one particular square in the unsolved puzzle area to reveal the piece that fits in that place. In the case of the visual puzzle, the individual help displays the image piece belonging to the tapped location; in the case of the music puzzle, the individual help plays the musical segment corresponding to that piece in the puzzle. In global mode, upon tapping the unsolved puzzle area, the whole solution is revealed. This means that in the visual mode, the puzzle figure is shown to the player. When playing the music puzzle, the whole music is reproduced for the player. The help type can be adjusted in the options menu prior to beginning a new puzzle.

2.3 Rules

A score based system is used to rank each puzzle solving attempt. Players are awarded 3 points when they place a puzzle piece in the correct position (for the first time per piece only). Positioning a puzzle piece incorrectly deducts one point from the current score. The intent of this system is to force players to think about their actions prior to executing them, avoiding unnecessary penalties for using, for instance, trial & error strategies.

Ranks are kept separately for each puzzle type and puzzle size. Games with the same score in the same category (puzzle size and type) are ranked according to the time spent completing the puzzle (with a lower time being better).

2.4   Interface

The game's interface can be observed in **Fig. 4** (visual mode and audio mode). The main region in the center is the unsolved puzzle area. Here we can see the segmented puzzle and all pieces which still remain to be discovered and the ones which are already placed. Correctly placed pieces keep their original colors, while incorrectly placed ones receive a subtle red transparent layer on top to reveal their current status. A correctly placed piece displays a green transparent layer on top of them for 2 seconds and then assumes its original image fragment (in the case of the visual mode).

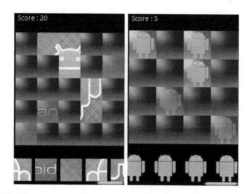

Fig. 4. Multimodal Puzzle Game: Visual Mode and Audio Mode

The lower section of the interface comprises a strip which contains the puzzle pieces. The order of the pieces in this strip is randomly generated prior to each game. In the case of the visual mode, the pieces showcase the image fragment they represent. In the audio mode, each piece has the same visual representation. To access its content, players need to tap once to play the audio segment. To place a puzzle piece in the unsolved area, players tap and drag the piece to the desired position and then let it go to execute the positioning action. During a game, and particularly in large puzzles, players may move a significant number of pieces from the strip to the unsolved puzzle area, causing it to be overcrowded and hindering the comprehension of which pieces are in place and which are not. We implemented a shortcut to make all incorrect pieces return to their original positions in the strip. By double tapping the strip area, the players are able to force all incorrectly played pieces to return to the strip in their original order.

The Multimodal Puzzle Game also comprises a Configuration menu which allows users to set their preferences, such as help type, puzzle size or default image and music library paths. The smartphone's home button opens a quick menu with several shortcuts, namely 'New Game', 'Configuration', quick access to 'Help Type' and

'Exit Application'. Scores and player preferences are stored in both the Android app and on a XML file for backup.

3   Experiment

We conducted an experiment whose goal encompassed identifying which puzzle solving strategies yielded the best performance according to a set of metrics. This experimental period lasted for two weeks, involving three researchers supervising the tests and providing support to subjects as requested.

3.1   Goals

The main goal pertained to the identification of which of the assessed strategies yielded the best results according to 3 different parameters: completion time, number of moves for completion and player score. This second overall research goal aims at reinforcing our previous results by providing empirical evidence on the advantages and disadvantages of specific puzzle solving approaches.

3.2   Research Goals

In this paper we will focus on performance while solving visual and audio puzzles:

- **RG1** – find the most appropriate strategy to solve the audio puzzle based on puzzle completion time.
- **RG2** – find the most appropriate strategy to solve the audio puzzle based on total number of movements for puzzle completion.
- **RG3** – find the most appropriate strategy to solve the audio puzzle based on the attained score.

3.3   Variables

In this study we controlled 4 different variables: the picture puzzle the players had to solve, the audio puzzle needed to be completed, the order in which puzzle pieces were displayed in the strip area of the game, and a fixed puzzle size for each mode. As for the dependent variables, we kept track the order in which pieces were placed in the unsolved area and the order in which each piece category was placed.

Independent Variables

- **Puzzle image** – To analyze whether players used the same solving strategy across different images we provided three different images for the players (the Multimodal Puzzle Game default ones: **Fig. 1**). Albeit three distinct images, their core components are similar in a sense that all include a prominent image of an android character, a small text area and then a simple background. We controlled the usage of the image in the experiment, alternating it between tasks.

- **Puzzle song** – Similarly to the previous variable, we provided three different songs for players (the Multimodal Puzzle Game default ones). Again, an excerpt of the background beat is represented in **Fig. 2** and is present throughout the whole song. At key instants (at second 2, 6 and 9), the initial segment of Beethoven's 5th Symphony is played. This segment acts as a Type-1 set piece, the transition between the two beats is considered a Type-2 set piece and the background beat is considered to belong to Type-3.

- **Puzzle strip order** – The third independent variable is the order in which puzzle pieces are presented in the strip area. We believe this order might influence the solving order of a puzzle. As such we controlled the way in which pieces are ordered in the strip. 3 variations were implemented: the first scatters the pieces randomly throughout the strip; the second places mostly all Type-1 and Type-2 pieces at the end of the strip; the last places mostly all Type-1 and Type-2 pieces at the beginning of the strip.

- **Puzzle Size** – Considering a trade-off between challenge and average time to complete each puzzle (in order to not alienate players) the puzzle size was fixed in 25 pieces for the visual mode and 16 pieces for the audio mode. The discrepancy in puzzle size is due to the amount of time spent in solving the audio mode puzzle which is significantly higher than in the visual mode.

Dependent Variables

- **Game time** – This metric will help us understand which strategy yields a faster completion time.

- **Total number of moves** – Total number of moves is also another way to discern one game from another. By analyzing the number of moves that was taken to complete the puzzle we can reveal the strategy that uses less movement to place pieces into proper place.

- **Player score** – Once more the rules for score are: +3 points for each piece in the right place, only for the first time, and -1 point for each one on the incorrect place; the score purpose is forcing players to think before acting.

3.4   Participants

19 subjects (aged 21 to 27; 18 male, 1 female) participated in this experiment. Individuals were students from different departments in our university. All of them had solved physical puzzles in the past (30% regularly still solve puzzles) and were proficient with modern smartphones, although the large majority had never played a puzzle game in a smartphone, let alone an audio version.

It is important to say that 40% of users had musical formation beyond the mandatory given at the high school level (either from specialized courses or through self-learning approaches).

3.5   Tools and Equipment

Participants were handed Android smartphones (Samsung Galaxy Mini) to play the game. All devices were previously loaded with the Multimodal Puzzle Game.

3.6   Procedure

The experimental period started with a pre-experiment interview to characterize the subjects (e.g. age, gender, experience with modern smartphones, music theory knowledge, etc.).

The main experiment's procedure was as follows: players were randomly assigned to play either 9 visual mode games or 9 audio mode games. The assignment resulted in 7 subjects playing the visual mode and 12 users playing the audio mode, leading to 63 and 108 play samples respectively, for a total of 171 games.

The 9 mandatory games subjects had to play had the following characteristics:

- Players played 3 games with each one of the 3 default images or songs, depending if they were assigned to the visual or audio mode. The differences between each image and song were disseminated previously in this paper.
- For each image / song players were confronted with a different piece order in the strip area:
  — In one of the games Type-1 and Type-2 pieces were randomly scattered throughout the strip.
  — In other setting, Type-1 and Type-2 pieces were forcefully put at the end of the strip.
  — In the last configuration, Type-1 and Type-2 pieces were forcefully put at the beginning of the strip.

The order of these 9 games was randomly assigned per participant. As an incentive for participation, users were given a download code for the version of the Multimodal Puzzle Game for their Android devices.

3.7   Results

Results related with the identification of the most popular strategies applied to solve both the visual and the audio puzzles were published in [19]. In sum, despite more puzzle solving strategies being found in the case of the audio mode, we can state that players primarily recur to 2 strategies when solving puzzles in a mobile device: they attempt to identify the most salient areas of the puzzle (e.g. particular images or segments of a song) and solve those first by prominence order. Secondly they solve the puzzle based on the order pieces are delivered to them even if they can navigate through all pieces. Both these conclusions hold true to the visual and audio modes of the Multimodal Puzzle Game. Nevertheless, we must emphasize that in visual mode only one strategy was clearly prominent and that was solving the puzzle based on the piece prominence in the puzzle. In audio mode, a third approach was found in which players solved the puzzle according to its natural presentation order.

Visual Mode. Given the existence of a single solving strategy (by piece prominence), in **Fig. 5** we can see the average time it took to complete each game in visual mode, also as the number of movements and the score achieved. In a way to recall, the game has a total of 25 possible correct moves. For each completion the average amount of time spent rounds 154 seconds, about 2 and a half minutes, and takes 47 moves. The average score obtained is approximately 54 points.

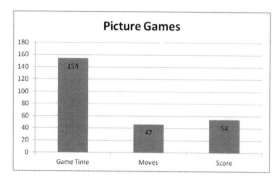

Fig. 5. Visual mode average metrics for time, moves and score

Audio Mode. Results for the audio mode can be observed in **Fig. 6**, **Fig. 7** and **Fig. 8**. **Fig. 6** contains a graph depicting the percentage of games solved according to three identified strategies: by piece category, by the piece strip order and by the puzzle's presentation order (e.g. first row, then second row, etc.). For 9% of the games we were unable to identify a noticeable strategy.

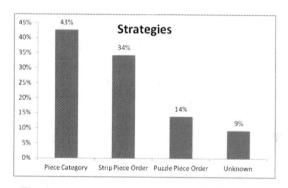

Fig. 6. Audio mode solving strategies distribution

In **Fig. 7** we have a simple comparative analysis for all musical puzzle solving strategies in regards to time, movements and score. The first graph shows the average time it took to solve the audio puzzle for each of the strategies; in the center we can see the average number of movements needed to solve the audio puzzle; the last graph holds the average scores reached with each strategy. We also point in each graph the respective averages for the games considered as "unknown", as a way of comparison and as a form of understanding the reasons for their exclusion from the data shown in the graphs above.

We also assessed if players switched strategies over the course of the 9 mandatory games of the experiment: the intent was to check if players adapted over time to the strategies which resulted in higher performance values. The variations of those strategies over time are shown in **Fig. 8**. In early games (1 and 2) there is an accentuation

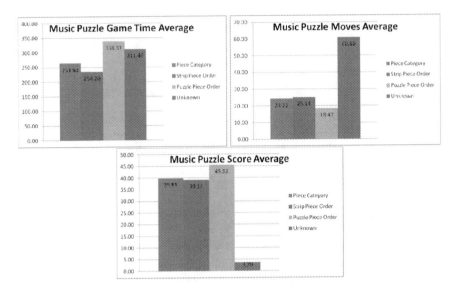

Fig. 7. Audio mode comparative analysis of the audio mode strategies for time, moves and score

of the piece category strategy. From game number 3 to game number 7, we can observe a high variation in the adopted strategies, possibly due to player experimentation with different approaches. However, in the last couple of games we can visualize a confluence towards the strategies which yield the best performance according to the assessed metrics.

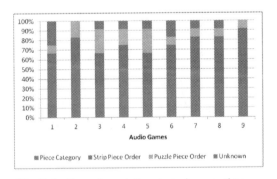

Fig. 8. Audio mode variation strategies over time

4   Discussion

We will now discuss these results, taking into consideration the data gathered from visual and audio mode separately.

4.1   Visual Mode

Here, players prioritized solving recognizable pieces immediately, forfeiting background sections of the puzzle to last. These results suggest visual cues are extremely important to solve a puzzle game as individuals will identify them first and attempt to put them together. Given that we attempted to fulfill these research goals with 3 different pictures (albeit and forcefully similar to each other) the gathered empirical data further emphasizes the usage of this strategy.

4.2   Audio Mode

Results for the audio mode were not as homogeneous as the ones stemming from the visual mode. By analyzing each game individually we ended up identifying 3 main strategies: piece category prioritization, solving by strip order and solving by puzzle order. Piece category prioritization was the most popular strategy with 43% of the games following this strategy. Even though a majority of at least 50% of samples was not reached for this strategy, it is plausible to state RG2 was met for the audio mode. This result emphasizes the importance that players give to prominent regions / segments of a puzzle, which ultimately leads to sharing puzzle solving strategies even across different interaction modalities.

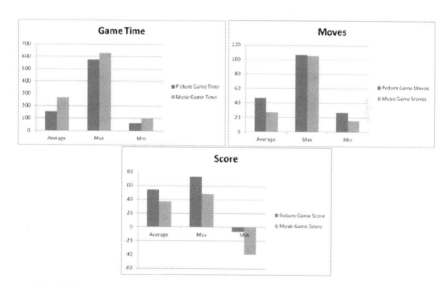

Fig. 9. Comparison between the visual and audio modes for team, moves and score

In order to answer to RG1, RG2 and RG3 we need to analyze **Fig. 7.** In terms of average time to solve the audio mode it is clear that puzzle piece order is the slowest one with almost 338 seconds (more than five minutes); the fastest is the strip piece order strategy with 234 seconds (nearly four minutes); the piece category strategy stood in the middle with an average of 264 seconds (a little more than four minutes). That being said, the RG4 answer is the strip piece order strategy. The middle graph in

Fig. 7 helps us figure out which strategy requires less moves to solve a puzzle in audio mode. On average, piece category and strip order strategies are virtually identical with 24 and 25 movements respectively, while puzzle piece order only requires 18 moves, thereby earning the right to RG5. The last metric we considered was the player's score. Here we can verify that on average, once again, piece category and strip order strategies display identical results, with 40 and 39 points respectively. Nevertheless, the answer for our RG6 research goal appears to be the puzzle piece order, providing players with the highest average score at 46 points.

By carefully analyzing the chart in **Fig. 8**, we can claim that there is no significant convergence towards a single strategy – the distribution for both piece categorization and strip order strategies constantly fluctuates over time; on the other hand the puzzle order strategy obtained a relatively stable number of followers. It is also important to state that four players did not alter their strategy across all 9 games, and the game in which most users altered their strategy was game number 6. This may have occurred for two reasons: a) due to player fatigue – since the audio version of the experiment lasted for a significant period (averaging more than 40 minutes per subject) we believe a few players were looking for a fast way to end the experiment, and thus changed strategies halfway through it (at around the 22 minute mark of the experiment); b) due to the questionnaire break introduced in game 5 - we asked users to respond to a short survey after game 5, leading us to assume this pause prompted players to explore alternative strategies when they resumed the experiment. In **Fig. 9** we present a comparison between visual and audio modes. These charts show that even though the audio puzzle was smaller in size compared to the visual (16 against 25, respectively), it took much longer to complete. However, the average number of moves performed to complete the audio dropped abruptly when compared to the visual mode. This led us to believe that players in the visual mode recur to "trial and error" approaches more often than in the audio mode.

5   Conclusions and Future Work

This paper presented the Multimodal Puzzle Game for Android devices. For the design of this application, we capitalized on the lackluster offer of puzzle games involving challenges beyond visual images. As such we created a game for Android devices which allows players to solve not only image puzzles, but also audio puzzles. The application allows users to tackle on a set of puzzles (both image and audio) created specifically for this game or pick images and songs from the device's own library.

Through this study we can state that there are different strategies for different results, some being more suitable to finish quickly and others to achieve higher scores. The main contribution of this study is the insight on player strategies which can prompt developers and designers alike to build puzzle game UIs to accommodate the users' preferred strategies or those which can maximize player performance.

A cooperative and competitive version of the multimodal puzzle game has already been developed and is currently under usability evaluation. Our intent is to deploy this new version and to assess collaborative and competitive puzzle solving strategies, using an experimental approach similar to the one presented in this contribution. Additionally a new modality is also being explored and currently under evaluation: haptics. The intent is to assess the viability of haptic puzzles recurring to vibratory patterns to provide new and innovative challenges to players.

Acknowledgements. This work was funded by FCT, through Individual Scholarship SFRH / BD / 39496 / 2007, through project PTDC/EIA-EIA/103676/2008 (InSIThe) and the Multiannual Funding Programme.

References

1. Battocchi, A., Pianesi, F., Tomasini, D., Zancanaro, M., Esposito, G., Venuti, P., Ben Sasson, A., Gal, E., Weiss, P.L.: Collaborative puzzle game: a tabletop interactive game for fostering collaboration in children with autism spectrum disorders (ASD). In: Proceedings of the ACM International Conference on Interactive Tabletops and Surfaces, ITS 2009, pp. 197–204. ACM (2009)
2. Diakopoulos, N., Luther, K., Essa, I.: Audio puzzler: piecing together time-stamped speech transcripts with a puzzle game. In: Proceedings of the 16th ACM International Conference on Multimedia, MM 2008. ACM (2008)
3. Duh, H.B.-L., Chen, V.H.H., Tan, C.B.: Playing different games on different phones: an empirical study on mobile gaming. In: Proceedings of the 10th International Conference on Human Computer Interaction with Mobile Devices and Services, MobileHCI 2008. ACM (2008)
4. Ginat, D.: Elaborating heuristic reasoning and rigor with mathematical games, pp. 32–36. ACM (December 2007)
5. Hill, J.M.D., Ray, C.K., Blair, J.R.S., Carver Jr., C.A.: Puzzles and games: addressing different learning styles in teaching operating systems concepts. In: Proceedings of the 34th SIGCSE Technical Symposium on Computer Science Education, SIGCSE 2003, pp. 182–186. ACM, New York (2003)
6. Hoggan, E., Brewster, S.A.: Crosstrainer: testing the use of multimodal interfaces in situ. In: Proceedings of the 28th International Conference on Human Factors in Computing Systems, CHI 2010, pp. 333–342. ACM, New York (2010)
7. Korhonen, H., Koivisto, E.M.I.: Playability heuristics for mobile multiplayer games. In: Proceedings of the 2nd International Conference on Digital Interactive Media in Entertainment and Arts, DIMEA 2007, pp. 28–35. ACM, New York (2007)
8. Lee, S., Zhai, S.: The performance of touch screen soft buttons. In: Proceedings of the 27th International Conference on Human Factors in Computing Systems, CHI 2009, pp. 309–318. ACM, New York (2009)
9. Levitin, A.: Analyze that: puzzles and analysis of algorithms. In: Proceedings of the 36th SIGCSE Technical Symposium on Computer Science Education, SIGCSE 2005, pp. 171–175. ACM (2005)
10. Levitin, A., Papalaskari, M.-A.: Using puzzles in teaching algorithms. In: Proceedings of the 33rd SIGCSE Technical Symposium on Computer Science Education, SIGCSE 2002, pp. 292–296. ACM, New York (2002)

11. Bell, M., Brown, B., Hall, M., Sherwood Matthew Chalmers, S., Barkhuus, L., Tennent, P.: Gaming on the edge: Using seams in pervasive games. In: PerGames 2005 Proceedings, Munich, Germany, pp. 11–18 (2005)
12. Paelke, V., Reimann, C.: Vision-based interaction - a first glance at plazing MR games in the real-world around us. In: PerGames 2005 Proceedings, Munich, Germany, pp. 92–97 (2005)
13. Poupyrev, I., Maruyama, S.: Tactile interfaces for small touch screens. In: Proceedings of the 16th Annual ACM Symposium on User Interface Software and Technology, UIST 2003, pp. 217–220. ACM (2003)
14. Reufer, T., Panknin, M., Geiger, C.: Sensodroid: multimodal interaction controlled mobile gaming. In: Proceedings of the 13th International Conference on Humans and Computers, HC 2010, Fukushima-ken, Japan, pp. 32–36 (2010)
15. Ross, J.M.: Guiding students through programming puzzles: value and examples of java game assignments, vol. 34, pp. 94–98. ACM (December 2002)
16. Sedano, C.I., Laine, T.H., Vinni, M., Sutinen, E.: Where is the answer?: the importance of curiosity in pervasive mobile games. In: Proceedings of the 2007 Conference on Future Play, Future Play 2007, New York, NY, USA, pp. 46–53 (2007)
17. Holleis, A.W.P., Kranz, M., Schmidt, A.: Playing with the real world. In: PerGames 2005 Proceedings, Munich, Germany, pp. 43–50 (2005)
18. del Blanco, A., Torrente, J., Marchiori, E.J., Martiınez-Ortiz, I., Moreno-Ger, P., Fernandez-Manjon, B.: Easing assessment of game-based learning with <e-adventure> and LAMS. In: Proceedings of the Second ACM International Workshop on Multimedia Technologies for Distance Learning, MTDL 2010, pp. 25–30. ACM, New York (2010)
19. Carvalho, J., Duarte, L., Carriço, L.: Puzzle Games: Players Strategies Across Different Interaction Modalities. In: Proceedings of Fun & Games 2012 (2012)

Cell Phone Puppets: Turning Mobile Phones into Performing Objects

Michael Nitsche and Sanjeev Nayak

Georgia Institute of Technology/ Digital Media
85 Fifth Str. NW TSRB
Atlanta, GA 30332-0165, USA
{michael.nitsche,snayak8}@gatech.edu

Abstract. We introduce *Puppettime*, a digital puppetry project that uses mobile phones as interfaces to control virtual puppetry via motion gestures. The goal of the project is to explore cell phones as performative objects in novel interaction designs. Combining the evolution of mobile devices into tangible interfaces with traditional puppetry, the paper discusses the connections between these domains. It describes the design rationale behind the *Puppettime* project as well as its implementation and first feedback, focusing on the core thesis that puppetry provides a valuable and underused metaphor for interface design that supports digital entertainment between co-present players.

Keywords: Puppet, tangible user interface, virtual character.

1   Introduction

The potential of gestures as intuitive input feature was recognized early on [1] but only the recent inclusion of advanced sensors in smart phones has made motion gesture recognition available to the larger audience of phone users. The inclusion of numerous sensors to smart phones allowed them to evolve into tangible controllers (as defined by [2]). But even though today's devices are stacked with accelerometers, compass, gyro, touch screens, and camera(s), all of them valuable features to support tangible interaction, the dominant interaction design for cell phones remains focused on the use of screens, buttons, microphones, and speakers.

The potential of mobile devices clearly encourages increased motion-based interaction but it remains woefully underused. The problem is not one of technology but one of design metaphors. We argue that in order to embrace the new opportunities a fundamental change of our understanding of mobile phones as media devices is needed. Through motion-based design, cell phones turn from audio-visual media devices into performing objects. They evolve from input/ output devices to objects, whose physical condition becomes prevalent not only to the player but every bystander. Designing for this form of mobile play cannot exclusively rely on audio-visual representation rendered by the phone, but it has to include the object itself in the design. This mirrors main arguments of earlier research on embodiment and

M. Herrlich, R. Malaka, and M. Masuch (Eds.): ICEC 2012, LNCS 7522, pp. 363–372, 2012.

situatedness of ubiquitous interaction [3]. Within the larger field, the goal of this paper is to address particularly the recognition of the device itself as performing object and explore the opening design space through an example project.

Parallel to our past work with digital puppetry [4] we have developed *Puppettime*, a prototype for a cell phone based digital puppetry system. It addresses a number of prevalent questions in the development of mobile interaction design for co-located digital entertainment, including design for multiple devices and for multi-user conditions, as well as testing of the underlying technology for fine grain control mechanisms. In this paper we will present the background, design, implementation, and some initial responses to the system.

2   Background

2.1   Mobile Phones and Tangible Interaction Design

A number of innovative projects have started to use phones as tangible objects in themselves. Phones have been used as controllers for Wii-like interaction with large screens [5], as well as controllers for 3D mobile games [6], co-located social games based on motion gestures [7], and multi-modal approaches that combine touch and motion [8]. First frameworks for the design of tangible interaction with phones are emerging [9] but the question remains how the interaction design and user experience will change as interactions with phones evolve further into a shared, movement-based, and co-located user experience. Does the design follow generic tasks, such as text input supported by accelerometers [10] or develop particularly phone-related gestures, like the DoubleFlip [11]?

This mirrors the challenge seen earlier in the transition of other interfaces to increasingly motion-based interaction design, particularly the focus on motion gestures in game consoles (Microsoft's Kinect, Sony's Move, Nintendo's Wii). Video games have discovered the social space in front of the console and designed particular interaction conditions for this space. But a key difference between gaming and general mobile phone usage is the different social context for gesture based interaction [12].

Motion gestures are performative. Unlike a screen-based gesture system, a motion input is clearly visible to others and constitutes an expressive action in itself. The Kinect transforms the living room into a performance stage for gaming and Sall/ Grinter have found that "physical gaming often brought an awareness of other householders" [13]. Likewise, motion gestures for mobile devices add a performative element to the interaction. Instead of a hidden input, as seen with keyboards or touch screens, bystanders are able to read and interpret the gestures. But because the surroundings and bystanders are often less familiar in the public use of smart phones, the resulting awareness of others is not always wanted. Technically, we might be able to use our smart phones like Wii controllers, but conceptually we have to revisit the motion gestures when we apply them to public use. How, then, can we develop performative gestures for innovative cell phone interaction design?

2.2   Value of Puppetry

To address this question we turned to puppetry. Puppetry presents a highly developed form of expressive interaction and over the course of its 4000-year old history it has developed rich and culturally complex performative practices [14]. It depends on motion gestures – what we would call "input" – to control a wide range of expressions. Thanks to its long tradition of outstanding artistry, the granularity and efficiency of this "input" is remarkably higher in traditional puppetry than it is in most current digital technology. The most delicate movement can have the power to evoke highly effective expressions in traditional puppetry formats. Thus, it provides a valid testing goal post for new interface technology and builds on a critical overlap between entertainment technology as a form of creative expression.

Puppetry has been identified as a metaphor for interaction with digital worlds before. For example, it has been claimed that puppetry supports storytelling, improvisation, and public engagement in digital media [15]. The relationship between puppeteer and puppet is used to describe the relationship between user and avatar, starting in early HCI concepts [16], to more current educational projects [17], and tangible interfaces [18]. At the same time, traditional puppetry has started to explore and theorize its relation to the digital, gradually building frameworks to include it better [19].

In commercial entertainment, digital puppetry is at work in a range of projects such as Disney's *Turtle Talk with Crush* exhibit at their Epcot theme park or the Henson studio's puppeteering set up for the TV show *Sid, the Science Kid* [20]. The problem is that these installations and other related work, like *ShadowStory* [21] use custom-built hardware controllers or expensive high-end commercial controllers [22]. This limits their accessibility to consumers and instead focuses on expert users. These high end installations do not allow visiting players to easily turn into puppeteers or set up their own puppet shows but instead keep most visitors in the role of traditional audiences that can only contribute at a certain location and with the help of certain technology. *Puppettime* aims to explore and open up the performative range of digital puppetry to these large groups, test how well modern phones can deliver on the fine granularity of puppet controls, and provide the basis for a discussion of new design concepts for phones as performing objects in mobile entertainment. To do so, it set out to provide a simple, and highly accessible mobile-phone-based puppet interaction system.

3   Puppettime

3.1   Designing a Puppet Interface for Mobile Phones

Puppettime is a digital puppetry project that uses multiple mobile phones as objects to control puppet performances on a projected 3D virtual stage. It is multi-player, allowing different players to join at any time and participate locally in a shared performance. Once the players have logged on to the central virtual stage, each one can customize their puppets on the mobile devices before they launch them into the performance. During such a performance, each player can either control their puppet with a single device – much like a simple rod puppet – or with two devices that allow for more detailed animation control of body and a puppet limbs.

Fig. 1. Stage application at work; lower menu presents stage director options; both puppets are controlled by players

The core principle is to use mobile devices as performative objects much like puppeteers use rods or strings. Puppets are controlled by spatial movement of the devices and players can directly engage with the virtual performance on stage "through" the device and not "on" the device. The goal was to direct attention away from the phone as a traditional focal point of the interaction and toward the performance of the puppets and their puppeteers themselves. Because the interaction is spatial and shared, players realize that they are collaborating with other players during the puppet play. Their collaboration happens not only on the virtual stage but also in the shared physical location. Other players are not hidden behind some interface but their physical behavior – how they move their hands to control the puppet – is obvious and the co-located collaboration spreads between virtual stage and physical control space.

3.2   Implementation

Puppettime functions across two platforms. Android smart phones are utilized as tangible motion controllers, and a laptop running *Unity3d* serves as a display device that receives the phone input and renders the virtual puppet show. The Android phones communicate with the Unity application over a local Wi-Fi network.

The Unity application serves as a digital counterpart to the physical stage. A 3D stage environment is rendered in real-time, giving a backdrop for the virtual puppet performance. A set stage, complete with props, lighting, and curtains gives the digital puppets a place to act our their stories. Unity's built in physics engine adds a sense of realism to the environment as puppets collide with stage geometry, as they would in the real world. Using a cloth simulator, the curtain geometry was made to flow realistically and could be manipulated by the puppet bodies as they moved through the cloth. The puppets themselves were built as rag dolls with their bodies anchored to an invisible rod. The puppets' arms, legs, and heads, were free to move, bounce, and flail along with the simulated gravity depending on how the puppeteer directed the puppet's body. The basic physics simulation helped to help make a tangible connection between the real world mobile device and the digital puppet.

The Android application (Android 2.1 and higher) allows players to log on to the Unity application via the IP address of the host computer, enter a user name to identify their phone, and select between two control schemes: single and dual control (fig. 2 left). Once logged on, players can customize their virtual puppets from a given selection (fig. 2 right). We provided puppets for the classic fairytale setting of Little Red Riding Hood: a wolf, a hunter, a grandmother, and a puppet for Little Red Riding Hood. To support the aforementioned playful engagement and customization, *Puppettime* allows participants to create their own puppet versions from these basic figures. Players can select a certain body part, and then swipe over the screen to flip between different elements (head, chest, arms, legs) from varying puppets to form their own character. This interaction is not unlike using a children's playbook with split pages that can be turned independently to create new combinations of shapes.

Fig. 2. Android app: selecting a control scheme (left) and puppet customization (right)

Once the player finishes the puppet assembly and activates the puppet, the phone turns into a tangible motion controller that allows the user to control their digital puppet in real-time. Motion data is gathered via the phone's accelerometer and magnetic sensors. The sensor data is turned into orientation values and is then sent via UDP packets over a local wireless network to the Unity application. The UDP protocol was chosen for its speed advantage over TCP. Fast reaction times are necessary to generate the impression of real-time control.

In the single phone scheme, the puppet's orientation will match the phone's orientation, and rotating the phone away from the vertical position will move the puppet in that direction (fig. 3). A quick vertical jerk makes the puppet jump. This is the most basic form of interaction with the system, and gives a similar style of control to that of a single rod puppet.

The dual phone control adds a second phone that controls either the arms or the head in addition to the main body. The secondary phone provides an interface to allow the user to select which additional limb to control: head, any single arm, or both arms (fig. 2 left). Rotations of this second phone will rotate whichever limb is selected. The access in this case is more complex, since the limbs are restricted to only rotate around a fixed joint, and the arms and head cannot match the orientation of the phone directly because they remain attached to the virtual avatar's main body.

Fig. 3. Single phone control scheme; movements are directly projected onto the puppet body

A challenge of digital technology is the lack of any direct connection to the controlled avatar. Puppeteers interact not only with the main control device but might operate individual strings on a marionette or even more directly, the expressions of a hand puppet with their own hand movements. The mapping applied in *Puppettime's* single rod control scheme is a direct translation of the phone's orientation onto the body of the virtual puppet. Players do not control a rod above or underneath the puppet but instead holds the puppet in their hands. This allows for a direct mapping of the phone as object to the virtual avatar as the virtual puppet.

All 3D objects were modeled in Maya and imported into *Unity3d*. *Unity3d* is a widespread platform for development of 3D applications and we used it here to code the stage for the puppet show. One laudable feature of Unity is its accessible multi-player option. It allowed us to implement multiplayer performances relatively easily. The sessions are designed to be free form and users can log on and out as they please. They can also rebuild their puppets as they wish.

The virtual stage application also provides icons that control aspects of the performance that are not related to the puppets themselves, such as lights, sound, and the opening and closing of the curtains. These element control specific stage effects and can be activated on the laptop, which turns into a form of a digital stage manager.

4   Discussion

The project has been demonstrated at a number of occasions and different participants from minors to professional puppeteers have played with it. Users immediately understand the single phone mapping. They recognize their customized puppet on the stage and instantaneously map the phone as control device on the puppet's movements. The phone was readily accepted as a performing object and the responsiveness of the system was sufficient.

However, we also recognized emerging complex conditions that were initially not anticipated. Technically, the bi-manual control that allows players to control body and any selected limb with two phones at a time, works as smooth as the single phone control. However, it took players longer to adjust to the dual device control and to figure out how the rotations of the secondary phone affected the movements of the body parts. To improve performance, we limited the rotation range to avoid unnatural clipping. Still, operating the second phone in synch with the primary controller can be challenging for first time users. This corresponds with earlier work on bi-manual interaction, particularly when the actions of both hands are not mirrored but instead asymmetric and often more complex in their relation to each other. Guiard's model of the "kinematic chain" [23] indicates a higher level of gestural manipulation and expression through a hierarchical relationship between the hands' performances. This model has been discussed in interface design for entertainment technology but his concept of the non-dominant hand (usually left) to guide the general reference frame and the dominant hand to affect smaller scale effects within this frame changes in animation. Animation easily shifts the frame – e.g. from a full body movement to a detailed hand gesture – depending on the motion to be enacted. This challenge has already been noted by 2D puppetry approaches [24]. In our case, the asymmetric condition of one phone controlling the body and the other controlling a single limb allowed for a hierarchical and differently scaled interaction, as mentioned by Guiard, but players had to adjust to that condition, which itself was fixed once the devices were launched.

What this seems to call for is a bridging between different states of mapping. For example, one player commented that the initial positioning of the phones in relation to the virtual puppet is not intuitive. Because the virtual puppet remains frozen upright in the middle of the virtual stage until the phone controls are activated, recognizing the initial mapping before this launch is impossible. Consequently, the performing object of the phone did not match the representation on the virtual stage at the moment of activation. Control started with a kind of shock effect.

Another comment pointed to the device and its physical affordances. An expert puppeteer had no problems with the orientation of the devices but mentioned a lack of weight for the digital puppet. For example, the center of gravity is an important element in physical puppet controls and it is not developed in the current version of *Puppettime*. This mismatch distanced the virtual puppet from the expert puppeteer. He expected certain affordances that the hardware could not provide. One goal of the project was to test available cell phone hardware for the particular puppetry metaphor. Except for this expert statement, we encountered little to no problems with the role of the cell phone hardware itself. However, we added a "freeze in location" feature that allowed players to freeze the virtual puppet's position in space by pressing the touch screen of the phone. This allowed for a gradual exploration of the puppet's animation and the controls. While it is not possible to adjust the weight of the device to that of the virtual puppet, this kind of multimodal interaction design might offer a possible solution for more nuanced control.

Our system can track movement along two axes, which meant that we had to include limitations in the animation control on the 3D stage. All puppets perform on a 3D stage but their movements upward or downward are limited to jumping. It is worth noting, that only the expert puppeteer commented on this limitation and suggested changes to the puppet designs and not necessarily to the control schemes. No other player noticed this seemingly obvious restriction and commented on it negatively. This indicates a possibly useful restriction for future designs for mobile phones as performative objects and indicates that the consistency and simplicity of the mapping is more important than the sheer range of animation effects called by it.

5   Conclusion and Future Work

We propose that puppetry provides a useful metaphor to explore mobile phones as performing objects using motion gestures. But the here introduced example project, *Puppettime*, also highlights limitations of the technology and challenges for future design. The system currently uses accelerometers and magnetic sensors to generate motion data. Most recent phones also include gyroscopes, capable of providing better orientation data. As they become more commonly available in smart phones, *Puppettime* and other gesture-based input concepts might very well implement the here explored interaction methods in their design. This does not necessarily mean more gestural input but instead better-designed transitions between possible states during this input.

The current interaction design for *Puppettime* showed a number of friction points for such a design. These include the initial orientation of phones in relation to a virtual character and the bi-manual control scheme. The transformation of the mobile device from a traditional cell phone to a performative object seems to cross a threshold moment that needs to be clearly understood by the puppeteer/ player. Future design iterations should improve this transition to support the mental projection by the player and lead into a less rapid feeling of sudden control (or loss of control). Although mobile devices are turning increasingly into tangible objects with new interaction design, they are likely to keep some of their more traditional interface structures. Thus, these thresholds between different interaction paradigms will remain in the case of the mobile phone and lead to a kind of double identity.

Acknowledgements. Puppettime was initially implemented by Sanjeev Nayak, Austin Denoble, and Vincent Zunga. We are thankful for in kind support by AT&T and assistance by Mark Guzdial.

References

1. Wexelblat, A.: Research Challenges in Gesture: Open Issues and Unsolved Problems. In: Wachsmuth, I., Fröhlich, M. (eds.) GW 1997. LNCS (LNAI), vol. 1371, pp. 1–11. Springer, Heidelberg (1998)
2. Ullmer, B., Ishii, H.: Emerging frameworks for tangible user interfaces. IBM Syst. J. 39(3-4), 915–931 (2000), doi:10.1147/sj.393.0915
3. Dourish, P.: What we talk about when we talk about context. Personal Ubiquitous Computing 8(1), 19–30 (2004), doi:10.1007/s00779-003-0253-8
4. Mazalek, A., Chandrasekharan, S., Nitsche, M., Welsh, T., Clifton, P., Quitmeyer, A., Peer, F., Kirschner, F., Athreya, D.: I'm in the Game: Embodied Puppet Interface Improves Avatar Control. In: Proceedings of the Fifth International Conference on Tangible, Embedded, and Embodied Interaction, pp. 129–136. ACM, New York (2011)
5. Vajk, T., Coulton, P., Bamford, W., Edwards, R.: Using a Mobile Phone as a "Wii-like" Controller for Playing Games on a Large Public Display. International Journal of Computer Games Technology (2), 1–7 (2008)
6. Chehimi, F., Coulton, P.: Motion controlled mobile 3D multiplayer gaming. In: Proceedings of the 2008 International Conference on Advances in Computer Entertainment Technology, pp. 267–270. ACM, New York (2008)
7. Fan, M., Li, X., Zhong, Y., Tian, L., Shi, Y., Wang, H.: Surprise Grabber: a co-located tangible social game using phone hand gesture. In: Proceedings of the ACM 2011 Conference on Computer Supported Cooperative Work, pp. 625–628. ACM, New York (2011)
8. Hinckley, K., Song, H.: Sensor synaesthesia: touch in motion, and motion in touch. In: Proceedings of the 2011 Annual Conference on Human Factors in Computing Systems, pp. 801–810. ACM, New York (2011)
9. Edge, D., Blackwell, A.F.: Bimanual tangible interaction with mobile phones. In: Proceedings of the 3rd International Conference on Tangible and Embedded Interaction, pp. 131–136. ACM, New York (2009)
10. Jones, E., Alexander, J., Andreou, A., Irani, P., Subramanian, S.: GesText: Accelerometer-Based Gestural Text-Entry Systems. In: Proceedings of CHI 2010, pp. 2173–2182. ACM, New York (2010)
11. Ruiz, J., Li, Y.: DoubleFlip: A Motion Gesture Delimiter for Mobile Interaction. In: CHI 2011: ACM Conference on Human Factors in Computing Systems, pp. 2717–2720. ACM, New York (2011)
12. Rico, J., Brewster, S.: Usable Gestures for Mobile Interfaces: Evaluating Social Acceptability. In: Proceedings of CHI 2010, pp. 887–896. ACM, New York (2010)
13. Sall, A., Grinter, B.: Let's Get Physical! In, Out and Around the Gaming Circle of Physical Gaming at Home. Computer Supported Cooperative Work (CSCW) 16(1-2), 199–229 (2007)
14. Blumenthal, E.: Puppetry: A World History. Harry N. Abrams, New York (2005)
15. Bottoni, P., Faralli, S., Labella, A., Malizia, A., Pierro, M., Ryu, S.: CoPuppet: Collaborative Interaction in Virtual Puppetry. In: Adams, R., Gibson, S., Arisona, S.M. (eds.) Transdisciplinary Digital Art. Sound, Vision and the New Screen. CCIS, vol. 7, pp. 326–341. Springer, Heidelberg (2008), doi:10.1007/978-3-540-79486-8_27
16. Walser, R.: Elements of a Cyberspace Playhouse. Paper Presented at the Proceedings of the National Computer Graphics Association, Anaheim, CA, March 19-22 (1990)

17. Marshall, P., Rogers, Y., Scaife, M.: PUPPET: Playing and Learning in a Virtual World. International Journal of Continuing Engineering Education and Life-long Learning 14(6), 519–531 (2004)
18. Mayora, O., Costa, C., Papliatseyeu, A.: iTheater Puppets Tangible Interactions for Storytelling. Paper Presented at the Intelligent Technologies for Interactive Entertainment, pp. 110–118. Springer, Heidelberg (2009)
19. Tillis, S.: The Art of Puppetry in the Age of Media Production. TDR 43(3), 182–195 (1999)
20. Eide, P.: Digital Puppetry. The Puppetry Journal 60(1), 12–13 (2008)
21. Lu, F., Tian, F., Jiang, Y., Cao, X., Luo, W., Li, G., Zhang, X., Dai, G., Wang, H.: ShadowStory: Creative and Collaborative Digital Storytelling Inspired by Cultural Heritage. In: Proceedings of the 2011 Annual Conference on Human Factors in Computing Systems, pp. 1919–1928. ACM, New York (2011)
22. Kim, S., Zhang, X., Kim, Y.J.: Haptic Puppetry for Interactive Games. In: Pan, Z., Aylett, R.S., Diener, H., Jin, X., Göbel, S., Li, L. (eds.) Edutainment 2006. LNCS, vol. 3942, pp. 1292–1302. Springer, Heidelberg (2006)
23. Guiard, Y.: Asymmetric Division of Labor in Human Skilled Bimanual Action: The Kinematic Chain as a Model. Journal of Motor Behavior 19, 486–517 (1987)
24. Kipp, M., Nguyen, Q.: Multitouch puppetry: creating coordinated 3D motion for an articulated arm. In: Proceedings of the ACM International Conference on Interactive Tabletops and Surfaces, pp. 147–156. ACM, New York (2010)

Brain-Computer Interface Games: Towards a Framework

Hayrettin Gürkök, Anton Nijholt, and Mannes Poel

Human Media Interaction, University of Twente, Enschede, The Netherlands
{h.gurkok,a.nijholt,m.poel}@utwente.nl

Abstract. The brain-computer interface (BCI) community started to consider games as potential applications while the games community started to consider BCI as a game controller. However, there is a discrepancy between the BCI games developed by the two communities. In this paper, we propose a preliminary BCI games framework that we constructed with respect to the research conducted in both the BCI and the games communities. Developers can situate their BCI games within this framework and benefit from the guidelines we provide and also extend the framework further.

Keywords: Brain-computer interface, games, flow, presence, challenge, fantasy, sociality, concentration.

1 Introduction

A brain-computer interface (BCI) is an input modality that can infer certain actions, intentions and psychological (e.g. cognitive, emotional) states by analysing the brain activity it captures. Besides its classical purpose of redressing the communication and mobility of disabled people, BCI has been proposed as a candidate modality for a range of recreational HCI applications to be used by the general population [7]. Among these, BCI games [17] attract the interest of researchers and developers from both BCI and games communities. However, we see a discrepancy between the BCI games developed by the two communities.

Many of the BCI games developed by the BCI community aim at testing some psychological hypotheses or evaluating the performance of signal analysis and classification techniques. Thus, less attention is paid to game characteristics than to technical aspects. These games do not usually have any narrative or rich feedback or visuals. User (i.e. player) experience evaluations are almost never carried out. This leads to BCI games that are reliable but often not enjoyable. On the contrary, BCI games from the games community are developed with respect to game design principles. However, the neurophysiology and signal analysis techniques they rely on are largely unknown. Because, these games mostly make use of the commercial BCI headsets which have their private technical details. This leads to BCI games that are potentially entertaining but unsatisfactory in terms of feeling of control.

M. Herrlich, R. Malaka, and M. Masuch (Eds.): ICEC 2012, LNCS 7522, pp. 373–380, 2012.

In this paper, we will try to transfer some knowledge from the games and the BCI communities into a shared preliminary framework to make them aware of each other's research. From the games community, we will show some game playing motivations which can be satisfied by the features of BCI. From the BCI community, we will take the current interaction paradigms used in general and show the ways they can be used in games. This way, we hope to contribute to bridging the gap between the two communities and promoting the development of entertaining and reliable BCI games.

2   A Framework of BCI Games

In the framework that we propose, we represent a BCI game using two descriptors. The first descriptor specifies the player motivation(s) the BCI game satisfies. In other words, it answers the question: *'Why is the game played?'*. The second descriptor specifies the interaction paradigm(s) the BCI game is built upon. So, it answers the question: *'How is the game played?'*. Next, we will elaborate on these descriptors and provide some guidelines for each. For the former descriptor, we will mainly benefit from research in the games community while for the latter in the BCI community. Finally, we will discuss the relation between the two descriptors.

2.1   Motivations Satisfied by the BCI Game

People play games which potentially fulfill their psychological needs. We see a correspondence between some psychological needs [20] and some game playing motivations [19], such as competence and challenge or relatedness and socialisation. In this section, we will provide some example game playing motivations (or needs) in which BCI can make a difference and discuss the ways to make the difference.

Challenge. Challenge is one of the elements of flow, which is the optimal experience for any activity and described as *"so gratifying that people are willing to do it for its own sake, with little concern for what they will get out of it, even when it is difficult, or dangerous"* [4]. Sweetser and Wyeth [22] proposed a model describing which elements a game should have in order to provide flow. Their model suggests that a game should offer challenges matching player skills and both must exceed a certain threshold.

BCI is an imperfect recognition technology and this is partly because there are no guidelines nor ground truth (e.g. an internal feedback mechanism such as a human sense) for generating particular mental activity. But, people can manipulate and learn to improve their voluntary mental actions as well as involuntary reactions as they keep interacting with a BCI that provides accurate feedback [24]. So, BCI game players need to show continuous effort and even repeat their actions until they are understood by BCI. Not only the successful end result leads to a positive affect but also the purposeful repetition brings fun [1].

Fantasy. Games let players do things that they cannot do -at least safely or without being criticised- in real life, such as flying or smashing cars. However, in a virtual world, it is not trivial to provide the very same sensation resulting from doing something in the real world. Such a sensation is known as presence and defined as *"the perception in which even though part or all of an individual's current experience is generated by and/or filtered through human-made technology, part or all of the individual's perception fails to accurately acknowledge the role of the technology in the experience"* [9]. Riva [18] claims that rather than our perception, it is our chain of actions that create the presence. He explains that a user *"is more present in a perceptually poor virtual environment ... where he/she can act in many different ways than in a real-like virtual environment where he/she cannot do anything."* In achieving this, it is essential to have a one-to-one correspondence between player actions (as well as reactions) in the real world and those in the game world, as provided by the Kinect.

We take the claim of Riva further and propose that 'to act' is not our ultimate goal. We actually aim 'to be' in the virtual world and to act is one way of satisfying our aim. So, we are more present in a virtual world in which we can represent ourselves more. We would like to be represented with our emotions and thoughts. In cases such as these, BCI can provide a translation between the psychological state of the player in the real world and the dynamics of the game world, just as Kinect provides correspondence between real-world and game-world actions. So, the additional inner state information can strengthen the feeling of presence.

Sociality. Some people enjoy playing computer games with other people. They play not necessarily for the challenge but just to be with others. They enjoy spending time with friends, seeing their reactions and expressions, and gloating or feeling proud upon winning [22]. Any multi-player version of a BCI game can provide such an interactive environment. Players may cooperate or compete using BCI or they can share their experiences, such as difficulties or enjoyment with control, while playing the game. These are, of course, not specific to BCI games. But, there are other ways in which BCI can provide sociality and which cannot be replicated easily or at all by other controllers.

Many social actions are related to expressing and perceiving emotions. Previous studies have shown that communication of heartbeat, which is a reflection of emotional activity, can improve the co-presence [3] and intimacy [10] of players. Heartbeat is certainly not the only nor the best indicator of emotion. BCI can recognise certain psychological states and let us share them. Since involuntary brain activity, such as emotional response, is not easily controllable, BCI can provide objective information about our emotional state. For this reason, BCI can also be used in game situations where players would like to hide their psychological states from each other. For example, in a bluffing game, players can restrict their bodily movements and to some extent even their physiological activity but not their brain activity. So, BCI can be used for emotion-awareness or, more generally, psychological awareness in two opposite game logics.

2.2   Interaction Paradigms Used by the BCI Game

BCI applications rely on brain signals originating from player actions and reactions to events. We call these actions and reactions interaction paradigms and collect them under three categories: mental state regulation, movement imagery and evoked response generation.

Mental State Regulation. Mental state games are usually played via two activities: relaxing or concentrating. Most of the mental state games let players move objects [8] but there are other uses such as changing the game avatar [17].

Relaxing is a preferable activity in a game as it leads to a positive affective state that players would like to reach while playing games [12]. Therefore, even if the game environment is not an affective one, people may play such games for the end effect of being relaxed. Moreover, they might easily refer their acquaintances and even children to play such games. Concentration is also a preferable game activity due to its absorbing effect. According to the flow [4,22] and immersion theories [2], concentration is the key to successful games. Therefore, games requiring concentration or paying attention, which is one of the activities leading to concentration, ought to provide a positive play experience.

Mental state regulation games should either be slow paced or in these games BCI should be used as an auxiliary controller along with a primary controller which is faster than BCI. Because, the speed with which we can change our state of relaxedness or concentration is much slower than the speed with which we can press buttons or use any other modality. Mental state games usually allow only binary control. For example, in a relaxation game, players can either be relaxed or not relaxed so they can communicate a maximum of two discrete commands. It is possible to fit a continuous scale between these two states but validating such a scale is non-trivial. Therefore, mental state regulation is less suitable for games that require large numbers of distinct commands.

Movement Imagery. Movement imagery games require no physical movement but imagery of limb movements, mostly the hands, fingers or feet. Players imagine movements to navigate [11] or to make selections [23]. To provide intuitive interaction, the mapping of imaginary movements to game commands should be coherent. For example, grasping an object at the left or right hand side can be matched to left or right hand imagery while walking can be matched to foot imagery. Such intuitive mappings can create the illusion that the game is recognising player's actions, even before they move.

Movement imagery can be recognised quickly, without needing to average the signal [23]. Therefore, movement imagery games are suitable for fast interaction. On the contrary, the number of commands in these games is limited to the number of distinguishable imaginary actions players can perform. Using other modalities in combination with BCI can increase the number of commands. However, the movements made to control other modalities, such as pushing a button or speaking, might contaminate the movement imagery signal. Especially when the signal is not averaged, the signal-to-noise ratio (SNR) is very low.

Evoked Response Generation. This class of games is dominated by steady-state visually evoked potential (SSVEP) games, accompanied rarely by P300 games (e.g. [6]). SSVEP is a brain response to flickering light or images. When we observe visual stimulus, say an image, that is constantly re-appearing at a frequency of f then the amplitude of the signals measured from our visual cortex are enhanced at frequency f and its harmonics ($2f$, $3f$, and so on).

One way of using SSVEP is to map the strength (amplitude) of SSVEP that is evoked by single stimulus to game actions. For example, a weak SSVEP can steer a virtual plane to the left while a strong one to the right [15]. Research has shown that sustained attention can strengthen SSVEP [5]. Sustained attention is an activity which can lead to a state of concentration [14]. This makes SSVEP suitable for concentration games. Another, and the more popular, approach is to use multiple stimuli each of which is associated with a command. With this approach, BCI is usually used to select a direction, for example to steer a racing car [13]. With this approach, a greater number of commands can be issued.

Evoked response generation is less suitable for fast games due to the signal averaging process, which requires signals to accumulate for some time. But they are suitable for multimodality thanks to their high SNR. The number of distinct commands in evoked potential games depends only on the number of stimuli. So, as long as the stimulation space is large enough to accommodate, (finitely) many stimuli can be presented to the player. But, a computer screen is a limited space so the number of stimuli that can be placed on the screen is also limited.

2.3   The Complete Picture

In this section, we will discuss the relation between the two descriptors of our framework. Specifically, we will discuss *which interaction paradigms can satisfy which player motivations and in which ways?* Where possible, we will mention existing or hypothetical BCI games supporting our discussion.

As any game can do, a BCI game can satisfy more than one set of player motivations (the first descriptor) at the same time. It might not satisfy any player motivations, for example if it is just an experimental game. This is illustrated by

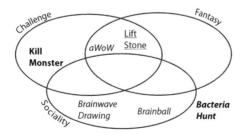

Fig. 1. Diagram showing the set of player motivations and example BCI games. The italic, underlined and bold fonts denote mental state regulation, movement imagery and evoked response generation games respectively.

the set diagrams in Figure 1. A BCI game can make use of multiple interaction paradigms (the second descriptor). The font stylings of the games in Figure 1 indicate the different interaction paradigms and their combinations. For example in the game Bacteria Hunt [16] the players chase fleeing bacteria by controlling an amoeba. It is a mental state regulation game because when the players are relaxed, the bacteria flee more slowly. It is also an evoked response game because when the amoeba catches a bacterium the players concentrate on a flickering circle to eat the bacterium. While there is no restriction on using any interaction paradigm to satisfy any player motivation, there might be preferred and non-preferred matchings.

A BCI game can offer a positively affective challenge if the game can hide BCI recognition errors under the game tasks or story. The game should provide the players with the illusion that when they encounter an error, this is not simply a technological fault of BCI but rather an expected situation given the player tasks and game environment. This way, they should be motivated to repeat the tasks until they learn how to generate the desired brain activity. In the mental state regulation game alpha World of Warcraft (aWoW) [17], the players play a druid that transforms from a bear to a humanoid when the players are relaxed and back again when they are stressed. The level of relaxedness is determined according to the alpha band power. But the players always think of the high level tasks of getting relaxed or stressed to transform. There might be times when players cannot transform desirably in the game. Especially for players who are familiar with the game World of Warcraft or similar games, this is not an unexpected situation. These players would consider that it should take some effort and time for a druid to transform. So, they would keep trying to find the right strategy to transform. The same principle may be applied to movement imaginary games. For example, in a game (let us call it Lift Stone) the players might lift a stone by imagining arm movements. Players familiar with the phenomenon of telekinesis would find this mapping (imagining arm movement and lifting) an intuitive one and consider that it should take some effort to lift something from far. For evoked potential games, due to the explicit stimuli, offering meaningful challenges is more difficult though not impossible. For example in a game (let us call it Kill Monster) players might try to kill a monster by concentrating on its heart which flickers like an SSVEP stimulus. People know that, though it does not flicker, the heart beats and it is the organ of vitality. So, they may accept that killing a monster should require some effort. In contrast, in the Bacteria Hunt game, the flickering circle is not related to bacteria so provides no motivation to concentrate on the stimulus.

To provide fantasy, a BCI game should incorporate additional, inner state information from the players to improve their sense of presence in the virtual world. In the game World of Warcraft, players play the role of a druid. So, the idea is that the players should put themselves in the place of their avatar. The original game translates players actions (e.g. pressing the key W) into game actions (e.g. moving the avatar forward) but it cannot go beyond that. In aWoW, players are represented not only by their actions but also by their psychological states. This way, they can feel more present in the game world. Movement imaginary games cannot convey psychological state information but they can represent covert player intentions. For example in the hypothetical Lift Stone game we mentioned in the previous paragraph, the players might feel as if the game is understanding their intention without having them move.

In a BCI game, sociality might emerge from the explicit social behaviours (e.g. vocalisations, gestures) of co-players while they are competing against or cooperating with each other. In this sense, any interaction paradigm is suitable for use. For example in the game Brainball [8], in which co-players regulate their mental states to roll a ball on the table toward each other, players might, for instance, talk to tease each other or generate facial expressions to manifest the difficulty they are experiencing. Sociality might also be formed through communication of implicit player states. For this sort of sociality, mental state regulation is the natural paradigm of choice. For example, in the game Brainwave Drawing [21], co-players try to synchronise their mental states in terms of their brain signals in different frequency bands.

3   Conclusion

In this paper, we proposed a preliminary framework for BCI games formed partly by research in the BCI community and partly by research in the games community. We represented a BCI game with two descriptor. One of these specifies which player motivation(s) the BCI game can satisfy. We mentioned three example player motivations which are challenge, fantasy and sociality. We showed the ways BCI games can satisfy each of these motivations and provided some guidelines for them. The other descriptor specifies which interaction paradigm(s) the game is built upon. We described three types of interaction paradigms which are mental state regulation, movement imagery and evoked response generation. We relied on literature on BCI and games research while constructing our categories. But there may be many more player motivations that a BCI game can fulfill or interaction paradigms it can make use of. So, obviously, developers should not feel restricted by our categorisations while developing their BCI games. On the contrary, they should investigate the alternative categories.

Acknowledgments The authors gratefully acknowledge the support of the BrainGain Smart Mix Programme of the Netherlands Ministry of Economic Affairs and the Netherlands Ministry of Education, Culture and Science. They would also like to thank L.E. Packwood for her help in improving the language of the article.

References

1. Blythe, M., Hassenzahl, M.: The semantics of fun: Differentiating enjoyable eeperiences. In: Funology, pp. 91–100. Kluwer Academic Publishers (2003)

2. Brown, E., Cairns, P.: A grounded investigation of game immersion. In: CHI 2004 Extended Abstracts, pp. 1297–1300. ACM (2004)
3. Chanel, G., Pelli, S., Ravaja, N., Kuikkaniemi, K.: Social interaction using mobile devices and biofeedback. Presented at BioS-Play 2010 (2010)
4. Csíkszentmihályi, M.: Flow. Harper Perennial (1990)
5. di Russo, F., Spinelli, D.: Effects of sustained, voluntary attention on amplitude and latency of steady-state visual evoked potential. Clinical Neurophysiology 113(11), 1771–1777 (2002)
6. Finke, A., Lenhardt, A., Ritter, H.: The MindGame: A P300-based brain-computer interface game. Neural Networks 22(9), 1329–1333 (2009)
7. Gürkök, H., Nijholt, A.: Brain-computer interfaces for multimodal interaction. International Journal of Human-Computer Interaction 28(5), 292–307 (2012)
8. Hjelm, S.I.: Research+design: the making of Brainball. Interactions 10(1), 26–34 (2003)
9. International Society for Presence Research: The Concept of Presence: Explication Statement (2000), http://ispr.info/about-presence-2/about-presence/
10. Janssen, J.H., Bailenson, J.N., IJsselsteijn, W.A., Westerink, J.H.D.M.: Intimate heartbeats. IEEE Transactions on Affective Computing 1(2), 72–80 (2010)
11. Krepki, R., Blankertz, B., Curio, G., Müller, K.R.: The Berlin Brain-Computer Interface (BBCI). Multimedia Tools and Applications 33(1), 73–90 (2007)
12. Lazzaro, N.: Why we play games: Four keys to more emotion without story (March 2004), http://www.xeodesign.com/xeodesign_whyweplaygames.pdf
13. Martinez, P., Bakardjian, H., Cichocki, A.: Fully online multicommand brain-computer interface with visual neurofeedback using SSVEP paradigm. Computational Intelligence and Neuroscience 2007, 94561 (2007)
14. Mateer, C.A., Sohlberg, M.M. (eds.): Cognitive Rehabilitation: An Integrative Neuropsychological Approach, 2nd edn. The Guilford Press (2001)
15. Middendorf, M., McMillan, G., Calhoun, G., Jones, K.: Brain-computer interfaces based on the steady-state visual-evoked response. IEEE Transactions on Rehabilitation Engineering 8(2), 211–214 (2000)
16. Mühl, C., Gürkök, H., Plass-Oude Bos, D., Thurlings, M., Scherffig, L., Duvinage, M., Elbakyan, A., Kang, S., Poel, M., Heylen, D.: Bacteria Hunt. Journal on Multimodal User Interfaces 4(1), 11–25 (2010)
17. Plass-Oude Bos, D., Reuderink, B., van de Laar, B., Gürkök, H., Mühl, C., Poel, M., Nijholt, A., Heylen, D.: Brain-computer interfacing and games. In: Brain-Computer Interfaces, pp. 149–178. Springer (2010)
18. Riva, G.: Is presence a technology issue? Virtual Reality 13(3), 159–169 (2009)
19. Rouse, R.: Game Design: Theory & Practice. 2nd edn. Wordware (2005)
20. Sheldon, K.M., Elliot, A.J., Kim, Y., Kasser, T.: What is satisfying about satisfying events? Journal of Personality and Social Psychology 80(2), 325–339 (2001)
21. Sobell, N., Trivich, M.: Brainwave drawing game. In: Delicate Balance: Technics, Culture and Consequences, pp. 360–362. IEEE (1989)
22. Sweetser, P., Wyeth, P.: Gameflow. Computers in Entertainment 3(3), 1–24 (2005)
23. Tangermann, M., Krauledat, M., Grzeska, K., Sagebaum, M., Blankertz, B., Vidaurre, C., Müller, K.R.: Playing Pinball with non-invasive BCI. In: Advances in Neural Information Processing Systems, vol. 21, pp. 1641–1648. The MIT Press (2009)
24. Wolpaw, J.R., Birbaumer, N., McFarland, D.J., Pfurtscheller, G., Vaughan, T.M.: Brain-computer interfaces for communication and control. Clinical Neurophysiology 113(6), 767–791 (2002)

Semiautomatic and User-Centered Orientation of Digital Artifacts on Multi-touch Tabletops

Lorenz Barnkow and Kai von Luck

Department of Computer Science, Hamburg University of Applied Sciences,
Berliner Tor 7, 20099 Hamburg, Germany
lorenz.barnkow@haw-hamburg.de, luck@informatik.haw-hamburg.de

Abstract. The orientation of objects on tables is of fundamental importance for the coordination, communication and proper understanding of content in group work. Similarly, the roles of orientation have to be taken into account when implementing software for multi-touch tabletops. This paper describes a combined approach to help with the orientation of artifacts, composed of both automatic and manual orientation methods. Using a custom test application, this study investigates the effects of automatic orientation of artifacts towards users.

Keywords: Multi-touch tabletops, Orientation of artifacts, territoriality, group work.

1 Introduction

The growing availability of commercial and low-cost multi-touch hardware in the recent years has led to increased research interest in this area [1]. As a result, several new techniques have been presented to support individual and collaborative work on multi-touch tabletops. In addition to supporting collaborative work, interactive tabletops are also suitable as a base of digital conversions of classic board games [2] or as novel input devices for computer games (e.g. real-time strategy [3]). The spatial proximity of people at tables allows for direct eye contact, communication using speech and gestures as well as direct perception of what is happening on the table [4]. One of the key challenges to support groups on multi-touch tabletops is the correct orientation of digital artifacts to meet the different perspectives of the participants arranged around the table [5]. Numerous techniques for the technical implementation of the orientation of digital artifacts can be found in the literature of the HCI and CSCW fields. In this paper, a combination of automatic and manual orientation is presented, which reduces the manual effort while also providing a high degree of flexibility. In a preliminary evaluation both the facilitation of the work and the acceptance of this solution was examined quantitatively and qualitatively.

2 Related Work

While working at tables the people involved usually show a distinctive territorial behaviour, partitioning the table into three regions: personal, group and storage

M. Herrlich, R. Malaka, and M. Masuch (Eds.): ICEC 2012, LNCS 7522, pp. 381–388, 2012.

territories [6]. The group territory refers to the shared table space in general, while the areas immediately in front of each person are called personal territory in which personal and private tasks are performed. Storage territories are mainly used to store artifacts for later use or to pass stacks of artifacts to other people [4]. The orientation of artifacts on the table serves three roles: comprehension, coordination and communication [5]. Comprehension refers, among other things, to the readability of text, which may decrease significantly in case of poor orientation [7]. Having artifacts face users supports coordination in such a way that personal territories and ownership become visible. Likewise, the active reorientation of artifacts towards one or more users usually initiates a communicative exchange.

Methods for the orientation of artifacts on multi-touch tabletops can be divided into three categories: manual, automatic and combined. Using means of manual reorientation each person is given the freedom to specify an arbitrary orientation for every artifact. These methods include explicit definition of angles, use of handles, physics-based approaches and multi-touch gestures [8]. All of them generally offer the same flexibility on multi-touch tabletops that would be expected from the real world, but they differ in terms of learnability and usability. On multi-touch tabletops, work can also be facilitated in such a way that the system automatically performs reorientation of the artifacts and thus relieves the users from this task. Such automatic orientation can be performed towards the spatially nearest table edge, based on established territories [9], towards the table edge of the spatially nearest user [10] or based on the position of the users [11]. However, entirely automatic orientation is rarely optimal [12] and negates the communicative role of orientation. Combined (or semiautomatic) methods complement the support of automatic systems with the flexibility of manual reorientation. One example is the use of vector fields and gestures to manipulate these vector fields [12]. However, since only regions rather than artifacts can be manually reoriented, the orientation is not preserved when artifacts are moved thus its coordinating role is compromised [5].

The presented automatic and combined methods pose difficulties regarding the flexibility, awareness as well as the communicative and coordinating roles of orientation. A facilitation of work due to automatic methods was elaborated on in the literature [12], yet it has not been proven or measured. On the contrary, one study suggests that a fully automatic orientation offers no measurable speed advantage over manual orientation and also restricts the freedom of users [11]. This paper presents a combined method of orientation, which was evaluated in a preliminary study to measure the facilitation of work and assess the usability based on the data collected from logs, questionnaires and interviews.

3   Evaluation of Semiautomatic Artifact Orientation

The semiautomatic orientation method examined in this paper combines automatic orientation towards the spatially nearest user with multi-touch gestures for manual rotation of digital artifacts. To reflect the previously described territorial behavior in the system, a personal territory at the table edge is created for each user, similar to [13] (see Fig. 1). However, these personal territories are each associated with a different color and are manually created, moved and removed. By default, the digital artifacts (i.e. interactive widgets such as pictures or news articles) on the tabletop are automatically oriented towards a focal point relative to the spatially nearest personal territory, thus facing the appropriate user, and assume the color of that personal territory in order to strengthen the perception of ownership (see Fig. 1). At any time and for each artifact this automatic behavior may explicitly be turned on or off using a button on the artifact or be overridden by manually rotating an artifact using multi-touch gestures. Manually rotated artifacts do not change their orientation by themselves, unless the automatic orientation feature for this artifact is switched on again by the user. Also mapping the color of an artifact to the corresponding personal territory of its owner is only carried out with activated automatic orientation. The colors also indicate whether the automatic orientation is activated, thus make the current mode (see [14]) visible at all times for each interface item.

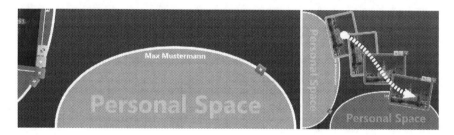

Fig. 1. Screenshots of a personal space (left) and automatic orientation towards the user (right)

3.1 Participants

Ten groups with three unpaid participants each (24 males, 6 females) were recruited. The subjects were between 18 and 45 years old and 24 of them were students. All used computers frequently and most of them (86%) used touch-screens frequently, though few (13%) had experience with large digital tabletops.

3.2 Apparatus

The experiments were performed on a custom built, rear-projected multi-touch tabletop with an interactive surface of about $200cm \times 65cm$ and a screen resolution of 2560×800 pixels (see Fig. 2). The connected computer runs Windows 7 and the test application was built using C# and WPF. In addition to capturing interaction logs, all sessions were recorded using three cameras.

Fig. 2. Experimental setting

3.3 Task

To evaluate the semiautomatic orientation method, an appropriate task was prepared, based on a realistic use case. Based on an interview the workflows in an editorial office were studied, with particular focus on group work involving two or more persons. These included firstly joint sifting through potential pictures for news articles, and secondly an editorial meeting in which the status of the upcoming issue was reviewed and discussed. The developed test application implemented similar use cases loosely based on these workflows and provided tools to browse for news articles and pictures on the internet, using Google News, Flickr and Google Images. The search tools also offered a function to create synchronized and connected copies of these widgets, so that, for example, search results could be jointly browsed. Furthermore, a newspaper widget was made available, which could be compiled into a virtual magazine, using drag-and-drop gestures (see Fig. 3).

In this study, the participants worked in groups to create a newspaper. This task included both loosely coupled phases during which the participants worked on their own as well as tightly coupled phases with strong emphasis on communication and the exchange of artifacts. There were no explicit role assignments, thus all participants had equal rights during the tightly coupled phases.

During the first part of the task every participant was instructed to search for three news articles on two given topics (e. g. "sports" and "entertainment") and pass these articles on to their neighbors in counterclockwise direction. Upon receiving articles from their neighbors each participant reviewed the articles and selected one article for each subject, discarding the rest. The remaining articles were presented and discussed to determine the sequence in which they should be added to the newspaper. This initiated the second part of the task, during which every participant searched one picture for each article of the newspaper. These pictures were also presented to the group and discussed to jointly choose the most appropriate picture for the corresponding article.

Fig. 3. Dragging a picture from the search tool into the newspaper widget (left) inserts it into the corresponding page (right)

3.4 Procedure

Each group performed the aforementioned task in two configurations which differed in the given topics for the newspaper and whether the automatic orientation was available or not. Using questionnaires before the experiments, the demographic characteristics of the subjects and their computer skills were gathered. In addition, all groups received an introduction to the system prior to the experiments and then had 10-15 minutes to test it on their own and ask further questions. Due to the limited scope of the application and small number of tools and widgets available to the user, this initial trial phase could be kept relatively short. The combined amount of time spent working on both task configurations was between 40 and 100 minutes ($mean = 69.5$, $SD = 21.7$). With further questionnaires after the experiments, the usability and collaboration at the table was assessed. The experiments were concluded with an interview with each group.

4 Results

4.1 Effects of Automatic Orientation on the Spatial Use of the Tabletop

Figure 4 shows an example of the spatial use of the tabletop by a group in both test conditions based on the logged interactions. This plot illustrates that the use of automatic orientation has no apparent effect on the spatial use of the tabletop, in contrast to the available space, which visibly restricts the operating radius of the two users on the right side of the plot. This indicates a lack of table size, which was criticized in later interviews as well. The same usage pattern could be seen for all 10 groups across the experiments.

4.2 Facilitation of Work

Based on a statistical analysis of the interaction logs, the facilitation of work by the automatic orientation was measured. For this, the interactions were distinguished as to whether they involved a manual rotation gesture or not. For

Fig. 4. Use of the tabletop by region using automatic orientation (left) or manual rotation only (right)

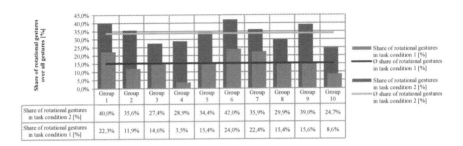

	Group 1	Group 2	Group 3	Group 4	Group 5	Group 6	Group 7	Group 8	Group 9	Group 10
Share of rotational gestures in task condition 2 [%]	40,0%	35,6%	27,4%	28,9%	34,4%	42,0%	35,9%	29,9%	39,0%	24,7%
Share of rotational gestures in task condition 1 [%]	22,3%	11,9%	14,6%	3,5%	15,4%	24,0%	22,4%	15,4%	15,6%	8,6%

Fig. 5. Use of manual rotation during both task conditions

the task condition using the combined method for orientation (task condition 1) an average of 15.4% of all interactions also involved manual rotation. Within the task condition using only manual rotation (task condition 2), the share of rotational gestures was, on average, at 33.8%, thus more than twice as high. Figure 5 shows that this difference was visible across all groups and proved to be statistically significant ($F_{1,18} = 45.041; p < 0.00001$).

4.3 User Experience

The postexperiment questionnaire consisted mainly of statements with a 6-point Likert scale (*fully agree* to *fully disagree*). Further open questions were omitted because of the subsequent interview. Overall, the subjects rated the operation of the test application to be easy (*mean* = 2.1; SD = 0.9). This was also reflected in the interviews, where the direct touch based interaction was described as an intuitive and fun experience. The assignment of colors to indicate ownership was both intuitive (*mean* = 1.2; SD = 0.5) and useful (*mean* = 1.8; SD = 1.1), which was reaffirmed in the interviews. The manual rotation of digital artifacts was easy to perform (*mean* = 1.9; SD = 1.0), while the automatic orientation was both useful (*mean* = 2.2; SD = 0.9) and satisfactory (*mean* = 2.2; SD = 0.9). The interviews revealed broad support for the automatic orientation, since it could be overridden at any time and thus offered both flexibility and facilitation of work. The automatic orientation was found particularly helpful while passing digital artifacts between the users. However, the continuous orientation towards a focal point proved to be unpopular, because artifacts were slightly reoriented with every movement. Firstly, some users felt this was a loss of control and secondly they thought a perpendicular alignment (with respect to the table borders) might be more orderly and space-saving.

5   Conclusions and Further Work

Given the falling prices for commercial multi-touch hardware (e. g. Samsung SUR40) and its growing number of users, multi-touch tabletops present a great potential for a wide range of applications in very different areas, such as professional collaboration, learning together and entertainment software in both private and public spaces (e. g. in bars or hotel lobbies). This paper presents a combined method for orientation of digital artifacts on multi-touch tabletops and analyzes its effects on the spatial use of the tabletop, the facilitation of work and the user experience through a preliminary study. The analysis of interaction logs showed no discernible effect on the spatial use of the available table space, with and without automatic orientation. A statistical analysis revealed that the share of manual rotation gestures is doubled when no automatic orientation is available. The survey of test subjects by questionnaires and interviews indicated a high acceptance for the combined orientation method. The automatic orientation especially helped in the transfer of artifacts between the users, since they were able to concentrate on the actual task at hand. This might help to improve the usability and user experience of collaborative work on digital tabletops including joint browsing and organizing holiday pictures [15] or exchanging and sharing resources in digital board games [2].

Because of the hardware used it was not possible to unambiguously assign every touch contact to the right user. At this point, further investigations are needed because the facilitation of work could not be proven for each individual person. Moreover, the experimental tasks included both loosely and tightly coupled phases, meaning it is unclear whether the combined approach for orientation is appropriate in both situations.

References

1. Schöning, J.: Touching the future: the rise of multitouch interfaces. PerAdaM-agazine (April 2010)
2. Wallace, J.R., Pape, J., Chang, Y.L.B., McClelland, P.J., Graham, T.N., Scott, S.D., Hancock, M.: Exploring automation in digital tabletop board game. In: Proceedings of the ACM 2012 Conference on Computer Supported Cooperative Work Companion, CSCW 2012, pp. 231–234. ACM, New York (2012)
3. Chaboissier, J., Isenberg, T., Vernier, F.: Realtimechess: lessons from a participatory design process for a collaborative multi-touch, multi-user game. In: Proceedings of the ACM International Conference on Interactive Tabletops and Surfaces, ITS 2011, pp. 97–106. ACM, New York (2011)
4. Pinelle, D., Gutwin, C., Subramanian, S.: Designing digital tables for highly integrated collaboration. Technical Report HCI-TR-06-02, Computer Science Department, University of Saskatchewan (2006)

5. Kruger, R., Carpendale, S., Scott, S.D., Greenberg, S.: How people use orientation on tables: comprehension, coordination and communication. In: Proceedings of the 2003 International ACM SIGGROUP Conference on Supporting Group Work, GROUP 2003, pp. 369–378. ACM, New York (2003)
6. Scott, S.D., Sheelagh, M., Carpendale, T., Inkpen, K.M.: Territoriality in collaborative tabletop workspaces. In: Proceedings of the 2004 ACM Conference on Computer Supported Cooperative Work, CSCW 2004, pp. 294–303. ACM, New York (2004)
7. Wigdor, D., Balakrishnan, R.: Empirical investigation into the effect of orientation on text readability in tabletop displays. In: Proceedings of the Ninth Conference on European Conference on Computer Supported Cooperative Work, pp. 205–224. Springer-Verlag New York, Inc., New York (2005)
8. Hancock, M., Vernier, F., Wigdor, D., Carpendale, S., Shen, C.: Rotation and translation mechanisms for tabletop interaction. In: First IEEE International Workshop on Horizontal Interactive Human-Computer Systems, TableTop 2006, 8p. (January 2006)
9. Shen, C., Vernier, F.D., Forlines, C., Ringel, M.: Diamondspin: an extensible toolkit for around-the-table interaction. In: CHI 2004: Proceedings of the SIGCHI Conference on Human Factors in Computing Systems, pp. 167–174. ACM, New York (2004)
10. Rekimoto, J., Saitoh, M.: Augmented surfaces: a spatially continuous work space for hybrid computing environments. In: Proceedings of the SIGCHI Conference on Human Factors in Computing Systems: the CHI is the Limit, CHI 1999, pp. 378–385. ACM, New York (1999)
11. Schiavo, G., Jacucci, G., Ilmonen, T., Gamberini, L.: Evaluating an automatic rotation feature in collaborative tabletop workspaces. In: Proceedings of the 2011 Annual Conference Extended Abstracts on Human Factors in Computing Systems, CHI EA 2011, pp. 1315–1320. ACM, New York (2011)
12. Dragicevic, P., Shi, Y.: Visualizing and manipulating automatic document orientation methods using vector fields. In: ITS 2009: Proceedings of the ACM International Conference on Interactive Tabletops and Surfaces, pp. 65–68. ACM, New York (2009)
13. Klinkhammer, D., Nitsche, M., Specht, M., Reiterer, H.: Adaptive personal territories for co-located tabletop interaction in a museum setting. In: Proceedings of the ACM International Conference on Interactive Tabletops and Surfaces, ITS 2011, pp. 107–110. ACM, New York (2011)
14. Raskin, J.: The humane interface (book excerpt). Ubiquity 2000 (May 2000)
15. Hilliges, O., Wagner, M., Terrenghi, L., Butz, A.: The living-room: browsing, organizing and presenting digital image collections in interactive environments. In: 3rd IET International Conference on Intelligent Environments, IE 2007, pp. 552–559 (September 2007)

Towards a Brewery Educational Game:
Would Existence of a Game Goal Improve Learning?

Cyril Brom, Edita Bromová, and Martin Pergel

Charles University in Prague, Faculty of Mathematics and Physics
Malostranské nám. 2/25, Prague, Czech Republic

Abstract. One useful but neglected approach to investigating instructional effectiveness of digital games is to manipulate presence of a game element and compare how the game with and without the element promote learning. In this work-in-progress paper, we introduce a comparative study we are preparing on investigating whether presence of a motivating game goal has a positive effect on learning gains. We also present a brewery simulation/game, which we have developed for the study's purpose. The simulation is the same as the game and contains the same educational materials, but it lacks an explicit game goal: the learners acquire a mental model of the beer production in both applications, but the learning process is "gamified" in the game. We believe that this research approach could help to identify useful features of educational applications.

1   Introduction

It has been argued that digital games can bring many advantages as educational aids, e.g. [5, 10]; however, empirical studies substantiating these claims remain limited and tend to generate mixed results, e.g. [1, 2, 6, 9, but also 11]. In addition, many of these studies, most notably comparative ones, are designed to answer the question whether the digital game based learning approach (DGBL) outperforms so-called "traditional" teaching methods. That complicates generalization of results because a "traditional" method used for a comparison often differs from an employed DGBL method in several dimensions, each of which can influence the learning outcome in either way.

A complementary approach to investigating instructional effectiveness of DGBL is to focus on game elements instead of whole games and ask a question what game features have the highest potential to promote learning. Isolating these features could help developers to develop more instructionally effective games. In comparative "feature isolating" studies, e.g. [9], different versions of a game are compared against each other, and the versions differ in just one or two elements. Similar approach has brought fruits in the close field of multimedia learning [8].

The goal of this work-in-progress paper is to present our brewery simulation/game, designed for the purpose of investigating instructional effectiveness of existence of a game goal and introduce our on-going study on this topic. Games are arguably most fun to play when the goal is personally meaningful and reasonably challenging, cf. [7]. One can hypothesize that that increases engagement of a player and that, in turn, cognitive processing of the player, which, in case of an edu-game, may increase

M. Herrlich, R. Malaka, and M. Masuch (Eds.): ICEC 2012, LNCS 7522, pp. 389–392, 2012.
© IFIP International Federation for Information Processing 2012

learning gains. At the same time, the gaming activities may compromise learning by distracting the learner's attention from the learning, a trade-off, cf. [9]. In Netlogo toolkit [12], we have developed an interactive simulation of the process of brewing, in which a learner acquires the mental model of the beer production. The learner can set various parameters at various points during the brewing process, influencing the outcome. The program has two versions: while the first is merely a simulation, the second is presented as a game in which the player can sell the beer, improve the brewery and buy better ingredients such as better yeast. Both versions have nearly the same interface (Fig. 1) and exactly the same supplementary instructions. Would the learning gains be higher for learners working with the game as opposed to learners working with the simulation? Note the application is not a "drill-and-practice" tool; the learning happens during interfacing with the simulated brewery.

The paper proceeds as follows: in Sec. 2, we introduce the process of brewing as modelled by our simulation. In Sec. 3, we detail the simulation and the study.

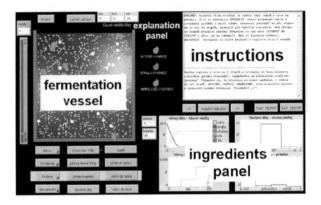

Fig. 1. Brewery simulation screenshot

2   Process of Brewing

The process of beer-brewing is a rather complicated one as in the beer there were isolated around 2 000 chemical compounds [4]. Thus we focused only on the main topics that can be used, for example, as the first step by a homebrewer and we focused only on the technology for bottom-fermented lagers of pilsner type. We omitted all the processes that can be outsourced (without loss of quality), like malted barley preparation. In general, our aim was to keep the whole simulation reasonably complex for an educational experiment, i.e. neither too short, nor too long.

To briefly describe the process, it consists of mashing, lautering, boiling, whirlpooling, wort cooling, (cool) fermenting and conditioning. As lautering and whirlpooling are simple procedures which one intuitively passes correctly (with an appropriate technology), we focused on the remaining ones only. Also filtering and packaging are not simulated. The mashing got simplified and thus we implemented the infusion mashing. The boiling process is restricted to the hops-addition. The fermentation and conditioning tries to simulate the life of the yeast in the wort.

We focused on typical points in each of the procedures, during which an error can be made, and knowledge of which can be tested easily. During the infusion we simulate how the enzymes in the malt are breaking down the starch into sugars (one "universal" sugar) with respect to the temperature. During the boiling we check just whether it lasts suitably long and how the hops-addition corresponds to a particular recipe. During the fermentation the yeast (*Saccharomyces cerevisiae*) reacts sugars to the alcohol and other chemicals (fusel). We simulate the activity of yeast with respect to the temperature, including the yeast's thermal shocks and change of its metabolism. We simulate also a parasitic bacteria falling into the fermentation tank (*Clostridium acetobutylicum*). From the yeast's by-products we focus only on ethanol, CO_2 and generic fusel. For the bacteria we focus on the acetone. During the conditioning a slight change of taste should take place. This moment we omit but it does not matter too much as we simulate the concentration of CO_2 (whose absence causes for a beer an adequate penalty) and the fusel concentration (which increases if the yeast produce CO_2 too quickly). Before the conditioning it is possible to make a sugar-surrogation.

3   Study on Instructional Effectiveness of a Game Goal Presence

The application models the brewing process as described in Sec. 2 and it has been developed using Netlogo toolkit [12] solely for research purposes. The application has two versions: a) an interactive simulation; b) a single-player game in which the player can sell the beer and improve his/her brewery by earnings from selling the beer.

There are many ways how a simulation can be "gamified" by adding a goal, and many of these ways can actually compromise learning [9]. Our first aim is to develop a game so that it instructionally more effective than the simulation, and only later pinpoint instructional effectiveness of various game goal types. Why have we chosen the brewing process? Brewing beer is a source of a national pride and a personally meaningful task for many Czechs. In addition, many people actually do not know how to brew beer and low previous knowledge can be expected.

For the study, we aim at employing between-subjects design with immediate and delayed post-tests (with over 18 years old subjects). Besides manipulating presence of the game goal, a third, "non-computer" group will be employed. Our plan is that in both research groups, the learners will first go through a tutorial (10 minutes), then proceed to "walk-through" the whole brewing process and inspect its branches (50 minutes), and finally, after a break, will be either assigned a task to brew several types of beers from a fixed list (simulation group) or proceed to the game on improving the brewery, in which they will brew the same types of beers as they would do in the simulation group (game group) (30 minutes). Learners in the non-computer group will study paper materials combining the simulation images and instructions (60 minutes) and participate in worksheet activities concerning the topic (30 minutes). In each group, the learners will be exposed to the materials for 90 minutes. All the groups' participants will work with the same texts and images during the whole study and have the same tasks for the last 30 minutes.

We have already conducted a feasibility study with 16 subjects, which helped us to refine the simulation and instructions. This study pinpointed one possible problem, the duration of the intervention: the initial exposure of 60 minutes is long for some learners. The open question is how many materials should be removed: the more we remove, the worse mental model of the process can be expected to be acquired.

Concerning the knowledge tests, we aim at employing Mayer's type of retention and problem-solving transfer tests [8], which we are presently piloting.

4   Conclusion

We have introduced an educational study we are currently preparing on investigating whether an interactive simulation is instructionally more effective if an explicit goal "gamifying" the learning content is added (and in a more remote future, what kind of goal should be added to maximize learning gains). Although our research question may seem trivial, empirical results elucidating this issue are very limited. For the study's purpose, we have already developed a brewery simulation/game and we are currently piloting the study. The application is not a "drill-and-practice" instructional program in which the learning part is separated from the gaming part; learners should learn directly when interfacing with the application.

Acknowledgments. This research is partially supported by project nr. P407/12/P152 supported by Czech Grant Science Foundation (GA ČR).

References

1. Brom, C., Preuss, M., Klement, D.: Are Educational Computer Micro-Games Engaging and Effective for Knowledge Acquisition At High-Schools? A Quasi-Experimental Study. Computers & Education 57, 1971–1988 (2011)
2. Clark, R., et al.: An Analysis of the Failure of Electronic Media and Discovery-based Learning: Evidence for the Performance Benefits of Guided Training Methods. In: Handbook of Training and Improving Workplace Performance. Instructional Design and Training Delivery, vol. I, pp. 263–297. Wiley, Somerset (2009)
3. Egenfeldt-Nielsen, S.: Beyond Edutainment: Exploring the Educational Potential of Computer Games. PhD thesis. University of Copenhagen (2005)
4. Esslinger, H.M. (ed.): Handbook of Brewing: Processes, Technology, Markets. Wiley (2009)
5. Gee, J.P.: What video games have to teach us about learning and literacy. Palgrave/St. Martin's, New York (2003)
6. Hays, R.T.: The Effectiveness of Instructional Games: A Literature Review and Discussion, Technical Report 2005-004, Orlando: Naval Air Warfare Center Training Systems Division (2005)
7. Malone, T.W.: Toward a theory of intrinsically motivating instruction. Cognitive Science 5(4), 333–369 (1981)
8. Mayer, R.E.: Multimedia learning. Cambridge University Press, New York (2001)
9. Mayer, R.E., Clark, R.C.: Simulations and Games in e-Learning. In: E-Learning and the Science of Instruction, 3rd edn., pp. 369–400. John Wiley & Sons (2011)
10. Prensky, M.: Digital Game-Based Learning. McGraw Hill, New York (2001)
11. Sitzmann, T.: A meta-analytic examination of the instructional effectiveness of computer-based simulation games. Personnel Psychology 64, 489–528 (2011)
12. Wilensky, U.: NetLogo, Center for Connected Learning and Computer-Based Modeling. Northwestern University (1999), http://ccl.northwestern.edu/netlogo/ (accessed March 11, 2012)

Player Control in a Real-Time Mobile Augmented Reality Game

Mareike Picklum, Georg Modzelewski, Susanne Knoop, Toke Lichtenberg,
Philipp Dittmann, Tammo Böhme, Volker Fehn, Christian John,
Johannes Kenkel, Philipp Krieter, Patrick Niethen, Nicole Pampuch,
Marcel Schnelle, Yvonne Schwarte, Sanja Stark, Alexander Steenbergen,
Malte Stehr, Henning Wielenberg, Merve Yildirim, Can Yüzüncü,
Frederic Pollmann, Dirk Wenig, and Rainer Malaka

Research Group Digital Media, TZI,
University of Bremen, Bibliothekstr. 1, 28359 Bremen, Germany
Projekt Movirwelt
http://movir.informatik.uni-bremen.de

Abstract. Controlling virtual characters in AR games for modern
smartphones is even more challenging than controls for 'pure' VR games
because the player has to keep the AR world in view. We propose six
interaction concepts based on combinations of both physical and virtual
buttons and sensor input and suggest an evaluation according to game
experience criteria.

Keywords: mobile gaming, augmented reality, AR, user interaction,
gestures.

1 Introduction

On smartphones, controlling characters in augmented reality games has a lot in
common with touch-based games but there is an additional problem: To receive
visual feedback of his actions the player needs to keep the AR world in view, so
one is not entirely free to choose his device's position.

Within a students' project we developed a real-time mobile augmented reality
game in which two virtual characters fight against each other. Each player controls a character in the AR world, which is created by having both devices track
the same marker (Fig. 1) and communicate wirelessly. While each player can
see both characters, one only controls his own. Additional information about
the current game state as well as buttons to initiate actions are displayed on
the screen (Fig. 1). The player can control the avatar's movement and initiate
primary and secondary attacks. He is also able to block the enemy's attacks. Primary attacks have a short range, e.g. kicks or punches while secondary attacks
can be long ranged e.g. fireballs. The movement speed of the character is limited
to prevent the avatar from moving instantly to the point the user clicked on.

In this paper we suggest different input options for the best game experience
in our AR game and propose further research to evaluate them.

M. Herrlich, R. Malaka, and M. Masuch (Eds.): ICEC 2012, LNCS 7522, pp. 393–396, 2012.
© IFIP International Federation for Information Processing 2012

2   Related Work

Hürst and van Wezel [1] developed a system in which the user's own hands
or fingers are used to interact with the 3D objects. Avatars can be moved or
knocked over by using the finger behind the device to 'push' the models instead
of touching the display. Usability tests showed that users interacting with objects
while holding a mobile device with one hand and moving the other one in front
of the camera results '... in an awkward hand position or even forces people to
switch the hand in which they hold the device.' Harviainen et al. [2] used camera
movement and accelerometers to control virtual characters. In one example an
animated model of a dog reacts to the camera movement, while another implementation uses the accelerometer to detect shaking or tilting of the phone. Gu
et al. [3] developed a game similar to ours and used the accelerometer to move
a character and touches on the screen to initiate actions. They did not evaluate
the effects of different input options on the game experience. Calvillo-Gámez et
al. [4] developed a questionnaire to measure game experience.

Fig. 1. left: AR mockup; middle: actual prototype; right: screen capture of the prototype. a) player/device 1, b) player/device 2, c) character of player 1, d) character of
player 2, e) AR marker, f) GUI buttons, g) AR arena

3   Interaction Concepts

When developing mobile interaction concepts several factors need to be considered to provide the best user experience. Often the screen is both input and
output device. The more control elements are placed on the screen the higher is
the risk of occluding important parts of the game with the user's fingers. This
might have a negative effect on the game experience and make it difficult to
control it in a real-time environment. As the touch screen provides no inherent
haptic feedback, the user has to actively make sure his fingers are in contact
with the displayed control elements which lowers the immersion by forcing him
to focus not on game content but on input modalities. An additional difficulty
in AR games on smartphones is to permanently keep the tracked marker in the
field of view of the device's camera.

The control of character movement in a game can be relative, with respect to
the position of the player, or absolute, with respect to absolute coordinates of the
AR world. Absolute control means that the player sets the goal of the movement
and the avatar moves to the destination by itself without further interaction of

the player. For continuous control the input is read in each update cycle of the game, forcing the player to give continuous input until the desired position is reached. Discrete input starts a perpetual movement until it is interrupted by further user input or the destination is reached. To improve user experience, feedback can be provided, e.g. to notify the player if his fingers are no longer in contact with the control elements on the touch screen or if the marker can no longer be tracked. While this feedback could use all output channels of the device it is important that the user can distinguish between the provided input feedback and the regular game output at any time. Feedback can be provided using vibration, audio signals and visual hints like a flashing screen or a some kind of in-game feedback of the character (e.g. stumbling).

The following concepts concentrate on controlling the movement of the character. Primary and secondary attacks as well as blocking are initiated by touching buttons displayed on the screen. The concepts focus on the touch screen and other built-in sensors of the devices.

Touch-Based Virtual Joystick. Some mobile games use a concept similar to a joystick but without the need for the actual hardware device. A circle is drawn on the corner of the screen and the position of a touch in relation to the center of the circle defines the position of the virtual joystick. It is usually used with a thumb. Virtual joysticks provide movement control relative to the character's position. They require the continuous and correct placement of the player's finger on the control element, occluding only a small part of the screen. Feedback can be provided if the finger is no longer touching the control element.

Touch-Gesture Control. Swipe gestures are well established to interact with smartphones. They are used to initiate the movement of the character in the indicated direction. Tapping on the screen stops the movement.

Physical Control Buttons. Some Android devices like the Motorola Milestone have physical keyboards which can be used to move the player model relatively to its current position with a set of predefined keys, analogous to many desktop games. This easy and intuitively understandable technique is established in many other applications. As most of the common devices currently on the market do not have a physical keyboard integrated, this concept is not suitable in general but provides the best haptic feedback.

Touch-Based Absolute Control. The user sets the location in the AR world by tapping on a point on the screen, occluding it only for a short period of time. The destination is set in the AR world, so moving the device does not change the target position. Depending on the distance between the current and the desired position of the avatar it might take some time before the movement is finished. It could be helpful to place a visual hint such as a flag or cross-hair in the AR world to remind the player about the current destination.

Field-of-View-Based Continuous Control. Instead of requiring the user to select a specific point, the destination is continuously updated to the center of the camera's current field of view. Moving the device and thereby the AR viewport allows the player to control the character. This is even true if the player does not intend to move the character. An alternative to the continuous updating could be realized by pressing a button to set the new destination. Again a visual hint can be helpful to indicate the current movement target.

Physical Gestures. Modern smartphones offer additional sensors like gyroscopes or accelerometers which can be used as input in games. They react to movements like tilting, rotating or shaking of the device. These gestures would also change the viewport on the AR world because the camera is fixed on the device. Further research has to show if the accompanying viewport change has a detrimental effect on the game experience in a real-time game.

4   Conclusion and Future Work

We presented several possible concepts for player control in mobile AR scenarios. Using visual, auditive or haptic feedback might mitigate the shortcomings of some of these concepts. Prototypical implementations will be used to conduct further game experience studies.

References

1. Hürst, W., van Wezel, C.: Multimodal Interaction Concepts for Mobile Augmented Reality Applications. In: Lee, K.-T., Tsai, W.-H., Liao, H.-Y.M., Chen, T., Hsieh, J.-W., Tseng, C.-C. (eds.) MMM 2011 Part II. LNCS, vol. 6524, pp. 157–167. Springer, Heidelberg (2011)
2. Harviainen, T., Korkalo, O., Woodward, C.: Camera-based interactions for augmented reality. In: Proceedings of the International Conference on Advances in Computer Enterntainment Technology, ACE 2009, pp. 307–310. ACM, New York (2009)
3. Gu, J., Duh, H.B., Kitazawa, S.: 7. In: A Platform for Mobile Collaborative Augmented Reality Game: A Case Study of "AR Fighter", pp. 99–108. Springer, New York (2011)
4. Calvillo-Gámez, E.H., Cairns, P., Cox, A.L.: 4. Human–Computer Interaction Series. In: Bernhaupt, R. (ed.) Assessing the Core Elements of the Gaming Experience, pp. 47–71. Springer, London (2010)

Evolution of GameBots Project

Michal Bída, Martin Černý, Jakub Gemrot, and Cyril Brom

Charles University in Prague, Faculty of Mathematics and Physics,
Department of Software and Computer Science Education
Malostranské nám. 2/25, Prague, Czech Republic

Abstract. GameBots is a project started in early 2000s by A. N. Marshall and
G. A. Kaminka. The project aims at providing researchers a real-time virtual
environment testbed for their agents. GameBots utilized environment of Unreal
Tournament first-person shooter game providing several scenarios for the
agents. GameBots project was continued by several research groups resulting in
many interesting applications. In this paper we summarize evolution of the
GameBots project and contributions made since the first appearance. We focus
on Pogamut GameBots branch which has been steadily developed for six years
with many improvements and optimizations.

1 Introduction

The intelligent virtual agents (IVAs) research community grows increasingly
interested in the use of computer games as primary evaluation testbeds. The
advantage of this approach is that contemporary computer games provide ready-made
rich environments with many properties of the real world without exposing
developers to difficulties inherent to robotics. However, the implementation of
interfaces between games and research software is a repetitive, time consuming task
and introduces many caveats.

The GameBots (GB) project [1] aimed at solving this problem regarding a 3D
first-person shooter game. In particular, the original GB provided access to the
environment of the first Unreal Tournament (UT) [2] by TCP/IP text-based protocol.
This allowed the researchers to directly connect agents written in high level languages
to a complex virtual environment.

The 3D engine behind Unreal Tournament called Unreal Engine (UE) was further
developed while keeping the same scripting language (UnrealScript). Thus the GB
code could be ported to its newer versions without any great effort. The UE is used in
the Unreal Tournament series as well as many other popular games.

Since the inception of GB, several research groups built upon the GB codebase,
resulting in multiple quite different platforms for communication with the
environments of various versions of the games and platforms built upon UE.
Currently, there are versions of GameBots for a) the original UT, b) its sequel Unreal
Tournament 2004 (UT 2004), c) its sequel Unreal Tournament 3 (UT 3), d) Unreal
Engine 2 Runtime Demo (UE 2) – a free version of UE and e) Unreal Development
Kit (UDK) – a free version of the latest UE.

M. Herrlich, R. Malaka, and M. Masuch (Eds.): ICEC 2012, LNCS 7522, pp. 397–400, 2012.

The JavaBot project [3] features a Java library for communication with GB, allowing a user to control agents in UT. JavaBot comes with a relatively simple application for running and observing the agents. The Rochester Institute of Technology GameBots project (RIT GB) [4] ported GB to UT 2004. While RIT GB supported multiple game types, the code was not optimized for performance and did not cover all of the possible bot actions. USARSim [5] is a robotic simulator built for UT 2004, UDK and UT 3. The communication protocol is based on the original GB. USARSim extended UT 2004, UDK and UT 3 by adding multiple robots (Khepera, Aibo, flying drones, etc.) with complete physics and sensor simulation, e.g., laser, infra and sonic. To our knowledge, none of the above projects features any IDE for debugging and only USARSim project is still being actively developed.

The Pogamut project [6] ported and extended GB for UT 2004, UE 2, UT 3 and UDK, optimizing its performance, adding many more features and building an extensive Java front-end (a NetBeans plugin).

The rest of this paper discusses the Pogamut GameBots, its advantages, new features, optimizations and research applications.

2   Pogamut GameBots Improvements

A major issue in previous GB implementations was performance. Our experience is that Unreal Engine in general is slow in concatenating strings and exporting large amount of textual data. This greatly limited the number of bots that could be run in parallel. By optimizing the amount of data exported by the engine, we have increased the number of bots running in parallel from approximately 4 to approximately 10 (depending on actual hardware configuration) measured in UT 2004. In this comparison, synchronous data containing updates of bots' sensory information were exported with the frequency of 4 Hz in both cases. Among the modifications made is a filtering mechanism preventing the bot to be flooded with hear sound events and we have also reduced the amount of exported synchronous data (e.g. positions of most navigation points are static and need to be exported only once).

One of common techniques used in robotics is to detect nearby obstacles by various kinds of sensors. We have added automatic raycasting for bots in Pogamut GB. This allows for steering research [7] with Pogamut GB.

To ease the development of IVAs with Pogamut GB we have introduced various debugging features into the graphical interface of the Unreal Engine for UT 2004, UT 3, UE 2 and UDK. Those include navigation graph visualization, agent information visualization (health, field of view, focus, etc.), raycasting visualization and general game info (Fig. 1).

In order to be able to make scientific comparison between bot and human behavior, a new type of connection called Observer connection was implemented. The connection a) enables listening to events triggered by a human player or a bot, and b) exports all movement and visibility information of the observed entity.

Following the interest in believable IVAs and interactive digital storytelling we have created a standalone package for UE 2 and UDK consisting of a virtual city and numerous agent avatars suitable for non-violent everyday life scenarios [8]. We also introduced a simple communication model driven by displaying comic-like balloons with icons. This package is freely distributed at our site[1] for research and educational purposes.

To develop a human-like bot for the BotPrize competition [9] Pogamut GB were extended to better interact with moving projectiles and to allow the bots to double jump and dodge-jump. This allows for complex human-like movement in the environment that (to our knowledge) no other GB version is capable of.

Fig. 1. Debugging features of Pogamut GB include navigation points and navigation grid visualization, raycasting visualization, bot health, armor and field of view visualization, general game information, etc. The screenshot is from UT 2004.

3   Conclusions

According to Google Scholar the use of Pogamut GB branch has been reported in nearly 100 published papers (23 by our group), including [7, 10, 11]. We believe this is a strong proof of versatility of the Pogamut GB for IVA research in general and also of their quality, stability and comprehensive documentation. While Pogamut GB are a standalone project (and are used as such), one of their main strength is the tight integration with the Pogamut platform [6], which introduces many higher level agent-oriented features on top of Pogamut GB. Porting Pogamut GB to newer versions of Unreal Engine brings opportunities to combine research with cutting-edge

---

[1] http://pogamut.cuni.cz/main/tiki-index.php?page=Download

entertainment computing technologies. The many new features ease the IVA development process and widen the usability spectrum to further research topics.

In general, Pogamut GB opens complex and challenging environments for IVAs research while letting the researchers focus on the implementation of the actual agent logic instead of the technical details.

Acknowledgments. This work was partially supported by a project P103/10/1287 (GACR), by student grants GA UK No. 0449/2010/A-INF/MFF and GA UK No. 655012/2012/A-INF/MFF and partially supported by SVV project number 265 314. Development of graphical content created for GameBots in Unreal Engine 2 Runtime Demo and Unreal Development Kit was supported by the project CZ.2.17/3.1.00/33274 that is financed by the European Social Fund and the Budget of the Municipality of Prague. We would also like to thank Zbynek Krulich who created majority of this graphical content using Mayang's Free Textures library: http://mayang.com/textures/.

References

1. Adobbati, R., Marshall, A.N., Scholer, A., Tejada, S., Kaminka, G.A., Schaffer, S., Sollitto, C.: GameBots: A 3D virtual world test bed for multiagent research. In: Proceedings of the Second International Workshop on Infrastructure for Agents, MAS, and Scalable MAS, Montreal, Canada (2001)
2. Epic Games, Inc.: Unreal Tournament (2001), http://en.wikipedia.org/wiki/Unreal_Tournament (May 30, 2012)
3. Marshall, A.N., et al.: JavaBot (2002), http://utbot.sourceforge.net/ (May 30, 2012)
4. Bayliss, J., Garwood, T.: GameBots for Unreal Tournament 2004. Rochester Institute of Technology (2005), http://www.cs.rit.edu/~jdb/gamebots/ (May 30, 2012)
5. Carpin, S., Lewis, M., Wang, J., Balakirsky, S., Scrapper, C.: USARSim: a robot simulator for research and education. In: Proceedings of the IEEE International Conference on Robotics and Automation, pp. 1400–1405 (2007)
6. Gemrot, J., Kadlec, R., Bída, M., Burkert, O., Píbil, R., Havlíček, J., Zemčák, L., Šimlovič, J., Vansa, R., Štolba, M., Plch, T., Brom, C.: Pogamut 3 Can Assist Developers in Building AI (Not Only) for Their Videogame Agents. In: Dignum, F., Bradshaw, J., Silverman, B., van Doesburg, W. (eds.) Agents for Games and Simulations. LNCS, vol. 5920, pp. 1–15. Springer, Heidelberg (2009), http://pogamut.cuni.cz
7. Popelová, M., Bída, M., Brom, C., Gemrot, J., Tomek, J.: When a Couple Goes Together: Walk along Steering. In: Allbeck, J.M., Faloutsos, P. (eds.) MIG 2011. LNCS, vol. 7060, pp. 278–289. Springer, Heidelberg (2011)
8. Bida, M., Brom, C., Popelova, M., Kadlec, R.: StoryFactory – A Tool for Scripting Machinimas in Unreal Engine 2 and UDK. In: André, E. (ed.) ICIDS 2011. LNCS, vol. 7069, pp. 334–337. Springer, Heidelberg (2011)
9. Hingston, P.: The 2K BotPrize. In: Proceedings of CIG 2009, Milano, Italy (2009), http://www.botprize.org (May 30, 2012)
10. Gemrot, J., Brom, C., Bryson, J., Bida, M.: How to compare usability of techniques for the specification of virtual agents' behavior? An experimental pilot study with human subjects. In: Proceedings of Agents for Games and Simulations, AAMAS Workshop, Taipei, Taiwan, pp. 33–57 (2011)
11. Arrabales, R., Ledezma, A., Sanchis, A.: Towards Conscious-like Behavior in Computer Game Characters. In: Proceedings of the IEEE Symposium on Computational Intelligence and Games 2009, pp. 217–224 (2009)

A Framework for Usability Evaluation of Mobile Mixed Reality Games

Charley Gielkens[1,2] and Richard Wetzel[2]

[1] Utrecht University, Princetonplein 5, 3584 CC Utrecht, The Netherlands
charley.gielkens@gmail.com
[2] Fraunhofer FIT, Schloss Birlinghoven, 53754 Sankt Augustin, Germany

Abstract. This research presents a framework that supports usability experts in determining which method to use when evaluating Mobile Mixed Reality Games (MMRGs). These are games that combine the real and virtual world by means of e.g. a smartphone and require the player to change their geographical location. As some different styles of MMRGs exist, e.g. running versus cunning or multiplayer versus single player, not every method is suitable for each style. The results of the methods are benchmarked against a heuristic evaluation and it is shown that using Instant Data Analysis (IDA), Diary, interaction logs combined with audio diary and retrospective think aloud combined with IDA perform statistically comparable, but that the latter is not favorable based on qualitative merits.

Keywords: mixed reality,augmented reality,games,usability evaluation.

1 Introduction

A game that mixes the real and virtual world to some degree is called a Mixed Reality Game [7]. If this is done using a mobile device such a game is called a Mobile Mixed Reality Game (MMRG). If the player has to change their location, the game is considered a truly mobile MMRG [13]. Mixed reality is interpreted rather freely, so that it does not only include Augmented Reality by means of a magic lens [1] but also by means of a map. Such games are also known as location based games.

As MMRGs are migrating from research projects [6,12] to consumer products, they are also migrating from specialized hardware to common hardware like smartphones, i.e. phones with advanced sensors. As the input and output capabilities on these devices is limited compared to a static desktop computer, a high degree of usability is of even greater importance. In current literature little is known about how to measure usability of MMRGs. For both games in general [2,9,10] and MMRGs [4] heuristic evaluation is a tried and tested method. In [4] a definition for the usability of MMRGs is given, which will also be used here: *"usability for MMRGs is the degree to which a player is able to learn, control, understand and safely play a game in the environment it was designed for."*

M. Herrlich, R. Malaka, and M. Masuch (Eds.): ICEC 2012, LNCS 7522, pp. 401–404, 2012.

2   Method

After studying both the Android Marketplace [4] for games and literature on usability evaluation methods [4], it was surmised that different styles of games exist and postulated that each had usability evaluation methods that were better suited to their needs. Four methods were identified that merited testing for certain styles of games which are described using questions. Their relation is visualized in figure 1. As the focus of this study are MMRGs in a context sensitive manner, the evaluation of mock ups (**question 1**) is not further investigated.

Question 2: Game Length. If a game is played over a longer period of time, the interface is most likely also complicated. In such a case it is advantageous if the player can also actually play it over a longer period of time. Therefore, using a diary is suggested. [11]

Question 3: Amount of Players. If more players are needed to play the game than there are experts available to observe them, direct observation becomes impossible. In this case it is suggested to use interaction logs (IL) and a spoken diary. The latter means that the participants vocalize their likes and dislikes, but not every single thought like in a think aloud (TA) [3] session.

Question 4: Session Length. When enough experts are available to observe players, but a play session takes a long time, e.g. over an hour, one may want to consider not having the experts present all the time as this is expensive. In order to make evaluating such a session easier, it is suggested to use IL and a spoken diary again.

Question 5: Physical Activity. If you have enough experts and the game doesn't last too long, e.g. less than an hour, the last thing to take into account is the amount of physical activity required to play the game. If one needs to run a lot, performing a concurrent TA becomes very difficult both for the participant as for the expert. It was therefore suggested to use retrospective TA and IDA [5] when a lot physical activity is involved and just IDA when it isn't.

To validate the suggested methods they are applied to relevant games which are also evaluated using heuristics for MMRGs [4]. For each list all issues will be rated on severity using he five-point scale introduced in [8]. The median severity ratings were compared between methods, within games using a Mann-Whitney test and the amount of issues were compared within games, between methods using a χ^2-test.

For the diary study Parallel Kingdom (http://www.parallelkingdom.com/) was used, for the slow paced game Tidy City [14] was chosen and for the other options Portal Hunt (http://www.totem-games.org/?q=portalhunt) was selected.

3   Results

In table 1 the amount of issues that have been identified using each method is shown per game, method and severity rating. For IDA ($Mdn = 1$) the median

Table 1. Issues per severity rating, per game, per method

(a) Parallel Kingdom

Severity	Heuristics	Diary
0	0	0
1	6	7
2	11	15
3	17	16
4	2	3
Total:	36	41
Median:	3	2

(b) Portal Hunt

Severity	Heuristics	RTA/IDA	IL/AD
0	0	1	0
1	0	5	3
2	19	13	11
3	18	11	32
4	13	9	10
Total:	50	39	56
Median:	3	3	3

(c) Tidy City

Severity	Heuristics	IDA
0	0	10
1	4	17
2	17	12
3	9	4
4	1	0
Total:	31	43
Median:	2	1

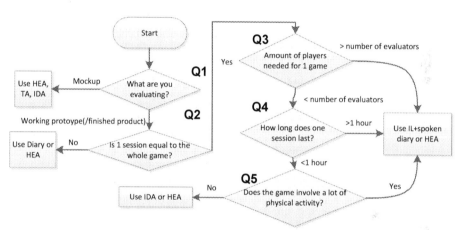

Fig. 1. ARGUEMENT – Augmented Reality Usability Evaluation Method ElectioN Tool

severity was significantly different from the heuristic evaluation ($Mdn = 2, U = 286.00, z = -4.372, p < .01$), but not for the other methods. The amount of issues did not differ significantly in any case.

4   Discussion

Notwithstanding the lack of significant differences, the extra effort that's required for RTA combined with IDA makes a strong case for replacing this method by interaction logs combined with audio diary as that methods resulted in more issues being identified with similar effort. The final version of the framework is visualized in figure 1.

Some limitations should be taken into account when reading this. E.g. the limited amount of participants, the use of the same usability expert in multiple evaluations and the fact that the results presented here are all based on a single observation. This means that further validation is required to make sure the results presented here are completely reliable.

Acknowledgements. The authors would like to thank Herre van Oostendorp, Christof van Nimwegen, their colleagues of the Mixed and Augmented Reality Solutions department of Fraunhofer FIT and TOTEM, the German-French project on Theories and Tools for Distributed Authoring of Mobile Mixed Reality Games under the Programme Inter Carnot Fraunhofer from BMBF (Grant 01SF0804) and ANR (http://www.totem-games.org).

References

1. Bier, E.A., Stone, M.C., Pier, K., Buxton, W., DeRose, T.D.: Toolglass and magic lenses. In: Proceedings of the 20th Annual Conference on Computer Graphics and Interactive Techniques - SIGGRAPH 1993, pp. 73–80. ACM Press, New York (September 1993)
2. Desurvire, H., Caplan, M., Toth, J.A.: Using heuristics to evaluate the playability of games. In: Extended Abstracts of the 2004 Conference on Human Factors and Computing Systems - CHI 2004, pp. 1509–1512. ACM Press, New York (2004)
3. Ericsson, K., Simon, H.: Protocol analysis: verbal reports as data. 1st paperb edn. The MIT Press, Cambridge (1985)
4. Gielkens, C.: A Framework for Usability Evaluation of Mobile Mixed Reality Games. Master, Utrecht University (2012), http://igitur-archive.library.uu.nl/student-theses/2012-0607-200545/thesis_charleygielkens_final.pdf
5. Kjeldskov, J., Stage, J.: New techniques for usability evaluation of mobile systems. International Journal of Human-Computer Studies 60(5-6), 599–620 (2004)
6. McCall, R., Wetzel, R., Löschner, J., Braun, A.: Using presence to evaluate an augmented reality location aware game. Personal and Ubiquitous Computing 15(1), 25–35 (2010)
7. Milgram, P., Kishino, F.: A taxonomy of mixed reality visual displays. IEICE Transactions on Information and Systems E Series D 77(12), 1321–1321 (1994)
8. Nielsen, J.: Severity Ratings for Usability Problems (1995)
9. Pinelle, D., Wong, N., Stach, T.: Heuristic evaluation for games. In: Proceeding of the Twenty-Sixth Annual CHI Conference on Human Factors in Computing Systems - CHI 2008, pp. 1453–1462. ACM Press, New York (2008)
10. Pinelle, D., Wong, N., Stach, T., Gutwin, C.: Usability heuristics for networked multiplayer games. In: Proceedings of the ACM 2009 International Conference on Supporting Group Work - GROUP 2009, pp. 169–178. ACM Press, New York (2009)
11. Sharp, H., Rogers, Y., Preece, J.: Interaction Design: Beyond Human-Computer Interaction. Wiley (2007)
12. Thomas, B., Close, B., Donoghue, J., Squires, J., Bondi, P.D., Piekarski, W.: First Person Indoor/Outdoor Augmented Reality Application: ARQuake. Personal and Ubiquitous Computing 6(1), 75–86 (2002)
13. Wetzel, R., Blum, L., Broll, W., Oppermann, L.: Designing mobile augmented reality games. In: Furht, B. (ed.) Handbook of Augmented Reality, 1st edn., pp. 513–529. Springer (2011)
14. Wetzel, R., Blum, L., Feng, F., Oppermann, L., Straeubig, M.: Tidy City: A Location-based Game for City Exploration Based on User-created Content. In: Proceedings of Mensch & Computer 2011, Chemnitz, Germany, pp. 487–498 (2011)

Therapeutic Presence - Virtual Illusions for Neurorehabilitation

Thomas Schüler

Institute for Cognitive Science, University of Osnabrueck
thschuel@uni-osnabrueck.de
http://www.thomasschueler.de

Abstract. The poster presents a project in which a computer game for neuro-rehabilitation is developed and its application explored. The development is based on the principles of mirror therapy and draws on recent findings in research on the concept of presence. Specifically, it is assumed that artistic virtual environments (VE) induce high presence experiences and thus enhance the treatment of neurologic diseases.

Keywords: virtual rehabilitation, neuro-rehabilitation, presence.

1 Introduction

Visual illusions may be used in neuro-rehabilitation to achieve therapeutic effects. This has been shown in 1995 by Ramachandran, Rogers-Ramachandran and Cobb who developed the "mirror therapy" based on these findings [1]. In mirror therapy patients with unilateral neurologic diseases are treated by a visual illusion that establishes the impression of control over the affected side. A mirror is placed on the sagittal body axis in front of the patient such that the reflected image of the unaffected body side overlays the actual position of the affected body parts. The patient is then asked to perform movements with both sides while watching into the mirror. This way the coupling between intended and perceived actions gives the impression of actually performing these actions with the affected body parts, thus leading to therapeutic effects on different neurologic diseases [2].

In recent years, systems have been proposed that transfer the idea of mirror therapy to virtual reality. [3] and [4] developed systems for patients with upper limb disabilities. In both systems the patients control an avatar through their natural movements and perform tasks, e.g. hitting flying balls with the avatar's hands. When these systems are used for mirror therapy, the movements of the patients' unaffected limb are used to control both limbs of the avatar, thus displaying symmetrically mirrored movements. The tasks are chosen such that symmetrical movements are needed to perform successfully. This way the visual illusion of a moving humanoid limb at the patients' affected side is established in a VE. In pilot studies, patients suffering from phantom limb pain and hemiparesis following a stroke have been successfully treated with these systems (ib.).

An explanation for the effectiveness of the mirror therapy is "the brain's predilection for prioritizing visual feedback over somatosensory/proprioceptive

M. Herrlich, R. Malaka, and M. Masuch (Eds.): ICEC 2012, LNCS 7522, pp. 405–408, 2012.

feedback concerning limb position" [5]. The visual illusion of a moving limb triggers those motor cortex regions of the observer that usually control the corresponding limb [6]. The degree to which the illusions are experienced as real plays an important role in the effectiveness of the treatment [7]. Using VEs for the therapy, the visual illusions can be modified in various ways to enhance the effect. This may be inspired by the area of computer game design. In research on VEs the term "presence" refers to the subjective experience of an agent that perceives and reacts to sensorial stimuli of a VE in a way similar to real life [8].

It is hypothesized here that the presence experience is central to the effectiveness of mirror therapy. The poster presents a project in which a computer game for neuro-rehabilitation is developed following this hypothesis. The game builds on the principles of mirror therapy and will be used with amputees to alleviate phantom limb pain. Specifically, it is assumed that artistic VEs induce high presence experiences and thus enhance the treatment of neurologic diseases.

2   Presence and Action

In the framework proposed by [9] and [10], presence is related to "the (prereflexive) perception of successfully transforming intentions in actions" [9]. For a strong experience of presence in relation to a VE, a correspondence between actions and intentions is more important than visual realism. Even a perceptually poor VE may constitute a strong experience of presence if it successfully supports an agent in carrying out his/her intended actions.

The framework is grounded in the view that all human behaviour in any environment is hierarchically composed of low-level operations that form actions and high-level activities [11]. These layers are all driven by some form of intentions and the successful (hypothetical) execution of the intentions by the agent generates presence as a sense of being-in-the-world [9]. Low-level operations (e.g. motor operations) and their intentions are usually highly automated and unconscious. However, if an intended operation fails to produce the expected result, higher-level cognitive processing is needed to reflect and alter the plan. This puts the agent in a more internal cognitive state and is experienced as a break-down in presence.

According to this framework, a patient with phantom limb pain experiences low presence regarding the phantom, when he/she is not able to enact his/her intentions with that limb. However, the visual illusion described above may provide the impression of successful action for the patient. It is important to mention that an agent evaluates the execution of behaviour mainly through monitoring its effect on an external world. Recent studies have demonstrated that an agent can in fact feel physically present even in a tool, if this tool is fully controlled by him/her [9].

Implications for Neuro-rehabilitation

Following this understanding when designing a VE for neuro-rehabilitation, it is particularly important to support the execution of all behaviour that can possibly be intended by patients. This can, however, be a sheer impossible task, because of the infinite amount of behavioural intentions a patient can have. Although intentions become more predictable when a concrete task is given and when it is clear which operations are necessary to accomplish the task, especially low-level operations are highly subjective and individual when patients have to accomplish these task by controlling humanoid limbs in a realistic VE. Moreover, if real-world movement of the patients is used to interact with the VE, the recording of this movement is limited by hardware needs. Patients will experience low presence and thus will have difficulties to believe in the illusion.

On the other hand, an artistic VE consisting of simple objects that are controlled by natural movement of patients will not lead to these problems. The artistic feedback can be generated based on the continuous flow of movement data in various ways. The behavioural possibilities within the VE need to be explored by the patients and their intentions are then based on this experience. The illusionary movement of the arm itself does not need to be displayed in order to feel that the observed behaviour was initiated by such a movement. Such artistic VE may still be based on mirror therapy principles and display bilateral behaviour that is controlled by unilateral movement. Using this kind of VE seems promising for the purposes of neuro-rehabilitation.

3   Artistic Virtual Environment for Neuro-rehabilitation

The assumptions presented above form the basis of a research project. It is investigated whether the use of an artistic VE, which provides a strong experience of presence, will be beneficial for the rehabilitation of neurologic diseases. A computer game for upper limb amputees with phantom limb pain is developed and therefore an artistic VE is designed that will be controlled according to mirror therapy principles. Figure 1 shows a an early prototype of the VE in application.

Fig. 1. A virtual environment for neuro-rehabilitation

The artistic feedback in the VE is generated using the movement of the patients' healthy limb and this movement is recorded using a motion capturing device. The body posture and gesture is recognized in the software and used as input data for generative design algorithms [12],[13]. These algorithms transform structured input data into expressive artistic output. For the above described application algorithms are developed that generate the output continuously, such that every movement of the patient results in an immediate effect on the virtual environment. The algorithms are chosen to produce expressive bilateral output based on symmetrically mirrored unilateral input. While controlling this VE the experience of presence will be strong and the alleviation of phantom limb pain is assumed.

4 Future Directions

The VE will be evaluated in summer 2012 with a small sample of amputees suffering from phantom limb pain. During and after the sessions the patients will be asked to report on their presence experience and their level of pain.

The scientific focus of the project is on the application of the theoretical framework of presence presented above. The project will be completed by the end of 2012. The poster presents the theoretical framework, the developed game and presumably preliminary results of the sample study.

References

1. Ramachandran, V.S., Rogers-Ramachandran, D., Cobb, S.: Touching the phantom limb. Nature (1995)
2. Ramachandran, V.S., Altschuler, E.L.: The use of visual feedback, in particular mirror visual feedback, in restoring brain function. Brain (2009)
3. Murray, C.D., Pettifer, S., Howard, T., Patchick, E.L., Caillette, F., Kulkarni, J., Bamford, C.: The treatment of phantom limb pain using immersive virtual reality: Three case studies. Disability & Rehabilitation (2007)
4. Eng, K., Siekierka, E., Pyk, P., Chevrier, E., Hauser, Y., Cameirao, M., Holper, L., Hägni, K., Zimmerli, L., Duff, A.: Interactive visuo-motor therapy system for stroke rehabilitation. Medical and Biological Engineering and Computing (2007)
5. Moseley, G.L., Gallace, A., Spence, C.: Is mirror therapy all it is cracked up to be? Current evidence and future directions. Pain (2008)
6. Iacoboni, M., Mazziotta, J.C.: Mirror neuron system: basic findings and clinical applications. Annals of Neurology (2007)
7. Rothgangel, A.: Spiegeltherapie – mehr als nur eine visuelle Illusion? pt_Zeitschrift für Physiotherapeuten (2008)
8. Slater, M.: A note on presence terminology. Presence Connect (2003)
9. Riva, G.: Is presence a technology issue? Some insights from cognitive sciences. Virtual Reality (2009)
10. Waterworth, J.A., Waterworth, E.L., Mantovani, F., Riva, G.: On Feeling (the) Present. Journal of Consciousness Studies (2010)
11. Kaptelinin, V., Nardi, B.A.: Acting with Technology: Activity Theory and Interaction Design. The MIT Press (2006)
12. McCormack, J., Dorin, A., Innocent, T.: Generative design: a paradigm for design research. In: Proceedings of Future Ground. Design Research Society (2004)
13. Bohnacker, H., Groß, B., Laub, J.: Generative Gestaltung. Verlag Hermann Schmidt (2009)

Integrated System for Automatic Platform Game Level Creation with Difficulty and Content Adaptation

Fausto Mourato, Manuel Próspero dos Santos, and Fernando Birra

Faculdade de Ciências e Tecnologia-Universidade Nova de Lisboa, Portugal
p21748@campus.fct.unl.pt, {ps,fpb}@di.fct.unl.pt

Abstract. This article presents an overview over our system for the creation of platform game levels. It consists of a framework with a generic and flexible approach that integrates most of the concepts that can be found in this type of games. In addition, some procedural techniques are employed allowing automatic level generation, dynamic difficulty adjustment, optional content creation and item gathering or triggering related challenges. The system can be extended by adding new plugins to support other games or generation algorithms.

1   Introduction

In the last few years, *Procedural Content Generation* attracted the attention of researchers, in particular under the context of videogame development. In this document we will focus content generation for platform videogames like *Super Mario Bros.* and *Sonic – The Hedgehog*. Generating levels for a platform game raises some complex aspects such as level viability, challenge suitability and aesthetic coherence. An interesting ongoing commercial work based on these topics is the game *Cloudberry Kingdom* [2], with focus on the generation of valid and challenging gaming environments. Our particular system, hereby presented, directs attention to the inclusion of optional content and contextualized challenges. For the scope of this article, we will focus the following contributions:

- Generic framework that supports level representation for multiple existing games.
- Configurable rule-based structure for graph generation and path estimation.
- Multi-step algorithm featuring a novel approach to complement level content.
- Plugin based system that allows the integration of further generation techniques.

2   Related Work

Primal work related with platform games focused the identification of the main features in this type of games and how the global context could be characterized, in works presented, respectively, by Compton and Mateas [1] and Smith et al. [8].

Following these ideas, first efforts on creating prototypes that could create platform game levels appeared. Two different approaches are particularly noteworthy, namely rhythm and chunk based. Rhythm based generation consists on creating levels to follow an adequate input or movement pattern [9]. For other studies related to this idea

M. Herrlich, R. Malaka, and M. Masuch (Eds.): ICEC 2012, LNCS 7522, pp. 409–412, 2012.

we refer to [10]. The chunk based generation consists on procedurally combining pre-authored small level parts, designated as chunks [4].

Personalization in this field has also been tried, in particular to perceive user feeling [6] and match user skills to inherent level difficulty [3].

3   System Overview

3.1   Level Representation

For the purpose of this work we will concentrate on PC versions, considering also some console inspired implementations. In particular, our system is suitable for the following games:

- *Infinite Mario Bros.*, an open source adaptation of the classic videogame *Super Mario Bros.*, frequently used as a research tool [7].
- The original videogame *Prince of Persia*, which allows interesting considerations in trigger related challenges.
- *XRick*, a remake of the original videogame *Rick Dangerous*.
- *Open Sonic*, an adaption of the game saga *Sonic – The Hedgehog*.

In its basis, a level is represented as a two-dimensional matrix. This discretized approach brings some advantages on later processes such as the analysis of possible paths. Each cell can be filled with a certain *Block Type* from a hierarchy defined by the game designer. The system allows defining *Groups* to refer particular cells that only make sense when used together, such as pipes in *Infinite Mario Bros.* (Fig. 1). To allow representing additional specific features, such as the ramps and loops of *Open Sonic*, it is also possible to define objects that fill a range of cells, which have been designated as *Contraptions*. In addition, *Categories* might be defined representing a set of blocks calculated using logical operators. For instance, in *XRick,* one can define a category named "support" with the expression "solid block □ platform".

3.2   Analysis

A path related level analysis tool is provided by the system. The designer defines a set of rules for the creation of a graph representing a network of available paths for the avatar. A rule is defined with a cell pattern and the corresponding graph entries. For instance, in *XRick*, one can define the basic horizontal movement with the pattern presented in Fig. 2. The lower two cells represent the *category* support previously referred. In the whole level, for every occurrence of each pattern, the corresponding entries are added to the level graph. In the end it is possible to observe the final graph as shown on Fig. 3 in the context of the game *Prince of Persia*.

3.3   Automatic Level Generation and Content Adaptation

The system includes the possibility of incorporating algorithms for automatic level generation, based on a plugin architecture, to ease the development of further techniques.

Currently we have tested simple heuristic generators and the genetic algorithm implementation presented in [5].

In order to improve level content we have also been developing some algorithms to adapt a basic level structure into a more complex gaming environment. Currently, the system analyses the produced graph and detects which nodes are mandatory and optional in the avatar path from the beginning to the end of the level. Also, dead end segments are detected and are used to provide power ups, collectibles or specific items that will be needed in the main path, improving content richness. Finally, difficulty is estimated based on graph transitions in a similar approach as proposed on [10], allowing an iterative process to search for a desired difficulty value.

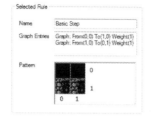
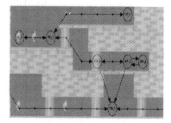

Fig. 1. Pipe in *Infinite Mario Bros.*, defined by a group of 2x2 cells

Fig. 2. Example rule defining possible bidirectional horizontal movement in *XRick*

Fig. 3. Graph generated for the first level of the game *Prince of Persia*

4   Usage Examples

In Fig. 4 we show a screenshot of the system's main window depicting a level for the game *Infinite Mario Bros.*. That level was generated with a plugin that implements a simple random algorithm. Fig. 5 presents again the main window, now displaying a level from the game *XRick*, extracted from the original game with a level importer plugin. Finally, Fig. 6 shows a level for the game *Prince of Persia*, created with a genetic algorithm (left part) and followed by the content adaptation process presented in the previous section (right part).

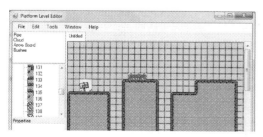
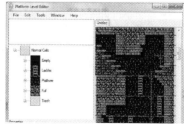
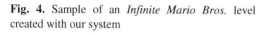

Fig. 4. Sample of an *Infinite Mario Bros.* level created with our system

Fig. 5. Editing a level for the game *XRick*

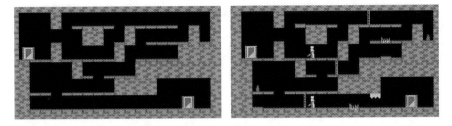

Fig. 6. Two steps on a composed generation process for the game *Prince of Persia*

5   Conclusions and Future Work

We presented a system that features a flexible and adaptable representation scheme that is compatible with different platform games. The architecture is extensible to allow the creation of additional plugins for different games or to implement new procedural content generation techniques. Some of the included algorithms are still under development but, however, the results are motivating. On the next steps we aim to extend the set of compatible games and also to expand the generation algorithms to include personalization, namely integrating user data obtained from gaming sessions.

References

1. Compton, K., Mateas, M.: Procedural level design for platform games. In: Proc. of the Artificial Intelligence and Interactive Digital Entertainment International Conference, AIIDE (2006)
2. Fisher, J.: How to Make Insane, Procedural Platformer Levels, http://www.gamasutra.com
3. Jennings-Teats, M., Smith, G., Wardrip-Fruin, N.: Polymorph: Dynamic Difficulty Adjustment through Level Generation. In: Proc. of the Workshop on PCG in Games (2010)
4. Mawhorter, P., Mateas, M.: Procedural Level Generation Using Occupancy-Regulated Extension. In: CIG-2010 - IEEE Conference on Computational Intelligence and Games (2010)
5. Mourato, F., Próspero dos Santos, M., Birra, F.: Automatic level generation for platform videogames using Genetic Algorithms. In: 8th International Conference on Advances in Computer Entertainment Technology, ACE 2011 (2011)
6. Nygren, N., Denzinger, J., Stephenson, B., Aycock, J.: User-preference-based automated level generation for platform games. In: IEEE Symposium on Comp. Intelligence and Games (2011)
7. Shaker, N., Togelius, J., Yannakakis, G.N., Weber, B., Shimizu, T., Hashiyama, T., Soreson, N., Pasquier, P., Mawhorter, P., Takahashi, G., Smith, G., Baumgarten, R.: The 2010 Mario AI Championship: Level Generation Track. Special Issue of IEEE Transactions on Procedural Content Generation (2010)
8. Smith, G., Cha, M., Whitehead, J.: A Framework for Analysis of 2D Platformer Levels. In: Proceedings of the 2008 ACM SIGGRAPH Symposium on Video Games (2008)
9. Smith, G., Mateas, M., Whitehead, J., Treanor, M.: Rhythm-based level generation for 2D platformers. In: Procs. of the 4th International Conference on Foundations of Digital Game (2009)
10. Smith, G., Whitehead, J., Mateas, M., Treanor, M., March, J., Cha, M.: Launchpad: A Rhythm-Based Level Generator for 2D Platformers. IEEE Transactions on Computational Intelligence and AI in Games (TCIAIG) 3(1) (March 2011)

Web-Based Graphic Environment to Support Programming in the Beginning Learning Process

Carlos J. Costa[1], Manuela Aparicio[1,2,3], and Carlos Cordeiro[4]

[1] ADETTI-IUL/ISCTE-IUL, Lisboa, Portugal
[2] IADE, Lisboa, Portugal
[3] UNL, Lisboa, Portugal
[4] Springfield Collegiate Institute, Manitoba, Canada
{carlos.costa,manuela.aparicio}@iscte.pt,
ccordeiro@sunrisesd.ca

Abstract. The present paper focus on the computer programming for a beginning level of learning. Students´ learning challenges were identified through literature review. We propose a solution that enables students to interact with an editor that gives an output as a response. We also analyze the impact of the use of this framework and identify that some support tools. Preliminary evaluation shows that some of the support tools are more effective than others.

Keywords: Computer science education, engineering education, computer programming education.

1   Introduction

Learning is a process of acquiring knowledge. In the area of computer programming, also known as computer coding is often regarded as a difficult task. In order to improve programming learning, Richard E. Pattis developed an alternative method that enabled an easy way for introducing students in computer programming[6] named Karel. It introduces a language repertoire to imperative commands whose actions can be visually displayed. Several environments have been developed to introduce younger students to the concepts of programming through robotics (whether real or virtual). These include Papert's Turtle Graphics[34], Pattis' Karel [6] and Lego Mindstorms [9],[10]. The use of robots is inherently attractive to many young students (even more attractive than 2D graphics). However, the constraints imposed here by the real (or virtual) world have to do with the available kits that give these environments an essentially compositional focus, and restrict the opportunities for exploration and extension by students, such as the robot construction itself and technical domain of hardware assemblage. There have been many efforts over time to develop initial learning environments to beginners, focused on either through direct manipulation of objects or through data and structure visualization. Following in this paper we describe the main problems faced by students. We describe a solution evaluation phased and present results on that evaluation.

M. Herrlich, R. Malaka, and M. Masuch (Eds.): ICEC 2012, LNCS 7522, pp. 413–416, 2012.

2   Programming Learning Problems

Students face diverse problems when they are learning programming [3] mainly because programming is dynamic and abstract. Several authors have identified which are the main difficulties in learning programming ([5]; [1]; [8]; [4]). Teachers deduce more difficulties than the perceived problems by the students. Programming novices often tend to focus on specific aspects rather than general ones. These results are verified by several studies ([4]; [5]). To start, student and teacher perceptions on programming's knowledge base are rather different, as teachers understand better the student´s limitations than themselves. Learning programming contains several activities, such as learning a language features, variables, program design and program comprehension. A study conducted by Rist [11] demonstrates that syntax understanding is not the main difficulty. Students may know the syntax and semantics of individual statements, but they do not know how to combine those elements in order to produce valid programs [12]. The cognitive domain plays an important role in the process of learning programming [7]: data recall (forget to declare initialize variables), understanding of the meaning of the problem, difficulty in translating that into a logic program, difficulty in algorithm design and applying a concept in a new situation, analysis of the program structure, and synthesis difficulty in integrating different modules. Furthermore, there are a myriad other reasons programming is difficult to learn [2],[14] like originality, many skills, program design and comprehension, choice of language, timing and course structure, and varied individual student abilities.

3   Proposed Solution

We propose a solution in which students are able to visualize and interact within one screen, in a dual interface, having a programming instructions, each has a graphical icon, at the same time they can also see a dragon moving according to the commands. A manual was developed with samples as supporting documentation, consisting of a list of procedures [13]. The manual describes basic procedures, conditional constructs, looks and variables, with simplified examples. On the right side of the screen, students visualize a dragon moving accordingly to the given instructions on the left side of the screen. If a student wants the dragon to move to the right, he/she must push the green right arrow. Students have a small number of available instructions to accomplish a specific task, as required by the teacher. The left side of the screen also displays programming command lines they appear automatically as the buttons are pushed. This is an important feature in order to allow the student to become familiarized with lines of code. The system also has different patterns or labyrinths that correspond to various levels of difficulty, within the exercises.

4   Evaluation

In order to evaluate opinions, this system was used by a group of first year computer science students. Students were asked to fulfill a questionnaire, using a 7 point Likert scale; the number of valid answers is 78. Concerning types of support, the manual was considered to be the least preferred type of support. Examples and the manual were most preferred by the students. This indicates that the students were not familiar with the subject.

Table 1. System support according to basic programming concepts

	Example (M)	(SD)	Manual (M)	(SD)	Stat t	Sig.
Basic procedures (move, turn left...)	5.56	1.58	5.12	1.45	2.47	.02
conditional constructs	5.04	1.55	4.96	1.47	.47	.64
Loops	4.78	1.65	4.79	1.61	-.08	.94
Functions	5.18	1.31	4.91	1.43	1.86	.07
Variables	5.01	1.32	4.88	1.40	.87	.39

M – Sample Mean, SD – Standard Deviation.

Also, the system was evaluated on what extent it supports writing of a specific type of code. On the other hand, the results of the system support were also evaluated.

Table 2. System support perceived by the students, and system result

	System Support (M)	(SD)	System Result (M)	(SD)	Stat t	Sig.
Complete program	4.73	1.33	5.27	1.40	-3.64	.00
Basic procedures (move, turn left...)	5.34	1.14	5.32	1.30	.09	.93
conditional constructs	4.88	1.40	5.03	1.33	-1.09	.28
loops	4.83	1.32	4.88	1.32	-.41	.68
functions	4.83	1.26	5.08	1.27	-1.72	.09
variables	4.78	1.32	4.94	1.40	-1.19	.24

M – Mean, SD – Standard Deviation.

The system support is based on manuals and exercises. The students were asked to perform the exercises, and the system displayed the dragon moving across the screen. Students found that the system provided good for supporting exercises´ construction, according to the values in Table 2. The students' results provided by the system were more positive regarding the perceived systems' support. But t Stat shows that means are not statistically different, except in the issue of complete program.

5   Conclusions

According to the literature review, there are several challenges related to the learning of computer programming. Some of them may be partially answered by utilizing virtual robots. We proposed a solution (dragon-robot) and than we analyzed the impact of the system usage. We found that that some support tools are more effective than others.

Acknowledgments. Research presented here is partially financed by FCT – Portuguese Research Ministry.

References

1. AlaMyka, K.: Problems in Learning and Teaching Programminga literature study for developing visualizations in the CodewitzMinervapoject. Codewitz Needs Analisys, lIteratur Study (2005)
2. Cummings, S.: Feedback 2.0: An Investigation into using sharable Feedback tags as Programming Feedback. Ph.D. Thesis, Durham University (2010)
3. Donmez, O., Inceoglu, M.M.: A Web Based Tool for Novice Programmers: Interaction in Use. In: Gervasi, O., Murgante, B., Laganà, A., Taniar, D., Mun, Y., Gavrilova, M.L. (eds.) ICCSA 2008, Part I. LNCS, vol. 5072, pp. 530–540. Springer, Heidelberg (2008)
4. Lahtinen, E., AlaMtka, K., Jarvinen, H.: A Study of the Difficulties of Novice Programmers. In: ITCSE 2005 Proceedings. ACM, Portugal (2005)
5. Milne, I., Rowe, G.: Difficulties in Learning and Teaching Programming— Views of Students and Tutors. Education and Information Technologies 7(1), 55–66 (2002)
6. Pattis, R.: Karel the Robot: A Gentle Introduction to the Art of Programming. John Wiley and Sons, New York (1981)
7. Renumol, V., Jayaprakash, S., Janakiram, D.: Classification of cognitive difficulties of students to learn computer programming. Indian Institute of Technology, India (2009)
8. Sajaniemi, J., Hu, C.: Teaching Programming: Going beyond "Objects First". In: 18th Workshop of the Psychology of Programming Interest Group, pp. 255–265. University of Sussex (September 2006)
9. Papert, S.: Mindstorms: Children, Computers, and Powerful Ideas, New ed. Basic Books (1993)
10. http://Lego.com
11. Rist, R.: Teaching Eiffel as a first language. Journal of Object Oriented Programming 9, 3041 (1996)
12. Soloway, E., Spohrer, J.: Studying the Novice Programmer. Lawrence Erlbaum Associates, Hillsdale (1989)
13. Costa, C., Aparicio, M., Cordeiro, C.: A solution to support student learning of programming. In: Proceedings of the Workshop on Open Source and Design of Communication (OSDOC 2012). ACM, New York (2012)
14. Piteira, M., Costa, C.: Computer programming and novice programmers. In: Proceedings of the Workshop on Information Systems and Design of Communication (ISDOC 2012), pp. 51–53. ACM, New York (2012)

Interactive Music Recommendation System for Adapting Personal Affection: *IMRAPA*

Keigo Tada[1], Ryosuke Yamanishi[2], and Shohei Kato[1]

[1] Dept. of Computer Science and Engineering, Graduate School of Engineering,
Nagoya Institute of Technology,
Gokiso-cho, Showa-ku, Nagoya, 466-8555 Japan
[2] Dept. of Media Technology, Ritsumeikan University,
1-1-1 Nojihigashi, Kusatsu, 525-0058 Japan
{ryama,shohey}@katolab.nitech.ac.jp

Abstract. We have so various types of entertainment, and music is one of the most popular one. In this paper, we proposed music recommendation system that interactively adapts a user's personal affection with only a simple operation, in which both acoustic and meta features are used. The more a user uses the proposed system, the better the system adapts the user's personal affection and recommends the suitable songs. Through the evaluational experiment, we confirmed that the proposed system could recommend songs adapting user's personal affection even if the personal affection variated.

Keywords: Music retrieval system, Interactive system, Affection, Personalization.

1 Introduction

Music is one of the most beloved entertainments and has attracted much attention as one of media to enrich human life. The large capacity of storage has enabled users to keep and carry a lot of music, then a user generally selects song using the given bibliographic data such as song name, artist name and so on; however it is cumbersome to select songs using only the bibliographic data. Moreover, music distribution services are becoming more widespread, thus users can get music by a single song and enjoy their favorite songs that match their personal affection. On the other hand, getting music by a single song poses a lack of coherence in their music databases, and to select songs using only bibliographic data has become more cumbersome.

From these facts, we believe that more intuitive and usable music entertainment system is needed. In this paper, we propose the music recommendation system adapting user's personal affection which has advantages of both random-play and using play-list. The proposed system dynamically recommends songs that adapt user's personal affection from user's own music database, then only a simple and natural operation is needed to listen and evaluate the songs.

M. Herrlich, R. Malaka, and M. Masuch (Eds.): ICEC 2012, LNCS 7522, pp. 417–420, 2012.
© IFIP International Federation for Information Processing 2012

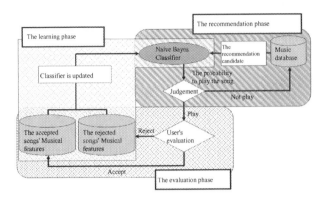

Fig. 1. The flowchart of the proposed system

2   The Proposed System: *IMRAPA*

We propose a music recommendation system named *IMRAPA* (Interactive Music Recommendation system for Adapting user's Personal Affection). Fig. 1 describes the architecture of the proposed system. In the recommendation phase, a candidate song estimated to be acceptive for a user's personal affection is recommended from the music database. The recommended candidate song is randomly selected from music database and input to Näive Bayes Classifier [4], and the probability of that the song is acceptive for the user's personal affection (probability of playing the song) is calculated. Based on the calculated probability, the system determines whether the song is played or not. Because we believe that a user's personal affection can be varying with time, therefore the stochastic mechanism was used in the proposed system for the recommendation, and even once rejected song has a chance to be recommended again. As the recommended song is played, in the evaluation phase, a user evaluates the song with simple operation: to keep listening and skip the song each means "accept" and "reject," respectively. Each latest N accepted and rejected songs' musical features are respectively stored in the user's personal affection database; N for adapting the variation of a user's personal affection is verified through pre-experiments and set $N = 30$. In the learning phase, Näive Bayes Classifier is updated with each usage, and the next recommended candidate song is determined by the updated Näive Bayes Classifier in the next recommendation phase. So the more the system is used, the better the system adapts the user's personal affection.

In our previous studies, we proposed the musical fluctuation features that cover sound variation on music which is confirmed to influence human affective evaluation of music [5]; we use these features as acoustic features in the proposed system. Also, we use bibliographic data such as artist and album name as meta features. By using both acoustic and meta features, we believe that the proposed system can adaptively recommend music adapting any types of personal affection. The proposed system is different from the existing systems [2,1] in that we use both acoustic features concerning musical variation with time which influence human affective evaluation of music and meta features such as artist and album name, and the other [3] in that the proposed system interactively and dynamically adapts a variable user's personal affection with only a simple operation. That is to say, the point of the proposed system is not recommendation mechanism, which is well known and used in varied systems, but specialized features to adapt personal affection on music recommendation and its system architecture.

3   Evaluational Experiment

In the experiment, we asked sixteen participants to demonstrate the proposed system based on their own personal affections with the experimental interface on the common computer and speaker. Though the proposed system needs only simple interface that has only "skip button," absolutely for verifying the usability of the proposed system, we prepared the experimental interface shown in Fig. 2; actually the system leans user's personal affection with only 2 options: accept or reject. We prepared 909 songs for the experimental music database which are selected from participants' music compact disks and then the genres and affective evaluations of songs were not biased. The participants were asked to listen to 200 songs, and then the evaluative criterion was "aggressive song or not" during 1-100th song (section 1), and the one was "calm song or not" during 101-200th song (section 2). In the two sections, each the 1-20th and 81-100th songs were assumed as the early and closing periods, respectively.

At first, we discuss about the evaluation of the recommended songs in section 1 (Fig. 3). The percentage of each evaluation was calculated from all participants' evaluations. The evaluation on the closing period tended to be higher than the one on the early period, and the significant differences were confirmed on "Definitely accept" and "Reject" using 2-sample test for equality of proportions. This result showed that the proposed system could become to recommend the aggressive song with time: the proposed system adapted the user's personal affection. Next about section 2 (Fig. 4), it was confirmed that all evaluations between the early and closing periods significantly differed. In the early period, despite the proposed system recommended the aggressive songs from the learning in section 1, the user accepted calm songs; naturally, the percentages of "Definitely accept" and "Accept" were very low and the one of "Weak reject" and "Reject" were high. However the percentages were reversed in the closing period, it was reasonable to consider that the proposed system became to recommend calm songs. These results suggested that the proposed system recommended songs adapting the user's personal affection at each time and could adapt its variation.

Fig. 2. Experimental interface

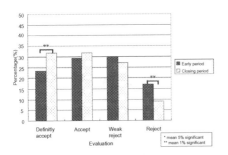
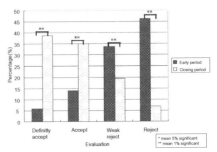

Fig. 3. The percentages of each evaluation on the early and closing periods in the section 1 (%)

Fig. 4. The percentages of each evaluation on the early and closing periods in the section 2 (%)

4   Conclusion and Future Works

In this paper, we proposed music recommendation system that interactively adapts user's personal affection in which both acoustic and meta features were used. Through the evaluational experiment, we confirmed the usability of the proposed system: the system became to recommend more acceptive songs for variable user's personal affection with time. The proposed system enables users unconsciously evaluate the recommended songs with only a simple operation: continuing to listen or skip, thus the proposed system can be useful especially where the operation using graphic interface should be difficult such as driving.

As using lyric, we expect that the proposed system becomes to catch user's personal affection more truthfully and be more usable. In our future, we will address this challenge and develop more intuitive and high efficiency music recommendation system.

References

1. Bogdanov, D., Herrera, P.: How much metadata do we need in music recommendation? a subjective evaluation using preference sets. In: Proceedings of 2011 International Society for Music Information Retrieval Conference, pp. 97–102 (2011)
2. Flexer, A., Gasser, M., Schnitzer, D.: Limitations of interactive music recommendation based on audio content. In: Proceedings of the 5th Audio Mostly Conference: A Conference on Interaction with Sound, pp. 96–102 (2010)
3. Knees, P., Pohle, T., Schedl, M., Seyerlehner, D.S.K., Widmer, G.: Augmenting text-based music retrieval with audio similarity. In: Proceedings of 10th International Society for Music Information Retrieval Conference, pp. 579–584 (2009)
4. Langley, P., Iba, W., Thompson, K.: An analysis of bayesian classifiers. In: Proceedings of the 10th National Conference on Artical Intelligence, pp. 223–228 (1992)
5. Yamanishi, R., Ito, Y., Kato, S.: Relationships between emotional evaluation of music and acoustic fluctuation properties. In: Proceedings of IEEE Symposium on Computers & Informatics, pp. 721–726 (2011)

Value-Based Design for Gamifying Daily Activities

Mizuki Sakamoto, Tatsuo Nakajima, and Todorka Alexandrova

Department of Computer Science and Engineering,
Waseda University
{mizuki,tatsuo,toty}@dcl.cs.waseda.ac.jp

Abstract. Computing technologies allow us to gamify our daily activities by embedding computers in our environments. In this paper, we propose a value-based gamification framework for increasing intrinsic motivation in our daily life. We introduce five values and a conceptual framework based on these values. Then, as an example we show how the values are used in Augmented Trading Card Game during its design.

1   Introduction

Daily digital objects are becoming more and more usual and widely sold as commodities. For example, recently televisions developed in Japan have become cheaper and cheaper despite of their excellent product quality and rich functionality. However, on the contrary new furniture and fashion goods attract us every year and they do not become commodities that are sold at cheaper prices with the time. The reason for this is the fact that they offer additional values to users. Especially, the prices for such products are kept high if the products offer the sense of rarity. The fact that the product quality does not become the main value for many of us to buy the product shows that we need to consider another way to design daily digital objects. Digital technologies are effective to make digital objects   usual commodities and as a consequence to decrease their prices, but they are also effective to add more values to products by customizing the products for each user.

In this paper, we present a value-based gamification framework in order to gamify daily activities. The central concept in our framework is *values*. A user's intrinsic motivation increases when he/she feels real or virtual goods or figures used in his/her activities valuable. Our framework introduces *five values* that are design tools to develop attractive gamification services. Then, we show how the *values* are used in *Augmented Trading Card Game* (*Augmented TCG*) [1] during its design as an example.

2   Value-Based Gamification Design Framework

This section briefly introduces the proposed five values, and presents a conceptual gamification framework to use these values.

The first value is the *informative value*. The value offers sufficient information to a user, and helps him/her to make a better decision. A typical example is an augmented

M. Herrlich, R. Malaka, and M. Masuch (Eds.): ICEC 2012, LNCS 7522, pp. 421–424, 2012.

reality service that superimposes useful information on an image captured by a camera. The service gives the user detailed information about the surrounding daily environment such as shopping information and route information. If a user does not find the necessary information, he/she may get lost and confused what to do, which might decrease his/her motivation to achieve his/her current goal.

The second value is the *empathetic value*. This value is achieved and enhanced by adding a virtual character or a pet to a service. For example, if a pretty virtual girl navigates a service, a typical male user usually feels the service more attractive. In a similar way, when a user takes care of a virtual pet in a service, he/she considers to continue using the service for a longer time. Especially, when a user maintains a long relationship with a virtual character or a pet, he/she could not give up using the service because he/she does not like to part from the character or the pet.

The third value is the *persuasive value*. The value gives a user feedback information according to his/her current situation. Also, the feedback information shows the future effect of a user's current activity. For example, a package of cigarettes shows photos of unhealthy lungs that are a result of long time smoking. Thus, while showing negative information might lead to a user stopping his/her current undesirable activities, showing positive information to a user would increase his/her motivation to engage into desirable activities.

The fourth value is the *economic value*. The value gives a sense of ownership to a user. Especially, physical tangibility is important to increase the sense of the ownership of an object. For example, people like to possess expensive jewelry or artworks. The rarity is a key to increase the sense of the ownership, and collecting rare objects increases the social status of a user as well. The sense of the ownership of an object is very important for a user to create his/her own original "empathetic story" with the object, which describes the user's feelings and attachment to the object and how the user's daily life has changed after he/she owns the object.

The fifth value is the *ideological value*. The value reminds a user important ideological concepts like friendship, justice and so on. However, the value is not explicitly presented to a user, but special stories carrying important ideological messages are used to explain the importance of such concepts implicitly. If a user knows the stories, then the characters appearing in the stories can be used as metaphors to show the ideological value.

Gamification offers the possibility to solve many real social problems. Current existing gamification frameworks take into account only game mechanics to motivate people and do not take into account the increase of the user's intrinsic motivation, which would lead to only partial solutions to the aimed social problems. A design with the proposed five values may enhance the current gamification frameworks and help people increase their self-efficacy that would make them believe that they are able to achieve their goals and to motivate them by themselves.

Fig. 1 shows how the five values are used to increase people's self-efficacy and to make them to think positively. The empathetic, economic and persuasive values offer people extrinsic incentives, and the informative value shows the reason to change human attitude or tips and tactics for making a better decision. Our framework is based on the *transtheoretical model* that is a psychological model to change human attitude. The four values are used as tools in the *transtheoretical model* to change a user's current behavior by reminding the importance and encourage his/her behavior change. On the other hand, the ideological value makes people's dream and expectation explicit to teach how changing a user's attitude realizes his/her dream. The combination of the extrinsic motivation and the ideological value enhances the intrinsic motivation and changes people's attitude, and makes people think more positively by increasing their self-efficacy. Therefore, the hurdles for people to solve some hard social problems become lower, and they become more confident and enthusiastic in taking an action to solve the problem through their increased self-efficacy and positive thinking.

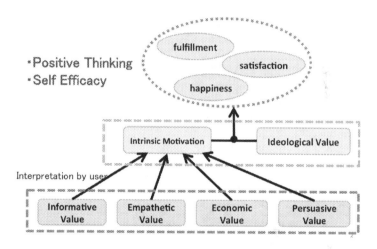

Fig. 1. Value-based Design Framework

3   A Case Study: Augmented Trading Card Game

Augmented TCG enhances the *Yu-Gi-Oh!* trading card game (http://www.yugioh-card.com/en/) performed remotely by two persons. The two players are located in different places. Each player's cards in his/her battle field on the table in front of him/her are captured by a camera and projected on the opponent player's table. Also, each player is represented as the 3D model of a virtual character used in popular animations and games, and this character is shown to the opponent player. The virtual character is controlled using *MS Kinect*, its movement is synchronized with the movement and the behavior of the player it represents.

We briefly describe how we consider the presented five values while designing *Augmented TCG* as follows. The first is the *informative value*. Detailed information about the card that the opponent player currently holds in his/her hand is shown on a small display near a player. Especially, the information about the strength level of the card is hard to see during the game so showing the detailed information about the cards is useful to support the player's better decision making and strategy choice. The value encourages a player not to give up the game.

The second is the *empathetic value*. In *Augmented TCG*, the virtual character representing players provokes their empathetic feeling and motivates them to play and enjoy the game better if that is one of their favorite characters. Currently, *Link* from *The Legend of Zelda* (http://zelda.com/) is chosen as a favorite character for players, but they can choose other favorite virtual characters for themselves as well. For some young players in Japan, favorite virtual characters are like close friends to them, so that they like to play with the character for a long time.

The third is the *persuasive value*. A small display shows a virtual character, that is illustrated on one of the cards in the player's deck, and encourages the player to win during the game. In TCG, trading cards are collected by each player with significant efforts. So, the player feels that his/her cards are very precious, and thus empathy with the characters depicted on the cards is easily initiated. Therefore, the encouragement by such character becomes a strong incentive to win the game.

The fourth is the *economic value*. In *Augmented TCG*, a player can use the physical paper cards from the TCG in the play. On the other hand, in the online version of TCG, cards are digitally represented in a virtual world. The player cannot touch the cards in the virtual world directly so he/she does not feel the strong sense of the ownership of cards. Using the physical paper cards is important to increase the sense of the ownership, and thus increases the motivation to collect more favorite cards to enjoy the game better. Especially, the rarity of the cards becomes a strong incentive to collect and own the favorite cards.

The last is the *ideological value*. *Augmented TCG* shows *Yugi* and *Kaiba* who are main heroes in the *Yu-Gi-Oh!* animation story and opponent players. The characters represent some ideological concepts like friendship and justice in their background story. So, playing against *Yugi* and *Kaiba* reminds players the importance of such ideological factors because the players know the stories behind the characters. The extrinsic motivation established by the previous four values encourages enjoying a game, and the ideological value teaches a player the importance of friendship to really enjoy the game. The five values leads to the self-efficacy to improve a player's gaming skills with his/her friends' cooperation and support.

4   Future Direction

When using the *transtheoretical model*, growing intrinsic motivation is essential to raise a user's current stage. However, traditional approaches require a large amount of information that will make a user feel values to change his/her current attitude. We like to exploit the idea of using a character from a fictional animation or a game story, and thus by reminding the user the leitmotif of the character's story [1] to reduce the necessary information to grow his/her intrinsic motivation.

Reference

1. Sakamoto, M., Nakajima, T., Tokunaga, E., Alexandrova, T.: Augmenting Trading Card Play with Empathetic Virtual Characters. In: HumanCom 2012 (2012)

Real Story Interaction:
The Role of Global Agency in Interactive Storytelling

Christian Roth and Ivar Vermeulen

VU University, De Boelelaan 1081, 1081HV Amsterdam, The Netherlands
roth@spieleforschung.de, i.e.vermeulen@vu.nl

Abstract. Interactive Storytelling (IS) is a promising new entertainment technology synthesizing pre-authored narrative with dynamic user interaction. Research on user experiences in IS is sparse. The current experiment tested whether different player expectations regarding the impact of their actions yield different user experiences by framing user agency as "local" vs. "global" in the introduction to the story. Local agency influences character behavior and story events, whereas global agency influences story development and outcomes. A between-subject design involved $N = 46$ participants playing the interactive story "Dinner Date". Findings suggest that experiential qualities (autonomy, flow, curiosity) reached higher levels when players believed to have an impact on the story outcome (global agency). Enjoyment did not differ between conditions. Systematic gender differences in user experiences are discussed.

Keywords: Interactive Storytelling, User Experience, Global Agency.

1 Introduction

Interactive Storytelling is a new promising field in interactive entertainment media. In a digital interactive story the player creates or influences a dramatic storyline by either controlling a protagonist or by issuing events as a director. IS envisions uniting two popular entertainment concepts: interactivity and narratives, thus producing a shift of focus from linear narratives to non-linear, interactive narratives. However, little is known about the user experience of playing such interactive stories. Popular works in the field (e.g. [1]) point out to the concept of agency as being crucial for meaningful interaction in interactive stories. Agency, the sense of control, can be experienced on a local and global level: Local agency focuses on what the user can do in a particular scene and environment setting. On a global level users have influence on the evolvement of a story, also including the ending. To perceive meaningful interaction, it is crucial for players to perceive the consequences of their actions. Generating feedback about local agency is relatively easy since it happens almost immediately after the user action. In contrast, generating feedback about global agency is hard. In

M. Herrlich, R. Malaka, and M. Masuch (Eds.): ICEC 2012, LNCS 7522, pp. 425–428, 2012.
© IFIP International Federation for Information Processing 2012

Interactive Storytelling systems, complex algorithms compute how single local actions have impact on a global scale, rendering it almost impossible to the user to differentiate the effect of all his inputs. Nevertheless, Interactive Storytelling differentiates itself from traditional video games by focusing on the influence that users have on the evolving story (e.g., global agency). So, to really appreciate IS for what it is, users should be aware of their global agency. In an experimental study, we investigated whether (1) focusing players' attention to their local vs. global influence on a narrative influences their experience of playing an interactive story and whether (2) providing feedback signals about successful user interventions on a local or global scale make perceptions of agency tangible. Players used the interactive story "Dinner Date", where they assumed the role of the subconscious of a character desperately waiting for his dinner date to arrive. For half of the respondents, potential agency was framed as merely local (influencing character behavior and local events), whereas for the other half, potential agency was framed as global (influencing story development and outcomes). To make perceptions of agency tangible, we added sound signals when, supposedly, user actions yielded significant impact.

2   Method

A total of 46 university students (18 males, 28 females; average age $M = 20.96$ years, $SD = 2.64$ years) played the interactive story "Dinner Date". In this system, users interact with a protagonist who is waiting for his dinner date to arrive, by pointing his attention to different objects present in the virtual environment. By directing his attention, thoughts and actions of the protagonist are triggered, leading to a new situation where, again, influence can be exerted. Participants were randomly assigned to one of two introductions. In the local agency introduction, participants were told that, by focusing the protagonist's attention, they could influence immediate character behavior and local story events. In the global agency introduction, they were told that they could influence the development of the protagonist's "life story" and future. Dinner Date provides hardly any feedback on user agency – feedback on user influence on a local level is ambiguous at best (the protagonist seems to mull around in circles, despite users' attempts to change his line of thought), whereas feedback on global agency (story outcomes, future events) is non-existent. To make agency tangible in both conditions, we introduced sound signals (beeps) that supposedly give feedback about user actions having a significant impact on either local events (in the local agency condition) or global events (in the global agency condition). After carefully reading the introductions, participants played Dinner Date for about 20 minutes. Subsequently, they completed a pre-established and validated questionnaire on user responses to interactive stories [3], which includes short scales in the following order: positive and negative affect, suspense, aesthetic pleasantness, system usability, curiosity, local agency, global agency, flow, enjoyment, presence, character believability, effectance, identification, user satisfaction, autonomy. All measurement dimensions were measured with a 5-point-Likert scale using between two and five items each. Reliability scores (see

Table 1) for all scales were acceptable. Finally, participants received credit points or 10 EUR as compensation, were debriefed and dismissed.

3 Results

Within-subject comparison by means of independent samples T-tests reveals that framing agency as local vs. global before play indeed affected user experiences (see Table 1 for results). First, a manipulation check showed that users in the global agency condition perceived significantly more global agency. Furthermore, when playing under the assumption of having global agency, participants were significantly more curious about the story progress, experienced significantly stronger flow, and significantly higher autonomy. Finally, participants in the global agency condition perceived the protagonist as significantly more believable. Prior research [2] showed significant gender differences in preferences for local vs. global agency in interactive storytelling environments whereas men tend to enjoy the perception of empowerment associated with global agency, women tend to enjoy the character involvement provided by local agency. Looking at gender differences using a factorial ANOVA in the current data set, we found that effectance was higher for male players in the global agency condition than in the local agency condition ($M = 3.60$, $SD = .65$ vs. $M = 2.75$, $SD = .67$), while female players showed inverted effects ($M = 2.92$, $SD = .71$ vs. $M = 3.12$, $SD = .77$; $F(1, 42) = 2.98$, $\rho = .017$). In addition, identification was higher for female players in the global agency than in local agency condition ($M = 3.02$, $SD = .76$ vs. $M = 2.64$, $SD = .96$), while for male players it was the other way round ($M = 2.70$, $SD = 1.00$ vs. $M = 3.51$, $SD = .47$; $F(1, 42) = 5.54$, $\rho = .023$). This finding puts earlier findings in a new perspective: it seems that men dissociate more from a protagonist when they have power over his providence, while women identify stronger when they feel more responsible for the protagonist's fate.

4 Discussion

The experiment showed the impact of induced perceptions of global agency on users' experiences of interactive storytelling environments. Results showed IS was more reciprocal (autonomy), interesting (curiosity), and immersive (flow) for participants in the global agency group. However, experience dimensions such as presence and suspense were not affected by the manipulation. Moreover, general enjoyment and affect did not differ between groups, so we must conclude that playing IS under the assumptions of global (vs. local) agency is different, but not necessarily better. Possibly, these non-findings can also be explained by the rather sad and contemplative nature of the Dinner Date environment. Analyses of gender differences showed, in line with prior research, that male participants experienced more effectance in the global agency condition, while for women it was vice versa. Women maintained character identification (in fact, it got stronger) when they felt in charge of the character's fate, while men tended

Table 1. Comparison of user ratings between local agency and global agency group

		Local Agency		Global Agency		
Experience dimension	Reliabilities	M	SD	M	SD	ρ
System usability	$\alpha = .89$	3.65	.89	3.87	.88	.41
User satisfaction	$r = .48$	3.26	.76	3.37	.71	.62
Presence	$\alpha = .81$	3.31	.80	3.44	.54	.52
Character believability	$r = .36$	3.19	.77	3.65	.68	.04[*]
Effectance	$\alpha = .76$	2.98	.74	3.19	.71	.34
Autonomy	$\alpha = .80$	2.16	.72	2.65	.75	.03[*]
Local Agency	$\alpha = .73$	3.00	.75	3.40	.82	.08
Global Agency	$\alpha = .74$	2.55	.78	3.39	.80	.00[*]
Curiosity	$\alpha = .73$	3.40	.57	3.78	.52	.02[*]
Suspense	$\alpha = .64$	3.75	.70	3.67	.43	.69
Flow	$\alpha = .72$	2.77	.67	3.12	.36	.01[*]
Aesthetic pleasantness	$\alpha = .72$	3.00	.66	3.03	71	.89
Identification	$\alpha = .82$	2.98	.90	2.89	.86	.74
Enjoyment	$r = .79$	3.36	.76	3.36	.69	1.0
Affect: positive	$\alpha = .77$	2.03	.50	2.22	.74	.33
Affect: negative	$r = .38$	3.52	.71	3.43	.77	.69

Note: [*] significant difference at $\rho < .05$. Reliabilities of scales with only two items were assessed using Pearson's r correlations (all significant at $\rho < .05$).

to dissociate. A general problem for IS environments is that they revolve around the idea of granting users global agency on story progress and outcomes, yet it is very hard to give users feedback about such agency. We introduced a new way of making perceptions of global agency tangible by providing sound signals when such agency was achieved. Although our design does not grant testing the impact of the sound signals itself, we did achieve higher levels of perceived global agency in the global agency condition, which means that – to some extent – our participants found this agency tangible. Future research could use a feedback vs. no-feedback experimental design to assess to what extent direct feedback on global agency adds to IS users' experiences.

References

1. Mateas, M., Stern, A.: Structuring content in the faade interactive drama architecture. In: Proceedings of the First Artificial Intelligence and Interactive Digital Entertainment Conference, pp. 93–98 (2005)
2. Roth, C., Vermeulen, I., Vorderer, P., Klimmt, C., Pizzi, D., Lugrin, J., Cavazza, M.: Playing in or out of character: User role differences in the experience of interactive storytelling. Submitted to CyberPsychology, Behavior, and Social Networking (2012)
3. Vermeulen, I.E., Roth, C., Vorderer, P., Klimmt, C.: Measuring User Responses to Interactive Stories: Towards a Standardized Assessment Tool. In: Aylett, R., Lim, M.Y., Louchart, S., Petta, P., Riedl, M. (eds.) ICIDS 2010. LNCS, vol. 6432, pp. 38–43. Springer, Heidelberg (2010)

Adaptive Difficulty with Dynamic Range of Motion Adjustments in Exergames for Parkinson's Disease Patients

Sandra Siegel and Jan Smeddinck

TZI Digital Media Lab, University of Bremen
Bibliothekstraße 1, 28359 Bremen, Germany
{siegel,smeddinck}@tzi.de

Abstract. Motion-based video games offer great promise in the support of traditional physiotherapy and are currently explored in a growing number of research projects. With a focus on Parkinson's disease (PD) patients, their therapeutic needs and strong individual differences in capabilities, this work describes an approach to dynamic difficulty adjustments in an exergame tailored for PD patients. The automated ongoing adjustment of the required range of motion, the amplitude parameter, is introduced as an important aspect of such adaptations. Results from a first case study suggest that the approach is viable and appreciated by therapists, yet could benefit from increased flexibility.

Keywords: serious games, parkinson's disease, motion-based games, exergames, difficulty adaptation, elderly entertainment.

1 Introduction

Parkinson's disease (PD) is characterized by a variety of motor and non-motor symptoms [1]. Regular physical activity in therapy sessions and auxiliary exercises at home play a central role in slowing down the progression of the neurological disease and in improving the patients' quality of life [2]. It is important to motivate patients to participate in these activities and to put effort into performing the often repetitive exercises. Exergames, as motion-based video games, offer great promise in augmenting existing therapy sessions and home exercising by providing additional guidance, feedback and motivation. Our work is based on the *WuppDi!* exergames suite for PD patients (cf. [3]). Evaluations of this project have shown that the chance of enriching the spectrum of tools around physiotherapy is appreciated by patients and therapists alike.

However, the target group of PD patients has very specific requirements that are dominated by the need to cater for strong individual differences in the mental and physical abilities and limitations of the players that result from different states of disease and symptoms, effects of normal ageing and fluctuations over the course of a day [2]. Typical game-difficulty modes (e.g. easy, medium, hard) encompass multiple game-play variables and do not allow for the required fine-grained control.

M. Herrlich, R. Malaka, and M. Masuch (Eds.): ICEC 2012, LNCS 7522, pp. 429–432, 2012.
© IFIP International Federation for Information Processing 2012

We introduce a system that implements an ongoing adaptation of difficulty parameter settings for individual players, focusing on the automated adaptation of their range of motion (ROM). The system, which also adapts parameters for speed and accuracy, was tested in an initial case study over the course of three weeks, in order to determine whether the individual settings can successfully be adjusted over time, aiming for an improved range and quality of motion, while providing a positive game experience.

2   A Brief Overview of DDA for Exergames and a PD Specific Implementation

Dynamic Difficulty Adjustments (DDA) are an important matter of research in relation to motion-based games for the support of physiotherapy for PD patients. The need for personalization in order to accommodate for strong differences in capabilities between individuals is a core requirement that has been identified in prior research [3] and related research with other heterogeneous target-groups, such as institutionalized older adults [4] and stroke patients [5]. This adaptation needs to be automated, because therapists cannot afford to make frequent manual adjustments for every individual patient. To date, related research seldom focused on the specific use-case of exergames for PD and largely omitted the aspect of automatic ROM adaptations, which we discuss here as the game-difficulty parameter *amplitude*. In addition to the more commonly studied difficulty parameters for *speed* and *accuracy* [5,6], the amplitude is an important aspect, since wide fluent movements are a crucial component of PD physiotherapy [3].

We implemented and tested DDA for *Sterntaler*, one of the WuppDi! games [3]. In the game, the player is tracked by a Kinect[1] sensor and follows differently shaped trails of stars with one hand. The position of the playing hand is mapped to a hand-shaped cursor that is used to collect the stars for points. Here, game difficulty is composed of the time available to collect all stars before they automatically disappear (*speed*), the size of the cursor with which the player has to hit the stars (*accuracy*) and the *amplitude* of movements the player has to perform to reach all stars. The latter is controlled by a scale factor that is applied to the mapping of tracked movements to the cursor, making it easier or harder to reach stars further away from the player.

The three difficulty parameters are automatically adapted after each game round based on the player's performance in that round and additionally slightly decreased for the first game of a new game session in order to provide for a warm-up round. Speed and accuracy settings change based on the rate of collected to non-collected stars and the completion time. For the adaptation of the amplitude setting, the collection rate is weighted by the distance of stars from the rest position of the play hand. Additionally, the motion profile of the play hand is consulted for inferring if non-collected stars were not accessible or if they could have been reached by the player (i.e. the player has moved his hand to the

---

[1] http://www.kinectforwindows.org

respective position before). Optionally, a calibration based on three predefined poses can be performed to determine a suitable amplitude setting for the first game and to constrain dynamic amplitude adaptation to a reasonable maximum. This process must be monitored by therapists and the results can be manually adjusted to match therapeutic constraints or goals.

3   Case Study

The system was applied in a case study with three male PD patients aged 64, 76, and 76, spanning five sessions per participant over a period of three weeks. Each participant played 16 game rounds with either hand. The evaluation was based on observational data, self-reported ratings of participants concerning the perceived difficulty and their game experience, game logs (difficulty settings, performance data and motion profiles) and video recordings that were analyzed together with associated physiotherapists. Due to the limited scope of this paper we focus on presenting the results related to amplitude adaptation (cf. [7]).

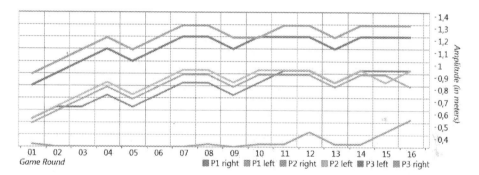

Fig. 1. The amplitude settings, which correspond to the diameter of movements necessary for covering the screen, for the three participants over all game rounds

The course of the amplitude settings is depicted in figure 1. The starting settings applied in the first round were determined by calibration and settled 40cm below the calibrated amplitude. These settings are quite distinctive as they respond to the different motion capabilities of the three participants and their body height (ca. 1,7m for P1/P2 and 1.98m for P3). As expected, due to the easy start settings, the required ROM steadily increases in almost all cases during the first game rounds until the calibrated constraints are reached. P2 (right) differs from the general trend due to the participant's individual problems in raising his right arm vertically and reaching the central upper area of the screen. Physiotherapists, when analyzing video recordings at different amplitude levels, underlined the importance of the provided individual and dynamic amplitude settings. The high level settings were seen as increasingly suitable and effective as participants needed to fully stretch their arms and their back.

While the upward trend in amplitude settings clearly illustrates the adaptation mechanism at work and therapists confirm that the adaptation approach generally provided suitable amplitude settings for our participants, some issues remain that demand for more flexibility in the adaptation mechanics: For P2 raising his right arm vertically was difficult, while stretching it to the sides was well possible, resulting in a low amplitude setting that did not get him to exploit his whole horizontal ROM. P1 suffers from a severely flexed spine (camptocormia) and an important focus in his exercises lies on stretching his trunk. Therapists therefore recommend to select star trails that motivate vertical movements and require a large range of motion while restricting the range horizontal movements, since these could possibly compromise his balance.

4   Conclusion

DDA in exergames have the potential to make them more useful and efficient, especially for heterogeneous target-groups with shifting needs like PD patients. The case study illustrated how such adaptations can work based on heuristic performance measures and highlighted the importance of an amplitude parameter in exergames for PD patients. However, the data analysis and therapist comments suggest that the system needs to be more flexible and allow for fine-grained control to encompass individual strengths and weaknesses (e.g. vertical vs. horizontal ROM). A more distinctive area-based performance analysis and more frequent live adaptations, based on a wider spectrum of feedback metrics, could be viable approaches to these challenges. Lastly, improving and evaluating DDA in exergames requires long-term studies with more subjects and the possibility to correlate game-performance data to reliable medical data.

References

1. Goldenberg, M.: Medical management of parkinson's disease. P&T 33(10) (2008)
2. Parkinson's Disease Society: The Professional's Guide to PD, London (2007)
3. Assad, O., Hermann, R., Lilla, D., Mellies, B., Meyer, R., Shevach, L., Siegel, S., Springer, M., Tiemkeo, S., Voges, J., Wieferich, J., Herrlich, M., Krause, M., Malaka, R.: Motion-Based Games for Parkinson's Disease Patients. In: Anacleto, J.C., Fels, S., Graham, N., Kapralos, B., Saif El-Nasr, M., Stanley, K. (eds.) ICEC 2011. LNCS, vol. 6972, pp. 47–58. Springer, Heidelberg (2011)
4. Gerling, K.M., Livingston, I.J., Nacke, L.E., Mandryk, R.L.: Full-Body Motion-Based game interaction for older adults. In: CHI 2012: Proceedings of the 30th International Conference on Human Factors in Computing Systems (2012)
5. Alankus, G., Lazar, A., May, M., Kelleher, C.: Towards customizable games for stroke rehabilitation. In: Proceedings of the 28th International Conference on Human Factors in Computing Systems, pp. 2113–2122 (2010)
6. Geurts, L., Vanden Abeele, V., Husson, J., et al.: Digital games for physical therapy: fulfilling the need for calibration and adaptation. In: Proceedings of the Fifth International Conference on Tangible, Embedded, and Embodied Interaction, TEI 2011, pp. 117–124. ACM, New York (2011)
7. Siegel, S.: Adaptive Difficulty in Exergames for Parkinsons Disease Patients. Unpublished master's thesis. University of Bremen, Bremen (2012)

The Influence of Music on Player Performance in Exergames for Parkinson's Patients

Damian Lilla, Marc Herrlich, Rainer Malaka, and Dennis Krannich

Digital Media Group, University of Bremen, Bremen, Germany
{lilla,mh,malaka,krannich}@tzi.de

Abstract. Music therapy and music and rhythm in general can support standard physiotherapy for people suffering from Parkinson's disease to improve the motion performance and quality, sometimes even helping to overcome motion blocks. With the availability of cheap motion-tracking devices, exergames have become an interesting option to complement traditional physiotherapy. However, the role of music and rhythm in the context of games for this special audience is still largely unexplored. Based on a prototype exergame we developed, a user study was conducted to compare the effects of different auditory clues and their absence in exergames for this target group. The results show significant performance differences with music versus without music, but surprisingly no differences were found between music synchronized with the interaction and unsynchronized background music.

Keywords: exergames, auditory cues, kinect, Parkinson's disease.

1   Introduction

The most common occurring symptoms of Parkinson's disease (PD) are reduced movement in amplitude and speed, problems in initiating movement, freezing, postural control difficulties, resting tremor or rigidity [1]. Physical therapy (PT) can slow down the progression of PD [2], but due to its repetitive nature, it can quickly bore and tire patients [3].

Music therapy (MT) can greatly enrich traditional PT and help to improve the precision, range, speed and quality of upper body movement [4]. By instructing PD patients to step to the beat of music, significant improvements for stride symmetry, length, gait velocity and cadence were achieved [5].

Exertion games (exergames) can motivate and immerse patients to facilitate repetitions [6] which are crucial in order to rebuild functional abilities [7].

To utilize the advantages of auditory cues and exergames, we developed a prototype which blends both approaches into one system. We hypothesize that the auditory cues will have a performance enhancing effect in this game-like environment. To validate this hypothesis we contrast the performance of three groups of patients with PD. In the first group, the music's rhythm is directly connected to the timing of the movement. In the second, the music does not correlate with the movement. In the third, no music is used during gameplay.

M. Herrlich, R. Malaka, and M. Masuch (Eds.): ICEC 2012, LNCS 7522, pp. 433–436, 2012.
© IFIP International Federation for Information Processing 2012

Fig. 1. Gameplay screen and an extract of movements for the mole game

Our results indicate that music can, in fact, have a performance enhancing effect when used in a game-like environment. In our particular setup it did not matter whether the music had a clear, easily followed beat or a more fluid, calming tempo.

2   Related Work

Assad et al. developed a collection of mini-games specifically for PD patients in order to train memory as well as upper and lower extremities. Within this collection the game "Cinderella" makes use of auditory cues in order to motivate and guide the patient's pace of movement [8]. However, these auditory cues are not directly connected to the timing of the motion. A system for PD patients by Yu et al. lets the user interact with the system by wearing a motion suit and also makes use of auditory cues in order to help the patients to pace their movements [3]. However, the timing of these movements is not directly synchronized with the beat of music. Contrary to both systems, ours strongly connects the beat of the music with the timing of the movement in the attempt to help train its temporal precision as well as to reduce motion blocks.

3   The Mole Game Prototype

While standing in front of the camera, the player's hands are tracked by the camera and represented as cartoon hands on the gameplay screen (cf. left side of figure 1). The game's goal is to grab a worm and feed the moles appearing from the holes repetitively. The earlier the player hits the appearing moles the higher the score, ranging from 100% to 0%. Visual cues, small helmets peaking out of the holes, act as a hint for the player where the next mole will appear.

4   Evaluation

We conducted nine meetings over the duration of three months at three places where Parkinson's disease patients meet for physiotherapy or socializing. Every meeting lasted for approximately 1 to 2,5 hours.

4.1   Procedure

We tested for differences between the groups' performances by logging their scores. Additionally, we videotaped the motion of the participants. They were randomly assigned by us into one of three groups. The participants played a training round which had no music, followed by three gameplay rounds with the same movement patterns and with the specific background song settings for their group. Each round lasted one minute and 14 seconds. The choreography for all three rounds was the same and consisted of simple one and two-handed reaching tasks (cf. right side of fig. 1). Group one's beat of the music exactly matched the timing when a mole appeared and should therefore have helped with the temporal precision of the movement. We did not, however, explicitly instruct the participants in both music groups to use the auditory cues to pace their motion.

4.2   Results

A total of 24 participants with a mean age of 70.4 ± 6.9 took part in the evaluation. 62,5% were males and 37,5% were females. All three groups had the same proportion of males (5) to females (3).

We conducted Kruskal-Wallis tests in order to reveal significant differences in the performances among the groups. In round one ($H(2) = 2,885$, $p=0,236$) as well as round three ($H(2) = 4,56$ $p=0,102$) no significant differences among the groups could be found, whereas the test revealed significant differences among the groups in round two ($H(2) = 6,5$ $p=0,039$). In this round, the participants of group one achieved an average score of $77,59\%\pm22,84$. Slightly lower was the score of the participants of group two with a mean score of $76,72\%\pm10,92$. Lastly, by nearly 20% less compared to the previous groups, the control group achieved a mean score of $57,18\%\pm20,50$.

Afterwards, we conducted pairwise Mann-Whitney U post-hoc tests in order to evaluate which pairs of groups had significant differences in round two. The difference between group one and the control group was significant (Mann-Whitney $U=10,0$, $n1=n2=8$, $p=0,021$ two-tailed). By analyzing the differences between group two and the control group, we found a tendency (Mann-Whitney $U=14,0$, $n1=n2=8$, $p=0,059$ two-tailed) for group two to score higher than the control group. Lastly, the differences in scores between the two groups with music were not significant.

Exclusively based on the observations, we could not identify any participants from group one rocking themselves or noticeably nodding their heads to the beat of the music.

5   Discussion

Our results show that music indeed effects player performance positively, even if the players are not explicitly instructed to regard the auditory clues. In contrast to our assumptions, the participants did not follow the specific beat in group one. We conclude that explicitly instructing players about the synchronization of the beat and the interaction might further increase performance.

6   Conclusion and Future Work

We have presented first experimental findings that music can improve the performance of PD patients in a game-like environment. For a follow up study we particularly recommend to explore if PD patients would time their movements with the help of auditory cues when explicitly instructed to do so. Further research could also discover the other attributes of music that could have positively affected performance in gameplay and why.

Acknowledgements. We thank the "Deutsche Parkinson Vereinigung", particularly the physiotherapists Katharina von Sauken, Rieke Tischkewitz, Brigitte Kloker, Marlis Böger and Renate Stöver. We further want to thank all the participants who patiently and with great effort took part in this study.

References

1. Morris, M.E.: Movement disorders in people with parkinson disease: A model for physical therapy. Phys. Ther. 80, 578–597 (2000)
2. Suteerawattananon, M., Morris, G.S., Etnyre, B.R., Jankovic, J., Protas, E.J.: Effects of visual and auditory cues on gait in individuals with parkinson's disease. Journal of the Neurological Sciences 219(12), 63–69 (2004)
3. Yu, W., Vuong, C., Ingalls, T.: An interactive multimedia system for parkinson's patient rehabilitation. In: Proc. MMSys 2010, Scottsdale, AZ, USA. Springer (2010)
4. Bernatzky, G., Bernatzky, P., Hesse, H.P., Staffen, W., Ladurner, G.: Stimulating music increases motor coordination in patients afflicted with morbus parkinson. Neuroscience Letters 361(1-3), 4–8 (2004)
5. Thaut, M.H., Kenyon, G.P., Schauer, M.L., McIntosh, G.C.: The connection between rhythmicity and brain function. IEEE Engineering in Medicine and Biology Magazine 18(2), 101–108 (1999)
6. Flynn, S., Palma, P., Bender, A.: Feasibility of using the sony playstation 2 gaming platform for an individual poststroke: a case report. Journal of Neurological Physical Therapy 31(4), 180–189 (2007)
7. Rand, D., Kizony, R., Weiss, P.L.: Virtual reality rehabilitation for all: Vivid GX versus sony PlayStation II EyeToy. In: Proc. ICDVRAT 2004, pp. 87–94 (2004)
8. Assad, O., Hermann, R., Lilla, D., Mellies, B., Meyer, R., Shevach, L., Siegel, S., Springer, M., Tiemkeo, S., Voges, J., Wieferich, J., Herrlich, M., Krause, M., Malaka, R.: Motion-based games for parkinson's disease patients. In: Proc. ICEC 2011, pp. 47–58 (2011)

The Soundtrack Of Your Life

Oliver Kierepka, Constantin Brosda, and Christian Geiger

University of Applied Sciences Düsseldorf,
Josef-Gockeln-Str. 9, 40474 Düsseldorf, Germany
{oliver.kierepka,constantin.brosda,
geiger}@fh-duesseldorf.de

Abstract. The rush of nowadays life turned travelling into a means to an end. Commuting people follow the same routes over and over and know less about the places they pass by. In this paper we present our approach of an interactive location-based audio application that invites users to explore alternative routes by sharing location-based song playlists. Therefore a prototypical smartphone application is developed that guides users through existing soundtracks and enables them to share their own playlists, their own Soundtrack Of Your Life.

Keywords: Location-based audio, mobile application, interactive multimedia.

1 Introduction

Mobility has become a part of our daily life and is more comfortable, less expensive and less exhausting than ever since. Today it is more extrinsic motivated and stronger bound to destinations and timely goals. Instead of interpreting travelling as an experience that offers new perspectives on the world, it often gets reduced to time optimized transportation from one point to another. Some people just know the microcosms of their home place, their workplace and the fastest route between them.

With our project we aim to increase the attractiveness of the surrounding by connecting pedestrian trails and places to an audio experience. The user leaves a virtual trace of the songs one is listening to along the route. This generates what we call the Soundtrack Of Your Life (STOYL).

2 Related Work

Tracking solutions enable users to log their individual routes and to share them with a community. Standalone GPS trackers or applications [1] for smartphones with integrated GPS sensors are examples of such services. Other services like Google Latitude [2] use the data to provide real-time information about the current global position of friends. Navigation devices provide assistance based on the current position while travelling to a specified location. Sounds or synthetic voices and graphical user interfaces signal new directions to the user. Warren et al. showed that instead user navigation can be implemented through continuously adapted music [3]. The "Central Park" as a location-aware album extends the idea of a location-based experience by a

M. Herrlich, R. Malaka, and M. Masuch (Eds.): ICEC 2012, LNCS 7522, pp. 437–440, 2012.

dynamically changing composition depending on the user's current position [4]. The SoundTracking application [5] enables users to share the song-title they are listening to and their current position with others.

3   Concept

Listening to music while walking or travelling has become a popular way of entertainment on the go. As we walk around we are able to carry our own individual music library with us. In STOYL the ability of nowadays smartphones is used to increase the appreciation of individual places and to explore the surrounding environment. Therefore real geolocations are linked with song playlists. Each user can leave a virtual track (sound channel) of the songs one listens to while walking. Every channel is unique as it consists of the individual preferences in music and paths. Other users walking along these sound channels are invited to step on new paths besides their well-known ones. As music is able to influence the way we see the world listening to an existing track offers an alternative point of view.

3.1   User Interaction

The user is guided through a binaural audio feedback that keeps one on track (see Figure 1). With this audio feedback synthetic voice overlays for navigation are unnecessary. In general the usage of graphical user interfaces is reduced to a minimum to enable the exploration and the visual perception of the surrounding world. Therefore vibro-tactile feedback signalizes other sound channels in proximity.

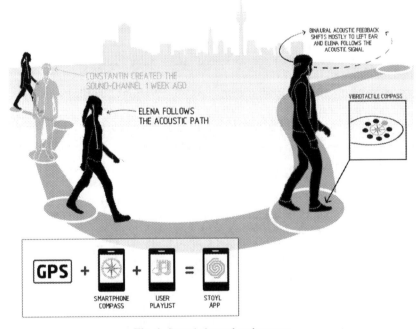

Fig. 1. Sound channel and system

3.2   Logging and Exploration

When in logging mode the application detects the current song the user is listening to. This information is combined with the GPS sensor's data as well as the internal compass. Those sound points are logged periodically and transferred to a server as a unique sound channel.

In exploration mode the user can listen to existing sound channels. If one approaches an other sound channel the vibration motor signalizes this to the user. Afterwards a short stop in walking starts an audio preview of the other channel and the current song is faded out. The user can now decide to enter the sound channel or to stay on the current track and walk on.

The guidance is based on a balance controlled, binaural mapping. If the user is walking straight ahead towards the next point of the sound channel, the current file is played on the right and the left earplug balanced. This rebuilds the perception of real sound sources depending on the angle between direction and the direct way to the source. To ensure a smooth directional navigation the sound channel's positions are interpolated and then used for the directional calculation. If a user walks outside of the channel one is smoothly guided to the next point.

3.3   Application

The smartphone is the central element of the application. It manages all incoming data that are gathered by the sensors. Based on this information the current position and direction is calculated and either logged or compared to existing sound channels. Additionally the visual interface and the internal vibration motor are controlled. For audio output a pair of headphones is used that is plugged directly into the smartphone. A web server provides storage and manages all logged sound channels. It can be accessed by the smartphone through standard network connections. For testing all audio files are hosted on the server and streamed to the clients on demand. The system has been implemented as a prototypical smartphone application.

4   Conclusion

We introduced the STOYL project that enables users to explore the world in relation to an individual musical playlist. It invites them to explore the environment and thereby to have a closer look besides their well-known paths. This is meant to broaden the user's horizon in two dimensions: first by the different music one is listening to and by the different routes one follows. In future work the prototypical application will be extended and evaluated as a system of multi user interaction.

References

1. Open GPS Tracker, http://code.google.com/p/open-gpstracker/ (accessed March 15, 2012)

2. Google Latitude, http://www.google.com/intl/de/mobile/latitude/ (accessed March 15, 2012)
3. Warren, N., Jones, M., Jones, S., Bainbridge, D.: Navigation via continuously adapted music. In: CHI 2005: CHI 2005 Extended Abstracts on Human Factors in Computing Systems, pp. 1849–1852. ACM, New York (2005)
4. Bluebrain, CentralPark, http://bluebrainmusic.blogspot.de/2011/07/blog-post.html (accessed Mrz 18, 2012)
5. Soundtracking, http://www.soundtracking.com (accessed March 13, 2012)

Mobile Gaming with Indirect Sensor Control

Daniel Böhrs, Dirk Wenig, and Rainer Malaka

Research Group Digital Media, TZI,
University of Bremen, Bibliothekstr. 1, 28359 Bremen, Germany

Abstract. The rapid growth of the mobile gaming market and the steadily improved hardware of mobile phones enable developers to create complex and extensive 3D games on mobile phones. While most current casual games have simple interfaces with few buttons, 3D games require new control interfaces to providing sufficient control options without limiting the field of view on the screen. This is important to improve the user experience. Within this work new ideas based on the use of the accelerometer as indirect control mechanism are presented. The accelerometer is used to switch between different interaction layers, which are also different game views for the player. Combined with this concept a buttonless touch area interface is used. We are planning to evaluate the ideas with a 3D game prototype running on Android devices.

Keywords: mobile gaming, sensors, mobile devices, labyrinth game.

1   Introduction

Controls for mobile phones are mostly touch screen and sensor interfaces. Currently this results in an adaption of conventional hardware elements from computers or consoles to build similar game controls on mobile phones. In games with various interaction possibilities, problems can occur while trying to map all needed controls on the display because the field of view can be limited substantially. Another approach is the use of sensors like the accelerometer, which is built into nearly all modern devices. This technique is especially popular in the racing game genre. A problem is that turning the device to the sides or shaking it can cause a lack of the overview. Both concepts limit the field of view in different ways. In order to tackle this challenge, we present the concept of an adapted combination of a accelerometer and a touch interface. The touch controls are integrated as a buttonless interface by using touch areas while the accelerometer is used as an indirect control mechanism. It enables the player to switch not only between different views, but also between controls. The overall result should be a clear interface with no disruptive objects on the screen and providing as much control as possible.

2   Related Work

Chu, K et al. [1] showed that mobile games on touch devices generally have a lack of comfort in the control system because of not existing hardware controls. New approaches must be found or existing ones have to be improved. Chui Yin Wong et al. [3] published study results demonstrating advantages of optimized touch interfaces in

M. Herrlich, R. Malaka, and M. Masuch (Eds.): ICEC 2012, LNCS 7522, pp. 441–444, 2012.

comparison to hardware controls. For example, the best scores while playing were arrived on touch interface and the amount of miss clicks was very low. An alternative approach is the use of the accelerometer which is already well established. This solution is mentioned by Kevin Browne et al. [2]: They used a touch based interface, one with an accelerometer and a gesture based system within a 2D scroll shooter game. The accelerometer interface was preferred by the testers and led to the best results in experience measurements. The use of accelerometers in 3D game is demonstrated by Fadi Chehimi and Paul Coulton [4] and is analogical to 2D games while using more axes for calculating movements within the game. The use of the accelerometer was rated mostly positive. Paul Gilbertson et al. [5] used the same approach but realized the game tunnel run without any buttons. The evaluation showed that players favor this type of control interface and the user experience ratings increase.

3   Concept

The developed prototype is a time based ball-through-labyrinth game with two different perspectives. Within the labyrinth corridors are objects, which must be passed by the user. The ball moves forward continuously without users control. One view is the top-down view, which is active if the device is placed horizontally (fig. 1). In this view the player can rotate left or right. The other view is a third-person view which allows the player to navigate around obstacles inside a corridor. In this view the player shifts the ball to the left or right.

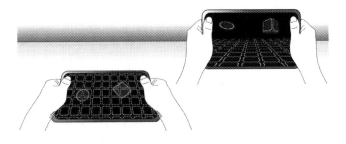

Fig. 1. Concept of a pitch gesture

The player is not forced to switch the view because he is able to see the map and the obstacles in both views. But the ability of swiftly moving around an obstacle by translating is a huge benefit which should motivate the players to switch the views by themselfs. This game is the basis for the idea of buttonless interaction in games with different control layers and views switched with the accelerometer. Within the concept multiple controls can be applied to smartphones without obstructing the players view and reducing screen-space by placing numerous visible buttons.

4 Control Concepts

Overall three concepts were implemented as parts of this work. A touch area and sensor interface, a touch area interface and a traditional touch button interface. The last one is used as control compare with the evaluation results of the other two approaches.

4.1 Touch Areas with Accelerometer Support

The first concept provides no visible objects on the touch screen (fig. 2). It is is divided vertically in two areas. Pushing the left side will trigger an action to the left and similar behavior is triggered on the right side. In the top view rotation is done by pushing the areas while in the third person view pushing leads to translations to move around obstacles. The switching between the two views is done by pitching the device. Holding it horizontally brings up the top view while holding it obliquely will switch to the third person view. The result is a clean screen and an intuitive way to switch the views.

Fig. 2. Touch areas with accelerometer support

4.2 Touch Areas without Accelerometer Support

The second concept is based on the first one but without sensor interactions. Instead of switching the views by tending, another touch area is inserted at the bottom (fig. 3). This concepts reduces the interaction to touch controls without limiting the field of view.

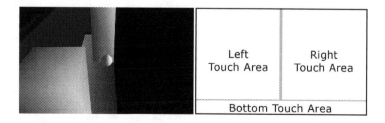

Fig. 3. Touch areas without accelerometer support

4.3   Traditional Touch Button Controls

The third concept is based on the known techniques by placing visible buttons on the screen to allow interaction (fig. 4). The number of buttons for this concept is 6: Two buttons to rotate, two to translate and two to switch the view. The buttons for switching the view are toggle buttons. The translation and view switching can be done in all views while the rotation is only possible in the top view.

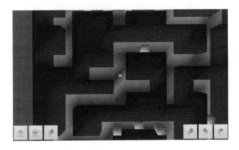

Fig. 4. Traditional touch button controls

5   Conclusion and Future Work

Currently we are planning an evaluation of the three concepts. Therefore, the presented prototype logs the interactions and sends them to a database for evaluation. At the end of the game a questionnaire is presented to get feedback about the users experience. The evaluation will investigate the advantages and disadvantages of the three control concepts and tests if the sensor support and the touch area concept could be approved as working. Every participant will play all three modes in random order. Future studies could adapt the concept for more complex games like shooters or role playing games.

References

1. Chu, K., Wong, C.Y.: Mobile input devices for gaming experience. In: User Science and Engineering (i-USEr), 2011 International Conference, November 29-December 1, pp. 83–88 (2011)
2. Browne, K., Anand, C.: An empirical evaluation of user interfaces for a mobile video game. Entertainment Computing 3(1), 1–10 (2012) ISSN 1875-9521
3. Wong, C.Y., Chu, K., Khong, C.W., Lim, T.Y.: Evaluating playability on haptic user interface for mobile gaming. In: Information Technology (ITSim), 2010 International Symposium, June 15-17, vol. 3, pp. 1093–1098 (2010)
4. Chehimi, F., Coulton, P.: Motion controlled mobile 3D multiplayer gaming. In: Proceedings of the 2008 International Conference on Advances in Computer Entertainment Technology (ACE 2008), pp. 267–270. ACM (2008)
5. Gilbertson, P., Coulton, P., Chehimi, F., Vajk, T.: Using tilt as an interface to control no-button mobile games. Comput. Entertain. 6(3), Article 38, 38:1–38:13 (2008)

Heuristics for Social Games with a Purpose

Aneta Takhtamysheva[1] and Tim Decker[2]

[1] Digital Media Lab, TZI, University of Bremen, 28359 Bremen, Germany
aneta@tzi.de
[2] 386 Main street, Oneonta, New York 13820, USA
tim@wanderingmanproductions.com

Abstract. Current project introduces a prototype of a game with a purpose constructed using heuristics of social game genre to attract long-term player involvement, and user content generation, to meet the constrains of time and budget.

Keywords: social gaming, playful applications, games with purpose, human computation, image tagging.

1   Introduction

Social games have experiencing unprecedented success rate. Millions of players, encompassing a large range of age categories play social games to relax, socialize and compete with Facebook friends on daily basis[1]. Social games are known for comparatively *small costs* of development, *minimalistic graphics*, *simple game mechanics*, and *viral promotion*, that seem to have fit the goals and development facilities of developers of games with a purpose (GWAP) [2].

In the current work we will discuss the heuristics of social games that can be utilized by games with purpose (human computation games) and propose a prototype of social game with purpose that also incorporates mechanisms that allow to deal with the financial and time constraints of researchers.

2   Social Game Heuristics Principles for Games with Purpose

Most games with purpose (GWAP) published on social networks so far have not been developed using heuristics specific for social network games; rather they were developed as *simple casual games* (i.e. Digitalkoot [3]), or gamified *playful environments* like Sentiment Quiz [4] that utilize social platforms only for the purpose of game deployment. This issue resulted in the lost opportunities of maximizing the reach and engagement of players that social networks like Facebook can potentially offer.

While existing game heuristics frameworks offered by Desurvire[5] and Pinelle [6], cover many elements that are also related to social games, some elements that are related specifically to the social game genre must be added. Paavilainen [7] suggests a

M. Herrlich, R. Malaka, and M. Masuch (Eds.): ICEC 2012, LNCS 7522, pp. 445–448, 2012.

set of Heuristics for Social Games, based on the guidelines developed by Järvinen [8], which besides the points common to all classic games, includes the following additional elements: *rewards for coming back; interruptability; using themes from popular culture; virality and sharing (rewarding players for inviting and gifting friends); narrativity (broadcasting of ingame events as a narration on the player's social network news timeline).* Also, other authors mention sophisticated *return mechanisms* [9] *rhythm design* [10] *ampleness of positive feedback* and very *clear game visuals* and *next step guidelines* [11] as part of a successful social game model.

We believe that in order to benefit from social game genre, social GWAP should strive to incorporate above mentioned elements whenever relevant.

In addition, Kirman [12] suggest utilizing *user empowerment mechanism* for asset creation and management of the game, to save efforts, time and money for researchers, and yet creating an engaging experience for players. This tactic has been successfully used in some commercial multi-player online games like *Second Life*, or *Spore* and might prove to be a valuable approach in research environment where developers might be limited in expertise, time and budget.

3   World Architect Game Prototype

While so far games with purpose were constructed so that the major challenge of the game is the serious tasks itself, we propose a concept of a serious game constructed using the heuristics of social games, where serious tasks are alternated with purely fun tasks.

The goal of this approach is test whether prioritizing fun tasks can leverage the overall sustainability of players' interest to the GWAP and actually increase the number of "serious" contributions of players in the long-run.

We present a concept/prototype of a game called *World Architect,* which represents a social network game with elements of serious tasks (image tagging). The game consists of variety of quests, some of which are related to serious tasks and others are not but serve the purpose of maintaining the attractiveness of the game.

Players have to set up villages, cities, states and countries by constructing buildings. To avoid costly process of game asset development (buildings) we incorporate user asset generation (*Construction Quest*). Users should create their own buildings (using graphic tools provided by the game) and can submit those for competitions. Each player is rewarded for participating in the evaluation of submitted pieces (*Judgment Quest*), the results of which serve as a ground for personalized game reminders. The next *Shopping Quest* requires users to create shipping tags for construction materials that were purchased to be "transported" to the construction location. The process of creation of shipping tags involves generating image tags. The quality of image tags is verified in the *Gardening Quest* where players have to match generated tags with images that they were created for. Each successful matching will bring the "gardener" a virtual tree, certain number of which is required to accomplish the construction process, and the "shippers" that created the successful image-tag combination will "safely" receive their construction materials at the construction spot.

Thus, both sides will reach perfect equilibrium only when providing honest image tagging and validation.

The game environment includes elements that are typical to many existing social network games: a popular culture theme, never-loose multi-session game play; return mechanics; simple strategy genre with simple puzzle elements; user's own unique space with a autonomous management rights; freedom to progress through the game at the desired pace; narrativity; social network login with open access to the user's profile data; and sociability (friends invitations and propagation mechanisms).

In addition to the above, the following guidelines were developed:

- Serious tasks positioned as secondary material to help deliver fun experience to the players rather than being a primary reason for playing the game.
- Serious tasks constructed as light "puzzles" that adds to the engagement of the game.
- Serious tasks deconstructed into smaller pieces and spread among several quests, thus decreasing the risk of breaking the flow of the game [13].
- Game consist of a variety of fairly independent blocks (mini quests) that are connected through storytelling, but can be replaced, improved or removed without destroying the whole game. This makes the game space more flexible for further improvement and extension.
- Mini quests represent a variety of playful activities to chose from – rating, selecting, drawing, puzzle solving, etc, thus giving user freedom of choice in activities instead of limiting to one type of activity.
- The voting scores that each user receives for works submitted for voting competition will in its turn serve two important points: boost efforts and motivation for the players, and:
- Serve as a ground for anticipated updates on how well the submitted works are performing in terms of ratings (narrativity element), and inconspicuously remind players about the game itself.

4   Further Steps

The next stage of the work is to conduct user studies and test the usefulness of the proposed approach where serious tasks are presented only as secondary elements of social games, and see if proposed guidelines, in particular those related to serious tasks, prove effective in terms of soliciting long term players' contributions. Also, the studies should help to find a proper balance between the number of serious tasks in proportion to the number of playful tasks so that to keep sustainable interest of players while receiving useful input at a pace and quantity that makes the game worth the investments that it required.

References

1. PopGames: Social Gaming Research. Research Report. Information Solutions Group (2011), http://www.infosolutionsgroup.com
2. Von Ahn, L.: Human computation. In: Proceedings of the 46th Annual Design Automation Conference (DAC 2009), pp. 418–419. ACM, NY (2009)
3. Chrons, O., Sundell, S.: Digitalkoot: Making Old Archives Accessible Using Crowdsourcing. In: HCOMP 2011 Proceedings of the ACM SIGKDD Workshop on Human Computation (2011)
4. Weichselbraun, S., Gindl, A., Scharl, A.: Using games with a purpose and bootstrapping to create domain-specific sentiment lexicons. In: Proceedings of the 20th ACM International Conference on Information and Knowledge Management (CIKM 2011), pp. 1053–1060. ACM, New York (2011)
5. Desurvire, H., Wiberg, C.: Game Usability Heuristics (PLAY) for Evaluating and Designing Better Games: The Next Iteration. In: Ozok, A.A., Zaphiris, P. (eds.) OCSC 2009. LNCS, vol. 5621, pp. 557–566. Springer, Heidelberg (2009)
6. Pinelle, D., Wong, N., Stach, T.: Heuristic evaluation for games: usability principles for video game design. In: Proceedings of the Twenty-Sixth Annual SIGCHI Conference on Human Factors in Computing Systems (CHI 2008), pp. 1453–1462. ACM, New York (2008)
7. Paavilainen, J.: Critical review on video game evaluation heuristics: social games perspective. In: Proceedings of the International Academic Conference on the Future of Game Design and Technology (Futureplay 2010), pp. 56–65. ACM, New York (2010)
8. Järvinen, A.: Game design for social networks: interaction design for playful dispositions. In: Proceedings of the 2009 ACM SIGGRAPH Symposium on Video Games (Sandbox 2009), pp. 95–102. ACM, New York (2009)
9. Thornton, W.M.: 7 - FarmVille, Making Great Games, pp. 101–113. Focal Press, Boston (2011), doi:10.1016/B978-0-240-81285-4.10007-8, ISBN 9780240812854
10. Tyni, H., Sotamaa, O., Toivonen, S.: Howdy pardner!: on free-to-play, sociability and rhythm design in FrontierVille. In: Proceedings of the 15th International Academic MindTrek Conference: Envisioning Future Media Environments (MindTrek 2011), pp. 22–29. ACM, New York (2011)
11. Isbister, K., Schaffer, N.: Chapter 10 - The Strange Case of the Casual Gamer, Game Usability, pp. 143–158. Morgan Kaufmann, Boston (2008)
12. Kirman, B., Casey, S., Lawson, S., Rowland, D.: User Powered Games for Research. In: Proceedings of the Games Design and Technology Workshop and Conference (GDTW), Liverpool (2008)
13. Jones, M.G.: Creating electronic learning environments: Games, flow, and the user interface. In: Proceedings of Selected Research and Development Presentations at the National Convention of the Association for Educational Communications and Technology, AECT (1998)

Serious Questions in Playful Questionnaires

Aneta Takhtamysheva and Jan Smeddinck

Digital Media Lab, TZI, University of Bremen, 28359 Bremen, Germany
{aneta,smeddinck}@tzi.de

Abstract. Conducting surveys is a time consuming and often expensive process. One of the main hurdles is motivating people to participate. The project presented herein proposes a playful approach, distributed via social network environments, where participants are intrinsically motivated to participate. A first evaluation showed an increased incentive to recommend friends to participate in the survey, as well as a preference of the playful approach to conducting surveys in general.

Keywords: Social networks, social gaming, social media, playful applications, opinion-mining, survey.

1 Introduction

Collecting feedback and opinions through playful applications is an approach that remains largely unexplored [1]. We argue that playful questionnaires, which attract users/gamers mostly through their playful aspect rather than through requests for a favor, can aid in circumventing some of the common challenges of human subject research, such as low response rates and survey fatigue [2]. In a wide range of research fields, opinion mining / surveys and quizzes [3] [4] [5] are tools are potential subjects to applying gamification for serious tasks which don't intend to bring any personal benefit to the users other than engaging experience. The finding that users play games not because they are useful, but mostly because they are fun [6] has already been applied to the games with a purpose [7] [8] [9] [10].

In order to evaluate the method of embedding serious questions in playful surveys and distributing them via social networks, we have created a sample playful application and conducted an explorative user experience study that involves having social network users interact with two versions of a survey: a playful one and a standard one.

2 Playful Questionnaire Design

The social network playful application called *Bake Your Personality* contains six serious questions about the video gaming preferences of the users. Following a pattern that has proven successful in the development of social networks applications, the playful questionnaire was developed relying on a universal theme that a wide

M. Herrlich, R. Malaka, and M. Masuch (Eds.): ICEC 2012, LNCS 7522, pp. 449–452, 2012.

audience can connect with [7]; in this case the process of cooking. Questions are asked using the metaphorical concept of a cooking process and of choosing ingredients for a final product (here: a cake). Figure 1 shows the quest to select 3 game genres that the player prefers to play most. Each question is presented as an action the player may perform; possible answers are represented by items that users interact with. At the end the "cake" is submitted for tasting, and user receives a playful personality report based on the "taste" of the cake. The players are motivated to be truthful with their answers in order to receive their correct personality report. In the background, the decisions made by users are recorded.

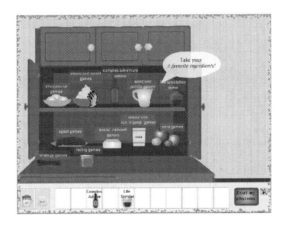

Fig. 1. Snapshot of the *Bake your Personality* application

The earnestness of the answers provided is checked by introducing a control question (a question that was asked before but appears again later on in a rephrased fashion).

In order to evaluate the validity and reception of the playful questionnaires approach presented herein, a questionnaire with a generic visual style and with an identical set of questions was developed. It contains single- and multiple-choice questions that correspond to the same questions and answers embedded in the playful application. After completing the standard questionnaire the users receive a playful personality report that contains the same text as in the playful version.

The major differences between these two questionnaires thus are in visual style, presence/absence of storytelling, and the amount of time necessary to complete the questionnaire. The playful application requires around 3 minutes on average, while the simple application takes less than 1 minute to finish.

3   Evaluation

The evaluation involved 20 students from 15 different study departments of the University of Bremen. The participant pool consisted of 10 males and 10 females, ranging in age from 20 to 35 years (M=25, SD=3.3 N=20). In order to counterbalance the order in which subjects participated in the conditions the sequence was randomly selected. Once participants completed both applications, they were asked to complete a feedback form, which covered the following issues:

1. Whether the playful elements of the playful questionnaire distracted users from their major task.
2. How users perceived each application: as a survey, serious personality report, playful personality report, or a game.
3. Whether users would recommend any of the two applications to friends on a social network (or verbally if they have no social network account).
4. Which one of the two versions the users would prefer to use in the future?

   1. The participants were asked whether the visual elements of the playful application notably distracted them from the major task of answering the "serious" questions. The results were compared to the responses given to the same question concerning the control application. A Wilcoxon Signed Rank test was applied to test the significance of the difference between the self-reported amount of influence of aesthetic and ludic elements on the answers provided by the users. It did not show any statistically significant differences between the degrees of "distraction" of these two applications: $Z=1.26$ (Mdn=4) $p>.05$ and showing a mild effect: $r=.21$.
   2. The analysis of the responses received regarding the question "*How do you perceive the application?*" - given the answer options: *game, playful personality report, serious personality report, survey and undecided* - revealed significant differences in how participants perceived both applications ($Z=-3.88$, $p<.00$). The majority of players perceived the playful questionnaire as a *playful personality report*, closely followed by *game*. The other version was perceived mostly as a *survey*.
   3. The question "*Which of the applications would you recommend to a friend on a social network?*" revealed significant differences in replies ($Z=-2.67$ $p<.00$), with the majority of participants being positive about the idea of spreading the playful questionnaire further to friends, while showing significantly less intention of doing so regarding the short questionnaire.
   4. Concerning the question "*Which application would you prefer to deal with*", most females expressed a preference of the playful questionnaire, while male players could be divided into two categories: those who would prefer the playful format and those who would distinctively prefer the short format.
      Finally, when asked to estimate the degree of earnestness that they displayed while interacting with each application, the majority of the users believed that they considered their answers more seriously when filling out the short survey, rather than when interacting with the playful questionnaire.

While self-reported accounts of earnestness are bound to be biased and the observed difference can likely be explained by the playful mood of the playful questionnaire that inevitably sets a more relaxed approach to answering questions, it is important to further investigate the data provided by quality control questions, once the survey is run on a social network.

4   Discussion and Conclusion

The user experience evaluation of both applications suggests that the majority of the experiment participants prefer to deal with the longer playful applications rather than generic short surveys. The experiment participants showed distinctively more willingness to recommend the playful version to their friends. They also expressed the belief that the playful elements do not distract them from the main task of answering serious questions.

The approach of playful questionnaires offers intriguing benefits in terms of motivation, cost and demographic control. Yet, for the time being, further studies need to be executed in order to investigate the potential biases, to improve filtering techniques and, in the long run, to determine whether the approach can be generalized to the point where businesses and research institutes can target certain demographics by design, while the extend of bias can be quantified. At the same time, a playful and fun experience must be offered to potential users, customers and players if they are to be confronted with playful surveys more frequently.

References

1. Schmidt, L.A.: Crowdsourcing for Human Subjects Research. In: Proceedings of CrowdConf 2010 (2010)
2. For some consumers, surveys breed feedback fatigue, USA Today (2012), http://www.usatoday.com/money/story/2012-01-07/consumer-feedback-fatigue/52432412/1 (last viewed: July 05, 2012)
3. Krause, M., Smeddinck, J., Takhtamysheva, A., Markov, V., Runge, N.: Playful Surveys: Easing Challenges of Human Subject Research with Online Crowds Challenges of Human Subject Research. In: HComp 2012 Proceedings of the AAAI Workshop on Human Computation (2012)
4. SlaveryFootPrint, http://slaveryfootprint.org (last viewed: July 05 2012)
5. Weichselbraun, A., Gindl, S., Scharl, A.: Using games with a purpose and bootstrapping to create domain-specific sentiment lexicons. In: Proceedings of the 20th ACM International Conference on Information and Knowledge Management (CIKM 2011), pp. 1053–1060. ACM, New York (2011)
6. Hsu, C.L., Lu, H.P.: Why do people play on-line games? An extended TAM with social influences and flow experience. Information and Management 41(7), 853–868 (2004)
7. Von Ahn, L.: Human computation. In: Proceedings of the 46th Annual Design Automation Conference (DAC 2009), pp. 418–419. ACM, New York (2009)
8. Cooper, S., Khatib, F., Treuille, A., Barbero, J., Lee, J., Beenen, M., Leaver-Fay, A., Baker, D., Popović, Z.: Predicting protein structures with a multiplayer online game. J. Nature 466, 756–760 (2010)
9. Kawrykow, A., Roumanis, G., Kam, A., Kwak, D., Leung, C.: Phylo: A Citizen Science Approach for Improving Multiple Sequence Alignment. PLoS ONE 7(3) (2011)
10. Chrons, O., Sundell, S.: Digitalkoot: Making Old Archives Accessible Using Crowdsourcing. In: HCOMP 2011 Proceedings of the ACM SIGKDD Workshop on Human Computation (2011)
11. Mahajan, A.: Zynga: Building Big Social Games. In: Game Developers Conference Presentation, Game Developers Conference (2009)

Interactive Installation Design to Enhance Audience Immersion and Informational Behaviour

Michaela Buchtová

Informational Science and Librarianship, Faculty of Art,
Charles University in Prague, U Krize 8, Prague-Jinonice, Czech Republic
michaela.buchtova@ff.cuni.cz

Abstract. The paper presents a technical and dramaturgical concept of two interactive installations proposing a complex dramaturgic approach to physically and emotionally immerse an audience. The concept was firstly presented as "Memorial for survivors and victims of holocaust" in 2011 in Prague, Czech Republic. The first installation is based on a technique of life illusion applied on a life-size statue, while using a combination of video portrait and video mapping techniques. The second installation offers an interactive presentation of historical photos and videos. By physical movement, an audience enters a visual 3D space with multimedia gallery arranged in historical order. The dramaturgy of both installations depends on presence and active movement of an audience, and aims to create an immersive space and personal relationship to presented story. The human-computer interaction (HCI) system was developed to propose alternative forms for active and/or passive informational behaviour of public museum exhibits and educational projects.

Keywords: Interactive museum, Immersive installation, Video mapping, Kinect.

1 Introduction

Two installations presented here were created to propose an innovative approach to interactive installation dramaturgy. Moreover we aimed to offer a platform which can be used and adapted by museums or galleries to create immersive environments supporting an audience experience and learning through intuitive elements for informational seeking behaviour. Our intention was to present an installation which immerses an audience into the story, and creates a personal relationship with a viewer. Some authors [2] additionally claim that emotional engagement can stimulate willingness to future informational seeking and learning activities. By implementing various interactive elements, both installations emphasize immersive and deeply personal experience.

The technical concept of two installations ("Timeline" and "Talking statue") was firstly presented as "Memorial for survivors and victims of holocaust" and brought a story of Marketa Novakova, a woman who went through ghetto Theresienstadt and extermination camp Auschwitz-Birkenau.

M. Herrlich, R. Malaka, and M. Masuch (Eds.): ICEC 2012, LNCS 7522, pp. 453–456, 2012.

While creating the interactive and technical concept we got inspired by our long-term collaboration with French artist Dominik Barbier and mainly by his scenography of museum "Mémorial de la Marseillaise" in Marseille [5]. There he used an inside video mapping on walls and on statues of main French revolution partakers. Our first installation – temporary called "talking statue" – was created by Kristof Slussareff with consultations with Dominik Barbier. The interactive user interface and overall dramaturgy of both pieces was built mainly upon interactive elements using a motion sensing hardware Kinect. The interface was built upon NxGraphics [4], multimedia framework software developed by Stephane Kyles for projects using 3D visualization, audiovisual materials and Kinect controller.

2   Life Illusion

In the first installation – "talking statue" – we have built the interactive principles on a life-size statue (more precisely a bust) in combination with classic video-portrait. We got inspired by the ancient Greeks, who never left their statues white, but they covered them with bright colours instead - they drew an orange coloured skin and clothing [6]. Therefore we manufactured a bust of Marketa Novakova, on which we mapped a video of Marketa telling her life story closely connected with her life in extermination camp Auschwitz-Birkenau. Literary speaking, we "let the statue talk". The video mapping was done real time with software Adobe After Effects [1], the audio was recorded during several personal meetings with Marketa, in the installation is used a 6 minutes long record.

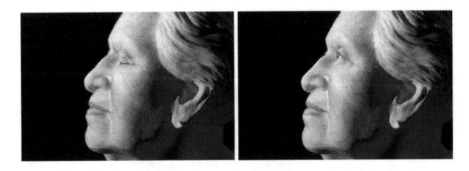

Fig. 1. Video mapping on the bust – effect of opening eyes

To enhance a personal engagement of audience, we added interactive elements reacting on mere presence of a viewer. In a sector of circle with approximate radius of three meters there is an interactive zone built upon Kinect. A viewer entering the interactive zone "awakens" the sculpture which tells its story in person. The audio rec-ord of Marketa's narration starts and Marketa's eyes open and blink (video mapping). While the viewer moves away from the interactive zone, the statue falls silent and white. As in absence of an active listener, stories of our past remain quietly forgotten.

3   Timeline

The second interactive installation set nearby proposed additional information and embedded Marketa's testimony in global historical context. The installation called "Timeline" is basically a video projection using visual 3D space to create an optic illusion of physical distance. It allows audience to "travel in time" and seek in historical material by a mere movement. A multimedia presentation on projection consists of historical audiovisual material, mainly sequences of photos in loops and short videos with explanatory texts. Moving towards or away from the multimedia presentation, a viewer depicts historical events of the years 1922 – 2011 and the photos or videos are showed in front.

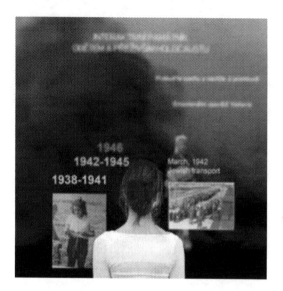

Fig. 2. Illustration of Timeline Installation

To strengthen the audience's immersion and physical illustration of "moving in history", as the presentation was inherited in 3D space, the audiovisual material from older time needs to be discovered by movement further to the presentation. On the floor there is a line highlighting historical periods so an audience can easily control the multimedia presentation and search information or material needed.

4   Audience Feedback, Future Opportunities

A technique of life illusion applied on the statue has shown as the key element while many people stayed stunned by a plasticity and vividness of bust visage and narration. According to audience comments, the interactive zone, which immediately reacts on a viewer's presence and leaving away, creates very personal relation with the story told by the statue. In the same way, the "Timeline" was appreciated because of its immersive 3D space. Both installations won a price of "The best interactive project built on Kinect" [3], audience decided about the winner.

Both installations can serve as a platform adaptable to other content and thematic. We used the platform to present a story of holocaust while "Talking statue" presented the history through a real testimony of one survivor and "Timeline" depicted the social and historical context by interactive audiovisual collage of real documents. The content, video mapping and statue can be changed, thus the platform can be used in museums and galleries. It brings a new interactivity and personal experience while reacting on the audience presence and movement.

Acknowledgements. The project was supported by Grant Agency of Charles University in Prague – project no. 5810/2012 "Digital Technologies in Education: Specification of the elements positively affecting learning and information behaviour".

The interactive installations were created with a support of non-profit organization „M77 – Arts, Digital Creation & Training": Kristof Slussareff (scenography, video), Stephan Kyles (programer, new media artist), Michael Gimenez (scenography, graphics), Stanislav Kokoška (historian, supervision), Michaela Buchtová (dramaturgy, project management). In collaboration with contemporary artist Dominik Barbier (Fearless Medi@terranée, France, www.fearless.fr), Foundation for Holocaust Victims (www.fondholocaust.cz), Post Bellum (www.postbellum.cz), Prague College (www.praguecollege.cz) and National Archive (www.nacr.cz).

References

1. Adobe: Adobe After Effects® (Version CS5) (Computer software)
2. Fredericks, J.A., Blumenfeld, P.C., Paris, A.H.: School engagement: Potential of the concept, state of the evidence. Review of Educational Research 74, 59–109 (2004)
3. Kovalík, J.: Jak jsme hackovali Kinect. Datarama online magazine Aktualne.cz (January 12, 2012) http://datarama.aktualne.centrum.cz/clanek.phtml?id=723589 (ac-cessed: April 3, 2012)
4. Kyles, S.: NxGraphics (Computer software), http://code.google.com/p/subnetworks/source/browse/#svn%2Ftrunk%2FNxGraphics%2FNxGraphicsSdk%2FNxVideo (accessed: April 3, 2012)
5. Mémorial de la Marseillaise. Museum paresentation, http://www.vert-marine.com/memorial-marseillaise-marseille-13/ (accessed: April 3, 2012)
6. Rosenthal, E. (ed.): Gods in Color: Painted Sculpture of Classical Antiquity. Harvard university versity Art Museums (2007)

Emotional Interaction with Surfaces - Works of Design and Computing

Larissa Müller[1], Svenja Keune[2], Arne Bernin[1,4], and Florian Vogt[1,3]

[1] Department Informatik, University of Applied Sciences (HAW) Hamburg, Germany
[2] Department Design, University of Applied Sciences Hamburg, Germany
[3] Innovations Kontakt Stelle (IKS) Hamburg, TuTech Innovation GmbH, Germany
[4] School of Computing, University of the West of Scotland, UK

Abstract. Here we present three interactive artworks that showcase the abilities of active textured surfaces to enable new qualities of surface interactions. Giving the surfaces different sensing abilities, ways to act and behaviors, then allows us to explore emotional attributes and character perceived by an observer. The three designs reflect artworks emotional perception of the observer and the resulting effects on behavior. The surfaces sense it's surrounding in terms of physical presence by proximity and emotional state based on facial expression. The surface can express its emotion with a change in movement and sound. The three surface designs explore further combinations of textile surfaces, sensors and reactive actuation to draw on the emotion of observers.

1 Introduction

Surface interfaces are predestined for manual and visual interaction, since they merge the modalities of physical input and visual output. Now, commonly used multi touch screens, particularly for mobile applications, enable physical interaction with planar rigid surfaces. Recent works have developed deformable interaction surface systems, which allow the incorporation of passive material attributes with surfaces in the physical interaction to enhance tactile feedback [1,2]. In our work we explore concepts of active surfaces, which are composed of interactive elements, inspired by repeating features in nature, in our case of animal scales, to find a trade-off between manufacturability and to form elaborate complex behavior of the overall surface structures. We see the potential to exploit these extended surface design spaces to form character, emotional attributes, and physical sensations to create compelling interaction.

We build on interactive works which combine emotional models and reactive objects based on facial [3], characteristic [4] and animalistic [5] physical artifacts. A number of emotional models have been developed to analyse human behavior and to create interactive systems. While in many existing works a strong association with prior experiences exists, we explore the mapping of behaviors. Less established associations are tread as degrees of freedom in a design space and let us guide by the affordances the designs provoke to find compelling mappings,

M. Herrlich, R. Malaka, and M. Masuch (Eds.): ICEC 2012, LNCS 7522, pp. 457–460, 2012.

with the goal to explore the ability of active surfaces to provoking and further respond to emotions of observers.

The works we developed are a part of an iterative process, based on the ideas from Mitch Resnick of a "'Lifelong Kindergarten"' [6]. A circle with the steps Imagine, Create, Play, Share and Reflect leads to fast prototypes. It also offers the possibility of creative working. The works we present consists of three different degrees of interaction. The first surfaces operates without any kind of sensor. The second one uses a distance sensor and the third is triggered by a visitors emotion, recognized from his face. We made tests with hundreds of visitors in which we were provoking some kind of interaction.

(a) Estoban   (b) Mocoleme   (c) Lomelia

Fig. 1. Emotional interaction triggered by: (a) random movements (degree one), (b) distance to the object (degree two), and (c) facial expression (degree three)

2 Description of Three Surface Designs

In the following we describe the three interactive artworks: Estoban, Mocoleme, and Lomelia that were created by the authors team with design and computer science backgrounds in terms of design concepts and interaction technology. Estoban and Mocoleme are focused on a relationship between sound atmosphere, movement und textile surface. Estoban affects the atmosphere in different urban spaces (private or public), and also has presence, the communication with Mocoleme is very simple. The intention is to have an affect on urban spaces and private rooms. Nature and urban sounds are calming, better than silence, which is often perceived as unpleasant and better for concentration or worklife than music. She reacts to distance with emotions, which are expressed by sounds and movement. Lomelia is based on a more complex kind of communication between an object and its observer. She includes the emotions of the observer to the interaction.

2.1 Estoban - Urban Stories

Estoban tells stories with sound. He creates a relaxed atmosphere and tells about his adventures from time to time. He shows his emotions in a subtle way. The border between reality and virtuality becomes fluently blurred. A direct contact to his surrounding is not what he looks for. He deals perfectly well with minimal attention. The attention received by listening to his stories is quite surprising.

We produced this first surface without any sensory input as an emotion backchannel. The displayed emotions are selected randomly. The output is using sound and movements to express and trigger emotions.

2.2   Mocoleme - Come Closer

Mocoleme likes to receive attention. If she feels neglected her mood changes quickly. She gives her opinions free running and is hardly affected. Once understood, you can play with Mocoleme in a wonderful way.

In this object we use distance as sensory input. The expression of emotions also appropriates sound and movements. The objective of this is to find out about preferences with respect to the input.

2.3   Lomelia - Emotional Dialogue

The emotions of an observer should not just be mirrored by the surface, but affect actions and emotions of visitors. It may get bored, for example, if a person is happy or be surprised following an anger outburst. She tries to frighten someone if the person is scared or gets annoyed by a lack of interest. The aim here is to express emotions by its movement.

The third surface, Lomelia, uses the SHORE library [7] from the Fraunhofer Institut of Integrated Circuits IIS as sensory input. This Software recognizes emotions from a visitors face. It gives a conclusion of the emotional states angry, happy, sad, or surprised. The camera placed on top of the surface is used to obtain an accurate picture of the current user. The servo motors are triggered by the assumed emotional states.

The overall system is separated into two modules with different functions: emotional display and emotional backchannel. The interfacing between these two modules is implemented via a central message broker that employs the publish-subscribe pattern. This enables the design to be flexible for further enhancements such as adding more modalities for input or output. The input module is implemented with infrared distance sensors and a camera that captures the faces of observers. The resulting images are emotion interpreted based on facial expressions implemented with the SHORE library [7]. The output module consists of a microcontroller to manage the servo motors of the interactive surfaces. All three active surfaces are constructed from fabric covered shell like base elements (Shown in Fig. 1c).

3   Summary

The three surface artworks demostrates the concept of active surface to facilitate the possibilities of emotional interaction. The benefit of our interactive installations is that they are made of textiles. By an invisible technique the observer becomes focused on haptic allure, physical qualities and movements. The degree of emotional perception of the artworks exhibited here allow different forms to engage the observer. Informal exhbits of the artworks have provided much positive feedback, demonstrating that active surfaces can produce emotional experiences. The concepts presented here show that emotional awareness interfaces, inspired by human-human communication, with basic expressions can be highly engaging for participants. This technology could be transfered to enterainment computing through the exchange with researchers in the field.

Acknowledgement. We thank Kai von Luck, Renata Brink, Gunter Klemke, Birgit Wendholt and Franziska Hübler for their feedback and their support for this work. Further we express our gratitude to the members of our Emotion-Lab for supporting the construction of the artworks. In addition, we thank the Fraunhofer Institute of Integrated Circuits IIS for providing the SHORE library.

References

1. Vogt, F., Chen, T., Hoskinson, R., Fels, S.S.: A malleable surface touch interface. In: Sketches and Applications at ACM SIGGRAPH (2004)
2. Smith, J.D., Graham, T.C.N., Holman, D., Borchers, J.: Low-cost malleable surfaces with multi-touch pressure sensitivity. In: IEEE Workshop on Horizontal Interactive Human-Computer Systems, TABLETOP 2007, pp. 205–208 (2007)
3. Becker, C., Prendinger, H., Ishizuka, M., Wachsmuth, I.: Evaluating Affective Feedback of the 3D Agent Max in a Competitive Cards Game. In: Tao, J., Tan, T., Picard, R.W. (eds.) ACII 2005. LNCS, vol. 3784, pp. 466–473. Springer, Heidelberg (2005)
4. Breazeal, C.: Emotion and sociable humanoid robots. International Journal of Human-Computer Studies 59, 119–155 (2002)
5. Wada, K., Shibata, T., Saito, T., Tanie, K.: Analysis of factors that bring mental effects to elderly people in robot assisted activity. In: IEEE International Conference on Intelligent Robots and Systems, pp. 1152–1157 (2002)
6. Resnick, M.: All i really need to know (about creative thinking) i learned (by studying how children learn) in kindergarten. In: Proceedings ACM SIGCHI Conference on Creativity & Cognition (C&C 2007), pp. 1–6. ACM (2007)
7. Kueblbeck, C., Ernst, A.: Face detection and tracking in video sequences using the modified census transformation. Journal on Image and Vision Computing 24(6), 564–572 (2006)

The Empathy Machine
Generated Music to Augment Empathic Interactions

David Kadish, Nikolai Kummer, Aleksandra Dulic, and Homayoun Najjaran

University of British Columbia,
Kelowna, Canada
dkadish@interchange.ubc.ca,
{nikolai.kummer,aleksandra.dulic,homayoun.najjaran}@ubc.ca

Abstract. The Empathy Machine is an interactive installation that augments a visitor's empathic sense during a social conversation. Empathy is a key component of interpersonal interactions that is often neglected by modern communication technologies. This system uses facial expression recognition to identify the emotional state of a user's conversation partner. It algorithmically generates emotional music to match the expressive state of the partner and plays the music to the user in a non-disruptive manner. The result is an augmentation of the user's emotional response to the emotional expression of their partner.

Keywords: emotional music synthesis, facial expression recognition, empathic interaction.

1 Introduction

Empathy, the ability to share feelings with others, is an important part of interpersonal communication and plays an essential role in human relations. Many communication technologies such as telephones and e-mail inhibit one or more of the senses, becoming barriers between the communicators that reduce the opportunity for empathic interaction.

This paper presents a proposed demonstration of a system that augments empathy in live interpersonal interactions. The installation will allow a user to experience a conversation, while receiving direct feedback regarding the emotional state of the conversation partner in the form of music.

2 Empathy, Emotion and Music

The conceptual basis for the installation is rooted in the hypothesis that music can trigger an empathic response, similar to the response that occurs when one views an emotional expression. Empathy is the ability to identify with the feelings and emotions of another person or being. The neurological basis for empathy is the existence of so-called "mirror neurons" [4]. Mirror neurons are activated both when a subject sees an action or emotional display and when they perform that

M. Herrlich, R. Malaka, and M. Masuch (Eds.): ICEC 2012, LNCS 7522, pp. 461–464, 2012.
© IFIP International Federation for Information Processing 2012

same activity. Emotional empathy, then, can manifest as a person feeling the same emotion as someone they are observing simply by seeing an emotional gesture on the part of the observed.

In addition to visual stimulation, music is often cited as a method of evoking an emotional response in a person[5]. In that way, music provides a secondary pathway to the emotional centres of the brain, which can be used to augment the emotional response derived from visual imput. The various properties of music that elicit or represent certain emotions have been studied by scientists since the 1930s[2].

3   Proposed Installation

3.1   Overview

The Empathy Machine augments a social interaction between a user and their conversation partner. The emotional state of the partner is assessed using automatic facial expression recognition (FER) software and the feedback to the user is played back to the user in the form of emotional music. The music is generated using an emotional music synthesis (EMS) system.

The user and their conversation partner sit at a table in the demonstration area. A webcam peers over the shoulder of the user at their partner. Video of the partner's face is input into the FER system, the expression is recognised, appropriate music is generated, and the result is played at background levels to the user through small speakers.

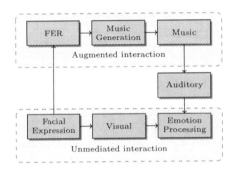

(a) System diagram showing how the Empathy Machine augments a user's empathetic understanding of a situation

(b) The Empathy Machine plays music to the user (green backpack), reflecting the expression of the partner (plaid shirt)

Fig. 1. Overviews of the Empathy Machine system

Table 1. Association between the emotions and musical features

	Tempo	Pitch	Rhythm Roughness	MIDI Instrument	Additional Parameters
Anger	Fast	High	Few repeated notes	#2 Piano	Stoccato, Phrygian mode
Fear	Fast	High		#100 FX 4 Atmosphere	Atonality
Happiness	Fast		Few repeated notes	#47 Orchestral Harp	Stoccato, Lydian mode
Sadness	Slow	Low	Repeated notes	#2 Piano	Legato

3.2 Facial Expression Recognition

The FER system is a modified version of the system described by Valstar and Pantic [7]. FaceTracker, an OpenCV-based algorithm for face registration and tracking based on [6], is used to track 66 points on a face across a series of frames.

The python machine learning package `scikit-learn` is used to perform classification on the features. For each facial action unit (AU) — the basic unit of facial motion — principle component analysis (PCA) is performed on the extracted features and a support vector machine (SVM) classifier is trained on the principle components to determine whether that AU is active. A second classifier is trained to map AU activation to the displayed emotion, using a multiclass one-versus-one SVM. This is used to distinguish between the display of one of four basic emotions and a neutral state.

3.3 Music Generation

The music used to represent the emotions is computer generated. Computer generated music lends itself to continuous generation and does not require an in-depth knowledge of musical composition. The music is generated using the AthenaCL algorithmic music generator. Algorithmic composition allows for the creation of non-repetitive music, thereby reducing strain on the user's ears. Musical parameters for the emotional music were selected from literature[1,3,8]. A summary of the parameters used for the music generation in the user study can be found in Table 1.

4   Future Development

The initial prototype of the Empathy Machine focuses on four emotions in a discrete sense. Future implementations will consider a more nuanced notion of degrees of emotion and will seek to add more basic emotions to the set of four. More effort will also be put into making the FER system more robust and to adding further complexity to the EMS system.

5   Conclusion

The use of music to create an emotional response is common in film and performance. The Empathy Machine represents the first attempt to use music generated in real-time to augment the emotional response to a live interaction.

The authors hope to provide an engaging demonstration of the possibilities that arise from the combination of real-time emotion detection and music generation.

Acknowledgments. The authors would like to acknowledge the assistance provided by Dr. Sidney Fels as well as the support of the Advanced Control and Intelligent Systems Lab and the Centre for Culture and Technology at UBC.

References

1. Gabrielsson, A., Lindström, E.: The influence of musical structure on emotional expression. In: Juslin, P.N.E., Sloboda, J.A.E. (eds.) Music and Emotion: Theory and Research. Series in affective science, pp. 223–248. Oxford University Press, New York (2001)
2. Hevner, K.: Experimental Studies of the Elements of Expression in Music. The American Journal of Psychology 48(2), 246 (1936)
3. Juslin, P., Laukka, P.: Expression, Perception, and Induction of Musical Emotions: A Review and a Questionnaire Study of Everyday Listening. Journal of New Music Research 33(3), 217–238 (2004)
4. Preston, S.D., de Waal, F.B.M.: Empathy: Its ultimate and proximate bases. Behavioral and Brain Sciences 25(01), 1 (2003)
5. Rickard, N.S.: Intense emotional responses to music: a test of the physiological arousal hypothesis. Psychology of Music 32(4), 371–388 (2004)
6. Saragih, J., Lucey, S., Cohn, J.: Deformable model fitting by regularized landmark mean-shift. International Journal of Computer Vision, 1–16 (2011)
7. Valstar, M., Pantic, M.: Combined support vector machines and hidden markov models for modeling facial action temporal dynamics. In: Proceedings of the 2007 IEEE International Conference on Human-Computer Interaction, pp. 118–127. Springer (2007)
8. Wallis, I., Ingalls, T., Campana, E.: A Rule-Based Generative Music System Controlled by Desired Valence and Arousal. In: SMC 2011 (2011)

Blending Real and Virtual Worlds Using Self-reflection and Fiducials

Martin Fischbach[1], Dennis Wiebusch[1], Marc Erich Latoschik[1],
Gerd Bruder[2], and Frank Steinicke[2]

[1] Human-Computer Interaction
[2] Immersive Media Group
University of Würzburg
martin.fischbach@uni-wuerzburg.de,
{hci,img}.uni-wuerzburg.de

Abstract. This paper presents an enhanced version of a portable out-of-the-box platform for semi-immersive interactive applications. The enhanced version combines stereoscopic visualization, marker-less user tracking, and multi-touch with self-reflection of users and tangible object interaction. A virtual fish tank simulation demonstrates how real and virtual worlds are seamlessly blended by providing a multi-modal interaction experience that utilizes a user-centric projection, body, and object tracking, as well as a consistent integration of physical and virtual properties like appearance and causality into a mixed real/virtual world.

Keywords: Mixed Reality, Self-Reflection, Fiducials, Fish Tank Virtual Reality, Interactive Virtual Art, Multi-Touch.

1 Introduction

Milgram and Kishimo define Mixed Reality (MR) to be located on a continuum between Augmented Reality (AR) and Augmented Virtuality (AV) [1]. While AR superimposes the real world by computer-generated images, AV enhances virtual worlds using real-world data. The general idea blends real and virtual objects into a combined real/virtual space which shares certain perceptive attributes like consistency of geometry, time, or illumination [2].

Merging real and virtual worlds using computer technology is challenging. One of the most important tasks concerns placements of superimposed objects to be consistent with the real world. Likewise, lighting effects like reflections and shadows have to match to obtain a consistent perception of a shared illumination space. In addition, movements of real/virtual objects have to be consistent and follow a plausible simulation of cause and effect between both worlds.

The combined synthetic and real illumination of objects to produce blended high quality images works only under specific limitations. Such limitations include renouncement of real-time performance, requirement of a geometric computer model of the real scene, light sources to be static [3], or special hardware usually not accessible in most MR system environments [2].

M. Herrlich, R. Malaka, and M. Masuch (Eds.): ICEC 2012, LNCS 7522, pp. 465–468, 2012.

This paper presents an enhanced version of the smARTbox [4,5], a portable out-of-the-box platform for semi-immersive interactive applications in promotional, artistic, or educational areas. The enhanced version blends real and virtual worlds using self-reflection of users and fiducial physical interaction objects to manipulate the virtual content. In addition to the stereoscopic visualization, marker-less user tracking and direct interscopic touch input of the smARTbox, the enhanced version provides two new key features demonstrated using a virtual fish tank simulation: (1) Interacting users perceive a self-reflection of their physical presence in the virtual world, i.e., on the simulated liquid surface of the fish tank and (2) real physical objects modify the simulation behavior, i.e., the virtual fishes react to objects placed in vicinity of the fish tank.

2   System Setup

The smARTbox's [4] metal frame provides the skeleton for a $112 \times 90 \times 63$ cm ($w \times h \times d$) wooden box. The top side is a back-projection surface fed with stereoscopic 3D images at 720p by an Optoma GT720 DLP-projector via a wide-angle converter lens and a mirror mounted at the bottom of the box at a 45° angle. The demonstration uses an Intel Core i7 @3.40GHz processor with 8GB of main memory and an nVidia Quadro 4000 graphics card. One Microsoft Kinect multi sensor system is utilized in combination with a set of IR-lights and an IR-camera in order to track the user's body and the physical objects, respectively. The hardware setup (without the computer) was constructed at a total cost of less than € 2,500 during a students project. The smARTbox is driven by Simulator X [6], a Scala-based software framework for intelligent interactive applications.

3   Touch and Fiducial Marker Tracking

In recent years, multi-touch interaction in combination with stereoscopic display has received considerable attention [7,8,9]. Hence, we constructed the smARTbox in such a way that the screen serves as a multi-touch-enabled surface using the Rear-DI principle [10]. Therefore, six clusters of IR-LEDs illuminate the screen from the inside with infrared light, which is reflected by objects in contact with the surface. The contact points are sensed by a Point Grey Dragonfly®2 digital video camera with a wide-angle lens and infrared band-pass filter. Touch positions and gestures are analyzed by a modified version of the NUI Group's CCV software [11]. In addition to tracking multiple touch points, CCV supports tracking of small fiducials, which can be pre-registered with corresponding real-world objects. For instance, a fiducial marker can be placed at a can for fish feed (see Figure 1 right). When the can (respectively the fiducial) is in contact with the touch surface, it gets recognized and its touch area serves as attractor for the fish. Other fiducials may be associated to objects, which serve as detractors to the virtual fish such as predators.

4   Self-reflection

The augmentation of the virtual scene with real world information additionally enhances the sense of presence for mixed reality environments [12]. Continuing this approach, the smARTbox setup utilizes 2.5D models of the real scene obtained from the Kinect to realize virtual self-refections of the user:

A triangulated 2.5D mesh with corresponding normals, faces, and texture coordinates is processed using the nestk library [13]. The related texture, a 640×480 pixel color image, is captured from the Kinect's RGB-camera. The communication between the native library-based image processing and the Scala-based Simulator X is handled by the Scala Native Access (SNA) framework. Simulator X' built-in renderer is used to appropriately position the textured mesh data in the virtual scene. The mesh contains the necessary spatial (geometric) data which is used to calculate a reflection at a virtual surface aligned with the water surface. The result is blended by a custom water shader with the interactive water surface (see Figure 1 left).

Fig. 1. Reflections on water surface (left) and interaction with a fiducial marker (right)

5   Conclusion

The smARTbox has great potential for presentations and exhibitions, since it is less expensive, easier to set up and transport than typical virtual reality installations. For this demo we have enhanced the smARTbox by an advanced blending of virtual and mixed reality concepts, which considerably increases realism of virtual objects. The lack of obtrusive instrumentation in combination with presence-enhancing visual and tangible interaction improves the engagement with users, e. g., in exhibition scenarios. The utilized software platform

Simulator X provides a state-of-the-art simulation engine with an integrated AI-core and several multimodal interaction components. Its scalable architecture provides an ideal platform, e. g., to experiment with alternate sensors, possibly enhancing accuracy or precision. An evaluation that we plan during the demo session will show in how far the usage of virtual reflections and tangible object interaction increases the users sense of presence and improves object interaction.

Acknowledgements. The authors want to thank Christian Treffs, Alexander Strehler and Anke Giebler-Schubert for supporting the implementation and realization of the presented work.

References

1. Milgram, P., Kishino, F.: A taxonomy of mixed reality visual displays. IEICE Transactions on Information Systems E77-D(12) (1994)
2. Naemura, T., Nitta, T., Mimura, A., Harashima, H.: Virtual Shadows in Mixed Reality Environment Using Flashlight-like Devices. Transactions of Virtual Reality Society of Japan 7(2), 227–237 (2002)
3. Jacobs, K., Loscos, C.: Classification of illumination methods for mixed reality. Comput. Graph. Forum 25(1), 29–51 (2006)
4. Fischbach, M., Latoschik, M., Bruder, G., Steinicke, F.: smARTbox: Out-of-the-Box Technologies for Interactive Art and Exhibition. In: Virtual Reality International Conference (VRIC). ACM (2012)
5. Fischbach, M., Wiebusch, D., Latoschik, M.E., Bruder, G., Steinicke, F.: Smartbox: A portable setup for intelligent interactive applications. In: Mensch und Computer Demo Papers (2012)
6. Latoschik, M.E., Tramberend, H.: Simulator X: A Scalable and Concurrent Software Platform for Intelligent Realtime Interactive Systems. In: Proceedings of the IEEE VR 2011 (2011)
7. Steinicke, F., Benko, H., Daiber, F., Keefe, D., de la Rivière, J.B.: Touching the 3rd dimension (T3D). In: Proceedings of the Conference extended Abstracts on Human Factors in Computing Systems, pp. 161–164. ACM (2011)
8. Valkov, D., Steinicke, F., Bruder, G., Hinrichs, K., Schöning, J., Daiber, F., Krüger, A.: Touching floating objects in projection-based virtual reality environments. In: Proceedings of Joint Virtual Reality Conference, pp. 17–24 (2010)
9. Valkov, D., Steinicke, F., Bruder, G., Hinrichs, K.: 2D touching of 3D stereoscopic objects. In: Proceedings of the Conference on Human Factors in Computing Systems, pp. 1353–1362. ACM (2011)
10. Schöning, J., Hook, J., Bartindale, T., Schmidt, D., Oliver, P., Echtler, F., Motamedi, N., Brandl, P., Zadow, U.: Building interactive multi-touch surfaces. Tabletops-Horizontal Interactive Displays, 27–49 (2010)
11. Cetin, G., Bedi, R., Sandler, S.: Multi-touch technologies. Natural User Interface (NUI) Group (2009)
12. Steinicke, F., Hinrichs, K.H., Ropinski, T.: Virtual Reflections and Virtual Shadows in Mixed Reality Environments. In: Costabile, M.F., Paternó, F. (eds.) INTERACT 2005. LNCS, vol. 3585, pp. 1018–1021. Springer, Heidelberg (2005)
13. Burrus, N.: NESTK Library (2012), http://nicolas.burrus.name/index.php/Research/-KinectUseNestk (last accessed: May 30, 2012)

The Animation Loop Station: Near Real-Time Animation Production

Benjamin Walther-Franks, Florian Biermann,
Nikolaas Steenbergen, and Rainer Malaka

Research Group Digital Media
TZI, University of Bremen, Germany

Abstract. We present the animation loop station, a near real-time animation production system. It brings the concept of loop stations or loopers commonly used for live music performances to the animation domain. Our system allows a single animator to build an animation layer by layer by capturing his own movement and building up complex motion through several passes or takes. In order not to interfere with capture and not break the performer's flow, control commands are handled by a speech interface.

Keywords: computer animation, computer puppetry, performance animation, layered animation, loop stations, performing arts.

1 Introduction

Motion capture is a method for fast, cost-efficient computer animation. It is widely used in the film, television and computer game industries. The increasing availability of low-cost full-body and facial capturing devices such as Microsoft's Kinect even moves motion capture in the reach of novices and small companies [2]. But while this approach already speeds up production times in comparison to offline animation practices such as keyframe animation, the motion capture workflow is still complex, requiring animators to clean, edit and apply capture data to rigged characters. Thus, while mocap includes real-time elements, the entire workflow production is still far from real-time.

In the music industry, changing consumer behavior has shifted the emphasis from selling studio productions toward live events. Simple devices, loop stations, enable small bands or even single person acts to create high fidelity songs on stage without pre-recorded material. By recording samples on stage, looping them, and cleverly layering multiple sample loops a single artist can create complex pieces entirely on his own, live, in front of an audience. The realtime music production becomes as much part of the experience as the "resulting" piece.

Looper workflows enable a rapid production style with a "live" quality that other areas of media production, such as animation, can benefit from. All that is lacking are the right concepts and interfaces. As a first step in this direction, we present the animation loop station, a near real-time animation production system. It enables a single artist to create complex animations just by acting

M. Herrlich, R. Malaka, and M. Masuch (Eds.): ICEC 2012, LNCS 7522, pp. 469–472, 2012.
© IFIP International Federation for Information Processing 2012

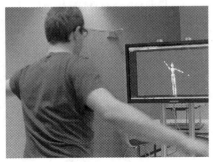

Fig. 1. The animation loop station in *Puppeteer* (virtual reality-style remote hand interaction; left) and *Performer* (body-to-body mapping; right) control modes

out and layering the animation, much like a musician constructs a song on stage by layering tracks. Building on recent developments in the area of computer puppetry [1,3], we have developed an environment that truly moves computer animation into the domain of real-time production.

2   The Animation Loop Station

Loop stations, loopers, or live looping samplers, are hardware or software devices that enable easy recording, playback and layering (overdubbing) of samples. They usually take the form of small hardware boxes, with pedals for foot activation, such as the *DigiTech JamMan* series[1]. Software loopers, such as *Sooper-Looper*[2] (which is in turn based on the *Echoplex Digital Pro LoopIII and LoopIV* hardware devices) run on common operating systems and only require the appropriate audio I/O to produce the same functionality.

These devices enable recoding and editing in the production domain (audio), while control (record, play, undo, stop, clear) is administered through hardware or software pedals and buttons, essentially low-fidelity spatial input. For animation, we need to record spatial input to bring virtual characters to life, occupying spatial input for the production domain (3D motion). In our animation looping system, we thus switch the modalities to aural input for control and gestural input for content creation. Since only 3D body motion is recorded, the aural channel is free for recording, layering and playback control.

2.1   Capture

The animation loop station offers two control modes, based on distinct animation metaphors. For "classical" full body motion capture we have the *Performer* mode, which maps the movements of the loop station user's skeleton onto a

---

[1] http://www.digitech.com/

[2] http://essej.net/sooperlooper/

humanoid-like character's skeleton. This is how most motion capture works and it enables a user with a certain capability of bodily expression to create a wide variety of character motion. For animation of non-humanoid characters or other scene elements we have the *Puppeteer* mode that employs manipulation techniques from virtual reality and computer puppetry. Our current implementation focuses on 6DOF capture for 3D animation, although the loop station concept could be applied to other input devices such as multi-touch interactive screens.

2.2   Control

For control via the aural modality we use spoken commands that are detected by state-of-the-art speech detection technology. These are simple one or two word commands that change the mode of the loop station. We implemented commands for basic recording and playback control much like audio loopers offer: "Record", "Play", "Stop", "Undo", and "Clear".

3   Live Animation Techniques

For both capture modes, we employ the principle of animation layering [1]. In each pass, certain features will be controlled live by captured input. If these features already have motion, there are three modes of layering:

- *Destructive* layering replaces the existing motion with the new motion.
- *Additive* layering adds the new motion to the existing motion (cf. [1]).
- *Blended* layering combines new and existing motion with a given weighting.

our system also includes timing modes that use spatiotemporal input to only drive the timing of a previously defined motion, without changing its component. Say the animator is happy with a trajectory but wishes to speed up parts of the motion while slowing down others. The animation loop station offers *Dragimation*-style performance timing [4] that allows the animator to drag an object through time along its trajectory at the desired pace, and use the new pacing as the new timing.

4   Implementation

Our current implementation of the animation loop station is written in python as an add-on to the open source 3D modeling and animation software Blender[3]. We chose to write an extension for Blender as it offers a powerful python API and a full classical animation pipeline. We use a Microsoft Kinect sensor for full-body motion capture and audio input. A server application translates skeleton data and detected speech to Open Sound Control[4] commands which are sent to the python add-on client. For speech recognition we use the Microsoft Speech Platform SDK.

---

[3] http://www.blender.org/
[4] http://opensoundcontrol.org/

5   Use Cases

As a main use case for the animation loop station we see hobbyist and semi-professional animation production. At little cost, even a single artists can achieve animation results in short time spans. Professional studios could also make use of the technology to quickly create animated storyboards or initial sketches that can then be refined by other animation methods. Combined with high precision tracking devices, it is conceivable that the loop station approach will find its way into professional motion capture workflows.

Another interesting aspect is that by moving animation production closer to realtime it becomes more of an art form that can be consumed for its own sake. Rather than only watching the resulting animation as part of a motion picture or computer game, audiences might find satisfaction in watching the act of production itself. Artists could use the animation loop station as a new means of expression, creating entire animated sequences on the fly in real-time, based on audience feedback and intuition.

6   Challenges

The key idea of the animation loop station is to enable fast meta-control for capture and layering modes via a different modality than actual capture input so that a single user can do both without having to leave the "flow". This approach does pose problems in certain scenarios. One such scenario is facial motion capture, where the same muscles for producing speech commands are used for creating capture input. Yet the overlap is minimal: After initiating capture with a speech command, facial motion capture can proceed unhindered. The spoken command for ending capture can be recognized and the relevant segment of the capture edited out automatically.

References

1. Dontcheva, M., Yngve, G., Popović, Z.: Layered acting for character animation. ACM Trans. Graph. 22(3), 409–416 (2003)
2. Leite, L., Orvalho, V.: Anim-actor: understanding interaction with digital puppetry using low-cost motion capture. In: Proc. ACE 2011. ACM, New York (2011)
3. Sturman, D.J.: Computer Puppetry. Computer Graphics in Entertainment (1998)
4. Walther-Franks, B., Herrlich, M., Karrer, T., Wittenhagen, M., Schröder-Kroll, R., Malaka, R., Borchers, J.: DRAGIMATION: Direct Manipulation Keyframe Timing for Performance-based Animation. In: Proc. GI 2012 (2012)

Exploring User Input Metaphors
for Jump and Run Games on Mobile Devices

Kolja Lubitz and Markus Krause

University of Bremen
{phateon,pinguin}@tzi.de

Abstract. Mobile devices are already an important platform for digital games. These devices need specialized input metaphors as they have various restrictions such as their own hardware capabilities and the lack of external input devices. Especially challenging are fast paced interactions as in Jump and Run games. This paper explores three user inputs for Jump and Run games on mobile devices along the game Somyeol.

1   Introduction

Games for mobile devices are already common and use a range of input methods. The most common input device for games on mobile devices is their touchscreen. Examples can be found here (Parhi & Karlson, 2006). Various games such as "Angry Birds" or "Cordy" use the touchscreen of mobile devices as the only input. The game "Angry Birds" for instance allows the player to shoot bird like characters with a simple sling metaphor. By dragging the sling around an anchor point the player chooses direction as well as strength of shot. Interaction in "Angry Birds" is reduced to this gesture. A classic Jump and Run game such as "Cordy" need more than one metaphor. The main challenge with a gamepad like input as this implemented for "Cordy" is that hitting the right movement button is difficult. In games like "Tiny Wings" or "Ninja Run" the problem is bypassed by letting the player run automatically.

Fig. 1. A screenshot of the Somyeols game. The overlay illustrates the multi touch input

M. Herrlich, R. Malaka, and M. Masuch (Eds.): ICEC 2012, LNCS 7522, pp. 473–475, 2012.

2   Input Methods

This paper investigates three different user input methods for Jump and Run games on mobile devices or simply JRGMs. It illustrates its findings along the mobile JRGM Somyeol. Somyeol is a puzzle Jump and Run game in which the player controls more than one character at a time. The goal is to control as much Somyeols as possible through the levels. Somyeol is a game which needs input metaphors for three different actions: move left, move right, and jump. The three following input methods were implemented for Somyeol.

1. **MultiTouch Input:** The multi-touch method uses only the touch screen for input. The screen is split into six areas as depicted in Fig. 1. The grid maximizes the actual button size as the whole screen is active. The lower left and right areas are used for walking, top left and right areas for jumping in the respective direction. In the top center a straight jump up action is triggered. The bottom center does not have an associated action.

2. **One-Finger Input:** The One-Finger input method getting the first touch point from the screen. If the touch point moves left or right the player moves. If the touch point moves up the player jumps, if the finger moves up and left the player jumps left. This approach was inspirited by gamepad analog sticks.

3. **Accelerometer Input:** This input method uses the accelerometer of many mobiles phones to get the device tilt. Left and right tilt allows for movement in the respective direction. A touch gesture is used to trigger jumping. We also tried to trigger the jump if the device moving up, but this easily moves the device out of the players focus. So we decide to use the whole touch screen as a jump button. This approach is inspirited by car driving games and "Doodle Jump" where the device tilt is used to going right or left. Gilberston et. al gives examples on tilt as an input method (Gilbertson, Coulton, & Chehimi, 2008).

3   Evaluation

The conducted study had 37 participants between 20 - 30 years old, 10 out of the 37 participants were women. Each participant played three test levels. Every level contains a certain challenge to test the input quality of the methods. After playing the participants answer a survey with 18 questions. These questions were integrated into the game and answered on the device the participant played with. The question whether the game was fun was answered on a 6-point Likert scale. The accelerometer input performed best with a mean of 4.27, multitouch (3.88) and one finger input (3.70) showed very similar results. The differences between the three input methods were however not significant. All p values measured with one tailed t-tests were >0.15. After publishing the game to a broader audience it turned out that accelerometer and multi-touch input were too demanding for players as both methods gained negative player feedback. This feedback was unexpected as questions in the survey about the usability of the input methods did not reveal any issues with any of the input methods.

References

Gilbertson, P., Coulton, P., Chehimi, F.: Using Tilt as an Interface to Control No-Button 3-D Mobile Games. Computers in Entertainment (CIE) 6(3) (2008)

Parhi, P., Karlson, A.: Target size study for one-handed thumb use on small touchscreen devices. In: Proceedings of the 8th Conference on Human-Computer Interaction with Mobile Devices and Services, pp. 203–210 (2006)

The Social Maze: A Collaborative Game to Motivate MS Patients for Upper Limb Training

Tom De Weyer[1], Karel Robert[1], Johanna Renny Octavia Hariandja[1,2], Geert Alders[3], and Karin Coninx[1]

[1] Hasselt University-tUL-IBBT,
Expertise Centre for Digital Media,
Diepenbeek, Belgium
[2] Parahyangan Catholic University, Bandung, Indonesia
[3] REVAL, PHL and BIOMED,
Hasselt University, Diepenbeek, Belgium
{tom.deweyer,karel.robert,geert.alders,
karin.coninx}@uhasselt.be,
johanna@unpar.ac.id

Abstract. Serious gaming is often used in the context of rehabilitation to increase the motivation of the patient to continue the rehabilitation program for a longer period. We investigate serious gaming in the context of rehabilitation programs for multiple sclerosis (MS) patients. Force feedback in combination with a virtual environment is used to establish a training environment supporting basic exercises and more advanced training games for the upper limb, in order to provide patients with an individual training program according to their capabilities. Based on our positive experiences with the use of individual games in this context, we explore "Social Gaming". More specifically, we designed and developed a "Social Maze", allowing patients to train together and to interact with the therapist. In this paper we clarify the game concept, setup and context in which the game is used, and report about the player experiences of patients and therapist.

Keywords: Rehabilitation, Serious Gaming, Social Gaming, Haptics.

1 Introduction

Social support can be beneficial for the engagement and motivation of patients to continue training. Patients' motivation during rehabilitation can be maintained and further enhanced through the incorporation of social interaction into the training exercises. Based on this belief, we have explored social rehabilitation training in a simple proof-of-concept game by designing and developing a simple collaborative game-like training exercise. The collaborative balance pump game is described in [1], which received the best paper award at GameDays 2010. An informal user study has revealed that most patients and therapists enjoyed training with this game. Inspired by

M. Herrlich, R. Malaka, and M. Masuch (Eds.): ICEC 2012, LNCS 7522, pp. 476–479, 2012.
© IFIP International Federation for Information Processing 2012

this positive experience, we developed Social Maze, a more advanced collaborative training setup with a more elaborated game concept which optimally fits in our I-TRAVLE [2] training approach and system.

Before describing the Social Maze concept, we briefly describe the structured training approach as supported by the I-TRAVLE system. Robot-assisted rehabilitation and virtual environment (VE) technologies are combined in our I-TRAVLE system [3]. Using a haptic robot as the central hardware component, a software and hardware system setup has been realized to support systematic and personalized training for MS and stroke patients. The module for therapists allows us to define, to personalize, and to monitor the training. The patient interface gives access to training exercises and games using haptic feedback. In our structured training approach we provide basic training exercises which include only one skill component that has to be trained in the context of the upper limb rehabilitation (namely lifting, transporting, turning, pushing and reaching), but also more advanced training exercises or games which combine multiple skill components.

The Social Maze, the collaborative training game described in the next section, was designed to combine several skill components. Furthermore, the collaborative nature of the game brings in a social aspect and stimulates interaction between patients and therapists.

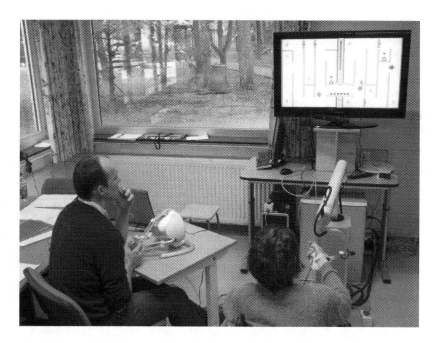

Fig. 1. System setup: with Novint falcon (therapist) and HapticMaster (patient)

2   Social Maze: The Game Concept

The Social Maze is a collaborative game played by two persons. Several scenarios are possible: two patients playing together (empathetic scenario), a patient playing with a healthy relative or with a therapist (sympathetic scenario). It is exactly this last scenario which we have most extensively tested during the therapy sessions in the rehab center.

In all scenarios the patient will use the HapticMaster (Fig. 1) as the input device to manipulate an avatar. In the case of the empathetic scenario, a fellow patient will also use the HapticMaster as the input device. In the sympathetic scenario, the healthy player (e.g. a family member or therapist) can have different possibilities of input devices, they can either use the Novint Falcon, which is a consumer haptic input device, a Wiimote, a balance board or the Microsoft Kinect, a motion sensing input device which enables operations using body gestures.

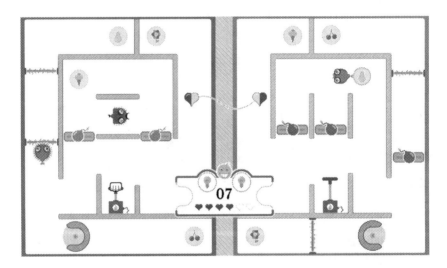

Fig. 2. Social Maze overview

Fig. 2 depicts our Social Maze with all game elements. The goal of this game is to collect all symbols, which represent points, by picking up each symbol and bringing it to the collecting bin. The elements of the game, with the pink background, were purposively designed so that two players (i.e. a patient and his/her training partner) have to collaborate as such to achieve the goal. Without collaboration, it is impossible to finish the game, so the game enforces so-called "closely-coupled collaboration".

The game area is divided into two. In each part the player, represented by a fish-like avatar (green for the left and purple for the right side), can move around his/her own maze to collect the symbols. Along the way there are some obstacles such as the laser beams that need to be avoided, the bombs that need to be demolished, the devil (red fish) that may not be encountered, and the rotators (with blue background) that need to be surmounted. Demolishing the bombs demands a tight collaboration between the players, where one player has to push the bomb trigger (push skill component) in order to destroy the bomb blocking the way of the other player. To pass the rotator, the players must enter it and perform the turning movement (turning skill component) to rotate it. When the players are hit by the laser beam or the devil, they will lose a life represented by a heart. To gain more lives, the players must attain the connecting heart (two connected half full hearts). Once the players pick up a symbol, they can place it in the collecting bin to earn points. After finishing collecting all symbols, a joint total score is shown to the players as depicted in the collective room.

The use of haptics makes sure that the patient's movement is kept within certain limits, for example it is not possible to go through the walls of the maze. Also, the haptic parameters allow us to control the complexity of the training depending on the physical performance of the patient, to make objects heavy or light etc., in order to strive for personalized training.

3   Discussion and Conclusion

The closely-coupled collaboration scenario as realized in the Social Maze turns out to be a successful (as shown in an RCT) and appreciated way to train. Besides providing the basic movements to be trained (skill components), the patient is immersed in a game concept that is challenging and stimulates social interaction. User tests, including observations, reveal that players discuss strategy and encourage each other. Pictures taken during the sessions show that social behavior is influenced by the game (e.g. mimicking each other's attitude). Patients and therapists also report more long-term social effects, such as teasing each other and referring back to gaming situations during previous sessions.

Acknowledgments. We acknowledge the INTERREG-IV program, project "Rehabilitation robotics 2", IVA-VLANED-1.14, Euregio Benelux, and the consortium partners.

See also www.i-travle.eu

References

1. Vanacken, L., Notelaers, S., Raymaekers, C., Coninx, K., van den Hoogen, W., Ijsselsteijn, W., Feys, P.: Game-Based Collaborative Training for Arm Rehabilitation of MS Pa-tients: A Proof-of-concept Game. In: Proceedings GameDays 2010, Darmstadt, Germany, pp. 65–75 (2010)
2. I-TRAVLE: Individualized, Technology-supported and Robot-Assisted Virtual Learning Environments, http://www.i-travle.eu
3. Feys, P., Alders, G., Gijbels, D., De Boeck, J., De Weyer, T., Coninx, K., Raymaekers, C., Truyens, V., Groenen, P., Meijer, K., Savelberg, H., Op, B.: Arm training in Multiple Sclerosis using Phantom: clinical relevance of robotic outcome measures. In: Proc. of ICORR 2009, pp. 576–581. IEEE (June 2009) ISBN 9781-4244-3789-4

HTML5 – Chances and Pitfalls

Demonstration for the Industry Track of the ICEC2012

Steffen Hees and Felix Faber

Bytro Labs GmbH
{steffen.hees,felix.faber}@bytro.com

Abstract. HTML5 is set to become the next standard in web applications, a key technology for the years to come. With its ability to handle multimedia and graphical content without the use of external plugins or APIs, it will play a crucial role in creating cross-platform content for both desktop- and mobile devices. Creating browser games using HTML5 is the logical next step on the evolutionary ladder of game development.

Realizing this potential, Hamburg-based game developer Bytro Labs has shifted all its resources toward developing their games in HTML5, incorporating the improved performance for complex graphics and the real-time aspect of communication between the player and the game. In the development of their newest game, they are not only creating a game fit for the future but they have been putting the new technology to the test.

1 Demonstration

In a presentation, Bytro Labs software developer Steffen Hees is going to provide an insight into the game creation process and the experiences with HTML5 [1–3]. He will illustrate where the potential [4, 5] and the pitfalls lie. Afterwards, he will discuss the most interesting issues with HTML5 in greater detail and demonstrate them directly on the prototype of our newest browser-based online game.

2 About the Company

Bytro Labs GmbH is an independent, owner-managed company, which develops and operates technically sophisticated, browser-based and mobile online games. By now, the games have over 1.5 Million registered users and are available in more than ten different languages. Bytro Labs was founded in 2009 by Felix Faber, Tobias Kringe and Christopher Loerken. They were decorated as "Founders of the Month" in June 2010 by the state of Baden-Wuerttemberg. With their 15 employees, Bytro Labs is located in the heart of Hamburg's Old Town.

M. Herrlich, R. Malaka, and M. Masuch (Eds.): ICEC 2012, LNCS 7522, pp. 480–481, 2012.

References

1. http://en.wikipedia.org/wiki/HTML5
2. http://www.whatwg.org/specs/web-apps/current-work/multipage/
3. http://www.w3.org/TR/2011/WD-html5-20110525/
4. http://www.browser-statistik.de/
5. http://gs.statcounter.com/

A Framework Concept for Emotion Enriched Interfaces

Arne Bernin

Department Informatik,
University of Applied Sciences Hamburg (HAW Hamburg), Germany
School of Computing, University of the West of Scotland (UWS), UK
arne.bernin@haw-hamburg.de

Abstract. The work presented outlines my doctoral research in emotion and
action based human computer interfaces, with the approach to create an open
source framework. The idea is to find the suitable abstractions and interfaces to
integrate different approaches to process input data to interpret user's emotions
and actions. Fusing and comparing alternatives for processing will help to find
the appropriate solution for a particular need for the next generation of interactive systems. Widening the sensing abilities of computers has the potential to
add new degrees of freedom to the design of human computer interaction and
ubiquitous entertainment computing.

1 Introduction

The level of interaction of today's computing systems lack various aspects that can be
found in human-human communication. One major difference lies in ability to communicate on an emotional level. Combining emotions and actions shows great potential for new applications by leveraging of humanlike communication skills. This is
particular relevant for communication centric applications such as gaming and learning. There are two fundamental designs to realize emotions in interactive Systems: 1.
observing systems facilitate an emotional monologue i.e. provide no feedback. 2.
Reactive systems have sensing and displaying abilities leading to an emotional dialog.
The dialog may be facilitated by a combination of one or more modalities. Humans
combine a variety of modalities as input channels for emotion recognition including
gesture, posture, and prosody of speech, semantic, context and facial expressions.

Combining different data sources is also a common approach in computer science.
Although there were some experiments in the field of combined channels for emotion
recognition in computer science, the decision, which aggregation of modalities are
more effective, is still an open research question. This decision also depends on
the application and needs to be determined on the basis of a particular application
scenario.

Currently there are many approaches in emotion interpretation and comparisons are
rarely performed. Therefore, integrating established algorithms in a common framework enables to compare application specific differences and find opportunities for
further research.

M. Herrlich, R. Malaka, and M. Masuch (Eds.): ICEC 2012, LNCS 7522, pp. 482–485, 2012.
© IFIP International Federation for Information Processing 2012

2   Framework

Current developments in entertainment computing go beyond the classic desktop scenario with one user in front of a display. Computer interaction has become ubiquitous. Therefore, the research scenarios should be developed in a ubiquitous context and laboratories, which we aim for in the livingplace hamburg, a smart home lab at the HAW Hamburg.[4]

The proposed framework enables to integrate different approaches in soft- and hardware and adds the ability to evaluate them on a scientific level. The requirements for the framework are:

1. Capability to log and replay all input data is needed for validation of an approach as well as comparison of different approaches with the same input data. Therefore, the complete data has to be written to data storage.
2. Processing of input data need to be performed at interactive rates. For this and to avoid bias due to fluctuating latencies, the framework has to be realtime orientated.
3. Concurrent processing of different modalities. The Framework needs the capacity to handle multiple input channels at the same time without fatal increase of processing time.
4. Facilities to analyze results for validation and comparison. In addition to logging of the input data, metrics of the system state, latencies, processing times and detection rate need to be saved for further analysis.
5. Easy exchange and integration of different processing components. This includes the requirements for an interface that works on different operating systems. Adapters for different programming languages are needed for flexibility.

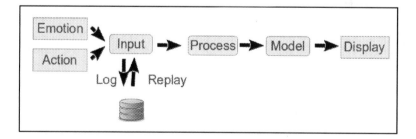

Fig. 1. Process flow

The flow model of processing is shown in Figure 1. The different components are:

Emotion: Sense describes the different input modalities as sensor input for different channels. Sense is gathered by observing the user with different technical systems. The user does not need to consciously act for expressing the sensed information as his current emotional state might be subconscious to him.

Action: Actions are performed by the user such as input to operate a game. Actions are actively and conscious expressions done by the user as part of his planned interaction.

Input: Input is an abstraction of Emotion and Action. Incoming data needs to be normalized for further processing. Input is also the step, where the data is first completely visible to the framework, so here is the place to log it.

Process: Input data needs to be filtered and processed. The aggregated Information is then used to update the emotional model.

Log/Replay: Capability to store all input data in a database for future evaluation.

Model: Emotional Model on Computational level. This model represents the current emotional state of the user as recognized by the system. It can also be used to validate state changes and avoid fluctuations caused by misattributed input data.

Display: Output modality. Appropriate Display is task for future research. The current interface for the livingplace as testing environment at the HAW is the central message broker.

3   Applications in Gaming

Sensing emotions opens a variety of applications for interactive systems. For my thesis work, i plan to evaluate my proposed framework in gaming scenarios. I envision two possible application domains in entertainment computing.

3.1   Serious Games

Serious games are used for learning. By Gamification of the learning context or by developing skills inside the game that also have a benefit in the real world. Emotion recognition has two major applications in the context of serious games: Feedback to the machine and feedback to the user. Feedback to the machine on an emotional level can be used to control the learning curve. Changing speed and level of presented facts in an automated learning system according to the speed of understanding can improve the efficiency of the learning process.[2] Provoking emotions can improve the user's motivation and memorization ability. Emotion recognition can be applied to verify the wanted effect. Further, emotional feedback to the user can improve can improve learning for public speaking and presentation skills.

3.2   Fun and Entertainment Games

There is an ongoing evolution in game controls from buttons and joysticks evolved to gestural input. In the future facial expressions and emotional state promise further enhancements. Expressed emotions can be transferred to avatar expression in game context. Like in serious games, Emotions can be applied to adapt the level of the game to user abilities and preferences. Current games use AI technologies, adding emotions have the potential to make them more believable.[1] Although, currently unknown, using emotion recognition technologies could increase immersion and embodiment on the user side.

3.3   Contribution to Entertainment Computing

The main purpose for the planned framework is to evaluate different approaches of sensing emotions and corresponding models for research. Nevertheless, the framework and exemplary procedure can be applied to integrate emotional sensing and to design into entertainment computing and games. Our complete prototype system can be directly integrated in game engines as additional source of input.

4   Current and Future Work

The main focus of the current work is to develop the basics of the framework. Therefore, methods and technical components evaluation for realtime messaging systems, facial expressions and prosody of speech is in process, the   procedure for framework development has been derived from this evaluations. Examples can be presented at the doctorial consortium. Suitable datasets for evaluation selected as well.

Future work includes the integration of a system for multi camera based determination of position and recognition of persons, currently developed at the HAW Hamburg. Integrating the results from the research done on terms of emotional surfaces at the HAW Hamburg are also part of future work. [3]

References

[1] Becker-Asano, C.: WASABI: Affect Simulation for Agents with Believable Interactivity. PhD thesis, Faculty of Technology, University of Bielefeld. IOS Press, DISKI 319 (2008)
[2] D'Mello, S., Jackson, T., Craig, S., Morgan, B., Chipman, P., White, H., Person, N., Kort, B., El Kaliouby, R., Picard, R., Al, E.: AutoTutor detects and responds to learners affective and cognitive states. In: Proceedings of the Workshop on Emotional and Cognitive Issues in ITS in Conjunction with the 9th International Conference on Intelligent Tutoring Systems (2008)
[3] Müller, L., Keune, S., Bernin, A., Vogt, F.: Emotional Interaction with Surfaces - Works of Design and Computing. In: Herrlich, M., Malaka, R., Masuch, M. (eds.) ICEC 2012. LNCS, vol. 7522, pp. 455–458. Springer, Heidelberg (2012)
[4] von Luck, K., Klemke, G., Gregor, S., Rahimi, M.A., Vogt, M.: Living place hamburg – a place for concepts of it based modern living. Technical report, Hamburg University of Applied Sciences (2010)

Expanding the Magic Circle in Pervasive Casual Play

Sofia Reis

CITI and DI, Faculdade de Ciências e Tecnologia,
Universidade Nova de Lisboa
2829-516 Caparica, Portugal
se.reis@campus.fct.unl.pt

Abstract. Typically, in digital entertainment, the screen is the center of the player's attention. If the real world was part of the gameplay, the player would also pay attention to what is happening around her. That is the case of pervasive games. Our objective is to find ways of making pervasive play available for a large casual audience, but in a way that casual games are not deprived of their intrinsic characteristics. Casual games are easy to play, have simple rules and easy to understand interfaces and the introduction of real world elements must thus not deprive them of these characteristics.

Keywords: pervasive games, casual games, interaction.

1   Introduction and Related Work

Playing is an activity that has been around for a long time. Games happen inside a magic circle, a sacred isolated space that totally immerses the players [1]. Digital games are games that make use of computers, mobiles phones or game consoles and such games suffer, in our view, of the following problem: the screen is the player's primary or even only focus of attention. It would be interesting if, at least during a few moments, digital games could be played without looking at a screen. Pervasive games have already accomplished that objective with the inclusion of real world elements in games. That way, instead of merely looking at a screen, the player also has to concentrate on what is happening around him or her.

A pervasive game is a *"genre in which traditional, real-world games are augmented with computing functionality, or, depending on the perspective, purely virtual computer entertainment is brought back to the real world"* [2]. Non pervasive games are played at a certain place, during a certain time and with certain people. In a pervasive game the magic circle is expanded spatially, temporally or socially, so pervasive games may be played everywhere, all the time and eventually with everybody [3]. Human Pacman, REXplorer and Heroes of Koskenniska are three examples of pervasive games. Human Pacman is a pervasive game inspired in the Pacman videogame. In this game, a Pacman player runs around in the real world and Ghost players hunt her down [4]. REXplorer is a spell casting game where tourists encounter spirits that are historical figures [5]. Heroes of Koskenniska is another pervasive game aimed at raising environmental awareness among visitors of a biosphere reserve [6].

M. Herrlich, R. Malaka, and M. Masuch (Eds.): ICEC 2012, LNCS 7522, pp. 486–489, 2012.

Our research focus is on casual pervasive games because we intend to include real world elements in games in a way that satisfies the requirements of a casual audience. Windows Solitaire, Tetris and Pacman are good examples of well known classic casual games. Casual games are easy in the sense that they have simple rules and simple to understand interfaces that make use of images and symbols, in detriment of long and fastidious text descriptions. In casual games the gameplay should be as obvious as possible. As a casual game usually runs in parallel with the player's other everyday activities the mental engagement necessary to play the game should be low [7]. In order to remain in the casual segment, the introduction of real world elements should not cause the games to become more complicated, else they will not be casual any more.

Merging casual and pervasive games is an ambitious and difficult objective [3]. Some games have already managed to fit both the requirements of casual and pervasive games. In Insectopia, a pervasive casual game, players use their mobile phones to hunt for rare bugs. Bluetooth devices around the player are the sources of the bugs [8]. Blowtooth also explores the detection of other Bluetooth devices to smuggle drugs [9]. Social Heroes is a game where players trade points by tagging each other using Twitter [10]. We intend to pursue the previous researchers' efforts in combining casual and pervasive games and to outline a framework to integrate real world elements in casual games.

2   Research Goal

Our objective is to develop ways of integrating real world elements in casual games and thus decrease the focus of the player's attention on the screen and divert that attention to the environment around the player. We, therefore, intend to introduce a pervasive twist in casual games in a way that complies with the following conditions:

- As casual games are easy and simple, the real world elements must thus be integrated in a way that is also easy and simple for the player.
- Casual players are usually not willing to invest in expensive or specialized hardware [11]. So the inclusion of real world elements will make use of functionality already available (or foreseen in the near future) in devices like computers, portable computers or mobile phones.

3   Results to Date

There are many real world elements that can be used in a casual game. So far, we have obtained results in what refers to the inclusion of sound, weather and the player's emotions, activities and location in games. For these real world elements we created games that merge naturally with the players' environment so that the magic circle blurs, expands and eventually overlaps with real life.

For the specific case of sound we created a game, The Castle of Count Pat that merges seamlessly with the activities of an educative setting. The game captures sound and shows the sound wave or the frequency spectrum, integrated with an animated character, to students in real time. The quieter the students are the higher the score. A video projector, connected to the computer where the game is running, shows the animated character to all students. The classes where the game was tested became quieter [12].

In another game, we created an Imaginary Friend that resorts to the player's emotions, activities and location. The player's physical activities are detected via the mobile phone's accelerometer so that the Imaginary Friend imitates the human friend, walking when the player walks and stopping and looking up when the player stops. The Imaginary Friend is projected on the floor via a pico projector that is attached to the player's backpack shoulder strap. The pico projector is connected to the mobile phone, where the Imaginary Friend's application is running. A significant increase or decrease in the arousal, detected via an electrodermal activity sensor, may indicate a change in the player's emotions. When this happens, the Imaginary Friend asks what the user is feeling and collects an emotion cookie that is stored inside a jar. The previously collected emotions cookies can also be consulted in a map [13].

Finally, in what refers to the weather, the player merely has to look out the window or step outside to check it without needing any sort of equipment, and that makes it a very pervasive, as well as casual, element. In Weather Wizards the player's powers vary according to the current real weather. The better the players adjust the spells in their grimoire to the real weather conditions the greater the chances of winning the duels [14].

All the mentioned games comply with our research objective of merging the real world with games, in a way that is easy for the player, and making use of functionality already available in devices such as computers, portable computers and mobile phones. The Castle of Count Pat only needs a low end computer, a microphone and a video projector to show the output of the game to students [12]. The Imaginary Friend resorts to a mobile phone, to an electrodermal activity sensor and to a pico projector. Electrodermal activity sensors may become widespread equipment in a near future as there are already companies commercializing such equipment [15, 16]. As for pico projectors, some mobile phones have already an incorporated projector [17]. For now, mobile phones with embedded projectors are not that widespread, but this may well be a possibility worth considering in the future as a way to solve the problems associated with the small size of mobile phones' screens. Finally, Weather Wizards needs only a mobile phone and a connection to the Internet [14].

4   Contributions of Our Work to Entertainment Computing and Conclusions

We are now at point in our research where results have already been collected, but where crucial decisions are still left to be made. Real world elements like the sound, the weather and the player's emotions, activities and location have already been addressed during our research but we are still planning to consider the opportunities provided by video and augmented reality. It is our plan to create a common conceptual or software framework that integrates all these real world elements. This framework will be a key result of our research as it may be of use to others who are also working towards binding games and reality. Finally, casual games are games for everyone and research done in this area will benefit a large number of persons. Our objective is to find ways of providing pervasive entertainment for a wide audience of causal players. This work was funded by FCT/MCTES (SFRH/BD/61085/2009) and by CITI (CITI/FCT/UNL - 2011-2012 - PEst-OE/EEI/UI0527/2011.

References

1. Huizinga, J.: Homo Ludens. Beacon Press (1971)
2. Magerkurth, C., Cheok, A.D., Mandryk, R.L., Nilsen, T.: Pervasive games: bringing computer entertainment back to the real world. Comput. Entertain. 3(4) (2005)
3. Montola, M., Stenros, J., Waern, A.: Pervasive Games: Theory and Design. Morgan Kaufmann (2009)
4. Cheok, A.D., Goh, K.H., Liu, W., Farbiz, F., Fong, S.W., Teo, S.L., Li, Y., Yang, X.: Human Pacman: a mobile, wide-area entertainment system based on physical, social, and ubiquitous computing. Personal Ubiquitous Comput. 8, 71–81 (2004)
5. Ballagas, R.A., Kratz, S.G., Borchers, J., Yu, E., Walz, S.P., Fuhr, C.O., Hovestadt, L., Tann, M.: REXplorer: a mobile, pervasive spell-casting game for tourists. In: CHI EA 2007, p. 1929. ACM Press, New York (2007)
6. Laine, T.H., Gimbitskaya, A., Sutinen, E., Choi, J., Yong, K., Lee, C.: Environmental sensor network for a pervasive learning space in a Finnish biosphere reserve. In: Proceedings of the 5th International Conference on Ubiquitous Information Management and Communication, pp. 88:1–88:6. ACM, New York (2011)
7. Kultima, A.: Casual game design values. In: Proceedings of the 13th International MindTrek Conference: Everyday Life in the Ubiquitous Era on - MindTrek 2009, p. 58. ACM Press, New York (2009)
8. Peitz, J., Saarenpää, H., Björk, S.: Insectopia: exploring pervasive games through technology already pervasively available. In: ACE 2007, p. 107. ACM Press, New York (2007)
9. Linehan, C., Kirman, B., Lawson, S., Doughty, M.: Blowtooth: pervasive gaming in unique and challenging environments. In: CHI EA 2010, p. 2695. ACM Press, New York (2010)
10. Simon, A.: Social heroes: games as APIs for social interaction. In: DIMEA 2008, p. 40. ACM Press, New York (2008)
11. Rohrl, D.: 2008-2009 Casual Games White Paper. IGDA (2008)
12. Reis, S., Correia, N.: The Perception of Sound and Its Influence in the Classroom. In: Campos, P., Graham, N., Jorge, J., Nunes, N., Palanque, P., Winckler, M. (eds.) INTERACT 2011, Part I. LNCS, vol. 6946, pp. 609–626. Springer, Heidelberg (2011)
13. Reis, S., Correia, N.: An imaginary friend that connects with the user's emotions. In: ACE 2011, p. 1. ACM Press, New York (2011)
14. Reis, S., Correia, N.: Engaging the Players with the Use of Real-Time Weather Data. In: Proceedings of the 4o Science and Videogames Conference-2011, Portuguese Society for Videogames Science (2011)
15. edaPlux | PLUX, http://plux.info/EDA
16. Q Sensor 2.0, http://www.affectiva.com/q-sensor/
17. Seeser laser pico projector, http://www.engadget.com/2011/10/15/seeser-laser-pico-projector-is-always-in-focus-powered-by-andro/

Time Simulator in Virtual Reality for Children with Attention Deficit Hyperactivity Disorder

Pongpanote Gongsook

Eindhoven University of Technology, Eindhoven, The Netherlands
p.gongsook@tue.nl

Abstract. This project aims at investigating how effective virtual reality is in manipulating and eventually training time perception for children with learning and/or behavior disorders. The interconnectivity of multiple brain regions is needed for time perception. Small dysfunctions in these brain regions may cause time perceiving problems. Likewise, children with attention deficit hyperactivity disorder (ADHD) appear to have comparable dysfunction in time orientation. However, the time perception can be trained in their early ages. In addition, research confirms the effectiveness of virtual reality in improving the sequential time perception of children with mental retardation. This paper presents the theoretical and empirical framework that uses a virtual reality time simulation game for training time perception of children with ADHD.

Keywords. Time Perception, Virtual Reality, Game, Attention Deficit Hyperactivity Disorder, Learning Disorders.

1 Introduction

Time is something humans cannot directly perceive with their senses. However, it can be perceived by reasoning on one's surrounding context or the sequence of events that happen within one's local environment [1, 2]. Children as young as 3 year old start developing their sensitivity to duration, and their time perception develops with age [3]. Time perception is a conceptual understanding that enables one's ability to predict, anticipate, and respond to events as past or present occurring in the environment [1, 2]. Children with attention deficit hyperactivity disorder (ADHD) have shown their difficulties in processing, reading, and telling time [4]. Although there are quizzes and tests on the internet that aim to improve children's time reading [5], most of them are designed for normal children. We aim at a virtual reality game that creates a time simulator for children with learning disorders and ADHD.

2 Connectivity between Time, Brain Functions and ADHD

Time perception needs the interconnectivity between multiple brain regions, including the cerebellum, basal ganglia, and prefrontal cortex. Individuals with cerebellar dysfunction may have difficulty with an event that requires precise movement timing

M. Herrlich, R. Malaka, and M. Masuch (Eds.): ICEC 2012, LNCS 7522, pp. 490–493, 2012.

[6, 7]. The basal ganglia, prefrontal cortex, and posterior parietal cortex have been suggested to be involved in interval timing [4].

The mentioned brain regions are found to be involved in the dysfunction of time perception during cognitive testing in the ADHDs [8]. ADHD is a behavioral condition identified by DSM-IV [9], which symptoms must be present before the age of seven, persist for at least six months, and be sufficiently severe to impact daily functioning across several settings such as home, school and interpersonal relationships. Children with ADHD have significantly smaller cerebral and cerebellar volumes, particularly the right cerebellum [6]. Besides, there are significantly lower levels of activation in the basal ganglia in children with ADHD [4]. However, rehabilitation as well as training could be done while they are in the early developmental stages [10].

3   Virtual Reality as a Diagnostic/Training Game

Virtual reality (VR) can be used in many aspects and application areas. VR simulations allow children with certain impairments to experience what could be difficult or even impossible for them to do in reality [11]. Fairley suggested that patients would feel more amused when they are rehabilitated using games that utilize VR [12]. Riva, Mantovani, and Gaggioli show that knowledge obtained in VR can be transferred into a real environment [13]. It is shown that participants who performed cognitive tasks that targeted on attention performance using VR did outperform scores of those who used the traditional methods [14]. However, we have found no existing effort in training time perception using a Game in Virtual Reality Environments (GVR).

4   Project Approaches

We aim at GVRs that children with ADHD can play in, and at the same time offers opportunities to train and improve their time perception. Gaming is chosen because it can immediately give them rewards, which they attract to [15]. GVR aims at improving the working memory of children with ADHD, which found out as one of their core cognitive deficits [16]. Improving the working memory might reduce some of their symptoms and associated behavior problems [17]. Mnemonic strategy, which encoding the information in a way other than directly remembering, will be used in this project [18].

The GVR uses linear storytelling so we can ensure that all the children experience the same branch of decisions. It includes mini games for specific memory tests for time estimation, production and reproduction. The game trains the children's time perception using various time teaching techniques such as clock faces or the appearance of the sky at different times of the day. It uses game-world time while teaching and uses real-world time while testing [19]. Before GVR is used as a psychological assessment tool, it must be evaluated by psychologists.

5   Conclusion

The goal is to investigate how effective time simulation in virtual reality is for children with learning disorders. Children with ADHD have time perception problems. However, their symptoms can be cured in their early ages. We believe that children with ADHD will have some benefits from learning time perception via GVR. The time simulator in virtual reality can be a candidate for the solution.

Acknowledgement. This work was supported in part by the Erasmus Mundus Joint Doctorate in Interactive and Cognitive Environments (ICE), which is funded by the EACEA Agency of the European Commission under EMJD ICE FPA n 2010-0012. We are also very grateful for the collaboration with Dr. Jos Hendriksen from Kempenhaeghe- centre for neurological learning disabilities.

References

1. Le Poidevin, R.: The Experience and Perception of Time, http://plato.stanford.edu/archives/fall2011/entries/time-experience/
2. Time Perception, http://www.britannica.com/EBchecked/topic/596177/time-perception
3. Droit-Volet, S.: Alerting attention and time perception in children. J. Exp. Child Psychol. 85, 372–384 (2003)
4. Hurks, P.P., Hendriksen, J.G.: Retrospective and prospective time deficits in childhood ADHD: The effects of task modality, duration, and symptom dimensions. Child Neuropsychol. 17, 34–50 (2011)
5. Learn to Tell Time Games & Websites for Kids, http://www.learningreviews.com/Telling-Time-Websites-Games-for-Kids.html
6. Toplak, M.E., Dockstader, C., Tannock, R.: Temporal information processing in ADHD: Findings to date and new methods. J. Neurosci. Methods 151, 15–29 (2006)
7. Casini, L., Ivry, R.B.: Effects of divided attention on temporal processing in patients with lesions of the cerebellum or frontal lobe. Neuropsychology 13, 10–21 (1999)
8. Smith, A., Taylor, E., Rogers, J.W., Newman, S., Rubia, K.: Evidence for a pure time perception deficit in children with ADHD. J. Child Psychol. Psychiatry 43, 529–542 (2002)
9. DSM-IV-R: Statistical Manual of Mental Disorders, Text Revision (DSM IV–R). Arlington, VA (2000)
10. Barkley, R.A., Koplowitz, S., Anderson, T., McMurray, M.B.: Sense of time in children with ADHD: effects of duration, distraction, and stimulant medication. J. Int. Neuropsychol. Soc. 3, 359–369 (1997)
11. Rose, F.D., Attree, E.A., Brooks, B.M., Andrews, T.K.: Learning and memory in virtual environments: a role in neurorehabilitation? Questions (and occasional answers) from the University of East London. Presence 10, 345–358 (2001)
12. Fairley, M.: Fun and Games: Virtual Reality Turns the Work of Rehab into Play, http://www.oandp.com/articles/2010-05_01.asp
13. Riva, G., Mantovani, F., Gaggioli, A.: Presence and rehabilitation: toward second-generation virtual reality applications in neuropsychology. J. Neuroeng. Rehabil. 1, 9 (2004)

14. Parsons, T.D., Bowerly, T., Buckwalter, J.G., Rizzo, A.A.: A controlled clinical comparison of attention performance in children with ADHD in a virtual reality classroom compared to standard neuropsychological methods. Child Neuropsychol. 13, 363–381 (2007)
15. Bioulac, S.S., Arfi, L., Bouvard, M.P.: Attention deficit/hyperactivity disorder and video games: A comparative study of hyperactive and control children. Eur. Psychiatry 23, 134–141 (2008)
16. Dehn, M.J.: Working Memory and Academic Learning Assessment and Intervention. Wiley (2008)
17. Klingberg, T., Forssberg, H., Westerberg, H.: Training of working memory in children with ADHD. J. Clin Exp. Neuropsychol. 24, 781–791 (2002)
18. Mastropieri, M.A.: Enhancing School Success with Mnemonic Strategies. Interv. Sch. Clin. 33, 201–208 (1998)
19. Zagal, J.: Temporal frames: a unifying framework for the analysis of game temporality. DiGRA, 1–8 (2007)

SGDA2012

Jannicke Madeleine Baalsrud Hauge[1], Heiko Duin[1], Minhua Ma[2],
and Manuel Oliveira[3]

[1] BIBA - Bremer Institut für Produktion und Logistik GmbH,
Hochschulring 20, 28359 Bremen, Germany
{baa,du}@biba.uni-bremen.de
[2] Digital Design Studio, Glasgow School of Art, Glasgow, UK
m.ma@gsa.ac.uk
[3] Sintef, Technology and Society, S.P. Andersensv. 5,
NO-7465 Trondheim, Norway
manuel.oliveira@sintef.no

1 International Conference on Serious Games Development and Applications

The **Third International Conference on Serious Games Development and Applications** is this year organised as a satellite conference to **IFIP-ICEC2012** in Bremen. **SGDA 2012** appears in the sequence of the successes of the First International Workshop on Serious Games Development and Application held in Derby in 2010 and Second International Conference on Serious Games Development and Applications, held in Lisbon in 2011. The aim of SGDA is to collect and disseminate knowledge on serious games technologies, design and development; to provide practitioners and interdisciplinary communities with a peer-reviewed forum to discuss the state-of-the-art in serious games research, their ideas and theories, and innovative applications of serious games; to explain cultural, social and scientific phenomena by means of serious games; to concentrate on the interaction between theory and application; to share best practice and lessons learnt; to develop new methodologies in various application domains using games technologies; and to explore perspectives of future developments and innovative applications relevant to serious games and related areas.

The emergence of serious games as a branch of video games has introduced the concept of games designed for a serious purpose other than pure entertainment. To date the major applications of serious games include engineering, education, health care, military applications, city planning, production, crisis response, and training. Serious games have primarily been used as a tool that gives players a novel way to interact with games in order to promote physical activities, to learn skills and knowledge, to support social-emotional development, to facilitate behavior transformation, to treat different types of psychological and physical disorders, etc. Many recent studies have identified the benefits of using video games in a variety of serious purposes. However, most Serious Games are still mostly focusing on the learning objective, and not so much in developing engaging and motivating user interfaces. In the world of entertainment games, there has been much more focus on the user experience. Therefore the organizational committee decided to co-locate SGDA with the 11th

M. Herrlich, R. Malaka, and M. Masuch (Eds.): ICEC 2012, LNCS 7522, pp. 494–495, 2012.
© IFIP International Federation for Information Processing 2012

International Conference on Entertainment Computer conference. This will give the opportunity of fostering the dialogue between the entertainment and serious games communities and will support a bi-directional knowledge transfer.

At SGDA 2012 around 20 presentations will be hold on different aspects of serious games design and use. The papers are published in LNCS. We are all welcoming you to participate in our discussions.

The Conference is supported by the **GALA Network of Excellence for Serious Games**, the **TARGET (Transformative, Adaptive, Responsive and enGaging EnvironmenT)** Project which is a Large-scale Integrating Project funded by the European Community under the FP7 (ICT-2007.4.3) and Digital Libraries & Technology-Enhanced Learning 2009-2011 (Grant Agreement N° 231717), BIBA - Bremer Institut für Produktion und Logistik GmbH, University of Bremen, Glasgow School of Art, INESC-ID, Technical University of Lisbon, and University of Derby.

GCI 2012 Harnessing Collective Intelligence with Games

1st International Workshop on Systems with Homo Ludens in the Loop

Markus Krause[1], Roberta Cuel[2], and Maja Vukovic[3]

[1] University of Bremen
[2] University of Trento
[3] Thomas J. Watson Research Center
phateon@tzi.de, roberta.cuel@unitn.it, maja@us.ibm.com

Abstract. With recent advances in harnessing the knowledge and skill of large groups of (unknown) network-connected humans, researchers and practitioners have been designing systems that make contributions of users entertaining and more engaging. Game mechanics are being applied to the traditional human computation tasks, such as transcription, classification and labeling. Seminal examples of such applications include ESP game and FoldIt. At the same time, companies seek strategies to include elements of gaming into business processes to increase productivity and engagement of employees. Framing a business goal in the form of a game is also a promising method for motivating newer generations in the workforce.

1 Introduction

The idea of designing systems that solve tasks and incorporate the playfulness of games has recently become an extensively discussed topic. Many Web 2.0 and crowdsourcing initiatives take advantage of the vast amount of hours spent on online playing, by extracting meaningful information, acquiring knowledge, or outsourcing production tasks. The workshop on "System with Homo Ludens in the loop" aims at providing a discussion forum for both researchers and practitioners in the fields of computer science, web technologies, and sociology, as well as psychology and business studies.

Many areas of knowledge acquisition inherently rely on the availability on large quantities of human input. The problem is that in many of these domains, users lack the motivation to contribute the required metadata. At the same time, there is a steady trend of people spending a substantial amount of time in playing games. As initially proposed by Luis von Ahn's "Games with a Purpose", one can benefit from the vast amount of hours spent on online playing, by applying mechanisms to extract meaningful information from game inputs. Since then, there have been many proposals to use casual games which capitalize on fun and competition as two key motivators for people, to willingly invest time and effort in knowledge acquisition related tasks hiding behind an entertaining collaborative game experience. The workshop will provide

M. Herrlich, R. Malaka, and M. Masuch (Eds.): ICEC 2012, LNCS 7522, pp. 496–499, 2012.

a forum for researchers and practitioners in Web technologies to discuss and exchange positions on the topic of using games for acquiring knowledge following the paradigm of human computation.

2   Areas of Interest

The objective of the workshop is to foster the thinking process about how to effectively involve the users in the loop of a production system or crowdsoucing initiative.

- Games for Collective Intelligence
- Human Computation Games (Games with a Purpose)
- Applications of games in science, industry and public sector
- Games for data collection, verification and classification
- Game-based surveys
- Task decomposition and gamification
- Quality management in collective play
- Cost-benefit analysis for collective play
- Games and new business models
- Commodification of play (uses and abuses of free time)
- Collective play as socialization (using social networks platforms)
- Game propagation in the social networks
- Game architectures and technology
- Incentives and adoption of games in enterprise environments

3   Accepted Submission Abstracts

Full submissions can be found in the proceedings of the 3'rd International Conference on Serious Games Development and Applications SGDA'12.

3.1   Value-Based Design for Gamifying Daily Activities

Computing technologies allow us to gamify our daily activity by embedding computers in our daily environments. In this paper, we propose a value-based gamification framework to increase pleasure in our daily life. Traditional gamification frameworks add game mechanics in our daily activities to motivate people. However, it is hard to maintain the motivation for a long time. Our approach is based on values to increase intrinsic human motivation. In this paper, we introduce five values, and how the values are used in Augmented Trading Card Game as a case study. Then, we show a framework to design gamification of daily activities to increase intrinsic human motivation.

3.2 Squaring and Scripting the ESP Game: Trimming a GWAP to Deep Semantics

The ESP Game, like other Games With A Purpose (GWAP), tends to generate "surface semantics" tags. This article first discusses why this is the case, then proposes two approaches called "squaring" and "scripting" to collecting "deep semantics" tags that both consist in deploying the ESP Game in unconventional manners. It also reports on a promising first experimental evaluation of the two approaches. It finally briefly discusses the relevance of squaring and scripting for other GWAPs than the ESP Game.

3.3 Logical Thinking by Play Using the Example of the Game Space Goats

The idea of "Serious Games" mainly describes games that generate overvalue. According to James P. Gee's learning theories, game worlds are some of the best learning environments imaginable as they encourage the utilization of the actively learned skills in other domains. The game "Space Goats" is designed according to these principles. It uses a graphical scripting interface to encourage the player to reason logically, while it stays a game all the time, and the player does not realize, that he has been taught.

3.4 Betaville - A Massively Participatory Mirror World Game

Betaville is an editable online mirror world designed to develop broader positive participation in development of new ideas for urban environments, particularly for new initiatives in public art, urban design, and development/redevelopment. A "mirror world" of any city, based on public terrain and GIS data supplemented by embedded links to background information, can be further developed by user-created proposals for additions and modifications to the environment. Multiple proposals can be offered, debated, and iterated for the same location. Betaville is a research and development collaboration between the Brooklyn Experimental Media Center of the Polytechnic Institute of New York University and the M2C Institute for Applied Media Technology and Culture at the University of Applied Sciences of Bremen

4   Organizing Committee

Roberta Cuel, University of Trento, Italy

Maja Vukovic, IBM T. J. Watson Research Center, USA

Markus Krause, University of Bremen, Germany

5   Program Committee

Denny Vrandecic, Wikimedia Foundation, Germany
Yaniv Corem, IBM Haifa Research Lab, Israel
Jon Chamberlain, University of Essex, United Kingdom
Robert Kern, Karlsruhe Institute of Technology, Germany
Jan Smeddinck, University of Bremen, Germany
Alexander Sorokin, Crowdflower.com, USA
Massimo Poesio, University of Trento, Italy
Christian Rozsenich, Clickworker.com, CEO, Germany
Otto Chrons, Microtask.com, CTO, Finnland
Simon Caton, Karlsruhe Institute of Technology, Germany
Francesco Schiavone, Parthenope University of Naples, Italy
Francesco Bolici, University of Cassino, Rome, Italy
Paolo Massa, Bruno Kessler Foundation, Trento, Italy
Tindara Abbate, University of Messina, Italy
Carl Goodman, Peppers Ghost Productions, United Kingdom
Claudio Bartolini, HP Labs, USA

2nd Workshop on Game Development and Model-Driven Software Development

Robert Walter[1], Maic Masuch[1], and Mathias Funk[2]

[1] Entertainment Computing Group
Department of Computer Science and Cognitive Science
University of Duisburg–Essen
Duisburg, Germany
{robert.walter,maic.masuch}@uni-due.de
[2] Designed Intelligence Group
Department of Industrial Design
Eindhoven University of Technology
Eindhoven, The Netherlands
m.funk@tue.nl

Abstract. Succeeding the 1st Workshop on GD&MDSD at last year's ICEC, this event continues the exchange of both novices and experts in the fields of game development and model-driven software development (MDSD). The overall goal is to further consolidate a platform for researchers and professionals who are interested in the topics of modeling, domain-driven design, and domain-specific languages in the context of game development. This year, we want to focus on future requirements in game design and development and how they can be addressed by MDSD techniques. The workshop covers questions like "how can game design benefit from the language engineering process?", "what are the pros and cons of visual and textual modeling languages?", and "how can model-to-model and model-to-text transformations be used to streamline game development workflows?".

Keywords: Game Development, Model-Driven Software Development, Domain-Specific Languages, Game Modeling, Game Authoring, Tooling, Prototyping.

1   Relevance of Workshop Topic

Games are highly interactive media applications within a hard to define common scope. Developed in multidisciplinary teams, they combine the artistic challenges of multimedia productions with the engineering challenges of IT-productions [1]. Hence, we face ambitious demands regarding the overall development process. However, the growing complexity and scale were not encountered by refined game development methods for many years [2]. Only recently, agile project management methods like Scrum were applied successfully in several productions [3],[4],[5].

M. Herrlich, R. Malaka, and M. Masuch (Eds.): ICEC 2012, LNCS 7522, pp. 500–503, 2012.
© IFIP International Federation for Information Processing 2012

In the last decade, MDSD has successfully made the transition from the academic sphere to industrial-grade software development and it provides many advantages [6] game development could benefit from. Key features of a system are formally described on a higher level of abstraction (the problem domain), omitting distracting details like the technical realization on a distinct platform (the solution domain). This allows for a better integration of domain experts (e.g. game designers, game writers, concept artists) in the development process, faster iteration times, and implicit system documentation. Using code generation, the transition from problem space to solution space can be automated, which is more efficient and less error-prone than the manual implementation in a third generation language. Moreover, games feature characteristics of software product lines. Since product-line engineering is an explicit application field of MDSD [6], we see a perfect fit of game development and MDSD. By means of expressive and engaging software tools such as DSLs and generative tooling content authors and game designers are strongly integrated into the development process. That is why we think that game development and MDSD should get in touch in an ICEC workshop, which is an excellent setting for the much needed professional exchange of ideas, feedback from diverse experts, and lively discussions.

2   Workshop Objective

The workshop's main objective is to bring together researchers and professionals of both fields to identify how game development could benefit from MDSD and vice versa. This year, we focus on upcoming requirements in game development fields like novel authoring tools, scripting and programming languages, and agile workflows.

2.1   Proposed Form and Schedule

In order to accomplish the described objective, we plan to provide a full day workshop that is divided into five sections.

8:30 AM *Introduction and Overview*: We start with welcoming all participants, presenting the results of last year's workshop, and giving an overview on the workshop's schedule and goals.

9:00 AM *Future Challenges and Possibilities*: This section comprises two keynotes. One keynote is meant to illustrate the future challenges in game development. The second keynote will introduce current and upcoming developments in MDSD. Markus Vlter, author of several articles and books on MDSD (e.g. [6]), already expressed his interest in doing this keynote.

11:00 AM *Position Papers*: Selected researchers and industry professionals present their experiences and opinions on "model-driven game development", covering theories, techniques, tools, infrastructure, and boundaries of MDSD. In combination with the former section, this builds the basis for the upcoming panel discussion.

2:00 PM *Panel Discussion*: The panel discussion will be a moderated talk with two invited experts of each field (game development and MDSD). They will discuss the application possibilities of model-driven techniques in the context of future challenges in game development and how the agile development nature of games might influence MDSD techniques. The audience is meant to take an active part in the discussion, raising questions, commenting statements, and giving answers.

4:30 PM *Retrospective*: The first three sections are going to be protocolled by the workshop organizers. In the final section, they present the protocol to identify and evaluate the findings of the workshop together with the participants. As a result, this should lead to a compilation of valuable research and development questions.

5:00 PM *Close*.

2.2   Expected Workshop Outcome

The organizers will compile the results of the workshop, especially the identified research and development questions, in a white paper which will be published on the website of the workshop. In addition, the accepted position papers are published as part of the conference proceedings. The workshop website shall continue to be used as a means to connect the participants, facilitate further discussions and information exchange, and promotion of subsequent events. Another concrete result could be the planning of a special issue devoted to the workshop topic in a suitable journal such as Entertainment Computing or Computers in Entertainment.

3   Bio Information of Workshop Organizers

Robert Walter received a diploma in Software Engineering and a Master of Science in Computer Science. In his Ph.D. studies, he examines the game development process with a focus on the creation and processing of narrative game content, develops concepts for domain-specific languages (DSLs)[1], and tools for an improved integration of all stakeholders-from game writers over artists and voice actors to localization studios-into the game development process. The goal is to find patterns that reduce development time, effort, complexity, and costs.

Maic Masuch holds the chair of Media Technology and Entertainment Computing at the Faculty of Engineering, Department of Computer Science and

---

[1] "[A DSL is] a computer programming language of limited expressiveness focused on a particular domain." [7]

Cognitive Science at the University of Duisburg-Essen. He received his Ph.D. with a dissertation on computer animation at the University of Magdeburg and, in 2002, became Germany's first Professor for Computer Games. He founded two companies, researches in the field of game design and game development for over twelve years, and is one of the pioneers of German video game research.

Mathias Funk is a Postdoctoral Researcher at the Designed Intelligence group in the Department of Industrial Design of the Eindhoven University of Technology (TU/e). After graduating from RWTH Aachen University in Computer Science he did a PhD at TU/e on the topic of adaptive data collection from commercial products in the field. He is cofounder of UXsuite, a startup company for product experience analytics software. Among others, his research interests are domain-specific languages for creative stakeholders, rapid prototyping, and user experience.

4   Further Information

Further information on the workshop can be found at the workshop site `http://gd-mdsd.blogspot.com/`.

References

1. Hight, J., Novak, J.: Game Development Essentials: Game Project Management. Delmar Cengage Learning (2007)
2. Petrillo, F., Pimenta, M., Trindade, F., Dietrich, C.: What Went Wrong? A Survey of Problems in Game Development. Comput. Entertain. 7(1), 13:1–12:22 (2009)
3. Esmurdoc, C.: Postmortem: Behind The Scenes Of Brütal Legend (November 2009), `http://www.gamasutra.com/view/news/25799/Postmortem_Behind_The_Scenes_Of_Brutal_Legend.php` (last access: July 4, 2012)
4. Graft, K.: Racing Evolution: Forza 3 and the Changing Driving Sim, `http://www.gamasutra.com/view/feature/4144/racing_evolution_forza_3_and_the_.php` (last access: July 4, 2012)
5. Nutt, C.: Q&A: Valve's Swift On Left 4 Dead 2's Production, AI Boost (July 4, 2012), `http://www.gamasutra.com/view/news/25701/QA_Valves_Swift_On_Left_4_Dead_2s_Production_AI_Boost.php`
6. Stahl, T., Völter, M.: Model-Driven Software Development: Technology, Engineering, Management. Wiley (2006)
7. Fowler, M.: Domain-Specific Languages. Addison-Wesley Professional (2010)

PULP Scription: A DSL
for Mobile HTML5 Game Applications

Mathias Funk and Matthias Rauterberg

Department of Industrial Design, Eindhoven University of Technology,
Den Dolech 2, 5600MB Eindhoven, The Netherlands

Abstract. As applications and especially games are moving to the web
and mobile environments, different tools are needed to design these applications and their behavior. HTML5 in combination with JavaScript
is a promising basis for such applications on a wide range of platforms.
Content producers and designers often lack the tools for such developments, or the expertise to operate existing, but too complex tools. This
paper presents work in progress about a novel domain-specific language
(DSL) PULP that aims at closing this gap. The language allows ty-
ing content such as images and media files together by modeling the
dynamic behavior, movements, and control flow. The DSL helps abstracting from asynchronous JavaScript, state machines, and access to
cross-platform media playback, which is generated in a final model-to-
text transformation. The DSL and tooling were created and evaluated in
close cooperation with content authors.

1 Introduction

The application domain targeted in this paper is simple educational games for
children from 3–7 years. These games aim for instance at improving foreign
language skills in a playful way. The games support simple touch gestures and
allow for guiding the players with sounds and videos.

Producers of interactive content and applications for mobile devices face a
huge diversity of platforms to develop for: from Apple's iOS or Google's Android
platforms to Windows Mobile, Symbian, WebOS, Blackberry, and others there is
a variety of systems available. This often involves major additions and changes
to the user interface and thus leads to huge efforts spent on device specific code
and testing. Apart from simply selecting a subset of platforms to target, a recent
trend is to target the devices' browsers with HTML5, which is commonly supported on most platforms. HTML5 in connection with CSS3 not only supports
transitions, animations, often hardware-accelerated, but also allows for native
media playback and local storage of application data. The browser as a platform
also requires programming in addition to the content authoring, and although
the programming model is relatively light-weight (consisting of HTML5 markup,
styling and JavaScript programming), this expertise is often beyond the abilities
of content producers.

M. Herrlich, R. Malaka, and M. Masuch (Eds.): ICEC 2012, LNCS 7522, pp. 504–510, 2012.

The central problem statement can be formulated as: how can the authoring of interactive content on the web for next generation platforms and novel input methods be supported by modeling in the form of domain-specific languages as means to enable end-user programming with rapid iterations? Tackling this problem by designing a language should mainly involve the content author and her expertise as a domain expert. What is behind this problem is the assumption that content authors and designers can benefit from domain-specific languages which represent a formal description of the final product, but allow to specify in a way that resonates well with the working habits and prior expertise of the domain experts.

The paper introduces the domain-specific language PULP that allows for scripting all structural and behavioral aspects of an interaction HTML5 application. While images and media files represent the content basis of the application, PULP provides a structural skeleton which is enriched with behavior and styling. In the end, a fully working interactive application is generated.

2   Related Work

Different techniques exist to *author* dynamic HTML5 content: on the one hand programming techniques based on either front-end scripting or domain-specific languages with code generation, and on the other hand there are light-weight prototyping techniques based on image slices that are annotated with links to support page transitions. Examples for the first techniques which involve modeling are the WebDSL and Mobl languages[2,3].

While WebDSL enables the development of generic web applications with a DSL, the Mobl language focuses on mobile application development. Both DSLs are supported by generators that ease quick iterations by generating respective HTML and JavaScript artifacts on-the-fly. The generated artifacts assemble UI elements and add interaction possibilities. The second technique of visual rapid prototyping is based on image slices that are assembled to form the screens of the application, and their annotation to allow for limited interaction support[5,4]. PULP's usage domain, however, is situated in-between: the focus is on applications without predefined interface elements but with image objects that serve as actors which can be manipulated and which structure the user experience. PULP aims at designing for (novel) interfaces with touch and gesture support, as well as native sound and video output. At the same time, PULP is a textual DSL and allows for more control over the application structure, collaborative working and version control.

3   The DSL

The design of an appropriate domain-specific language PULP for the purpose of rapid prototyping of interactive (touch-based) applications needs to involve concepts of the domain as first-class citizens, but also the user of such a language having a distinct set of skills. The language concepts are explained in the following, before turning towards the necessary skills to master the language.

3.1   Language Concepts

As mentioned before, the users of the PULP language are designers and content creators for different interactive media. They are trained, sometimes even formally, to think in terms of canvases and objects within. Behind this is the notion of coordinate systems and pixels as the basic measure of distance within such systems. Often, these users have good understanding of the size of screen objects and can reliably estimate the pixel size of objects or distances. The PULP DSL draws on these skills as all screen objects and the screens are measured and positioned according to pixel counts. For the sake of simplicity, only absolute positioning is used as relative positioning of elements could potentially lead to obscure dependencies between screen objects. The second important skill of language users is the ability to not only position elements in 2D space, but also according to a z-index, i.e. the notion of screen layers. The language supports this by first the straightforward convention to place objects in order of appearance, and second by layers which may group objects on the same (layer) z-index.

A PULP script contains essentially a number of screens, therein, screen objects, and definitions of interactions upon these screen objects. These interactions are expressed as action chains. The language was designed such that the number of structural tokens such as "=>" or "{" and "}" is kept to a minimum, whereas operative (or more verbal) keywords have a direct counter part in observable functionality like "show", "hide", "move", and "play". The general terminology originally aligned with the analogy of a theater stage with background, foreground, actors and requisites. It later evolved to a more open theme of screens, screen objects, and interactions.

3.2   Screen Primitives

An application in PULP is first defined with a few global constants such as "title", "width", "height" and background color. Furthermore it is structured into different *screens* which can contain screen objects and associated interactions. Screen objects are divided into layers, images, and text. Layers enable grouping other screen objects and expressing a z-order on the screen. Images and text are defined with coordinates and size parameters, as well as optional styling (according to CSS3). In addition to screens, different media objects can be defined in a PULP application: videos, sounds, and voices. The difference between sounds and voices is the convention that sounds can be played in parallel, whereas voices are played exclusively to ensure understandability. Finally, a start screen is given for starting up the application.

3.3   Action Chains

An action chain consists of at least one action trigger and one action result. More than one action trigger define either an ordered sequence of actions that have to be performed by the user to reach an action result, or an arbitrary sequence of actions that are needed to trigger the action result. In general, sets of combined action triggers are useful for setting with *scripted* behavior that is expected from the user, such as learning environments, whereas single actions triggers are incorporated most for user interface prototypes that strive for simplicity and good usability.

An action chain is defined as:

```
Trigger (=> Trigger)* => Result (=> Result)*
```

An example is a click action on a predefined image that triggers sound playback followed by a screen change. Note that the image defines "click" as a possible action:

```
image showResults (images/btnShowResults.png) width 200 height 40 click
sound buttonSound (media/btnSound.mp3)
click showResults => play buttonSound => screen resultScreen
```

Multiple triggers within an action denote a simple form of a state machine: the results are only triggered in case all specified triggers are performed in the right order by the user. An example is entering a code ("4321") on a graphical numeric pad to gain access to the result screen:

```
image numPad1 (images/buttons/numPad1.png) click
image numPad2 (images/buttons/numPad2.png) click
...
click numPad4 => click numPad3
        => click numPad2 => click numPad1 => screen resultScreen
```

This last aspect of action chains enables to quickly prototype interactive applications with complex interaction patterns that would require larger efforts to achieve with manual JavaScript programming. PULP hides this complexity, and instead presents a designer-friendly, more application focused view on HTML5 scripting.

4   Tool Implementation and the HTML5 Generator

The PULP editor tool (cf. Fig. 1) is based on the Eclipse platform[1], and makes use of the Xtext domain-specific language toolkit[2] to provide a textual editor with syntax coloring, auto-completion, and validation. The generation step is a model-to-text generation of HTML and JavaScript code and it is enabled by the Xtend2[3] tools. The editor allows browsing image and media files while creating PULP language elements.

When a PULP file is saved in the editor, the PULP generator (for HTML5) runs automatically and creates a hierarchy of files in an /html/ subfolder where also the images and media files reside. The generator creates a single HTML file

---

[1] Eclipse: http://eclipse.org
[2] Xtext: http://eclipse.org/Xtext
[3] A part of Eclipse Xtext.

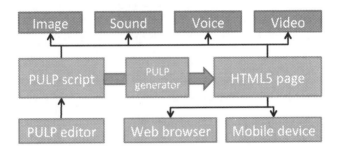

Fig. 1. Architecture of PULP tool chain with media and script artifacts

which first contains the declaration of all screens and screens object as HTML
`<div>`s and images, then the associated media files as HTML5 `<audio>` and
`<video>` objects. Finally, JavaScript is generated according to the given interaction capabilities and defined interaction of screen objects. The generated
JavaScript makes use of jQuery[4] and a few custom library functions.

5   Evaluation

A short informal evaluation of the tool has been carried out. In general, the
possibility to achieve small games with comparatively rich interaction and touch
gestures was received positively. During the evaluation, the participants were
presented first with an exemplary PULP script that demonstrates most of the
functionality and uses few pictures and media files to script an application.
Different items of the PULP script were explained and participants could ask
questions if necessary. This step took at most 15 minutes. In the next evaluation
phase the participants were asked to change minor parts of the PULP script, such
as positioning of images, and styling of text. Subsequently, the focus shifted to
modifying the interactions that were attached to the screen objects, e.g. changing
the click action on an image to a mouse-over action and triggering different
sounds after a drag and drop action. This second phase took at most 20 minutes.
In the third and last phase, participants were asked to be creative with their own
material that they brought to the evaluation. This last phase did not involve
extensive coaching anymore, and took about 25 minutes.

A more formal follow-up study is planned and will be carried out with a later
version of the tool. Interesting aspects of this evaluation will concern the creation of more complex control flows, visual positioning of elements, and embedding videos. Furthermore, tool iterations based on user feedback are expected to
motivate not only functional improvements, but also improvements of language
syntax and semantics.

---

[4] jQuery: http://jquery.org

6   Conclusions

This paper introduces a novel domain-specific language (DSL) for design and content authoring stakeholders in the domain of mobile games and other interactive applications. The potential range of applications is larger than shown in this paper, however, the gaming domain was chosen due to its focus and availability of professional users and testers. The emphasis is on enabling to script interaction flows, gestures and behavior in general. Combined with appealing visuals and supportive media such as object sounds and ambient atmospheres (potentially also video), applications created with PULP can convey a user experience that adequately matches the final product in its main lines. This rapid prototyped experience is important for showing the product vision as a clear goal during development, but also for demo purposes and early user feedback.

The presented DSL aims at simplifying programming tasks that would normally involve parallel and event-based programming paradigms, gesture handling, and handling of browser compatibility issues. The associated generator component takes a PULP file and linked media files as input and generates an entire HTML5 web application, which can be directly tested with a web browser.

Behind the PULP language and tools is the question whether DSLs can be applied successfully in the domain of design where the use of textual tools is not as common. DSLs naturally relate to modeling and formalization - therefore the question is extended to the applicability of (more or less formal) modeling in the design domain. The research on the PULP language aims at investigating this problem domain in the future. Further future work can be also derived from the evaluation, namely to ease the positioning of screen objects and to allow for prototyping other, more elaborate user interfaces that make use of gestures. Finally, prototyping efforts should be aligned with means to observe use flows[1] for the collection of user feedback during early stages of development.

References

1. Funk, M., van der Putten, P., Corporaal, H.: Analytics for the internet of things. In: CHI EA 2009: Proceedings of the 27th International Conference Extended Abstracts on Human Factors in Computing Systems, pp. 4195–4200. ACM, New York (2009)
2. Groenewegen, D.M., Hemel, Z., Kats, L.C.L., Visser, E.: Webdsl: a domain-specific language for dynamic web applications. In: Harris, G.E. (ed.) Companion to the 23rd Annual ACM SIGPLAN Conference on Object-Oriented Programming, Systems, Languages, and Applications, OOPSLA 2008, Nashville, TN, USA, October 19-13, 2007, pp. 779–780. ACM (2008)

3. Hemel, Z., Visser, E.: Declaratively programming the mobile web with mobl. In: Proceedings of the 26th Annual ACM SIGPLAN Conference on Object-Oriented Programming, Systems, Languages, and Applications, OOPSLA 2011, Portland, Oregon, USA. ACM (2011)

4. Hosseini-Khayat, A., Seyed, T., Burns, C., Maurer, F.: Low-fidelity prototyping of gesture-based applications. In: Proceedings of the 3rd ACM SIGCHI Symposium on Engineering Interactive Computing Systems, EICS 2011, pp. 289–294. ACM, New York (2011)

5. Jørgensen, A.P., Collard, M., Koch, C.: Prototyping iphone apps: realistic experiences on the device. In: Proceedings of the 6th Nordic Conference on Human-Computer Interaction: Extending Boundaries, NordiCHI 2010, pp. 687–690. ACM, New York (2010)

MDSD for Games with Eclipse Modeling Technologies

Steve A. Robenalt

Web Circuit, Cameron Park, CA 95682, USA
steve@webcircuit.com

Abstract. This paper describes an approach to be used to apply Model Driven Software Development (MDSD) techniques to the development of software for 3D games on multiple platforms, with additional usage in Scientific Visualization, Virtual Reality (VR), Augmented Reality (AR), and Animation applications. Specific areas of applicability for MDSD techniques include development tooling and artifact creation. The MDSD support for this functionality can be implemented as extensions to the Eclipse Platform augmented by a subset of the modeling projects that are available with Eclipse.

1 Introduction

The development of 3D game software presents some unique technical challenges when compared to other types of software. Principal among these challenges is the desirability of supporting multiple platforms with minimal effort and maximal (platform specific) performance. Supporting multiple platforms typically implies not only multiple programming languages (C, Objective-C, C++, Java, etc.), but also different graphics libraries (OpenGL, DirectX, OpenGL ES), different versions of those libraries (OpenGL 2.X, 3.X, and 4.X), and extensions that introduce features from later versions in conjunction with an earlier API version. Maximizing performance generally involves optimizing source code structure for specific target platforms, as well as taking advantage of newer graphics APIs or API extensions when they are available. In general, the selection of programming language has a lesser impact on performance when compared to the graphics libraries since the latter achieves performance improvements by exploiting hardware dedicated to the purpose (e.g. GPUs).

In practice, the choice of both programming language and graphics library are generally dictated by the hardware vendors and the supported operating systems for the target platforms.

The content of this paper is based heavily on the author's experience in developing and maintaining an Eclipse-based MDSD tool chain in an enterprise software environment, and on recent ongoing work to build Eclipse-based MDSD tooling for a new game engine architecture.

M. Herrlich, R. Malaka, and M. Masuch (Eds.): ICEC 2012, LNCS 7522, pp. 511–517, 2012.
© IFIP International Federation for Information Processing 2012

2   Existing Strategies

The conventional solution for supporting multiple platforms for game development involves the selection and modification (or less often, creation) of a game engine - a set of related software artifacts that have already been ported to multiple platforms - followed by customization of the result to include content based on the theme of the game under development. One of the earliest examples of a game engine was the Quake engine, used in the game of the same name. Other game engines are available as well, such as the Unreal engine, and the Unity 3D engine, which are both proprietary, and which provide a complete development environment and runtime for games that can be targeted to multiple platforms.

Cross platform support in these engines can be implemented using a variety of mechanisms, most of which are based on segregation of code into platform independent layers and platform specific layers, then using a combination of conditional compilation and conditional build steps to handle the targets.

Supporting multiple graphics (or other) libraries can use the same conditional compile/build facilities, or in more extreme cases, can cause the need to create separate but functionally equivalent (from the perspective of the game) versions of the same software, which can be maintained in parallel.

Alternatively, games can be implemented using a Virtual Machine approach with a common graphics API (e.g. Java Virtual Machine + Lightweight Java Game Library), in which case the game-specific code is platform neutral and the JVM and game library handle the platform specific differences. Note that in this case, the game library does not insulate the developer from handling multiple versions of the underlying OpenGL implementation, which is usually tied to the hardware and device drivers of the graphics adapter.

3   Model Driven Strategies

While the above methods for supporting multiple platforms have all been used over many years, and are successful to varying degrees, a newer approach involves the introduction of Model Driven Software Development (MDSD) techniques into the development process.

3.1   Idealized MDSD

In the idealized MDSD case, a single Platform Independent Model (PIM) of the game is created and maintained. For each target platform, the PIM is transformed into a Platform Specific Model (PSM), which reflects the constraints and capabilities of the target platform, then the PSM is transformed into source code that is specific to (and more optimized for) that particular target.[1]

3.2 Variations

There are many practical variations of this idealized case:

1. The transformation to PSM is omitted, and the required transformations are implemented in the source code templates.
2. The transformation from PSM to source code is omitted, and platform specific object code is produced directly from the PSM.
3. The PSM is interpreted directly by the game runtime, rather than compiled.
4. The transformation from PIM to PSM may also have multiple stages.

The use of these variations depends on a balance of complexity in the process relative to complexity in the tool chain (e.g. code templates). These variations generally do not impact the resulting generated code, but they do impact the creation and maintenance of the components of the MDSD tooling.

3.3 Advantages

The major advantages of the idealized case are:

1. The PIM becomes the single, definitive reference for all versions of the software.
2. The PIM is substantially simpler and more comprehensible than the source code it will eventually produce, thus it is quicker to create and easier to maintain.
3. The PSM provides an intermediate checkpoint where platform constraints can be validated and enforced.
4. The source code can also be audited to insure that it is complete, correct, and efficient.
5. The source code also provides the ability to debug code that contains errors, which can be traced back to the code templates.
6. Code consistency and quality improve quickly based on the use of few templates to generate many artifacts.

3.4 Disadvantages

The major disadvantages of the idealized case are:

1. A practical MDSD tool chain requires a consistent architecture in the PIM specification, and significant expertise in creating the code templates (i.e. most experienced personnel).
2. In practice, the PIM is often an incomplete model, which leaves parts of the application unspecified.
3. Compensating for an incomplete PIM generally means integrating generated and handwritten code, which requires care and planning.
4. Coordinating handwritten and generated code complicates the evolution of the software over time.

Compensating for these disadvantages can eliminate or substantially reduce their impact, but often, the insight needed to develop compensation only comes as a result of experience.

While the Idealized MDSD scenario has great potential, a more pragmatic approach is often appropriate. This approach involves applying MDSD selectively to parts of the development process. The artifacts that are selectively generated are then integrated into a standard development process involving code written by hand. This allows for selective introduction of MDSD into an existing development environment.

4   Using Eclipse for MDSD

Building an MDSD tool chain from scratch would be a very complex task. However, starting from existing tools which can be easily customized is much more feasible. The Eclipse Integrated Development Environment provides extensive support for MDSD tooling via numerous modeling related projects. Foremost among these is the Eclipse Modeling Framework [2], which provides the meta-model (Ecore) for many of the other projects, as well as for numerous non-modeling projects.

Some of the other relevant Eclipse modeling projects include:

1. CDO Model Repository - persistence and sharing of models.[1]
2. ATL - Model-to-model transformation (e.g. PIM to PSM).[2]
3. Xpand/Xtend - Model-to-text language for source code templates.[3]
4. Xtext - Domain Specific Language creation toolkit.[4]
5. Modeling Workflow Engine - Coordinated execution of the MDSD tool chain.[5]
6. OCL - Declarative specification of model constraints.[6]

By combining these projects, and optionally using some of the other related projects, a sophisticated MDSD tool chain for game development can be produced in a comparatively short period of time. In particular, the Xtext project provides good integration of text-based models into Eclipse itself, leveraging the support provided by the IDE when editing models and building artifacts from them.

Note that Eclipse has utility in the game development community outside of the above noted Modeling projects. Eclipse was created originally to integrate the diverse sets of tools used in software development into a common environment using a plug-in based architecture that simplifies integration. The same approach is feasible when applied to the many artifacts needed to create games.

---

[1] http://www.eclipse.org/cdo/
[2] http://www.eclipse.org/atl/
[3] http://www.eclipse.org/xtend/
[4] http://www.eclipse.org/Xtext/
[5] http://www.eclipse.org/projects/project.php?id=modeling.emf.mwe
[6] http://www.eclipse.org/modeling/mdt/?project=ocl

5   Applying MDSD Techniques

The next section describes how MDSD techniques and the Eclipse modeling projects can be combined and used in various parts of the game development cycle.

5.1   Development Tooling

The development of games requires the production and coordination of a large number of artifacts, both in the form of descriptive elements representing the game environment, and in the production of source code that renders the environment, allows player interactions, handles the progress of play, and renders the scene in the environment frequently enough to provide smooth animation.

Environment Creation. A large number of descriptive elements are used in the construction of game environments. The following are some major classes of these elements:

1. Geometry - Mathematical descriptions of the surfaces of the environment, players, and objects comprising the game.
2. Textures - Descriptions of surface textures, either through stored or dynamically created images projected onto the geometry.
3. Attributes - Details (e.g. material properties) added to the geometric elements to enhance the realism of the environment.
4. Lighting - Location and nature of light sources which affect the visible properties of the elements of the environment.
5. Animation - Definitions of how elements of the environment change over time, both independently, and in response to player actions.
6. Sounds - Used to enhance the realism of the environment; generally tied together with animations or player actions.

Development tooling can be provided to support the creation and maintenance of each of these classes of elements, while MDSD tooling can be used to project these elements to the target environment. For example, the PIM for surface geometry would store surface descriptions using double precision floating point numbers, while the transformation to the PSM and then source code would reduce the surface description to single precision or fixed point numbers based on the capabilities of the target.

Shader Programs. One of the major changes that has been driving improvements in the performance and realism of games for the last several years has been the introduction of programmable hardware, along with the development of Domain Specific Languages (DSLs)[3] that are used to write the programs. For historical reasons, these languages are commonly called shader languages, named for type of artifact they were originally used to create. More recently, these programs have been used to create animation effects, and even to handle more general workloads such as physics calculations.

One of the most common DSLs used for this purpose is GLSL[4],[5], which is part of the OpenGL specifications[6],[7]. Based on the need to keep up with performance improvements made possible by hardware enhancements, and to reflect the growing diversity of computational tasks that are being delegated to the GPU, the GLSL language itself has changed substantially in recent years. Also, the GLSL language has variants that are specific to specific parts of the programmable hardware.

MDSD techniques can be used for tooling support for shader programs in two distinct areas. The first area involves using the Xtext DSL toolkit to add support to the Eclipse IDE for GLSL as a language. This provides for productivity enhancements such as syntax highlighting in editors and code completion suggestions. The second area involves modeling the shader progams using a PIM, then adding PSMs and source templates to target the shader programs to multiple versions, or even to alternative shader languages.

5.2 Artifact Creation

One of the primary uses for MDSD techniques involves the ability to support multiple target platforms from the same PIM. Depending on the diversity of target platforms to be supported, source code artifacts must be created to account for many variations:

1. OS/Window System - Windows, OSX, Linux, IOS, Android, Firefox, Chrome
2. Platform Type - Desktop, Tablet, Phone, Browser
3. Programming Language - C, C++, Java, Objective-C
4. API Version - OpenGL 2.X, 3.X, 4.X, OpenGL ES 2.X, WebGL, DirectX

Creating these artifacts involves developing model-to-model transformations for the PIM to PSM phase, and model-to-text templates for the source code creation phase. The number and complexity of the transformations and templates can vary based on the valid combinations of the above factors, but in general, is a small fraction of the number of actual artifacts that are generated.

6   Summary

There are many areas of game software development where MDSD techniques can be exploited to streamline the development process and improve code consistency and quality. The Eclipse IDE and Modeling frameworks provide a solid foundation upon which a game-specific MDSD tool chain can be built, and the resulting tools can be integrated into Eclipse itself to augment existing development processes.

Since the application of MDSD tools in other software disciplines (notably enterprise and mobile) has yielded substantial benefits, there is certainly a strong motivation to pursue MDSD in game development as well.

References

1. Kleppe, A., Warmer, J., Bast, W.: MDA Explained. The Model Driven Architecture: Practice and Promise, pp. 5–8. Addison-Wesley (2003)
2. Steinberg, D., Budinsky, F., Paternostro, M., Merks, E.: EMF Eclipse Modeling Framework, 2nd edn. Addison-Wesley (2009)
3. Fowler, M., Parsons, R.: Domain-Specific Languages. Addison-Wesley (2010)
4. http://www.opengl.org/documentation/glsl/
5. Rost, R.J., Licea-Kane, B., et al.: OpenGL Shading Language. Addison Wesley (2010)
6. http://www.opengl.org/documentation/
7. Shreiner, D.: OpenGL Programming Guide, 7th edn. Addison Wesle (2010)

A Feature-Based Environment for Digital Games

Victor T. Sarinho[1], Antônio L. Apolinário Jr.[2], and Eduardo S. Almeida[3]

[1] DEXA – State University of Feira de Santana (UEFS),
Feira de Santana, Bahia, Brazil
vsarinho@gmail.com
[2] Federal University of Bahia (UFBA),
Salvador, Bahia, Brazil
[3] Reuse in Software Engineering (RiSE),
Salvador, Bahia, Brazil
{apolinario,esa}@dcc.ufba.br

Abstract. Digital games can be considered as an important software development area in our society. This paper proposes the Object Oriented Feature Modeling (OOFM) usage in the digital game domain. It aims to represent and manipulate distinct game features, defined by NESI and GDS models, in a parameterized and hierarchical way. As a result, a Feature-based Environment for Digital Games (FEnDiGa) is provided, a product line platform able to integrate and adapt represented game features in different types of available game engines.

Keywords: Digital game domain, game features, OOFM, FEnDiGa.

1 Introduction

Digital games can be considered as an important software development area in our society. Analyzing the digital game domain, it is possible to verify multiple examples of game genres and categories presenting common features among them [1], distinct modeling approaches able to represent digital games [2, 3], and a great influence of game engines during game design and implementation activities [4].

This paper proposes the Object Oriented Feature Modeling (OOFM) [5] usage in the digital games domain. It aims to manage distinct *game features* provided by NESI [2] and GDS [3] models in a specialized OOFM structure, providing the *game logic*, *rules* and *goals* (the G-Factor [4]) in a *parameterized* and *hierarchical* way. As a result, the *Feature-based Environment for Digital Games* (FEnDiGa) is provided, a software structure able to *integrate* and *adapt* represented *game features* in different types of available game engines.

The reminder of this paper presents three game development steps necessary to provide and use the FEnDiGa structure: 1) the variability documentation of digital games in a generic way; 2) the creation of a feature-based environment and process able to work with generic game features; and 3) the configuration of feature game resources in order to provide a final game.

M. Herrlich, R. Malaka, and M. Masuch (Eds.): ICEC 2012, LNCS 7522, pp. 518–523, 2012.

2   Step 1: Documenting the Game Variability

An interesting problem in the digital game domain is the representation of game characteristics. There are many types of game representation approaches in the literature presenting a lot of game elements, game behaviors and so on. In a previous work [2, 3], two distinct generic feature models were proposed (Fig. 1): the NESI model, documenting the conceptual variability of a digital game, and the GDS model, documenting the implementation variability of a digital game.

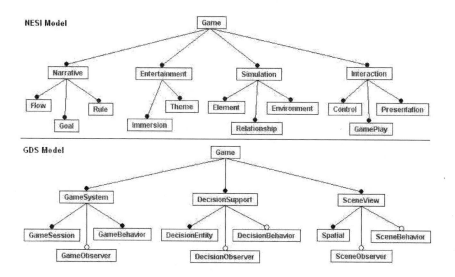

Fig. 1. The NESI and GDS models

The NESI model [2] defines a digital game as a combination of *Narrative, Entertainment, Simulation* and *Interaction*. A *Narrative* is a *Flow*, a dynamic script trying to achieve *Goals* following defined *Rules* of a game. *Entertainment* is represented by the player *Immersion* during the gameplay, following a *Theme* proposal to integrate the player and the game in the proposed reality. *Simulation* is a combination of *Elements* (resources to play) and respective *Relationships* that happen in a defined *Environment* (spaces to play). The human *Interaction* is represented by *Control* (game inputs) and *Presentation* (game outputs), consolidated by the *GamePlay* that represents a current game execution as a whole. With these main features, other sub-features related to game concepts were defined, providing more than 350 conceptual game features to be configured and manipulated by game designers.

On the other hand, the GDS model [3] defines a digital game as a combination of *GameSystem, DecisionSupport* and *SceneView* main features, generating more than 250 related sub-features. The *GameSystem* feature is the main joint point of a game. It is responsible to control the game execution, describing available *GameBehaviors, GameContext* and *GameObservers* for a digital game. The *DecisionSupport* feature is an effort to integrate some artificial intelligence strategies used by different digital games, presenting *DecisionEntities*, the *ContextState* of each *DecisionEntity*, *Decisio-nObservers* monitoring *DecisionEntities* values, and predefined *DecisionBehaviors* able to read and update *DecisionEntities* and *ContextStates* values during their execu-tions. The *SceneView* feature is a collection of *SceneNodes* distributed by *Spatial* sessions with various *SceneBehaviors* and *SceneObservers* able to perform scene actions in a game. A *SceneNode* represents a collection of information about the scene, describing specific *Location* and *BoudingVolume* for collision detection among other scene nodes, as well as hierarchical information about *AudioNode*, *Graphic-Node* and *PhysicsNode* simultaneously.

3   Step 2: Creating a Feature-Based Environment

NESI and GDS models describe generic and distinct Feature Models (FMs) and Fea-ture Configurations (FC) for digital games. OOFM provides basic elements (*Feature-Type*, *Feature*, and so on) to work with represented FMs and FCs. The *OOFM Framework* [5] is a combination of OOFM elements plus extra classes, interfaces and packages that follows the Model-View-Controller (MVC) architectural pattern [6]. It defines abstract *FeatureState*, *feature observer*, *FeatureBehavior* and *Adapter* struc-tures in order to organize the production of final system for represented FMs and FCs.

FEnDiGa is a concrete specialization of the *OOFM Framework* focused on the digital game domain (Fig. 2). It is a game development environment that: *represents game features* based on NESI and GDS models via OOFM resources; *combines game features* using the proposed OOFM Framework structures, and *implements game fea-tures* using specialized adapters of desired game engines.

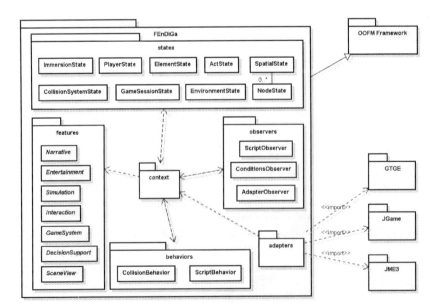

Fig. 2. The FEnDiGa architecture

The *representation of game features* are performed by *FeatureClass* structures [5]. They are created for each main feature of the respective NESI and GDS models (game feature containers), presenting feature methods that prepare each *featureModel* and respective *featureConfigurations* for games.

The *integration of represented game features* can be performed by *FeatureState*, *feature observer* and *FeatureBehavior* specializations. Using a *FeatureState*, different game features (but representing similar characteristics) can be used to model a common state. A good example is the *ElementState* class, which is a combination of *Element*, *Avatar* and *DecisionEntity* game features.

FeatureState instances can be monitored by *FeatureStateObserver* instances, which are triggered whenever a *FeatureState* update is applied. They verify collisions among *Element* instances or updates in current values of *Avatar Skills*, for example. When a *feature observer* is triggered, a *FeatureBehavior* instance is performed, providing support for game behaviors described by *game features*, such as *Action*, *Relationship*, *GameBehavior*, *DecisionBehavior* and *SceneBehavior*.

Finally, for the *implementation of game features*, it consists of preparing specific *Adapter* instances to reflect available *features* and *FeatureState* instances in the desired game engine. They are the main interface among game engines procedures and represented *game features* in order to execute the configured game.

Moreover, considering the FEnDiGa development steps, *features* and *states* can be configured by *Game Designers* and *Game Programmers*, *observers* and *behaviors* can be contextualized by *Game Programmers*, and *adapters* can be provided and used by *Game Engine Specialists* and *Game Programmers*, respectively. Fig. 3 illustrates this game development process, describing their game actors and important game development activities.

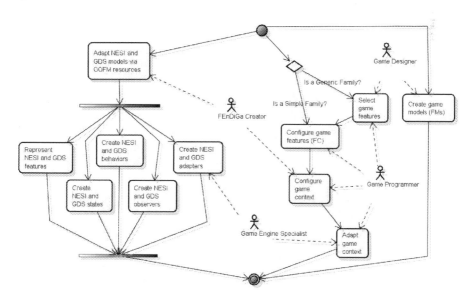

Fig. 3. The FEnDiGa development process

4   Step 3: Configuring the *SimplifiedPacman* Game

With FEnDiGa structures ready to be instantiated by the FEnDiGa development process, the next step is the development of a final game (*SimplifiedPacman* in this case) by the configuration and interpretation of adapted *game features*.

Initially, identified *game features* based on NESI and GDS models are instantiated via FEnDiGa by the game developer. Next, several game *states*, such as *pacmanState* and *pillState*, are created to represent and integrate instantiated *features*. *Feature* updates and the notification of *FeatureState* updates are performed by *behavior* instances, which are defined by *ScriptBehavior* (such as *pacmanDieBehavior*) and *FeatureBehavior* specializations (*movePacmanBehavior*, for example). Also, for feature *observer* instances based on condition evaluation (*collisionSystemObserver*) and defined *ScriptObserver* (*lifeEndEvent*) results, they evaluate desired game *states* and indicate which *behaviors* must be performed, according to *observer* results. Finally, for the adaptation process, *Adapter* interfaces are implemented, such as *SimplifiedPacmanSpriteAdapter* and *SimplifiedPacmanJGObjectAdapter*, in order to adapt available engine resources (such as *Sprite* and *JGObject*) for defined FEnDiGa structures. They are used by engine procedures (such as *init*, *start, render*, and so on) in order to associate an engine behavior for each adapted *state* in a game.

As a result, by the proposed configuration of *features*, *states*, *behaviors*, *observers* and *adapters*, a complete structure for the *SimplifiedPacman* game, ready to be performed, is provided. Fig. 4 illustrates the *SimplifiedPacman* final architecture, adapted to three distinct game engines (GTGE, JGame and JME3) [7].

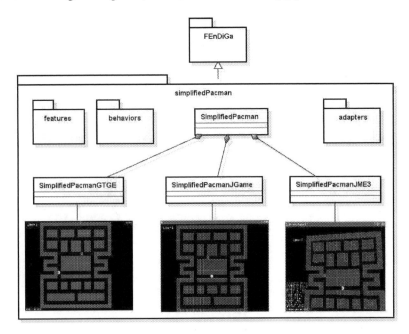

Fig. 4. The *SimplifiedPacman* game achitecture

5   Conclusions and Future Work

This paper presented the application of the OOFM technique in the development of digital games represented by NESI and GDS feature models. For that, the FEnDiGa structure and development process were defined, providing a game development environment able to integrate conceptual and implementation aspects of games.

By the FEnDiGa usage, the game development work can be resumed to: instantiate representative *features* of a game; define *states*, *observers* and *behaviors* to represent a game context based on instantiated *features*; and define which *states* will be worked by *adapters* during the game execution in a final game engine.

Several types of combinations among defined FEnDiGa structures can also be performed, allowing as a result a great level of reuse for game categories represented by *features* (the game mixing). In addition, NESI and GDS specializations can be also supported, allowing the production of customized frameworks for games and game sub-domains (FEnDiGa-RPG) according to designer interests.

In other words, by the FEnDiGa usage, the game logic becomes *standardized* (based on NESI and GDS models), *portable* (G-Factor [4] in an independent way via *Adapters* usage) and *reusable* (distinct combination of *game features*) in a new software development approach.

For future work, some extra activities will be performed, such as the evaluation and simplification of NESI and GDS models, the development of FEnDiGa supporting tools, and the FEnDiGa usage in different game development approaches (engines, frameworks), categories (RPG, FPS, Adventure) and complexities (complete games instead of simplified versions, collaborative development, etc.).

References

1. Wolf, M.: The Medium of the Video Game. University of Texas Press (2002) ISBN: 029279150X
2. Sarinho, V., Apolinário, A.: A Feature Model Proposal for Computer Games Design. In: Proceedings of the VII Brazilian Symposium on Computer Games and Digital Entertainment, Belo Horizonte, pp. 54–63 (2008)
3. Sarinho, V., Apolinário, A.: A Generative Programming Approach for Game Development. In: Proceedings of the VIII Brazilian Symposium on Computer Games and Digital Entertainment, Rio de Janeiro, pp. 9–18 (2009)
4. Binsubaih, A., Maddock, S.: Game Portability Using a Service-Oriented Approach. IJCGT 2008, Article ID 378485, 7 pages (2008)
5. Sarinho, V., Apolinario, A.: Combining feature modeling and Object Oriented concepts to manage the software variability. In: Proceedings of the IEEE IRI 2010, August 4-6, pp. 344–349 (2010)
6. Krasner, E., Pope, T.: A cookbook for using the MVC user interface paradigm in Smalltalk-80. J. Object Oriented Program 1, 26–49 (1988)
7. List of game engines. From Wikipedia, the free encyclopedia, http://en.wikipedia.org/wiki/List_of_game_engines

Automating the Implementation of Games Based on Model-Driven Authoring Environments

Christos Karamanos and Nikitas M. Sgouros

Department of Digital Systems, University of Piraeus
18534, Piraeus, Greece
ckar2006@yahoo.com, sgouros@unipi.gr

Abstract. In recent years the emergence of multiple game platforms (e.g., mobile, specialized consoles, PC) along with the rising interest in game creation by users with limited technical background calls for the development of high level authoring environments that base the creation process on abstract game models and automate their implementation. This paper describes our research towards the creation of such a development and execution environment that incorporates a graphical authoring environment based on an abstract model of common action RPG games along with a 3-D rendering client that automatically translates the resulting game into an OpenGL ES implementation.

Keywords: Authoring & Content Creation, Domain Modeling & Software Generation.

1 Introduction

In recent years the emergence of multiple game platforms (e.g., mobile devices, specialized consoles, PC) has placed a considerable burden on game development thus creating the need for authoring tools that can automate multi-platform implementation. In addition, the rising interest in game creation by users with limited technical background calls for the development of high level authoring environments that focus the development efforts on describing the game idea rather than on its specific technical implementation. This can be made possible through the development of abstract game models that capture the basic characteristics of whole classes of games and allow for different instantiations of this basic model through appropriate authoring environments.

As a first step towards the development of model-driven authoring this paper describes a game creation environment that seeks to provide high level authoring capabilities for a popular class of games we refer to as *action RPGs*. In these games the player moves in 3-D space having to face a series of enemies and escape from certain traps while collecting treasure items and various devices that boost his health and physical abilities. Collecting a certain amount of treasure items allows the user to terminate successfully the game, while decreasing its health level to zero after a series of unsuccessful battles leads to unsuccessful termination of the game.

M. Herrlich, R. Malaka, and M. Masuch (Eds.): ICEC 2012, LNCS 7522, pp. 524–529, 2012.
© IFIP International Federation for Information Processing 2012

The game environment provides a graphical authoring tool that allows a user with limited technical background to specify the plan of the 3-D space that comprises the game space and the location and attributes of the rest of the game elements (enemies, traps, treasures, health points, enhancement items), In addition, the specifications created by the user are then fed to a rendering client that automatically creates and manages the 3-D game environment based on the specifications it receives via the Web from the authoring system. The authoring and rendering systems run as separate applications. In particular, the authoring environment runs as a Web application, while the rendering client executes on a variety of computing devices that will eventually run the game since it is built using OpenGL ES.

While there has been significant work on general-purpose game engines (e.g. Unity, JMonkey, Unreal) the use of these engines require significant technical background and programming expertise. There has been considerable research in game authoring environments for users with non-technical background mainly centered on the development of scripting environments [1-2] and an interpreter for executing the scripts, or on the use of UML-based models [3]. While this approach can support simple games in 2-D environments, as we move to 3-D and/or increase the complexity of the games in terms of the characters and objects involved the amount of scripting grows significantly making the addition of functionality and debugging these scripts increasingly difficult. Our approach offers a more user friendly solution to users with limited technical background based on deciding what game model to use and providing graphical ways of configuring basic features of each game model. In addition, the rendering client can be used as a stand-alone game engine API allowing for in-depth modification of the resulting game.

Game Maker [4] is a popular development tool that provides a graphical front-end to an interpreted scripting language (GML) for game creation. Our approach seeks to create a development environment on a higher level of abstraction than Game Maker. In our system users graphically configure complete game models thus significantly reducing the need for scripting. In addition, there is no need for a special-purpose scripting language since the game models can be directly mapped to OpenGL implementations thus providing more efficient and portable implementations.

In the rest of this paper, section 2 describes in detail the graphical authoring environment while section 3 presents our work-in-progress in developing the rendering client. Finally, section 4 is a discussion and future work section.

2   The Authoring Environment

The authoring environment models game space as a 2-D grid that will be subsequently mapped by the rendering client to a 3-D space. There are two main character types (see Fig. 1) that can move around in game space: players (controlled by users) and enemies (that are opponents to the players and controlled by the rendering client). Each grid cell may possess one or more of the following nine primary attributes: (i) Clear (the cell has no attributes) (ii) Wall (the cell contains a motion obstacle) (ii) Trap (the cell contains a trap which has a negative effect on some of the player's attributes (e.g. speed, agility)) (iv) Enemy Control Area (the cell is within an area that an enemy can move into) (v) Player (the cell currently contains a player) (vi) Enemy (the cell currently contains an enemy) (vii) Treasure (the cell contains an effect that influences positively the material rewards obtained by a game character) (iix) Buff (the cell contains an effect that gives a beneficial boost to the performance of a game character) (ix) Health (the cell contains an effect that gives a beneficial boost to the health of a game character).

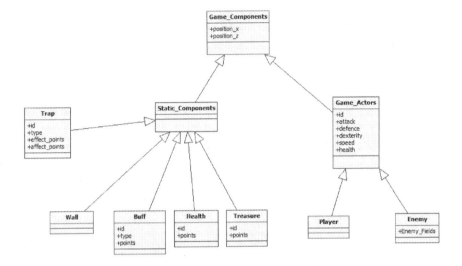

Fig. 1. Class diagram of the available game components

When combined these primary attributes give rise to fourteen composite attributes for each cell (e.g., Buff in Enemy Control Area, Health in Enemy Control Area, Player in Enemy Control Area etc). In addition, the author now has to set attribute values for the game characters (players & enemies) and the rest of the game features (health items, treasure items, enhancement items, traps). For the player type these include setting points in a numerical scale for: (i) Speed (how fast the player moves in game space) (ii) Health (how fit is the game character) (iii) Attack (the potential for winning a battle with an enemy as an attacker) (iv) Defense (the potential for winning a battle with an enemy as a defender) (v) Agility (the ability to escape from a trap).

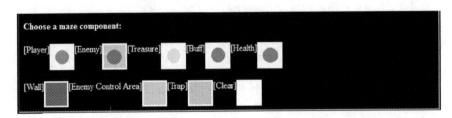

Fig. 2. Graphical representation of the available game components

For the enemy type the game author can set the same attribute values as the ones for the player type. In addition the author can set the value of the Enemy Areas attribute which describes the set of grid cells in which the specific enemy can move.

For health items, the game author can set the amount of health points the item would have in a numerical scale. The player's total health points will increase according to these points when player retrieves the health item.

For treasure items, the game author can set the amount of treasure points the item would have in a numerical scale. The player's total treasure points will increase according to these points when player retrieves the treasure item.

For enhancement items (buffs), the game author can set values for: (i) Buff Type (the player's attribute that will be enhanced if player retrieves the enhancement item – attack, defense, speed, agility) (ii) Buff Points (the amount of enhancement points).

For trap items, game author can set values for (i) Trap Type (the player's attribute that will be affected/decreased if player activates the trap) (ii) Trap Effect Points (the trap's activation threshold) (iii)Trap Affect Points (the amount of decreased points after trap activation)

A player and an enemy battle each other whenever their distance becomes less than an amount defined by the rendering client. In this case the rendering client randomly assigns to one of the characters the role of the attacker while the other one becomes the defender (the roles of the characters change consecutively while the battle progresses). A random value is added to the attack/defense attribute of the attacker/defender and the winner of the battle is the character with the larger value of his corresponding attribute which is then subtracted from the health points of the losing character. The encounter continues until the player escapes the battle by increasing the distance against the enemy more than the defined threshold or if one of the characters loses all its health points.

For each trap the game author specifies its activation and affect values. Each time a player/enemy enters a trap a random value is added to the value of his agility and their total is compared with the activation value for the trap. If this total is larger, the player/enemy escapes from the trap unharmed. Otherwise, the value of one of his attributes (attack, defense, speed, agility) defined by the author for this trap is reduced by the affect value of the trap.

While a trap reduces the value of a character attribute, a buff increases the value of a chosen attribute by an amount set by the game author. Finally, a treasure increases the value of a treasure item that is defined by the author. For each treasure item the author defines a specific amount for its successful collection. Successfully collecting all treasure items provides a winning terminating condition for a player in the game.

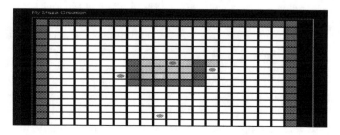

Fig. 3. A snapshot of the 2-D game grid with some of the components defined

Figures 2 and 3 provide snapshots of the graphical environment used during authoring. The technologies used for the development of the application are: Spring Framework MVC, Java, JSP, JSTL, CSS, Javascript – JQuery, AJAX. Execution of the editor is implemented using an Apache Tomcat web server. The Spring Framework MVC (Model View Controller) was used to make the application parts easier to recognize and manage. As a framework that is based on the MVC model, it consists of three distinct entities (model, view and controller) and provides a clear division between them. Business logic and user interface are treated as totally two different layers that are easy to manage. The use of Spring annotations makes request handling easy and straightforward. Furthermore, the ability to use features such as security and role management for future expansion of the editor, makes Spring fit for use as the base of the Web client. The operational logic of the application was implemented in Java while the client side (View) consists of a set of JSP pages formatted with CSS and using Javascript – JQuery. AJAX technology was used for the direct communication between the client and the server so that the request-response to materialize without being visible to the user during the construction of the game space.

3   The Rendering Client

The rendering client is responsible for creating and executing the game based on the specifications received by the authoring system. In addition it can be used as a stand-alone game management API as long as it receives game specifications that are compatible with the ones created by the authoring system. It is implemented in Java based on the OpenGL ES API. Figure 4 provides a snapshot of the game environment created by the client on a mobile device.

4   Discussion and Future Work

We describe our research towards the creation of authoring environments based on abstract game models that describe the basic characteristics for whole classes of games and allow their automatic instantiation in a variety of computing platforms. These game models provide configurable implementations for all the mechanics in each game type including player management, terrain generation, navigation and interaction among the game objects. Our approach seeks to eliminate the need for special-purpose scripting languages by providing direct mapping of the game models to OpenGL implementations. There are a lot of open problems that need to be addressed in order for this approach to become feasible. In particular, there is the need for the development of automated synthesis capabilities so that parts of different game models could be combined in order to automatically create implementations for new types of games not envisaged by the system. Furthermore, the complexity of the mapping between game specification and its implementation is expected to increase as the game models are extended to describe higher level behavior between game objects (e.g., conflicting goal-driven behavior between characters) and more complex plot structures (e.g. aristotelian plot conceptions). More immediate future work in this area is focused on running user trials of the authoring and rendering systems along with the development of abstract models for other classes of games (e.g., sports, business or social games) and the provision of multiplayer capabilities in the rendering client.

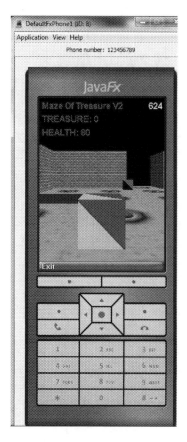

Fig. 4. Snapshot of the rendering client depicting the player (the blue & yellow cube) close to a trap (the green floor) facing an enemy (the black & purple cube) and a health item (the blue cube)

Acknowledgments. Presentation of this work was partially supported by the University of Piraeus Research Center.

References

1. McNaughton, M., Cutimisu, M., Szafron, D., Schaeffer, J., Redford, J., Parker, D., Scriptease: Generative design patterns for computer role-playing games. In: 19th IEEE Int. Conf. on Automated Software Engineering, pp. 88–99 (2004)
2. MIT, Scratch (2009), http://scratch.mit.edu
3. Reyno, E.M., Carsi Cubel, J.A.: Automated Prototyping in Model-Driven Game Development. Computers in Entertainment (CIE) 7(2) (2009)
4. Habgood, J., Overmars, M.: The Game Maker's Apprentice. APress (2006)

Game Developers Need Lua AiR
Static Analysis of Lua Using Interface Models

Paul Klint[1], Loren Roosendaal[2], and Riemer van Rozen[3]

[1] Centrum Wiskunde & Informatica*
[2] IC3D Media
[3] Amsterdam University of Applied Sciences*

Abstract. Game development businesses often choose Lua for separating scripted game logic from reusable engine code. Lua can easily be embedded, has simple interfaces, and offers a powerful and extensible scripting language. Using Lua, developers can create prototypes and scripts at early development stages. However, when larger quantities of engine code and script are available, developers encounter maintainability and quality problems. First, the available automated solutions for interoperability do not take domain-specific optimizations into account. Maintaining a coupling by hand between the Lua interpreter and the engine code, usually in C++, is labour intensive and error-prone. Second, assessing the quality of Lua scripts is hard due to a lack of tools that support static analysis. Lua scripts for dynamic analysis only report warnings and errors at run-time and are limited to code coverage. A common solution to the first problem is developing an Interface Definition Language (IDL) from which "glue code", interoperability code between interfaces, is generated automatically. We address quality problems by proposing a method to complement techniques for Lua analysis. We introduce Lua AiR (Lua Analysis in Rascal), a framework for static analysis of Lua script in its embedded context, using IDL models and Rascal.

1 Introduction

Game developers use script languages to develop and maintain game logic separately from game engine libraries. Lua is a script language [1] in the form of an ANSI C library[1] developed by Ierusalimschy, de Figueiredo and Celes. During its evolution [2] Lua has gradually matured and has remained light-weight. Moreover, it is an embeddable, minimalistic yet extensible, general purpose, dynamically typed script language. Its language design trade-offs, displayed in Table 1, have shaped the co-development of the embedding API and script features [3]. Lua is popular in game development. Using Lua, developers can quickly create prototypes. However, using Lua also comes at a cost. In later development stages, when larger quantities of engine library code and game script are available, developers encounter maintainability and quality problems.

---

* This work is part of the EQuA project. http://www.equaproject.nl/
[1] http://www.lua.org/

M. Herrlich, R. Malaka, and M. Masuch (Eds.): ICEC 2012, LNCS 7522, pp. 530–535, 2012.
© IFIP International Federation for Information Processing 2012

Table 1. Lua Design Trade-offs

Lua feature	Trade-off	Mitigating argument
Light-weight	Large responsibility to its users	Well-defined responsibilities
Dynamic typing	Lack of static type checking	Flexibility of use
Maintainable C	Lack of pure speed	Embedded in efficient C
General-purpose	Lack of domain-specific features	Extensible script language
Simple	High use of few APIs	Low learning curve
Embeddable	Need for interoperability code	This code can be generated

First, using a standard generator for the coupling between Lua and the game libraries sacrifices speed, and maintaining a hand-written coupling with domain-specific optimizations is labour intensive and error-prone. Second, assessing the quality of Lua scripts is hard due to a lack of tools that support source level *static analysis*, which entails computing information about scripts before run-time. The commonly used Lua scripts for dynamic analysis only report warnings and errors at run-time, and are limited to code coverage. Static analyses do exist, but are mainly applied to intermediate representations in Single Static Assignment (SSA) forms for run-time optimization, e.g. LuaJIT[2] and the run-time specializations of Williams *et al.* [4].

Both problems increase with scale and special measures are necessary for ensuring maintainability and code quality. A common solution to the first problem is to develop an Interface Definition Language (IDL) from which optimized *"glue code"*, interoperability code between interfaces, is generated automatically. However, code quality problems remain to be addressed. Quality problems are not unique to Lua. Blow [5] expresses increased complexity and lack of development tools and White *et al.* [6] describe the need for better script notation. Ramsey and Assis [7] express the need of the Lua community for machine-checkable APIs including types, whole-program and modular static analysis and static type inference. Providing practical methods for static analysis of Lua is hard because static analysis algorithms are subject to a trade-off between speed and precision and developers require exact and immediate feedback during development.

We address script quality problems by proposing a method to complement analysis techniques of Lua. We describe an approach in collaboration with IC3D Media that uses the Rascal Meta-Programming Language[3] [8]. IC3D Media is a Dutch SME located in Breda, active in games for entertainment and training. We introduce Lua Analysis in Rascal (Lua AiR), a framework for static analysis of Lua script in its embedded context, using IDL models.

2   Static Analysis of Lua

We can think of scripts as having many run-time states reachable via possibly many execution paths. Running every program path is infeasible, but abstracting

---

[2] http://luajit.org/
[3] http://www.rascal-mpl.org/

Table 2. Static Analysis: Features and Tools

	Tools				
	LDT	**Lua Inspect**	**Lua Checker**	**Lua for IDEA**	**Lua AiR**
tool characterization	Eclipse IDE	SciTE/VIM plug-in, HTML output	command-line simplifier & checker tools	IntelliJIDEA plug-in	Meta-Framework, Eclipse IDE
based on	Metalua	Metalua	lex/yacc, Lua	Kahlua	Rascal MPL
affiliation	Eclipse, Sierra Wireless	David Manura	Google	Jon Akhtar	HvA, CWI, EQuA project
1 globals & locals (definition and use)	yes	yes	strict declare before use	yes	yes
2 var use must be undefined	no	yes	yes (locals)	yes (locals)	yes
3 var use may be undefined	no	no	no, disallowed	no	not yet
4 link a definition to its uses	highlight all	yes	no	yes	yes (no color)
5 link a use to its definitions	occurrences	yes	no	yes	yes (no color)
4 definition must be unused	no	yes	no	yes	not yet
5 definition may be unused	no	no	no	no	not yet
6 duplicate local declaration	no	yes, mask(ed)	yes	no	yes
7 assignment discards expression	no	no	no	yes "unbalanced no. exps"	yes
8 assignment implicitly deletes var	no	yes, value nil	no	"unbalanced"	yes
9 operator applies coercion to operand	no	no	no	no	limited
10 constant folding	no	"infer value"	no	no	limited
11 dead code detection	no	not working	no	no	no
12 type inference	no	"infer value"	no (todo)	"infer nullity"	no
13 function signature inference	no	not working	no	no, call sites show definition	static IDL

from specific execution states enables us to reason about software properties and to compute them timely. *Static analysis* refers to the extraction of information about states and behavior from a software application without executing it.

Table 2 enumerates static analysis features applicable to Lua and compares existing analysis tools. Features include distinguishing between global and local variables (1) and relating declarations to uses (4), possibly using syntax highlighting. Many of these features (1-6) can be approximated by data flow analysis techniques [9] such as *reaching definitions*, which computes for each program point which assignments can reach it. Others features require no flow analysis (7, 8) or require more advanced inference techniques (9-13). Figure 1 illustrates features described in Table 2 using comments and references (f*n*), where (a) illustrates features 1, 2, 4, 7, 8 and 9 and (b) shows features 1-3.

```
1 function f(c)        --(f1) assign function to f
2   a      = 1         --(f1) creates global a
3   local b = true     --(f1) creates local b
4   a, b    = b, a     --(f4) swap a and b
5   a, b    = 1,2,3    --(f7) discards 3
6   a, b    = c        --(f8) implicitly deletes b
7   print(b)           --(f2) nil, undeclared b
8 end                  --      close scope
9 f("4")               --(f4) call f,bind c to "4"
10 print(a)            --(f4) 4, read global a
11 d = 2 .. a          --(f9) coerces 2 to string
12 d = d / "12"        --(f9) coerces 12 to number
13 print(c, d)         --(f2) nil 2, undeclared c
```

(a) Sequential Assignments

```
1 function hit(self, damage)
2   if self.health < damage then
3     isDown = true    --(f1) assign global
4   else
5     print(haelth)    --(f2) must be undefined
6   end
7   self.health = self.health - damage
8   print(isDown)      --(f3) may be nil or true
9   return self
10 end
11 unit = {health=10}          --create a test unit
12 unit = hit(unit, 4)         --call hit, bind unit, 4
13 unit = hit(unit, 8)         --call hit, bind unit, 8
```

(b) Event Handler

Fig. 1. Lua Script demonstrating potential errors that static analysis can find

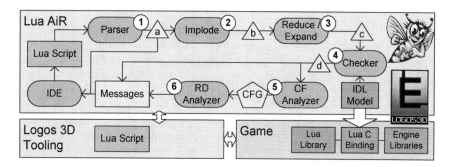

Fig. 2. Lua AiR Model Transformations

Koneki Lua Development Tools (LDT)[4] is an Eclipse plug-in that provides remote debugging and rudimentary static analysis for highlighting and refactoring. Lua Inspect[5] is an experimental static analysis tool that infers values, but incorrectly for conditional assignments. Lua Checker[6] is a basic command-line tool that checks local variable declarations against their uses. Lua for IDEA[7] enriches call sites with API structure (e.g. for World of Warcraft). LDT and Lua Inspect are based on Metalua [10], a Lua extension for static meta-programming.

2.1   Lua AiR Framework

This section explains the approach of the Lua AiR framework. IC3D Media has developed two languages for interoperability between Lua and their Logos3D game engine called Interface Definition Language (IDL) and Interface Generator Language (IGL). IDL defines function signatures and data types. IGL defines the generator format of the mapping between engine functionality defined in IDL models and Lua. Unlike other approaches shown in Table 2, we utilize information from the embedded context in our analysis. Functions and data structures exposed to Lua, and managed by the Logos3D engine, are statically defined and strongly typed. Sharing function signatures and data types modeled in IDL between the embedded environment and Lua enables checking function call site arguments against formal parameter types. Furthermore, it reduces the need for type inference and saves computation time in inter-procedural analysis. Additionally, code documentation can be shared between script proxies and the embedded context.

Lua AiR is a Rascal meta-program that implements the analysis as a pipeline, as illustrated by Figure 2. Rascal generates a specialized Eclipse IDE for Lua editing, highlighting, and static analysis. The analysis consists of the following model transformations. 1) The Lua script under analysis is fed into the parser generated by Rascal from our *Lua Grammar* (130 LOC). This produces a *parse*

---

[4] http://www.eclipse.org/koneki/ldt/

[5] https://github.com/davidm/lua-inspect

[6] http://code.google.com/p/lua-checker/

[7] https://bitbucket.org/sylvanaar2/lua-for-idea/wiki/Home

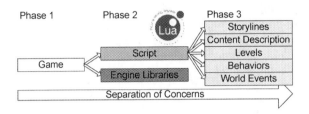

Fig. 3. Increased Complexity requires Separating Concerns

tree (a), depicted as a triangle. 2) The *implode* function matches the nodes of this tree to an Algebraic Data Type (ADT) that represents our Abstract Syntax Tree (AST) (b). This model transformation relies on compatible names and types between the Lua grammar and the ADT. 3) *Reduce* and *Expand* rewrite the AST to simplify the analysis (c). 4) The *Checker* provides static type checking and annotates the AST with scope information (d). 5) Given this AST, the *Control Flow (CF) Analyzer* generates a Control Flow Graph (CFG). 6) The *Reaching Definitions (RD) Analyzer* uses the CFG and performs fixed-point computation over *generate* and *kill* sets to generate the reaching definitions. Finally, the tool displays a log and the view in the IDE is updated by annotating the parse tree with results. The meta-program currently comprises approximately 3 KLOC.

3   Discussion and Future Work

This section discusses problems and describes opportunities for future work.

Empirical Validation. We believe that providing developers with better tools will improve code quality, but we have no proof yet this assumption is correct. Our approach can be validated by verifying if programmers can improve code quality by using our framework.

Improved Precision. Our analysis is *context insensitive* with respect to individual program states and execution paths and lacks type inference. Our analyis can be improved by using context sensitive techniques based generating and evaluating logical constraints [8, 9].

Tool Integration. Our framework cannot be used yet by existing tools. We plan to create a *Query API* to interface with other tools.

DLSs. Lua lacks the domain-specific notation which non-programmer game developers need to model software artefacts. A separation of concerns, as shown in Figure 3, is necessary to tackle challenges resulting from increased complexity in game development. Games can be modeled using sets of complementary lightweight little languages, one for each concern, as demonstrated by Palmer [11] and advocated by Furtado [12]. We observe that Lua AiR can be extended to support DLSs for higher level game concerns such as world events, character behavior and mission design, using IDL bindings to check if models conform to the interfaces of their library foundations.

4 Conclusion

In this paper we related Lua script quality problems to a lack of tools that support its static analysis. We evaluated the features of available tools and proposed a method to complement techniques for analysing Lua. We introduced Lua AiR, a framework for static analysis of Lua script in its embedded context, using IDL models and Rascal. Its main goal is to provide the immediate script analysis developers need to improve code quality. Preliminary results show that Lua AiR can provide additional information about Lua scripts. In future case studies we plan to use Lua AiR to analyse existing game code on a larger scale.

Acknowledgements. We thank the reviewers for their constructive comments.

References

1. Ierusalimschy, R.: Programming in Lua, 2nd edn (2006), Lua.org
2. Ierusalimschy, R., de Figueiredo, L.H., Celes, W.: The Evolution of Lua. In: Proceedings of the Third ACM SIGPLAN Conference on History of Programming Languages, HOPL III, pp. 2-1–2-26. ACM, New York (2007)
3. Ierusalimschy, R., De Figueiredo, L.H., Celes, W.: Passing a Language through the Eye of a Needle. Commun. ACM 54(7), 38–43 (2011)
4. Williams, K., McCandless, J., Gregg, D.: Dynamic Interpretation for Dynamic Scripting Languages. In: Proceedings of the 8th Annual IEEE/ACM International Symposium on Code Generation and Optimization, CGO 2010, pp. 278–287. ACM, New York (2010)
5. Blow, J.: Game Development: Harder Than You Think. ACM Queue 1, 28–37 (2004)
6. White, W., Koch, C., Gehrke, J., Demers, A.: Better Scripts, Better Games. Commun. ACM 52, 42–47 (2009)
7. Ramsey, N., Assis, F.: Almost Good Enough to Scale: A Lua Mail Handler and Spam Filter (presentation slides). In: Lua Workshop (2008)
8. Klint, P., van der Storm, T., Vinju, J.: RASCAL: A Domain Specific Language for Source Code Analysis and Manipulation. In: Proceedings of the 2009 Ninth IEEE International Working Conference on Source Code Analysis and Manipulation, SCAM 2009, pp. 168–177. IEEE Computer Society, Washington, DC (2009)
9. Nielson, F., Nielson, H.R., Hankin, C.: Principles of Program Analysis. Springer-Verlag New York, Inc., Secaucus (1999)
10. Fleutot, F., Tratt, L.: Contrasting Compile-Time Meta-Programming in Metalua and Converge. In: Workshop on Dynamic Languages and Applications (July 2007)
11. Palmer, J.D.: Ficticious: MicroLanguages for Interactive Fiction. In: Proceedings of the ACM International Conference Companion on Object Oriented Programming Systems Languages and Applications Companion, SPLASH 2010, pp. 61–68. ACM, New York (2010)
12. Furtado, A.W.B., Santos, A.L.M., Ramalho, G.L.: SharpLudus Revisited: from ad hoc and Monolithic Digital Game DSLs to Effectively Customized DSM Approaches. In: DSM 2011. SPLASH 2011 Workshops, pp. 57–62. ACM, New York (2011)

Future Trends in Game Authoring Tools

Florian Mehm, Christian Reuter, Stefan Göbel, and Ralf Steinmetz

Technische Universität Darmstadt, Multimedia Communications Lab (KOM)
Rundeturmstrasse 10
64283 Darmstadt, Germany
{florian.mehm,christian.reuter,stefan.goebel,
ralf.steinmetz}@kom.tu-darmstadt.de

Abstract. Authoring Tools for digital games are used to create games from
scratch, integrate content and game mechanics easily and can assist in a multitude of ways in the production chain of a game. For example, they can allow
non-programmers to work on the game logic by means of domain-specific or
visual programming languages, increase the collaboration between team members by integrating computer-supported collaborative work techniques, assist in
catching errors in the game by model checking and offer publishing to multiple
platforms by saving games in an intermediate format which can be run on various systems. This already interesting and viable approach can be extended in a
number of ways which we exemplify in this position paper to indicate possible
future directions for game authoring tools.

Keywords: Authoring Tool, Procedural Content Generation, Domain-Specific
Language, Multiplayer, In-Game Editing.

1   Introduction

The concept of providing an authoring tool that streamlines the workflow in a certain
area (may it be multimedia [1], e-Learning [2] or more recently games [3, 4]) has a
long history in computing. It is successful due to several factors: it allows non-
technical users to work on projects that would otherwise be out of their reach (due to
lack of expertise, especially concerning programming languages); it can bring structure into unstructured domains (such as game development) and it can speed up development by streamlining and automating common tasks. Authoring tools also reduce coordination effort between different groups involved in the game production
process such as writers and artists. They separate themselves from level editors in
most commercially available games as they support more development tasks up to the
creation of a complete game.

In the field of game authoring tools, several examples can be seen, each focusing
on a specific approach to authoring. The e-Adventure authoring tool is specialized for
the creation of educational adventure games [3]. The SHAI Scenario Editor described
by Est et al. [5] allows users to define educational scenarios using high-level logic
visualized in diagrams that is converted to low-level logic internally by the system.

M. Herrlich, R. Malaka, and M. Masuch (Eds.): ICEC 2012, LNCS 7522, pp. 536–541, 2012.
© IFIP International Federation for Information Processing 2012

The Alice [6, 7] tool uses a visual programming language to allow users to program their own game and learn about programming concepts simultaneously. The authors of this paper have provided the authoring tool StoryTec [4] targeted at the creation of Serious Games, combining several positive properties also found in the projects mentioned here, such as a visual programming approach and high-level logic for authors.

In the following, we focus on possible areas of innovation where authoring tools can be extended and thereby improved in the future. This includes the extension into the content generation process as well as domain specific languages and other novel authoring concepts that can make authoring tools more expressive without increasing their complexity for the user. The concept of model checking can assist users by detecting errors automatically. We also discuss multiplayer games, an area largely ignored by current authoring tools, and describe ideas on how the authoring process itself can be enhanced by using game concepts.

2   Areas of Innovation

2.1   Procedural Content Generation

While authoring tools have been demonstrated to be able to assist (non-technical) users in adding content to games, the next possible step is to assist users in creating content by the provision of procedural content generation tools.

Work in the field of procedural content generation for games has intensified in the last years [8]. Examples for this are systems creating infinite levels for platform games in the style of Nintendo's Super Mario Bros [9]. These systems aim at generating as many aspects of a game as possible (including the game's narrative[10] or rules [11] in some cases).

The vision of Procedural Content Generation is to allow users to enter a semantic description and receive a fitting assets, may it be a virtual character, 3D object or piece of music. Currently, research into authoring tools and procedural content generation is still largely separated, but the combination of both could help the work of authors tremendously by speeding it up and reducing the number of necessary experts in the production of a game significantly. Other approaches could reach similar results by using methods for semantic content retrieval, giving access to content already created for other applications. Among the possible challenges of this approach is the way in which the semantic description for the object under creation is to be given (as parameters in a restricted domain, as natural language, etc.) and if and how authors can manipulate the object after it has been created.

2.2   Domain-Specific Languages and Visual Languages

While domain-specific and visual programming languages are already used in current authoring tools, their leverage can be extended by increasing their expressiveness and applicability to game development. Examples of visual programming approaches can be found in the previously mentioned e-Adventure, Alice and StoryTec systems. A text-based domain-specific language for games is the Inform 7 language for the creation of interactive fiction [12]. Especially the latter language shows the elegance possible with this approach: reading the source files of a game created with it makes immediate sense to a person able to understand English, while being parseable by the computer at the same time.

Especially model-driven and component-based software engineering approaches fit together well with authoring tools, as they abstract from implementation details and offer users only the level of semantics and detail they want to work with. BinSubaih and Maddock [13] describe a system that separates a game's core logic from the actual implementation in a game engine. The EGGG language [14] is designed to describe games on a very high level of abstraction, realizing them using a set of re-usable software components.

Potential difficulties with Domain-Specific Languages in game authoring tools result from the definition of these languages themselves, including the scope as well as the granularity of the language constructs, possibly resulting in too restrictive languages on the one hand and too unwieldy languages for practical use on the other.

2.3   Novel Authoring Concepts

Departing from the paradigms of standard e-Learning or multimedia authoring tools such as timelines or 2D layouts, new authoring concepts can be embraced. A strong example is the block-based editing paradigm successfully used by the independent game Minecraft[1] [15], which has spawned whole worlds of user-created 3D models without the need for 3D modeling know-how.

By switching to such simple authoring concepts, novice authors and authors without technical expertise (commonly the main target users of authoring tools) have a very low threshold of learning compared to traditional 3D authoring tools, which require careful manipulation of the mouse and keyboard and complicated concepts such as cameras, lights and 3D meshes made of vertices and polygons.

2.4   Model Checking

Apart from streamlining and structuring content and game logic, authoring tools can support users in more ways by offering automatic checks for syntactical and especially semantic errors. An example can be found in the model checking capabilities described in the context of the e-Adventure authoring tool [16], which can inform users of potential problems in the game. Future versions of such mechanisms could employ methods of artificial intelligence such as machine learning in order to detect semantic problems in authored games and make the author aware of them, potentially even providing automatic correction advice. For example, an educational game authoring tool might alert the user whenever a certain learner type has been neglected in the game or whenever a dead end (a section of the game where no more progress can be made due to conflicting or missing game logic) has been created.

---

[1] Available from http://minecraft.net

2.5   Multiplayer Authoring

By the increasing number of (massively) multiplayer and social games, it can be seen that multiplayer games are becoming a larger and larger aspect of the game industry. Authoring tools can support this sector by making multiplayer mechanics (synchronization of players, collaboration, etc.) evident and manageable to authors.

This field of authoring has been largely neglected so far. In recent work, the authoring tool StoryTec has been extended for the authoring of multiplayer games, yielding a first prototype in this field[17]. It was then used to create an adventure game being playable for two players. The early state of research in this field shows that especially the puzzle design has to be supported in the authoring tool by offering mechanisms to synchronize or separate players. As an example from the associated demo, one player is set in the authoring tool to be restricted to one part of the game world due to being pinned down by a fallen-down tree, while the other player has to move around and find a way to free him or her. However, the first player is the only one in possession of a map, forcing the two players to collaborate. This interaction has been set up in the authoring tool by a set of constraints and conditions, showing a first version of this area of authoring tool improvement.

The aspect of adaptivity (based for example on player or learner modeling) found in current authoring tools such as StoryTec or e-Adventure will increase in complexity but also in potential reward in terms of added enjoyment and effectiveness by the addition of multiple players. Whereas in the single player case the game only has to be adapted for the needs of a single player, in the multiplayer case, the adaptation has to happen to each single player as well as for the whole group at the same time. A first approach including automatic and manual adaptation by a Game Master is shown by Wendel et al. [18].

2.6   In-Game Editing, Gamification and User-Generated Content

By dropping the classical authoring tool interface and allowing editing directly inside the game, users can easily work on the game while receiving immediate feedback. This concept has been touched upon by platforms such as Jumala[2] or games like Little Big Planet [19], as well as the already mentioned Minecraft. At the same time, this can be leveraged to incentivize user-generated content by means of gamification, giving players in-game rewards like achievements or items for building new content and extending games.

Again, this step lowers the threshold for novice authors tremendously by offering the authoring capabilities directly in the game environment. Usual authoring tools for games rarely have a true WYSIWYG (What you see is what you get) interface; instead, they rely on abstractions in order to maintain the overview for the author. With in-game editing, authors can immediately see the effects of their changes and try them out in the exact same context as their players. The closest authoring tools have gotten to this are systems like CryTek's Sandbox editor[3] or the Unity game editor[4], which allow starting the game right inside the editor interface for testing purposes.

---

[2] Available at http://jumala.com
[3] See http://mycryengine.com/

Problems that are commonly associated with User-generated content have to be addressed in the context of authoring tools as well, namely those of copyright infringements, quality control and management and retrieval of a possibly very large body of generated content [20] .

3 Conclusion

In the previous sections, we have outlined a set of areas where future authoring tools can go beyond the current state of the art, opening up authoring tools to new groups of users and improving the strong aspects of authoring tools further. These areas should not be seen in isolation. Instead, the combinations of areas can prove worthwhile and add new strengths of their own while mitigating the drawbacks of individual approaches. For example, in-game editing and procedural content generation in combination yield vast worlds that authors can change on the fly, without the need to create the basic layout of the world first. A large part of making multiplayer authoring feasible will probably lie in model checking, since the addition of more than one player in the game increases the space of possible actions and combinations of variables in the game exponentially, making it a hard problem for humans to keep all logical and semantic constraints in view at the same time.

At the same time, critical questions also appear due to these innovations. For example, procedural content generation could be seen as hindering the free creativity inherent in games. Automatic retrieval for content aggregation or user-generated content might give rise to copyright issues. It is also questionable whether the content produced by these methods yields enough quality compared to assets created by professional artists. We therefore see the further evaluation of these ideas as future work.

References

1. Bulterman, D.C.A., Hardman, L.: Structured multimedia authoring. ACM Transactions on Multimedia Computing Communications and Applications 1, 89–109 (2005)
2. Cristea, A.: Authoring of adaptive educational Hypermedia. In: Seventh IEEE International Conference on Advanced Learning Technologies ICALT 2007, pp. 943–944 (2007)
3. Torrente, J., Blanco, Á.D., Cañizal, G., Moreno-ger, P., Fernandéz-Manjón, B.: <e-Adventure3D>: An Open Source Authoring Environment for 3D Adventure Games in Education. In: Proceedings of the 2008 International Conference on Advances in Computer Entertainment Technology, ACE 2008. ACM, New York (2008)
4. Mehm, F.: Authoring Serious Games. In: Pisan, Y. (ed.) Proceedings of the Fifth International Conference on the Foundations of Digital Games - FDG 2010, pp. 271–273. ACM (2010)
5. Est, C.V., Poelman, R., Bidarra, R.: High-Level Scenario Editing for Serious Games. In: Richard, P., Braz, J. (eds.) GRAPP 2011 - Proceedings of the International Conference on Computer Graphics Theory and Applications, pp. 339–346. SciTePress (2010)

---

[4] See http://www.unity3d.com

6. Villaverde, K., Jeffery, C., Pivkina, I.: Cheshire: Towards an Alice Based Game Development Tool. In: International Conference on Computer Games, Multimedia & Allied Technology, pp. 321–328 (2009)
7. Kelleher, C.: Motivating programming: using storytelling to make computer programming attractive to middle school girls (2006)
8. Hendrikx, M., Meijer, S., Velden, J.V., Iosup, A.: Procedural Content Generation for Games: A Survey. ACM Transactions on Multimedia Computing, Communications and Applications 1, 1–24 (2012)
9. Shaker, N., Togelius, J., Yannakakis, G.N., Weber, B., Shimizu, T., Hashiyama, T., Sorenson, N., Pasquier, P., Mawhorter, P., Takahashi, G., Smith, G., Member, S., Baumgarten, R.: The 2010 Mario AI Championship: Level Generation Track. IEEE Transactions on Computational Intelligence and AI in Games 3, 1–16 (2011)
10. Cavazza, M., Lugrin, J.-L., Pizzi, D., Charles, F.: Madame bovary on the holodeck: immersive interactive storytelling. In: Proceedings of the 15th International Conference on Multimedia MULTIMEDIA 2007, pp. 651–660. ACM (2007)
11. Smith, A.M., Mateas, M.: Variations Forever: Flexibly Generating Rulesets from a Sculptable Design Space of Mini-Games. In: IEEE Conference on Computational Intelligence and Games (CIG), pp. 273–280. IEEE (2010)
12. Reed, A.: Creating Interactive Fiction with Inform 7. Course Technology PTR (2010)
13. BinSubaih, A., Maddock, S.: Game portability using a service-oriented approach. International Journal of Computer Games Technology (2008)
14. Orwant, J.: EGGG: Automated programming for game generation. IBM Systems Journal 39, 782–794 (2000)
15. Duncan, S.C.: Minecraft, Beyond Construction and Survival. Well Played 1, 9–22 (2011)
16. Moreno-Ger, P., Fuentes-Fernández, R., Sierra-Rodríguez, J.-L., Fernández-Manjón, B.: Model-checking for adventure videogames. Information and Software Technology 51, 564–580 (2009)
17. Reuter, C., Wendel, V., Göbel, S., Steinmetz, R.: Multiplayer Adventures for Collaborative Learning With Serious Games. Accepted at 6th European Conference on Games Based Learning (2012)
18. Wendel, V., Hertin, F., Göbel, S., Steinmetz, R.: Collaborative Learning by Means of Multiplayer Serious Games. In: Luo, X., Spaniol, M., Wang, L., Li, Q., Nejdl, W., Zhang, W. (eds.) ICWL 2010. LNCS, vol. 6483, pp. 289–298. Springer, Heidelberg (2010)
19. Westecott, E.: Crafting Play: Little Big Planet. Loading 5, 90–100 (2011)
20. OECD: Participative Web and User-Created Content. OECD Publishing, Paris (2007)

The Effectiveness and Efficiency of Model Driven Game Design

Joris Dormans

Amsterdam University of Applied Sciences

Abstract. In order for techniques from Model Driven Engineering to be accepted at large by the game industry, it is critical that the effectiveness and efficiency of these techniques are proven for game development. There is no lack of game design models, but there is no model that has surfaced as an industry standard. Game designers are often reluctant to work with models: they argue these models do not help them design games and actually restrict their creativity. At the same time, the flexibility that model driven engineering allows seems a good fit for the fluidity of the game design process, while clearly defined, generic models can be used to develop automated design tools that increase the development's efficiency.

1 Introduction

Games are hard to design and develop. Game audiences expect a higher level of quality year after year. For contemporary triple-A console titles this means that development teams easily consists of more than a hundred designers, programmers, and artist, and a production period that spans multiple years. Even for casual games, which up until a few years ago could be developed within a couple of months by a team of under five people, we see changes. The current generation of mobile and social games is already developed by experienced studios that assign twenty to thirty developers to the task and year-long development times are no longer uncommon. In order to keep producing better quality for less money, the games industry needs to find ways to either increase revenues, or improve the efficiency and effectiveness of the development process. This paper investigates how modeling techniques can be used to do the latter, but also at the obstacles that need to be overcome to get model driven techniques accepted by the game development community.

2 Abstract Game Development Tools

For a while, within the game design community there has been a careful push for the development of abstract tools and methods for game. In a 1999 article Doug Church called for the development of 'formal abstract design tools' [1]. Since then, a number of frameworks and tools have sprung up. Many of them

M. Herrlich, R. Malaka, and M. Masuch (Eds.): ICEC 2012, LNCS 7522, pp. 542–548, 2012.

are primarily design vocabularies, created to help understand and identify common structures in games, and avoiding to be prescriptive in their description of games.[1] Berndt Kreimeier suggested to apply the design pattern approach from architecture and software engineering to game design [2]. In contrast to vocabularies, design patterns are prescriptive; they describe 'good', generic solutions to common problems. However, the most prominent work on design patterns within the domain of game design to date [3], is explicitly distanced from a prescriptive approach, creating a hybrid approach that is closer to a design vocabulary than a pattern language. At the same time, Raph Koster experimented with a graphical grammar to express game mechanics [4], this approach was followed by [5,6,7]. In contrast to the design vocabulary approach, the focus of these grammars has not been the collections of descriptions they allow, but the design lore that they capture. For example, the Machinations framework [7] sets out to visualize the structures in game mechanics that create emergent gameplay; in other words, it departs from theoretical vision on quality in games, and constructs a tool set that allow game designers to interact with the structures that contribute to that quality more directly.

In the Machinations framework the diagrams expressing game mechanics act as a domain specific language (DSL) for a subset of game development; in this case for a game's "internal economy" [8]. Using similar DSLs for level design opens up the possibility of applying techniques and ideas from Model Driven Engineering (MDE) [9] to game design. Graph transformations might be used to transform machinations diagrams to graphs outlining interactive missions for level design or vice versa [10]. Similar ideas have been explored by Reyno and Carsí Cubel from a more technical perspective focusing on automatically generating code for games [11,12]. The techniques typically used in a MDE approach to game development (transformational grammars, UML, Petri nets, and so on) require a considerable effort to use for game designers that do not have a background in software engineering. In fact, one of the biggest challenges to introduce any abstract game development tool, is to convince game designers of its value in the first place.

3   Design versus Engineering

Leaving aside the much longer history of board games, game development is a very young field. The current generation of prominent game developers got to the place they are today because of hard work, entrepreneurship, and bravura. For the early pioneers of the field there were no abstract tools to guide them. Nonetheless, they have created an industry. As a result there is a certain level of animosity towards abstract design tools. A fair number of game designers dismiss design tools because they do not think the tools are effective enough, they fear the tools might actually harm the creative process, or both [13,14].

---

[1] Most notably among these are the Game Ontology Project (see www.gameontology.com and the 400 Project (see www.theinspiracy.com/400_project)

The lack of proven, effective design methods is a serious concern. The current DSLs and design vocabularies for games tend to have a steep learning curve, and are anything but widespread. Although many are designed for actual design work, few have found frequent use outside universities. However, effectiveness is not an argument against design tools, it is a requirement: the effectiveness of a game design tool versus the effort required to master it should be apparent. Typically, this means that using a design tool should lead to better games built in less time, and the time reduction should be more than the time required to learn the tool.

The negative effects on the creative process are trickier to deal with. Many advocates of game design tools argue that they are designed to support the creative process, while many designers experience tools as rigid and restrictive instruments. Although, it can be reasoned that this argument against abstract, theoretical methods for game design stems from a naïve perspective on art and creativity. After all, practitioners of any form of art, from painting and sculpture to cinema and performance, use abstract tools such as the theory of perspective, composition, and editing techniques, to teach and improve their form. However, it is equally important to make clear in what ways game design tools *support* rather than *restrict* game design.

By nature game design is a flexible process. It is impossible to plan and design a game on paper and expect good results from simply building the game as per specification. Too often, what looks good on paper does not work as expected, or simply lacks fun. Gameplay is the emergent result of players interacting with a dynamic system. Until that system exists in some prototype form, it is impossible to say whether or not it works. This means that an important task of the game designer is to spot opportunities as they arise during the development of a game. A famous illustration of this effect is the development of *SimCity* from the editor for another game (*Raid on Bungeling Bay*). While working with the editor, game designer Will Wright discovered that it was much more fun to build the urban environment than it was to fly around it and shoot enemies as the original game intended.

MDE is a suitable approach to deal with the dynamic process of designing games. By capturing different aspects of games in different models and describing how one model can be transformed into a different model allows for a sufficient level of agility: for one game mechanics might be the natural starting point, while for another game interactive missions might be. At the same time, using models forces designers to think about their game at an abstract level. In addition, different models foreground different structures in the game's design; in a way, each model acts as a different lens. Machinations diagrams foreground feedback loops that operate in a game's economy, by building such a diagram, the designer will have to deal with these structures consciously. Daniel Cook's skill chains [6] visualize the dependencies between the skills players must master to successfully play the game: it is a useful lens that should be used to investigate tutorial stages and learning curves in any game.

However, model driven engineering has not been applied to game design extensively. As discussed above, within the game design community there are no widely accepted abstract models for game development, not even for specialized tasks such as level design or interactive storytelling. Without clearly defined, widely accepted models that have a proven positive impact on the development process, it will be hard to convince the games industry to start applying model driven engineering techniques on a larger scale. Yet, it is the argument of this paper that the game development community would do good to investigate the opportunities presented by MDE, as these opportunities could lead to a more efficiently designed games which in turn leaves more room to elevate creative game design to the next level.

4   Applying Models Effectively

Looking at the common problems encountered during game development, problems regarding design and managing game features are the most prominent [15]. Traditionally, the content and scope of a game's design is recorded using a game design document. However, these documents have a poor track record: they are considered to be a burden to create while they are hardly consulted by the development team.

Using generic, abstract models can increase the effectiveness of game development far beyond the current practice of writing game design documents. Clearly defined, generic models are less open to different interpretations by different team members. In the most ideal case, the model's syntax is completely unambiguous. When done right it is even possible to use formal models such as Petri nets [16,17] to identify structural strengths and weaknesses of a design in an early stage. Although similar effects can be reach with relative simple and informal models such as the skill chain diagrams (see above). These diagrams expose a number of structural characteristics such as the number of connections between individual skill nodes and the relative width and depth of the diagram, which are indications of the relative steepness and length of the learning curve, respectively.

The Machinations framework is a good example a generic, abstract model that foregrounds structural qualities of a game's design. The number of nodes, connections, but also the number of feedback loops in a Machination diagram, are all important indications of the complexity of the game and the quality of the gameplay that emerges from it. The pattern library that is part of the framework catalogues common structures that are indicative of particular dynamic effects. The use of these patterns helps designers to understand and improve the dynamic gameplay. At the same time the patterns are flexible enough to enhance creativity. There are many ways to implement each single pattern, and the number of ways to combine patterns is infinite.

The wide range of levels of abstraction the Machinations diagrams are able to express can be leveraged to create a design strategy. A game designer can start out with a fairly simple model of the game and elaborate on it by slowly increasing the complexity by replacing simple constructions with more complex ones. The design patterns can be used as a guide for this process. Relative simple patterns can be replaced by more complex ones. Within the Machinations framework this process is referred to as elaboration, and each pattern in the library indicates what patterns it elaborates and by what patterns it is elaborated.

5 Applying Models Efficiently

The application of model driven engineering techniques also creates opportunities to increase the efficiency of the game development process. Generic, abstract models can act as quick, early prototypes that would normally require more time and effort to build. They can be used to simulate games and collect gameplay data at a very early stage. In addition, these models can be used to develop automated design tools that can speed up the process and freeing designers from manual work to focus on those aspects of the development process that benefit most from their creative labor.

These days, all game developers are convinced that prototyping is a critical aspect of developing games. Because gameplay is an emergent result of the game as a dynamic system, the best way to find out whether or not a game works is to build the system and set it in motion. Visual representations such as Machinations diagrams can help identify important structural features that create the emergent gameplay and help designers to shape the gameplay towards a target form, they can never fully replace a play test session using a playable prototype. Fortunately, Machinations diagrams can be executed and allow user interaction when running. This means that they can actually serve as abstract, low fidelity prototypes. At the same time, the diagrams allows the designer to define artificial players and quickly run many simulated play sessions to collect data. This helps designers to balance games in a very early stage. Although, there remains a gap between the model and the real game. Data collected in this way primes designers for gameplay effects that might occur, and already allows them to find out what measures can be taken to counter-act certain unwanted effects.

With sufficient sophisticated models and tools, MDE for game design can be taken much further. Recent experiments with mixed initiative procedural content generation (PCG) [18,19] sketch the possibility of creating design tools that automate certain tasks to speed up the process of design. Procedural content generation is already being used in commercial games, in most cases to generate levels either during design time, or every time the player starts a new session. The mixed initiative approach to PCG has the computer algorithm collaborate with a human designer in order to get better results. However, PCG techniques are typically tailored towards a specific game. Using generic and abstract models, the same techniques can be applied to multiple games, and hopefully will lead to the development of intelligent, generic design tools. MDE and model transformations seem to be a perfect match for this development as they offer enough flexibility to deal with the agility of the game development process while they are defined clearly enough to be automated [10]. Ideally a game designer will be able to go back and forth through and make changes to different, connected models of the same game, although it is a considerable technical challenge to create a system that allows a designer to step back to an early model of a game, make changes to it, and automatically reapply all transformations that generated the current state of the game.

6   Discussion

However promising the prospect of applying MDE to game design is, the current state of the art of MDE in game design still faces many challenges. A lack of widely accepted models to represent different aspects of games means that currently no one can expect game designers understand and apply these models. Successful models need to be expressive enough to be able to deal with an infinite variety of games, while still be intuitive to game designers. In addition, they should not require too much effort to master. At this moment is remains unclear whether or not models like this are going to surface soon. No one should expect one single model for the entire process of game development, or every aspect of a game, to emerge. It is better to focus on different models for particular aspects of games and game design. Using multiple models creates a more flexible frame work that and allows designers to adopt MDE techniques one step at a time. However, multiple models also present a problem. It is not always clear how transformations can be defined that allow a model of a certain type to be transformed into a model of another type. For example, a graph based model might be used to express mechanics or missions, but there is no transformational grammar that specifies how a graph can be transformed into a spatial map representing a game level.

MDE can be used to develop generic, automated design tools. These should be build to support designers in their task. Ideally a design tool manages trivial, repetitive task and foregrounds potential structural strengths and weakness of a design. No tool should require trivial, repetitive task from the designer. This allows the designer to focus on the creative tasks. It is critical that the designer stays in control of the creative aspect of the design process at all times. Model transformations are a good way of codifying design strategies for a particular game or a game genre. Using automated design tools, development teams should expect a considerable effort to get the tool up and running. For this reason it is unlikely that the entire process can be automated at once. Small steps should be taken for each new development cycle, starting with steps are more generic and can be easily reused in subsequent projects.

Finally, we have very little experience of applying these techniques to actual games. Currently, many game development studios have settled into particular ways to develop games that are not necessarily suited to MDE. They have set up content pipelines and follow milestone plans. Further research on how to integrate MDE techniques and automated design tools into this process is needed.

References

1. Church, D.: Formal abstract design tools. Gamasutra (1999)
2. Kreimeier, B.: The case for game design patterns. Gamasutra (2002)
3. Björk, S., Holopainen, J.: Patterns in Game Design. Charles River Media, Boston, MA (2005)
4. Koster, R.: A grammar of gameplay: game atoms: can games be diagrammed? Presentation at the Game Developers Conference (2005)
5. Bura, S.: A game grammar (2006)
6. Cook, D.: The chemistry of game design. Gamasutra (2007)
7. Dormans, J.: Machinations: Elemental feedback structures for game design. In: Proceedings of the GAMEON-NA Conference (2009)
8. Adams, E., Rollings, A.: Fundamentals of Game Design. Pearson Education, Inc., Upper Saddle River (2007)
9. Brown, A.: An introduction to model driven architecture (2004)
10. Dormans, J.: Level design as model transformation: A strategy for automated content generation. In: Proceedings of the Foundations of Digital Games Conference 2011, Bordeaux, France (2011)
11. Reyno, E.M., Carsí Cubel, J.Á.: Model-driven game development: 2d platform game prototyping. In: Proceedings of the GAME on Conference (2008)
12. Reyno, E.M., Carsí Cubel, J.Á.: Automatic prototyping in model-driven game development. ACM Computers in Entertainment 7(2) (2009)
13. Guttemberg, D.: An academic approach to game design: Is it worth it? Gamasutra (2006)
14. Sheffield, B.: Defining games: Raph koster's game grammar. Gamasutra (2007)
15. Petrillo, F., Pimenta, M., Trindade, F., Dietrich, C.: What went wrong? a survey of problems in game development. ACM Computers in Entertainment 7(1) (2009)
16. Brom, C., Abonyi, A.: Petri nets for game plot. In: Proceedings of AISB (2006)
17. Araújo, M., Roque, L.: Modeling games with petri nets. In: Proceedings of DiGRA 2009 (2009)
18. Smith, G., Whitehead, J., Mateas, M.: Tanagra: A mixed-initiative level design tool. In: Proceedings of the Foundations of Digital Games Conference 2010, Monterey, CA, pp. 209–216 (2010)
19. Smelik, R., Turenel, T., de Kraker, K.J., Bidarra, R.: Inegrating procedural generation and manual editing of virtual worlds. In: Proceedings of the Foundations of Digital Games Conference 2010, Monterey, CA (2010)

Proposal for the 4th Workshop on Mobile Gaming, Mobile Life – Interweaving the Virtual and the Real

Barbara Grüter[1], Holger Mügge[2], Leif Oppermann[3], and Mark Billinghurst[4]

[1] Hochschule Bremen, Flughafenallee 10, 28199 Bremen, Germany
barbara.grueter@hs-bremen.de
[2] Universität Bonn, Römerstraße 164, 53177 Bonn, Germany
muegge@iai.uni-bonn.de
[3] Fraunhofer FIT, Schloß Birlinghoven, 53754 Sankt Augustin, Germany
leif.oppermann@fit.fraunhofer.de
[4] HIT Lab NZ, University of Canterbury, Private Bag 4800, Christchurch 8140, New Zealand
mark.billinghurst@hitlabnz.org

Abstract. Over the last few years we have witnessed the smartphone dominating the market, the rapid growth of mobile apps, a surge in mobile augmented reality and location-based apps, and burgeoning mobile communities. While mobile topics continue to provide rich research challenges, people and companies outside academia already use these apps regularly. This is due to the increased availability of affordable devices, applications and technologies that support the creation of mixed reality experiences. Thus a core theme of our workshop at ICEC 2012 is authoring mixed realities, designing mobile games and creating mobile experiences. We would like to assess how professional designers and developers, as well as academics and end users, are using the technology to connect the digital and the real in a mobile context.

1   Introduction

This is the fourth workshop on Mobile Gaming since 2008. Recent developments in the mobile domain emphasize the vanishing border between mobile gaming and mobile life, and the emerging mixed reality worlds, so this fourth installment of the series introduces a revised title and a new member to the committee (Mark Billinghurst). The organizers are from four different organizations and have been actively involved in the field of mobile gaming for at least more than five years each.

1.1   Organizers Background

Barbara Grüter is Professor for Human-Computer Interaction (HCI) at the Hochschule Bremen and Associated Professor of the Graduate School Advances in Digital Media at the University Bremen. She is head of the research group Gangs of Bremen with the focus on interaction and mobile gaming experiences by exploring, developing, and play testing mobile game prototypes. She currently leads the BMBF project

M. Herrlich, R. Malaka, and M. Masuch (Eds.): ICEC 2012, LNCS 7522, pp. 549–552, 2012.
© IFIP International Federation for Information Processing 2012

Landmarks of Mobile Entertainment (2010-2013) and is spokeswoman of the research cluster Mobile Life at the Hochschule Bremen since February 2012.

Holger Mügge is a project manager at the University of Bonn and organizes the research group Software Architecture and Middleware which does research projects on context-sensitivity and mobile gaming. He is also co-founder and CEO of Qeevee, a young company that specializes in mobile distributed applications for entertainment, gaming and learning.

Leif Oppermann is deputy head of the Mixed and Augmented Reality Solutions group at Fraunhofer FIT. Through his current role at FIT and previously at the University of Nottingham's Mixed Reality Lab, he has been directly involved in various projects that researched into Mixed Reality and Pervasive Gaming.

Mark Billinghurst is director of the HIT Lab New Zealand at the University of Canterbury. He has a wealth of knowledge and expertise in human computer interface technology, particularly in the area of Augmented Reality and mobile AR. His research team developed the first collaborative AR application for mobile phones, and one of the first mobile AR advertising campaigns.

Together, the organizers have experience in organizing three previous editions of this workshop; two of them as part of the annual conference of the German "Gesellschaft für Informatik" (GI), and one at ACM ACE in 2011.

1.2   Goals

This workshop provides a forum for researchers and practitioners in the field of pervasive, mobile, and location-based gaming. The thematic focus is on mobile games and other social mobile applications that take location and context, and players' movements as important design parameters. The workshop particularly addresses mobile game designers, developers, and scholars who are concerned with current and future issues of mobile game design, development, staging, and evaluation. It aims to span the boundaries between play, research, and business.

1.3   Motivation

Mobile applications already pervade our everyday life. Mobile games allow their players to exploit the arising opportunities for mobile human-computer interaction in a playful fashion. The archetypical mobile game is Geocaching, which started immediately after the US government announced the discontinuation of the artificial degradation of GPS signals for non-military users on 1 May 2000. In this game, players hide caches, small treasures, and announce their locations as GPS coordinates over the Internet for other players to search for them. In a similar way, mobile games today utilize the location by means of mobile and pervasive technology. Small and portable devices are equipped with sensors and models of their environment that allow them to sense the emerging context of play and interact with the player.

These mobile games combine the real and virtual worlds. As outdoor games they continue the tradition of rallies and Geocaching. They use the outside real environment as playground but use computing devices to access a digital world and to enable and organize play activities. Thus they offer unique gaming possibilities. They enable communication and collaboration between players independent from their positions; they augment the real world by game-specific information and action possibilities; they allow the collection of game process data for analysis and complex feedback; they integrate the game interaction with other web-based services and perform complex game mechanics either on the client- and/or the server-side.

In this workshop, we explore the mobile games of tomorrow and their aesthetical, technological and conceptual assumptions. We have already seen the convergence of mobile, social, and map technologies. We are now witnessing the emergence of mobile game communities, the localization of social networks, a surge of mobile Augmented Reality (AR), social mobile gaming platforms, mobile game creators, and the development of dynamic map technologies. We further notice emerging ecosystems connecting mobile gamers, producers, researchers, and game technologies.

2 The Workshop

We solicit research or position papers, prototype demonstrations, and position statements and questions as contributions to the workshop. We will set up a program committee and organize at least three reviews for each contribution. Accepted papers and demonstrations will be presented at the workshop as part of the program. In addition we will invite one or two keynote speakers from academia and industry.

During the hands-on session, participants could also try out specific approaches to planning and creating their own mobile experiences under the supervision of an expert.

All contributions will be available to all participants in advance through a workshop webpage which will also be updated after the workshop to reflect the results.

We are expecting about 10 – 20 participants. We are aiming for attracting submissions from fitting research projects and student works. Moreover we intend to invite industry representatives, including also small companies.

2.1 Topics of Interest

Topics of interest include, but are not limited to:

- Authoring solutions and game creators
- Mobile game design and patterns of game play
- Mobile Augmented Reality/Mixed Reality
- Mobile play experience, design and evaluation
- Producing mobile games
- Interfaces and interaction techniques for mobile games
- Development processes and architectures
- Complexity of hardware, software, infrastructure – problems and solutions
- Mobile games and mobile projectors
- Casualty of mobile games
- Mobile Gamification, Serious Games and Games with a purpose

- The emerging context of mobile game play and context-sensitive technology
- Market strategies and business models for mobile games
- Staging and deployment strategies

2.2   Submission, Dates and Websites

All workshop submissions will be handled via our EasyChair account, which is linked in from the workshop website.

Submission Deadline	June	16	2012
Notification of acceptance	July	01	2012
Final version	July	15	2012
Workshop	September	26-29	2012

Workshop website	http://sam.iai.uni-bonn.de/moga2012/
Conference website	http://www.icec2012.org/

Presented papers will be archived at the workshop website and selected papers will be published with Springer.

"Do Not Touch the Paintings!" The Benefits of Interactivity on Learning and Future Visits in a Museum

Konstantinos Mikalef[1], Michail N. Giannakos[2,*],
Konstantinos Chorianopoulos[3], and Letizia Jaccheri[2]

[1] Hellenic Open University, Patra 26335, Greece
kostas.mikalef@gmail.com
[2] Norwegian University of Science and Technology (NTNU), Trondheim 7491, Norway
{mgiannak,letizia}@idi.ntnu.no
[3] Ionian University, Corfu 49100, Greece
choko@ionio.gr

Abstract. Educators and museum curators have recognized the value of interactivity, but it remains unclear what is the right level of interactivity in informal learning settings, such as museums. In this study, we explore the effect of increasing levels of interactivity on learning performance and students' intention for future museum visits. We developed an educational mobile application based on QR codes and quiz software, in order to augment visual arts comprehension during a visit to an art gallery. In addition to the mobile-based version of the game, a paper-based version was also employed followed by a controlled experiment. A total of 60 lyceum students (between 15 and 16 years old) participated in a between-groups evaluation that compared the performance of three levels of interactivity (passive guided tour, paper-based, mobile-based), as well as the perceptions among the groups. The results indicate that the mobile-based student group had higher performance in the post-assessment when compared with the paper-based one. Notably, perceived interest for the game affects students' perceptions for a future museum visit. Further research should consider the effects of higher-fidelity types of mobile applications, such as 3D graphics, as well as augmented-reality games.

Keywords: Mobile learning, informal learning, performance, perceptions, mobile devices, museums.

1 Introduction

Mobile applications are increasingly used nowadays to assist many scenarios (e.g., museums, cultural heritage locations, outdoor activities). Educational medium effectiveness

---

* This work was carried out during the tenure of an ERCIM "Alain Bensoussan" Fellowship programme. The research leading to these results has received funding from the European Union Seventh Framework Programme (FP7/2007-2013) under grant agreement no 246016.

M. Herrlich, R. Malaka, and M. Masuch (Eds.): ICEC 2012, LNCS 7522, pp. 553–561, 2012.

and students' perceptions for the medium highly affect the learning success. As the introduction of learning tools is often complex, students do not always use them as expected. For instance, students' perceptions regarding the importance and the interest for the medium are some of the most widespread barriers for the effective adoption (e.g. [5, 7]). In addition students' perceptions have an impact on what they have already learned and what they choose to do next [11]. Especially, for the mobile devices, due to their portability and functionality, they can be used outdoors, in exhibitions and in other non classroom settings, extending the depth and breadth of informal learning and the importance of students' perceptions.

Research in educational games argues that well-designed games can meet some of the needs of students and pursue them to enroll in learning procedures [13]. Evidence of learning performance of educational games has been shown in several areas, such as history, arts and cultural heritage [2, 3].

Portable devices have been successfully employed as learning tools in both formal and informal learning contexts. In the formal learning, handhelds have been used in teaching both within the classroom setting and out-classroom (i.e. [2]). In addition, the potential of handhelds to assist informal learning has been explored through different frameworks. For instance, handhelds have been used as museum guidebooks [6, 12] or as learning systems [8].

Researchers have often stressed the benefits of enhancing the functions of museums, parks and exhibitions by designing educational projects connected to learners' informal learning, [8] and making non classroom environments more enjoyable and motivating for learning [12]. In the context of museums, many researchers have employed new technologies and customized mobile devices for attracting and engaging visitors. On that direction visitors' beliefs is highly important [2]. For instance, one of the most successful projects was conducted in the Exploratorium of San Francisco [6]. This study was one of the pioneers in the direction of combining mobile technology and capturing experience in the real world.

Many studies have shown the potential of portable devices to increase learning opportunities. Informal learning with the real world experiences is some of the most remarkable advantages. Mobile devices' portability and functionality make them suitable for out-classroom learning, for instance bird-watching, plant hunting and museum guiding are some of the most successful case studies [6, 8]. As such, it is subsequent that the use of mobile devices would bring many benefits and opportunities for informal learning in future. In particular, in this study we aim to provide insights of the following question: (How) Can interactive mobile technology be exploited to implement informal education?

As such, we designed an interactive mobile-based and a paper-based game and we conducted a controlled experiment in order to explore the educational impact and students' performance and perceptions affected by interactivity and mobile technology.

2   Methodology

2.1   The Game Design

A quiz was designed to include several game elements, such as purpose, rules, score, and limitations (space-time). The main purpose of the quiz activity is to identify a series of paintings, at an Art Gallery (fig. 1), based on descriptions of visual elements. During our experiment, the quiz was played by teams of two players, who were given 25 minutes to answer 12 questions that lead them to certain paintings.

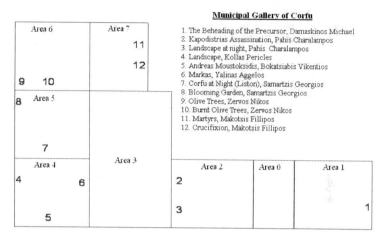

Municipal Gallery of Corfu

1. The Beheading of the Precursor, Damaskinos Michael
2. Kapodistrias Assassination, Pahis Charalampos
3. Landscape at night, Pahis Charalampos
4. Landscape, Kollas Pericles
5. Andreas Moustoksidis, Bokatsiabis Vikentios
6. Markas, Yalinas Aggelos
7. Corfu at Night (Liston), Samartzis Georgios
8. Blooming Garden, Samartzis Georgios
9. Olive Trees, Zervos Nikos
10. Burnt Olive Trees, Zervos Nikos
11. Martyrs, Makotsis Fillipos
12. Crucifixion, Makotsis Fillipos

Fig. 1. The layout of the public art gallery and the 12 correct answers (paintings)

Two free (one of them open-source) software tools were used for implementing the activity, a QR application and a quiz application. The only hardware requirement for running the software is a java enabled mobile phone. Camera feature was a requirement for the QR application1[1]. The design of the questions was implemented with MyMLE[2] application, which allows creating mobile learning content. Some of the basic advantages of this game is the low cost of the infrastructure and that there is no coding required in developing the quiz of questions.

There are two versions of the activity, a Mobile Based (MB) and a paper-based (PB) version. In MB version QR codes are placed next to paintings. Each team provided with two mobile phones, one where questions displayed and answers typed in, and a second one that was used to scan QR codes. When the players identify a painting as an answer to a question, they scan the QR code next to it and type a four digit number as the answer (Fig. 2). If the answer is correct they get a message indicating so. If the answer is wrong, they get a message indicating that they have one more chance to answer correctly. Hence in total each team was given up to two chances to identify a correct answer.

The PB version of the game was identical, except from the fact QR codes were replaced with numbered post-its and the questions were printed on paper. However the major difference in the gameplay between the two versions was that players do not receive any feedback regarding their answers, during the PB game.

---

[1] http://qrcode.sourceforge.jp
[2] http://mle.sourceforge.net

Fig. 2. The QR codes were placed next to the paintings (left), the mobile application (right)

2.2   Sampling

The research methodology included a survey composed by the four main measures and by score tests. The initial sample of the study was sixty 1st grade lyceum (upper general secondary school) students, aged between 15 and 16 years. All the students were attending an elective course in ICT and multimedia at a general lyceum at Corfu, Greece. Three groups were formed up with high similarity in their prior class performance. The three groups of twenty students each, corresponded to the three different classes of the aforementioned course. Group A consisted of 16 males and 4 females, Group B consisted of 17 males and 3 females and Group C consisted of 16 males, 4 females. It should be noted that according to the school's policy students were assigned to the classes of the elective course in a rather "random" manner. At the initial sample of 60 students, we had 5 drop-outs, one female student from Group A, two female students from Group B and two male students from Group C, leaving a total of 55 (19 for the first group, and 18 for the remaining two).

2.3   Procedures

The study was conducted over a three-week period from 10th to 28th of May 2010. During the first week formal classroom teaching was held. At the second week students visited the Art Gallery (Fig. 1) of the Municipality of Corfu and at the third week the posttest (questionnaire and assessment) took place. Upon completion of the tour students from Group A and Group B were briefed on the rules and played the game (mobile- and paper-based respectively). The students of Group A, were also provided with mobile phones with a sample quiz as well as sample QR codes in order to familiarize themselves with the software. The same devices were used during the game. Students of Group C where given instead 30 minutes extra time to spend at the gallery (extended tour), in order to identify visual elements on their own as they wished. For the final week of the study, the students from all three groups took the formal test (assessment) and answered the questionnaire.

2.4   Measures

In order to measure students' effectiveness, all groups completed the cognitive assessment at the end of the study. In addition, Groups A and B completed the survey with the four measures regarding students perceptions.

For the cognitive test a twelve-item assessment, consisting of multiple choice questions, was employed. Students were presented with a series of pictures and had to choose one out of the four descriptions that was more accurate. The description was referring to the same visual elements that were also employed during the game, which were combinations of all of the following: primary and secondary colors, warm and cold colors, geometric and organic shapes, depth and perspective. For instance, two questions were: "which painting has Religious Theme, Action Scene and Perspective in two spots?" (correct: The Beheading of the Precursor) and "which painting has Action Scene, Urban Landscape and Warm Colors?" (correct: Kapodistrias Assassination).

The second part included measures of the various questions identified in the literature from previous researches. These measures included Perceived Importance [9]; Perceived Comprehension [4]; and interest with the activity and the visit [1]. In particular the following constructs were employed: (1) How important do you believe that the activity is to your future visits (perceived importance of activity for future visit, **PIAFV**), (2) How well do you feel you understand the concepts taught (perceived comprehension, **PC**), (3) How interest did you find the visit (perceived Interest for the visit, **PIV**) and (4) How interest did you find the activity (Perceived Interest for the activity/game, **PIG**). For each statement, students have to mark their response on a five-point Likert scale in relation to four measures.

2.5   Data Analysis

Firstly, in order to examine the differences among mobile-based, paper-based game and extended tour guide on students' effectiveness, a post hoc test was conducted. A Games Howell criterion was used in order to examine separately for each group the influence of 1) mobile-based game, 2) paper-based game and 3) extended tour guide on students' effectiveness. In addition for identifying any differences in students' perceptions for perceived importance, perceived comprehension and interest with the activity and the visit a t-test was conducted among mobile-based and paper based game. Finally, for identifying any correlations among students' perceptions Spearman correlation coefficient was conducted.

3   Research Findings

To examine the hypotheses regarding students' performance, the Post-hoc analyses using Games – Howell criterion were conducted to verify whether the different learning procedures (Group) are related to the different effectiveness of the students. The results of three groups, Group A ($M_1=9.00$, $SD_1=2.08$), Group B ($M_2=7.28$,

$SD_2=1.67$) and Group C ($M_3=8.50$, $SD_3=1.97$), highlighted a significant difference only between Group A and Group B ($p<0.05$).

The results highlight that the enrolment with the mobile affects their performance. However, both (paper-mobile) games persuade the children in several ways. A team benefits from a strategy and game characteristics seem to motivate and excite them for the activity. In addition, based on the observations of the researcher students seemed to be more focused and immersed on the mobile application (fig. 3). Interestingly, mobile application did not push students to lose their interest for the museum as many paintings and its features are discussed from students by the end of the experiment and on the respective course on school. Another notable observation is that students from both groups spent approximately the same total time at the gallery (19 min on average). This may be derived from students' familiarity with mobile phones and the simple design of the game.

Fig. 3. Students of the mobile-based game were immersed in questions displayed on their mobile phones

Regarding students' perceptions among mobile-based and paper-based game, a t-test was used for identifying the differences, with four independent variables (PIAFV, PC, PIG, PIV) and the one dependent variable (Group) were included. All variables demonstrate very high levels on both groups (fig. 4), but no significant difference is identified on students' perceptions among the two groups.

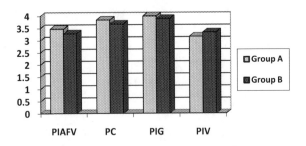

Fig. 4. Students perceptions among mobile-based and paper-based game

Spearman's correlation coefficient between the measures was used, which is about quantifying the strength of the relationship between the variables. Spearman's test suggests that some of the measures are related, in some cases relatively strong. More precisely, perceived interest for the game is strongly related with all measures. Perceived interest for the visit has correlation only with perceived interest for the game. Moreover, perceived importance of activity for future visit and perceived comprehension have significant relation with all measures except perceived interest for the visit. Table 1 indicates the exact results of the test.

Table 1. Spearman correlations between measures

	PIAFV	PC	PIG	PIV
PIAFV	1			
PC	.411**	1		
PIG	.342**	.355*	1	
PIV	.272	.213	.560**	1

* Correlation is significant at the 0.05 level. ** Correlation is significant at the 0.01 level.

4   Discussion and Conclusions

The current study is one of the few so far, where a mobile application assists an informal educational process. Conducting a field study, of this kind with a sample of a 55 students, was not an easy task, especially when social interaction threats are concerned. The overall results prove that the mobile application had a positive effect, on students' performance at the final test and also does not affect their interest for visiting the gallery.

The results of the study allow us to argue that the enhancement of mobile device in a learning game context benefits students' performance in a highly significant way. This result may be explained from previous findings in the literature [8] stating that the usage of mobile devices motivates students and offers sufficient learning opportunities to improve learning procedures. From research we do not have sufficient evidence to suggest that the usage of a mobile application affects students' perceptions regarding the non-classroom learning environment. However, students' perceptions for the game interest positively affect their beliefs for the visit, for a future visit and their comprehension. Hence, we can argue that the enrolment of mobile devise can improve the effectiveness of game based learning and can compete the extended guiding effectiveness in a non classroom environment. In addition, students' interest with the game helps them to understand the benefits of the visit and provide a vehicle for future visits.

These findings have important implications for understanding how students regulate their learning and achievement. Previous studies have shown that students' perceptions of what they have already learned affect what they choose to do next [11]; thus, the differences that entity and incremental theorists exhibit in their perceived comprehension could potentially have long-term effects on their achievement, even if these differences are not currently reflected in their actual comprehension (as was the case in our experiment).

The findings of this study must be interpreted in light of some potential limitations. First, the generalizability of this study must be carefully made, as it was conducted in a single context with specific instructions. Secondly, the sampling of the study apart from students at one grade level and was not longitudinal; therefore the data could not reveal the continuation of the MB game behavior. Despite these limitations, the findings generate valuable insights, which can be used as part of hypotheses for representative follow-up studies in technological tools' educational effectiveness and experience.

Further studies may consider aiming to reveal several insights. First investigating the effect of the game in students' performance under different context and for a long-term period might help on the overall understanding. Also, another study involving different educational levels and students with different levels of computer experience might draw several important conclusions. Further research also needs to examine students' intention to adopt Augmented Reality based learning.

Acknowledgements. The authors would like to thank all of the students, the schools' staff and the museum curator for their participation in the experiment. This work is also supported by project CULT (http://cult.di.ionio.gr). CULT (MC-ERG-2008-230894) is a Marie Curie project of the European Commission (EC) under the 7th Framework Program (FP7).

References

1. Berger, C., Carlson, E.: Measuring computer literacy of teacher trainers. Journal of Educational Computing Research 4(9), 289–303 (1988)
2. Cabrera, J.S., Frutos, H.M., Stoica, A.G., Avouris, N., Dimitriadis, Y., Fiotakis, G., Liveri, K.D.: Mystery in the museum: collaborative learning activities using handheld devices. In: Proceedings of the 7th International Conference on Human Computer Interaction with Mobile Devices & Services, MobileHCI 2005, pp. 315–318. ACM, New York (2005)
3. Costabile, M.F., De Angeli, A., Lanzilotti, R., Ardito, C., Buono, P., Pederson, T.: Explore! Possibilities and Challenges of Mobile Learning. In: Proceedings of CHI 2008. ACM Press, New York (2008)
4. Dunlosky, J., Lipko, A.R.: Metacomprehension: A brief history and how to improve its accuracy. Current Directions in Psychological Science 16, 228–232 (2007)
5. Giannakos, M.N.,, Vlamos, P.: Using Webcasts in Education: Evaluation of its Effectiveness. British Journal of Educational Technology (2012), doi:10.1111/j.1467-8535.2012.01309.x
6. Hsi, H.: A study of user experiences mediated by nomadic web content in a museum. Journal of Computer Assisted Learning 19, 308–319 (2003), doi: 10.1046/j.0266-4909.2003.jca_023.x
7. Hsu, C.-L., Lin, J.C.-C.: Acceptance of Blog Usage: The Roles of Technology Acceptance, Social Influence and Knowledge Sharing Motivation. Information and Management 45(1), 65–74 (2008), DOI= http://dx.doi.org/10.1016/j.im.2007.11.001

8. Huang, Y., Lin, Y., Cheng, S.: Effectiveness of a mobile plant learning system in a science curriculum in Taiwanese elementary education. Computers & Education 54, 47–58 (2010), doi:10.1016/j.compedu.2009.07.006

9. Joshi, K.D., Kvasny, L., McPherson, S., Trauth, E.M., Kulturel-Konak, S., Mahar, J.: Choosing IT as a Career: Exploring the role of Self-Eficacy and Perceived Importance of IT Skills. In: ICIS 2010 Proceedings, Paper 154 (2010), http://aisel.aisnet.org/icis2010_submissions/154

10. King, D.L., Delfabbro, P.H., Griffiths, M.D.: Video game structural characteristics: a new psychological taxonomy. International Journal of Mental Health and Addiction 8, 90–106 (2010)

11. Metcalfe, J., Finn, B.: Evidence that judgments of learning are causally related to study choice. Psychonomic Bulletin & Review 15, 174–179 (2008)

12. Sung, Y.T., Chang, K.E., Hou, H.T., Chen, P.F.: Designing an electronic guidebook for learning engagement in a museum of history. Computers in Human Behavior 26, 74–83 (2010)

13. Tarumi, H., Yamada, K., Daikoku, T., Kusunoki, F., Inagaki, S., Takenaka, M., Hayashi, T., Yano, M.: KEI-time traveler: visiting a past world with mobile phones to enhance learning motivation. In: Proceedings of the 7th International Conference on Interaction Design and Children, IDC 2008, pp. 161–164. ACM, New York (2008)

Mobile Application for Noise Pollution Monitoring through Gamification Techniques

Irene Garcia Martí, Luis E. Rodríguez, Mauricia Benedito, Sergi Trilles,
Arturo Beltrán, Laura Díaz, and Joaquín Huerta

Institute of New Imaging Technologies (INIT), University Jaume I (UJI)
{irene.garcia,pupo,mauri.benedito,sergi.trilles,
arturo.beltran,laura.diaz,huerta}@uji.es
http://www.geoinfo.uji.es

Abstract. Full data coverage of urban environments is crucial to monitor the status of the area to detect, for instance, trends and detrimental environmental changes. Collecting observations related to environmental factors such as noise pollution in urban environments through classical approaches implies the deployment of Sensor Networks. The cost of deployment and maintenance of such infrastructure might be relatively high for local and regional governments. On the other hand recent mass-market mobile devices such as smartphones are full of sensors. For instance, it is possible to perform measurements of noise through its microphone. Therefore they become low-cost measuring devices that many citizens have in their pocket. In this paper we present an approach for gathering noise pollution data by using mobile applications. The applications are designed following gamification techniques to encourage users to participate using their personal smartphones. In this way the users are involved in taking and sharing noise pollution measurements in their cities that other stakeholders can use in their analysis and decision making processes.

Keywords: Gamification, mobile applications, environmental monitoring, noise pollution, PPGIS, VGI.

1   Introduction

Many people on Earth are living in cities and it is expected that 70% of human population will live in cities by 2050 [1]. This fact influences in the growth of activities carried on in industrial parks and urban areas including traffic and other human activities that affect environmental conditions such as noise pollution.

In order to guarantee a sustainable development of our cities, European policies try to regulate the evolution of these environmental conditions. Among others, the European Noise Directive (END) [2], adopted in 2002, establishes a legal framework related to the assessment of environmental noise. In Article 3, it is defined *"environmental noise"* as *"unwanted or harmful outdoor sound created by human activities, including noise emitted by means of transport, road traffic, rail traffic, air traffic, and from sites of industrial activity"*. In the same article, other concepts like *"annoyance"* or *"harmful effects for health"* are defined.

M. Herrlich, R. Malaka, and M. Masuch (Eds.): ICEC 2012, LNCS 7522, pp. 562–571, 2012.
© IFIP International Federation for Information Processing 2012

There are authors who state that noise pollution could seriously affect human health: In [12, 13] it is discussed the set of issues a sustained exposure to noise pollution could trigger, ranging from less-severe sleep disturbances or hearing impairment to much serious cardiovascular disturbances or mental instability.

Daily city activities cannot be stopped, but it is important to continuously pinpoint noise observations to understand if there is any underlying problem that could be a cause of human health issues that should be solved by any government entity. Noise pollution could be measured through sensor networks, but it is a phenomenon that occurs in the entire city with different intensity throughout time and space. Therefore, data acquired with this method could not be enough to depict the city situation.

In this context, it is important to consider a different way for data collection with a high temporal and spatial noise data resolution and with a low deploying cost. The key for this noise pollution monitoring in cities is based in citizenship participation. Involving citizens in monitor noise pollution by using mobile applications is a very cheap method for administrations to acquire real-time data that may help local or regional governments to identify potential problems and therefore, try to solve them.

In this paper we present two mobile application prototypes to collect noise pollution data in urban areas. One of the issues that arise when developing a crowdsourcing monitoring application is the fact that we rely on the measurements taken by the users, but, how to engage users to use this application and provide observations? The main idea is to engage citizens to take noise samples by gamifying the process of acquiring data to obtaining a noise pollution map. One of the problems we identify in the traditional mobile noise measurement taking is that we have to convince the user he or she has to start taking noise samples and keep this practice through time. In this new data acquiring approach, it is crucial the massive and maintained participation over time from general public. This would help creating a huge noise pollution repository to be used for further and more accurate analysis. The difficulty arises from the boredom of doing repetitive tasks without an incentive or amusing elements.

Here is where gamification techniques take major importance, because they provide a mechanism to motivate users to use the application and provide information while they are using a gamified application. In this paper we propose a general approach for noise pollution data collection that implements a crowdsourcing noise pollution monitoring application based on gamification techniques. The main idea applying these techniques to environmental monitoring is to encourage users to participate in data collection process by using their personal smartphone devices. The output of this public participation is a high amount of georeferenced noise pollution dataset that can be later used for further analysis or decision making processes. We demonstrate the application of these gamification techniques by implementing two mobile application prototypes as a proof of concept. Therefore, *NoiseBattle* and *NoiseQuest* mobile applications will be presented as a new participatory way of noise pollution data collection.

The remainder of this paper is organized as follows: In section 2 we discuss the background of this work, including topics such as noise pollution monitoring, general gamification concepts and related work. In section 3 we describe how we applied to this project the gamification concepts. In section 4 we briefly describe the general architecture of this Project and present the two prototype applications in development and finally, in section 5, we present the conclusions and future work ideas.

2   Background and Related Work

2.1   Environmental Noise Pollution Monitoring

Environmental monitoring is a crucial task to control our planet status and development trends. With the adequate set of technologies and tools it is possible to monitor almost any measurable parameter. In our case, we are interested in controlling the noise levels on cities.

In [3] it is described and applied the concept of creating a GI system with Voluntered Geographic Information (VGI), called Public Participatory GIS. The authors define a PPGIS as the result of using GIS capabilities and techniques by the general public, although it was first described in [4]. Moreover, in this paper, scientist community is encouraged to break top-down strategies of delivering geographic data, where government entities, institutions or companies provide them at their own interest. The authors' state that is important to create new bottom-up data productions in order to create GI systems that really fits users' needs and availability. An example of PPGIS application it is found in [3], where Canela (Brazil) users can post comments about POIs related to health or education, such as complains for a school menu service or asking for information related to cultural heritage.

In [5] we could find a good description of the concept "Citizens as Voluntary Sensors". The author states that humanity as a collective, possesses a huge amount of knowledge about the Earth surface and its properties, such as place names, topographic areas or status of a transportation network. If we enable this people with electronic devices to digitize this information, we have a massive collection of raw data collected by volunteers that we can use in our analysis, services and geoprocesses.

Following the PPGIS and Citizens as Voluntary Sensors guidelines, we thought that it would be interesting to join both concepts to apply them in environmental noise pollution monitoring. In this field, some attempts already exist:

According to [6] there are three main approaches to assess noise pollution: simulation maps and data collection through sensor networks. First method consists in applying physical noise propagation laws considering well-known noise sources to get noise affection maps, while second method is based on acquiring data using a distributed network of sensor devices. Finally, there is another method they outline, based in the direct participation of citizenship by providing VGI.

In this paper, we are going to extend the idea described in [6] by developing two mobile applications to collect noise pollution data in urban areas by applying to its development Gamification concepts. Therefore, as users will collect their own noise samples, we are using the concept of citizens as sensors [5] and, as we are going to publish our data in a Noise Mapping Platform, we are contributing to the enlargement of a PPGIS.

2.2   General Gamification Concepts

The 'citizens as sensors' paradigm [5] implements the idea of crowdsourcing the sensor data collection. This is a straightforward way of collecting huge amount of data at a very low cost. Nevertheless, users need an incentive to make volunteers collect those data willingly. At this point here is where the gamification methodology plays its role. In [7] it is questioned how the general public can be motivated to voluntary participation by displaying noise data publicly on a Web GIS platform through maps or allowing tagging the noises measured to enrich this information in a subjective way. However, applications with no incentives will probably attract users highly motivated to collaborate with this platform, just for their satisfaction of contributing to science. Those users will gladly update their observations in the long term, but this set of noise data, although big, will not represent the entire city situation. Gamifying a repetitive or complex problem breaks this gap/wall between a scientific problem and citizenship and allows any citizen to contribute to science unconsciously.

The core concept for gamifying is engagement. As seen in [8], engaging users to do something is crucial to encourage citizenship to collaborate with a project. Engagement could be achieved by motivating people, so it is important to create nice and user-friendly applications that foster people to take the measurements we need.

According to [8] to do a good gamification process it is important to consider four key concepts: user status, access, power & stuff.

Status: Users usually like to compare or share their progress and achievements with other users, to see who is in a better or worse position than others.   To do this, it is necessary to split game progress in stages or levels, from easiest to hardest ones.

Access: This concept encourages allowing users to unlock new features depending on their contribution or participation in the game. It is important to make these features exclusive enough to engage the user who achieves them more attached to the application.

Power: With the transference of some power to some users, it is possible to encourage them to keep using the application. The power can be represented by letting them to do actions that are not allowed to users who have used less the application.

Stuff: In addition to all functional concepts stated above, it is important to provide a set of free rewards, badges or gifts for users as an incentive to keep playing. Those items are attractive to users because they can make the difference with others.

2.3   Related Work

Nowadays, there are many successful examples of gamified and purpose-oriented applications. It is the case of Phylo[1] an application that exploits the natural capacity of human being to recognize visual patterns, an operation with a high computational cost. Phylo presents DNA sequences in the mobile device screen in a gamified context and engages users preparing a race competition among them and providing awards and acknowledgment for winners.

Another example of gamification comes from automobiles' brand Nissan[2]. It includes in their new car models an application for monitoring gas emissions and featuring an automatic gaming system to provide real-time information about the gases

---

[1] http://news.cnet.com/8301-17938_105-20024075-1.htm
[2] http://news.cnet.com/8301-17938_105-20026662-1.html

emitted to the atmosphere. Users are then encouraged to drive responsibly to go up in drivers' rankings.

Regarding the collection of noise using public participation, several projects have been carried on. For example, in [15] is presented a project where the users can contribute to collect noise from the city and publish it in the NoiseTube platform. The platform offers a mobile application that consumes an API for sending the collected data. Later the user can see the maps with the noise data in a website. Other project worth to mention is presented in [14]. In this case the authors describes a mobile application for collecting noise data, and add the possibility of including extra information related with the perception of the noise measured (i.e. annoyance) or the location (i.e. home or work place).   In both cases the incentive for collecting data is the mere contribution.

Finally, it is also important to consider the gamification techniques applied to produce FourSquare application, as it is a successful social game oriented to business-purposes that breaks the wall between the virtual/real world by providing physical rewards to users.

3   Applying Gamification Concepts

After explaining the gamification theoretical concepts in section 2.2, we are going to explain how we carried on the gamification process in particular to our prototypes. Considering the two use cases we have developed, those concepts have been applied as follows:

Status: In our project, we have created this progress based on the number of noise observations: as users collect information, they get more points that will increase general score and therefore, their level.

Access: The access concept is grounded as unlocking quests or owning more city areas, depending on the prototype. Collecting noise observations is the key to progress in both applications. Data acquisition is rewarded: as long as the users collect more noise observations, access to different kind of things is granted.

Power: In one of the prototypes we provide power by giving the capability of sending noises (or sounds) to an enemy in the battle. This kind of actions are important to foster competition among users, so they feel motivated to keep progressing in the game to gain that special power another user has.

Stuff: A set of avatars and rewards have been created for both use cases.

Regarding the target users analysis, we followed the classification found in [9]. In this paper, the author divides users in four different types: killers, achievers, socializers & explorers. In our prototypes, we targeted the following users:

Noise Battle: The user profile we targeted is mainly *Achiever*. In this application, the idea is providing an environment where the user can win points and conquer areas, with the purpose to make the player feel rewarded just by winning and sending noises to the enemies. The competition factor is very important to make their achievements more satisfying.

Noise Quest: The type of user targeted in this second case is *Explorer*. Here the competition with other users is not as intense as the previous case. In this application it is more important walking around the city taking measurements than the score achieved by the number of observations taken. The "goodness" of the observation is more valuable than the number of measurements collected.

4   Architecture and Prototypes

4.1   General Architecture

This section describes in detail the conceptual architecture we used. Figure 1 depicts the general architecture of the project. The prototypes in-development for this project follows the same schema. As seen, the modules are divided in three parts: *Mobile Client-side application, Middleware Layer* and *Remote Server-side* that are described below these lines.

The *Mobile application* provides the functionality that allows user to take measurements, send them to the middleware and check the general progress of the battle in course. We suggest that the application should be divided in the following modules: *User Interface, Measurement, Mapping* and *Connection & Encoding*. For the *User Interface* we used Android SDK because it is a free and growing development platform and provides a good integration with Google Maps, the engine we used for our *Mapping module*. Regarding the *Connection & Encoding Module*, we decided to implement our own classes in Java to connect and send the data to the *Middleware Server*. For the *Measurement Module* we used part of the mobile noise pollution measurement application developed by IFGI (Institute for Geoinformatics, University of Münster) called **NoiseDroid**. NoiseDroid is an open-source mobile application that allows the user taking noise samples. This application has its own noise quality assessment system which provides information about the usefulness of the noise data collected [10, 11]. Due to the open-source condition of NoiseDroid, we reused source code related to the collection and assessment of the noise samples, and include it in our *Measurement Module*.

Middleware layer has as main goal to attend all incoming noise observations, store them in a noise database and send the measurements taken to a remote server. This layer, that should lay on an intermediate server, takes care as well of keeping the user's status up-to-date in real-time, writing in the database the new data and sending back the status to the user while notifying other users of the changes on the game they are playing. We have divided the functionality of this server in three different modules: *Client Communication, Transactional, Remote Server Connection*. For the *Client Communication Module* we decided to develop our own set of classes in Java. The *Transactional Module* is programmed in Java as well, but we used Hibernate for the communication with the database. In the case of the *Remote Server Connection Module* we used the API provided by the server for sending the noise data.

Remote Server-side is the module that will contain all retrieved VGI noise data from users and will allow the analysis by general public by providing some mapping layers. We think about the functionality of this server in these modules: *Mapping* and

Data Management. In order to reuse available resources, we decided to contribute to Open Noise Map Platform (ONMP) by sending our collected data to this noise mapping platform. ONMP was developed by IFGI and provides a Web GIS interface where it is possible to see uploaded noise measurements comfortably, using a map layout.

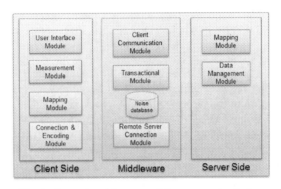

Fig. 1. General architecture of the proposed solution

4.2   Noise Battle Prototype

Noise Battle is a gamified mobile application developed for Android platform where users have to move around a city taking noise samples. Currently the game is on development and it is not entirely functional or available to download. The final goal of this game from the user's point of view is conquering the city by taking noise measurements.

The city is split into cells of a grid, so the user can conquer the cells by taking more and better measurements than other users in the area. During the game, the users are rewarded by different means: either by measuring in the proximity of one of the rewards placed in the grid or by conquering some cell of it. The rewards might include the possibility of sending noises or sounds to the foes. The sounds that can be sent to the rivals are used to show the power obtained by the sender of the noise. The rivals have the option of re-conquering previously conquered cells by performing better quality measurements or more recent measurements. These mechanisms should encourage the players to provide more accurate (based on a criteria taken from the API used) or updated noise data. Regarding the rewards, we have considered awarding measurements dispersion and data quality (based on NoiseDroid quality assessment) in order to assure a regular number of observations taken in the entire city area. Besides, we also took into account to place rewards (or having higher density of them) in zones where there is more interest about noise pollution conditions. The observations gathered are immediately uploaded to the middleware server, which further submit it to the ONMP platform. The ONMP platform can store it and make it available for visualization or processing.

In Figure 2 (left) it is possible to see a sample of the battlefield where a game is going to start. As seen, the city is divided in a grid where each cell represents an area the user can conquer through taking noise measures. For each measurement performed, it is possible to see the minimum, maximum and mean of noise measured. Then the player can decide to submit it as his move in the game. In this case there are some items placed for each cell that represent locations where the player can take a noise measurement and receive a reward. Figure 2 (centre) represents a more advanced state of the battle for that city, where some users have started using the application and conquered some areas. The areas conquered can be recognized by the colour of the cell. In this scenario there are three players, each of them with a different colour and avatar associated competing each other. Figure 2 (right) provides a higher level of detail of the image in the centre. In the next section we briefly describe the second prototype.

Fig. 2. Some images depicting **NoiseBattle** prototype working

4.3   Noise Quest Prototype

Noise Quest is a prototype of mobile application for Android platform that using quests, challenges and missions will guide a user around a city taking noise samples following a storyline. At this point, NoiseQuest application development is in a very early stage, so it is not possible to present any sample screenshot. The quests are focused in conquering different POIs by taking samples, making a competition with the different users playing the game and progressing in the story. The general idea of this application is to obtain noise measurements distributed uniformly around the city throughout time. For this purpose, the application will guide the user over all city area following a storyline where he or she is the main character. This game has different levels of difficulty so quests will be easier at the very beginning of the game and getting harder as long as the player advances in the game. The game starts in the user position and taking this point as a centre it draws three concentric circles with a determined radius whose size depends on the selected level: the higher the level, the bigger the circles are and therefore, the general difficulty of the game increases until covering the entire city area. First quests consist in obtaining measurements in the user's surroundings, located in the most inner circle. As long as the user completes the quests, the missions and challenges will lead the user to positions farther away, in the outer circles.

5   Conclusion

In this paper we presented an approach for designing environmental noise pollution monitoring applications based on crowdsourcing by means of applying gamification techniques. We presented a conceptual architecture and components to implement this kind of applications. For demonstration purposes two gamified mobile applications for noise pollution monitoring have been developed. The use of these applications by general public could contribute to increase urban society welfare through noise sampling, locating areas with a higher noise pollution to make some research or analysis and try to solve the problem.

Gamifying it is an interesting process to convert tiring and repetitive tasks in others lighter and more user-engaging ones that can provide huge amount of data to all-levels government entities and other decision makers. Logically, if a tool capable of spotting noise problems is created, it would be interesting from local authorities to consider this potential source of data to improve liveability of a city.

Developing purpose-oriented and gamified applications for mobile platforms it is very interesting due to its big range of possibilities and topics to create applications. Nevertheless, we think that in parallel, it is recommended to provide a pure GIS application where it would be possible to check and make operations with the set of data and make analysis.

As future work, it would be interesting to implement mechanisms for filtering and correcting VGI data, as per nature, some of them might be false or inaccurate for scientific analysis. On the prototypes functionality, two improvements could be done: at this point, both applications are spatially dividing the city in a grid in NoiseBattle case and in concentric and growing circles in NoiseQuest example. It would be interesting to change these geometric shapes into more real ones that fit a city district or neighborhood, so the user is competing in more natural divisions. The second idea would be implementing a noise measurements expiring policy for observations. A user would lose his/her score progressively in time with the aim of sticking the user to the application: the idea is encouraging them to keep them taking noise samples by slowly removing their conquers and score due to inactivity.

Acknowledgements. This work has been partially supported by the GEOCLOUD project ref. IPT-430000-2010-11, INNPACTO 2010 subprogramme, Ministry of Science and Innovation; OSMOSIS: Open Source Mobile Sensor Information System. IMPIVA Institute (Institute of Small and Medium-sized Enterprises from Generalitat Valenciana) and European Regional Development Fund (ERDF), ref. IMPIVA I+D IMIDTA/2009/793 and IMIDTA/2010/24.

References

1. United Nations: Report about State of the World's Cities 2010/2011: Bridging the urban divide (2011)
2. European Parliament: Directive 2002/49/EC of the European Parliament and of the Council of 25 June 2002 relating to the assessment and management of environmental noise (2002)
3. Bugs, G., Granell, C., Fonts, O., Huerta, J., Painho, M.: An assessment of Public Participation GIS and Web 2.0 technologies in urban planning practice in Canela, Brazil. Cities 27(3), 172–181 (2010)
4. Nyerges, T., Barndt, M., Brooks, K.: Public participation geographic information systems. In: Proceedings of Auto-Carto 13, Seattle, WA, American Congress on surveying and mapping. Bethesda, MD, pp. 224–233 (1997)
5. Goodchild, M.: Citizens as Voluntary sensors: spatial data infrastructure in the world of Web 2.0. International Journal of Spatial Data Infrastructures Research 2, 24-32 (2007)
6. Maisonneuve, N., Stevens, M., Ochab, B.: Participatory noise pollution monitoring using mobile phones. Information Polity 2010 15, 51–71 (2010)
7. Maisonneuve, N., Stevens, M., Niessen, M., Hanappe, P., Steels, L.: Citizen Noise Pollution Monitoring. In: Proceedings of the 10th International Digital Government Research Conference 2009 (2009)
8. Zichermann, G., Cunningham, C.: Gamification by Design. Implementing Game Mechanics in Web and Mobile Appls. O'Reilly Media, Inc. (2011)
9. Richard, B.: Hearts, clubs, diamonds, spades: Players who suits MUDs (1996), http://www.mud.co.uk/richard/hcds.htm
10. Foerster, T., Jirka, S., et al.: Integrating Human Observations and Sensor Observations – the Example of a Noise Mapping Community. In: Proceedings of Towards Digital Earth Workshop at Future Internet Symposium. Berlin, Germany, September 2010; CEUR-WS: Aachen, Germany, vol. 640 (2010)
11. Everding, T., Jürrens, E., Andrae, S.: In-stream Validation of Measurements with OGC SWE Web Services. In: Second International Conference on Advanced Geographic Information Systems, Applications and Services, pp. 93–98. IEEE Computer Society (2010)
12. Goines, L., Hagler, L.: Noise Pollution: A modern plague. Southern Medical Journal 100, 287–294 (2007)
13. Trombetta Zannin, P.H., BelisárioDiniz, F., Alves Barbosa, W.: Environmental noise pollution in the city of Curitiba, Brazil. Journal of Applied Acoustics 63, 351–358 (2002)
14. Bilandzic, M., Banholzer, M., Peev, D., Georgiev, V., Balagtas-Fernandez, F., De Luca, A.: Laermometer – A Mobile Noise Mapping Application. In: Proceedings of NordiCHI 2008 (2008)
15. Maisonneuve, N., Stevens, M., Niessen, M.E.: NoiseTube: Measuring and mapping noise pollution with mobile phones. In: Proceedings of the 4th International ICSC Symposium, Information Technologies in Environtmental Engineering (ITEE 2009), Thessaloniki, Greece, May 28-29 (2009)
16. D'Hondt, E., Stevens, M., Jacobs, A.: Participatory noise mapping works! An evaluation of participatory sensing as an alternative to standard techniques for environmental monitoring

AtomicOrchid: A Mixed Reality Game
to Investigate Coordination in Disaster Response

Joel E. Fischer, Wenchao Jiang, and Stuart Moran

The Mixed Reality Laboratory, University of Nottingham
{joel.fischer,psxwj,stuart.moran}@nottingham.ac.uk

Abstract. In this paper, we draw on serious mixed reality games as an approach to explore and design for coordination in disaster response scenarios. We introduce AtomicOrchid, a real-time location-based game to explore coordination and agile teaming under temporal and spatial constraints according to our approach. We outline the research plan to study the various interactional arrangements in which human responders can be supported by agents in disaster response scenarios in the future.

1   Introduction

Disaster response (DR) typically include groups of human, canine, computational and embodied agents (such as robots) coordinating a response to a disaster such as an earthquake, a flood, a terrorist attack, an epidemic outbreak or a nuclear disaster. Responders may have to coordinate and perform their operations potentially under critical temporal and spatial constraints, with limited resources and personnel, where failure may cost human lives. Particularly, coordination is an essential requirement in DR in order that groups of people can carry out interdependent activities together in a timely and satisfactory manner [1].

The ORCHID project[1] investigates the potential of human-agent collectives (HACs) in a DR scenario, where groups of humans and computational or embodied agents collaborate to achieve a common task. The critical nature of the DR domain makes it difficult to evaluate and study systems designed to support or enable HACs 'in the wild'. On the other hand, computational simulations of such scenarios are not only extremely difficult to construct, but the veracity of results may be impossible to verify [2]. In particular, simulations may misconceive the emotional response induced in realistic settings, such as stress, fear or panic [3].

Conversely, reports of Mixed Reality Games (MRGs) have unpacked people's interaction 'in the wild', for example how they achieve spatially distributed coordination to orchestrate a game [4]. More specifically, 'serious' MRGs have been suggested as an approach for exploring scenarios that are typically hard to study in the wild, such as DR [5]. To clarify, we do not interpret the prefix 'serious' to mean that the game itself is inherently serious – players could still find it fun to play – more that the underlying research objectives are 'serious'.

---

[1] www.orchid.ac.uk

M. Herrlich, R. Malaka, and M. Masuch (Eds.): ICEC 2012, LNCS 7522, pp. 572–577, 2012.
© IFIP International Federation for Information Processing 2012

We apply this approach to study HACs 'in the wild' by situating both agents and participants in real world environments, and presenting them with compelling game scenarios analogous to disasters. The objective is to study coordination, interaction and communication amongst actors while also having greater confidence in the efficacy of behavioural observations.

A shared understanding and situation awareness are key requirements for coordination in settings that involve human-agent interaction [1]. We are particularly interested in how the coordination of DR can be supported and designed for by studying and designing for coordination in MRGs. In particular, MRGs share a common set of characteristics with DR scenarios that we outline in the following section.

2   Coordination in DR and MRG

Drawing on related work, we now illustrate some key characteristics that highlight how coordination is achieved in MRGs, and how these key characteristcs are shared with DR.

1. **Bridging the physical and the digital.** Both DR as well as MRGs routinely bridge the phyiscal and the digital as part of their actors' coordination [6]. While DR for example makes use of the twitterverse to inform the real world response [9], MRGs provide hybrid spaces to enable playful and artistic performances and public experience [7], often across different media [8].
2. **Orchestration.** The work of managing a DR as well as MRGs are highly orchestrated activities. Authoring and orchestration tools 'behind the scenes' of an MRG as well as player interfaces provide managers, players and spectators with different temporal and spatial views of the game world in order to support the experience [4]. These settings are somewhat comparable to the 'control room' of a first response operation, if only in their collection of various technological arrangements to communicate and coordinate real-time information streams to create a holistic as possible picture of the setting of interest.
3. **On-the-ground and online.** In both DR as well as (many) MRGs people on the ground work with people online to solve a common problem [7]. In [9], the authors show how an understanding of online content can help to understand medical coordination challenges in DR from pre-deployment to on-the-ground action. MRGs often leverage the fact that people on the ground and people online have different views of the world that are turned into different abilities within the game. For example, Uncle Roy All Around You [6] involved online and physical players collaborating in order to achieve a common goal - finding the mysterious Uncle Roy in the back streets of London.

Despite not being a comprehensive list, these key characteristics illustrate the overlap between coordination in MRGs and DR that underlie our motivation to explore the approach of serious mixed reality games further.

3   AtomicOrchid

As a test bed for HACs in DR we designed and implemented an MRG called AtomicOrchid, that we continue to describe in this paper. In the following sections, we describe the game scenario, gaming and authoring interfaces, and the research-driven design rationale behind the game mechanics.

Game Scenario. AtomicOrchid is a location-based real-time MRG based on the fictitious scenario of radioactive explosions creating expanding and moving radioactive clouds that pose a threat to responders on the ground (the field players), and the targets to be rescued around the game area. Field responders are assigned a specific role (e.g. 'medic', 'transporter', 'soldier', 'ambulance') and targets have specific role requirements, so that only certain teams of responders can pick up certain targets. For example, an 'injured person' can only be picked up by an 'ambulance' and a 'medic'. Field responders must not expose themselves to radioactivity from the cloud for too long, else they risk becoming 'incapacitated'.

In their mission to rescue all the targets from the radioactive zone, the field responders are supported by (at least one) person in a centrally located 'headquarters' room.

Player Interfaces. Field responders are equipped with a 'mobile responder tool' providing them with sensing and awareness capabilities (see figure 1). The app shows them a reading of radioactivity, their health level, and a GPS-enabled map of the game area with the targets to be collected and the 'safe' drop off zones for the targets. They can also use the tool to broadcast message to the other field responders, and to headquarters.

Headquarters (HQ) is manned by at least one player who has at their disposal an 'HQ dashboard' that provides them with an overview of the game area, including real-time information of the players' locations (see figure 1). HQ can also broadcast messages to all field responders (not shown), and can review the responders' exposure and health levels. Importantly, only headquarters has a view of the radioactive cloud. 'Hotter' zones correspond with higher levels of radioactivity.

Authoring. We have designed a simple graphical authoring interface for AtomicOrchid that allows non-programmers to set up a game on the fly, including specifying GPS-locations of the game area, targets, and drop-off zones. An important feature is that the game can be played anywhere (in principle), which is an essential requirement for deployments 'in the wild'.

Design Rationale. It is worth mentioning that certain game mechanics are designed to allow us to explore specific aspects of coordination in HACs. Sensing and awareness of the environment are necessary requirements for coordination in DR. However, in order to create the need for more communication amongst HQ and field responders, the spatial position and movement of the cloud is only known to HQ. Furthermore, the specifics of role-target allocation creates the

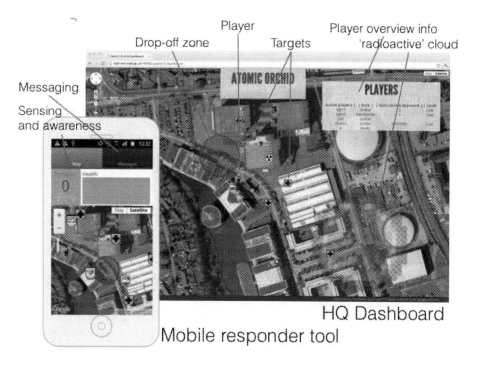

Fig. 1. Player interfaces in AtomicOrchid

requirement for field responders to form 'agile teams' – forming, disbanding, relocating and re-forming continously in order to complete the game objective. Agile teaming is seen as one of the key challenges of DR that can be supported by computational agents [10].

While the described game scenario does not include computational or embodied agents specifically, the scenario allows the creation of complex role-target allocations that, together with spatial and temporal constraints, provide an interesting use case for computational agent support. We will elaborate the integration of agents in AtomicOrchid in the next section.

Platform. AtomicOrchid is based on the open-sourced geo-fencing game Map-Attack[2] that has been iteratively developed for a responsive, (relatively) scalable experience. It is essentially a client-server platform relying on real-time streaming of location data built using the geoloqi platform, Sinatra for Ruby, and state-of-the-art web technologies such as socket.io, node.js, redis and Synchrony for Sinatra[3]. Open source mobile client apps that are part native, part browser based exist for iPhone and Android; we adapted the Android app to build the AtomicOrchid mobile responder tool.

---

[2] http://mapattack.org/
[3] http://bit.ly/rf4pQ7

4   Researching HACs with AtomicOrchid

Complexity in role-target allocation in AtomicOrchid can easily become a bottle-neck for human decision making, given the critical temporal constraints. Field responders may struggle to decide on the order of 'targets' to save, and how to efficiently coordinate re-grouping in the required teams. 'Coalition formation with spatial and temporal constraints' is a well-defined and difficult problem in the multi-agent systems community, for which a computational solution efficient enough to be applicable in a real-time scenario has been proposed [10].

As an exploration of human-agent interaction in AtomicOrchid, we plan to integrate a computational coordinator agent that instructs field responders on when to form coalitions and which targets to rescue based on real-time analysis of the location and distances of responders and targets on the ground. Through a series of deployments, we will explore the effects of different interactional arrangements. Initially we aim to explore the following arrangements:

– The agent 'instructs' only headquarters, detailing teaming and target allocations for all responders. This arrangement relies on HQ 'translating' and delivering the instructions to the field responders.
– The agent directly 'instructs' the field responders individually, detailing teaming and target allocations on an individual basis.

Further configurations of these arrangements include whether the instructions are delivered initially as a 'one-off' plan for the entire game, or whether the instructions are delivered 'just-in-time' after the completion of a sub-task, i.e. after a target has been dropped off in the safe zone. The configuration of interactional arrangements allows us to explore various ways in which human responders can be supported by computational agents.

The 2x2 factor research design achieved through the combination of interactional arrangement (agent–HQ vs agent–responder) and delivery mechanism (one-off vs just-in-time) can be enriched by considering further research questions of human-agent interaction, such as

– How (and when) does the agent need to present the information or instructions most effectively to supports the responders' tasks?
– Where do agents fit into existing human disaster response practices?
– What are the benefits and shortcomings of using a software agent to instruct and assist disaster response compared to a human coordinator?
– How can people best respond to agent instructions and how can the agent improve/learn from the human response?

5   Summary

In this paper, we proposed the application of serious mixed reality games to explore and design for coordination in disaster response scenarios. We introduced AtomicOrchid, a real-time location-based game to explore coordination and agile teaming under temporal and spatial constraints. We outlined the research plan by which we will study the various interactional arrangements in which human responders can be supported by agents in order to enable HACs in disaster response scenarios in the future.

Acknowledgements. This work is supported by EPSRC grant EP/I011587/1.

References

1. Bradshaw, J.M., Feltovich, P.J., Johnson, M.: Human-Agent interaction. In: Boy, G.A. (ed.) The Handbook of Human-Machine Interaction: A Human-Centred Design Approach, pp. 283–299. Ashgate Publishing Company, Surrey (2011)
2. Simonovic, S.P.: Systems Approach to Management of Disasters: Methods and Applications. Wiley (2009)
3. Drury, J., Cocking, C., Reicher, S.: Everyone for themselves? a comparative study of crowd solidarity among emergency survivors. British Journal of Social Psychology 48(3), 487–506 (2009)
4. Crabtree, A., Benford, S., Rodden, T., Greenhalgh, C., Flintham, M., Anastasi, R., Drozd, A., Adams, M., Row-Farr, J., Tandavanitj, N., Steed, A.: Orchestrating a mixed reality game 'on the ground'. In: Proceedings of the SIGCHI Conference on Human Factors in Computing Systems, CHI 2004, pp. 391–398. ACM, New York (2004)
5. Fischer, J.E., Flintham, M., Price, D., Goulding, J., Pantidi, N., Rodden, T.: Serious mixed reality games. In: Mixed Reality games. Workshop at the 2012 ACM Conference on Computer Supported Cooperative Work (2012)
6. Benford, S., Magerkurth, C., Ljungstrand, P.: Bridging the physical and digital in pervasive gaming. Commun. ACM 48(3), 54–57 (2005)
7. Flintham, M., Benford, S., Anastasi, R., Hemmings, T., Crabtree, A., Greenhalgh, C., Tandavanitj, N., Adams, M., Row-Farr, J.: Where on-line meets on the streets: experiences with mobile mixed reality games. In: Proceedings of the SIGCHI Conference on Human Factors in Computing Systems, CHI 2003, pp. 569–576. ACM, New York (2003)
8. Lindt, I., Ohlenburg, J., Babatz, U.P., Oppermann, L., Ghellal, S., Adams, M.: Designing cross media games. In: Proceedings of the 2nd International Workshop on Pervasive Gaming Applications (2005)
9. Sarcevic, A., Palen, L., White, J., Starbird, K., Bagdouri, M., Anderson, K.: "Beacons of hope" in decentralized coordination. In: Proceedings of the ACM 2012 conference on Computer Supported Cooperative Work - CSCW 2012, p. 47. ACM Press, New York (2012)
10. Ramchurn, S., Polukarov, M., Farinelli, A.: Coalition formation with spatial and temporal constraints. In: Proceedings of the 9th International Conference on Autonomous Agents and Multiagent Systems, AAMAS 2010 (2010)

A Ubiquitous Solution for Location-Aware Games

André Pinto[1,3], António Coelho[1,2,3], and Hugo da Silva[1,2]

[1] Departamento de Engenharia Informática, Faculdade de Engenharia,
Universidade do Porto, Porto, Portugal
{andre.da.silva.pinto,acoelho,hugo.da.silva}@fe.up.pt
[2] INESC TEC (formerly INESC Porto), Porto, Portugal
[3] 3Decide, Palcos da Realidade, Porto, Portugal

Abstract. Even though we now witness a popular use of location-based mobile games, the player experience in these applications is always limited by the errors of common location technologies, especially in indoor scenarios. This paper describes the way we minimize this problem in our game development platform, by levering the potential behind smartphone sensors to estimate players' trajectories. Our approach is based on a Pedestrian Dead Reckoning (PDR) algorithm that combines methods to determine orientation, detect steps and estimate their length. Other typical multiplayer mobile games problems, like network latency, are also briefly addressed.

Keywords: location-based games, mobile games, location-based services, ubiquitous, indoor, pedestrian dead reckoning.

1 Introduction

During the last years, the proliferation of smartphones with location capabilities enabled the creation of several categories of location-based services (LBS). Among them, the mobile social gaming phenomena ended up attracting more attention to the opportunities created by these technological advances in the entertainment field. At the same time, ubiquitous computing, a model in which information is omnipresent and contextualized, is now more prevalent than ever before [1].

Although enabling interesting use cases for mobile games, everyone who used a GPS-enabled device, has certainly experienced its accuracy and availability bottlenecks, whether caused by indoor usage, city canyons or other physical obstacles. Even the alternative solutions, like WLAN positioning, can get its performance critically deteriorated in dynamic non-line-of-sight situations. These limitations are restraining mobile games (and many other LBS) from exploring truly ubiquitous experiences.

The solution presented in this paper was motivated by the development of a serious game that helps the player to explore a faculty building by engaging the user in a "treasure hunt". During the gameplay the player gets to know the most

M. Herrlich, R. Malaka, and M. Masuch (Eds.): ICEC 2012, LNCS 7522, pp. 578–583, 2012.

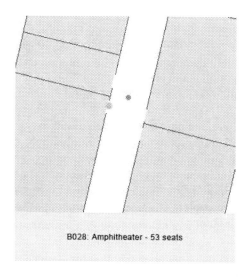

B028: Amphitheater - 53 seats

Fig. 1. Game screen showing the player (green) near a point of interest (yellow)

important places around him/her, whilst receiving basic useful information of the surroundings (Figure 1). By visiting specific points of interest within the faculty campus, the player collects points for his/her team. This use case implies some technical requirements such as indoor player positioning and intensive location reporting to the server.

To enable the development of this type of games, we propose a multiplayer mobile gaming platform that was developed to diminish the above inaccuracies by implementing a pedestrian dead reckoning method that uses the sensors usually available on recent smartphones (accelerometers, magnetometers and gyroscopes) to estimate the players' positions. Besides the location problem, our platform also offers a basic communication system created to minimize latency impact during the necessary data exchange in a multiplayer environment.

2   Platform Architecture

Our platform is composed by several client applications (one per player), which access one server application by using the available network technology in the place (e.g. WLAN, 3G, 4G). Both of these applications are written in Java. The client applications are responsible for reporting the player position to the server and engaging the user in the game mechanics. The server application manages the game communication and controls game-sensitive data, like the scoreboard. Finally there is a third entity, a PostGIS database, from which the client applications obtain the building plan data. In our test case, this data is used to render the plan and show information about the points of interest near the player.

Although we had used a Sparkfun Razor IMU with 9 Degrees of Freedom to gather the sensors data, the approach is equality valid for any smartphone which fulfil the necessary hardware requirements.

3   Related Work

The pedestrian dead reckoning approaches to location is not a new topic in the scientific community. From the various work already done, we highlight the 1996's patent [2], which provides an initial overview of the solution as a whole, and, more recently [3], that offers an implementation for handheld devices. Other solutions are also addressed in surveys like [4] and [5], which enable the reader to better understand the complete panorama of indoor location methods. On the other hand, communication problems like network latency, which are common in these situations, have also been targeted in [6].

4   Pedestrian Dead Reckoning (PDR)

PDR is a method used by Inertial Navigation Systems. In this kind of systems, the positioning process is based on a relative estimation. The previous known position of the subject/object's is used together with an estimate for its displacement to obtain an approximation of the current position. For PDR solutions, the displacement estimate intends to measure the distance of pedestrian locomotion. The method is composed by 3 main tasks:

– orientation determination,
– step detection,
– step length estimation.

In a "disturbance-free environment", orientation could be given directly by the magnetometer's readings. In the "real world", magnetic fields are very irregular which makes the former method a naive use of this sensor. On the other hand, electronic gyroscopes have offset and drift errors, so they can't be a reliable source for orientation without realizing further steps to treat their data. In order to fix this we combined the gyroscope's data with the values received from the magnetometers and accelerometers into a direction cosine matrix. This process includes several different methods that are generically described in [7]. Still, this process is not free from the negative effects of magnetic disturbances, so we implemented an additional technique to detect interferences on the magnetometer's signal [8]. We did this by monitoring sudden changes in the norm of the magnetic field, and temporarily ignoring the magnetometer's data while they are present.

The step detection process is based on a state machine that processes the accelerometer signal over the vertical axis and detects "step-like" waves. The state machine contains 4 states: *IDLE*, *ACC UP*, *ACC DOWN* and *STOPPING*. Each one of these states has its own transition conditions that reflect the mechanic of the different step phases.

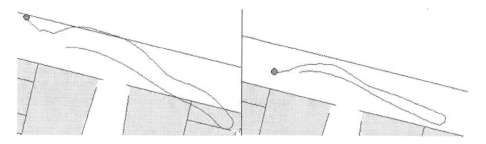

Fig. 2. Player's straight line trajectory (red) obtained by using our approach without (left) and with (right) magnetic disturbances detection

Finally, as a step length depends on multiple factors that can be associated with the subject (e.g. height, sex), the environment (e.g. inclinations, stairs) or the walk dynamics (e.g. step frequency and walk gait), we used various different metrics obtained from the accelerometer to estimate its value, namely: the double integral of acceleration's norm (without gravity), the maximum amplitude of vertical acceleration, the minimum anteroposterior acceleration and a step frequency estimate. An additional constant factor is added to represent a reference value. During an initial calibration phase, the weights (w_i) of each one of these factors (v_i) are estimated by using multiple linear regression. Afterwards they are combined to calculate the step length (sL) estimate for every detected step:

$$sL = \sum_{i=1}^{5} w_i \cdot v_i \tag{1}$$

5   Communication

There is a strong relation between the communication requirements and the game genre. When creating a platform for mobile serious games, it is not possible to predict the kind of games it will be used for, so the optimization work was focused on the system's reaction to the worst-case scenario. Many of the problems present in the worst-case scenario are greatly increased by mobile network characteristics, which are typically slower and more error-prone than the wired networks. This easily leads to package loss and latency. Considering the circumstances, different protocols (UDP and TCP) were assessed and ways to minimize the negative effects of latency (e.g. dead reckoning) were studied.

For location-based games that heavily rely on a continuous feed of messages reporting the player's position, the importance of a single message is very low as it becomes immediately outdated with the next one in the stream. Therefore, a protocol like TCP, whose methods for granting reliability introduce considerable delay on the network, is unsuited to our case. For instance, if one position update message fails to reach its target, skipping it and sending the new position instead, would be a better option than trying to send the obsolete position again.

Additionally, the bigger segment header (UDP: 8 bytes, TCP: 20 bytes) and the considerable weight of acknowledgement messages in the network transfers (38% [9]), are all strong drawbacks for TCP in its comparison with UDP. Thus we ended up using UDP to handle the communication between the different actors. Our conclusions are also supported by [6] where UDP invariably outperforms TCP in every tested network (e.g. UDP UMTS: 458 ms avg, TCP UMTS: 933 ms avg).

6   Conclusions and Future Work

Overall, the final solution produced encouraging results when compared with the naive approach, but even with all the previous corrections, the PDR displacement estimation's accuracy still depends on the sensors data reliability. As can be seen in Figure 2, our approach creates some deviation from the real trajectory. This is especially worrying, as these errors accumulate in each iteration (as is typical in INS), which can lead to useless estimates relatively quickly. In order to minimize this accumulated error we plan to implement restrictions on the possible trajectories performed by the player. By removing impossible moves, like a person crossing a wall, we can keep the total uncertainty within an acceptable level in regions with physical obstacles. Additionally, it might be useful to introduce support for TCP communication to accommodate other use-cases that need to assure reliable message delivery.

As an alternative, the developer could eventually adopt a "seamful" design approach by adapting the game mechanics and bringing these limitations into the game itself. In some cases, informing the player about the existence of problems and exploiting them as game features, can constitute a valid alternative [10].

The present method can be used as a stand-alone solution, or as an auxiliary component of another location technology, which makes it also useful for outdoor-only games that require higher precision than a GPS-only solution can provide. Nevertheless, other location-aware products and services can also gain from the use of these techniques. A migration to a smartphone platform and a more intensive end-user experience would definitely foster further refinements and help consolidating the solution.

Acknowledgments. This work is partially supported by the Portuguese government, through the National Foundation for Science and Technology - FCT (Fundação para a Ciência e a Tecnologia) and the European Union (COMPETE, QREN and FEDER) through the project PTDC/EIA-EIA/114868/2009 entitled "Eras - Expeditious Reconstruction of Virtual Cultural Heritage Sites".

References

1. Greenfield, A.: Everyware: the dawning age of ubiquitous computing. New Riders (2006)
2. Levi, R., Judd, T.: Dead reckoning navigational system using accelerometer to measure foot impacts. U.S. Patent Number 5, 583, 776 (1996)

3. Syrjärinne, J., Käppi, J., Saarinen, J.: MEMS-IMU based pedestrian navigator for handheld devices. Nokia Research Center (2001)
4. Liu, H., Darabi, H., Banerjee, P., Liu, J.: Survey of Wireless Indoor Positioning Techniques and Systems. IEEE Transactions on Systems, Man, and Cybernetics, Part C: Applications and Reviews (2007)
5. Koyuncu, H., Yang, S.: A Survey of Indoor Positioning and Object Locating Systems. IJCSNS International Journal of Computer Science and Network Security 10(5) (2010)
6. Wang, A., Jarrett, M., Sorteberg, E.: Experiences from implementing a mobile multiplayer real-time game for wireless networks with high latency. Hindawi Publishing Corp. (2009)
7. Premerlani, W., Bizard, P.: Direction Cosine Matrix IMU: Theory (2009), gentlenav.googlecode.com/files/DCMDraft2.pdf
8. Ladetto, Q., Merminod, B.: Digital Magnetic Compass and Gyroscope Integration for Pedestrian Navigation. In: 9th Saint Petersburg International Conference on Integrated Navigation Systems (2002)
9. Chen, K.-T., Huang, C.-Y., Huang, P., Lei, C.-L.: An empirical evaluation of TCP performance in online games. In: Proceedings of the 2006 ACM SIGCHI International Conference on Advances in Computer Entertainment Technology. ACM (2006)
10. Broll, G., Benford, S.: Seamful Design for Location-Based Mobile Games. In: Kishino, F., Kitamura, Y., Kato, H., Nagata, N. (eds.) ICEC 2005. LNCS, vol. 3711, pp. 155–166. Springer, Heidelberg (2005)

Workshop on: Exploring the Challenges of Ethics, Privacy and Trust in Serious Gaming

Rod McCall[1], Lynne Baillie[2], Franziska Boehm[1], and Mike Just[2]

[1] EMACS Research Unit & Interdisciplinary Centre for Security, Reliability and Trust, University of Luxembourg, Luxembourg-Kirchberg, L-1359
[2] Interactive and Trustworthy Technologies Research Group, Glasgow Caledonian University, Glasgow, G4 0BA
{roderick.mccall,franziska.boehm}@uni.lu,
{l.baillie,mike.just}@gcu.ac.uk

Abstract. The workshop will explore the core challenges associated with the increasing use of serious gaming in particular those systems that seek to persuade users to alter their behavior. The workshop will focus on three main areas: data privacy, trustworthiness and usability. The workshop particularly welcomes submissions from people who seek to bridge the divide between these topics.

1   Introduction

Serious gaming technologies are being used to address a number of societal challenges such as traffic congestion, e-health, cross cultural awareness and education. Furthermore, as these technologies become increasing mobile, social and ubiquitous in nature a number of core challenges arise.

Firstly, as has been documented within the media, mobile phone manufacturers and operating system developers often insert clauses that allow their platforms to store the location and other private information. As users frequently fail to read the full terms and conditions they are often unsure of precisely what is being stored about them and how it will be used. The problem of data retention also extends to massive multiplayer online games and worlds such as SecondLife. This leads to a perceptual gap in terms of what users believe they have signed up to and what they have actually agreed to.

As a result there is a need to explore the data privacy and protection issues that surround serious and persuasive gaming. For example, at present data is often stored by the provider or manufacturing company e.g., SecondLife, Google or Apple who have access to all the user actions and information. The data privacy issue is even more problematic in areas such as ehealth.

Currently many games platforms and technologies are being used for e-health and rehabilitation in particular e.g. the Wii, Kinect etc. This has shifted the gaming platforms from being technologies for play into being medical devices for rehabilitation and monitoring. What are the implications of this from a privacy and trust perspective? Further how can we ensure that we design ehealth serious games to ensure that they are fit for purpose?

M. Herrlich, R. Malaka, and M. Masuch (Eds.): ICEC 2012, LNCS 7522, pp. 584–585, 2012.
© IFIP International Federation for Information Processing 2012

User acceptance of games as a viable tool is necessary for users to fully engage in a consistent and accurate manner. A lack of acceptance or trust in how the games behave (the "rules") and how it treats them and information could reduce or nullify potential game benefits. In particular, proper design and interaction with the user are critical to ensure appropriate and acceptable game actions and responses, especially for applications such as e-health where some users might already be in sensitive or vulnerable situations. Trust may also be derived from the game results and how they are presented and conveyed, as can be seen in a workplace environment where colleagues may be able to see the results of others, especially if game results were to portray a user in a particularly negative way.

In multi-player games, trust in player authenticity is important to ensure that impersonators cannot access personal information, or attempt to receive game benefits belonging to other users. Trust also hinges upon games being played "within the rules", including the behavior of the game players and the game manager. Proper design and interaction with users is thus important in terms of a trustworthy design and in conveying this to participating users.

Pervasive Gaming as a Potential Solution to Traffic Congestion: New Challenges Regarding Ethics, Privacy and Trust

Vincent Koenig[1,2], Franziska Boehm[2], and Rod McCall[2]

[1] EMACS Research Unit &
[2] Interdisciplinary Centre for Security, Reliability and Trust
University of Luxembourg
Luxembourg-Kirchberg, L-1359
{Vincent.koenig,franziska.boehm,roderick.mccall}@uni.lu

Abstract. The following paper presents a review of the ethical, privacy and trust aspects relating to pervasive gaming in particular within the domain of traffic congestion. The paper deals explicitly with the challenges involved that fall between the gaps standard ethical practice and scientific research when studies comprise of those in the lab (where collection and use is heavily controlled) and those which take place in the wild where there is the requirement to share data possibly with external parties. Also where the nature of such work is at the borders of the concept of traditional study and a commercial running prototype.

Keywords: ethics, privacy, trust, game, car, traffic.

1   Introduction

The I-GEAR project (incentives and gaming environments for automobile routing) aims to understand the motivations that drivers have while undertaking their daily commute and then to provide them with a range of incentives to change their behaviour with the aim of reducing traffic congestion. A key aspect of the project is on ways in which the problem could potentially be solved without recourse to expensive roadside infrastructure. As a result our solution involves encouraging commuters to use their mobile devices within a serious pervasive (and persuasive) gaming context.

While technical and human-computer interaction aspects are highly relevant within this project a number of the challenges lie outside these areas. For example there is a complex interplay between the technical, human, legal and ethical issues that need to be dealt with. This paper illustrates how the I-GEAR project triggers questions pertaining to ethics, privacy and trust in the context of a serious game that is meant to reduce traffic within Luxembourg. Furthermore, while there are no doubt issues relating purely to Luxembourg the higher level ethical, privacy and trust issues should also be applicable in other countries. We start by outlining the main ideas behind our game model and describe in the second stage specific questions regarding ethics,

M. Herrlich, R. Malaka, and M. Masuch (Eds.): ICEC 2012, LNCS 7522, pp. 586–593, 2012.

privacy and trust. It is important to note that this is a sample game design concept and the final design will depend on early user requirements modelling. Additionally, rather than providing out-of-the-box answers, we discuss these issues under the light of specific expertise, that we believe goes someway beyond the traditional interdisciplinary approaches within IT research. Ultimately, we would like this paper to foster awareness for the importance of ethics and legal frameworks to be taken into account in pervasive gaming.

2   I-Gear: Sample Game Model

The game we intend to develop will run on smartphones for two reasons: firstly, the number of smartphones sold to adults has expanded significantly in recent years (thereby creating a ready potential user base) and secondly, the vast majority of smartphones come with localization (GPS most of the time) and data networking capabilities. Furthermore, in contrast to systems integrated into the cars, this allows us to build on the most recent and widespread technology, to easily bind the device to a specific user, to easily deploy updates and to have easy and instant access to a large number of potential users.

I-GEAR relies on the concept of incentives being provided to drivers within a game-like environment. Incentives have already been used within traffic management and studies have found that even for a comparatively low cost people will alter their driving behaviour [1]. I-GEAR does not claim to be able to remove costs completely, but instead aims to minimize costs by providing financial and non-financial incentives to encourage drivers to change their behaviour. I-GEAR will develop a pervasive game in the sense that it attempts to alter (or persuade) drivers to change their behaviour through the use of social, psychological, financial or game design incentives. Drivers for example may undertake individual actions such as: giving other drivers priority, taking the slow traffic lane, stopping in designated areas during peak times to reduce congestion, taking alternative routes or car sharing. Such behaviours may also benefit other drivers or groups to which the driver belongs. Part of the challenge within this approach is not only to identify relevant incentives but also gaming techniques that remove some of the need to provide purely financial incentives.

The project will utilize a contextual design [2][3] methodology in order to identify specific incentives and gaming strategies. It is our opinion that the nature of the project requires that we allow the end-users to identify and test the incentives that may work given their particular preferences, circumstances or hard requirements. It is also important to explore the order in which people are given incentives such that we encourage good driving patterns early on while also encouraging them to progress further up the ladder. For example we want to specifically avoid traps where one higher-grade incentive is perceived as being worth less than one which is easier to attain.

Motivations are a key part of the driving game that is proposed within I-GEAR, for example we do not envisage that one particular type of incentive will work for all drivers. Instead, through the contextual enquiry process, we will seek to identify combinations of incentives and motivations that are applicable either on an individual or group defined basis. Furthermore, we plan to use two main forms of incentive: immediate and status. Immediate rewards will be given when a driver undertakes an action e.g. stopping at a café for which they receive a ½ price coffee. Alternatively status rewards or points will be used to encourage longer-term behaviour where drivers collect points for consistently undertaking good actions.

As noted earlier, I-GEAR will also encourage drivers to collaborate and compete through the use of gaming approaches. This will be achieved by offering both individual and social incentives. The underlying main objective always aims to reduce traffic congestion and improve the quality of mobility in Luxembourg.

The originality of our approach is partially reflected by a combination of aspects, all of them potentially raising issues, if they are not properly dealt with, such as:

- Our game concept uses location data and requires users to be identified;
- It is meant to be pervasive as it aims to alter driver behaviour;
- It is meant to share data, enabling collaborative approaches and a shared incentive / reward system;
- It clearly combines real- and virtual-world scenarios and, as such, is a serious game;
- It is meant to integrate an environment of potential high risk, with complex human factors aspects.

3   E-P-T Issues

We are aware our approach sets several challenges in terms of ethics, privacy and trust. There are other challenges in addition, that will not be dealt with in the context of this paper (e.g. technical aspects, human factors and user acceptance). In the following section, we will discuss separately issues concerning ethics, privacy and to some extent also trust.

3.1   Ethics Issues

Ethics requirements and constraints are very strong in social sciences; this also applies to research contexts. [4][5]. The main ethical principles are [4]:

1. Respect for the person's rights and dignity
2. Competence
3. Responsibility
4. Integrity

The first principle strongly relates to legal aspects and aims at a person's privacy, confidentiality, self-determination, autonomy and consistency with the law [5].

The second principle describes how techniques of dealing with patients or conducting research need to meet the highest professional standards of current knowledge and training.

The third principle refers to scientific responsibilities regarding consequences of one's actions and work. It basically stipulates that a professional way of acting requires you to be accountable for your actions and the ways they are conducted.

The final principle describes how attitudes and actions should be in line with honesty, fairness and respect of others.

While some of these principles may rather obviously link to our use case, some others reflect the fact that they have been set up for defining rules in a therapeutic setup, typically how psychologists should deal with patients. There are other ethical frameworks that more explicitly fit a context of research; the best known and most cited with regard to research in social sciences is the APA code of conduct "Ethical principles of psychologists and code of conduct" [4]. The most relevant principle with regard to our context is that of informed consent. It should be noted that it strongly relates to the first principle described in EFPA. This principle defines that participants have to be thoroughly informed beforehand about the precise processes they are going to face, their outcomes and objectives. In addition, it stipulates that, once the participants have understood all these facets, they are required to express their consent or disapproval, free of any influences.

Relating the principle of informed consent with respect to our game concept, there are two sequential stages that need to be differentiated: the research stage with intermittent experimental setups (simulator in laboratory environment, later on the road) and the final game release. While ethics is quite well defined for research contexts [], we think this is less obvious for final game releases as planned within I-Gear. A crucial point that needs to be dealt with is the end user license agreement (EULA): this allows making sure (1) the user explicitly consents with all the information about the game provided and (2) certifies being of sufficient age. On the other hand, while we think the EULA is a crucial point, we are also convinced it is a very difficult challenge to constitute an EULA that is both sufficiently detailed with regard to information completeness and still sufficiently readable in order to improve chances the user really considered all the information before expressing his consent. Who has not yet been annoyed by "excessively long" EULA texts, scrolling through endless pages, looking for an "OK" button to hit? Of course, bridging between both aspects, explicitness and readability, may constitute an arguable compromise and legal requirements may conflict with those of readability and event ethics to some extent.

Finally, the ethics aspects could also be discussed under a perspective of freedom of choice (e.g. is a pervasive game, namely that developed in I-GEAR, impeding on the freedom of choice?). We think that this question is already covered by our discussion on informed consent und thus will not be treated as a separate question any further here.

3.2   Privacy Issues

While ethics requirements with regard to privacy play an important role in social science, they are equally codified in legal provisions. When collecting and analysing different kinds of information in the framework of the I-GEAR project, it is clear that there are legal implications. Questions arising in relation to the amount of data collected, the possibilities to share the data with third parties or the general legitimacy of data processing for research purposes are worthy of consideration.

As mentioned before, the I-GEAR project collects different types of information, amongst other, data related to the location of the smart phone, telephone or tablet, GPS data, user IDs, data related to the profile of the user (age, gender, car type, transport references etc.) and data derived from the location information (location data, which direction the users took, preferences regarding the driving behaviour etc.). However, before discussing how to process these data, it is important to distinguish between information and personal data collected during the project. Only when personal data is concerned, some legal limits, named in the following, are applicable. Personal data can be described as "any information relating to an identified or identifiable natural person; an identifiable person is one who can be identified, directly or indirectly, in particular by reference to an identification number or to one or more factors specific to his physical, physiological, mental, economic, cultural or social identity".[6] According to this definition of the EU Data Protection Directive 95/46/EC, many of the data collected during the I-GEAR project meet this definition and are therefore personal data. They are protected by the above mentioned Directive 95/46/EC and by various legal acts transposing this directive into the national law of the EU Member States.

With regard to the standards of processing, it is central that the purpose of the processing must be clearly defined before the processing, which should exclude both the processing for unspecified and unknown purposes and the possibility to subsequently change the original purpose[7]. In more concrete terms this means that the data collected in the framework of the I-GEAR project can only be used for the (predefined) purposes of the project and are not allowed to be used for other, not predefined purposes afterwards. Further, personal data must be "processed fairly and lawfully, collected for specified, explicit and legitimate purposes and not further processed in a way incompatible with those purposes; adequate, relevant and not excessive in relation to the purposes for which they are collected and/or further processed; accurate and, where necessary, kept up to date"[7].

Some other criteria for making data processing legitimate are further detailed in Directive 95/46/EC. One very important condition in the framework of the I-GEAR project is that the processing is legitimate, if the data subject has unambiguously given his consent[8]. The data subject's consent means "any freely given specific and informed indication of his wishes by which the data subject signifies his agreement to personal data relating to him being processed"[9].

Another element of a fair processing of data is the information provided to the data subject. Knowing that one's personal data are processed guarantees transparency and enables the person concerned to assess its own position and to adapt their behaviour to a given situation. The information includes (a) the identity of the controller and of his representative, (b) the purposes of the processing for which the data are intended and (c) any further information in so far as such further information is necessary having regard to the specific circumstances in which the data are collected and to guarantee fair processing in respect of the data subject[10].

On condition that the data are collected with respect to the above principles, the question of further use of the data arises. It is planned to share the data originally only used for research purposes with local business partners to ensure that the incentives (e.g. coffee for ½ of the price) are used and that the rewards are distributed. While taking into account that this change in purpose has to be communicated to the users from the beginning on and that consent is needed for such use, certain other conditions apply as well. Transferring the data to companies within the EU, which are also subject to the rules of Directive 95/46/EC, has to comply with national law provisions transposing the directive. Transfer to companies outside of the EU is regulated more strictly and requires more protection[1].

When however discussing the rules of Directive 95/46/EC, it should be taken into account that this instrument will be replaced by a new regulation in 2014[2]. This means that EU data protection law will be more effectively harmonised than before: if adopted, the regulation would apply directly in the EU Member States and its provisions would be directly binding. One important change would, for instance, relate to the fact that in case of data breaches, the responsible data protection authority as well as the individual would have to be notified[11].

3.3   Trust Issues

Trust issues are the least concrete to deal with and there are multiple valid ways of looking at trust. In contrast to ethics and privacy, it is more of a perceived quality than a tangible and easily controllable quality. In the context of I-GEAR, we think trust is mainly relying on two requirements:

1. Strict compliance with and transparency of that compliance with both ethics and legal aspects;
2. Specific emphasis on those principles that reassure a user our pervasive game is developed in a way that it will not jeopardize driving safety under any condition, provided the user behaves as a responsible driver;

While the first requirement may easily be generalized over a broader context, the second one is much more specific to high-risk domains. In addition, there remain questions about the trustworthiness of a system that intents to alter your driving behaviour: some people may perceive this property of a system as not acceptable and as a result not be in favour of pervasive games. This of course assumes they understand the term as a precise definition, especially when used in the public context this may not be immediately obvious. Finally, on a less general level, there may also be doubts regarding the performance of a system or game that has an impact on your driving waypoints: does this system suggest the best route in regard of the user's preferences

---

[1] For details, compare Article 25 and 26 of the Directive 95/46/EC, OJ 1995, L-281/31.

[2] Proposal for a Regulation of the European Parliament and of the Council on the protection of individuals with regard to the processing of personal data and on the free movement of such data (General Data Protection Regulation), 25 January 2012, COM (2012) 11 final.

and the system's expected behaviour? This applies to many properties that define a navigation path: travel time, travel distance, fuel economy, etc.

It appears, trust is a very specific property and, as a perceived property, may be extremely dependent not only on the system itself, but very much on the users' specific expectations. We think I-GEAR has to consider the two above-mentioned requirements and also look more specifically into the results on user acceptance testing in order to understand whether there may be issues of trustworthiness amongst those cases where user acceptance is not given.

4   Conclusion

While not all aspects of ethics, privacy and trust could be discussed in this paper, we believe that the brief discussion presented should inform people about these aspects with respect to serious gaming. At present it is our view that these issues are at times not sufficiently explored, and indeed this is due in part to the contradiction which arises between aspects such as informed consent and the basics of playing serious games. In other respects it is simply that such issues have not been considered in the context of serious gaming merely due to its often perceived fringe appeal or level of interest. Furthermore, another explanation could be that gathering the interdisciplinary expertise is a difficult challenge in a domain that often concentrates on technical aspects. Our work within this area is still evolving and we expect to publish more about our experiences within I-GEAR at a later date.

Regarding trust issues, we highlighted how we think trust is linked to both ethics and privacy within a conditional relationship while an important part of trust also falls into the domain of user acceptance. We explained why we think that ad-hoc approaches only work to some extent when it comes to guaranteeing trust; in contrast to ethics and privacy, there is no guarantee that respecting predefined requirements is sufficient for establishing trustworthiness.

Finally, it is interesting to note that most of the requirements regarding ethics and privacy call for the same underlying principles that are expressed in different terms while converging towards the same objective of protecting a person's rights.

Acknowledgements. The I-GEAR project is partially funded by Fonds National de la Recerche, Luxembourg under grant number 11/IS/1204159. The authors would also like to acknowledge other members of the I-GEAR project including: Thomas Engel, Nicolas Louveton, Tigran Avanesov and Martin Kracheel.

References

1. Bliemer, M.C.J., van Amelsfort, D.H.: Rewarding instead of charging road users: a model case study investigating effects on traffic conditions. In: Proceedings of the third Kuhmo-Nectar Conference (2008)
2. Beyer, H., Holtzblatt, K.: Contextual design: designing customer-centered systems. Morgan Kaufmann Pub. (1998)

3. Holtzblatt, K.: Rapid Contextual Design: A How-to Guide to Key Techniques for User-Centered Design (Interactive Technologies), p.324. Morgan Kaufmann (2004)
4. The Official EFPA meta-code of ethics, http://www.efpa.eu/ethics
5. The Official APA Ethics Code, http://www.apa.org/ethics/index.aspx
6. Article 2 a of the EU Data Protection Directive 95/46/EC, OJ 1995, L-281/31
7. Article 6 of the EU Data Protection Directive 95/46/EC, OJ 1995, L-281/31
8. Article 7 a of the EU Data Protection Directive 95/46/EC, OJ 1995, L-281/31
9. Article 2 h of the EU Data Protection Directive 95/46/EC, OJ 1995, L-281/31
10. Articles 10 and 11 of the Directive 95/46/EC, OJ 1995, L-281/31
11. Articles 31 and 32 Proposal for a General Data Protection Regulation, 25 January 2012, COM (2012) 11 final

Conducting Ethical Research with a Game-Based Intervention for Groups at Risk of Social Exclusion

Ian Dunwell

Serious Games Institute, Coventry University
United Kingdom
i.dunwell@cad.coventry.ac.uk

Abstract. With developers of entertainment games increasingly exploiting the potential the platform affords for capturing rich data on user behaviour, adopting similar paradigms for "serious" purposes such as positive social change or public health intervention is a tempting prospect. However, exploitation of this potential must be tempered by a careful consideration of how ethical principles can be adhered to and applied to foster and sustain trust amongst end-users. This is particularly the case for at-risk groups, who may be particularly vulnerable to misunderstanding or misinterpreting requests to participate in research activities. In this paper, several key areas in which serious games present unique ethical considerations are presented and discussed: the unique nature of play as a source of data for analysis, the motivating role of the game and its use as an incentive for participation, and the impact of the entertainment gaming industry and its conventions user expectations. A case is presented based on preliminary work in developing a serious game for European migrants, and a number of key areas for consideration described. Through discussion of the emergence of methods and techniques for the analysis of data arising through play, the technological urgency for development of mechanisms to support ethical capture and processing of data from game-based learning environments is noted. To conclude the paper, future ethical dilemmas brought by success in achieving technological platforms capable of stimulating and managing behavioural changes are discussed.

1   Introduction

Entertainment games, and their serious counterparts, have attracted a wide range of attention from various sectors of the research community. With a little over a quarter of 13,000 Europeans surveyed in 2010 agreeing they considered themselves "gamers" [1], the pervasiveness and widespread appeal of this emerging medium is apparent. Attempts to demonstrate the impact and value of these serious outcomes often seek to utilize data captured from interactions between user and game, however, as an emergent medium, how users perceive and trust games requires careful consideration to ensure both an ethical and methodologically-sound approach to research. Since the early 1990s, the potential negative impact of emerging technology on exclusion

M. Herrlich, R. Malaka, and M. Masuch (Eds.): ICEC 2012, LNCS 7522, pp. 594–599, 2012.
© IFIP International Federation for Information Processing 2012

through a "digital divide" has been well documented [2]. However, as technology has matured and become increasingly pervasive, interventions seeking to harness this same technology to promote inclusion and empower groups at-risk of social exclusion have equally been observed to emerge [3-5]. In this article, we refer to "at-risk" groups specifically in terms of their risk of social exclusion; itself a concept lacking a ubiquitous definition, though broadly described as a state in which individuals fail to contribute economically, socially, and politically to the society in which they live [6]. In Section 2, this paper presents from a pragmatic perspective a number of ethical considerations specific to serious games intended for these at-risk groups, reflecting on the unique case of game-based interventions, leading to discussion of both the need for trust, and routes towards obtaining it. Section 3 then reflects upon these considerations in light of the European Mobile Assistance for Social Inclusion and Empowerment of Immigrants with Persuasive Learning Technologies and Social Network Services (MASELTOV). The paper concludes by considering the broader ethical questions that must be confronted in the drive to create effective game-based methods for social, societal, and behavioural change.

2   Fostering Trust in At-Risk Groups through an Ethical Approach

The challenges posed in ethically assessing the impact of technology with at-risk groups have been explored in general terms in a wide range of frameworks [7]. What, then, makes serious games worthy of special consideration? Interesting is the ease with which games are labeled as either "serious" or "entertainment" when few other media are defined in such absolute terms (consider, for example, the notion of "serious television"). Yet does this distinction extend to the end-user? It is not uncommon for serious games to adopt a stealthy approach to their learning objectives [8], and in doing so particular care must be taken in ensuring fundamental ethical processes such as informed consent are adhered to. However, the issue here is self-evident: if the user is informed of the objectives of the game, the pedagogical method is compromised, and a study of users in a naturalistic context becomes impossible. The lack of immediate solutions to this problem is no doubt a contributory factor to the paucity of conclusive, generalizable and objective studies showing the impact of game-based learning in a natural usage context. Whilst a range of studies have demonstrated the situational benefits of such approaches [9-11], a need still exists for a fuller understanding of how the indirect nature of learning through play is best selected and applied to meet a given learning requirement.

The depth of interaction, and possibility games afford for increased connection and emotional investment from users [12] can be argued as one of the primary mechanisms through which they sustain engagement and foster intrinsic motivation to play [13]. In the case where the rationale behind the selection of a game-based approach stems from its perceived ability to reach at-risk groups outside of formal or structured contact, adhering to ethical principles can be particularly challenging when seeking to compete for screen-time in a leisure context. Commercial games such as

Farmville achieve success by adapting to the user [14], based on data capture methods that have been argued as unethical [15]. We may seek to implement our ethical approach, yet can we reasonably expect to attract users when we actively obstruct their access to ensure they are informed? Similarly, without the ability to customize and adapt our games without the express consent of the user, we should expect to provide an inferior service to those users who opt-out. If we allow users to opt-out of research activity, what incentive do we offer for them to participate, and if none, can we reasonably expect sufficient participants to ascertain whether our serious game achieves serious impact? Shifting context to a classroom, trial, or other environment where extrinsic motivation can be relied upon is an obvious solution, though if this is unrepresentative of the actual usage context, findings may be of limited value.

Fostering trust is therefore essential in guiding the decisions of participants to allow researchers access to their data, as well as allowing serious games to exploit the adaptive and iterative approaches shown to improve their efficacy [16]. In entertainment gaming, and more generally software development, an End User Licensing Agreement (EULA) commonly accompanies the process for installation and first access. Increasingly, these agreements include consent to have data analyzed and kept for marketing purposes. A study of 80,000 users found that 50% of users took less than 8 seconds to read the agreement. Such was the extent of over-familiarity with the EULA process, users were observed to be more inclined to blindly accept terms if the presented screen resembled an EULA [17]. In short, the majority of users have become accustomed to accepting these agreements without review; an unsurprising finding when considering that, in terms of perceivable impact on the user, the EULA is hard to recognize as more consequential than any other confirmation dialogue during an installation or startup process. Yet does this lack of attention from the user stem from a lack of understanding of what they are consenting to, or is it that these users understand the implications of a standard EULA and are happy to consent? Even presented with research addressing this question, it would be unlikely to apply to broader or generalized usage contexts.

An EULA is typically deployed with provision of service as an incentive: users unwilling to consent cannot typically access the software or game, therefore should we also consider the ethical implications of using a serious game as a vehicle to incentivize consent? For any intervention with intrinsic appeal, particular attention needs to be paid to the impact incentivisation may have on decisions to opt-out. A participant eager to play the game may not be a willing test subject; yet they may be willing to disregard this concern to gain continued access to the game. The extent to which this effect needs to be considered and planned for does, as with any other intervention, depend highly on the ability to ensure the participant makes the decision to participate in an informed manner, with the capacity to play the game whilst opting-out of the associated research activity. Thus, care should be taken when conducting research alongside users who are intrinsically motivated to play the game, but not necessarily to participate within the research programme. The title of this section acknowledges that an ethical approach is central in developing the trust required amongst end-users to perform effective evaluations. Important is not only the need to adopt an ethical approach, but how to communicate it effectively to the end-users without compromising the pedagogic or behavioural model at the core of the intervention's design. In the next section, we discuss how these principles might be applied in the specific case of a game-based intervention seeking to lower the risk of social exclusion amongst migrants entering the EU.

3   Game-Based Intervention for European Migrants

We consider specifically in this section the case of a serious game currently being developed to support migrants entering the European Union (EU) from non-EU states as part of the MASELTOV project. The audience, therefore, is typified by the need to develop an understanding of the language and culture of the host country, as well as form social ties which lead to inclusion. In such a case, it is suggested games can form an effective basis for cultural learning through playful scenarios, and the gamification of existing resources. In this case the ethical approach builds upon the established principles of informed consent, though also notes the difficulties that can be posed in achieving this with an audience whose linguistic and cultural skill-set is defined by their country of origin rather than destination. Key, then, is to limit the requirements for these skills within the game, and to make the consent process highly transparent and accessible, as well as giving reference to the cultural context of the user. Technology is increasingly allowing data from users to be monitored and assessed. As the game developed for MASELTOV will be employed through a mobile device, technological methods for gaining consent for tools such as location awareness can be capitalized upon. However, again consideration must be afforded to the evidence given in the previous section, which suggests consent achieved through user agreements may not be fully informed. To address this, secondary mechanisms for ethical validation and information must be fully explored.

In addressing the general problem of social exclusion, the game must also be considered in its wider context as a single tool amongst a broader set of applications. The motivation games can stimulate, as outlined in the previous section, must be carefully considered with respect to its implications for how users might interact with the broader MASELTOV platform. A technological need to ensure users retain ownership of the data the system generates on their behaviour therefore emerges; a complex challenge when considering the interactions between multiple applications as well as the social context of the platform. Work within the MASELTOV project will therefore explore the role the game can play as both a conveyor of content and stimulus of intrinsic motivation, and central to this work will be an understanding of how trust can be sustained through a transparent, accessible, and integrated approach to data capture.

4   Conclusions

This paper has focused primarily on the pragmatic aspects of implementing a game-based solution or intervention to a problem. Indeed, serious games are commonly put forth as a medium with high potential as a means of behavioural change in a public audience. Many games already exist seeking to shift behaviour to certain ends; for example stimulating healthier eating [18], treatment adherence [10], and behavioural science frequently underpins their design [19]. Taking the general goal of these approaches to be games capable of changing behaviour to any stated set of parameters, and ethical questions immediately emerge, particularly when one of the largest scale serious games to-date has functioned as a military recruiting tool [20]. More to the point, can, or should, we expect users to "trust" interventions which seek to covertly, or even insidiously, change their behaviour? Whilst games are by no means the sole technology for which these concerns must be raised, they are, based upon the above cited examples, one of the most powerful.

A future where these approaches are effective enough to require these questions to be answered fully is perhaps not as far away as we might like to think. Approaches to understanding "big data" [21] are increasingly allowing us to interpret meaning and models from complex systems and behaviours. Significant future investiture will undoubtedly enable research that explores how these techniques to be applied to iterate and adjust these complex systems to our own ends. Yet in the context of platforms for social, societal, or behavioural change, the ethical dilemmas these systems may raise cannot be understated. In fact, there can be little doubt that an information-driven approach capable of adjusting societies and behaviours on a large-scale is no less of an ethical conundrum, or, indeed, as potentially devastating, as Oppenheimer's bomb. We might, as well-meaning researchers, seek to shift behaviour for short term public health gain, such as promotion of healthier lifestyles, but we cannot truly understand the "butterfly effect" our actions might stimulate. Though digital technologies and other emerging media only constitute individual parts of the complex structures underlying changes in behaviour, it is important to be mindful of this wider picture. In doing so, we must ask ourselves not only how we achieve our goals of change, but how we can expect to understand fully their consequences.

Acknowledgements. This work has been supported by the European Commission under the Collaborative Project MASELTOV ("Mobile Assistance for Social Inclusion and Empowerment of Immigrants with Persuasive Learning Technologies and Social Network Services") funded by the European Commission under the eInclusion theme, project FP7-ICT-7 Grant agreement n. 288587.

References

1. ISFE, Video Gamers in Europe, in ISFE Consumer Survey 2010, Interactive Software Federation of Europe (2010)
2. Norris, P.: Digital Divide: Civic Engagement, Information Poverty, and the Internet Worldwide 2001. Cambridge University Press (2001)
3. Adams, A., Blandford, A., Lunt, P.: Social empowerment and exclusion: A case study on digital libraries. ACM Trans. Comput.-Hum. Interact. 12(2), 174–200 (2005)
4. David, M.: The politics of communication: information technology, local knowledge and social exclusion. Telemat. Inf. 20(3), 235–253 (2003)
5. Ureta, S.: Mobilising Poverty?: Mobile Phone Use and Everyday Spatial Mobility Among Low-Income Families in Santiago, Chile. The Information Society 24(2), 83–92 (2008)

6. Glenister, D., Tilley, S.: Discourse, social exclusion and empowerment. J. Psychiatr Ment Health Nurs 3(1), 3–5 (1996)
7. Wright, D.: A framework for the ethical impact assessment of information technology. Ethics and Inf. Technol. 13(3), 199–226 (2011)
8. Davis, L.: Liemandt Foundation launches hidden agenda contest: university students vie for a $25,000 prize by building video games that secretly teach middle school subjects. Comput. Entertain. 1(1), 4 (2003)
9. Knight, J.F., et al.: Serious gaming technology in major incident triage training: a pragmatic controlled trial. Resuscitation 81(9), 1175–1759 (2010)
10. Kato, P.M., et al.: A Video Game Improves Behavioral Outcomes in Adolescents and Young Adults With Cancer: A Randomized Trial. Pediatrics 122(2), 305–317 (2008)
11. Rebolledo-Mendez, G., et al.: Societal impact of a serious game on raising public awareness: the case of FloodSim. In: Proceedings of the 2009 ACM SIGGRAPH Symposium on Video Games 2009, pp. 15–22. ACM, New Orleans (2009)
12. Dormann, C., Biddle, R.: Understanding game design for affective learning. In: Proceedings of the 2008 Conference on Future Play: Research, Play, Share 2008, pp. 41–48. ACM, Toronto (2008)
13. Tychsen, A., Hitchens, M., Brolund, T.: Motivations for play in computer role-playing games. In: Proceedings of the 2008 Conference on Future Play: Research, Play, Share 2008, pp. 57–64. ACM, Toronto (2008)
14. Cikic, S., et al.: What FarmVille can teach us about cooperative workflows and architectures. SIGCAS Comput. Soc. 41(2), 18–31 (2011)
15. Zimmer, M.: But the data is already public: on the ethics of research in Facebook. Ethics and Inf. Technol. 12(4), 313–325 (2010)
16. Kam, M., et al.: Designing e-learning games for rural children in India: a format for balancing learning with fun. In: Proceedings of the 7th ACM Conference on Designing Interactive Systems 2008, pp. 58–67. ACM, Cape Town (2008)
17. Böhme, R., Köpsell, S.: Trained to accept?: a field experiment on consent dialogs. In: International Conference on Human Factors in Computing Systems 2010, pp. 2403–2406. ACM, Atlanta (2010)
18. Baranowski, T., et al.: Squire's Quest! Dietary outcome evaluation of a multimedia game. Am. J. Prev. Med. 24(1), 52–61 (2003)
19. Thompson, D., et al.: Serious Video Games for Health How Behavioral Science Guided the Development of a Serious Video Game. Simulation & Gaming 41(4), 587–606 (2010)
20. Zyda, M., et al.: The MOVES institute's America's army operations game. In: Proceedings of the 2003 Symposium on Interactive 3D Graphics 2003, pp. 219–220. ACM, Monterey (2003)
21. Cuzzocrea, A., Song, I.-Y., Davis, K.C.: Analytics over large-scale multidimensional data: the big data revolution! In: Proceedings of the ACM 14th international workshop on Data Warehousing and OLAP 2011, pp. 101–104. ACM, Glasgow (2011)

Cyber Security Games: A New Line of Risk

John M. Blythe and Lynne Coventry

Department of Psychology, School of Life Sciences, Northumbria University,
Newcastle-Upon-Tyne, UK
{john.m.blythe,lynne.coventry}@northumbria.ac.uk

Abstract. Behaviour change is difficult to achieve and there are many models identifying the factors to affect such change but few have been applied in the security domain. This paper discusses the use of serious games to improve the security behaviour of end-users. A new framework, based upon literature findings, is proposed for future game design. The trust and privacy issues related to using serious games for improving security awareness and behaviour are highlighted.

Keywords: Information security, Behaviour change, Security games.

1   Introduction

Organisations and individuals are becoming increasingly reliant on technology and the internet for the storage and processing of their information. Statistics reported by the Internet World Stats [1] indicate that the number of internet users worldwide has increased by 528.1% since 2000, and now represents 32.7% of the worldwide population. Whilst the globalisation of the internet and technology has brought many benefits for businesses and users, the increased dependency on cyberspace also creates vulnerability to security threats: for example, viruses, hacking attempts and malware. These threats present a major risk and so it is important that businesses and individuals protect themselves from the growing threats in cyberspace.

Attention has therefore been devoted to improving the security behaviour of end-users. In organisations, previous approaches have been adopted such as training, education and awareness campaigns. These approaches can take a number of different forms including presentations, newsletters, video games, and posters. A review of the existing literature on security interventions suggests that current approaches lack empirical evidence and a theoretical grounding with the majority of approaches being based upon practical experience [2]. To date, the use of serious games to improve security behaviour and awareness has received little attention, though the use of games for information security awareness has been proposed by researchers. However, in domains other than security, research into the use of serious games for behaviour change and knowledge impact has produced mixed results in research [3].

Serious games intending to change the behaviour of end-users need to incorporate models of behaviour change. Whilst there is relatively little research regarding behaviour change in security settings, there are a few examples. The research that exists

M. Herrlich, R. Malaka, and M. Masuch (Eds.): ICEC 2012, LNCS 7522, pp. 600–603, 2012.

has used behaviour models from health psychology literature. For example, one study used the Health Belief Model (HBM) to improve anti-phishing behaviour with the game 'Anti-Phishing Phil' teaching users to avoid phishing attacks. Using the HBM, this study manipulated participant's perceived susceptibility and found that tailored risk messages increased intentions to behave securely online regardless of whether participants were presented with at low risk or high risk message of being a potential victim of fraud. However, overall, the study found that the use of the game as a training program had no effect on actual secure behaviour [4]. Thus suggesting that intention to change did not lead to actual change. This study only manipulated one aspect of the HBM, perceived susceptibility, and generally more than one factor should be addressed simultaneously. Research from health has discussed the manipulation of behavioral determinants of models in great depth and meta-analyses have found behaviour change interventions for health behaviour to be efficacious [5].

We propose a framework based upon our current work investigating factors influencing security behaviour (see table 1).

Table 1. The behavioural determinants to be targeted in game design for behaviour change

Behavioural Determinants	Security context for the game player
Perceived vulnerability	Assessment of the probability of an event occurring as the result of a breach
Perceived severity	The severity of the consequences of a security breach
Response efficacy	Belief as to whether the recommended action will actually avoid the threat
Response cost	Perceived costs of performing the security behaviour
Self-efficacy	Belief they have the knowledge and skills to perform the security behaviour
Attitude	Their positive or negative feelings toward security behaviour
Subjective norms	Relevant others to the user are performing the security behaviour
Locus of control	The extent to which they believe that they can control events that affect them
Psychological ownership	Perception that they own what they are protecting by performing the behaviour

The framework is based upon two well-established theories of behaviour change; the protection motivation theory [6] and the theory of planned behaviour [7] with additional factors of locus of control and psychological ownership. We seek to address the practical efficiency of the framework in game design and argue that future serious game design should target the behavioural determinants (table 1) to increase the efficacy of behaviour change games. Games adopting this framework need concrete examples of how they are targeting each factor in the framework and how each determinant is manipulated in the game design. This will enhance the behaviour change effectiveness and further aid in the understanding of the use of serious games for behaviour change.

2   Security Games: A Double-Edge Sword?

Games designed to improve security behaviour have inherent trust and privacy issues. These games are designed with the intent to improve behaviour, yet they have the potential for people to expose their real life security behavior, its weaknesses and actual security data such as passwords. Firstly, users are pushed to a particular behaviour i.e. what the designers of the games target for a particular security issue. In the case of 'Anti-Phishing Phil', the game focuses on one generalized measure of behaviour which is the detection of fake URLs in phishing scams. In reality, users are more likely to face a range of phishing attacks so are required to use a number of heuristics to detect these attacks. Future security game design should ensure complete coverage of phishing attacks/security issues and required behaviour to ensure that a user is not left vulnerable.

A further issue surrounding the use of security games is that they can maintain logs of user behaviour, for example, the security resource management game cyberCIEGE [8]. The game requires the user to take the role of a decision maker for a fictional IT-dependent organisation and they must make choices regarding technical, procedural and physical security. Their role is to ensure that the organisation's employees are happy and productive whilst ensuring that security measures protect information. The game creates a log of the choices made by the user which can be viewed to provide summaries of progress and details of individual gameplay.

The content of these logs could potentially be very sensitive as they could provide information about the security behaviour of the individuals. For example, if a security game requires the development of more effective passwords, studies have shown that users manage around 8 passwords [9] and have on average 25 accounts protected [10]. When combined they have on average 25 accounts that require a password but only have 8, therefore they are more likely to re-use current passwords. In games, users are also likely to re-use and disclose their real world passwords in a scenario that requires them to develop more secure ones. Those who have access to these logs could therefore use this information for malicious intentions.

It is important that the access to these logs is reflected in the policies of the games and acceptable usage by organisations using security games for improving awareness in employees. Wrongful access to logs of behaviour can give indication of weak aspects of users' security practice and what resources individuals may protect (in the case of a resource management game). This could potentially highlight weak areas in organisational infrastructures which could then be comprised by hackers. The acceptable use of security games should also be addressed as the competitive nature of some of these games may mean that organisations may wish to create a leaderboard in which employees may compete with each other to achieve higher scores. Such an approach may improve engagement and the potential effectiveness of the game. However, in the context of organisations, this may lead to many trust and privacy issues. For example, if an employee is particularly careless regarding their security then a leaderboard could present them a negative manner. An employee could perceive this as being procedurally unfair and this can have implications for their productivity and their psychological contract with their company.

These issues are more concerning when games adopt a social media framework as they leave players vulnerable to social engineering attacks. For instance, researchers have designed a prototype security awareness game with a social media framework [11] that uses a leaderboard, so users have the ability to view their friend's scores and thus their friend's progression. They can share badges and achievements on their profile which can be viewed by friends. Users can select topics such as password security and social media security. A major issue with this sort of framework is that it leaves individuals open to a social engineering attack. By displaying an individual's security behaviour on their social network, it has the potential to highlight weak aspects of their security and those who score low could be the target of an attacker who could identify where to exploit based upon their score. Social engineers are known to use social media to gain information about users which they can then use to exploit them.

Phishing could also be potentially developed for security games, in which the user is tricked into thinking they are learning how to improve their security behaviour when the game is actually used to gather information regarding their security practice. It is therefore important that this sort of issue is addressed in future practice.

In conclusion this paper has presented a new framework for designing future games for security behaviour change based upon previous research findings. The paper has also identified potential trust and privacy issues with serious security games. In future work the framework presented will be validated and developed.

References

1. Internet World Stats, Internet usage statistics: the internet big picture (December 2011), http://www.internetworldstats.com/stats.htm (retrieved June 22, 2012)
2. Puhakainen, P., Siponen, M.: Improving Employees' Compliance Through Information Systems Security Training: An Action Research Study. MIS Quart 34, 757–778 (2010)
3. Connolly, T.M., Boyle, E.A., MacArthur, E., Hainey, T., Boyle, J.M.: A systematic literature review of empirical evidence on computer games and serious games. Comput. Educ. 59(2), 661–686 (2012)
4. Davinson, N., Sillence, E.: It won't happen to me: Promoting secure behaviour among internet users. Comput. Hum. Behav. 26, 1739–1747 (2010)
5. Johnson, B.T., Scott-Sheldon, L.A.J., Carey, M.P.: Meta-Synthesis of Health Behavior Change Meta-Analyses. Am. J. Public Health 100(11), 2193–2198 (2010)
6. Maddux, J.E., Rogers, R.W.: Protection motivation theory and self-efficacy: A revised theory of fear appeals and attitude change. J. Exp. Soc. Psychol. 19, 469–479 (1983)
7. Ajzen, I.: The theory of planned behavior. Organ Behav. Hum. Dec. 50, 179–211 (1991)
8. Thompson, M.F., Irvine, C.E.: Active Learning with the CyberCIEGE Video Game. In: 4th CSET Workshop, San Francisco, CA (2011)
9. Grawemeyer, B., Johnson, H.: Using and managing multiple passwords: A week to a view. Interact Comput. 23(3), 256–267 (2011)
10. Florencio, D., Herley, C.: A large-scale study of web password habits. In: Proceedings of the 16th WWW 2007, pp. 657–666 (2007)
11. Labuschagne, W.A., Burke, I., Veerasamy, N., Eloff, M.M.: Design of cyber security awareness game utilizing a social media framework. In: 10th Annual ISSA Conference ISSA 15-17 (2011)

Open Source Software for Entertainment

Letizia Jaccheri and Michail N. Giannakos

Norwegian University of Science and Technology (NTNU), Trondheim 7491, Norway
letizia@idi.ntnu.no
http://letiziajaccheri.com

Abstract. In this tutorial, we explore open source software practices and tools that are suitable for a growing number of creators of interactive and playful systems. The introduction of open source tools such as Processing and Arduino has motivated a broader participation of technical and non-technical users in the creative production of interactive systems. Maker communities meet regularly and they share resources and knowledge for creative hacking, fun, and networking. In this context there are two main issues: on the one hand, software creation practices, based on collaboration and sharing, on the other hand, the respective end-user programming tools for artists, hobbyists or children. This tutorial presents a coherent overview of related work and our own experiences in the organization and running of maker workshops. It encompasses creative sessions whose final goal is to inspire the participants to experience open software practices and tools. This goal can divided into three sub-goals: 1) Technical (Interactivity, multimedia) 2) Artistic (poetic message, playful, experimental) 3) Open (sharing, reuse and participation). As a side effect of the study, the participants will cooperate and get to know each other and learn examples of new media prototyping tools and sharing platforms. The tutorial proposes a set of initial research questions which will challenge the participants to explore the relationship between Open Source Software and Entertainment.

Keywords: Open Source Software, Art, Creative processes, Arduino, Scratch, Processing, Maker communities.

1 Introduction

Tools for creativity enable digital creators, professionals or hobbyists, to realize their desire for expression with powerful development environments that support animation, music, or video editing tools [10]. Open source tools for creativity, such as Processing (http://processing.org), Arduino (http://arduino.cc) [3], and Scratch (http://scratch.mit.edu) [9] have their roots in this inter-section of open source software (OSS) and creativity. These two fields of study and practice are important for the work presented in this tutorial. The aim of the tutorial is to stimulate participants to acquire knowledge and basic skills about creative, playful and open software engineering practices and tools. The goal of the tutorial is to disseminate knowledge on existing open software tools and community projects practices as well as facilitating simple practical activities with the purpose of stimulate reflection.

M. Herrlich, R. Malaka, and M. Masuch (Eds.): ICEC 2012, LNCS 7522, pp. 604–607, 2012.

2   Open Source Software

A software system is open source if its code is available to everybody for inspection, use, and modification. Users of OSS are not paying customers but potential software co-developers. OSS was born as a movement based on contributions of volunteers. However, an increasing number of companies are getting involved in OSS projects [2]. Use and further release of modified version of an OSS system are regulated by a license. OSS is much more than the possibility to change the code. The most important characteristics and success factor of OSS projects are associated with communities of users and developers. The degree of activeness of the community is crucial for an OSS project. Each user of an active community is not isolated but part of a community. Members of each community are connected and help each other via mailing lists, forum and IRC channels.

3   Joy of Creation as Entertainment

The role of the active user in entertainment has been explored in the entertainment computing literature. Nakatsu et al. [7] presents a framework for understanding entertainment which divide experiences in passive (like reading and watching movies) and active (like doing sports and creating art). The inner joy of creation and unselfish cooperation has often been identified as an important asset of the OSS developer culture. Around these issues of creation and cooperation, Castells [4] proposes analogies between the world of OSS and the world of art. Castells anticipates art as a growing area of the Internet, stating that 'open source art is the new frontier of artistic creation'. The Internet not only serves as a means for distribution of artifacts, but also serves as a shared platform for a process that aims to create new artistic artifacts. Several difficulties have been faced into the collaboration between distant persons. This is an issue shared with most intellectual activities. In previous work [11] this issue has been identified, when computer engineering students are working together with non-engineers or other branches of engineering. Applying and adapting methods from the field of social psychology have proven to be successful in optimizing the collaboration in heterogeneous groups. These methods approach the issues in a social manner and generally aim at optimizing the social issues and in effect optimizing the end results of the collaboration. This has proven successful when applied on students with a multi-disciplinary background working with innovative, new media, solutions. Innovative and creative businesses are often found within the field of computer science. These are often faced with similar issues, for instance when one or more stakeholders to a project have different backgrounds than the rest of a team. Or when the task is to "think outside the box" and develop creative solutions. The social issues experienced in these settings may be an obstacle that results in sub optimal solutions.

4   Description of the Tutorial

This tutorial builds on our experience in facilitating and studying creative processes. [4] [6] and focus on OSS and its intersection with entertainment.

Audience: The audience for this tutorial comprises software engineers, researchers and PhD students interested in creative technologies and processes. The participants will have to bring their own laptop (Windows, Linux, or Mac). It is an advantage if the participants have already installed Processing and Scratch tools, but this is not mandatory. No practical programming knowledge is required. Participants will be able to work in small groups to be able to test and experience the methods presented in the tutorial. The organizers will exploit their networks to improve recruiting to this tutorial.

Inspirational Questions: The tutorial is motivated by several *inspirational research questions* that are intended to be explored and be a basis for reaction. Examples of questions are:

RQ1. Which is the relationship between OSS and entertainment computing?
RQ2. How can an understanding of OSS communities enhance state of the art in entertainment computing?

Tutor Background: Jaccheri is a professor at NTNU, Norway. She has twenty years' experience of teaching and researching and she has been involved in the supervision of more than 12 PhD students. She has published book chapters and papers and has given presentations at several universities in Europe. Her motivation for developing this tutorial is to disseminate the bulk of knowledge and practical learning methods with an International audience. Preliminary versions of this tutorial have been tested with University students and in related tutorials [4].

Structure: The format is a full day tutorial. A preliminary structure of the tutorial is available at http://artentnu.wordpress.com/icec2011-tutorial/ together with all the slides, which can be downloaded and reused. See also Table 1. The first half of the tutorial will include presentations on the background of the topics included, different tools that leans well to OSS and art, several different strategies for enhancing creative collaboration in teams and an array of examples illustrating the potential in the intersection of OSS and art. The second half of the tutorial will include experience and creativity based learning sessions. The participants will work in teams on small creative tasks using the methods presented earlier. Several work sessions will be held with a reaction and discussion part at the end of each. This will introduce the participants to some of the obstacles that can occur when working in a creative team and several of the strategies that can either avoid or address these issues.

Table 1. Structure of the day

Time	Activity
09:15 – 10:00	Computer art and entertainment
10:30 – 11:15	Open source software
11:15 – 12:00	OSS, art and entertainment
14:00 – 15:30	Creative session 1: (a) Choose characters; (b) Experiment with motion, looks, sound, sensors (Pico Boards will be provided by the organizers).
16:00 – 17:15	Creative session 2: (c) Develop a story board; (d) Programming, (e) Share. 17:15 Final discussion and conclusions
Breaks are from 10:00 - 10:30 and 15:30 - 16:00; Lunch is 12:00 - 14:00	

References

1. Anacleto, J.C., Fels, S., Graham, T.C.N., Kapralos, B., El-Nasr, M.S., Stanley, K. (eds.): ICEC 2011. LNCS, vol. 6972. Springer, Heidelberg (2011)
2. Ayala, C.P., Cruzes, D., Hauge, Ø., Conradi, R.: Five facts on the adoption of open source software. IEEE Software 28(2), 95–99 (2011)
3. Buechley, L., Hill, B.M.: LilyPad in the wild: how hardware's long tail is supporting new engineering and design communities. In: Proceedings of the 8th ACM Conference on Designing Interactive Systems, DIS 2010, pp. 199–207. ACM, New York (2010)
4. Castells, M.: The Internet Galaxy: Reactions on the Internet, Business, and Society. Oxford University Press, Inc., New York (2001)
5. Chorianopoulos, K., Jaccheri, L., Nossum, A.S.: Creative and open software engineering practices and tools in maker community projects. In: Proceedings of the 4th ACM SIG-CHcI Symposium on Engineering Interactive Computing Systems, EICS 2012. ACM, New York (2012)
6. Høiseth, M., Jaccheri, L.: Art and Technology for Young Creators. In: Anacleto, J.C., Fels, S., Graham, N., Kapralos, B., Saif El-Nasr, M., Stanley, K. (eds.) ICEC 2011. LNCS, vol. 6972, pp. 210–221. Springer, Heidelberg (2011)
7. Nakatsu, R., Rauterberg, M., Vorderer, P.: A New Framework for Entertainment Computing: From Passive to Active Experience. In: Kishino, F., Kitamura, Y., Kato, H., Nagata, N. (eds.) ICEC 2005. LNCS, vol. 3711, pp. 1–12. Springer, Heidelberg (2005)
8. Noble, J.: Programming Interactivity: A Designer's Guide to Processing, Arduino, and Openframeworks, 1st edn. O'Reilly Media (2009)
9. Resnick, M., Maloney, J., Monroy-Hernandez, A., Rusk, N., Eastmond, E., Brennan, K., Millner, A., Rosenbaum, E., Silver, J., Silverman, B., Kafai, Y.: Scratch: programming for all. Commun. ACM 52, 60–67 (2009)
10. Shneiderman, B.: Creativity Support Tools Accelerating Discovery and Innovation. Communication of the ACM 50(12), 20–32 (2007)
11. Trifonova, A., Ahmed, S.U., Jaccheri, L.: SArt: Towards innovation at the intersection of software engineering and art. In: Proceedings of the 16th International Conference on Information Systems Development, pp. 29–31. Springer (2007)

Author Index